THE COLOR

KAI BIRD

OF TRUTH

McGeorge Bundy

and William Bundy:

Brothers in Arms

A BIOGRAPHY

Simon & Schuster

SIMON & SCHUSTER
Rockefeller Center
1230 Avenue of the Americas
New York, NY 10020

10 9 8 7 6 5 4 3 2 1

Library of Congress Cataloging-in-Publication Data

Bird, Kai.
    The color of truth : McGeorge Bundy and William
Bundy, brothers in arms : a biography / Kai Bird.
        p.   cm.
    Includes bibliographical references (p. 412) and
index.
    1. Bundy, McGeorge.   2. Bundy, William P.,
1917-   .   3. Political consultants—United States
—Biography.   4. United States—Foreign relations
—1945–1989.   5. National security—United
States—History—20th century.   6. United States
—Politics and government—1945–1989.   I. Title.
E840.6.B57   1998
973.92'092'2—dc21
[B]   98-24676   CIP
ISBN 0-684-80970-2

"Gray is the color of truth."

—McGeorge Bundy,
in a speech about Vietnam
at the Cosmos Club, May 1967

For Eugene and Jerine Bird

and for Susan and Joshua

Contents

Introduction

THE ROOM was hot and we were young and angry. Forty of us—students at Carleton College in Northfield, Minnesota—had packed ourselves into a small seminar room to hear John F. Kennedy's former national security adviser field questions about the ongoing war in Vietnam. I was twenty-one years old and this was my first encounter with McGeorge Bundy.

Two and a half years earlier, eighty-nine of us had been arrested in Minneapolis while blocking the doors of a draft-induction center. It had been the largest act of civil disobedience in the history of the state. Four students had just been gunned down by the National Guard at Kent State University while protesting the Nixon administration's invasion of Cambodia. That week 123 Americans were killed in Vietnam, bringing the total to 41,733 Americans killed. By then, upwards of two million Vietnamese on both sides had also died since the war had started in the late 1950s. Through numerous demonstrations and now by small acts of civil disobedience, many Americans from all walks of life had hoped to end a bloody and senseless war. In that spring of 1970, the anti-war movement shut down colleges all across the country. The president called us "bums" and the war went on for five more years.[1]

It was now November 9, 1972. American soldiers were still coming home in body bags. Just days earlier the peace movement's presidential candidate, Senator George McGovern, had been defeated in a landslide by President Richard M. Nixon. And now here was McGeorge Bundy—a man we all knew as one of the prime architects of the war—waiting to take our questions. His mere presence seemed an affront, an unspeakable act of arrogance.

Bundy stood in the well of this small amphitheater, beaming at us with a tight, clenched smile. Behind his clear-plastic frame glasses, his bright blue eyes gleamed with an icy intelligence. Trim and pink-cheeked, Bundy was a handsome, almost boyish man who looked much younger than his fifty-three

years. As president of the Ford Foundation, he now had the profoundly envi-
able job of passing out some $200 million a year to just about whomever he
wished. We probably would have been surprised to learn how much of this
money Bundy was funneling to black power advocates in the civil rights
movement, environmentalists and public-interest law groups around the
country.

But we knew little and cared less for McGeorge Bundy's current good
works. All that interested us about this man was his complicity in a senseless
and therefore immoral war that had divided America like nothing since the
Civil War a hundred years earlier. I can remember none of the actual words
we exchanged that day. But I still have a vivid memory of two things: our
anger and frustration, and his self-assurance. Bundy just stood behind the
lectern and calmly responded to our questions with the practiced clarity of the
Harvard dean he had once been. Clearly, he had done this before, deftly
responding to earnest questions with a display of clipped, cool logic, a bit of
wryness and, if necessary, a cold bucket of condescension.

He was not exactly defending the war—and certainly not the war as it
was still being waged by Nixon and Henry Kissinger. His answers were analytical and filled with historical asides to analogies which may or may not have
been relevant—we were too young and unread and too exasperated to judge
whether his arguments could withstand any real intellectual scrutiny. He was
certainly not apologetic. He confessed to nothing. Yet, neither did he reject
our passionate questions out of hand. He tried to engage us and tried to
explain, without actually saying so, that the war—his war—had been somehow inevitable. This was hardly a satisfying explanation for the death and
destruction our country continued to rain on Indochina. It still isn't.

Even so, I came away from this first encounter with Bundy perplexed and
curious to know how such an intelligent man had become so intimately associated with such a national disaster.

WHEN in 1992, I next met Bundy, he took me out to a French restaurant
around the corner from his Manhattan office at the Carnegie Corporation. He
listened politely as I explained my intention to write a full-scale biography of
him and his brother William. After a moment's hesitation, he remarked,
"Well, my mother would not have approved." Stunned, I asked why, and he
said, "Oh, she would have a one-word explanation: 'Halberstam.' "

He said it with a grin, but it was clear that the entire Bundy clan had
been mortified by what David Halberstam had written, first in a *Harper's*
essay with the mischievous title "The Very Expensive Education of McGeorge
Bundy," and later in his 1972 best-seller, *The Best and the Brightest*. Halberstam's portrayal of the Bundy brothers wounded them so deeply in part,
perhaps, because it was so close to the mark. Halberstam's Bundys were recog-
nizable even to men who counted themselves as friends and admirers. The
writer had captured a piece of the Bundys and then succeeded brilliantly in

using them—and Robert McNamara, Dean Acheson, John J. McCloy and other "Wise Men"—as metaphors for all the promises and failures of the foreign policy establishment that took the nation to war in Vietnam.

Nearly three decades later, passions about the war have cooled only slightly. This book is a full-scale biography of both McGeorge Bundy and his brother William Putnam Bundy. Seven years in the making, it is based on scores of interviews and tens of thousands of archival documents. Many of these documents were recently declassified by the Kennedy and Johnson Presidential Libraries or through the Freedom of Information Act.

Essential portions of this book, however, contain information from government documents that remain secret. Without these materials—culled from the private papers of Averell Harriman and Michael Vincent Forrestal—this biography of two brothers could not have been told.

THE Bundy saga is an emblematic story of the American Century. Smart and gifted, this Boston Brahmin family endowed their sons with all the privileges and opportunities of the American establishment. Educated at Groton, Yale and Harvard, the Bundys became Proper Bostonians, a class of aristocrats bred to public service in a democratic culture. Related to the Lowells and Putnams, the Bundys moved in the highest circles of Boston society. The patriarch of the family, Harvey Hollister Bundy, born in 1888, became an assistant secretary of state during the administration of President Herbert Hoover. His friends and mentors included Supreme Court Justice Felix Frankfurter, President Herbert Hoover, the poet Archibald MacLeish and—most significantly—Henry Lewis Stimson.

Two of Harvey Bundy's sons—William Putnam Bundy and McGeorge Bundy—chose to follow their father into public service. Both were educated at Groton and Yale, and both were extraordinarily clever boys. In temperament and character McGeorge took after his sharp-tongued, acerbic mother, while William seemed to model himself after his father. The sibling rivalry between these two sons was intense and lifelong—but properly circumspect, as befitting a polite Boston Brahmin family. Like their father, they were astute in cultivating establishment mentors like Stimson, Justice Frankfurter, Walter Lippmann, Dean Acheson, Judge Learned Hand, John J. McCloy, Joseph Alsop and Allen Dulles.

In an era dominated by the Cold War—a conflict often waged in the gray world of secret intelligence—it is significant that as young men during World War II both Bundy brothers were trained as signal intelligence officers. Assigned to Bletchley Park outside London, William Bundy became one of America's leading cryptographers, privy to the war's most closely guarded secret, the German military cipher, code-named Ultra. McGeorge Bundy served as Admiral Alan Kirk's "one-time-pad" man, decoding similar intelligence intercepts during the 1944 Normandy invasion. The experience left the Bundys with an appreciation for how important a weapon intercept intelligence could

be to those who had to make decisions about war and peace in a dangerous age.

After the war William Bundy followed his father's lead and received a
law degree from Harvard. For several years he practiced corporate law in
Washington, D.C., but the work bored him, and when the Korean War broke
out he joined the Central Intelligence Agency. Soon, William Bundy was one
of a dozen of Director Allen Dulles's closest advisers. As staff director of the
CIA's Office of National Estimates (ONE), Bundy was deeply involved in the
debate over whether the United States should intervene in Vietnam in 1954
when it became clear that the French were about to lose their bid to retain
their colonial hegemony in Indochina.

Meanwhile, his brother McGeorge—at the age of twenty-eight—had
written Henry Stimson's memoirs, On Active Service in Peace and War. Published in 1948, just as the Cold War was unfolding, the book became a bible
of the establishment's worldview, an argument for an activist foreign policy
in pursuit of liberal empire.

In 1949, having established himself as an up-and-coming young policy
intellectual, McGeorge Bundy began teaching government and world affairs
at Harvard. Though he lacked a doctorate in any field, he quickly received
tenure and by 1953, at the precocious age of thirty-four, he was appointed
dean of Harvard's Faculty of Arts and Sciences.

At Harvard throughout the 1950s, Dean Bundy had to defend the university from Senator Joseph McCarthy's political witch-hunts. He did so, protecting those few tenured Harvard professors who had once been members of
the Communist Party and who refused to "name names." But as a Cold War
anti-communist liberal, Bundy also sacrificed those few untenured scholars
who refused to cooperate with the FBI.

When John F. Kennedy occupied the White House in 1961, intellectuals
who had demonstrated a political instinct for what Arthur Schlesinger, Jr.,
called the "vital center" suddenly found themselves being courted by politicians. As Henry Kissinger put it with wry understatement, "professors for the
first time moved from advisory to operational responsibilities."[2] As classic vital
center liberals, the Bundys were obvious candidates for major jobs. McGeorge
Bundy was named the president's special assistant for national security affairs
and William Bundy became a deputy assistant secretary of defense.

In the early 1960s, they managed one crisis after another: the Bay of
Pigs, Laos, Berlin and the most dangerous nuclear confrontation of the entire
Cold War—the Cuban missile crisis.

As anti-communist liberals—and particularly as men steeped in Stimsonian internationalism—the Bundy brothers were instinctively goaded to meet
any Cold War crisis with the threat of military force. Having learned the
lesson of Munich too well, they feared appeasement more than ill-conceived
intervention.

On the central issue of nuclear weapons, McGeorge Bundy understood the danger these primordial weapons posed to all human civilizations. Notwithstanding Hiroshima, he knew these were weapons that should never be used by rational men. And he understood that if he could see that the atomic bomb was militarily useless, then even its value as a weapon of deterrence would ultimately lack credibility. The sensible course, therefore, lay in the negotiated elimination of nuclear weapons. In this, Henry Stimson and J. Robert Oppenheimer had been his tutors. He could grasp all this—a large contradiction that lay at the heart of the Cold War—and yet in the White House he often felt barred from acting upon what he knew.

In a similar fashion, when it came to dealing with Castro's Cuba or the Berlin crisis of 1961, the Bundys often seemed to know better than most of their peers that they had settled for a safe pragmatism when an intellectually more radical policy might have achieved so much more. They knew better, and therefore their story is tinged with vague self-regret. In this sense, ultimately the Bundys were policy intellectuals shackled by Cold War shibboleths which they could not quite bear to break.

Nowhere was this more true than during their deliberations over the war in Vietnam.

THIRTY-THREE years after the momentous decisions of 1965, we have before us newly declassified archival documents from Washington, Moscow, Berlin and elsewhere that add immeasurably to our understanding of the Cold War calculations that motivated men like the Bundy brothers to intervene in the Vietnamese civil war. The documents show that the Bundys and other decision-makers registered deep doubts about the American enterprise in Vietnam and did so far earlier than historians had thought. To be sure, they could be arrogant and maddeningly self-assured. In this sense, they earned David Halberstam's sly opprobrium as "the best and the brightest" of the Vietnam-era establishment. But they were not essentially shallow or ignorant. They understood and sometimes shared many of the basic assumptions of the war's fiercest critics. At critical turning points, they understood that there was an alternative to war—and at times they presented the case for neutralization and withdrawal. They knew far more than their critics thought they knew. And that makes their story far more tragic than any of us thought. Long before Robert McNamara privately turned against the war, the Bundy brothers understood what a dubious venture the Johnson administration had embraced. They knew how badly the war was going as early as 1964–65, yet they found a way to persist in folly.

They were Cold War liberals but they were not Cold War ideologues. They could be dismissive of the so-called domino theory. "I always lose my temper," Mac Bundy later said, "at the notion that a series of complex political organisms can be understood by comparing them to an inanimate set of black tiles."[3] They understood that Vietnam was a gamble. They knew from Vietnamese history that South Vietnam was not really a nation, and they understood the dangers of fighting a white man's war on the Asian mainland. They were aware of the long odds against an American force achieving what the French had already attempted and failed to do in Indochina. They had read critical accounts of the French defeat in Indochina, and as intellectuals they understood the importance of this history. As policy-makers, they surrounded themselves with aides like Michael Forrestal, James Thomson, Jr., and Chester Cooper who supplied them with highly pessimistic assessments of the war.

As national security adviser for Presidents Kennedy and Johnson, McGeorge Bundy tolerated a wide range of opinion from his aides. Indeed, he sought out men who were capable of dissenting from conventional wisdom. In 1964, as assistant secretary of state for the Far East, William Bundy could write a long memorandum marshaling all the reasons the United States should not make a stand in Vietnam—and he later anguished over the war in a way that few people around him appreciated.

The Bundys knew that Vietnam was not worth the American blood sacrifice that was paid during the Korean War, let alone anything that risked the use of nuclear weapons. They did feel that the preservation of South Vietnam was worth some carefully calibrated American effort. Perhaps, they reasoned, Hanoi would get the message through a bombing campaign. William Bundy used a musical analogy to describe the bombing: "It seems to me that our orchestration should be mainly violins, but with periodic touches of brass."[4] This was a perfect Bundyism: witty, but smartly detached from the human consequences of an act of war.

Similarly, when McGeorge Bundy initially recommended a sustained bombing campaign to President Johnson in February 1965, he warned him, "We cannot assert that a policy of sustained reprisal will succeed in changing the course of the contest in Vietnam. It may fail, and we cannot estimate the odds of success with any accuracy—they may be somewhere between 25 percent and 75 percent. What we can say is that even if it fails, the policy will be worth it. At a minimum it will dampen down the charge that we did not do all that we could have done, and this charge will be important in many countries, including our own."[5] This too, was an oddly cold, even bloodless calculation. How many Vietnamese and American lives were worth a failed demonstration of America's credibility in the Cold War?

During the pivotal decisions of 1964–65, both brothers urged President Johnson not to make an open-ended commitment of American ground troops. Mac Bundy warned Secretary of Defense Robert McNamara that his proposal to introduce large numbers of troops was "rash to the point of folly."[6] The president's national security adviser clearly understood the grave risks associated with any attempt to wage a ground war in Southeast Asia.

Both brothers understood that the French experience in Indochina was a critical bellwether. At some undefined point, William Bundy wrote, the presence of U.S. combat troops would begin to turn "the conflict into a white man's war with the U.S. in the shoes of the French."[7] So when in the summer of 1965, President Johnson and McNamara were contemplating a further deployment of ground troops, William Bundy proposed placing a ceiling on the number of American troops at around 85,000. This, he argued, should be seen as the point beyond which the war would become dangerously Americanized. "In a nutshell," William Bundy wrote on June 25, "if we assume that the situation is deteriorating so that we have at present perhaps no more than a 20% chance of stemming the VC gains so that Hanoi would come to terms, we believe that the introduction of major additional US forces would not increase the chances of success to more than 30%, and would run the overwhelming risk of a truly disastrous US defeat. We believe such a defeat would be far worse than defeat without such a major additional commitment. . . ."[8] Obviously, they knew the road ahead was perilous.

When the war was nevertheless escalated into a white man's war, the Bundy brothers nevertheless persevered and made Lyndon Johnson's war their war. If the historical evidence now makes it plainer why out of their skepticism the Bundys devised a strategy of gradual escalation, it makes it harder to explain why they persevered in a policy which they had known from the beginning was extremely dubious. But like Robert McNamara, they now defended the war in public even while in private they increasingly acknowledged that the war was not going well.

Two weeks before he left the White House in early 1966, McGeorge Bundy wrote a memorandum for his files in which he took issue with what he called the "Lippmann Thesis." Contrary to Walter Lippmann's assumption that the United States didn't belong in Southeast Asia, Bundy noted that "we have been the dominant power" there for twenty years. "The truth is that in Southeast Asia we are stronger than China." The war's casualties were terrible, but the "danger to one man's life, as such, is not a worthy guide. . . . If the basic questions of interest, right, and power are answered, the casualties and costs are to be accepted." As to Lippmann's frequent argument that where the French had failed, the Americans were no more likely to succeed, well, Bundy had a characteristically flippant response: "There has been no serious proof of French political effectiveness since 1919."[9]

How could Bundy warn against the "folly" of intervention and then barely nine months later tell himself that the "casualties and costs are to be accepted"? One explanation clearly seems to rest in the fact that as liberals the Bundy brothers feared the conservative alternative. As liberals, they did not fear the war's critics on the liberal left. They knew they could hold their own in any debating forum with the anti-war students and their critics in the academy. Indeed, some of the war's critics were their Cambridge friends and former colleagues, intellectuals like David Riesman, John Kenneth Galbraith, Stanley Hoffmann and Hans Morgenthau. The Bundys labeled as naive the youthful leaders of the New Left who were beginning to organize demonstrations against the war. But if they underestimated the political significance of the war's New Left critics, they nevertheless were not ignorant of the movement's intellectual arguments. They read—and quickly dismissed—the radical critiques of the war written by I. F. Stone, Noam Chomsky and Marcus Raskin. They knew this "verbally minded" class of intellectuals was bright and articulate but of no threat or even relevancy to the political realities of Washington.

If opposition to the war came from the left, the Bundys believed that the real threat lay to their right. Once President Johnson had decided to take a stand in South Vietnam, the job of men like the Bundys was to contain the war. If not managed by liberals, they felt this war could easily have become a Chinese-American war, a rerun of the Korean War. If the Chinese communists intervened with large numbers of ground troops, the Bundys knew that the pressures from the Joint Chiefs to use tactical nuclear weapons would become irresistible. There were, as McGeorge Bundy said, "wild men waiting in the wings." This, the Bundys thought, was unacceptable. Still, they fully believed that America's containment of Soviet and Chinese communism necessitated U.S. interventions around the globe. Containment in Vietnam therefore meant "limited" war.

We can now see that the American debacle in Vietnam had its origins in the early Cold War. As early as April 1950—before the Korean War—McGeorge Bundy and Arthur Schlesinger, Jr. (among others), had argued in the pages of the *New York Times* that the United States had to have the capacity to wage limited war.[10] Ideas matter. This was a war custom-designed by Cold War liberal policy intellectuals who prided themselves as disciples of Henry Stimson, the establishment's apostle for the twin gods of military preparedness and internationalism. In this sense, the same worldview that ultimately drove a reluctant President Woodrow Wilson to intervene in World War I was also the logic of intervention in Vietnam. The Bundys and other architects of Lyndon Johnson's war thought they could so calibrate their intervention against Vietnam's nationalist, anti-colonial revolution that America could be seen by the rest of the world to be taking a stand against communist-directed wars of national liberation. This perception that Washington was not "losing" another Asian country to communism without taking a stand—was all that was important to the Bundys. Cold War America, they believed, had to stand by its commitments under international law. It was a very Wilsonian notion.

THE liberalism of the Bundy brothers became even more pronounced with the passage of time. Caricatured in the 1960s by the New Left as war criminals, in the decades to come the Bundys remained liberals in every sense of the word. As president of the Ford Foundation, McGeorge Bundy lent intellectual and financial support to a whole range of liberal causes from affirmative action to arms control programs. Bundy became an eloquent critic of institutionalized white racism. It was, he wrote in 1968, the "white man's fears and hates that must have first place" in explaining the condition of the American Negro.[11]

Similarly, as editor of *Foreign Affairs*, his brother William defended all the tenets of a liberal, internationalist foreign policy.

By comparison to Walt Rostow, Henry Kissinger, Zbigniew Brzezinski and others who succeeded them as managers of the national security state, the Bundy brothers were consistent, vital center liberals who labored for most of their careers, as it turned out, against a tide of American conservatism. In their personal relations with their friends and family, they were decent men. As policy-makers, they defended decisions which caused the deaths of many Americans and many more Vietnamese in a war that shouldn't have happened. Though ambitious men, they were neither ideologues nor crass opportunists. In the increasingly partisan atmosphere of the foreign policy establishment of the post-Vietnam era, the Bundys were, to borrow a phrase from the scholar Richard Pells, invariably of a "liberal mind in a conservative age." [12] As such, their story is intimately bound up with the tragedy of American liberalism in the Cold War era.

1

Harvey Hollister Bundy: The Patriarch

"Don't Talk While I'm Interrupting!"

No MAN CASTS a longer shadow over the American Century than Henry Lewis Stimson. Today, his name is an ancient memory to much of the American public. But for those guardians of the American establishment groomed to manage U.S. foreign policy in the postwar period, Stimson was the ultimate mentor. Two generations of policy-makers, whether serving Republican or Democratic administrations, invariably considered themselves part of what they called the Stimsonian tradition. For men like John J. McCloy, Dean Acheson, Averell Harriman or Harvey Hollister Bundy, Stimson personified the bipartisanship and pragmatic idealism of the postwar policies they later pursued in the interest of American hegemony.

As Stimson's closest aide and most fervent advocate, Harvey Bundy reared his sons William and McGeorge Bundy to perceive America's role in the world through Stimsonian eyes. These intellectually gifted and ambitious brothers learned their Stimsonian lessons well—and decades later they tried to apply them with tragic results in Vietnam's civil war.

Even in his time, Henry Stimson was an archaic man of Victorian rectitude. As the journalists Drew Pearson and Robert Allen observed in a critical 1931 profile, "He paid $800,000 for a palatial estate in fashionable northwest Washington, yet he believes in the redistribution of wealth and advocates increased income taxes for the wealthy. He is cold, aloof, criticized as being snobbish, but does the most generous and thoughtful things for those around him. He is a strange mixture of conservatism and liberalism, of pacifism and militarism, of gentility and democracy . . . [he is] a combination of weird contradictions."[1] Where some saw a fastidious attention to high principles, others saw simple self-righteousness. Where some saw a sense of noblesse oblige, others saw the condescension of an American Tory. Stimson called himself a "progressive conservative" and favored vigorous enforcement of the

23

anti-trust laws during the administration of Theodore Roosevelt. On the other hand, he opposed the economic reforms of the early New Deal. He could defend the right of socialists to be seated in the New York Assembly, but in 1942 he vigorously supported the internment of 110,000 Japanese Americans —an act historians have since called the single most egregious violation of American constitutional civil rights during the twentieth century.[2]

Stimson was a highly complicated man, capable of both painful soul-searching wisdom and profound misjudgment. In establishment lore, a premium is put on what the ancient Romans called *gravitas.* As John J. McCloy —one of Stimson's later acolytes—put it, " 'Gravitas' did not imply age or brilliance, and, least of all, a style or school of thought. It means a core, a weight of judgment and honest appraisal."[3] This was the ideal which Stimson was supposed to personify.

On foreign policy, Stimson's instincts made him an internationalist and therefore an interventionist. In the face of Japan's aggression in Manchuria in 1931, for instance, Secretary of State Stimson wanted to impose stiff economic sanctions. President Herbert Hoover disagreed. However deplorable, Hoover told his cabinet, Japanese actions in Manchuria "do not imperil the freedom of the American people, the economic or moral future of our people. I do not propose ever to sacrifice American life for anything short of this." Economic and military sanctions "are the roads to war" and he would not go to war over Manchuria.[4]

Stimson himself was not prepared to intervene on the ground with troops to force the Japanese out of their neighbor's backyard. But he was angered that the president refused to wave Teddy Roosevelt's "big stick" around, that he had no sense of bluff. Instead, Hoover had undermined the credibility of any bluff by publicly ruling out force.

The Manchurian crisis was a turning point in the intellectual odyssey of Washington's fledgling foreign policy establishment. Men like Stimson, Harvey Bundy and the gentlemen of the Council on Foreign Relations believed America had been shown to be impotent by its response to Japanese aggression.

Stimson simply thought the world would be better off if America assumed the responsibilities of the British Empire. One day in 1932, after listening to Stimson explain why Washington should hold on to the Philippines despite the opposition of a vigorous independence movement, Hoover commented, "Well, that's [Stimson's argument] the white man's burden." Undaunted, Stimson shot back, "Yes, that's what it comes down to and I believe in assuming it. I believe it would be better for the world and better for us."[5]

Ultimately, much of America's foreign policy in the post–World War II era can be traced back to the Stimson Doctrine of the early 1930s: America could and should intervene unilaterally and impose peace on the world. Aggression would be met first by nonrecognition and trade embargoes, then by military threats and finally by overwhelming force. Peace would be restored by force of arms carried out with the sanction of international law. All of Stimson's successors as secretary of state, at least up through the Vietnam War era, embraced this strategy. It was Dean Acheson's rationale for the U.S. intervention in the Korean civil war, and it would very much guide Dean Rusk's management of the Vietnam War.

Stimsonians were complicated creatures. They always went to war for the most high-minded, Wilsonian reasons. They could be ever so self-righteous, yet coldly pragmatic. And though they invariably had at least a fig leaf of international law to cover their actions, their use of military force was always under American command and exercised unilaterally. More often than not they could convince themselves that if they sometimes behaved like imperialists, they were nevertheless imperialists by invitation. Ultimately, their goal was American hegemony in an open global marketplace—not territorial expansion.

Needless to say, they had their critics. George Kennan would later deplore the "legalistic-moralistic" flavor of the Stimsonian approach to foreign policy.[6] So, too, in a different generation, would Henry Kissinger. But Harvey Bundy was very much of the Stimson school.

Harvey Bundy loved Herbert Hoover the man, but he agreed with the interventionist instincts of his "Colonel" Stimson. Naturally, his adolescent boys were exposed around the family dinner table to these same arguments about America's role in the world. Inevitably, they too would become young Stimsonians.

IF Henry Stimson was the grand patriarch of the American foreign policy establishment, Harvey Bundy was its preeminent clerk. Though he was to become a living caricature of the Boston Brahmin lawyer, Harvey was, in the words of a friend, "A Bostonian not born in Boston."[7] In the late nineteenth century, the Bundys lived in Grand Rapids, Michigan, but culturally they were still a family of middle-class expatriate New Englanders. The first of the Bundys came to Connecticut as an indentured servant.[8] Harvey's grandfather, Solomon, had been a Republican congressman from the little town of Oxford in upstate New York during the Hayes administration. Even so, the family was not particularly well off and had only enough money to send one son to college. McGeorge Bundy, Sr., Harvey's father, was selected because he had earned high grades from the Oxford Academy, the local prep school. He was sent to Amherst College and graduated in the class of 1876. After serving an apprenticeship in his father's law firm, he passed the bar in September 1878. Two years later Congressman Solomon Bundy used his political connections to obtain for his son a one-year appointment as vice-consul in Le Havre, France. McGeorge came back speaking excellent French and enthralled with everything Continental.

Soon afterwards, a family friend offered him work in his law practice in Grand Rapids. Eager to get out from under his father's shadow, McGeorge

Bundy, Sr. accepted and moved west. He would spend the rest of his life in Michigan, but his heart was always in the East. In 1885 he met Mary G. Hollister, the daughter of the largest banker in Grand Rapids, at the local Congregational Church. Soon afterwards, they were married. The Hollisters had migrated from central Massachusetts to upstate New York and then on to Michigan. Mary's mother, a member of the Goodhue clan that landed at Plymouth Rock in the 1600s, was a leading spirit of the Society of Colonial Dames and a member of the Daughters of the American Revolution.

Harvey Hollister Bundy was born in Grand Rapids on March 30, 1888. Grand Rapids in those years was not much more than a glorified sawmill on the Grand River, containing a general store, a post office and, gradually, a few furniture factories. The factory workmen were initially skilled artisans brought in from Holland. The Dutchmen quite literally constituted the working class.

As a youth Harvey Bundy grew up quite conscious of the social divide. Dutchmen worked in the furniture factories, and men of New England stock managed the companies, ran the banks and provided professional services. The Dutch went to public schools. Only those of New England stock could afford to send their sons and daughters to Major Powell's Private School. The Bundys and Hollisters lived up on the hill, along with others who had "got along" in life, and the Dutch lived down by the river. The Dutch and the Yankees did not mix. "The whole of Grand Rapids seems to be based," Bundy recalled, "primarily—at least the group that we were part of—on a New England background. The traditions of Christmas and many other traditions that I now recognize as essentially the same traditions that my wife's family were brought up with for two hundred years in New England. . . . Of course, there was also the Dutch community, which we didn't see."

Harvey and his older brother, Nathan Hollister Bundy, were raised by an overly protective mother who prohibited them from hunting or fishing with their father, or even from learning to swim, for fear that they might drown. Instead, Harvey and his brother grew up on a tennis court built by their wealthy grandfather on a stretch of land dividing their two homes. "From the time we were five or six years old," Bundy recalled, "we had tennis rackets and played on that court. . . . We were there, surrounded by our own friends, and nobody could bother us."

Out of this exquisitely sheltered existence, young Harvey Bundy grew up to be something of a snob. In 1902, when he was fourteen, he was sent away to the Hackley School, a prep school run by a dreamy old Unitarian minister in Tarrytown, New York. Because he had two uncles who were enthusiastic alumni of Yale, Harvey and his brother "were sort of brought up to believe we'd go to Yale." And so, in 1905, Harvey, by this time a gangly, six-foot one-inch boy who weighed only 128 pounds, boarded the train for New Haven. Yale was, as he put it, "just my cup of tea."

"Life was easy for me." He filled his hours with plenty of extracurricular activities, playing tennis "violently all the time." It surprised him how little he had to study: "an infinitesimal amount of work. It was ridiculous. Ridiculous." He had a ready smile and made friends quickly. Robert Moses, the future powerbroker of New York City, was a friend and classmate. So too was George Harrison, who thirty years later would work so closely with Harvey on the Manhattan Project. In his junior year Harvey was selected to the most exclusive and ritualistic of fraternities, Skull and Bones. Only fifteen men were tapped for membership each year in the secretive club. Bundy was enormously pleased. "It was a success story," he recalled years later. "But it wasn't very much justified. Personality is a curious thing. I had an easy time."⁹

Nothing affected him more at Yale than the people he met at Skull and Bones. They met twice a week, and Bundy claimed the friendships he formed were such that Skull and Bones "did more for us than any other single experience in our lives."

All in all, however, Bundy didn't learn much at Yale. He decided to study law almost by default. "I fell back to the law because my father and my grandfather had been lawyers." But like his father before him, Harvey first wanted to explore the world a bit. He decided to take a job for just a year teaching at St. Marks, a church prep school, which educated, as Harvey put it, "boys from a particularly narrow group of people of one social status, mostly from the Eastern seaboard." Teaching proved to be a miserable experience, so when halfway through the school year his father came to him with a proposition from a rich friend, he immediately jumped at it: to take the friend's son on a *Wanderjahr* around the world for the extraordinary sum of $3,000.

At the age of twenty-two, Harvey set off in 1910 with this young man, avoiding the temptations of Europe, and instead taking the less-traveled roads to places like Moscow, Cairo, Bombay, Calcutta and Shanghai. In the Philippines, Bundy met George Putnam, a young man from a wealthy old Bostonian family. Putnam took them around the American colony, and, after Bundy returned to America, invited him for long weekends out to the Putnam country home. There, in 1911, Harvey met George's sister, Katharine Lawrence Putnam, a woman as loquacious and lively as Harvey was discreet and reserved.

Like his father before him, Harvey was to marry the daughter of a wealthy and powerful leader of the community. Related to the Cabots, Lowells and Lawrences, the Putnams were very Proper Bostonians, meaning they too spoke only to God and one another.*

---

* A 1910 ditty captured the Proper Bostonians thus:

> And this is good old Boston
> The home of the bean and the cod,
> Where the Lowells talk to the Cabots,
> And the Cabots talk only to God.

(CLEVELAND AMORY,
The Proper Bostonians [New York: Dutton, 1947], p. 14.)

■

KATHARINE PUTNAM, born in 1890, was the favorite niece of A. Lawrence Lowell, the president of Harvard University. He once said of her, "She's not a pretty child, but she's somebody I'd like to know." [10] Katharine was indeed a headstrong woman who, even as a child, knew her place in the world. "I had a terrible temper," she later remembered. Once when she was five or six years old, a neighbor caught her picking blackberries on his property adjoining the Putnam summer home in Manchester, Massachusetts: "What are you doing, little girl, picking blackberries on my place?"

The little girl responded, "I'm Katharine Putnam. I'll go pick blackberries on my own place." She then tipped the whole basket of blackberries on the dirt road and stomped on them. "I can remember the feeling of those black-berries coming through my toes and his looking perfectly terrified. Absolutely horrified—he'd never seen such a spitfire."

By character and blood Katharine lived in a different universe from the Bundys. The Lowells traced their lineage in Boston back to 1639, and Katharine's great-grandfather was John Amory Lowell, who in his time had selected six presidents of Harvard. His son, Augustus Lowell, not only more than quadrupled the family's already considerable wealth, but also gave Boston four renowned children: A. Lawrence Lowell, another Harvard president; Amy Lowell, the poet; Percival Lowell, a well-known astronomer; and Elizabeth Lowell, who married the son of another Boston scion, William Lowell Putnam. This Putnam, Katharine Bundy's father, was a name partner in the law firm of Putnam, Putnam & Bell. For many years he sat on the board of AT&T, and late in life he greatly added to his fortune by buying bankrupt companies and putting them on their feet.

As a young girl, Katharine was driven around in a Rolls-Royce, and her parents bought a Monet and at least one Renoir to hang in their home. Her mother ran their Boston household and the summer home in Manchester with the aid of eight maids and a butler. Every spring Katharine traveled abroad, and at sixteen she ordered three dresses from Paris for her coming-out party. In the winter of 1910, at the end of the debutante season, she traveled with her father to Luxor, Egypt, where they rented a villa for two months and Katharine memorized the hieroglyphs from the Tomb of the Kings.

Never very close to her often bedridden mother, Katharine nevertheless learned from her father to speak her mind and never, ever to fear the outra-geous. In the summer of 1910 she traveled all over Europe with her father, who took her everywhere, including the best burlesque Europe had to offer. "He [Father] bought me a gold [wedding] band so he wouldn't be embarrassed to take me to these strip tease places. . . . He liked them and I . . . oh, I love that kind of thing." (Sixty-eight years later, she took great delight in shocking her interviewer by describing the differing "styles" between French and Ger-man strip-tease techniques.) As a Boston aristocrat, she could afford to be a little bit eccentric, to shock people just like her aunt Amy Lowell, the poet and biographer of John Keats, who regularly appeared in Boston society smoking a cigar.

This was the Katharine Putnam who in 1911 became "pretty well smitten with my blond law student." Harvey Bundy, however, was not at all thinking of marriage. After his year-long travels, he had firmly decided on a law career. Because his father had tied up whatever money he had in an ill-advised investment in Michigan lumber, family finances were tight. Then his father died of cancer during a business trip to Brussels in the autumn of 1911. Nevertheless, Harvey had saved a couple of thousand dollars from his *Wanderjahr*, and this was enough to get him started at Harvard Law School.

Katharine realized Harvey would not consider marriage until he could afford it. "It took me a long time to get him," she recalled many years later. "I worked hard . . . I knew he was much more interested in the law than he was in me."

Partly in order to escape this impasse, and partly because she knew she wasn't ready for marriage herself, she soon decided to take a trip around the world with two girlfriends. "Uncle Lawrence wrote letters to all the British diplomats and we were pretty well escorted," Katharine remembered. "Oh, it was a marvelous trip." They went all over Europe, Russia, China and the Philippines. In Shanghai, Katharine persuaded a friend, Peter Bowditch, to take her to a Chinese opium den. "I loved [Thomas de] Quincy's books," she recalled in 1978, "and I thought I was going to have all the nice dreams he had. Of course, I was too scared to take enough to really get going. I'd love to smoke pot now."

Upon her return in the summer of 1913, she enrolled in Radcliffe to be near Harvey. "I think he was furious when I bothered him. . . . Nobody wanted less to get married than Harvey to me." The truth was that he enjoyed her company. "He adored Boston dances, and he went to them all and danced very well, and he had loads of other girls. He's had other girls all his life. He didn't want to marry me a bit. But he done it! He done it!"[11]

Katharine's exuberance was not to be resisted. Years later, after Bill and Mac had become public personalities, people would remark on the forcefulness of her personality and the obvious influence she held over her sons. "Very much a personage," said one of her friends to the journalist David Halberstam. "Very bright. But she also has this extraordinary sense of being an intellectual, the consciousness of being part of a great intellectual tradition. . . . But she's never done anything herself, never written anything, or acted anything, but she's so aware that she's linked with a great intellectual tradition, an intellectual heiress really, that she feels and lets you feel that she's accomplished something."[12]

Katharine's behavior over the years was invariably outrageous, calculated to scandalize or at least to shock people, particularly strangers. She was sharp-tongued and opinionated in a manner which either immediately gave offense or charmed her audience. And the more one got to know her, the less her behavior gave offense and the more she charmed. The contrast between the unreserved, even indiscreet Katharine and her future husband was always stark.

WHILE at Harvard, Harvey immersed himself in the law, studying under such legal giants as Ezra Thayer, Samuel Williston, Joe Warren and Joseph Beale. In 1914, Bundy stood at the head of his class when he graduated from Harvard. Though he had no money to his name, his prospects were bright. They became brighter when Dean Ezra Thayer called him into his office and said he had chosen him to clerk with Supreme Court Justice Oliver Wendell Holmes. Bundy was taken by surprise, but quickly accepted, knowing the experience would give him "a special mark on my record." [13]

The associate justice, it just happened, was known to Kay Putnam, as Cousin Wendell, since he had married her grandmother's first cousin. Holmes paid Bundy $2,500 a year, a generous sum for a recent graduate, basically to serve as a social secretary and collector of gossip. "He wanted his secretary to dine out every night," recalled Bundy, "and come back and tell him the latest gossip." [14] All of Washington used to drop in to see Holmes at teatime, including Justice Louis Brandeis, the eminent biologist Tom Barbour, an assistant secretary of the navy named Franklin D. Roosevelt and many writers from the *New Republic* crowd.

Holmes was already a legend, and Bundy worshiped him. "I had the rare privilege yesterday afternoon," he wrote Kay one day in 1915, "of hearing the Justice and Justice [Charles Evans] Hughes talk about cases and the philosophy of life and many other things for about an hour. I suppose it would be very hard to find any other two men in the country as big as those two, and the closer one comes to them the bigger they seem." But if he stood in awe of the justice, he nevertheless was capable of the most difficult thing for a loyal aide, offering criticism. "This morning," he confided in another letter to Kay, "the Justice pleased me a lot by remarking that my criticism of his opinion yesterday had been both acute and valuable. Just for your ears." [15] The relationship of a loyal servant to an unquestionably powerful authority figure was a role Harvey Bundy would often play in his long career. He could be unreservedly loyal, yet still speak to power.

For a time Bundy lived in the city's most famous bachelor quarters, the "House of Truth," located at 1727 Nineteenth Street in northwest Washington. This group house had been founded in 1911 by Felix Frankfurter together with a number of other young men who were intellectually minded and on the threshold of notable public careers. The House of Truth was so named by Justice Holmes, somewhat facetiously, for the allegedly high-minded conversation that regularly took place around its large dinner table. Holmes thought this redbrick, Victorian town house had "the fastest talkers, the quickest thinkers" in all of Washington. Walter Lippmann, Louis Brandeis, various cabinet members, diplomats and artists like the sculptor Gutzon Borglum (who one night drew his plans for Mount Rushmore on the dining room table) were also frequent guests.[16]

"Life was by no means monastic," Bundy remembered. "One had a blizzard of invitations to everywhere. . . . There were the enormous dinner parties with six butlers and three kinds of wine, and diplomats and this, that and the other, and young girls coming out." Neither was his work for Justice Holmes at all demanding: "It was in a sense a loafer's life. I spent a lot of time out at the Chevy Chase Club playing tennis."[17]

Bundy was living a charmed life. And he was still being pursued by Kay Putnam. On the evening of October 16, 1914, he took Kay to the Willard Hotel for dinner and proposed. Still short of money, he had borrowed enough from his brother to buy Kay an engagement ring. She eagerly accepted and promptly quit Radcliffe. "I was a nest builder by nature," she recalled. "So thrilled to get the man I really wanted." There was still an obstacle in the form of Justice Holmes's firm rule against employing any married clerks. Harvey felt compelled to tell the justice of his engagement, but he promised he would not get married until after his clerkship was finished.

Kay then went to work on Cousin Wendell, first by flirting with him and second by ingratiating herself with Mrs. Holmes. Every Monday was the justice's at-home day, when tea was served to callers. "You'd stop in," Kay remembered, "and if you're an old lady you leave your card, and if you're a young lady you'd stay and flirt with the Justice and give him a good time." Kay remembered him greeting his female company one day with the ditty, "The proper geese have left the proper ganders to come and play with the old man."[18]

By Christmas, Mrs. Holmes was saying, "I think this is just too silly for anything. I want you married and down here helping me." They were wed in April 1915.

If Kay was happy with her "blond law student," Boston society was somewhat nonplussed. *Town Topics*, the local society rag, ran a notice on their engagement which wryly noted that Grand Rapids was "a very far cry from the peculiarly aristocratic surroundings of the Putnams and Lowells." Harvey thought this delightful, and for years afterwards he carried around a crinkled copy in his wallet and took great pleasure in pulling it out and reading aloud from it on every anniversary.

"Grand Rapids was very hard to live down," Kay confessed. "I mean, you don't know what it *sounds* like. You'd do much better coming from Los Angeles or Santa Barbara. . . . But Grand Rapids was cheap furniture!"

After marrying, Harvey and Kay moved into what Kay called a "cunning house" on Jefferson Place near Dupont Circle. With Harvey's $2,500 salary from Justice Holmes and Kay's $2,400 yearly allowance from her father, the new couple considered themselves "rich." Kay promptly hired herself a full-time maid at $3 a week.[19]

When his clerkship with Holmes expired in the summer of 1915, Bundy took his bride back to Boston, where Harvard's Dean Thayer persuaded him to accept a position with Hale & Grinnell for an annual salary of $1,000. The experience was not a happy one. Kay thought the lead partner, Richard Hale, "stingy" and a "dreadful man." [20] Fortunately, a year later an opening occurred in his father-in-law's firm, so Bundy joined Putnam, Putnam & Bell as an associate in the autumn of 1916. That summer he had spent a month up at the Plattsburg, New York, military camp, otherwise known as the millionaire's club. There he received military training in the company of men like Henry Stimson, the young John J. McCloy, Lewis Douglas and dozens of other corporate lawyers enamored of the "military preparedness movement" sweeping the country that year.

Nine months later the United States entered World War I, and though Bundy tried to join up, the army rejected him. They said his eyesight was inadequate, and that at 128 pounds he was severely underweight. Instead, Bundy went to work for the Justice Department in Washington, monitoring FBI reports on the alleged spying activities of German enemy aliens. Bundy was bored by the work, and when the opportunity arose to work under Herbert Hoover, he eagerly changed jobs. Even then the Great Engineer had a loyal following in elite circles. When Hoover was appointed food administrator, Felix Frankfurter and Bob Taft arranged for their mutual friend, Bundy, to work as one of Hoover's four assistants. "Felix was the greatest placer of men who ever lived," Bundy said.

"To me, Hoover was one of the great heroes," Bundy recalled. "The Chief," as they called him, inspired them to work eighteen-hour days organizing shipments of food to the front, writing regulations on the control of important commodities and otherwise managing much of the U.S. economy. The experience nevertheless left Bundy highly skeptical of the government's ability to regulate the economy. "I pretty near got to the point where I thought the government ought to have an army and a navy and run the lighthouses, and nothing else." [21]

By this time, Bundy was a father. Harvey and Kay's first son, Harvey Hollister Bundy, Jr., was born on May Day 1916, in Cambridge. Kay and her baby boy followed Bundy down to Washington when the United States entered the European war, and that's where William Putnam Bundy was born on September 24, 1917.

Kay often took her two baby boys to Dupont Circle in northwest Washington, a short walk from their home, where she would sit on a park bench with other mothers. Martha Taft (married to Robert Taft) had two sons as well. Eleanor Roosevelt brought her sons to Dupont Circle on the one day of the week when her nanny did not work. While they had dear friends in common, particularly Corinne Alsop, the mother of Stewart and Joe Alsop, Eleanor and Kay did not take to each other. Kay called Eleanor a "scummer" —a person of bad character. "I thought she was the worst mother I ever saw," Kay said years later. "She was very rude, I thought, to me constantly. Eleanor didn't like me and I didn't like her." [22]

When the war was over, Harvey returned to his Boston legal practice in February 1919. He and Kay rented a charming little house on Hilliard Street in Cambridge for $50 a month and hired a maid for $6 a week. Their closest friends, Archibald and Ada MacLeish, lived across the Harvard campus, on Phillips Place. Like Harvey, Archie was a Skull and Bones man (Yale class of 1915) and a middle westerner who was just graduating from Harvard Law. By 1920, MacLeish was working in a law firm well known to Harvey, while their wives were the best of friends. "Ada and Kay got along just like a pair of ducks," Archie recalled. Kay quickly introduced this future Pulitzer Prize–winning poet and his beautiful wife to Boston society. After one memorable dinner at which Kay introduced Archie to her aunt Amy, Archie sent a poem of thanks which ended thus:

> Perhaps I've not seen Shelley plain,—
> That gift was not in God's bestowal,
> But I can overcome the pain,—
> I dined at Kay's with Amy Lowell.[23]

The Bundy-MacLeish friendship would endure a lifetime.

In 1918–1919, the years of the great flu epidemic, none of the Bundys were spared. Nearly eight months pregnant, Kay was hospitalized for three weeks; she was so ill that no one thought it wise to tell her that her eighteen-month-old son, William, had almost died. Only later did she learn that "Billy was just hanging by a hair." She recovered just in time to give birth to their third son, McGeorge, on March 30, 1919—the thirty-first birthday of her husband. It was a normal birth in every way but one.

Kay and Harvey had checked into the hospital around 2 A.M., but because there had been a previous false alarm, the doctors were in no rush to get her into the delivery room. Three hours later, when Kay's doctor had still not shown up, the head nurse became convinced that the time had come. The nurse, Harvey and the elevator boy managed to slide Kay onto a three-wheel dolly stretcher, which promptly tipped over, throwing her, screaming, to the floor. "I fell on my head," Kay later recalled, "while Mac was trying to get into the world." Repositioned on the stretcher, Kay was then put into the elevator for the ride up four floors. She kept thinking about the elevator boy —"He'll be so embarrassed if this baby is born in his face"—but they made it to the door of the delivery room only to find that there was no key. The nurse ran like a demon back down four flights of stairs to retrieve a key, leaving Harvey with his screaming wife.

In the next few moments Mac was born, in the hallway outside a locked delivery room. When Kay shouted, "Beat it, beat it, beat it," Harvey calmly replied, "I know all about babies." (He had attended the birth of two previous sons.)

Four days after the birth Archie MacLeish wrote a congratulatory (and

prophetic) poem entitled "An Ode in Reminder of Adversity," warning Harvey
—a loyal Yale man—that he might

> live to see (O fate too hard!)
> Thy sons in sequence crossing Harvard Yard. [24]

Harvey nicknamed his third son Sliv, short for sliver. [25] But if there was
any special rapport between Mac and his father it quickly became evident that
Mac had dipped into his mother's gene pool, while Harvey, Jr., and Billy were
growing up in their father's mold. The two older sons would mirror their
father's tall, rail-thin physique and serious, disciplined demeanor. Mac, by
contrast, grew into a short, feisty, sharp-tongued little boy, clearly bursting
with Lowell pride and Putnam sense of self.

The boys, however, would not long be alone. In May 1920, Harriet was
born, the fourth child in as many years. "A daughter!" Kay recalled. "I couldn't
believe it. [I] made them go and look again." [26] Daughter Laurie, the fifth and
last child, came as an afterthought in September 1923. The Bundys were now
quite the Boston family. Initially, they lived on Marlborough Street, but when
Laurie came they moved to a spacious, four-story town house at 133 Beacon
Street, within walking distance of the Boston Commons.

The Bundy siblings had an exquisitely idyllic childhood. Every Sunday
morning Grandfather Putnam came to the house on Marlborough Street and
read them the comics. "He had a lovely, gentle manner," recalled Bill. "The
Putnams figured much more in our lives than the Bundys. Growing up, we
heard stories about Israel Putnam, a Revolutionary War general. We were
very much aware of the Lowell family history." A. Lawrence Lowell, president
of Harvard from 1909 to 1933, was a regular presence. Every Christmas night
Uncle Lawrence hosted a dinner for the whole family. Christmas Day dinner
was always at Grandmother Putnam's house overlooking the Commons at 49
Beacon Street.

Bill's earliest memories included the seasonal migration of the whole
family out to Manchester in the summer and the return to Boston in the
autumn. In Manchester, the Putnams owned a large tract of land on Smith
Point, overlooking the tiny harbor from which working fishermen still took
their trawlers out to sea. Grandma and Grandpa Putnam lived in a nineteen-
bedroom "cottage" nestled in the woods. A three-minute walk through the
forest brought you to another, smaller house which the Putnams deeded to
their daughter. This is where the Bundys spent their summers. Though not as
large as Grandma Putnam's house, it had a splendid view of the tree-lined bay
with its rocky shoreline.

The household staff consisted of a nurse, a cook and a maid. "They were
all Irish, of course," Bill said. During the summers the children were also
supervised by a couple of Yalies who served more as companions than tutors.
"We had God's quantity of fun," recalled Bill, who for several years had his
own horse, which he named Mississippi Missouri. There were two tennis

courts on the property and all the boys learned to play hard, fast games, as their father had. The courts attracted boys from all over the village, including Benjamin Crowninshield Bradlee, the future editor of the *Washington Post*. By the time Mac was fifteen, he was regularly trouncing his father.

And as if the horseback riding and tennis were not enough, the family had a fifteen-foot wooden sailboat and a rowboat. "Grandfather took us rowing on this absolutely filthy pond," Bill remembered. "And every Sunday afternoon there was a baseball game." Though this was in the days before softball, Grandmother Putnam had a sporting goods store make up a stock of soft "hardballs." They were regulation-size baseballs, but so soft that no one could get hurt. Grandmother Putnam was always the scorekeeper, while Kay often served as the umpire.

"We pitched overhanded and played hard," Bill recalled, "but the general understanding was that you were not to 'show off.' I remember a cousin who habitually let the ball drop so that the younger kids could get on base." During one game Bill came sliding hard into home plate, only to be called out by his mother. He got up and angrily said, "You're a fool." Kay responded, "And you're the son of a fool."

This was a family that did a lot of talking back. "Everyone talked all the time, and there was a lot of teasing," Bill said. "It was a very noisy family." Later, Harvey Bundy, Sr., ordered stationery embossed with what he announced was the family motto: "Don't Talk While I'm Interrupting!"[27]

All the children were bright and noisy, but Billy and Mac were seen as something special. The two younger boys were both handsome, quick-witted, full of energy and obviously brothers. But there were some striking contrasts between them as well. Their sister Harriet—or Hattie, as she was called—remembered how different they could be: "Bill prized his similarity to his father. Both were high-energy men who would give out in the early evening. Mac would stay up late, just like his mother." Mac was the mischievous child. One summer day in Manchester he taunted Hattie, daring her to jump from the porch to the lawn below, a fall of nine feet. "Well, I jumped," Hattie recalled. "Mother saw me do it, this little girl in a white dress flying down through the air. I broke my foot."[28]

Kay was the disciplinarian in the family. "Father would always retreat in that situation," said Hattie. "Mother was the central switchboard in the family," Harvey, Jr. recalled many years later. "She always knew what everyone was doing." Except for Sundays, Harvey Bundy, Sr. rarely spent much time with the children. After a long day in the office, he would, however, make a point of saying goodnight to each of his children in their rooms. "The nurse," Hattie remembered, "used to say to us, 'Now, thank your father for your bread and butter.' It was a little joke."[29]

From Mac's perspective, his father seemed somewhat distant. "He was very much a father, very much the final court of authority. . . . He could be friendly and kind, but I think his interest in people grew later in life. I became more aware of him as I grew older." The dissimilarities between his parents were very evident: "Father would be more of the judicious conciliator and the seeker of the common path. My mother, by contrast, was quite peppery, strong in her arguments and quicker to judgment."[30]

Mac was, of course, also describing his own total self-assurance. "Mother's sense of righteousness was very deep," Hattie said, "and so's Mac's. Mother always conveyed to us her profound belief in the clear difference between right and wrong. How well I remember our fights over the dining room table. . . . For her, things were black and white. It's an outlook that descends directly from the Puritans and we all have it. But Mac has it more than the rest of us."[31]

The Bundy boys dominated the dinner-table shouting matches, and whether the subject was politics or history—as it often was—they insisted on cold logic, and facts and more facts. Hattie remembered one of her brothers dismissing her female intuition with the remark, "You haven't done your homework, dear, so please be quiet." There was nothing dreamy about these boys, but between Bill and Mac, Bill was clearly the more introspective. He was the one interested in ideas as ideas, while Mac was simply more inclined to learn what worked and what didn't. Mac was the pragmatist and Bill was the deeper thinker. Mac was also fiercely competitive, and it quickly showed in his school marks, for however well Bill did, Mac the next year was always a point or two above him.

Kay encouraged this sibling competition, but when it came to her first son, she soon had cause to worry that it would come between the brothers. The eldest, Harvey, Jr., was reading so well in kindergarten that when it came time to send him to school he jumped into second grade. That turned out to be a mistake because the boy had an undiagnosed case of dyslexia. His grades deteriorated; he would get a 100 in math and then fail the history exam. "I was terribly worried," Kay remembered, "whether to send Billy to the same school, [he] was so much quicker reading. I mean, Billy can open a page— Billy and Mac, either of them—can open a page and read the page at a glance."

Up to then all three boys had been going to the Dexter Lower School, a private elementary school founded in 1924 by Harvey Bundy, Sr., and several of his friends. The school was run by three spinsters, Miss Myra E. Fiske, Miss Josephine P. Dow and a Miss Green. Bill Bundy always regarded these three women as "among the greatest teachers I ever had. They damn well expected you to measure up. . . . We cruised through on the academic side. I was passionate about history." Each morning Miss Fiske would have the class recite the school motto, "Our best today, better tomorrow."

Bill was in the same class for one year as the young John F. Kennedy, and they became good enough friends for Bill to attend the future president's tenth birthday party. "Jack didn't have the physical disabilities that plagued him as an adult. I have a clear picture," Bill recalled, "of a quick-witted, resourceful, spry young boy, while his brother Joe was just very solid."[32]

■

By the late 1920s, the Bundy household was well established in Boston society. Bundy had become an expert trusts and estates man, earning around $25,000 annually. This was a considerable sum, but he was pulling in much more for the law firm. He was becoming a rainmaker—the partner in a law firm who is able to generate large sums of money. One year he made a small fortune of $150,000 on a single property transaction.[33] In all his years at the bar, Harvey would pride himself on the fact that he never had to litigate a case. He kept his clients out of court and in the money. He also acquired a reputation for keeping his clients' assets out of the hands of the tax man.[34]

In the midst of the great market boom of the 1920s, Bundy became the personal investment adviser and counsel for one enormously rich client, the Lyman family trust, headed by Arthur Lyman, the leader of Boston's Yankee Democrats and one of the most important men in the city. The Lyman estate was worth millions, and gradually Harvey Bundy found himself working exclusively on that account. In 1929, Arthur Lyman—who just happened to be a cousin of William Putnam's—appointed Bundy a trustee of the Boston Personal Property Trust, the oldest investment trust in the country. This institution took monies from some of Boston's First Families and invested in what we would call today a mutual fund. Such responsibilities put him in the company of old wealth Bostonians like Charles Francis Adams and Robert F. Herrick, who also served as trustees. These were men who planned things, "who did the sort of thing that Elihu Root did so much, advising businessmen on how to accomplish their purposes, either financing or [advising them on] what dangers to avoid. . . ." About the same time, Harvey switched law firms and became a senior partner at Choate, Hall & Stewart, a larger firm with twenty-three partners. Choate, Hall was known as a Yalie firm, and, as Kay put it, that was a "queer thing in Boston."[35] It was also unusual for a firm to recruit an outsider as a new partner, but Bundy had known the firm's managing partner, John L. Hall, from Yale and the two men both summered at Manchester. At the relatively young age of forty-one, Bundy was, as he later put it, "greasing the wheels of this industrial enterprise system, that's what it is, so that the whole moved smoothly, and so that you don't get into a law suit."[36]

Bundy joined Choate, Hall just before the October 1929 stock market crash, and for the next two years he spent most of his time trying to raise loans for clients standing on the verge of bankruptcy. This in turn brought him into the company of J. P. Morgan and other Wall Street financiers. As the depression deepened, these contacts would prove to be invaluable.

In the spring of 1931, Harvey and Kay Bundy took a trip to Washington, D.C., to visit one of Harvey's old Yale friends, Allen Klots. A special assistant to Secretary of State Henry Stimson, Klots had worked in Stimson's law firm, Winthrop & Stimson, and the childless Stimson treated the young man as a son. As Kay Bundy remembered it, Stimson came into their lives quite "accidentally." The secretary of state and his wife, Mabel, came to lunch one day at Klots's home and left having "fallen in love with Harvey" and his peppery wife. In talking with Bundy, Stimson realized he had the perfect candidate to fill the then-vacant job of assistant secretary of state. Bundy was obviously a clever lawyer, Yale- and Harvard-trained, and his Boston practice had already equipped him to deal with the pressing issues of international debt. Moreover, his political credentials were impeccable. Not only had he worked for Hoover during the war, but Bundy had even campaigned for him at the 1920 Republican convention in Chicago. "I was an original Hoover boy," Bundy recalled.[37] Though Stimson barely knew him (they had met briefly at Yale functions), the secretary knew he could sell Bundy to the Hoover administration in every direction.

Soon after this luncheon meeting, Stimson called Bundy and asked him to consider the job. On May 10, Bundy arrived in Washington and had a long talk with Stimson. The next day, the secretary went by the White House to propose Bundy's name to Hoover. The president said he knew Bundy well and was "favorably impressed with him."[38] The appointment was announced to the press on May 15, and Bundy assumed his duties in early July, though his confirmation by the U.S. Senate would not happen until the end of the summer.

At forty-three years of age, Bundy was taking a drastic pay cut—down to a government salary of $9,000—but this was more than sufficient to rent a stately home at 6 Kalorama Circle, located in Washington's Embassy Row. The financial sacrifice would be brief, and in return he would have the opportunity to work for the man who would come to define the American foreign policy establishment.

HENRY STIMSON must have reminded Harvey Bundy very much of an earlier mentor, Justice Holmes. Both men were solid, charismatic products of Tory America, though Stimson, like Harvey himself, had none of the justice's playfulness. Harvey was as stiff and correct in his dealings with people as Stimson. They had much in common. Both men prized loyalty and deference to authority; both were Hoover Republicans, politically conservative on domestic issues and confirmed internationalists of the Hoover, not Wilsonian stripe. Both served as trustees for some of the most powerful private interests in the country. And both viewed their stints as public servants in Washington in the same manner, as trustees for the public interest.

Harvey's loyalty to Stimson would become legendary. The Bundys in turn became the Stimsons's most frequent dinner guests. And whenever Mabel retreated to their Highhold estate on Long Island, Stimson would dine with the Bundys. Kay charmed the old man as she had charmed Holmes. After one such dinner Stimson dictated to his diary, "Mrs. Bundy is particularly attractive."[39] When one day a mutual friend commented that Stimson said grace before every meal, Kay confronted Stimson and said, "You don't say grace."

Stimson replied, "Kay, dear, the first time you ever came to dinner you talked so much that Mabel and I decided we'd drop grace every time you came." The relationship was so "cozy" that over time Stimson seemed to become part of the Bundy family. When they were home from boarding school, Bill and Mac Bundy occasionally played deck tennis with Stimson at his Woodley Park estate up off Connecticut Avenue.[40]

The Bundys had a feverish social life. Three or four times a week Harvey Bundy would come home from the office and change into a boiled, starchy shirt with white vest that was the standard uniform for white-tie dinners. One evening his eldest son, Harvey, Jr., was seated next to Justice Holmes, who leaned over and told the boy, "You have talked to a man who has talked to a man who fought in the Revolutionary War!"[41]

Those were also the days of Prohibition, and the Bundy children remembered the bootlegger coming regularly to the kitchen back door to sell his liquor. "Both Mother and Father drank in moderation through the years," said Bill Bundy. In Boston, obtaining liquor and drinking it socially was not a problem. But in Washington, one had to drink with a measure of official hypocrisy. "I was breaking it [Prohibition] all the time, secretly," Kay said. Their dinner parties were two-tier affairs; your "wet friends" would be invited a half hour before those officials who could not afford to be seen drinking. "Occasionally," Bill recalled, "we boys would help serve the drinks."[42]

Kay rather disapproved of Herbert Hoover, and not only because he had refused to drop his support for Prohibition. "Mr. Hoover was a great man with serious limitations," Kay said. Her husband may have been a Republican, but Kay was a Democrat, and sometimes even a socialist. In 1920 she voted for Eugene Debs. "I vote Democratic in national elections and Republican in state elections," she explained. "I can't vote for the Irish, I'm sorry. Crony, crony, crony."[43]

It was the depths of the depression, and the Bundy children remembered that poor people knocked on their back door, begging for food. "People were coming and asking for a handout of bread and milk at my house in Washington," Harvey Bundy, Sr., later recalled. "Nobody could get a job and everybody was going busted. . . . It was a terrifying time."[44] Kay had the cook make butter and bacon sandwiches to feed the panhandlers, and the children's nanny patched old clothes for the poor.

During the two years that Harvey and Kay lived in Washington, their three boys were already in boarding school. But the boys visited frequently and spent some part of the summers in Washington. They would visit their father in his office and then wander through the hallways of the State Department, then located in what is now known as the Old Executive Office Building, next door to the White House. "I think we got government service in our blood during these Washington visits," Bill Bundy recalled. "There wasn't much to do, so we often went up to Capitol Hill and watched the politicians perform. I remember seeing Huey Long, who was then considered the scourge of the Senate." [45]

For two years Harvey worked at Stimson's side, dealing with war debt renegotiations, the 1931 Manchurian crisis and a host of other foreign policy issues. "The whole financial house was falling around us," recalled Bundy. Stimson was constantly praising Bundy to his diary, underscoring what a "great comfort" it was to have a man like that with the initiative to do a "very good piece of work. . . ." But it was a frustrating period because however much the crises at home and abroad demanded action, President Hoover was disposed to do nothing. Late in 1930, Stimson confided to his diary that he had complained about "the President's peculiarities" to one of his old mentors, Elihu Root. "I told him that the President being a Quaker and an engineer did not understand the psychology of combat the way Mr. Root and I did." [46]

Hoover and Stimson also disagreed strongly over how to deal with the question of war debts. Stimson thought that given the depression it was foolish to demand payment from the Europeans; Hoover firmly believed the Europeans could and should pay their obligations. One day Stimson gave Bundy the task of convincing Hoover to give his approval to a refinancing of French debt. "If the President doesn't agree with me," Stimson warned, "he will have my resignation." Bundy met with Hoover in the Lincoln Study of the White House and, to his relief, the president gave his assent. Bundy thought of himself as a lawyer serving his client, and that often meant trying to restrain Stimson. "I was more of a confidant and advisor, and somewhat of a cautioning influence." [47]

If Hoover's instincts were isolationist, he was in all fairness also an internationalist, but of a different stripe than Stimson. The president, for instance, supported the idea of disarmament, and bedeviled Stimson with his proposal in June 1932 that global armaments be reduced by nearly one-third. Stimson favored an increased defense budget and thought Hoover's proposal a "proposition from Alice in Wonderland." The secretary of state did not believe the United States could rely on the League of Nations. The lesson he learned from the Manchurian crisis was that the United States could not "dispense with police force. And the only police force I have got to depend upon today is the American Navy." [48]

By election eve November 1932, there was little doubt that Franklin Roosevelt would soon be replacing Hoover in the White House. As the Bundy family sat around the radio, listening to the early results, Hattie remembered thinking that her father "still had a glimmer of hope that Hoover would be reelected, but we knew Daddy was going back to Boston regardless of the outcome." [49]

The night before Hoover left the White House, the Bundys were invited by the president to a last supper. At one point late in the evening Kay found herself sitting alone with Hoover in his Oval Office study, making small talk.

The following morning Kay and Harvey attended the inauguration of Franklin Roosevelt, and that afternoon Bundy handed in his resignation. In the evening he hosted a farewell dinner for Stimson. It was a relaxed, even jovial affair. Toward midnight Bundy stood up and toasted his boss, then everyone gathered around the piano and sang songs. Later that spring Kay packed up the house and moved the family back to Boston.[50]

Bundy's second stint as a public servant had been a frustrating experience. However much he admired the Great Engineer, he was not blind to Herbert Hoover's faults. The president was overly ponderous and often as dull as his chosen game of medicine ball. No one ever cracked a joke in a Hoover cabinet meeting. Temperamentally, Bundy admired Hoover's steady calm in the face of what had been two years of bitter disappointments. But contrasted with Stimson's often passionate arguments on behalf of more openly intervention-ist policies—whether it be answering Japanese aggression in Manchuria or intervening in the financial crisis—Bundy had to admit that the Hoover administration had failed to meet the challenges of the day. Years later, when Mac and Bill Bundy were discussing Arthur Schlesinger's new history, *Crisis of the Old Order*, their brother-in-law Don Belin argued that the Hoover administration couldn't have been as inept as Schlesinger painted it. "Father interrupted," Bill recalled, "and said, 'If anything, Schlesinger has painted too gentle a portrait.' "[51]

2

Groton:
A Very Expensive
Education

We few, we happy few, we band of brothers.

Henry V

In THE BLACK-AND-WHITE photograph, twelve-year-old
McGeorge Bundy stares coldly, defiantly, straight into the camera. It is a
startling portrait of a young boy wearing a mask of fear and conceit, intelligence and aloofness. The boy-child seems ever so young to be wearing such
adult emotions, just as his grown-up clothes hide the child within. The severe,
horn-rimmed glasses, the dark, three-piece suit and a tightly knotted tie
around a white starched collar make him look like a little boy playing the
stage role of a proper English schoolboy, dressed for Eton or Rugby. It is all so
British. But such was the attire of all the boys of Groton, an exclusive preparatory boarding school that by 1930 was quietly regarded by members of the
eastern seaboard establishment as *the* place to prepare their sons for Harvard
or Yale (and only rarely Princeton or Stanford) and then a career in one of the
Wall Street professions.

By the time Mac Bundy arrived at Groton in 1931, his brothers, Harvey
and Bill, were already part of the Groton family, ruled by an intimidating
patriarch, Dr. Endicott Peabody. This son of a merchant banker had spent five
years of his youth enrolled in the British public school of Cheltenham and
three years at Trinity College, Cambridge, an education which made him a
lifelong Anglophile. Soon after being ordained as an Episcopal minister, Peabody decided his mission in life was to bring to American youth the same
opportunities he had found at Cheltenham. In 1884 he founded Groton "to
cultivate manly, Christian character, having regard to moral and physical as
well as intellectual development."[1] It was no accident that Groton was built in

the same decade as the first publication of the *Social Register*, which one social historian has called "a convenient index of this new associational aristocracy."[2]

Forty-seven years later Peabody still presided over the small school, located on ninety acres thirty miles northwest of Boston. He had managed to keep the school's enrollment to fewer than 190 boys, 90 percent of whom came from families listed in the *Social Registers* of Boston and New York.[3] Modeled after Cheltenham, there were six forms—Peabody insisted on using the English word for classes—of about thirty boys each, running from ages twelve to eighteen.

In the first twenty years of the school's existence, Peabody had managed to collect the enormous sum of $700,000. A good portion of these funds came from John Pierpont Morgan, Sr., who had given Peabody's father, S. Endicott Peabody, a lucrative partnership in his investment banking firm. With access to such well-heeled financing, Endicott Peabody eventually built a schoolhouse, two dormitories, a gymnasium and faculty residences, all in classic red brick with white wooden columns. These buildings are spaced around a gracious commons simply called the circle.

Everywhere, the boys are reminded of their lineage. The schoolhouse contains one enormous room large enough for a desk for every boy in the school. Massive wooden beams hold up a vast cathedral ceiling, which gives the room an atmosphere of solidity and simple grandeur. Adorning the walls are wooden plaques listing the names of each graduating class in gold letters.

But the most striking feature of the campus is an exquisite Gothic chapel built of white stone blocks in 1900. Fourteen glittering, arched stained-glass windows—all constructed by English artists—line the walls, and eight magnificent chandeliers hang from the darkly lacquered wooden ceiling. The floor gleams with black-and-white marble squares, and off to the side of the altar is a floor-to-ceiling organ. An American flag stands adjacent to a pulpit sculptured in the form of a brass eagle, its wings pulled back, as if ready to take flight.

Known to his boys as The Rector, Peabody had an extraordinarily formidable personality. His bright blond hair had turned white by the time the Bundy brothers arrived at Groton, but his "terrifying blue eyes"—as Archie Roosevelt, class of 1936, called them—could still fix a boy with a gaze so steady as to be unnerving. "I think if we had ever been asked what God was like," recalled Marshall Green, a classmate of Bill Bundy's, "Peabody would have come to mind."[4]

His physical stature alone caused more than one first form Grotonian to cower in the shadows. Wearing a dark blue suit, with a starched collar and white bow tie, Peabody could be seen every day, striding about his campus, inspecting everyone and everything. He was a tall, broad-shouldered man, and the boys learned to brace themselves for his jovial and, he thought, gentle slap on the shoulder, which as often as not sent the uninitiated reeling from the blow.

When presiding in church or lecturing his boys, his penetrating voice fairly boomed. He spoke with the accent of a cultivated man; it was not a British accent, but then neither was it identifiably American. "His annual reading of the *Christmas Carol* by Dickens was just a tremendous experience," Bill Bundy remembered. "The whole school would crowd into his large study and listen to him read the story with great clarity and expression." His preaching, by contrast, was "undistinguished"—he never tired of saying that "obedience is one of the greatest of human virtues."[5]

And when he was angry, his reprimands so terrified his boys that they would remember these encounters for the rest of their lives. A classmate of Bill's, Louis Auchincloss—who became a great novelist of American manners —later wrote of Peabody, "when he reprimanded, he was simply terrifying, like God in a Blake watercolor." Averell Harriman (class of 1909) once told his father, "You know, he [Peabody] would be an awful bully if he weren't such a terrible Christian."[6]

Within two weeks of his arrival at Groton in 1930, Bill Bundy had the first of many vivid encounters with the Rector. He was standing in the school's student newspaper office when he accidentally dropped a rack of type. After loudly exclaiming, "Damn!" he quickly found himself ushered into Peabody's cavernous office. Cursing usually earned a boy six black marks, which meant endlessly walking around the great circle that formed the heart of the campus. But this time the Rector looked at Bundy with a hard glint in his eye and said, "Boy, did your mother and father teach you to use such language?" When Bundy mumbled, "No," Peabody paused, drawing out the drama of the moment, and said, "Don't do it again."

Only later did Bundy learn that Peabody had some years earlier visited the Bundy household: "He knew perfectly well," Bill recalled, "that my mother was capable of all sorts of language."[7]

Mac Bundy was himself "scared to death" those first few weeks at Groton but, he recalled, "probably less so than most boys because I had two elder brothers in the school. One didn't expect to be happy." Groton had its grim side. "Six years in a place like Groton," recalled Marshall Hornblower, a classmate of Bill's, "is a long siege."[8]

Each dormitory had about twenty-five boys, supervised by a bachelor master, as Peabody called his faculty. The boys had the barest of amenities, though they never had to make their own beds, do their laundry or wait on tables. These daily necessities were performed for them by dowdy maids and waitresses, chosen "not to arouse the lust of growing boys."[9] Girls were not seen, though not a few boys were smitten by the Rector's tall, blond and very lovely granddaughter Marietta, who occasionally came to see her grandfather.*

---

* Marietta Peabody Tree grew up to become a U.S. delegate to the United Nations during the 1960s. She was a notable figure in the liberal wing of the Democratic Party and the mother of Frances FitzGerald, the author of *Fire in the Lake*, a book critical of the American experience in Vietnam.

The boys slept in one large room partitioned by simple curtains around each bed. There was just enough space for a bed, a small bureau and a wooden, straight-back chair. No pictures were allowed on the walls, perhaps because the Rector suspected the arts in general bred self-indulgence, "gushiness" and "sentimentality." [10] The windows were kept open at night, even during the coldest of winters.

The day began with a loud wake-up bell at 6:55 A.M., followed by a compulsory cold shower. Breakfast was sharp at 7:30. Everyone—the boys and all the masters—ate in the dining room of Hundred House, the largest dormitory. The Rector and his wife presided at all meals, sitting at a raised head table. The boys were seated by form in assigned seats at long wooden tables. Every week each boy would move one place around the table, keeping the same companions on either side. This way there was a new face across the table each week. Breakfast was followed by morning chapel services. By 8:25 A.M. classes began. Throughout the day the deep clanging tone of the school-house bell told the boys when to eat, when to study and when to pray. At noon they broke for lunch in a common cafeteria. The food at both lunch and dinner could not be touched until the boys stood and Peabody said a prayer. (The words of the prayer never varied.) In the afternoon there were various seasonal team sports, followed by study halls and detention periods. At bed-time the Rector and Mrs. Peabody would again lead the school in evening prayers and then shake hands with each boy. As they filed by, dressed in starched Eton collars, blue suits and pumps, Peabody would occasionally single out a student and say, "I want to speak to you for a moment, my boy." [11] The subject might be a boy's academic performance, his rowdiness, a dirty collar or news from home.

Some boys thrived under the Rector's regimen, and some boys thought Groton a "nightmare," "an austere monastery, full of prayer and devoid of women." Louis Auchincloss later wrote in his memoirs, "Groton was like the salt that Keats is supposed to have rubbed on his tongue to intensify the delights of wine." [12] President Theodore Roosevelt's son Archibald was summarily expelled when the Rector, who routinely screened all the boys' mail, intercepted a postcard sent to another Groton boy in which Archibald had asked, "How is the old Christ Factory?" And the young Dean Acheson, an unrepentant nonconformist in the eyes of the Rector, escaped expulsion only because his mother managed to shame Peabody into taking him back. Franklin Roosevelt got by at Groton, but did so as a nonentity. He later confessed to a friend, "I always felt hopelessly out of things." Altogether, it sometimes seemed as if the school's most successful graduates were those boys who suffered most from the Rector's insistence on obedience and conformity. [13]

But the Bundys were not troublesome "mollycoddles," as Peabody called those boys who needed excessive attention. From the beginning both Bill and Mac conformed to the Rector's expectations, shining academically and taking an active role in Groton's community life. "I was awfully cocky my first year," Bill remembered. "Someone asked me how I thought I'd do the next year and

I said somewhere between 89 and 92. Well, I actually got a lower grade than 89, and they made a note of it in the yearbook."

Only recently had Peabody finally abolished hazing. Even so, younger boys were often roughed up. "There were bullies around," Bill recalled, "and it could be an intimidating place. . . . It helped that I had an older brother on campus. I never really had a confidence problem." [14]

Bill was nothing if not disciplined. He, Marshall Green and Marshall Hornblower always vied with each other for the top position in their class. Bill consistently received marks of 88, while Hornblower and Green were always right behind him. "I think Bill always deplored my relaxed way," recalled Green, "and that I took life much less seriously than he did." Bill was studious, but he also didn't have to be a grind. Assigned to the same study room, Hornblower remembered how annoyed he felt when Bill would finish his work in an hour and a half, and "I'd be stuck there for hours longer." [15]

Bill loved history and current events. At Groton he began reading *Time* magazine religiously and took part in a whirlwind of extracurricular activities. He became a member of the debating team, editor of the weekly school newspaper (which was printed by the students themselves) and secretary of his form.

Peabody's notions about "muscular Christianity" led him to raise his estimation of a boy if he was robustly athletic. Rigorous sports, he believed, was a "sacrament" that might distract an adolescent boy from sin. His mission was not to create intellectuals, but merely upstanding young men. "I am not sure," he once said, "I like boys to think too much." [16] His Episcopalian religious sensibilities were simpleminded. "He had a never-sleeping sense of imminent corruption," Auchincloss later wrote, "lurking in idleness, in tobacco, in alcohol, in loose women, and in something he darkly defined as 'sentimentality' which presumably embraced all forms of pederasty, physical or sublimated." [17] Peabody was fond of all sports, but especially football, precisely because it required the rugged physical courage that he thought built character in a boy. If a Grottie wasn't football-minded, he had a hard time winning the respect of his peers.

Lanky, bare-boned Bill Bundy had no chance of making the grade in such a game. "Bill had bad eyes and he just wasn't athletically inclined," remembered Hornblower. "But in his methodical manner he had decided that he was going to play goalie on the hockey team. He insisted on taking me down to the lake, where I would shoot pucks at him for hours on end. His legs would fly all over the place, but he was determined." [18] He may have been awkward, but he made the hockey team for four years. "He wanted to make himself an athlete," remembered another classmate. "Anything he did, he wanted to do terribly, terribly well. And he was very frustrated when he didn't do it well." And while he may not have been a first-string football player, he more than made up for it with his team spirit.

"Bill was much more intensely emotional than McGeorge," recalled Auchincloss. "Much more. When Bill goes out for something, he goes out almost too hard, you know."[19]

IN their first few years at Groton, Mac followed Bill, both academically and in his extracurricular activities. If Bill, however, was receiving grades in the high 80s, Mac would invariably score a couple of points higher. "Mac was consistently brighter than I," Bill said. "I was bright, but he was super-bright." "I was a clever little boy," Mac confirmed.

Like his brother, Mac was not an athlete. "I played in the backfield in football, and badly," Mac said. "I was terrible at football." But just as Bill found a place for himself on the hockey squad, Mac created a niche for himself on the tennis team, and like Bill, he wrote furiously for the school paper, but also became editor in chief of the monthly *Grotonian*. He was president of the drama society, active in the Missionary Society (a campus charity group), a member of the Civics Club and captain of the Groton Debating Team.[20]

Peabody required all the boys to take one hour of public speaking a week, so the competition for making the debating teams was fierce. Both Bill and Mac, however, not only excelled at debate, but also put on performances that were remembered years later. "The Bundys were perhaps the best debaters I ever had," recalled Richard K. Irons, a Groton history teacher (and a 1929 Rhodes scholar) who coached the teams.

Irons taught all the Bundy boys and was a singular influence on the development of their political outlook. "I was a semi-socialist," recalled Irons, in retirement after forty-two years of teaching at Groton. "I took Walter Lippmann at his word that FDR was a moderate country squire who wasn't likely to be a great president. But then, I was apt to take even more extreme positions precisely because so many of my students were such ardent Republicans." Irons encouraged his students to come to his study and argue politics. "You had to knock some sense into these boys and challenge their preconceptions," Irons said.[21] One of Bill Bundy's classmates, William McCormick Blair, Jr., argued with Irons all the time. "At Groton," recalled Blair, "I was such a Republican."[22] A nephew of Robert R. McCormick, the notoriously conservative publisher of the *Chicago Tribune*, Blair became Adlai Stevenson's campaign manager, an ambassador to the Philippines during the Johnson administration and a confirmed liberal.

Mac Bundy, too, recalled being a "good little Hoover Republican when I first went to Groton." But one could not be an adolescent in the 1930s and not be influenced by the upheavals of the New Deal. Bill remembered that he quickly drifted "leftward" toward the Democratic Party, even as his father complained that the New Deal was unfairly changing the rules. Mac recalled Roosevelt visiting Groton during the 1932 campaign and telling an assembly of Grotties what fun he was having on the campaign trail. When FDR came back again in 1934, Mac was the designated winner of the "FDR debating prize." "The prize," said Bundy, "was a copy of *Paradise Lost* by John Milton, and while I didn't get a chance to meet Roosevelt, I gave the book to one of his Secret Service men, who got the president to sign it. I still have it."[23]

Roosevelt's 1934 visit to Groton—on the occasion of the school's fiftieth anniversary—came at a time when most alumni considered the president a traitor to his class. Passions were running so high that Peabody felt compelled to send out a circular to the alumni warning them that they should not attend the festivities unless they were prepared to be civil to the nation's president.[24] Peabody, who had voted for Hoover in 1932, was now sufficiently enamored of his most famous graduate to vote for Roosevelt's reelection. He thought Roosevelt sincere, but disapproved of the New Deal's structural reforms. He was, nevertheless, concerned about the poor, and in the midst of the depression he encouraged his boys to participate in local charity works for the needy. If he was a bit of a "Christian socialist," then it was a socialism that borrowed from the political sensibilities of his old Cambridge instructor Charles Kingsley, "who ended up more interested in better sanitation than in economic or social reform."[25] Like Kingsley's, the Rector's interest in the poor ultimately came down to a concern for their mere cleanliness and morals. Naturally, this gap between his liberal Christian ideals and his conservative political stance did not escape the notice of his boys. "He was determined," one Grotonian later wrote in *Harper's*, "to be a liberal—if it killed him. And so, of course, he was not a liberal, he was only determined."[26]

Still, if the Rector's politics were touched with Puritan hypocrisy, he managed to convey to the boys his profound devotion to the principle of personal loyalty. One must never turn your back on family, friends, Groton —or particularly a president. He demonstrated this one evening in 1937 at a dinner held in his honor at the Union Club in New York City. Nearing his eighty-first birthday, he stood up and gave a warm and lighthearted talk about Groton and its place in the world. The assembled alumni listened and responded with applause until suddenly the Rector abruptly changed his tone:

> Something has troubled me a good deal lately. Personally I don't pretend to know much about politics or economics. [The audience here laughed politely.] But in national crises like the present one, we get pretty excited and perhaps give vent to expressions that later on we are sorry for. I believe Franklin Roosevelt to be a gallant and courageous gentleman. I am happy to count him as my friend."[27]

As George Biddle (class of 1904) recalled the incident, the stunned Grotonians sat in silence at this declaration of loyalty to the despised class traitor. These words took courage to speak, and his audience of Grotonians was perhaps stunned into silence as much by their admiration for the Rector's loyalty as by their distaste for Roosevelt.

By early 1935, young Mac Bundy—by now a fifth former—thought of himself as a socialist. He was reading *The New Republic* and *The Nation* in the school library, and late that year he wrote a "juvenile essay on socialism" which his teacher arranged to have read by a Groton trustee. "I remember,"

Mac said, "the word came back, 'This young man is a socialist.' As a result, I was given a two-volume edition of *Das Kapital*. I don't know anyone who has read it all, but I read a lot more of it than many of my late socialist friends."

Actually, in a letter to Scott Buchanan, the trustee who gave him the book, Mac claimed to have read the entire text. "I finished it yesterday," he wrote, "and although I found it as great as the authorities say it is, I am in some ways glad that our Karl did not complete his series. I have never read a book which required more intense concentration . . . the reading of the first chapter proceeded at the rate of about ten pages an hour."

Written in August 1935, this letter to Buchanan is delightfully revealing of Bundy's sixteen-year-old charms. On display are Bundy's gumption, arrogance and wit. He writes almost as if to an equal, though Buchanan is not only an elder but also a college president: "Having read *Kapital*, I can begin to sympathize with Marx's dislike (dislike is too weak a word, but I want to hide the passionate temperament which is almost Marx's only fault as a scientist) of those dabblers who, without any understanding whatever of the underlying laws of economy, take it upon themselves to explain anything and everything. . . . The more I think about it, the less I blame Marx for his passion. . . . It is high time that we had some more such works as *Kapital*." In passing he discusses the works of Harold Laski, Aldous Huxley, H. G. Wells and Archibald MacLeish, then confesses that though he considers himself an atheist, he is particularly struck by Huxley's social pacifism ("It's nothing more than the philosophy of Jesus, stripped of theological trimmings and put forward by an anthropologist, but it struck me as something new and very impressive").[28]

Mac's flirtation with Marx and Huxley was not taken very seriously by his father. "I was aware," Mac said, "that my father was busy not being intrusive when it came to his sons' opinions." Harvey wasn't worried, and indeed, by the end of the year Mac had published a short story in the school magazine in which a foolish businessman becomes a convert to socialism and ends by losing not only his wife, but his company as well, to the greed of his workers.

Mac's talents as a writer were cultivated by another Groton teacher, Malcolm Strachan, who taught English and had both Bundys reading writers like T. S. Eliot and Virginia Woolf. "He gave me a sense of the importance of thinking about words and how they go together," Mac recalled.[29] Strachan had spent five years in Cambridge, England, and like the Rector, he had steeped himself in everything English. But unlike the Rector, he was a man of no pretensions. He simply loved literature, and teaching for him was a matter of imparting to the boys his basic enthusiasm for the words. To the consternation of some, he often passed out copies of a piece of writing without the author's name attached. This forced the boys, sometimes to their bafflement, to discuss a work without knowing whether they were reading a Tennyson, an Eliot or the words of an unknown. He rarely bothered to grade his students; what counted was bringing life to the words.[30]

One year Strachan directed a production of Shakespeare's *Henry V* and selected Mac to play the leading role. "Mac only had to read the play once and then, like a computer, he gave it right back to you," remembered Auchincloss. "He did it very splendidly and emphasized the militaristic part very well. He played the king."[31]

Strachan later became an ordained minister and remained a good friend of the Bundys to the end of his life. Both Strachan and Irons—and other teachers like the future sculptor George W. Rickey and Louis Zahner, who taught English for forty years—were lively, demanding teachers. They had the Bundys reading twice as much literature and history as a sophomore at Harvard. When Bill ran out of history courses he received permission from the Rector to take a private tutorial on English history with another Groton master, Ronald Beasley. This elderly Englishman had Bill writing weekly papers of six to eight typed pages. A year later Mac did the same thing, electing to drop Latin in favor of an advanced course on European history.[32]

However coolly intelligent Bill seemed, Mac always displayed the sharper wit, together with that sometimes abrasive Lowell decisiveness and the jarring self-confidence of a Putnam. His ability to think on his feet was sometimes uncanny. When called upon to read a composition on the Duke of Marlborough, Mac promptly stood up and began reading what seemed to his teacher a perfectly well-written essay. But as he read, Mac's classmates began giggling at his performance, and only afterwards did the teacher ask a student what was so funny. "Didn't you know?" replied the student. "He was unprepared. He was reading from a blank piece of paper."[33]

Mac was a bit of the imp; unlike the more self-consciously serious Bill, he was the kind of Grottie who could get away with things without being labeled a slacker or a mollycoddle. "Bill was the Bundy who got along with everyone in his class," Stanley Resor recalled. "He always had the wider cross section of friends." Mac's friends, by contrast, were always more like him, boys who had a flair. "People liked Mac because he was so quick, but at times he was too quick." His classmates knew Mac was fun to be around, but they were also wary of his bite. "Mac was always the more glib of the two brothers," Marshall Hornblower remembered. "He was the sharp-tongued one."[34]

There were other differences. Mac may have been the family wit, but it was Bill who early on established a reputation for himself as a lady's man. "He loved the girls," said his sister Harriet. "So much so that I remember a local society hostess telling me that she made a point of sitting Bill at the dinner table away from the women, with men at his left and right." Bill was a "wonderful dancer," Harriet recalled, while Mac never danced and rarely went to parties as a teenager. Though there was only one occasion a year, on Washington's birthday, when girls from surrounding schools would be shipped in to Groton for a day or two, Mac never invited a girl to these dances. "I was shy," he admitted.[35]

During one summer vacation Mac and his brothers were taken by their mother to the Folies-Bergère in Paris. Kay Bundy turned this little adventure into a staple of Bundy family lore by recounting to friends how twelve-year-old Mac had "become terribly bored" by the spectacle of French burlesque. During the second act, when Kay realized Mac had disappeared, her frantic search for him ended when Mac was discovered outside the theater, sitting under a palm tree, reading a Rover Boys book.[36]

Girls must have been the only area in which Mac chose not to compete with his brother. "You couldn't have two boys as bright as all that without some rivalry," Stanley Resor recalled. "Whether Bill felt that Mac was pushing him, I don't know."[37] In some ways the competition between the two was too obvious. Solid, steady Bill was always leading the way, fulfilling the role his strong-willed mother had cast for him. Because Harvey, the eldest, had never excelled in school, Kay Bundy had pinned her ambitions on Bill, yet, there was Mac, right on his heels, and always excelling a little bit more a year or two later. "No mother would have to push Mac," Kay recalled. "He was a self-starter."[38] It was a pattern set early in life and never to be varied throughout their long careers. Bill was forever the bright, responsible boy, while Mac was the even brighter, charmingly aggressive brother.

BILL received 100 in his college entrance exam in English history and high marks in other subjects. Mac did even better, scoring 100s in math, history and English. His handling of the English exam, however, occasioned an unusual dispute among the teachers assigned to grade his work. The exam required a student to choose one of three topics and write an essay. "The three topics," Irons recalled, "were coeducation, school athletics and something else, I forget. Instead of choosing one topic, Mac wrote an essay on all three, criticizing the question and the topics as banal." He even suggested what kind of topics should have been offered. One of the three readers of the exam gave him a low mark for failing to follow instructions. But the other two readers threw out this penalty.[39]

Cheekiness had paid off. By the time Mac was seventeen years of age, he had spent six years at Groton perfecting a behavior that charmed adults by its sheer audacity. As a sixth former, he told Peabody that his beloved football program was "bad, that it was encouraging boys to lie and cheat."[40]

Mac used his editorship of *The Grotonian*, the school's monthly magazine, to write sassy editorials on everything from "the question of pacifism in an over-armed world"—he seemed to be against the disarmers and for the advocates of military preparedness—to the nature of snobbery at Groton. The latter issue arose when Henry Luce's *Fortune* magazine suggested that the typical private school graduate "pictures life as one long country-club piazza with a hot baby on the railing and a super-charged Mercedes at the other end." Mac defended Groton: "Groton is not snobbish; snobbery is of all things the last which can be called a part of Groton's teaching; the fact is that Groton has been betrayed by those of her graduates who have been more influenced by their home environment than by Groton."[41] The editorials extolled the virtues of open-mindedness, liberalness and rationality. Like Peabody, his first great mentor, Mac Bundy was determined to be a liberal, but he often ended up being only very determined.

PEABODY's influence on these young boys was altogether overbearing. He quite literally haunted their lives even after they left Groton, writing them postcards on their birthdays and otherwise congratulating or reprimanding them on the occasion of their successes or defeats. When they married, he expected to officiate, and when they had sons, he expected to teach them.[42]

The values and peculiar worldview of the Rector permeated generations of upper-class Americans who by no accident would become, in the words of Dean Acheson, "present at the creation" of the American Century. Many of these Peabody boys wielded considerable influence over public affairs, particularly in the field of foreign affairs. Of the fifteen hundred or so boys who passed through Groton during the Rector's time, there were one U.S. president, two secretaries of state, one national security adviser to the president, one deputy special assistant to the president for national security affairs, one secretary of the treasury, one secretary of the army, one secretary of the navy, seven assistant secretaries, seven ranking CIA officials, three U.S. senators, five U.S. congressmen, ten ambassadors, six generals and two admirals. Many more of Peabody's students went on to become lawyers, bankers or businessmen on Wall Street, quietly building the modern law factories and corporations of twentieth-century America.[43]

The large number of Groton boys populating the foreign policy establishment may in part be naturally attributed to their class backgrounds. "The Rector was always preaching that we were children of privilege," recalled Marshall Hornblower, "and therefore we should aim for a career in public service." This theme was reflected by the school's motto, emblazoned on a coat of arms with a sword, a crown and three open-faced books: "To serve is to rule." But while Peabody preached a sense of noblesse oblige, what he meant, first and foremost, was a career in service of the church. "To the church first, to the nation second," recalled Richard Irons. "Of course, half the boys went into banking."[44]

Indeed, Groton may have given the boys so much religion that they became inoculated against the church.* The entire Anglophilic atmosphere created by Peabody tended to reinforce the boys' natural class prejudices— which in turn led them to choose the professions of their fathers. Groton certainly bred a brand of *Social Register* conformity. "Independence, in almost any form, was punished," Joe Alsop writes. The school "taught us a certain arrogance of manner," recalled Marshall Green. "A conceit. And in the end, a

---

* Nathan Pusey, who as president of Harvard was Mac Bundy's boss, explained Bundy's aversion to churchgoing by saying, "Groton boys got so much of church at Groton that afterwards they felt they needn't ever go again."

lack of identification with people of other races. Indeed, we were not only brought up to feel a sense of public duty, but also a sense of our own superiority. And all of us learned later in life that we should have learned some humility. We should have paid more attention to the needs of less privileged peoples and Groton should have taught us more about other peoples, in Asia and Africa."[45]

If the Groton experience for the Bundy brothers was undoubtedly formative, it was also a bundle of decidedly mixed blessings. Like the Rector himself —whom George Biddle once called "a somewhat great man, whom I find incompatible with my own conception of the adequate"—Groton provided an admirable education. Peabody imparted to them such lifelong values as a firm sense of personal loyalty, a certain Christian liberalism and a dedication to public service. But the Groton education also contained the seeds of intellectual inadequacy, a myopia to anything outside the Anglophile world and a certain distasteful arrogance that settled around the shoulders of its young men. This marriage of intellectual self-assurance and condescension toward other cultures was ill-fated. Indeed, Groton gave the Bundys—and the establishment they were to serve—a very expensive education.

3

Yale:
The "Great Blue Mother"

> We are taught at an early age to salute the flag, to be
> patriotic, and to believe a lot of lies.
>
> McGeorge Bundy, 1940

FROM GROTON, the Bundy brothers were ordained for
Yale. They did not bother to apply to another college. "In those days," explained Mac, "if your father was an alumnus and you had a warm body, you really didn't have to worry about not getting admitted."[1] But before heading for the Old Eli in New Haven, Connecticut, Bill was given a special graduation present: a cruise ship tour of the Mediterranean. In late June 1935, he and Groton classmates Marshall Green and Louis Auchincloss boarded a small, 9,000-ton freighter—the SS *Exochorda*—in Jersey City and shipped out for the French Riviera. By day, the boys swam, played shuffleboard or Ping-Pong, and by night dined on eight-course dinners and danced. One evening, after viewing the film *Klondike*, Green scribbled in his diary, "Bill was going in great form, and made audible running comments all through the talkie film. He had everybody quite in stitches. . . .[2]

Upon docking in Marseilles, they transferred to the *Prins Olav*, an exquisite two-funneled Norwegian yacht formerly owned by King Edward VII. Bill and Marshall bunked in the servants' quarters. For the next three and a half weeks they and a number of other young Americans sailed to Corsica, Tunis, Malta, Crete, Rhodes, the Dardanelles, Constantinople, Troy, Corfu and various other spots in Greece. It was billed the "Odyssey Cruise."

At eighteen years of age Bill was finally losing his adolescent gawkiness and had turned into a rather handsome young man. Green wrote in his diary that summer that Bill "looked the same old shot, perhaps a bit worse for the wear with a pineapple haircut which accentuated his six foot, three inch height." He looked very much like his father at the same age: a finely chiseled face with prominent cheekbones, a long, sharply defined nose and small gray-blue eyes. Like all the Bundy boys, he wore glasses most of the time, and invariably dressed in a well-tailored, if rumpled, suit and tie.[3]

By his own recollection, this summer cruise afforded Bill his first real opportunity to socialize with women and engage in the kind of carousing that was forbidden at Groton. The boys danced and bantered with the young women on ship, and tried, as Green noted in his diary, to convince them that "all Grotties were not alike." One evening in the ship's bar, someone wagered Bill that he couldn't drink four large planters' punches—swimming in rum— and then recite all the monarchs of England, together with the dates of their reigns. Bill accepted the wager, downed the rum, named all the kings down to the current reign of George V and then promptly collapsed on the floor. Later he leaned out over the ship's railing and retched what he had drunk.[4]

"All in all it was a wonderful trip," Bill recalled, "a time of socializing." The cruise was operated by an American couple who hired a number of youngish Oxford dons to lecture the travelers each night after dinner on what they would see ashore the next morning. "In Athens," Bill said, "we had the whole Parthenon one night to ourselves. There was a full moon and I just wanted to sit there and take in the scene in complete silence. When my companion, Antoinette Perry [the actress after whom the Tony Awards were to be named], started chatting about how lovely it was, I told her to 'shush up.' "

Most of their sightseeing focused on the artifacts of the ancient Greek and Roman Empires. But in Italy they also received a taste of the current political scene: "We could not help but feel the oppressive atmosphere," Bill recalled. "Mussolini was at the height of his powers and one night we got into a near row with some Italians who thought we had made improper comments about their leader."[5]

Bill would remember it as a most idyllic summer, a Groton boy's coming out into a world of Turkish antiquities, Adriatic sunsets and innocent flirtations. Some nights he stayed up until three in the morning, playing bridge, dancing and drinking Greek ouzo. Passing through the Strait of Otranto, the gateway to the Adriatic Sea, he and his companions sat on deck mesmerized by the "most remarkable of all" sunsets. "The setting sun behind the billowy, grotesquely-shaped clouds cast a glory in all directions," Green jotted in his diary. "The shores of the Albanian coast were streaked with waterfalls. The surf was dashing high on one of the bleakest coasts the Mediterranean has to offer."[6]

When the time came to go home, Bill and Marshall met up with the rest of the Bundy clan aboard another ocean liner, the SS *President Garfield*, bound for New York. Marshall recalled that when a group of Egyptian students on the ship asked them the difference between Republicans and Democrats, sixteen-year-old Mac Bundy answered, "We Republicans believe in family and property and all those reactionary things." They also believed in a Yale education, the "great Blue Mother," as Mac would later call it.[7] That autumn Bill enrolled at Yale, to be followed a year later by Mac. The country was in the midst of its longest and deepest economic depression.

THE autumn of 1935 was also the autumn of the reign of James Rowland Angell. Inaugurated in 1921, this good-humored, former professor of psychology was the first Yale president not to be an alumnus, and he immediately took the university in a new direction. Where his predecessors had generally thought of their tasks in terms Endicott Peabody would have approved—to educate gentlemen, not scholars—Angell announced that he intended to make Yale a haven for intellectual scholarship: ". . . where the great investigators and scholars are gathered, thither will come the intellectual elite from all the world."

Fourteen years later, by the time Bill Bundy arrived, his father, Harvey, class of 1909, would not have recognized the campus. Angell had built eight new residential quadrangles, a massive new library and twenty-six other new buildings. A college for rich boys had become a richly endowed university boasting a completely refurbished medical school, a law school and other graduate facilities that really did attract the intellectual elite of the Western world. The number of faculty had increased by over 60 percent, and the university endowment had spiraled from $25 million to $93 million. As one historian of the university put it, "Yale was largely rebuilt under Angell. He found it in brownstone, and he left it in granite."[8]

A campus looking like a pristine piece of Oxford or Cambridge had suddenly materialized in the midst of Connecticut. Gothic spires adorned every building, and narrow English archways and high garden walls kept the campus turned inward, intimate and isolated from the town outside. By 1935, nine residential colleges, all built in the form of quadrangles, were open. Each was ruled by its own master, and each came equipped with its own dining room, library and meeting rooms. Whereas previously students identified themselves by class, now they would see themselves as a member of a particular college. Only the freshmen were initially kept together, all eating in the freshman dining hall. As sophomores they chose one of the residential colleges, where they lived and dined every day with students from the two higher classes and also with their master and various members of the faculty. White linen tablecloths, silver and china "added an indefinable distinction to an atmosphere that seemed to one observer midway between that of an Oxford hall and an American club."[9]

Bill embraced Yale life in a way that he never had with Groton. "I had not realized how much I had been oppressed by the atmosphere at Groton," he recalled. Nearly 75 percent of the boys came from similar upper-class backgrounds and large numbers came from preparatory schools like Groton, Andover and Hotchkiss. But the residential college system and the fact that the freshmen all ate together tended to break up these cliques. "I took to going over to the Freshman Commons," Bill recalled, "and sitting at whatever table was open. You met lots of new people that way."[10]

Though they remained friends, Bill and Marshall Green drifted apart. Bill gravitated toward a group of boys who included Robert Taft, a future senator; William Scranton, a future governor; Cyrus Vance, the future secretary of state, and Gaspard d'Andelot "Don" Belin, Jr., a pleasant young man who would become his brother-in-law.

Bill made the freshman soccer team and, somewhat to his surprise, won the post of goalie on the hockey team. He was elected chairman of the Freshman Forum, and he joined numerous campus clubs and committees, including The Pundits, the drama club, the Political Union and the debating society, where his debating coach was Walt Rostow. As his class yearbook noted, "There were committees to join, and Bill Bundy joined all of them." [11] All this, and he still managed to excel in his class work. He became engrossed by a course on the French Revolution, taught by Sherman Kent, a charismatic lecturer who fifteen years later would be Bill's immediate superior at the Central Intelligence Agency.

"By the end of my freshman year," Bill recalled, "I had broken the ice in a lot of ways." In the spring, he heeled at the *Yale Daily News*, together with Don Belin, Stan Resor and Bill Scranton. Under the chairmanship of Jonathan B. Bingham (the future congressman), the *News* that year shocked the alumni by expounding a pro–New Deal editorial line. Bill was drawn to the excitement of daily journalism. "Learning to write like a journalist wasn't terribly difficult," he said. "I remember spending hours talking with the wonderful guys who ran the presses."

That summer Bill and three of his classmates, Resor, William Blair and William Roth, drove out west in a Buick convertible. Resor had invited them to visit his parents' ranch at Jackson Hole, Wyoming. Along the way, the boys stopped off in Cleveland to attend the Republican convention. "Somehow," recalled Bill, "we got official badges as sergeants of arms that allowed us into the convention. We were all from Republican families and we all ended up life as Democrats. It was a totally dispirited occasion, as the Republican Party was readying itself to be trounced. . . . I left the convention feeling no great affection for the Republicans."

When they got to Wyoming, Bill was awed by the beauty of the Resors' Snake River Ranch, nestled alongside a rushing river and surrounded by the Grand Tetons. He and his friends spent the rest of the summer riding horses up into the mountains, branding cattle, piling hay and repairing the fences on the Resors' sizable ranch. "It was rough work in the outdoors all day and I really felt fit," Bundy recalled.[12] In the evenings Bundy had friendly arguments about the New Deal with Resor's father, who was head of the J. Walter Thompson advertising agency. "I recall to my shame," Bundy later wrote Stan Resor, "giving a thoroughly sophomoric speech on how the advertising business was the root of all evil. . . ." At the end of this "glorious summer" the boys competed in a couple of events in the local rodeo, then headed back to Yale.[13]

Bundy had already known Stan Resor for six years at Groton, but it was this trip to Wyoming that cemented their lifelong friendship. At Yale, Bundy suggested to him that they room together. Bill had chosen Jonathan Edwards, the residential college known as the "hot-house of brighties."[14] The smallest and most intimate of the colleges, its master, Robert D. French, also happened to be an old family friend. Bill and Stan each had a bedroom and shared a small sitting room. A maid kept the place tidy. Because Stan's mother was a trustee of the Museum of Modern Art in New York, the boys had paintings on loan from the museum to decorate their rooms. Bill had a drawing by Salvador Dali in his room.

"Bill was a big man on campus," recalled Resor, who sometimes felt he was riding Bundy's coattails during his years at Yale. Resor was welcomed into such esoteric clubs as the Pundits Club and the Elizabethan Club, organizations "for which," he later wrote, "I had no apparent qualification, except being Bill Bundy's roommate."

"I remember him," Resor said, "sitting in this big armchair in our room, balancing a typewriter on his lap, while he effortlessly banged out a thoughtful editorial for the Yale Daily News."[15]

Bundy seemed to have time for everything. "I was something of an activities-aholic," he said. "I did too much."[16] But Yale rewarded those who did too much, particularly if they did it effortlessly. The novelist John Leggett described the social atmosphere at Yale during the 1930s in this way: "Yale was a goldfish bowl in which we fluked about, earnestly unfurling our aspirations. The telling marks on a man were his prep school, his dress and what he did with his leisure. Grace, detachment, not seeming to care and, above all, being with acceptable companions—these were prized."[17]

Bill had all of these qualities—and later, so too did his younger brother. Mac had arrived on campus with instant fame: at the freshman convocation, the dean of students announced that their class was distinguished to have the first Yale student to achieve three perfect scores on his college entrance exams.

"People immediately identified Mac as the guy in the class," recalled Gordon Grayson, who became his best friend. Like his brothers coming from Groton, Mac thought Yale was "great fun." "There were movies, poker games and just taking in people." Mac also lived in Jonathan Edwards College, on a floor below Bill. But they didn't mix much, even though Mac followed his brother on the debating team, the Yale Daily News, the Pundits Club and the Elizabethan Club. Later, Mac began contributing pieces to the monthly Yale Literary Magazine, whose editors described him in the class history as "sly of wit and with a wicked gleam in his eyes. He came to us in the guise of a book reviewer but turned out to be much more lethal."

Academically, he was ranked even better than Bill, though he hardly studied. "Study was an on again, off again affair," Mac recalled. "When you were writing a paper, it could be very intense. But in general, it wasn't very hard work. In fact, much of it was a terrible waste of time." Though he still loved history, he decided to major in mathematics.

Mac was dubbed Mahatma Bundy by the class prankster, partly because he was such a Boston Brahmin, and partly because he was constantly speaking out on the issues of the day. His class history wryly noted, "This week passed without Mahatma Bundy making a speech."[18]

In Yale's caste system, it was inevitably the well-bred boy who already had a wide acquaintanceship with his fellow prep school mates who would be chosen for membership in the hierarchy of clubs, fraternities and extracurricular activities that defined campus life. The Elizabethan Club, which accepted both Bill and Mac as members, was one such exclusive watering hole, where Elis drank tea with various faculty and discussed art criticism and literature. Like other campus organizations, the Lizzie existed to set its membership apart. Jews were not banned, but it was the rare Jew who was ever invited to join.*

There was no secret to the formula for social success. A boy's dress, his ability to sit down and take tea with the master of his college, and the ease with which he threw himself into such activities as the *Yale Daily News* signified to all that this was a boy marked to be set apart from others. For years the local clothier, Rosie the Tailor, demonstrated a discerning eye for these telltale characteristics by accurately predicting who would be chosen on Tap Day for one of the elite secret societies. There were three important senior societies—Wolf's Head, Scroll and Key, and Skull and Bones—and altogether they honored no more than 15 percent of each class.[19]

Of all the social networks at Yale, Bonesmen were thought to be the elite of the elite, chosen for their achievements. Invariably, the most important men on campus were tapped: the football captain, the chairman of the *News*, the chairman of the annual Budget Drive. "Bonesmen were selected for their demonstrated worldly success," recalled Richard Bissell, class of 1932. "And I rather disapproved of that. Most of the people I knew were happy that I turned them down." Bissell was the rare exception. Selection by Skull and Bones may have been a reward for extracurricular achievements, but it also was a virtual passport to even greater worldly rewards. If influence can be measured in numbers, this particular secret society has had a spectacular record. At Yale itself, self-perpetuation was the rule. From the 1860s through the early 1920s, all of the university secretaries and 80 percent of the faculty were Bonesmen.[20] Outside Yale, Bonesmen can boast a couple of U.S. presidents (William H. Taft and George Bush), and dozens of notable figures from the world of politics and business.†

---

* Eugene and Walt Rostow were both Lizzies, but Richard Ellmann, a classmate of Bill Bundy's, was rejected. Ellmann later became a literary critic and biographer of James Joyce.
† Notable Bonesmen include Secretary of State Henry L. Stimson, Governor Averell Harriman, Assistant Secretary of War Robert Lovett, Henry Luce, Archibald MacLeish, Senator Robert A. Taft, Percy Rockefeller, Governor Gifford Pinchot, Justice Potter Stewart, J. Richardson Dilworth, William F. Buckley, Jr. (and his son Christopher T.

Bill Bundy—the ultimate big man on campus—was an obvious candidate for Tap Day. He was confident of being tapped by the society of his choice, Skull and Bones. He knew members were "selected on the basis of merit and civic performance." And given his record, "I didn't bite my nails in suspense." [21] So on the second Thursday of May 1938, he joined a couple hundred of his fellow juniors on the grass courtyard of Branford College. Also milling about were hundreds of spectators, come to see who would be chosen and who rejected. As the Battell Chapel clock struck five, senior members of the various societies, dressed in black ties and blue suits, bolted from doorways facing onto the court and strode rapidly through the throng of white-faced, nervous young men. Bill was first approached by a representative from Scroll and Key and soundly struck on the back. But he turned and firmly shook his head, signifying a rejection. Next came a senior Bonesman. Again Bill was tapped solidly in the small of his back and told, "Go to your room." This time Bill wheeled about and walked to his room, with the Bonesman right on his heels. In private, the formal invitation was made and accepted.

Even as Bill was participating in this honorific ritual, his younger brother was using the pulpit of the *Yale Daily News* to denigrate the secret societies. Mac had refused to heel for the paper (he said it took too much time), but Bill (as vice chairman) and Don Belin (as chairman) had nevertheless offered him the rare privilege of writing a column. Just a week before Tap Day, Mac wrote of the secret societies that "their secrecy is ridiculous, and they do turn too often merely to 'the boys.' As a result, they help to set a warped standard of college success; they ignore many a man of real mark, selecting many others of dubious quality." He went on to say that "both their Tap Day and their black magic are openly and justly mocked."

In the same editorial, and in a second piece written the day before Bill's Tap Day, Mac pointed out that prominent critics of the society have nevertheless often become members themselves. Is this, he asked, a betrayal of their views? Well, not really. After all, "to be tapped for Skull and Bones is still an honor at which no man need sneer." The selection process may be corrupt and Tap Day itself may be unnecessarily brutal and humiliating, but "such honors still have meaning; this may be irrational, but it is true."

Mac started out attacking the elite societies, but he ended with a call for higher standards. The societies should reward scholarship and select "eminent men only when they are justly eminent." In other words, if Skull and Bones was becoming "justly mocked," it was because standards had slipped. [22]

A year later, when Mac was faced with the decision of whether to participate in Tap Day, he was torn. In the end, he followed Bill into Skull and Bones only because "it became clear to me that it would be a blow to my father if I didn't join. He believed then in the institution as I do now. But at the time a

---

Buckley), the Reverend William Sloane Coffin, Jr., Ambassador Winston Lord, Senator John H. Chafee, Senator John Kerry and Senator David Boren.

big part of me was ambivalent. If my father hadn't been a member of Skull and Bones, I am sure I would not have joined."[23] Some were astonished that Mac had relented. Marshall Green scribbled a line down from a Tennyson poem, "Just for the price of gold," and pinned it on Mac's door. "Some of us," explained Green, "had founded a little club called the Donkey's Ear, the sole purpose of which was to disparage the secret societies. At one event, fourteen of us dressed up all in black and carried a coffin around. This was clearly not Bill's cup of tea, but Robert French, the master of Jonathan Edwards, thought it terribly funny."[24] Three of Mac's classmates refused Bones, and in the spring of 1940, when it was his turn to do the tapping, an unheard-of number— nine men—including one of his best friends, Kingman Brewster (the future president of Yale), rejected a tap from Skull and Bones.

Skull and Bones had been founded in 1832 by a group of disgruntled Phi Beta Kappa members. William H. Russell, valedictorian in the class of 1833, persuaded fourteen other Elis to found a rival, but secret society. Russell later endowed Skull and Bones with a considerable fortune, managed by the Russell Trust Association. By 1856, an intimidating, windowless granite crypt had been built to accommodate the society's enigmatic activities.[25]

Aside from the camaraderie, Bonesmen were entitled to certain material privileges. The clubhouse and its dining facilities were one thing, but the Russell Trust also owned a summer house on Deer Island, a rustic retreat in the Thousand Islands region of upstate New York. The Russell Trust also reportedly had a special fund from which any Bonesman could withdraw up to $15,000 in a lifetime for any purpose.[26]

Some of what we know about Bones traditions have the ring of authenticity, and some things seem to have been purposely embellished. As an anonymous Bonesman told the *New York Times,* "The myths surrounding the society are far more interesting than the actuality. So one likes to keep them afloat."[27] Rumor has it that the tomb contains the skull of the Mexican revolutionary Pancho Villa, who was assassinated in 1923 and whose grave was desecrated in 1926 by persons unknown. If not Pancho Villa, then we are told —not by Bonesmen, of course—that the tomb contains the skull of the Apache chief Geronimo, and that this particular artifact was obtained by Prescott S. Bush, who later became a U.S. senator and the father of President George Bush.[28] Initiates supposedly wrestle naked in the mud and later recount their sexual histories while lying naked in a coffin. Whatever the case, all Bonesmen agree that behind the padlocked door of the tomb, lifelong bonds are cultivated. The Bones ethos is a means to an end; without the cloak of secrecy, Bonesmen seem to be saying, one cannot fathom the nature of human friendship.

For the Bundy brothers, Skull and Bones was always some kind of touchstone; it taught these future keepers of national secrets a code of absolute discretion. But they valued it as a door to simple human friendship. "It was a very intense experience," Bill recalled. "It stretched you. You had to think for yourself and you learned a lot about human beings and the different qualities of men. It became a lot of fun. It was an important part of my life."[29]

Mac felt the same way. "It was and is an important part of my life," he said. "It does focus around the intense experience of learning to trust your colleagues. In our case, it was fifteen white, Anglo-Saxon Protestants.* Even today we meet irregularly as a group and individually. It is a remarkable institution."[30]

Skull and Bones was not a political vehicle except in the narrowest sociological terms. It was simply a club of like-minded and usually privileged young men who made a point of keeping in touch with each other. As an anonymous Bonesman told the *New York Times*, "Members are supposed to be selected on the basis of being the best and brightest, so there's a natural affinity to do business together. There's a certain trust, a certain comfort level, they develop in the club." Mac denied it was ever "a vehicle for influence peddling."[31] Far from becoming public figures—or even powerful men behind the public stage —his fellow Bonesmen had respectable but unremarkable careers in business, law or one of the other professions. In this sense, the criticisms Mac leveled at the secret societies before he joined one himself still rang true long afterwards. Far from being a broadening experience, Skull and Bones merely reinforced the paradigms of the Bundy brothers' Boston Brahmin upbringing. "It was not a level board," Bill Bundy said later. "I was certainly conscious of it, but not as much as I should have been. The social structure was loaded." He remembered meeting Jews, for instance, at the Political Union or at the *Yale Daily News*. "But in the fraternities, the ethos of the boarding schools tended to prevail."[32]

For Mac in particular, who had a more abrasive personality than his elder brother, Skull and Bones probably wore off some of his rough edges. Or as Gordon Grayson later explained, "This precocious boy made true friends for the first time in Bones."[33]

If Skull and Bones was where the Bundys explored their interiors, the Political Union was where they staked out their positions on the great issues of the day. Bill served first as secretary and then chairman of the Political Union, while Mac was its secretary and then leader of the Liberal Party. "Even as a sophomore," said one classmate, "Mac had a coherent worldview."[34]

By 1938, Mac recalled, "I was a New Dealer, a leader of the Liberal Party on campus and it was our duty to defend the New Deal." Politics at Yale was a serious vocation, conducted through the campus Political Union, which was in turn divided into three factions: the Labor Party, the Liberal Party and the Conservative Party. Though the Liberals dominated the Political Union, this was no reflection of Yale in general, since fully 75 percent of all Yale under-

---

* In the spring of 1991, Bonesmen decided to defy tradition and their elders by tapping some women for the first time. In the ensuing furor Bill became a proponent of admitting women, and persuaded Mac and other alumni to ratify the decision.

graduates favored Alfred Landon in the 1936 election.[35] Those who were politically active at Yale, however, tended to be Liberal. In the context of the 1930s, this particular liberalism was cerebral, rational and nonideological—in other words, it was the haven of centrists.

Despite the depression Yale in these years was, as Kingman Brewster later wrote, "pleasantly fat and essentially untroubled." True, the depression had "broken the promise of self-perpetuating privilege," Brewster wrote. "In personal terms, this meant that very few could bank on success by inheritance. More fundamental, the assumptions, values and goals of our fathers' time were up for rejustification."[36] But most students nevertheless tried to avoid grappling with these facts.

Not the Bundys. Bill, in his unsigned editorials, and Mac, in his twice-weekly column, remonstrated against complacency. "Compete, freshmen," Mac wrote in one sarcastic column, "compete, meet the right people; compete and get on the inside; compete and win. As for your education, forget it; you probably didn't come here for a higher education anyway." In another column, he had the audacity to call for the abolition of Yale football. Commenting on a survey of Princeton seniors which registered an overwhelming optimism, Mac warned, "they are living in a false world, shrouded in the mists of their own confusion."

In their writings in the *Yale Daily News* and in speeches before the Political Union, both brothers were adept as they picked their way through the political minefields of the 1930s to position themselves in what Arthur Schlesinger, Jr., later described as the "vital center." They defended the Wagner Act and the rights of organized labor, but attacked *The New Republic* and *The Nation* as representative of the "blind and angry left." Mac skewered the American Legion as "composed largely of the same class of people as those who brought Hitler to power—the penny-proud, ignorant petit bourgeois folk who detest the left-wing labor movement, fearing to see their prized (and largely imagined) 'social superiority' vanish in something vague called communism." But lest he be seen as too left-wing, Mac was always careful to weigh in against demagoguery of any stripe. "Collectively, the lower classes are potentially destructive," he wrote in the autumn of 1938, "(so, of course, is any overly self-conscious class). . . ." As liberals, the Bundys scorned class politics. And as liberals, they supported civil liberties, academic freedom, and "religious and racial tolerance."[37] In walking this fine line, the brothers set themselves apart from most of their peers.

To begin with, most Elis were apolitical. Those who had strong opinions were either rabidly anti-Roosevelt or had cast their lot with one of the left-wing factions on campus. There were very few communists; more Elis identified themselves as socialists.

William Kunstler, class of 1941, was leader of the left-wing Labor Party when he met Bill Bundy. "I admired him," Kunstler recalled. "He seemed to personify the ideal Yale student."[38]

Walt Rostow, who would later work with Mac in the Kennedy and Johnson administrations, first met the younger Bundy while studying Keynesian economics under Richard Bissell. The son of a Russian immigrant, Rostow had received one of Yale's eight scholarships given to New Haven's public high school, and in the late 1930s, Rostow was considerably to the left of most of his contemporaries. Though not a member of the Communist Party, Rostow was recommending to his classmates books like *The Coming Struggle for Power* that presented an orthodox communist worldview. "As economists, we thought the New Deal was rather sloppy," Rostow said.[39]

David Dellinger, who would later become a leader of the protest movement against the Vietnam War, came to the left out of philosophical and moral convictions. Dellinger got to know Mac Bundy in his senior year at Yale, and as a Yale counselor from 1937 to 1939. "I thought him likable," Dellinger writes in his memoirs, "but sharper and quicker than he was reflective or deeply exploratory. Unlike Rostow, he did not consider himself a 'revolutionary,' but like Rostow his emphasis seemed to be on being a chess master, brilliantly moving the pieces (human beings) around and always being one of those in charge. . . .[40]

Students like Dellinger, Kunstler and Rostow cared passionately about their politics. And by comparison, they perceived the reasoned, cautious liberalism of the Bundys as antiseptic. Bill and Mac were smart, witty and fun to be around, but not committed. They prided themselves on being nonideological.

But there was an exception, one cause in which they were moved by instinct and therefore felt compelled to write about with passion: war and peace in Europe. In this they stood against the *Yale Daily News*'s editorial line, which was loosely isolationist. Far from being fervent followers of the America First line emanating from Charles Lindbergh in Chicago, most undergraduates simply thought nonintervention was the best policy for Europe and America. As Kingman Brewster, a leader of the isolationist camp on campus, explained, "isolationism at Yale was not of the inland variety." Instead, Brewster argued that the "disastrous" undertow of World War I suggested to many people that German hegemony in Europe was the best of the worst. Mac's own roommate, Gordon Grayson, asked, "Why should we be involved? I was a pro-British pacifist. That was the atmosphere around campus, except for a very few politically active students like Mac."[41]

Bill's conversion to interventionism came in the autumn of 1938. In competition for the class oratory prize, he had selected as his topic, "What is an Individual's Obligation in the Event of War?" "My first draft," he recalled later, "was teeter-tottering on the pacifist line. And then Kristallnacht came. After reading about those events, I changed the speech to say that there was only one answer: you had to fight."[42]

By this time, both brothers had experienced Hitler's Germany firsthand: Bill spent ten days in the summer of 1937 in Berlin and Munich, and Mac followed him in the summer of 1938, using the Bundy family station wagon to drive all over Europe in the company of several other Yale students. While in Germany they tracked down the Jewish mother of a Yale classmate who had been denied permission to emigrate. At her urging, they took possession of her small fortune of hidden diamonds and smuggled them back to America. Not long afterwards, their classmate was able to buy his mother's way out of Germany.[43]

Just days after the September 29, 1938, Munich agreement whereby the British acceded to Hitler's occupation of the Sudetenland, Mac used his column to express his profound disapproval of appeasement. The war scare was over, he wrote, but "war would have been better than what we have now. . . . Over and over again in the last few weeks I have heard my friends say that they wish the English and French and Russians would smash Hitler now. I have said it myself. And while we who said it were painfully surprised by our own belligerence, our sentiments were quite sober and sincere."[44] For this generation, Munich would become one of those unchallengeable paradigms, the historical analogy of what not to do in the face of aggression. It would be a lesson the Bundys learned well, and even too well.

EVEN after war finally came to Europe in September 1939, the debate in America between isolationists and interventionists would remain unsettled until Pearl Harbor. And long before that event, all the Bundys believed they were already at war. In his senior year Bill began taking a correspondence course in cryptology from the army Signal Corps. (He persuaded Bill Kunstler to join him.)[45] After graduating with honors in June 1939, and given his certainty that war would be coming to America, Bill decided not to travel to Oxford for postgraduate studies in European history, as he had intended. He decided it would be best to stay closer to home. History was and always would be his first love, so that autumn he moved to Cambridge and enrolled in a masters history program. (His elder brother, Harvey, Jr., was also at Harvard that year, finishing his masters in business administration. Harvey, Jr., later served for five years in the army and then went on to a career in business.)

At Harvard, Bill studied under William Langer, a crusty, temperamental professor of diplomatic history who spoke with a thick South Boston twang that betrayed his Dorchester working-class origins. "A fabulous speaker," Bill recalled, "he would often end his lectures to a standing ovation. But he was also a relentless interrogator. If you survived the Langer treatment, you felt you had passed muster." In just a few years Langer would become Bundy's boss in America's first peacetime intelligence agency. But at Cambridge, he was Bill's intellectual mentor, stimulating his interest in the history of European foreign relations. At the end of the academic year, however, bowing to his father's wishes, Bill applied to Harvard Law School and was admitted for the fall session.

That summer he worked in Washington under Archibald MacLeish, who had been appointed the librarian of Congress. An old family friend, MacLeish was becoming a mentor to both Bundy brothers. Through similar family connections, Bill found a room in a bachelor's house, known as the Hockley estate, that then served the same social-political purpose for his generation as the House of Truth had for his father's time. Bill's housemates included Bill Sheldon, John Ferguson, John Oakes (a future *New York Times* editor and liberal columnist), and two bright and gregarious New Deal lawyers, Adrian Fisher and Edward Pritchard. Philip Graham (the future publisher of the *Washington Post*) had just left to marry Katharine Meyer (the daughter of the newspaper's owner, Eugene Meyer), but he still occasionally came by for a drink. "To be with this crowd for the summer," Bill said, "and take in their conversation was quite an experience. These young guys were already part of the Frankfurter-Acheson circle. I shared a bathroom with Ed Pritchard. He was the kind of man who had his best ideas during his morning constitution, and he did not hesitate to share them with you." [46]

Something else happened of a personal nature during that summer in Washington. Throughout his childhood Bill had occasionally socialized with the Dean Acheson family. While at Yale, he had sometimes run into the Achesons at hockey games; Bill had even carried on an informal correspondence with Acheson. [47] The veteran lawyer, for his part, was quite taken by Bill Bundy. In any event, Acheson called Bill one day that summer and invited him to spend a weekend at the Acheson Harewood farm in Maryland, located eighteen miles north of Washington. Because it was convenient, Acheson asked Bill to swing by his law office on the way to the farm and pick up his daughter Mary. "I was immediately struck by Mary," Bill recalled. "She was just pushing sixteen and I remember making a mental note to myself to keep an eye on her. She was lively, outgoing and very nice looking. Sprightly in every way. Well, I could describe her with just one word, 'unique.' " Mary Acheson was indeed a beautiful and lively young teenager. Like her father, she had a sharp tongue and a roguish sense of humor. She would often remind people who knew both the Bundys and the Achesons of Kay Bundy: a smart, emotional and sometimes sassy woman. Bill was quite smitten.

In the autumn of 1940, as the Battle of Britain hung in doubt, Bill returned to Harvard to study the law. "The first year," Bill said, "was a shakedown, a fixed course of classes. It was a pleasant year, but I was increasingly preoccupied by the war news. For that reason, I barely squeaked by to make it on the law review." Bill was still an interventionist, and together with Charlie Porter, a classmate and future congressman, he led a campus organization with the ringing name of Fight for Freedom. They were a marked minority in the student body. "Our rallies were always controversial affairs," Bill said. When confronted with a throng of hecklers at one such rally, William Yandell Elliott, a Harvard professor and an ardent interventionist, dismissed their concerns with the wave of a hand and the words, "War is no more dangerous than crossing Harvard Square." [48]

Mac finished his studies at Yale and graduated in June 1940. During his senior year he had written a thirty-page essay on the looming question of war. The essay was published that year by a major New York firm in a collection of essays entitled *Zero Hour: A Summons to the Free.*[49] (The book includes contributions from the poet Stephen Vincent Benét, the journalist William L. White and the historian Walter Millis.) Mac's essay is an argument on behalf of intervention against European fascism.

He makes it clear that "we are in the war already; the question that remains is how to fight." It was not hard to see, he writes, "that every part of our lives is going to be affected. Already we can feel the changes coming. Friends of mine who never worked in their lives are training for the army and navy reserves. Girls who by their own admission were not made for physical exertion are scrubbing floors and shaking thermometers as they painfully acquire the elements of nursing. My family, which had not for years seen anything in short pants or pigtails, has made room for a couple of very small subjects of King George.

"There is nothing funny, any more, about Adolf Hitler," he continues. "Let me then put my whole position in a sentence. I believe in the dignity of the individual, in government by law, in respect for the truth, and in a good God; these beliefs are worth my life, and more; they are not shared by Adolf Hitler, and he will not permit them to me unless he has to; I therefore believe that my efforts, and those of the countrymen with whom I share my beliefs, must be energetically given to their defense. . . . It was a long sentence, and even now the picture is incomplete." War, he writes, is evil, but "it is occasionally the lesser of two evils."

Having staked out his position, Bundy then goes on to explain why he found himself in the minority. Why were so many of his peers skeptics? His answer is to recall "somewhat painfully" the first American history book he read in grammar school. The text made all of America's history "a series of triumphant victories," from the Revolution all the way down through the years to when America went off to war in 1917 to "make the world safe for democracy, and to take our rank as the richest, wisest, bravest, kindest, strongest and most civilized of nations on the earth."

America was indeed a great and astonishing country, but it was also a country, Bundy says, with "imperfections" in its past. "We are taught at an early age to salute the flag, to be patriotic, and to believe a lot of lies. It is therefore not surprising that when our eyes are opened, we react rather strongly against the innocent credulity of our childhood.

"I remember wondering a little, when I first studied American history, at my mother's lack of interest in the Daughters of the American Revolution, to membership in which her ancestry entitles her; it seemed to me that she was rather cold and unpatriotic about it all. As I learned more, I understood better; I forgave my mother. . . ."*

---

* Kay Bundy, in fact, had resigned her membership in the DAR because they had the gall to ask her to verify her ancestry.

As they studied the history of America's intervention in World War I and the collapse of Wilsonian ideals in the postwar peace, boys of Bundy's generation had every reason to become skeptical of an intervention in another European war. "When one's first steps in patriotism turn out to be misguided," Bundy suggests, "it is only natural that one should become a skeptic."

By labeling his isolationist opponents skeptics, Mac was claiming for himself the reasonable center. To be sure, there was plenty of "propaganda" used by all sides, but the reality was the threat of fascism. "As for civil liberties and the Bill of Rights," he writes, "they must not be suspended under any circumstances. It is one thing to be firm towards fifth columnists and quite another to suspend the ordinary rights of ordinary Americans. I myself do not include members of the Communist Party or the German-American Bund in the category of ordinary Americans; it seems to me perfectly evident that both groups are essentially owned and controlled by unscrupulous foreign governments."

Foreshadowing the position taken by many liberal anti-communists during the McCarthy era, Bundy concludes, "this is a vexed issue, largely because so many people cannot see the difference between a Communist and other types of Leftists, but the facts of Communist action and thought speak clearly for themselves. . . . Even in these cases, however, we must proceed by law and with restraint . . . it is our business to distinguish carefully between traitors and people we don't like." Civil liberties were for all Americans, except those who joined the Communist Party or the German-American Bund.

Coming of age at twenty-one, Mac already possessed a full-blown political worldview. He was a pragmatic liberal, an early anti-fascist but also an early anti-communist liberal. On domestic issues, he was staking his ground in the vital center; he would be a liberal Republican. On foreign policy issues, he was a premature advocate of a pax Americana, a benevolent free-market empire that would replace the world order represented by the worn-out British Empire by opening trade doors around the world to U.S. business interests, promoting democracy and ending colonialism.

UPON graduating, Mac was uncertain about what to do with himself. He had a major in mathematics, but he knew he didn't want to be a mathematician. "I was good at it, but not great, and I remember exactly the moment when I discovered this fact. I was a senior and met a man named Andy Gleason. He could do logarithms in his head."[50] And though he had taken the trouble to get himself admitted to Harvard Law School, he felt certain the war would interrupt such studies. Earlier in the year, on advice from Archie MacLeish, he had turned down a job offer from Ted Weeks at The Atlantic magazine to work as an editor.[51]

Finally, by way of postponing any such career decision, he and one of his Skull and Bones comrades, Gordon Grayson, decided to take time off and travel throughout South America. "We wanted something fun and different to do before the army got us," Grayson said. But instead of just being tourists, the two friends persuaded the State Department to let them work as volunteers on a project to disseminate books on American culture and literature through U.S. embassies in Latin America. (The idea may have come to them from MacLeish, to whom Mac wrote, "We are going as Americans and Hitler-haters; we want to be as useful as possible in both categories.") Altogether, they spent ten months traveling through Mexico, Colombia, Peru, Chile, Argentina and Brazil. Mac learned passable Spanish, though he was annoyed when the locals said he spoke it with a German accent. On a tight budget, they stayed in third-class hotels and traveled steerage. "Mac was an easy person to travel with," Grayson recalled. "He has both intellectual and worldly interests. He loved to take in the local scene. Unfortunately, he had a horrendous sense of direction. He was so absentminded, he'd walk out the door and invariably walk in the wrong direction." [52]

Upon their return in August 1941, Mac accepted a rare invitation to become a junior fellow at Harvard. This elite Harvard institution, modeled after Oxford's All Souls Society, had been founded in 1933 by his great-uncle A. Lawrence Lowell, who used $1.5 million of his estate to endow the society. Six to eight junior fellows—"the ablest men from an able field"—were selected each year for three-year terms. Each fellow received a personal stipend of $1,500 plus free room, board and books. Fellows usually lived in Lowell House near Harvard Square and met twice a week for lunch and once for dinner. They were free to choose a project and study it in their own fashion. There were no exams, papers to write or obligations of any kind. According to the society's oath, they were supposed to "practice the virtues, and avoid the snares, of the scholar." [53]

Their special status gave them unusual access to virtually any of the faculty; in principle, they could invite to their regular Monday-night dinner table the most interesting men in Cambridge. T. S. Eliot joined them one evening, and Vladimir Nabokov came to dine ten years before *Lolita* made him famous. Theoretically, such a mini-cauldron of intellectual fermentation could be beneficial to the university, broadening the faculty's interests and serving as a disruptive force against mediocrity. Yet, the society could also descend to the petty. Some fellows would later regard it as "a cruelly self-confident group of undeniably talented men who paraded their knowledge of wines and other esoteric things after the stag manner of a British common room. . . ." [54]

Fellows were selected in a candidly subjective fashion; typically, a candidate would be told, "There is no one in this room competent to examine you. The purpose is for us to get acquainted, and the best way to do that is to talk. So talk." [55] Mac Bundy was not at a loss for words. He told Henry Lee Shattuck, the senior fellow who interviewed him, that he was interested in exploring the "theory and practice of politics." Politics was a topic certain to interest Shattuck. As treasurer of the Harvard Corporation since 1929, Shattuck was one of the most powerful and respected men in Boston. In addition, he occupied the only safe Republican seat on the Boston City Council, representing the well-heeled Back Bay–South End district. He also just happened to be an old family friend.

Needless to say, Mac was selected as a junior fellow.* (It probably didn't hurt that another old family friend, Archie MacLeish, had promoted Bundy's candidacy.)[56] Shattuck quickly became yet another of a long line of older men who would serve him as a mentor, role model and friend. A lifelong bachelor, Shattuck was everyone's idea of the proper Boston Yankee. As Harvard's treasurer during the worst years of the depression, Shattuck saved much of the university's stock portfolio by prudently withdrawing from the market before the big crash. Like Mac's father, Shattuck was a money manager for Boston society families, but compared to the Bundys, he was enormously rich. He was an odd combination—a practical man of finance yet also an intellectual who collected post-impressionist paintings. When his bachelor's club at Dover, Massachusetts, was going broke, Shattuck bought the place as his private retreat and frequently invited junior fellows out to take long walks in the woods with him. "He was excellent company," recalled one junior fellow. "He was always reading all kinds of things, a fascinating fellow." The Harvard philosopher Alfred North Whitehead, who had helped Lowell plan the Society of Junior Fellows, still frequented the fellows' dinner table. At one such gathering, he remarked in his funny, high-pitched voice, "I have lived with academic and intellectual men all my life, and they are not very sensible. Now that man [pointing to Shattuck] is very sensible."[57]

Soon after Bundy's selection as a junior fellow, Shattuck phoned with a request. "He asked me to his office and then suggested that I run for his city council seat," Bundy recalled. The assumption was that if the senior Republican ward leaders tapped Bundy for the seat, then the voters would elect him.

"I was twenty-two years old, reading Plato and running for the Boston City Council," Bundy remembered with a laugh. His first and only experience with electoral politics ended in an upset defeat. "Well, to my surprise, I lost," Bundy said. "I went door-to-door campaigning, but not nearly enough. I also didn't spend enough on the campaign. There was a local newsletter that wanted me to take out advertising. I thought it was a shakedown and so refused to buy any ads. Of course, that didn't make them happy." The experience cured Bundy of any appetite for electoral politics. "It would, in any case," he recalled, "have been a very odd thing to have spent the war on the Boston City Council."[58]

---

* Other alumni of the Society of Fellows include Arthur Schlesinger, Jr., Noam Chomsky, Daniel Ellsberg, Carl Kaysen, Cord Meyer, Ray Cline and James Tobin.

4

The War Years, 1941–1945

We went for a walk in the gardens one day and the subject of my impending transfer to the Pacific came up. Father told me, "We have this new weapon coming into use that will end the war. You probably won't have to go to Japan." Father was in the know.

WILLIAM P. BUNDY

B<small>Y THE SPRING OF</small> 1941, the war in Europe was a daily concern to all the Bundys. In April, Harvey Bundy moved to Washington to serve as special assistant to Secretary of War Henry L. Stimson. Harvey had turned down Stimson's earlier request that he join him the previous summer, saying, "I don't really want to, Mr. Stimson, I don't want to start again, because I have to make a living for my family." But after the fall of France, when the "phony war" became what Kay Bundy called "a perfectly awful war," Stimson called again: "I need a special assistant, just to stay with me, Harvey, all the time. All the time. I've decided the other boys [Assistant Secretaries Robert Lovett and John J. McCloy] are great and doing a wonderful job, but I need help and you're the only person who can do it."[1]

At seventy-four Stimson was both physically energetic and always tired. His daily regimen of long afternoon horseback rides and regular naps usually kept his depressive temperament in check. Still, he was always ailing and worrying. And since he had been hired by Franklin Roosevelt to run the War Department as if the United States was already at war, he indeed had many legitimate worries.

Harvey Bundy was the perfect foil for such a man. With his innate reserve, Bundy served as a ballast in the war secretary's office. He was the man who could tell Stimson "no." "He might give you hell for disagreeing with him," Bundy recalled, "and then the next day he'd call you up on the telephone and apologize." Bundy's cautiousness sometimes so infuriated Stimson that he would call his old friend, in jest, "a lily-livered coward." But for the next five years Stimson would refer to him as "my closest personal assistant." And in this capacity Bundy would serve, as his son Mac later wrote, "as [Stimson's] filter for all sorts of men and problems," including such closely guarded war secrets as the Manhattan Project, the development of radar and the management of intercept intelligence.[2]

Intercept intelligence, also known as signal intelligence, shortly became a Bundy family vocation. While Harvey sat in the War Department reading the highly classified final product, his wife and sons soon became involved in the arcane business of cryptology, toiling away at deciphering the radio codes of various foreign powers. Oddly enough, the first Bundy to become a cryptologist was Kay. In 1941, at the age of fifty-one, with all five of her children off on their own, Kay thought she ought to get a job. By happenstance, an old friend and neighbor, Lydia Chapin Kirk, the wife of Admiral Alan Kirk, had also moved to Washington and was organizing a group of wives to volunteer their time for the navy. Years earlier Kay had chaperoned Lydia's dates with Kirk. At Lydia's urging, Kay agreed to take a course with the U.S. Navy on open codes, meaning she was taught how to discern whether there was a hidden message in plain-text letters or telegrams sent abroad. "I smoked like a chimney," Kay recalled, "and I got absolutely absorbed in code-breaking."

Kay worked initially for Naval Intelligence out of Arlington Hall, and later switched to code-breaking for the army. The work required a quick, analytical mind capable of picking out suspicious-looking cables and passing them on to the Federal Bureau of Investigation. Kay made light of it, but the work could save lives; on one occasion, she identified a United Fruit acquaintance in Honduras who was carelessly sending cables that allowed German submarines to track and sink American freighters. She and Lydia were good enough at it that they were later decorated with a silver medal emblazoned with the words "Silence Means Victory." Kay thought this highly amusing, "considering we were the two most garrulous women in the United States."[3]

Meanwhile, two of her sons, Bill and Mac, were both employed for a short time in the newly created Office of Facts and Figures, a skeleton intelligence and propaganda agency housed in the Library of Congress and run by Archie MacLeish. At the end of the summer of 1941, Bill Bundy, having finished his first year at Harvard Law School, received his "presidential greetings" from Roosevelt and was drafted into the army. After one eighteen-hour stretch of KP duty—which "sure felt like a week"—and ten days of basic training, Bill was given the standard army aptitude test. His scores were so high that he was selected for the army's Signal Intelligence Corps. Harvey Bundy had suggested to Bill that he apply to the Signal Corps's school at Fort Monmouth, New Jersey. "But I can honestly say," Bill recalled, "I don't know if my assignment was arranged with a word from my father. It could have been, but I don't know. . . . I did the basic crypt course that fall, and we were just about ready to do some field exercises when Pearl Harbor hit." Over the next year, Bill underwent further cryptology training and emerged from officer candidate school as a first lieutenant.

In the autumn of 1942, while honing his talents as a cryptologist, Bill was quietly courting Dean Acheson's daughter Mary. The attraction he had felt for her in the summer of 1940 had been nurtured by occasional dates in the summers of 1941 and 1942. Now, he began to pursue her in earnest. Mary was by then studying art at Sarah Lawrence College, a private liberal arts school for women located outside New York City. Bill was twenty-five and determined not to lose his chance of a life with Mary simply because of the war. "I'd take the train up Saturday, arrive in the evening, and we'd just have Sunday together before I'd have to get back on the train again. By December we were engaged. She was eighteen. Our parents were quite taken aback, but we had achieved a tactical surprise."[4]

The couple surprised everyone by announcing their engagement on December 5, 1942, at a party for Kay Bundy's fifty-second birthday. Dean Acheson was startled, to say the least, by the news. In contrast to Mac, whose youthful arrogance annoyed Acheson, Bill had always seemed the most pleasant and gracious of Harvey Bundy's boys. But Mary was so young, and the war was so certain to disrupt their lives, that Acheson firmly tried to discourage the event. "I explained most lucidly to Mary . . . that they should wait until the end of the war to get married. So they got married at once. All in all, the father of the bride is a pitiable creature. . . . His only comforter is a bottle of good bourbon."[5] These words were written (to Harry Truman) in 1956, when the passing years allowed him to view the marriage with some detachment. At the time, according to one family friend, "Acheson felt that Bill was a child picking a child bride from the Acheson household." So in the beginning Acheson sometimes treated his new son-in-law with disdain; on one occasion he entertained guests by making barbed comments about Mary's paintings, criticizing those oil landscapes that were "post-Bill" in contrast to those she had painted "pre-Bill." Acheson's attitude toward Bill would change; indeed, with time his affection and respect for him grew markedly.[6]

Only a month after announcing their engagement, Bill was informed by the army that he would be shipping out for an undisclosed foreign posting in a matter of months. He and Mary quickly decided to be married on January 30, 1943. "Everything was done on the spur of the moment," Bill recalled. "Mary wore her sister's dress." They were married in St. John's Church in Georgetown in a ceremony marked by what the Boston Globe called "wartime simplicity." Only relatives and close friends attended, but these included such notables as Henry Stimson, Robert Lovett, John J. McCloy, Richard Bissell and Felix Frankfurter. McCloy hosted the wedding luncheon. "I read somewhere," Bill later complained, "that it was described as the social event of the year. Ridiculous. I suppose I can see how some might see it, a secretary of war, two assistant secretaries, a Supreme Court justice. But these were our family friends. No one was there by virtue of their public position."

Afterwards, Bill and Mary quickly bought and moved into a Georgetown brownstone on Thirty-third Street. "It was tiny," Bill said, "just ten and a half feet wide. We lived there for a few months before I shipped out and Mary went back to live with her parents. We sold the house after the war."[7]

Even at eighteen Mary was an opinionated young woman, but she also had the reflective temperament of an artist. Bill's persistence had led her to an early marriage, which in turn ended her college studies. When Bill left for London in August 1943, she got a job, like her mother-in-law, at Arlington Hall, deciphering Japanese army materials. There she was befriended by Zeph Stewart, another Yale graduate and family friend of the Bundys', who was also working as a cryptologist. For a time in 1943–44, Stewart boarded in the Acheson home, and in these circumstances he and Mary became close friends. "Mary was not as opinionated nor as managerial as Kay Bundy," Stewart recalled. "Kay was so intimidating, so dominant and overbearing. Mary, on the other hand, was a gentle butterfly, so ethereal in nature. She and Kay were as distinct as night and day. Perhaps they did have the same sense of humor, but whereas Mary had a soft tone, Kay could be so blunt and sharp-tongued."[8]

In many ways, Bill and Mary were themselves opposites, in temperament and interests. Bill was always serious, while Mary could be engagingly whimsical. She loved a good party and the company of people who laughed a lot. Wartime separations would not make it any easier for this couple to put their marriage on an even keel.

Even in these first few months of married life, Bill was absorbed in his work. Before going abroad, he grappled with a cryptology problem which decades later happened to be popularized by Ken Follett in a best-selling novel, *The Key to Rebecca*. "A hostile nation—which I should not name—was using a cipher based on pages from a book which the FBI knew had been checked out of the Library of Congress. My job was to use the same book, interpret the key and break this particular code. I and a very able colleague were successful."[9]

After this exploit Bundy and a few other officers were summoned to a rare briefing, which amounted to a ritualistic baptism into that narrow circle of men party to the war's most closely guarded secret. "A small group of us at Monmouth," Bill recalled, "were one day called into a soundproof room and briefed on Yellow, which was our code word for Enigma. By that time, I had already worked on Purple, the Japanese code. We were told, 'No one will leave this room a free man. You will never talk about this to anybody who isn't cleared, and you will never hereafter go anywhere where you can be captured.' This was a damn important secret, a secret for life."[10] The young Bonesman had been tapped a second time.

SHORTLY afterwards Bundy was selected to be the commanding officer of a token American contingent of cryptologists who were to work with the British at their highly secret decoding facility at Bletchley Park, England. Harvey

Bundy had been negotiating for months with the British to decide how the two allies would share their respective intercept intelligence. It had finally been agreed that the Americans would have primary responsibility for the Japanese material (code-named Purple) and the British would take the lead on the German ciphers (code-named Ultra). Now that this division of responsibilities had been settled upon, the Americans would be allowed to send a small team of their own cryptologists to monitor the British take of German intercepts. It was this team which Harvey's son was now to lead over to Britain.

Lieutenant William P. Bundy had been teaching cryptology for some time now, so when he was told, "You get the pick of the litter," he already knew who were the best students: "I went over the list and picked a hell of a good team." He named nine officers and ten enlisted men. Among the officers were seven cryptologists (including Bundy) and two translators. These men came from a variety of backgrounds, none as Bostonian as Bundy's. Second Lieutenant Arthur J. Levenson came from a lower-middle-class Jewish family in Brooklyn and had graduated from City College. "I'd never met anyone like Bill Bundy," Levenson recalled. "He was smart, and I had thought only Jews were smart. So he was a surprise." [11]

They sailed in early August 1943 aboard the USS *Aquitania*, landed in the Scottish port of Greenock and made their way to London. After three weeks they were dispatched to Bletchley Park, a once-sumptuous Victorian estate located on fifty-five acres of land forty-six miles north of London. Bundy was the only one of his team who had been fully briefed on their mission. After being picked up at a dreary railroad junction, Bundy and his men were driven to the gates of Bletchley Park, where their papers were carefully checked by armed guards. They then drove inside the park, past a grassy oval, a duck pond and a "ghastly" old Tudor Gothic, oak-paneled manor house, which was itself surrounded by dozens of ugly, low-slung prefabricated wooden huts and concrete bunkers.[12] This was the headquarters of England's "looking-glass war" of deception and interception against the Germans. Soon, more than six thousand clerks and a thousand boffins—cryptologists—were overflowing the grounds of Bletchley Park.

Bundy's team was taken into a newly constructed brick building with several wings, each running about sixty feet. There, the Americans were split up, the translators escorted to the right wing of the building, known as Hut Three, while Bundy and his fellow cryptologists were taken to the left wing, known as Hut Six. Inside Hut Six, they were introduced to its chief, Gordon Welchman, thirty-three, a ruddy-faced Englishman who was rather nervous about these Americans. The British had agreed to their presence, but they were not entirely sure if these Americans would have the necessary talents, and worse, they dreaded the possibility that some of them might be so unsuitable as to require them to be shipped home. It took one of the Americans, Lieutenant Bill Bijur, a blunt-speaking advertising man from Manhattan, to break the ice. As Welchman began a rather stiff welcoming speech, Bijur interrupted to ask, "Do you mind if we smoke?" He then pulled out the largest cigar the Englishman had ever seen and lit it with a flourish. Amused, Welchman promptly dispensed with his speech and began to talk informally. "From there on," he recalled, "the party was easy. . . . They simply wanted to know what they could do to help. They were such a damn good group of people. . . . Their leader [Bundy] joined our management group and before long he became a major contributor to the key-breaking activities of the Hut Six watch." [13]

It helped enormously that the British quickly saw that the Americans were well prepared. "They had no idea who we were," Bundy recalled. Unfortunately, the U.S. Army had lost their test scores. "We had to take the tests all over again," Arthur Levenson recalled. "To work on signals intelligence you had to have a score of 125 or higher. When the scores came back this time, I remember a British officer saying, 'My God, what scores.' Bill scored 160 out of 161." [14]

Bundy quickly became one of five rotating "heads-of-watch" in Hut Six, responsible for ensuring the quick decoding of intercepts, which were then placed onto a conveyor belt and trundled off to Hut Three, where they were translated and then analyzed by a team of intelligence officers. Bundy's counterpart in Hut Three was a bright young lawyer named Telford Taylor, who later became a war crimes prosecutor at Nuremberg, and—much later—a prominent critic of the Vietnam War.* British or American, the men assigned to Bletchley were all bright and well educated. And they knew it. "The Ultra community at BP [Bletchley Park]," wrote a British veteran, "saw itself as— perhaps was—an elite within an elite." [15] The entire British prewar chess team, including Stuart Milner-Barry, who was then ranked number one in the country, was part of its group.

Bundy ran his command in a most informal manner: "There never was a more complete meritocracy than Hut 6," he recalled. [16] He assigned men by their ability, even putting lieutenants and captains in positions where they reported to better qualified sergeants and corporals. What mattered was a man's ability to quickly and accurately break the daily code.

Bletchley already had an Enigma machine smuggled from Poland. Looking something like a portable typewriter, the Enigma was used by the Germans to encode their wireless messages. But each German service had its own ciphers, and those ciphers were changed on each Enigma machine on a daily basis. In order to read the German intercepts, Bletchley's men had to look for

* All sorts of extraordinary people were drawn into Bletchley's circle: Alfred Friendly later became editor of the *Washington Post;* Langdon van Norden became a prominent businessman and chairman of the Metropolitan Opera Association; Lewis Powell was to become a Supreme Court justice; Alan Turing, the eccentric British mathematician, helped create the modern computer and later committed suicide; Ian Fleming later wrote the James Bond spy thrillers; Roy Jenkins became a prominent member of Parliament.

what they called cribs—a string of letters which formed a familiar pattern, such as a known phrase, title or geographic name—which then allowed them to break the cipher for the day. Often, a routine weather report would provide enough of a crib to achieve success. Bundy remembered one sixteen-letter message—*Lage unveraendert* ("situation unchanged")—that was an "absolute giveaway." Spotting these cribs was the first step; the second was to then run the crib through a simple mechanical computer called a bombe that would test what settings on the Enigma could produce a message with that result.

Each morning the first order of business in Hut Six was to break the Luftwaffe cipher, nicknamed Red. This cipher was used by every German air force unit on every front, and from May 1940 through the end of the war, the men at Bletchley broke this code, usually before breakfast. But since the Germans used some forty different keys each day, there was always plenty of work for those in Hut Six. The intelligence produced on a daily basis, in terms of the volume of messages intercepted, translated and forwarded to Allied commanders, was astounding. In the calendar year 1944, for instance, some 44,000 such messages were thought important enough to forward to commanders in the field.[17]

To process this volume of intercepts, everyone rotated on three eight-hour shifts; each watch consisted of a dozen men sitting around wooden tables in a cold and damp room, reading reams of intercepts. As head of the watch, Bundy paced around the table, "like a hockey coach," recalled Levenson, "walking up and down behind his players," intervening with his own hunches when one man would get stuck on a particularly difficult code. "The watch had the job of putting, figuring out what was worth trying on the machines [the bombes]—which cribs you would use, how much priority you would give them, which was the likelihood of your having the right answer versus the importance of breaking that particular key, that particular network on that day. . . . The machines would then say this setting [on Enigma] would do it. . . . Those would be tested and, if you got it right, bing, the watch would spring up and this austere British voice would say, 'Wallflower is up.' " * [18]

Levenson thought Bundy was "usually pretty much of a genius." Another American cryptologist, Louis Smadbeck, later concluded, "Technically, Bundy was probably the best mind we had over there." He was also popular. "He was a superb commanding officer," Smadbeck said.[19]

By the winter of 1943–44, Bundy's unit—the 6813th Signal Service Detachment—had grown to forty-five professionals, plus another twenty-five enlisted men who served as drivers, cooks and clerks. They settled into Little Brickhill, a former girls school located three miles from Bletchley. Life then began to slip into a routine. For security reasons, once posted to Bletchley Park, no one was ever permitted to transfer out for the duration of the war. Bundy tried to turn Little Brickhill into a home—or at least a cozy college

* "Wallflower" was Bletchley Park's designation for a particular German key.

fraternity. "We probably had by all odds the finest library of any American outfit any size anywhere in the world," Bundy later wrote. He abolished the officers' mess and decreed that officers and enlisted men would eat together. The food was excellent because of two "magnificent cooks" from Worcester, Massachusetts, and Philadelphia.[20] He allowed his men to dress casually unless military brass were visiting. When off duty, his men could read, or play volleyball or tennis. Invariably, in the evenings, there was a bridge or poker game. Over at Bletchley itself, there was a small auditorium where movies were shown in the evenings and in which frequent dances were held. The atmosphere was positively donnish. "On a superficial glance," wrote Malcolm Muggeridge, the British journalist and intelligence officer who spent some time at Bletchley, "it might have been taken to be a Fabian summer-school."[21]

Few of these men were chosen for their military comportment. Alfred Friendly later observed, "Some of the Bletchleyites were, it must be confessed, a queer lot." Alan Turing rode around the English countryside on a bicycle wearing a gas mask, on the theory that this would protect him from the pollen that affected his hay fever. Josh Cooper, another British mathematician, was on one occasion seen walking out of Bletchley's gates, absentmindedly holding his hat in his hand and wearing an open briefcase atop his head. "It was a bad place," Friendly later wrote, "in which to play chess for money." At lunchtime, one could sometimes see men sitting blindfolded, and from the nature of the conversation it was clear they were playing three-dimensional ticktacktoe.[22]

The British military establishment tolerated such curiously unconventional men precisely because of the enormous contributions they were making to winning the war. Despite the rigid secrecy these boffins knew they were making a difference. "We rarely had a chance to read a whole message," Bundy recalled. "Everything was compartmentalized. But every now and then you'd get an inkling that something important had been discovered." Morale was always high. "[Bletchley] was the one place in the military," Friendly wrote, "where there was no sense of futility, of useless work or of nonsense."[23] By the time Bundy arrived, Bletchley could already take credit for having broken the German submarine codes, which probably turned the tide in the deadly battle for control of the Atlantic. Likewise, Hut Six could claim a fair measure of credit for the successful Allied campaign to push Field Marshal Erwin Rommel out of North Africa, starting with the critical Battle of El Alamein. And between September 1943—when the Americans arrived to share in Ultra —and June 1944, Bletchley was preparing to play a critical role in D day.

"We had no real warning of D day," Bundy recalled, "but everyone knew it was coming. As it happened, a big dance was scheduled for the night of June 5 at Bletchley. The people in charge decided not to cancel it as that might have tipped someone off. It was a very fine party. The vermouth in our martinis was replaced with sherry, but they were good. That night, after the party, I went directly on the midnight shift. I remember being surprised to see Stuart Milner-Barry—the chief of Hut Six—there in the hut. He would occasionally drop by, but it was unusual for him to show up on the midnight shift. Well, by 1 A.M. we began picking up messages in the clear that parachutes were dropping. This was part of the deception operation. By 6 A.M. everyone knew that the landings were on. So we had about five hours advance notice." [24]

WHILE Bill Bundy played a critical, if secret role in D day, Mac Bundy had a front-row seat. Initially, Mac's draft board had rejected him because of poor eyesight. So for a time in early 1942 he followed Bill to Archie MacLeish's Office of Facts and Figures in Washington. By then, MacLeish had assembled a small staff of intellectuals that included Arthur Schlesinger, Jr., Charles Poore of the *New York Times*, Allen Grover from *Time* and Malcolm Cowley of *The New Republic*. Almost immediately, the FBI's J. Edgar Hoover tried to force MacLeish to fire Cowley because of his left-wing politics. MacLeish defended Cowley, but was eventually forced to let him go. Throughout the spring MacLeish was the target of nasty attacks by the *Chicago Tribune*, the Hearst papers and other right-wing papers whose editors believed him to be too sympathetic to Roosevelt's wartime alliance with the Soviet Union. Finally, after eight months, Roosevelt disbanded the office.

Bundy was appalled. After learning of MacLeish's removal, Mac wrote him that June, "There are so few whole men in the world—so very few. Great men have always weaknesses—Mr. Roosevelt's is that in trying to hurt no one's feelings he takes advantage of the great of heart. Which is why there are so many small things done in Washington, and so many small people busily inflating their own balloons. In such an atmosphere an honest man, and a man who *cares*—and not about himself—is a shining light. To such a man others owe more than they can express—and kids who have a chance to work for such a man know a lot if they merely know that they are lucky. I know a lot."

MacLeish replied warmly, "It may sound a little excessive to you, but . . . I would rather have had that letter from you than anyone in this country—and I include the gentleman on Pennsylvania Avenue." Mac was, MacLeish gushed, "one of the two or three people who really understand what I mean." [25] Clearly, Mac had cemented an important friendship; MacLeish would prove to be the first of a long line of older, powerful men who found themselves charmed and dazzled by Mac Bundy.

By this time, Mac had got himself into the army by memorizing the eye chart.[26] Like his brother, he trained at Fort Monmouth in signal intelligence. But in the spring of 1943, instead of being assigned to Bletchley or some other cryptographic slot, Mac was presented with what he called "a crazy opportunity" to join up with Rear Admiral Alan R. Kirk, commander of Allied amphibious forces. The Bundy-Kirk family connections were innumerable: Kirk's wife, Lydia, was Kay Bundy's best friend; Kirk himself had been a close friend of Kay's brother Roger during World War I; and, more recently, Mac had dated one of the admiral's daughters in Washington. So when Kirk was looking for a personal aide, Mac Bundy was an easy choice. "Kirk wanted someone in a brown uniform, an army man, as his aide," Mac recalled. "We met and talked about it briefly, and then he asked me to be his Ultra officer for the Western naval forces. This meant I was the only officer who always accompanied Kirk and was authorized to work the 'one-time pad.' I would decipher these German intercepts received through the operation at Bletchley. It was amazing how accurate the information was; it would tell you when the German air force was going to attack our ships, and from what direction they would fly in. . . . I was probably faster at working the one-time pad than the average signal officer."[27]

Mac Bundy had joined Kirk just in time to ship out for the invasion of Sicily in July 1943. After Sicily was secured, Kirk was transferred to London, where he became the U.S. Navy commander for the Western Task Force of Overlord, the code name for the much-delayed invasion of France. Bundy went with him, where he remembered enduring a "long London winter of staff work . . . we were so busy not remembering things—everything was so classified . . . I came to be the 'guy at the door,' as it turned out. Watching Admiral Kirk's copy of the Overlord plan was my problem."[28]

Mac had a lovely flat facing onto Grosvenor Square and he managed to get out quite a bit in London society. Twice during these months he made an appearance at Harold Laski's salon, where British intellectuals met to argue politics and exchange war news. He also lunched with Laski on at least one occasion. A close friend of Frankfurter's, Laski was a socialist who made a habit of cultivating the sons of wealthy and influential Americans.[29] Bundy was no socialist, but he enjoyed Laski's wit, and in any case, the professor— who frequently wrote speeches for the American ambassador—was hardly a pariah.

Admiral Kirk introduced Bundy to one of the more famous London society hostesses, the American-born Lady Astor. "I did get to know her rather well," Mac said. "She asked me back to her very pleasant country home more than once. She was a wonderfully eccentric person." One day the American ambassador, John Winant, phoned to say that Lady Astor wanted Princess Elizabeth to meet some presentable young Americans. "He asked if I and Jack Perry, a naval officer, would meet the princess," Bundy recalled. "So Jack and I went down to Clivedon and had tea one afternoon with Elizabeth. She was very shy."[30]

Shortly before the invasion of France, Admiral Kirk, General Omar Bradley and their staffs boarded the heavy cruiser Augusta and sailed to a point twelve miles offshore from Normandy—just out of range of German artillery. Though the weather was foul, General Dwight D. Eisenhower had given the order for the invasion to proceed early in the morning of June 6, 1944. At 3:35 A.M. the Augusta's clanging bells sounded the alarm to general quarters. Soon afterwards, amphibious landing craft began moving toward the darkened beaches.

Together with Kirk, Bradley and a dozen other officers, Lieutenant Bundy crowded onto the *Augusta's* bridge to view the impending landing. Distant explosions could be heard and occasionally splotches of red light erupted from the sky. At 4:55 A.M. a burning plane plunged into the sea just off the *Augusta's* starboard bow. As the darkness lifted, Bundy could see silhouetted in the half-light hundreds of ships of all shapes and sizes as far as the eye could see. Just before 5:50 A.M., Bundy and the others on the bridge stuffed their ears with bits of cotton, and moments later the heavy shipboard guns all around them began lobbing round after round of artillery shells toward the shoreline.

Twenty minutes later the *Augusta's* own guns began firing; Bundy could feel the ship shudder beneath his feet with each explosion. By 6:45 A.M. the group barrage was over, and the *Augusta* moved closer to shore, where Bundy could vaguely see through binoculars the amphibious landing craft disgorging frightened young men into the surf off Omaha Beach. Standing on the bridge was surreal; nibbling at K rations, staring out at the beaches, Bundy could see and not see the battle. "Seen through binoculars on the large ships," wrote one of Bundy's fellow officers, Lieutenant John Mason Brown, "the shore is an anthill in turmoil. The death cries do not reach us. The falling bodies we do not see. The first desperate dash through the water is beyond our vision. ... We do not even hear the sulphurous stammering of the machine guns. The initial confusion is not ours. We know only this unholy and disquieting calm. And learn that the destroyer *Corry* has been sunk, And thank our stars that so far we have been missed." [31]

As Kirk's Ultra man, Bundy was not supposed to put himself in a position where he might be captured. His job on June 6 was to use his "one-time pad" to deliver timely pieces of intercept intelligence to his admiral. But later on D day, as their curiosity got the better of them, a group of officers were given permission to take a small boat in for a closer look. "We wanted to see firsthand what was happening on Omaha Beach. We got close to the beach but did not actually land." Upon their return, Kirk interrogated the officers on what they had seen. Bundy thought they were giving his admiral more information than they really had, so when it came his turn he said, "To tell you the truth, I didn't see anything, and I don't think anyone else did either."

On D day plus four, when the landing sites were fully secure, General Bradley moved his headquarters ashore in preparation for the effort to break out from the beachheads and run for Paris. Though Bradley's aides had been amazed by how curtly Bundy had interrupted their general on several occasions during the past few days, Bradley now turned to recently promoted First Lieutenant Bundy and said with a slight smile, "You're now the senior Army officer present afloat." [32]

Mac spent the rest of the European war as Kirk's aide, following him to France, where he managed the admiral's headquarters in a comfortable mansion on the outskirts of Paris. He found Paris "tremendously depressing." The euphoria of liberation had passed and all that Bundy could see was "the misery of a population without food or heat, caught in the clutches of a vast black-market." It was there in January 1945 that Mac received a copy of a thin volume, a war memoir written by his fellow officer and best friend at the time, John Mason Brown. After reading it, Mac wrote his friend, "I wish also that I could feel that by our occasional experience of an ineffective air raid we had been in any real sense a part of the battle. A part of the operation, we surely were, and we have a right to be proud of it, but in larger terms, when you have been four months in Paris, you cannot but admit that the war belongs to Ernie Pyle's men more than to ours." He confessed to Brown, who by then was already stateside, waiting to be discharged, that he hoped his next assignment would entail "real soldiering."[33]

By the end of the European war, neither Bill nor Mac had seen any combat; as officers privy to the secret of Ultra, they were barred from getting anywhere near the enemy. But precisely for this reason, their war experience impressed upon them the value of both secrecy and intelligence.

Ultra was an extraordinary weapon. That the Allies were reading the most secret communications of the Nazi war machine—including Hitler's instructions to his generals and the Nazi war machine's daily operational plans—made the war winnable, and at a cost far cheaper in blood and treasure than would have been the case otherwise. As Bletchley veteran Peter Calvocoressi later wrote, "Ultra created in senior staffs and at the political summit a state of mind which transformed the taking of decisions. To feel that you know your enemy is a vastly comforting feeling. It grows imperceptibly over time if you regularly and intimately observe his thoughts and ways and habits and actions. Knowledge of this kind makes your own planning less tentative and more assured, less harrowing and more buoyant."[34] The Bletchley boys, in other words, made it possible for Roosevelt and Churchill to prosecute this enormously destructive war with an extraordinary confidence.

Any evaluation of Ultra's role must also take note of the quite astounding fact that the secrets of Bletchley Park were kept for thirty-one years after the end of the war. In the case of the Bundy brothers, who never spoke of it even to each other, perhaps this secrecy is not surprising. Keeping mum about Ultra was no different than bearing the secrets of Skull and Bones.

Years afterwards, Bill Bundy would evaluate the role of Ultra in this fashion: "I find it very hard to imagine how the war would have unfolded without what Bletchley did. There are those who say it shortened the war by nine months or by this or by that. I think it would have been just a totally different war in every respect, and the fact that this was done by an operation that maintained security has always made me kind of a bug on security with very strong feelings. These were not diminished, I may say, by having participated in the management of a very tragic war in Vietnam, where it was clear that the other side always knew much more than we did, not through any communications techniques, but by a host of human agents."[35]

■

WHILE two of his sons served as Ultra warriors abroad, Harvey Bundy had spent the war harboring numerous secrets of his own. He was Stimson's chief filter for intercept intelligence: "All the 'Magic' intercepts came across my desk." And when Pearl Harbor happened, he knew for a fact that there had been an enormous intelligence failure. Critical Magic intercepts had hinted at Japanese intentions: "The intercepts showing that the Japanese were very interested in the position of every ship in Pearl Harbor, all of those intercepts came across my desk—and I spoke to G-2 about it. I said, 'The Japs are showing an enormous interest.' And G-2's reply was, 'Oh, they always do that everywhere in the world.' "[36] Though he was one of the few who saw all the intercepts, and though he had raised the matter, Bundy felt no personal responsibility. The system had failed, not him. A few months later the head of G-2 was quietly transferred and a Wall Street lawyer, a friend of Bundy's, was brought down to revamp the procedures for evaluating Magic intercepts.

Stimson relied on Bundy to supervise a wide variety of War Department activities. Though Bundy had no scientific training, his boss, being a lawyer himself, was of the opinion that any field of human activity was just another case. So Bundy was appointed Stimson's personal representative to the Office of Scientific Research and Development. Over the reluctance of the military, which thought new inventions took years to develop, Bundy used his position to needle the generals to develop radar and other technological innovations.

And then, just a month before Pearl Harbor, on November 6, 1941, he was given a top-secret briefing on the Manhattan Project. Bundy thought it a "perfectly appalling thing." But if they could get it, "we'd win the war and damn quickly, too, if it was what they said it was." This conviction was borrowed in part from James Conant, the Harvard president and a member of the president's special Top Policy Group on the Manhattan Project. A few days after the Japanese attack, Bundy had gone up to Harvard to see Conant, who was in bed with a heavy cold. Bundy was in a pessimistic mood, and all he could talk of was the tremendous naval losses sustained at Pearl Harbor. "I couldn't see how the devil we were going to win the war," Harvey said. Conant allowed Bundy to "spread the gloom" for a while and then interrupted to say, "Don't worry. We'll win the war unless the Germans get S-1 [the atomic bomb] first." Bundy had not thought of this nightmare. Conant had meant to reassure him, but Bundy walked out of the Harvard president's bedroom with yet another worry.[37]

Thereafter, Bundy paid close attention to the progress the scientists were making on the bomb. For the remainder of the war, he was "the Secretary's eyes and ears on the whole atomic project." When the Manhattan Project's General Leslie Groves selected a site at Los Alamos—that ironically had an internment camp for Japanese Americans—it was Bundy who pulled the bureaucratic strings to get the internment camp summarily moved. When there were security problems with some of the foreign-born scientists working on the project, Bundy handled it.

When it came time to decide what to do with the atomic bomb, Harvey Bundy played a key role in clarifying Stimson's thinking. "My impression was everybody assumed it [the bomb] was going to be used," he recollected years later. To Bundy's mind, the issue was a purely "tactical" question, best left to the military. They were waging total war, where conventional doctrines of morality were held in suspension. The atomic bomb was not anything different from the firebombing of Tokyo or Dresden: "War was death, and the question now was to get it over with." As to the firebombing, he knew that Stimson ". . . was horrified by the idea, but he wasn't in a position—nor did he want—to stop it. He had reached a point where now the borderline between armies that fight in the field and civilians at home had gone, particularly with the power of these weapons. So that I think he had passed the point of no return."

At Potsdam in July 1945, when Stimson was informed of the results of the first atomic bomb test at Alamogordo, New Mexico, Bundy remembered how his boss's attitude toward the Russians changed. Until then many officials assumed the military wanted Russian entry in the war against Japan, if only because the shock value of such a move might well force Tokyo to surrender terms. Now, things were different. "Damn it," Stimson told Bundy, "we don't need the Russians in the war." It was a new world, and the Americans had a monopoly on a weapon of mass destruction. Bundy was a witness to how the existence of the bomb inevitably became a factor in the minds of those responsible for conducting relations with the Soviet allies. "Apparently," recalled Harvey Bundy, "it changed entirely Truman's attitude in negotiating in Potsdam with Stalin."[38]

Bundy also knew that at this point in the Pacific war, the issue was not whether the Japanese were going to surrender, but how soon. Numerous peace feelers had been received. OSS director William Donovan, for example, had reported on May 12 that Japan's minister to Switzerland, Shunichi Kase, had communicated his wish "to help arrange for cessation of hostilities." Kase reported that "one of the few provisions the Japanese would insist upon would be the retention of the Emperor." Bundy had also been reading Purple intercepts of Japanese cable traffic which made it very clear that Tokyo was looking for a way to surrender. President Harry S. Truman himself referred to one such intercept as the "telegram from [the] Jap Emperor asking for peace."[39] Bundy was also well aware that a large number of his colleagues in the War Department, the State Department and the White House—including Assistant Secretary of War John J. McCloy, Secretary of the Navy James Forrestal, Acting Secretary of State Joseph C. Grew, Navy Under Secretary Ralph Bard and Admiral William D. Leahy—were strongly urging the president that the war could be quickly ended by merely clarifying what Washington meant by unconditional surrender.

Just before accompanying Stimson to the July 1945 Potsdam Conference —or perhaps early in the conference itself—Bundy sat down and wrote a short undated memorandum for his boss. Classified top secret, the memo provides an astonishing insight into the highly controversial issue of whether the atomic bombings of Japan were necessary to bring about an end to the war. Perhaps because the document was not declassified until 1973, and because it was unsigned and undated, historians have overlooked its significance. But it indicates that Bundy and Stimson had good reasons to think that the Pacific war would end without an invasion of the Japanese home islands.

The first question Bundy asked was: "Do we need Russia in the Japanese war?" By way of answer he notes the "effect of S1 [the atomic bomb]" and writes, "There would be great advantages if the Russians did not have their entrance [into the war] as a great bargaining point." The second issue at hand, according to Bundy, was "the warning to Japan." Here, Bundy refers to the debate over whether there should be an "inclusion of reference to the Emperor" in the Potsdam Proclamation. And he asks, "Can we get this across [to the Japanese] privately in time[?]" A warning that included a guarantee for the emperor would have "the advantage to us in dealing with Russia in having an orderly authority in Japan instead of a vacuum into which Russia and Russian philosophy so easily move."

The rest of the memo—points three, four, five and six—are entirely absorbed with "the increasing Russian demands all over the world."[40]

Two conclusions can be drawn from this memo: First, Stimson and Bundy were absorbed with the problem of how to deal with Russia in the postwar period, and the atomic bomb, they knew, was a critical factor in this relationship. When they thought of the bomb, they automatically thought of the Soviet Union. Second, they could only afford to speculate about ending the Pacific war without the Soviets if they thought the Japanese were approaching an early decision to surrender. If the war were to go on for many more months, then Soviet entry was crucial. But the assumption was that either the bomb would end the war or the Japanese would surrender once they were given a guarantee for their emperor. Either solution was preferable to Soviet entry into the war, which could only complicate the planned American occupation of Japan.*

At Potsdam, Bundy knew, McCloy and Stimson had lobbied hard to persuade Truman to include in the Potsdam Proclamation specific wording that a postwar Japanese government "may include a constitutional monarchy under the present dynasty."[41] But they had lost this argument with the president, who, under the influence of Secretary of State James F. Byrnes, had clearly decided to let the clock run out. The bomb would be dropped as soon as it was ready, which Truman and Byrnes knew would happen well before the August 15 date on which the Soviets had now promised to enter the Pacific war.

---

* Forty-three years later, when McGeorge Bundy published his study of the atomic bomb, *Danger and Survivial*, he made no mention that his father had been so intimately involved in the internal debate over whether to use the weapon against Japan.

Accompanied by Bundy, an exasperated Stimson abruptly departed Potsdam on July 25. Stopping off in London, Harvey took a day off to visit his son Bill at Bletchley Park. By this time, Bill had received the news that he and other American cryptologists were scheduled to be sent to the Pacific. "We went for a walk in the gardens one day," Bill recalled, "and the subject of my impending transfer to the Pacific came up. Father told me, 'We have this new weapon coming into use that will end the war. You probably won't have to go to Japan.' Father was in the know." [42]

BILL was not the only Bundy so forewarned of the atomic bombings. Kay Bundy was at that very moment extremely worried about Mac, who in early 1945 had volunteered for Pacific duty and had already been transferred to the 386th Regiment of the 97th Army Division.* "Though it was a very green division," Mac said, "we were nevertheless assigned to the campaign to invade the Japanese home islands." Technically, as an Ultra officer, Mac should not have been allowed anywhere close to combat. His mother claimed he "lied himself into an infantry regiment." Mac said he just thought it was the right thing to do, and suggested that the army bureaucracy just let it happen. [43]

While Kay was frantic with worry about Mac's news, Harvey seemed completely unperturbed. Writing from Potsdam on July 21, he told Kay, "I see by *Stars and Stripes* that the 97th Division will not reach the combat zone until December 1st. Early enough for me. I continue [to be] optimistic in that theatre." Harvey was optimistic precisely because he and other Truman administration officials knew the Japanese were trying to surrender and would no doubt find their way to capitulating long before an invasion could be mounted. [44]

In late July, shortly after Mac shipped out for the Philippines, Harvey Bundy and Stimson returned from Potsdam. Kay soon had Stimson over for dinner and in her usual fashion she minced no words. When Stimson politely asked, "Did you have a good holiday?" Kay blurted, "It was all perfectly horrible, Mr. Stimson." She explained that Mac had been on leave, and they had gone up to the Manchester house, "but it was just a perfectly horrible time, and I didn't enjoy seeing him go off on that train [to invade Japan]."

"Well, Kay," Stimson replied, "I tell you, I promise you something. He'll never have to land in Japan." [45] Stimson was confident that the Japanese were likely to surrender long before an invasion could be mounted. If the atomic bomb did not end the war, the Soviet Union's scheduled entry into the Pacific

---

* On February 9, 1945, Captain McGeorge Bundy had formally requested a demotion to the grade of first lieutenant specifically in order to facilitate his transfer to a combat division in the Pacific. When the cable, signed by General Eisenhower, reached Stimson's desk, the war secretary issued personal instructions that Bundy's request should be "treated as a perfectly routine matter" but that if Bundy's eyesight was still defective no special waiver should be granted which would "imperil the boy's command or himself." Stimson noted that he was "impressed" by the "spirit of the telegram" (Stimson diary, Feb. 12, 1945, with attached cable).

war by August 15, 1945, would surely shock the Japanese warlords into an early surrender.

Without warning, on August 6, Hiroshima was incinerated. Three days later a second atomic bomb destroyed Nagasaki. Some 200,000 people, mostly women, children and old men, were killed. Many of these were vaporized instantly; some died slowly over days or weeks from radiation poisoning. Thousands survived, only to live for decades with the painful aftereffects of radiation-induced cancers. This was a legacy that worried Stimson and all the men around him. Even after the atomic bombings, the Japanese still insisted on assurances for the preservation of the monarchy. Stimson now spent two tense days, assisted by McCloy and Bundy, drafting a new protocol of surrender that included language that Truman and Byrnes had rejected only a few weeks earlier. The Japanese then surrendered on August 14.[46]

THE war was finally over, but Stimson, even in his exhausted state—his doctors believed he had suffered a mild heart attack on August 8—could think of little else but the "primordial weapon." McCloy later recalled that in the days following the surrender, he and Stimson had "long and painful thoughts about the atomic triumph."[47]

Late in August, Stimson gave a little sermon to his friends at the St. Hubert's Club in the Adirondack Mountains which hints at his moral unease. He warned that another war could "end our civilization."[48] In mid-September, he sent Truman a long memo laying out his concerns: "In many quarters it [the atomic bomb] has been interpreted as a substantial offset to the growth of Russian influence on the continent." In other words, the U.S. atomic monopoly—and of course, the fact that Washington had demonstrated a willingness to use it against Japan—was already being perceived by friends and foes alike as a diplomatic weapon. The Russians were very likely to respond with their own atomic program. The result, Stimson argued, would be "a secret armament race of a rather desperate character." The survival of civilization itself required that Washington do everything possible to avoid such an arms race. "For if we fail to approach them [the Soviets] now and merely continue to negotiate with them, having this weapon rather ostentatiously on our hip, their suspicions and their distrust of our purposes and motives will increase."

Stimson concluded by recommending to Truman that the United States make a dramatic and sweeping proposal directly to the Soviet Union to share control over atomic technology. He even suggested that this would "specifically lead to the proposal that we would stop work on the further improvement in, or manufacture of, the bomb as a military weapon, provided the Russians and the British would agree to do likewise."[49]

Written barely a month after Hiroshima, this extraordinary memo was obviously a product of "long and painful thoughts about the atomic triumph." Soon, Stimson would revisit the controversial issue of Hiroshima in a major magazine article, using as his ghostwriter a junior fellow at Harvard, the twenty-seven-year-old McGeorge Bundy.

5
Stimson's Scribe

I think we deserve some sort of medal for reducing these particular chatterers to silence.

McGeorge Bundy
February 18, 1947

McGeorge Bundy's late bid to experience some "real soldiering" was foreclosed by the Japanese surrender in August. But if Mac had seen the war entirely through the eyes of an admiral's aide, he nevertheless did not leave the army with romantic notions about the nature of war. "When the war is over," he wrote John Mason Brown, "I'm going to get away from all crowds of all kinds for a while. . . . I don't think I'll wait around for any triumphal marches, either. I suppose they are as necessary as people say they are, but I don't want any part of it myself—wars are full of glory and greatness, but they are not of themselves as a whole, either one or the other—they are ugly." [1] So at war's end, Bundy returned to take up his residency at Harvard as a junior fellow, living in Eliot House, far from the madding crowds.

At the same time, his father, Harvey, resigned his position at the War Department and returned to his Boston law practice. Stimson resigned on the same day, September 21, 1945, and literally collapsed at his Highhold estate on Long Island, exhausted and yet still worried by the drift in policy toward the atomic bomb. The Colonel's diaries make it clear that he understood that Jimmy Byrnes had atomic diplomacy in mind. He noted in early September: "I found that Byrnes was very much against any attempt to cooperate with Russia . . . he looks to having the presence of the bomb in his pocket, so to speak, as a great weapon to get through this thing. . . ." [2]

But if Stimson was unhappy with Byrnes's policy, there was little he could do about it as he recuperated in his Highhold estate. Throughout the autumn and early winter he was a very sick man. Only a month after leaving office he suffered a massive coronary occlusion that kept him in bed until Christmas. [3] But by the spring of 1946, he had recovered enough that his old friend, next-door neighbor and sometime publicist Arthur Page encouraged him to begin writing his memoirs. He warned Stimson, however, that he needed a young man to talk him through the book and to do the actual writing.

Page talked to Stimson's closest wartime aide, Harvey Bundy, who in turn talked to Rudolph Winnacker, a War Department historian. In March and April both Bundy and Winnacker exchanged correspondence with Stimson on the subject of who should assist him. The three men quickly settled on a logical and easy choice, a bright young man in whom they all could trust to work with great discretion, none other than Harvey Bundy's twenty-seven-year-old third son, Mac Bundy. As a junior fellow at Harvard, the younger Bundy was free to make Stimson's memoirs his own project. Already known to Stimson as the son of his trusted aide, Bundy had also proved himself a lively and publishable writer for *The Atlantic*.

Cass Canfield, an editor at Harper & Brothers, assured Page that Bundy was the right choice for the job: "He has a clear, crisp style and should be an excellent choice of person to assist Col. Stimson in preparing the memoirs."[4] Early in the summer of 1946, Canfield signed a contract to publish the memoir in return for an advance of $3,000, half of which was to go to Bundy.

That summer Mac moved into a little red cottage on Stimson's Highhold estate and began work. Each morning Stimson would come by, accompanied by his longtime secretary, Elizabeth Neary. Mac would interview Stimson on the porch of the cottage, while Neary took notes. The main source for the memoir, aside from Stimson's reminiscences with Bundy, was Stimson's diary.

Only three months into the project, however, Stimson and Bundy were diverted by a more pressing task—a defense of the decision to use the bomb. A Gallup poll in late August 1945 had shown that 85 percent of the American people supported the atomic bombing of Japan.[5] But within a year Stimson was alarmed by reports in the media that some elite opinion-makers were beginning to voice criticism of the decision.

• On March 6, 1946, Reinhold Niebuhr and twenty-one other Protestant clergymen and philosophers published a statement in the *New York Times* which characterized the Hiroshima and Nagasaki bombings as "morally indefensible."[6]

• In July the U.S. Strategic Bombing Survey report concluded that "certainly prior to December 31, 1945, and in all probability prior to November 1, 1945, Japan would have surrendered even if the atomic bombs had not been dropped, even if Russia had not entered the war, and even if no invasion had been planned or contemplated."[7]

• On August 31, *The New Yorker* devoted an entire issue to John Hersey's devastating description of Hiroshima. The article soon became a widely read book.

• On September 9, Admiral William F. Halsey, commander of the Pacific Fleet, was quoted by the Associated Press as saying the bomb was used because the scientists "had a toy and wanted to try it out" despite the fact that "the Japs had put out a lot of peace feelers through Russia long before."[8]

• On September 14 the editor of the *Saturday Review of Literature*, Norman Cousins, published an impassioned editorial on the "crime of Hiroshima and Nagasaki."[9]

While it would be a mistake to suggest that a sea change was about to occur in the American public's opinion of the bomb, these critical stirrings were enough to worry the men associated with the decision to use the weapon. No one in 1946 was more worried than James B. Conant, the Harvard University president and a member of the Interim Committee that recommended using the weapon on a city. Conant had been shocked in March 1946 when he read in the *New York Times* that his favorite theologian, Reinhold Niebuhr, had signed the Federal Council of Church's statement condemning the Hiroshima and Nagasaki bombings.[10]

He was also annoyed in the summer of 1946 with the release of the U.S. Strategic Bombing Survey report and Admiral Halsey's critical comments on the atomic bombings. But it was Norman Cousins's editorial in the general circulation *Saturday Review of Literature* that spurred Conant to write Harvey Bundy. Enclosing a copy of the editorial, he wrote that he was "considerably disturbed about this type of comment which has been increasing in recent days."[11]

The Harvard president realized that this was no academic debate. If a shroud of guilt were to envelop the public's perception of the decision to use the atomic bomb, this alone might be enough to so relegitimize deep-rooted isolationist sentiments that it would be impossible for the Truman administration to carry out its internationalist agenda.

"You may be inclined," Conant wrote Bundy on September 23, "to dismiss all this talk as representing only a small minority of the population. . . . You will recall that it became accepted doctrine among a group of so-called intellectuals who taught in our schools and colleges that the United States had made a great error in entering World War I, and that the error was brought about largely by the interests of the powerful groups. Of course, there is little relation between these two types of fallacies, but I mention the history after World War I only to emphasize that a small minority, if it represents the type of person who is both sentimental and verbally minded and in contact with our youth, may result in a distortion of history."[12]

It was, therefore, of "great importance" that "someone who can speak with authority" write something that would set the record straight. To Conant's mind there was only one obvious candidate: Henry Stimson. Conant was aware that Harvey's son McGeorge was at that very moment assisting Stimson in the writing of his memoirs. Could Harvey, he asked, and perhaps Stimson's other good friend, George Harrison, persuade the retired war secretary to have young Bundy ghostwrite a magazine article "pointing out the conditions under which the decision was made and who made it?"[13]

Upon receiving Conant's letter, Harvey contacted his son at Stimson's Highhold estate and broached the idea. Over lunch one day early that autumn Stimson reluctantly agreed to author the piece as long as Mac did the actual writing.

Stimson was depressed by the whole topic; he genuinely feared that a written narrative of the decision-making that led to Hiroshima would only inflame passions. Even after he had a draft of the proposed article in hand, he wondered whether to publish it. "I have rarely," Stimson wrote Frankfurter, "been connected with a paper about which I have so much doubt at the last moment. I think the full enumeration of the steps in the tragedy will excite horror among friends who heretofore thought me a kindly-minded Christian gentleman but who will, after reading this, feel that I am cold blooded and cruel. . . ."[14]

Mac understood the special nature of the assignment, and though he had been relying strictly on Stimson's own recollections for the memoir, he now interviewed a number of people for the magazine piece. He talked to his father, who wrote him a memo on the subject, and he also interviewed Conant, General Leslie Groves [the Manhattan Project's chief], George Harrison and the secretary of the Interim Committee, Gordon Arneson.[15]

But it was his father's memo which set the tone and theme for the article. Drafted on September 25, Harvey Bundy's "Notes on the Use by the United States of the Atomic Bomb" contained all the arguments used by his son in the *Harper's* article, including many assertions which in hindsight we can see were just not true. Harvey asserted, for instance, that the Interim Committee had "discussed intensively whether the bomb should be used at all" and whether a demonstration of the bomb should be held before Japanese observers. Both of these assertions were greatly exaggerated. Harvey also wrote in his memo that there was no evidence—then or in 1946—that the Japanese were weakening and might surrender without an invasion. The atomic bombing was ordered, Harvey wrote, "primarily on the belief that the use would save American lives by terminating the war as rapidly as possible. . . ."[16]

Harvey also claimed that the Interim Committee had rejected using the bomb on targets "where the destruction of life and property would be greatest . . ." in favor of targets "primarily military in character where the nature of the building construction would show completely the devastating effect of the bomb." And he incorrectly asserted that the petition of those scientists opposed to the use of the bomb on Japan had been discussed by Stimson with Truman.[17]

Significantly, Mac chose to ignore that portion of his father's memo which argued that the timing of the Hiroshima bombing was in no way tied to the Russian entry into the war. He saw that even broaching the subject of winning the war without the Russians would invite difficult questions about possible atomic diplomacy.

By the end of November, Mac had a draft of the article, which by now was destined to appear in *Harper's*. On the afternoon of November 29 he left Highhold for Cambridge, where he delivered the manuscript to Conant. Within a day the Harvard president had blue-penciled the article, deleting some material, adding paragraphs and revising the tone of the piece. Conant specifically urged Bundy to cut out any detailed discussion of whether the decision-makers had debated a modification of the terms of unconditional surrender. This, of course, was central to the issue, but Conant advised Bundy that "the problem of the Emperor diverts one's mind from the general line of argumentation" and would be both "unnecessary and unwise."

In a brief and even perfunctory fashion, the Interim Committee had discussed the merits of a warning or a demonstration of the bomb's power before Japanese observers. But even though this was hardly remembered by Stimson and never mentioned by Truman as a factor in their decision-making, Conant wished Bundy to emphasize this fact since "both these points are stressed strongly by the people we are trying to impress with this article."[18] By way of deflating the destructiveness of the bomb, Conant also wanted Bundy to emphasize that this was a weapon like any other, and that the destruction inflicted on Hiroshima was similar to that suffered by Tokyo during the firebombing raids.

Bundy soon wired Conant that he was "personally delighted" with his suggestions. The published article made all these points and incorporated wholesale some of Conant's paragraphs. Conant was greatly pleased, and when he read a galley of the *Harper's* piece in late January 1947, he wrote Stimson, "It seems to me just exactly right, and I am sure will do a great deal of good." Conant thought it essential that the American people "stay tough" in their attitude toward the bomb's use: ". . . if the propaganda against the use of the atomic bomb had been allowed to grow unchecked, the strength of our military position by virtue of having the bomb would have been correspondingly weakened. . . ."[19]

Conant's expectations were more than met. When *Harper's* published the cover story in its February 1947 issue, the *New York Times* treated it as front-page news. Stimson had the only byline on the piece. Years later Bundy would tell historian James Hershberg that the final article was "basically all his [Stimson's] arguments; the prose is mine."[20] Nevertheless, Bundy's authorship was kept a secret from the public at large. In the weeks and months after the piece was published, Stimson received letters of congratulations from Truman, Groves and dozens of other members of the atomic establishment. Writing from Cambridge, Mac told Stimson, "Boston I find humming with activity and interest—the *Harper's* article has been read by everyone I meet, and it seems to have covered the subject so well that I find no follow-up work needed. This is of particular interest in the case of one or two of my friends who certainly fall in Mr. Conant's unkindly classification of the 'verbal minded'—I think we deserve some sort of medal for reducing these particular chatterers to silence."[21]

Bundy's essay would stand for at least two decades as the definitive explanation of the decision to use the atomic bomb. Even today, it remains the orthodox view. To those "chatterers" who had no special knowledge of these events, the piece seemed wholly reasonable. The atomic bombing of Hiroshima and Nagasaki was made to seem inevitable—"this deliberate, premeditated destruction was our least abhorrent choice." And the alternative was authoritatively described as an invasion of the Japanese home islands at a heavy cost to American lives.[22]

The *Harper's* article became the source for one central myth about the decision, namely Stimson's assertion that "I was informed that [the invasion of the main Japanese home islands] might be expected to cost over a million casualties, to American forces alone." Where did Stimson and Mac find this figure? Bundy had asked the War Department for any casualty estimates given to Stimson in the summer of 1945, but he never got them. Instead, he and Stimson simply agreed to use the nice round figure of one million casualties.[23]

IF these arguments were convincing to the public, men with special knowledge of these events differed. Joseph Grew, for one, knew the piece had neatly sidestepped the central question: could the war have been brought to a close in August or earlier by clarifying the terms of unconditional surrender? According to his good friend William R. Castle, Grew was "very angry" after reading the *Harper's* piece.[24] On February 12, 1947, he wrote Stimson to complain that his article contained no real discussion of the advice he had given him in the spring and summer of 1945 on this question: "I and a good many others will always feel that had the President issued as far back as May, 1945, the recommended categorical statement that the Japanese dynasty would be retained if the Japanese people freely desired its retention, the atom bomb might never have had to be used at all. . . ."[25]

Oddly enough, Stimson sat on this letter, written by a man he genuinely respected, for more than four months. On June 19, he finally responded to what he called Grew's "very interesting letter about the Japanese surrender. . . .": "The *Harper's* article did not seem the place for any discussion as to what might have happened if the position you so early and ably urged had been adopted sooner than it was or stated more clearly in the Potsdam ultimatum. My own views, as you know, were very much in accord with yours all the way through, with perhaps the small exception that in May 1945 I was not convinced that the right moment for a strong public statement on the Emperor had yet come."

Stimson then assured Grew that in his forthcoming memoirs he and "young Bundy" have "tried to make clear in some detail the cross currents which put so much difficulty in the way of the course you and I advocated before it was finally and clearly accepted by the President." In an apparent allusion to Jimmy Byrnes, Stimson went on to say, "This is a difficult and rather touchy business because, as you know, feelings ran high and there were very fine men, who should have known better, working on the other side."[26]

There were other critics of the *Harper's* article. William R. Castle, who had served—with considerable irritation—under Stimson as under secretary of state during the Hoover administration, was another nonbeliever. After reading the *Harper's* article, Castle wrote in his diary of February 9: ". . . He [Stimson] knew that Japan was suing for peace, that its economy had been destroyed and he must have had the Navy statement that surrender was only a matter of days. I wonder whether Stimson, with Marshall, wanted war to continue long enough to give them a chance to try out the atom bomb on Japanese cities."[27]

As Stimson now turned his attention back to the task of completing his memoirs, he and Mac had a discussion about how they should handle the "rather touchy" issue in *On Active Service in Peace and War,* the eventual title of their collaborative book. Stimson had serious qualms about revealing any more than he already had in the *Harper's* article. To say any more "would very likely embarrass Byrnes . . . my personal relations with the President are under a veil as to the relations with the Russians."[28] So Mac finally concluded, "Maybe the thing to do is just reprint the *Harper's* article. . . ."[29] Stimson agreed.

There were, however, a few differences.

WHEN Bundy and Stimson had finally agreed upon a draft manuscript of the memoir, they decided to send the chapters concerning the war years to General George C. Marshall, who by then was serving as Truman's secretary of state. Marshall in turn passed the manuscript to George Kennan, who was then serving as head of the Policy Planning Staff at the State Department. In their draft, Bundy and Stimson had included the following two passages about the post-Potsdam period: ". . . the War Department civilian staff was thinking long and painful thoughts about the atomic triumph. Meanwhile in the State Department there developed a tendency to think of the bomb as a diplomatic weapon. Outraged by constant evidence of Russian perfidy, some of the men in charge of foreign policy were eager to carry the bomb for a while as their ace-in-the-hole."

And in another entry, Bundy had stated that Stimson's September memo on controlling the bomb had been: ". . . [p]resented at a time when some American statesmen were eager for their country to browbeat the Russians with the atomic bomb 'held rather ostentatiously on our hip.' "

Kennan read these passages as nothing short of inflammatory. He wrote Bundy that he was not aware of which officials in the State Department might have held these views, but he did know that the publication of these words would "play squarely into the hands of the Communists who so frequently speak of our 'atomic diplomacy.' . . ."[30]

Upon receipt of Kennan's complaint, Bundy immediately conceded that "the language you question was incautious and exaggerated." But while reassuring Kennan that Stimson would rework the offending passages, Bundy proceeded to explain to Kennan why what had been written was nevertheless correct: "The divergence between Mr. Stimson and Mr. Byrnes in September 1945 was a real one, and Mr. Byrnes' *reported* [Bundy's emphasis] attitude (for purely short-term negotiating purposes) was not far from the one described. . . ."

It is also my feeling, however, that the basic *attitude* [Bundy's emphasis] of Mr. Stimson's September paper was not shared at the highest levels in the direct line of foreign policy making. . . . Do you suppose that perhaps the President felt a little secret relief in Potsdam when Stalin showed little interest in the bomb. *I* [Bundy's emphasis] would have—and I think I'd have been wrong.

But these are mere personal speculations—I should hate to have them taken as historical analysis and even less as Mr. Stimson's judgment. And in any event the situation now has changed and we do not want to play into the hands of the Kremlin's hired liars.[31]

Though he had accurately described Byrnes's view of the atomic bomb as a diplomatic weapon, Bundy would now redraft the language to exclude this information. When he was done, he wrote Kennan to thank him for his assistance: "In effect, you have merely improved our manners, and I am grateful."[32]

IN his "note of explanation and acknowledgment" at the end of Stimson's memoirs, Bundy provides a brief description of how the book was written. He states that Stimson's "diary has been liberally quoted. . . ." And yet, curiously, when his narrative comes to dealing with the decision to use the bomb against Japan, Bundy quotes from the diary very little. The omissions are so startling that one must conclude that Bundy and Stimson were intent on suppressing any suggestion in the memoirs that the bomb was used for any reasons other than military necessity. In the diary, Stimson repeatedly refers to the atomic bomb and Russia in the same breath: "Over any such tangled weave of problems the S-1 [the code word for the atomic bomb] secret would be dominant" (May 15, 1945). The bomb is called a "mastercard," a "royal straight flush" and "a weapon which will be unique" (May 15–16, 1945). With regard to prospects for Japan's surrender, Stimson says, "I told him [Grew] that I was inclined to agree with giving the Japanese a modification of the unconditional surrender formula and some hope to induce them to practically make an unconditional surrender without the use of those words" (May 29, 1945). And later in June, he comments, ". . . it became evident today in the discussion that we all feel that some way should be found of inducing Japan to yield without a fight to the finish . . ." (June 19, 1945).

Perhaps influenced by Grew's criticism of the magazine article, Stimson had Bundy add one caveat to his larger argument in defense of the atomic bombings. In the memoir, Bundy writes, "Only on the question of the Emperor did Stimson take, in 1945, a conciliatory view; only on this question did he later believe that history might find that the United States, by its delay in stating its position, had prolonged the war."[33] This was a startling admission, which most readers in 1948 seem to have ignored then and ever since.

ONLY much later would such establishment figures as John J. McCloy, James V. Forrestal, Lewis Strauss, Herbert Hoover, Admiral William D. Leahy and General Dwight D. Eisenhower decide to speak on the record about the Hiroshima decision. They would write brief notes to each other (and in their diaries) which made it clear that they knew the account given by Bundy and Stimson was incomplete, particularly with regard to the Japanese attempts to negotiate a surrender with their monarchy intact. But in 1948, the year of the Berlin airlift, the emerging Cold War made it seem prudent to hold one's tongue about what was past.

Not surprisingly, given Stimson's long and distinguished career, On Active Service in Peace and War became a moderate commercial success when it was published in early 1948. The 698-page memoir, which Bundy had written in just eighteen months, was quickly deemed authoritative on a host of historical events associated with Stimson's life. Foreign Affairs called it, "One of the most important biographical works of our generation." The New Republic judged it a "central document of our times," and the Saturday Review of Literature gushed, "The honesty of this book stands out on every page." One reviewer concluded, "McGeorge Bundy has made an excellent Boswell. He enters the great tradition of the secretaries of famous men (typified perhaps by John Morley) who have had the great privilege of writing the biography and editing the papers of a top-flight figure under the personal direction of the hero-historian."[34]

Like the Harper's essay, published just a year earlier, the book further helped to establish the official explanation for the decision to use the atomic bomb against Japan. As literary executor of Stimson's papers, Bundy kept the Stimson diaries closed to independent researchers until 1959. Only when historians began digesting the diaries and other declassified State Department papers would a markedly different history begin to emerge. This process began with the publication in 1965 of Gar Alperovitz's book Atomic Diplomacy: Hiroshima & Potsdam. In subsequent years, the scholarship of Martin J. Sherwin, Barton J. Bernstein, Gregg Herken, James Hershberg and Robert L. Messer, among others, further undermined the main tenets of the orthodox school. The revisionists used such previously unknown sources as Truman's handwritten diary (discovered only in 1978), Magic intercepts of Japanese diplomatic cable traffic and the diaries of Walter Brown, James Byrnes's private secretary, to discredit the main line of argument presented by Bundy and Stimson in 1947.[35]

Ironically, McGeorge Bundy was to some extent himself part of this new consensus. In 1988, after working for eight years on the subject, Bundy published Danger and Survival: Choices About the Bomb in the First Fifty Years, which basically defends the use of the bomb as "understandable," but takes into account the archival evidence produced by later historians. He labels as "false" the notion that "a desire to impress the Russians with the power of the bomb was a major factor in the decision to use it." But he concedes: "What is true—and important—is that these same decision makers were full of hope that the bomb would put new strength in the American power position."[36]

There were other concessions. A delay on the atomic bombing of Nagasaki "would have been relatively easy, and I think right." Regarding the undocumented casualty estimate of "over a million," Bundy writes that "defenders of the use of the bomb, Stimson among them, were not always careful about numbers of casualties expected. Revisionist scholars are on strong ground when they question flat assertions that the bomb saved a million lives."[37]

As to his own role in drafting the *Harper's* essay for Stimson, Bundy acknowledges, "After the war Colonel Stimson, with the fervor of an advocate and with me as his scribe, wrote an article intended to demonstrate that the bomb was not used without a searching consideration of alternatives." To suggest that Stimson had written the *Harper's* piece with the "fervor of an advocate" is an extraordinary admission since at the time Conant had recruited Bundy to serve as Stimson's ghost with the very precise instruction that the resulting essay should appear to be anything but a piece of advocacy.[38] As to the substance of the *Harper's* argument, that a "searching consideration of the alternatives" had been conducted, Bundy carefully writes, "That some effort was made, and that Stimson was its linchpin, is clear. That it was as long or wide or deep as the subject deserved now seems to me most doubtful."

Bundy's conclusions are mixed. "I have argued my own present belief that there were things that might have been done to increase the chance of early surrender, but I have also had to recognize how hard it was to decide to do those things as matters actually stood in May, June, and July [1945]. And if perhaps, or even probably, there were better courses, we are measuring a real decision against might-have-beens." Historians should not indict leaders with knowledge obtained long after the fact. But by the time Bundy was writing his book in the 1980s, historians had evidence that Stimson, Byrnes and Truman had been in possession of the facts, which have led to questions about the necessity for the bombings.

In his very last word on the subject, Mac writes, "Whether broader and more extended deliberation would have yielded a less destructive result we shall never know. Yet one must regret that no such effort was made."[39]

Three years before publishing his book, Bundy explained his "regrets" in language which explicitly posed the crucial question raised by the revisionists. Interviewed on the *MacNeil/Lehrer NewsHour* on the occasion of the fortieth anniversary of the atomic bombing of Hiroshima, Bundy said, "I am not disposed to criticize the use of the existence of the bomb to help to end the war, but it does seem to me, looking back on it, that there were opportunities for communication and warning available to the United States government which were not completely thought through by our government at that time.

In July and early August 1945, the United States government knew three things that the Japanese government did not. One was that the bomb was coming into existence, had been successfully tested. One was that the United States government was prepared to allow the emperor to remain on his throne in Japan, and the third was that the Russians were coming into the war. And the question, it seems to me, that was not fully studied, fully presented to President Truman, was whether warning of the bomb and assurance on the emperor could not have been combined in a fashion which would have produced Japanese surrender without the use of the bomb on a large city, with all the human consequences that followed." [40]

As a precocious young scholar, Mac had effectively seized, in the apt phrase of the historian Barton J. Bernstein, "the contested terrain of nuclear history." [41] The ghosted *Harper's* article defending the bomb had silenced the "verbal-minded" critics of Hiroshima. Nearly forty years later Bundy was asking the very same questions as Stimson's critics. By then, the history he had written in 1946–47 had become a pillar of popular opinion about both the end of the war and the beginning of the Cold War. As Stimson had written (in his own hand) in the foreword to his ghosted memoir, "I have lived long enough to know that history is often not what actually happened but what is recorded as such." [42]

6

Portrait of a Young Policy Intellectual, 1948–1953

> *I prefer Mr. T [Truman] in victory to his pursuit of it. He will disappoint his more repulsive followers as much as Dewey would have fooled the fat cats. But this leads only to Arthur Schlesinger's dynamic center!*

> McGEORGE BUNDY
> to Justice Felix Frankfurter
> December 3, 1948

McGEORGE BUNDY'S relationship with Henry Stimson did not end with the publication of their book. Mac continued to see the Stimsons, not just socially, but almost as a family member of this childless household. He regularly stopped by for dinner or to spend a long weekend, and otherwise served as the old man's discreet conduit to the world outside Highhold. The relationship was not that of father and son, but something rarer, that of genuine friendship between men of different generations. While, to his peers, Mac's manner with his elders might seem impertinent, some old men were charmed by such directness. By his late twenties, Mac had a striking collection of such men in his orbit. They were invariably powerful men like his father; indeed, initially, they were his father's friends: Archibald MacLeish, Admiral Alan Kirk, the prominent book editor Cass Canfield and, of course, Henry Stimson. Stimson trusted young Bundy utterly, and so did Justice Felix Frankfurter.

In 1946–47, Bundy had corresponded or talked with Frankfurter on numerous occasions concerning the Stimson memoir. The justice had read (and edited) chunks of the manuscript. But their relationship had progressed far beyond the scope of that work. Frankfurter was beginning to consult Bundy regularly on all sorts of issues, including some of the cases before his court.

Bundy's letters contained commentaries on the justice's published opinions—and some none too gentle criticisms of the Court's other opinions.

When Frankfurter's simmering philosophical differences with Justice Hugo Black erupted in the summer of 1947, Bundy wrote, "What I find doubly astonishing is that in trying to make a case Black has adopted what he himself in one passage rejects—the notion that the Court can now find that the XIVth Amendment includes the first 8 [sic]." The case in question—*Adamson v. California*—was the occasion for a fierce dispute between Justices Black and Frankfurter. In a dissent which he would later regard as his finest hour on the Court, Justice Black had argued that the passage of the Fourteenth Amendment had made the Bill of Rights (the first ten amendments) applicable to the states. In just a few years, Black's dissent would prevail, and the Fourteenth Amendment would be used to justify a wave of civil rights and civil liberties rulings against a range of state laws. But the once liberal Frankfurter of Harvard University had gradually become a conservative constitutionalist on the Court, and he found Black's judicial activism a brazen attempt to read into the Constitution what he thought ought to be there. Twenty-eight-year-old Bundy wrote Frankfurter that he was "impressed by the subtle but devastating attack on Blackism," and unconvinced by Black's assertion that freedom from self-incrimination [and by extension other provisions of the Bill of Rights] were "essential to due process."[1] Many years later Bundy's views on judicial activism would be unrecognizable to those who read his briefs in support of affirmative action, but in 1947 he was still very much a rare political animal: a Frankfurter Republican.

Frankfurter welcomed Bundy's commentaries and flattered the young man with his attentions. That September, knowing of Bundy's indecision about his future, Frankfurter made him an unexpected offer. Why not join him the following year as one of his two clerks? Clerking for a Supreme Court justice had become far more prestigious—and certainly it entailed more substantive legal work—than when Bundy's father had clerked for Holmes in 1915. And Mac was not even a lawyer! Even so, Bundy hesitated, not for just a few days, but for several weeks.

When he finally replied to Frankfurter's letter, he declined the offer. "I know my ignorance better than you, but I should be willing to let you stew in the juice of your own kindness if I honestly felt that it would be good for me to do so. But I think it would be wrong for me next year to take another job as personal assistant, to anyone." He explained that he had spent the war years as an aide, and now had spent nearly two years as Stimson's assistant. "By next Spring it will be time for me to go to work on my own, for awhile at least."*

---

* Disappointed, Frankfurter was determined to get a Bundy as his second clerk, so after receiving Mac's decision, the justice turned around and offered the position to Bill, who had just graduated from Harvard Law School. Unaware of the offer to Mac, Bill also refused Frankfurter's invitation, partly because he was a little wary of being the

Frankfurter nevertheless had strong opinions about what young Bundy should do with his life and continued to pursue him. One autumn day in the late 1940s, the justice took Mac for a walk in the Berkshires and had a long talk with him about his prospects. Both men were visiting Archie and Ada MacLeish in their country home. "Felix told me," Mac recalled, " 'It is time you do something sensible. You ought to become a lawyer.' " He pressed Mac very hard, so hard that when Mac firmly demurred, Frankfurter left feeling miffed. Mac thought it "late in the day, by my standards" to go back to square one on a completely new career. He was approaching thirty, and while he wasn't quite sure what he wanted to do, he was attracted to writing history. His brother Bill—whose first love was also history—had nevertheless accepted his father's advice and gone back to law school after the war. By 1947, Bill was a rather unhappy associate at the Washington law firm of Covington & Burling. Mac would not make that kind of "sensible" calculation; he might not have a professional degree, but he had other things going for him.[2]

That autumn he confided to Frankfurter that he had made a "short-term commitment to Walter Lippmann for a job that is shrouded in publishing secrecy." Early in 1948, Bundy met Lippmann in New York to discuss the idea of collaborating on a book. (Lippmann's wife, Helen, took such a liking to Mac Bundy that she tried to match him up with her twenty-three-year-old daughter, Gregor Armstrong. Mac wasn't interested and neither was Gregor.)[3]

Lippmann had been for many years the nation's most influential columnist. Thirty years Bundy's senior, Lippmann—like Stimson, Frankfurter, MacLeish and other old men in young Bundy's orbit—had such a high opinion of this twenty-eight-year-old that he invited Bundy to help him reedit and update his 1937 book, The Good Society.[4] Lippmann told him, "You should come at it thinking of yourself as the owner of an old house which you are free to remodel in any way that you see fit so as to make it habitable for yourself."[5]

Why Lippmann would want to reissue a book which the critics had panned a decade earlier is perplexing. But that Bundy was interested in the project sheds some light on his political views of the time. The Good Society was read by many as an indictment of collectivism. Any degree of state planning of the economy, Lippmann argued, inevitably undermined liberal democracy, a form of government which could flourish only within the market economy. Up to this point, the book could be read as an unqualified defense of laissez-faire capitalism; but then to the confusion of many readers, the second half proceeded to make the case for a welfare-state liberalism—including social insurance, income equalization through progressive taxation, and Keynesian countercyclical government spending—that seemed very much to be the kind of New Deal program characterized as collectivist and authoritarian in the first half of the book. In the midst of the 1930s, this argument satisfied neither partisans nor critics of the New Deal.

"second clerk," and also because "I was thirty years old, and I decided it was time for me to make a living" (WPB interview, Mar. 11, 1993).

A decade later, perhaps Lippmann thought the message could be reworked to appeal to political sensibilities ready for compromise and moderation. Neither Lippmann nor the young McGeorge Bundy liked the collectivist aspects of the New Deal. But as liberals they desperately wished to tame and civilize the market economy, preferably through the judiciary, by means of regulation and law. "Liberal remedies require the liquidation of some, and modification of many, vested rights," Lippmann had written in 1937. But neither in 1937 nor a decade later was Lippmann prepared to sanction the kind of radical steps that would have liquidated some of these "vested"—read "property"—rights. Lippmann's liberalism was too rarefied to be practical. As Henry Steele Commager later wrote of *The Good Society*, it was "an effort to find not so much a compromise as an escape, and the escape was into that eighteenth century past which had laid so firmly, as Lippmann felt, the foundations of true liberalism." [6]

Off and on over the next year Bundy tried to rethink *The Good Society*, but he never produced more than an outline and a few fragments of draft chapters. Eventually, he confessed to Lippmann that he had taken the book apart but could make little or no progress in putting it together again. The problem, he thought, was that the original book was written when it was important "to demonstrate that the logic of full planning was the logic of war and dictatorship; now, among responsible men, the escape from thinking into socialist utopia is no longer prevalent or even very popular." To be sure, there were still socialists, but even those in Britain practiced something quite different from their rhetoric. The danger now was no longer so much from the left as from the right, specifically, from a "revival of Mr. Hoover's philosophy." For Bundy, the true believers in central planning and the "do-nothings" were "equal enemies." The challenge was to make the case for the liberal state operating within a "modern free market." Unfortunately, the market system, Bundy observed, seemed notoriously unstable: ". . . we are now watching our boom slide off under the impact of forces so vague and yet so massive that they might as well be from another world."

Even more worrisome, Bundy confided, was the clear evidence provided by the previous war that "the responsibility of government has outrun the most centralist of theories." It had been big government, using the tactics of a command economy, that had won the war, and this fact had left an indelible imprint on postwar America. By the spring of 1949, with the Cold War shifting into high gear, the state was not about to wither away. But Bundy told Lippmann that he was hopeful, at least, that "there may be a distinction between the interim fortress state of the present and the desired welfare-market society to whose development we even now look forward. . . ."

He couldn't spell out the details for Lippmann, but Bundy was sure that their "desired welfare-market society" could be "reconstructed" precisely because the ideological contest had ended and liberalism had prevailed. "Thus, in 1949," he wrote Lippmann, "as I think we agreed, the battle between right and left, on ideological terms, has become a battle in the clouds revolving around theoretical issues between socialism and capitalism which have little or nothing to do with the practical problem of effective economic organization in a free society. The significant battle-ground has shifted to far more difficult and less exciting problems of degree and form." * 7

INTELLECTUALLY, Lippmann's and Bundy's political roots were buried in eighteenth-century liberalism, but as a practical matter, both men were quietly working to elect Thomas Dewey president of the United States. Bundy had come down to Washington in the summer of 1948 to work with Richard Bissell on the Marshall Plan. "I was just getting my feet wet," Bundy recalled, "when I got an invitation to join the Dewey campaign." Bissell encouraged Bundy to do it because he thought Dewey would win and he would need contacts in the new administration to push the Marshall program. So Bundy moved to New York's Roosevelt Hotel, where for the next few months he virtually lived out of the fifteenth floor suites of the Dewey campaign headquarters. Working under the close supervision of Wall Street lawyer Allen Dulles, Bundy wrote foreign policy speeches for the candidate and briefed Dewey on foreign policy issues. Together with the financier Douglas Dillon and Christian A. Herter, a Massachusetts congressman, Bundy and Dulles served in effect as Dewey's state department. They were also Dewey's central intelligence agency. Allen Dulles's brother John Foster Dulles, who was then a member of the Truman administration's U.S. delegation to the United Nations, regularly leaked classified cables on various foreign policy issues to the Dewey campaign. Foster Dulles, Dewey's presumed secretary of state, was in Paris for much of that autumn, attending the U.N. General Assembly meeting. The U.S. delegation was then involved in delicate negotiations with the Soviets over Allied rights in occupied Berlin, but this did not stop Foster Dulles from leaking classified cables on the negotiations. He had them dispatched to a U.S. government office in New York where they were decoded and then sent by messenger over to the Dewey campaign headquarters in the Roosevelt Hotel. Bundy used this material to prepare daily briefing papers for Truman's opponent.†8

---

* Here, Bundy is anticipating Daniel Bell's 1960 book, *The End of Ideology*, and Francis Fukuyama's 1989 essay "The End of History."
† Ironically, two decades later, Henry Kissinger imitated Dulles's act of political espionage by leaking classified information from Paris on the status of the Vietnam peace negotiations to the Nixon presidential campaign in 1968. What Kissinger did had far more serious implications since the information conveyed through this back channel may have been a factor in Nixon's narrow victory and it certainly facilitated Kissinger's promotion to national security adviser. By contrast, the back channel run by the Dulles brothers (and Bundy) had no influence on the outcome of the 1948 election and was apparently condoned by Secretary of State George C. Marshall. (Walter Isaacson, *Kissinger: A Biography* [New York: Simon & Schuster, 1992], pp. 129–33.)

Mac enjoyed the campaign enormously. He liked the speechwriting and on at least one occasion persuaded Lippmann to collaborate. "There was only one rule," Bundy recalled, "never write anything that the governor hasn't said before." Caution pervaded the campaign. Determined to appear as reasonable as Truman was shrill, Dewey refused to respond to Truman's jabs even when the president accused him of being a "front man" for the same kind of "powerful reactionary forces" which had encouraged German and Japanese fascism in the last war.[9]

Everyone Bundy knew—including his father, Frankfurter and Lippmann —thought Dewey was a sure winner. Lippmann thought Truman a small, insecure man who "does not know how to be President . . . does not know how to conduct foreign relations or how to be Commander-in-Chief." He was certain Truman would be defeated. When asked about the campaign by his colleagues at the Society of Fellows, Bundy had replied with breezy certainty, "We're just riding the polls in." Mac recalled, "I had long lunches with people who wanted ambassadorships in the coming Dewey administration. The results of the election were a complete shock."[10]

Afterwards, Frankfurter tried to persuade Bundy to write an analysis of the Republican defeat. Mustering all his legendary flattery, the justice wrote Bundy that what he had in mind was an inquiry written "by that aspect of you which for me is a combination, *in posse*, of the earlier Henry Adams and the later Brooks Adams." The comparison to the Adamses—exemplars of intellectual aristocrats in nineteenth-century America—was certainly pretentious, but not inaccurate. The young chronicler of Henry Stimson's life was, like the Adamses, a product of Boston, a deist, a skeptic, yet a political idealist, a young man with a young man's ambition to move in the world of action while, paradoxically, still preserving his sense of ironic detachment.

If flattered, Bundy nevertheless thought Frankfurter's proposal unwise. "I think Bundy of Eliot House might have done it and may do it later," he wrote Frankfurter, "but it would come ill from Bundy late of the Roosevelt Hotel, however olympian and Adamish his approach." At the very least, he needed time to restore his perspective. But even then, he asked the justice, "must I cease from partisan 'aspiration'? Which Adams should one imitate after all? Are not the elder and better ones such partisans as might affright their student offspring?"[11]

By partisan, Bundy meant that he still thought of himself very much as "one of those Republicans who wanted to rescue Theodore Roosevelt's party." He and Frankfurter might be friends, but Bundy knew the justice to be both a very partisan Democrat and a man who relished pulling political strings. "How funny," Bundy said decades later when reminded of the incident. "That's a very Felix suggestion. Find his only friend in the enemy camp and tell him to explain why they were tangled up!"[12]

The political lesson Bundy learned from the Dewey debacle was simple: "A Warm Heart & A Willing Hand will almost always beat Competence &

Economy. And should." The candidate was flawed, not the politics. Still, Bundy thought the victorious Democrats would move to the center. He told Frankfurter, "I prefer Mr. T [Truman] in victory to his pursuit of it. He will disappoint his more repulsive followers as much as Dewey would have fooled the fat cats. But this leads only to Arthur Schlesinger's dynamic center! Do you like the word dynamic? . . . Have you written any good opinions lately? Send me one to keep me in touch with your own dynamic center."[13]

Earlier that year Arthur Schlesinger, Jr., had published an essay which later became the core of his 1949 book, *The Vital Center*. Schlesinger's thesis that political power in America was usually and rightfully claimed by the party that managed to seize the ideological "vital center" was a message that a Boston Republican like Bundy could embrace easily.

Schlesinger defined his liberalism by emphasizing what it was not. At a time when liberals were being labeled by the Republican right wing as pro-communist, some liberals were desperate to disassociate themselves from the Communist Party and those considered to be its fellow travelers. Postwar America was a very conservative society, and by the late 1940s red-baiting was becoming a national spectacle.

In self-defense, anti-communist liberals began loudly to proclaim their anti-communist credentials. In January 1947, Schlesinger became a founding member of a new caucus called the Americans for Democratic Action (ADA). Joining him were other like-minded anti-communist liberals such as John Kenneth Galbraith, Joe Alsop, Joe Rauh, James Wechsler, Hubert Humphrey and Reinhold Niebuhr. (Schlesinger described Niebuhr as the "architect of the ADA foreign policy.")[14] As a "Frankfurter Republican," Mac Bundy had no need to join something like the ADA. His anti-communist credentials were already in order. Yet neither did he really believe the communists were a threat to anyone but themselves: ". . . although we are tempted to think of Communism as the dynamic religion of the age," he wrote Lippmann in 1949, "I think it is more accurate to assess Communism as a currently virulent heresy [the word "parasite" was crossed out] operating in a turmoil generated by the impact of the West as a whole on itself and the rest of the world."[15]

By the time *Vital Center* came out in 1949, Schlesinger was a widely recognized public intellectual. He and Bundy were also the closest of friends. They were in many ways very much alike. Both were junior fellows—and therefore never received doctorates—yet they would become prominent figures in the academe. Both were recognized for their brilliance at a young age. Schlesinger had won a Pulitzer Prize at the age of twenty-eight. And like Bundy, he was sometimes, particularly from a distance, seen as arrogant. One of his friends, Richard Rovere, later wrote of Schlesinger, "Partly, I think, because of his precocity and partly because he tended toward overkill in controversy, he was widely held to be a rude and arrogant young man, intolerant of those who disagreed with him and contemptuous of those who knew less than he did." He also had Washington fever. "Cambridge was all very well," he once told Rovere, "but the real world was in Washington." Felix Frankfurter, no stranger to power himself, later told Rovere, "I'm very fond of Arthur, but he is not like us. You and I have no interest in power, but Arthur loves it. He likes to be near it, he likes the feel of it, the smell of it."[16]

MUCH the same thing could be said for Mac Bundy. By the spring of 1949, Mac had accepted an appointment as a lecturer at Harvard, a job arranged in part by Frankfurter's "helpful counsel."[17] But since his classes would not begin until September, Mac took on a project with the Council on Foreign Relations in New York to study Marshall Plan aid to Europe. It wasn't Washington, but it might as well have been. The council's study group on aid to Europe included some of the foreign policy establishment's leading figures. Working with young Bundy on the project were Allen Dulles, David Lilienthal, Dwight Eisenhower, Will Clayton, George Kennan, Richard M. Bissell and Franklin A. Lindsay. Dulles, Bissell and Lindsay had been members of OSS during the war and would shortly become high-ranking officials of the newly formed Central Intelligence Agency. Eisenhower was about to become president. Kennan was a high-ranking State Department official. Their meetings were considered so sensitive that the usual off-the-record transcript was not distributed to council members. There was good reason for the secrecy. These were probably the only private citizens privy to the highly classified fact that there was a covert side to the Marshall Plan. Specifically, the CIA was tapping into the $200 million a year in local currency counterpart funds contributed by the recipients of Marshall Plan aid. These unvouchered monies were being used by the CIA to finance anti-communist electoral activities in France and Italy and to support sympathetic journalists, labor union leaders and politicians.[18]

Both Bundy brothers were also good friends of Frank Wisner, the legendary intelligence officer who ran these covert programs in Western Europe. They socialized with Wisner and his pretty wife, Polly, often at dinner parties hosted by Joe Alsop. "Everybody knew everybody else, of course," recalled Schlesinger. "All old personal friends. [Chip] Bohlen, the Alsops, Dick Bissell. You couldn't help feeling the institutional dynamic at work. . . ." Phil and Kay Graham of the *Washington Post* were also part of the same social scenery. In short, the council's study group placed Mac Bundy among a small group of like-minded men who fully understood and endorsed the necessity for waging psychological warfare against the Soviet Union.[19]

The policy paper Mac wrote that summer, "Working Paper on the Problem of Political Equilibrium," assumed that such covert activities in Western Europe were worthy endeavors. Indeed, his paper points to the achievements of this political warfare as an argument against those right-wing Cold Warriors who favored a preventive war against the Russians.[20]

The one significant disagreement Bundy had with Schlesinger in these years was over the Alger Hiss case: Schlesinger was certain of Hiss's guilt, while Bundy contributed early on to the Hiss defense fund. In January 1949, when Secretary of State–designate Dean Acheson forthrightly told his Senate confirmation committee that he and Hiss had "become friends and remained friends," Bundy applauded him: "Your statement today as a friend about a friend is one of the two or three really clear things that have been said by any one at any time in the Chambers affair. I know that hundreds who have watched men hedge will cheer—and I hope that millions will now think twice before they judge by headlines. Anyhow, they will know that the new Secretary of State is a man."[21]

In September 1949, Mac left New York to take up his new job as a lecturer in the government department at Harvard. His patron in the government department was William Yandell Elliott, a legendary figure at Harvard for years and perhaps the most powerful member of the department. A domineering man, Elliott had strong opinions and demanding expectations of his students and junior faculty. (In addition to Bundy, he was a mentor to the young Henry Kissinger.) A Rhodes scholar and a product of Oxford, Elliott favored the tutorial system, and as such was enamored of those like Bundy who came out of the junior fellow program. The fact that thirty-year-old Bundy had never taken a class in government was not a problem for Elliott.

Bundy's first course, "Government 180: The U.S. in World Affairs," was an immediate hit. When some students complained about the length of his reading list, Bundy replied, "If the lists are long, that is intentional."[22] He was a natural talker, and when he lectured he often paced about the room, stabbing the air with accusatory fingers to underscore his point. It was usually a performance that kept his students awake. His lecture on the Munich sellout of 1938 was often given to an audience of standing room only. He made it clear that the prudent use of force early in the Munich crisis would have succeeded where appeasement certainly failed. Such Stimsonian themes of interventionism were, of course, by then a pillar of conventional wisdom. But the verve and colorful manner with which Bundy retold the Munich calamity helped to popularize an outlook which influenced a whole new generation of postwar policy intellectuals.

John Kenneth Galbraith, however, was one Harvard professor who was unconvinced of the universal lessons of Munich, and he often argued with Bundy about interventionism. An exasperated Bundy would exclaim, "Ken, you always advise against the use of force—do you realize that?"[23] Despite their political differences—Galbraith was a liberal Democrat—he and Bundy soon became the closest of friends.

Like Galbraith, Bundy made a point of being brash and informal, and he acted as if he had no patience for the university's bureaucracy. Less than a month after arriving on campus, Mac wrote Frankfurter, "My first brushes with the Harvard bureaucracy give me an internal sense of astonishment that the university has accomplished anything ever since it first hired a dean." Yet, far from complaining, he wrote the justice just a few days later that he was ecstatic about his new environment: "Harvard is wonderful. I find myself having such a good time that I wonder why I didn't point toward all this before...."[24] He did not admit it to Frankfurter, but there was a personal reason Bundy may have been feeling particularly happy about his new situation.

Not long after arriving back in Cambridge, Mac went out on a blind date with Mary Buckminster Lothrop, the associate director of admissions at Radcliffe. A pretty, twenty-five-year-old brunette, Mary had won some kind of bet with Louisa Clark, the daughter of Grenville Clark, a legendary Wall Street lawyer, and her reward was a blind date. Louisa, then a law student and a friend of Mac's, arranged the date. Ironically, Kay Bundy had tried to introduce Mac to Mary two years earlier, but Mac had refused to be fixed up by his mother. Kay had known Mary's mother, Eleanor, for years and the Lothrops had even summered at Manchester. Mac's younger sister Laurie had been a playmate of Mary's when the two girls were ten or eleven years old. So it was something of a mystery as to why Mac had never met Mary Lothrop. Now he lost no time. "After that first date," Mac recalled, "I called her the very next day." He took her out once more, then sat down and wrote her a letter proposing marriage. Mary was charmed by this impetuousness and accepted. When a mutual friend later told her he had always thought Mac to be a gifted but austere young man, Mary laughed and said, "Austere? Then he must have changed before I met him. How could I call a man austere who took me out twice and then wrote a letter proposing marriage? I call that impulsive."[25]

Three months later Mary Lothrop surprised Kay by showing up at the Bundy family Christmas party. Soon afterward, Mac announced their engagement. Mac described Mary to his old friend John Mason Brown as "a beautiful, laughing, bright and wonderful gal from Boston and Manchester that I never met until three months ago." The wedding date was set for June 10, 1950. (Later, Brown would say that Mary had "the face of Lorna Doone.")[26]

Mac made a point of taking Mary to Stimson's Highhold estate, where she was introduced to the penultimate Bundy family mentor. Though in failing health, the Colonel was busy trying to put together a collection of his speeches for publication. Many of Mac's Boston friends had known her for years. Six years younger than Mac, she was a distant cousin of Ben Bradlee's; the future editor of the *Washington Post* had known her as a childhood friend. Mary's father, Francis B. Lothrop, was another Groton boy (class of 1917) who had gone on to Harvard and then accumulated a substantial fortune. He was a quiet, eccentric man. Mary, however, took after her outgoing mother. Unlike Mac, who was always putting people on edge with his biting wit, Mary was the kind of person who made even strangers feel at ease. She was warm and gracious with everyone, and though pretty, was not the kind of woman who was ever flirtatious. She was, in short, Mac's temperamental opposite.[27] But she was also very Boston Brahmin. Years later, when McGeorge Bundy was a household name in the 1960s, a friend went to Shreve, Crump & Low Co., Boston's exclusive jewelry shop, and bought a gift for Bundy. When informed that the gift—a pair of silver dice—was to be inscribed to one McGeorge Bundy, the elderly clerk in a black suit scratched his head for a moment and then said, "Oh, I know that Bundy name, he was the fellow who married Mary Lothrop."[28] Obviously, the Lothrops were Bostonians of substance in a way that the Bundys had been only for a generation. Mac had followed his father's lead by marrying well.

Mary Lothrop continued to work that winter and spring of 1950, but quit Radcliffe the day she was married at Beverly Farms, in St. John's Episcopal Church. Groton's Malcolm Strachan performed the service, and afterwards they had a large reception. As a wedding gift, Frankfurter gave Mac a complete bound and boxed collection of *The New Republic.** Stimson was too ill to attend the wedding, and died a few weeks later.

That summer Mac and Mary moved into a small one-bedroom, one-study apartment in Winthrop House overlooking the Charles River. Mac was more than a little satisfied: "We were a couple of baked beans ready to get married."[29]

LESS than a year later the government department recommended Bundy for tenure as an associate professor. When Harvard president James B. Conant was asked to approve the appointment, he hesitated. Conant knew and admired Harvey Bundy's son, and he certainly felt in Mac's debt for the stellar service he had performed as Stimson's ghostwriter on the defense of the bomb in *Harper's.* But as he looked over Bundy's qualifying papers, Conant asked whether it was true that Bundy had never taken an undergraduate or graduate course in government. "That's right," replied the representative from the government faculty. "Are you sure that's right?" asked Conant. "I'm sure" was the answer.

"Well," responded Conant as he signed off on the appointment, "all I can say is that it couldn't have happened in Chemistry."[30]

By 1951, Bundy was well on his way to becoming a "public intellectual." In May 1945, Captain McGeorge Bundy had published a short essay in *The Atlantic* entitled "A Letter to Twelve College Presidents" in which he made the case for universal military service—even in peacetime. He had then ghostwritten Stimson's February 1947 *Harper's* essay, and coauthored the Stimson memoirs. Now, in November 1951, Bundy published in *The Atlantic* a review of the young William F. Buckley's first book, *God and Man at Yale.* He savaged the book. Bundy called it a "dishonest" attack on Yale as a "hotbed of 'atheism' and 'collectivism.' " After soundly ridiculing the notion that Yale's economics department was somehow subversive, Bundy charged that Buckley was a "twisted and ignorant young man whose personal views of economics would have seemed reactionary to Mark Hanna."[31]

In reply, Buckley charged that "haughty totalitarians" like Bundy, under

---

* Sometime later Mac lent the volumes to his neighbor Edmund Wilson, who never returned them.

the guise of "academic freedom," were leading the country inexorably "towards collectivism." Bundy, wrote Buckley, would no doubt live to see the country suffer the ravages of this collectivism, "even from his privileged position of minor Court Hatchet-Man. . . ."[32]

Reporting on the controversial exchange, the *Saturday Evening Post* thought Bundy had been too tough on Buckley and suggested that if "McCarthyism" was abroad, so too was "McGeorge Bundyism." Dwight Macdonald, writing in *The Reporter*, labeled Bundy's review an "apoplectic denunciation." Liberals like Bundy, Macdonald wrote, had reacted to Buckley with all "the grace of an elephant cornered by a mouse."[33]

Buckley, of course, turned out to be wrong that his conservative crusade was "losing" against the inexorable tide of "collectivist" liberalism. Over the next few decades Buckley's political philosophy would be embraced by commanding elements of the Republican Party, while Bundy's "haughty" liberalism would come to be blamed for a host of the nation's ills. The bitterness and personal invective that characterized their encounter in the pages of *The Atlantic* in 1951 would serve as a harbinger of the intemperate times to come.*

At the same time that Bundy found himself sparring with young Bill Buckley, he was busy editing an annotated collection of speeches and public statements by Dean Acheson. He finished writing *The Pattern of Responsibility* in October 1951 and the volume appeared to somewhat critical reviews in December. Unlike his work for Stimson, this volume is neither biography nor history. It reads like a lawyer's brief on behalf of a client accused of high crimes and political misdemeanors. By 1951, Acheson was a lightning rod for McCarthyites, so by any measure it was a mark of political courage for Mac to associate himself in print with the secretary of state.

And that, of course, is Bundy's point, that to question the loyalty and patriotism of a man of Acheson's stature is in itself a mark of irresponsibility. In the "hue-and-cry against Mr. Acheson," Mac explains in his introduction, there was "room for a book whose evidence might set the more irresponsible attacks in a perspective of fact, while providing Mr. Acheson's own answer on arguable matters."[34]

The book originated from a phone call Bundy received from Paul Brooks, a friend who worked at Houghton Mifflin. "He knew I was upset about the attacks on Acheson," Bundy later recalled, "and asked me if I could put together something by way of reply."[35]

Bundy quickly produced a book by taking excerpts from Acheson's speeches, organizing them by subject and splicing his own commentary into the "Red Dean's" prose. The result was a meandering defense of Acheson's record as secretary of state with chapter titles that included the "Soviet

* The two men didn't meet until years later when Buckley invited Bundy to lunch. "It was not a great success," Bundy recalled. "He just doesn't strike me as an interesting man. He's just a mélange of propositions hotly defended and attacked."

Threat," "The Great Debate on Troops to Europe," "Germany," "Security and Loyalty in the Department of State" and "Korea."

Whatever its depiction of Acheson, the book reveals much of Bundy's worldview. Mac was adamant that Acheson was not "soft or pink," but he volunteered that he had some honest differences of opinion with the great man, and he painstakingly listed these in his preface:

• Mac disagreed with Acheson's decision to rearm the Germans in the autumn of 1950.

• Acheson's China policy had not "adequately assessed the probable character of a Communist regime. . . ." Nevertheless, Bundy quickly added, "That does not imply that I think Nationalist China could have been saved; I do not."

• Bundy criticized Acheson's defense of the State Department's loyalty and security program, charging that it had been "clumsily administered" and had "produced some unfairness to individuals. . . ."

• Regarding the "vexed issue of Alger Hiss," Bundy writes, "I think it entirely understandable that Mr. Acheson should have felt it right and necessary to say everything that he said, but I also think it plain that Alger Hiss, even on the difficult assumption that he was wrongly convicted, has not honorably or candidly repaid his friendship and compassion." Bundy's purpose here—rather neatly accomplished—was to defend Acheson for defending Hiss, and simultaneously, to put himself on record as doubtful of the innocence of a man to whose defense fund he had contributed.

• Lastly, Bundy attempted to deal with the larger charge that Acheson had been soft on the Soviet threat: "If the charge against him is that in 1944 and early 1945 he was hopeful of Russian good intentions, then I believe he must plead guilty, along with most of his countrymen, myself among them."[36] In other words, most Americans, Acheson and Bundy included, had been merely naive about Soviet intentions. But Bundy knew that this alone was not sufficient. Indeed, the subtext of Bundy's commentary for the next several hundred pages is to argue the merits of a liberal strategy for dealing with the Soviets.

His logic borrowed heavily from the dark pragmatism of the Reverend Reinhold Niebuhr, a friend whom he later called "our favorite moral philosopher."[37] Acheson's Soviet policy too often promised "definite results in an indefinite world."[38] As a good Niebuhrian, Bundy seemed to be saying, Acheson should have known better. The world was evil, but being part of this world, man must learn to live with the evil within him and in his neighbors. From this theological insight came the underpinnings of a foreign policy based on coexistence with an essentially evil neighbor, the Russians. In this vein, Bundy quotes Acheson from an April 1950 speech: "It does not follow from this [moral conflict] that the two systems, theirs and ours, cannot exist concurrently in this world. Good and evil can and do exist concurrently in the whole great realm of human life. They exist within every individual, within every nation, and within every human group."[39]

In Bundy's account, it was easy to say what Acheson's foreign policy was not: it repudiated isolationism, appeasement and preventive war. As to what it was for, that was harder to define, but "basically the position can be summarized in the following propositions: Resist Communism, and build 'situations of strength'; work for an eventual settlement without war, accepting the fact that the course ahead is long, hard, and dangerous; stick to our ideals." In the long run, Bundy argues, the "Communist and non-Communist worlds may be able to live together in the same world, without war." And if war can be averted, over time the Soviet empire might evolve into something less oppressive and aggressive. Borrowing from the realism of George Kennan, Bundy points out that the Soviets' imperial behavior stemmed as much from its czarist roots as from its communist ideology. And if so, it was important to remember that the Russian state has historically "displayed considerable caution" in their drive to achieve hegemony.[40]

Essentially, Bundy's defense of Acheson's policies amounts to a liberal interpretation of Kennan's containment strategy. War was to be avoided, preventive war was regarded as an insanity, and every opportunity would be seized to negotiate accommodations with the Soviets. As such, containment was not to be regarded as a military strategy, but rather a political strategy to persevere against an evil, but essentially inefficient—and therefore ultimately weak—rival economic system. Acheson's goal was not a violent "rollback" of the Soviet sphere of influence, but an uneasy accommodation that hopefully would plant the seeds of evolution and liberalization. "We do not propose to subvert the Soviet Union," Acheson said. "We shall not attempt to undermine Soviet independence."

But Bundy hastened to explain, "This disclaimer of any effort to destroy Soviet independence should not be taken as a refusal to employ certain methods of political and psychological pressure to weaken Soviet totalitarianism. The public record on this subject is necessarily and properly obscure, but it would be rash to assume that in the present phase of Soviet imperialism Acheson has rejected the notion of acting where possible to weaken the Kremlin's grip on the Russian people."[41] A sophisticated response to the Soviet challenge, Bundy suggested, would include a vigorous menu of covert operations and psychological warfare.

NOT very long after the publication of *The Pattern of Responsibility*, Mac Bundy received a phone call from Acheson. Would Mac have time, asked the secretary of state, to serve as the recording secretary to a State Department "panel of consultants on disarmament"? Bundy accepted the assignment, not only as a courtesy to Acheson, but also because the panel was to be chaired by the famous Manhattan Project physicist J. Robert Oppenheimer.*

---

* The Oppenheimer Panel included Vannevar Bush, Dartmouth president John S. Dickey, Allen Dulles and Joseph Johnson, president of the Carnegie Endowment for International Peace.

Bundy was eager to meet the physicist. To prepare for his job as rapporteur, he traveled to Oppenheimer's offices at the Institute for Advanced Study in Princeton, New Jersey, and subjected himself to one of the physicist's famous lectures for novices on the atom. Bundy was enthralled; "Robert" was "marvelous, fascinating and complicated." Afterwards, he wrote an uncharacteristically humble note to his new friend, saying, "I find it hard to thank you enough for the patience with which you undertook my education last week; I only hope that somehow I can be useful enough to make it worth your effort." [42] It is not hard to understand why the two men suited each other temperamentally; both were the kind of smart men who enjoyed the company of other smart men. Both were skeptics and interested in politics, and neither suffered fools. In no time at all the two men were exchanging handwritten notes to each other addressed as "Dear Robert" and "Dear Mac" in which they discussed everything from the merits of Harvard's physics department to the health of their respective wives. [43]

By 1952, Oppenheimer was engaged in a losing battle to thwart the building of a thermonuclear bomb, the H-bomb. The Korean War was raging, and with Cold War tensions at a peak President Truman had already made the decision to go ahead with the "super bomb," largely on the grounds that if the Russians could produce it, then Americans had to build it first. The decision, made in secret, was vigorously supported by the Joint Chiefs and, most notably, Oppenheimer's rival and critic within the community of atomic physicists, Edward Teller. When these supporters of the super bomb learned of the creation of the Oppenheimer Panel, they regarded it as another effort to stop the super. For all these reasons, Bundy's service as Oppenheimer's note-taker would be an eye-opener.

For one thing, the matters under discussion were so highly classified that Bundy was required to obtain the highest possible security clearances. Because Harvard lacked the proper security vaults for classified papers, he was given an office at MIT's newly founded Center for International Studies (which was funded indirectly by the CIA). In one of their first meetings in early June the Oppenheimer Panel agreed that their brief was first and foremost the "problem of survival" in which the United States and Russia faced "a scorpion stalemate —which might or might not involve active war. . . ." [44]

A month later Bundy hosted a second meeting in the living room of his new quarters, a rambling nineteenth-century Cambridge house within bicycling distance of Harvard Square. Oppenheimer, Joe Johnson and John Dickey were present, while Harvard president James B. Conant attended as an unofficial observer. Conant led the discussion, which focused on how oblivious most Americans were of the very real dangers of atomic warfare. According to Bundy's notes, Conant complained that the "ordinary American" thought of the bomb as a weapon threatening the Soviets, "while the more significant fact was that now and in the future such blows could be delivered by others on the United States." Even without the H-bomb, Conant argued, all but the largest of U.S. cities could easily be wiped out with a single atomic weapon.

No one on the panel disagreed that such weapons were by definition militarily useless. Once the American monopoly over such weapons had been broken in 1949, the atomic bomb essentially became more of a threat to America than a weapon that any president would ever want to use again in combat. The problem was that the American public did not recognize this fact. Even worse, Conant said, was "the attitude of the leaders of the American military establishment." Our generals were relying almost exclusively upon these weapons as "their principal hope of victory in the event of all-out war." If Americans could have confidence in the strength of their conventional defenses, "it would become possible for the United States to dispense with its present reliance on atomic bombs." But for this to happen, Conant argued, U.S. military leaders "must be persuaded that atomic weapons in the long run are on balance a danger to the United States."[45]

That the bomb was a useless military weapon because it could not be used without inviting nuclear retaliation and that its mere existence represented a threat to American cities was not, of course, a concept unfamiliar to Bundy. He had known for some years now of Stimson's own very early misgivings about atomic weapons. He knew Stimson had believed that it was in the U.S. national interest to place all such weapons of mass destruction under international control. The irony could not have escaped Bundy that the men sitting in his living room—who just seven years earlier had worked practically night and day to build the bomb—now shared all of Stimson's fundamental misgivings. They too favored some sort of nuclear disarmament regime. That June evening Conant even suggested that as a first step perhaps the United States should issue a "no first use" declaration: it might, he said, "be a good sign if the United States could reach a stage in its military position in which it would become possible for us to announce officially that we would not be the first to use atomic weapons in any new war."[46]

Not only did Conant now favor no first use, but according to his biographer James Hershberg, he also supported Vannevar Bush's proposal to announce a tacit moratorium on any testing of a thermonuclear bomb. The first such test was already scheduled for that autumn, and any postponement was sure to meet with staunch opposition from the military establishment.

Conant, Bundy and the others on the Oppenheimer Panel that summer knew, however, that they had no means of advancing these ideas to the political arena. Ironically, they were caught in the veil of secrecy that they had themselves draped over atomic matters. They could not go public with their concerns without violating their security clearances. In a sense, they knew that the greatest secret was that there were no atomic secrets. Any nuclear weapons that could be developed by the United States could also be developed by the Soviet Union and in very short order. But these were not the kind of men who could contemplate throwing their security clearances to the wind and taking their case to the public.

The Oppenheimer Panel continued to meet that summer and autumn, but their deliberations were clearly academic. Bush's proposal for a moratorium on testing the super bomb was flatly rejected on October 9 by the National Security Council. Defense secretary Robert Lovett angrily said "any such idea should be immediately put out of mind and that any papers that might exist on the subject should be destroyed." Three weeks later the United States exploded a 10.4-megaton thermonuclear bomb in the Pacific, vaporizing the island of Elugelab. A clearly depressed Conant told a *Newsweek* reporter, "I no longer have any connection with the atomic bomb. I have no sense of accomplishment."[47]

Bundy nevertheless wrote up a report of the panel's recommendations, which was forwarded to departing Secretary of State Acheson just as Dwight D. Eisenhower moved into the Oval Office. It is a prescient document, and Bundy was obviously proud of his authorship. He later took the trouble in 1982 to publish an edited version of the document in an academic journal, entitled "Early Thoughts on Controlling the Nuclear Arms Race."[48]

At the time, of course, this paper was highly classified and circulated among only a handful of Eisenhower administration officials. Had it been released in 1953, it surely would have created a firestorm of controversy. Bundy paints a bleak portrait of a world in which nuclear weapons would soon threaten all civilization. "The riven atom," he quotes Stimson saying in 1947, "uncontrolled, can be only a growing menace to us all." The Soviets, Bundy writes, could have one thousand atomic bombs in just a "few years," and "5,000 only a few years further on." This was the power to win not an ordinary military victory, but "the power to end a civilization and a very large number of the people in it." Bundy concedes that this nuclear stalemate might lead to a "strange stability" in which both sides would refrain from using a suicidal weapon. But if so, "a world so dangerous may not be very calm, and to maintain peace it will be necessary for statesmen to decide against rash actions not just once, but every time." In conclusion, he suggests that "unless the contest in atomic armaments is in some way moderated, our whole society will come increasingly into peril of the gravest kind."

In the face of such peril, Bundy (and the Oppenheimer panelists) placed as their primary recommendation the simple idea of "candor." Americans were complacent and ignorant of the nuclear peril largely because a policy of excessive secrecy had kept them that way. To rectify matters, Bundy urges that ". . . the United States Government should tell the story of the atomic danger . . . the rate and impact of atomic production . . . and that it should direct attention to the fact that beyond a certain point we cannot ward off the Soviet threat merely by 'keeping ahead of the Russians.' "[49]

Logically, Bundy argues, a policy of candor would alert the American people to the nuclear peril and simultaneously signal the Soviets that we did not intend to use this weapon in a preemptive first strike. Washington could then begin to pursue a policy of dealing with both the Soviet Union and the arms race. He puts no stock in the current U.N. disarmament talks, which had dragged on interminably with no progress. But he urges direct, continual communication with the Soviets. The Kremlin should know roughly the size of the American nuclear arsenal and that we were interested in bilateral talks on reducing this arsenal. All in all, this was a policy prescription that Bundy himself only tentatively explored in the 1960s, and which Henry Kissinger very belatedly and reluctantly acted upon in the 1970s.

If the recommendations of the Oppenheimer Panel's Bundy report had been followed by the Eisenhower administration in 1953, the Cold War might certainly have taken a different, less militarized trajectory. This is a speculation Bundy himself later posed in his 1982 *New York Review of Books* essay on "The Missed Chance to Stop the H-Bomb."[50] Eisenhower's National Security Council initially agreed that a policy of candor would not constitute an unacceptable security risk, but ultimately, the result was a presidential address, "Atoms for Peace," which probably served to reinforce the country's complacency, and jump-started a program of atomic energy that inadvertently became a source for nuclear weapons proliferation.

Over the remainder of the 1950s the Eisenhower administration's erratic policies on arms control and nuclear defense greatly annoyed Bundy and fueled his growing disaffection from the Republican Party. But that was to come later. By early 1953, when Bundy passed on his highly classified findings to the State Department, he had established his credentials among Washington insiders as one of a handful of policy intellectuals privy to the highest of security clearances. And that fact would be critical to his career at Harvard in the midst of McCarthyism.

7

Dean Bundy of Harvard, 1953–1960

> *. . . in our search for excellence, once we are satisfied that a man is not a rascal (a standard which in Harvard's view excludes Americans who still surrender to Communist discipline), we do not worry much about his politics. . . .*
>
> DEAN MCGEORGE BUNDY
> 1955

B Y THE END OF 1952, America was in the grip of what one historian later called the "Great Fear." Thousands of civil servants, teachers, scientists, journalists, Hollywood scriptwriters and ordinary working-class citizens had lost their jobs in a government-orchestrated anti-communist purge. Federal loyalty boards, the attorney general's list of subversive organizations, congressional committees, loyalty oaths, Smith Act prosecutions and the FBI's extensive network of informers constituted a machinery of repression that operated with devastating efficiency.[1]

Universities were not immune from the witch-hunts. Congressional investigators knew that Harvard had been home to a network of Communist Party cells. Right-wing critics sneeringly called Harvard the "Kremlin on the Charles."[2] Long-awaited congressional hearings to investigate subversion in universities were now scheduled for February 1953, and more than a dozen former Harvard students or teachers were on the witness list. Understandably, the faculty was nervous about the impending confrontation, but at the same time many felt confident that Harvard would be well defended by its president, James B. Conant.

So it was with considerable distress that the Harvard community learned that on the first day of the New Year 1953, Conant had informed the Harvard Corporation of his decision to step down from the presidency. After nearly twenty years Conant was tired of "flexing the same muscles all the time." Eager for a complete change of pace, Conant had accepted President-elect

Dwight D. Eisenhower's offer to name him high commissioner to the newly sovereign Federal Republic of Germany. "Where will I be 4 years from now?" Conant noted in his diary. "Heaven knows, but at least not on this job."[3]

Conant appeared to be abandoning Cambridge just as a battle over academic freedom was about to begin. This was bad enough, but it was particularly galling that he was leaving for a mere ambassadorship. "It seemed ten steps down," said Mac Bundy, "for the president of Harvard to merely run Germany."[4]

Rumors quickly circulated around Cambridge about who might replace Conant. And when in April, Bundy was appointed the new chair of the government department, his name was added to the short list of candidates for the presidency. He had just celebrated his thirty-fourth birthday. Bundy's rapid promotion from lecturer in 1949 to a tenured position in 1951 to chair of a department in which he didn't even have a degree suggested he had been ordained for higher office. Why not the presidency? Conant himself had been only forty years old when he assumed the presidency in 1933. Though a Yale undergraduate, Bundy had no fewer than thirty-three direct Harvard ancestors in his family tree. His personal association with Harvard now dated back to 1941, when he had begun his stint as a junior fellow. And, of course, his great-uncle was none other than Conant's predecessor, A. Lawrence Lowell.

Unbeknownst to the Cambridge rumor mill, Charles E. Wyzanski, Jr., the head of the Board of Overseers, was lobbying the Harvard Corporation to pick Bundy. So too was the New York patriarch, Judge Learned Hand, who argued that Bundy—whom he called "the brightest man in America"—would be an authentic successor to Presidents Eliot and Lowell. Another eminent member of the Harvard Board of Overseers, Walter Lippmann, was also urging Bundy's appointment.[5]

Not unaware of the speculation, Bundy laughingly referred to the color of his Eli pedigree and quipped that such talk was nothing more than a "blue herring."[6] Still, he must have felt at least a pang of disappointment when the Harvard Corporation instead gave the nod that spring to an outsider, Nathan Marsh Pusey, then the president of Wisconsin's Lawrence College.

Pusey was in every respect Bundy's opposite, an apparent nobody, an unexceptional fish in the backwaters of Wisconsin. Forty-six years old and a Harvard graduate, Pusey had grown up in Iowa, and he still exuded a certain midwestern moral certitude scorned by Cambridge cynics. He was frugal of word and polite to a fault. He was a believer, not a cynic. Decrying postwar America's materialism, at Lawrence he had demanded that religion should play a prominent role in campus life. An ardent believer in the value of a liberal arts education, he had required that physics majors read Shakespeare and art historians read John Stuart Mill. "College people," he wrote in 1949, "believe that something can be done about the state of the world, not blatantly, crudely or self-righteously, but quietly, intelligently, and persuasively, and especially in and through individual lives."[7]

He was a teacher's teacher, a professor who had never written a book, a fact which alone suggested to some that he was not qualified for tenure at Harvard, let alone the presidency. "Pusey had a great reputation for religiosity," Arthur Schlesinger, Jr., said, "and he did not seem to have the kind of incisiveness and skepticism which some of the faculty felt a Harvard president ought to have."[8]

But after the mercurial figure of James Conant, who had ruled Harvard as if he were the nation's number one educator, the Harvard Corporation believed they had in Pusey a president who would be a full-time administrator, whose very un-Cambridge qualities would require him to focus on Harvard's business and not the nation's. He had one additional quality which made him particularly attractive to the Harvard Corporation in the spring of 1953: he was a liberal educator from Wisconsin who had publicly criticized Senator Joseph McCarthy in his own home state. In 1951, Pusey had joined a bipartisan group, the Wisconsin Citizens' Committee on McCarthy's Record, which had published a small book attacking McCarthy's record. It was thought by the Harvard Corporation that this act of political courage would endear the new president to Harvard's faculty.

When Pusey's appointment was announced in July, McCarthy announced that "Harvard's loss is Wisconsin's gain." The senator had not forgotten Pusey's stand against him in the 1952 election, and now told a reporter, "I don't think Pusey is or has been a member of the Communist Party, but he is a rabid anti-anti-Communist."[9]

The unflappable Pusey didn't even bother to respond: "That I was being attacked by McCarthy immediately gave me a standing I otherwise never would have had in the Harvard community. As it was, the *Crimson* referred to me as 'Pusey, Pusey, Who's he? Who's he?' "

Shortly before taking office, while vacationing on a Wisconsin lake, Pusey was briefed on his new duties by David Bailey, Harvard's secretary. Bailey told him that his first order of business would be to select a new dean for the Faculty of Arts and Sciences. "Dave had a list of five candidates," Pusey recalled. "At the bottom of the list was Mac Bundy. I didn't know Bundy, but the name rang a bell with me. I'd read William F. Buckley's *God and Man at Yale* . . . it made me sick to my stomach. . . . And then I'd found an article by Mac Bundy in *The Atlantic* attacking Buckley. So I pointed to Bundy's name on the list and told Dave, 'He's the first fellow I want to see.' "

Later that summer, when Pusey finally met Bundy, he felt an immediate rapport. "I asked him then and there if he would become dean," Pusey said. "I never interviewed any of the other candidates."

Pusey and Bundy jointly announced the news on August 19. Typically, Mac's mother, Kay, was unimpressed. When someone that summer congratulated her on having a son become dean of Harvard at the age of thirty-four, she snapped, "It's a terrible idea. Mac should be an author."[10] Mac, however, had no real qualms. He knew, of course, that it was in some ways a thankless job. "A friend advised me," Bundy recalled, "that I had better take it, because, 'If you don't, someone else will, and then you will be angered by his stupid mistakes.' "[11] One of his closest friends, Kingman Brewster, had a wreath of funeral lilies delivered to his home, symbolic of Mac's demise as a scholar and his resurrection as a university administrator. (Bundy later returned the favor when Brewster abandoned the teaching of law at Harvard to become provost and later president of Yale.) But if this promotion meant putting any personal scholarship on hold, this was a cross he could bear easily. He had been thinking of doing a biography of Woodrow Wilson, a scholar-politician whose internationalism and interventionist spirit evoked his sympathies, but he thought this project could be pursued later. Besides, he could tell himself that with two published books to his credit, he'd already done the scholarly thing. It was time to add a managerial experience to his résumé.*

A Yale colleague wrote a piece of doggerel that neatly summed up Mac's career to date:

> *A proper young prig, McGeorge Bundy,*
> *Graduated from Yale on a Monday*
> *But he shortly was seen*
> *As Establishment Dean*
> *Up at Harvard the following Sunday.*[12]

With uncharacteristic modesty, Bundy told a reporter, "Right now, I propose to learn my job, and for awhile I'll stick to my knitting."[13] A few days later he took as his office a large room in the northeast corner of University Hall that once served as President Lowell's office. It contained a built-in safe, a cavernous fireplace and two distinctive worktables on which Bundy stacked piles of papers and books. Across a granite threshold and down the hall, Bundy could walk to the faculty room, an immense chamber where as many as several hundred faculty would soon gather to hear his maiden address as dean. The walls were plastered from floor to ceiling with oil portraits of eminent Harvard figures, including Henry Wadsworth Longfellow, Charles William Eliot and A. Lawrence Lowell. By tradition, the dean presided over these faculty meetings while sitting at an enormous round oak table, placed at the head of the room. It was a theatrical setting and called for a man with a stage presence.

While preparing for this speech, his first performance as dean, Bundy told a friend that he had recalled Macaulay's description of how the younger Pitt, at the age of twenty-four, awed the House of Commons with a speech that made him a legend in his own time. Bundy said he was determined to do

---

* A few weeks later he turned down an offer from the Eisenhower White House to serve as special deputy assistant to the president's national security adviser, Robert Cutler. "I was still wet behind the ears," Bundy explained, "and a grown-up like Cutler wouldn't have wanted me" (MB interview, Apr. 5, 1993).

the same. When the time came, he spoke without notes, and gave a speech which most remembered as eloquent and peppered with facts and figures. Some called it masterful, and most of these sometimes cantankerous Harvard scholars were persuaded that Pusey had made a brilliant choice for the dean-ship.

Soon afterwards, Archie MacLeish, by then a Pulitzer Prize–winning poet, wrote his young friend a note gushing with pride and optimism about the new Harvard regime: "I feel in my bones a new age—a new era. It is not only the President's [Pusey's] youth and yours. Not only the vitality you both have and the complementary intelligences which so patently create a new kind of thinking. Not only the courage and candor which make the air good to breathe. It is more than all those things and the many others I can think of. It is the fact that this Harvard cares about values."[14] That autumn Mac recruited Archie to serve as acting master of Eliot House.

DEAN BUNDY quickly became a busy man. But in the autumn of 1953 there was one distinctly unacademic topic which commanded his attention, and it was called McCarthyism. Almost every week the Republican senator from Wisconsin was hurling some new allegation that Harvard was harboring subversives. The *Crimson's* headlines that autumn portrayed a university under siege: "Pusey Rebuts Red Baiting Education Critics"; "Furry Lawyer Hits McCarthy Charges"; "Army Prevents Professor Fairbank from Travelling to Japan to Teach"; "3 Professors Deny Backing Chinese 'Reds.' " (East Asian scholars like John Fairbank, who was falsely accused of being a Communist Party member, were particular targets of congressional investigators.)

On one level, the headlines underscored the absurdity of McCarthy's charges. By almost any definition other than McCarthy's, Harvard always has been a bastion of conservatism, a training ground for young men who invariably grow up to take their places in elite institutions, whether it be in big business, the law, the teaching professions or the government. Harvard is the last place in America to look for subversives. Bundy knew this, Pusey knew it, indeed, most conservatives knew this.

But then everyone knew that McCarthy's charges had less to do with larger truths than with the sheer political power of his message. All that mattered was that postwar America was in the grip of a witch-hunt. And very few men of either liberal or conservative persuasions thought it necessary or prudent to challenge any of the assumptions behind the witch-hunt. McCarthyism, after all, had gotten its start during the Truman administration. President Harry Truman's loyalty-security program had targeted critics to his left within the Democratic Party—followers of Franklin Roosevelt and Henry Wallace—who believed that the early Cold War with the Soviet Union was being mismanaged and needlessly militarized. Designed to avert more drastic action by congressional conservatives, Truman regarded the loyalty checks as a distasteful but politically defensive measure.[15]

In this sense, McCarthyism was very much a bipartisan affair, particularly in the late 1940s. Anti-communist liberals believed the radical New Dealers had gone too far in socializing the economy and that the Wallacites were naive to think an accommodation with the Soviets was still possible. Most good liberals condemned only McCarthy's tactics, not his goals. The witches—the communists and their fellow travelers—were beyond the pale, even, and perhaps particularly, for liberals who feared being painted with the broad crimson brush of the popular front. Throughout the 1930s the Communist Party of the United States had earned the grudging admiration of some Americans simply by pressing energetically for long overdue reform in such volatile areas as race relations and labor rights. The number of party members, however, was always infinitesimal, and by the early 1950s the communists were a spent political force.

By the time McCarthy began making his outlandish charges in February 1950, Conant and many other university administrators around the country had already surrendered to the notion that being a communist barred one from teaching. In June 1949, Conant signed on to a public statement by the Educational Policies Commission of the National Education Association which flatly concluded that a Communist Party member should not be employed in the schools. In private, Conant later modified his position to say that he only meant this ban to apply to public schools. The university campus, he thought, should be kept "free for all manner of heresy." It was not the role of the university to investigate a professor's political beliefs. On the other hand, Conant believed that if the proper governmental authorities on their own initiative found and passed information which could identify an academic as a clandestine communist, well then, that information could and should be used by universities to clean house.

Like Bundy at the time, Conant was not motivated by any genuine worry that communists posed a serious threat. The ban on public school teaching, he said, would probably affect a "terrifically small number" of teachers, no more than one in a thousand. It was necessary only on tactical grounds. "If you were willing to take the stand against members of the [Communist] party," Conant argued, "you could make a strong defense against anybody who is being persecuted as belonging to popular front or front organizations, which is a different thing."[16]

This was a slippery slope. Conant would not argue that communists should be barred a citizen's right to vote, but he would argue that they should not be allowed to teach. In March 1949, he and Dwight Eisenhower, then president of Columbia University, agreed that universities should not "knowingly" employ communists as teachers. But then, neither did they want to investigate whether a teacher was a communist. "We ought not to be Gestapo agents," Eisenhower said. Obviously, once educators conceded that communists should not be teaching children, this concession opened the door to all sorts of possible government intrusion in academic affairs. Indeed, it was not long before Harvard established a relationship with the Federal Bureau of Investigation. FBI records show that by June 1950, J. Edgar Hoover was noting that "arrangements have been perfected whereby information of interest will be made available to the Bureau on a confidential basis . . . in connection with Harvard College and the Graduate School of Arts and Sciences." [17]

By late 1952, congressional committees were calling academics with radical credentials and demanding that they testify both about themselves and their colleagues. "Naming names" became the litmus test. When in December 1952, Rutgers University decided to fire two professors who took the Fifth Amendment against self-incrimination rather than be forced to name names, Conant decided that Harvard would follow suit. After reviewing a seven-page legal brief with the university's counsel, Conant informed the Harvard Corporation that he now believed that invoking the Fifth Amendment should be grounds for dismissal. [18]

Shortly afterwards, however, Conant announced his impending resignation, and as a consequence a policy which might have led to the firing of a handful of Harvard professors was placed in limbo. Instead, a debate emerged on campus on how to handle those who took the Fifth Amendment. Surprisingly, Conant succeeded in persuading one of Harvard's legendary civil libertarians, Zechariah Chafee, Jr., to publish a letter in the *Crimson* (with Arthur Sutherland, another Harvard Law professor) which concluded, "The Fifth Amendment grants no privilege to protect one's friends." [19] In the ensuing furor, Chafee privately began backpedaling, telling friends that he had not meant his letter to become university policy.

Eventually, Mac Bundy—not yet dean, but a newly promoted associate professor in the government department—waded into the debate. On April 23, 1953, he sat down and wrote a long letter to Provost Paul Buck. Bundy basically agreed with Conant's presumption that Harvard should not "knowingly" hire a communist professor. But what about those faculty members who took the Fifth? On this question, Bundy argued that if faculty members took the Fifth before a congressional committee, yet candidly told university authorities that they were no longer (or had never been) under the influence of the Communist Party, then they should not be dismissed. But if they refused to deny party membership and otherwise refused to deal with the Harvard Corporation in a candid fashion, then dismissal might well be an appropriate action. Bundy concluded that "without supposing that there will be no exceptions, I offer the opinion that Harvard should consider the use of the Fifth Amendment in cases such as those which have lately occurred as a serious obstacle to appointment or reappointment to the University." [20]

Provost Buck immediately realized the significance of Bundy's letter, and quickly informed the Harvard Corporation that it could be considered a fair reflection of faculty opinion. Bundy's letter represented a step back from Conant's harder line. But it still left the door open to the possibility that Harvard could fire a scholar, ostensibly for a lack of candor with his colleagues.

So long as they were candid with the university, Bundy seemed to be suggesting that the university should stand by those scholars who took the Fifth Amendment—if their motivation was solely to avoid having to name names.

Bundy's position in the spring of 1953 may well help to explain why his subsequent selection as dean was greeted so warmly by a majority of the faculty. As dean, however, Bundy's views evolved.

By the autumn of 1953, Harvard had only three public Fifth Amendment communists: Dr. Wendell Furry, a tenured associate professor of physics; Leon Kamin, an untenured teaching fellow in the department of social relations; and Helen Deane Markham, an untenured assistant professor of anatomy. Pusey and Bundy decided to lodge a formal reprimand against each of these scholars, but their "misconduct" was not grounds for immediate dismissal. Later, however, the contracts of the two untenured individuals, Kamin and Markham, were not renewed.

Only Furry survived, but barely. Bundy thought Furry's previous insistence on taking the Fifth was harmful to Harvard precisely because the communist activities in which he had participated were so utterly prosaic. After considerable pressure, Bundy persuaded Furry to waive his Fifth Amendment rights and testify at a televised hearing staged by Senator McCarthy in Boston. At the same time, the dean encouraged Furry to give an interview to the *Crimson*'s J. Anthony Lukas. Published on February 3, 1954, this interview— which was widely reprinted by newspapers across the country—portrayed Furry as an unlikely political threat to Harvard, let alone the country. Lukas later recalled Furry as "mild, self-effacing, eager to clear himself with his colleagues and students, but nonetheless insistent that everything he'd done had been consistent with loyalty to America." Essentially apolitical, Furry had joined the Communist Party in 1938 out of an emotional concern to do something about the rise of German fascism. The party's Harvard unit, he claimed, did no more than meet twice a month to discuss current events and various books. He quit in 1947, he asserted, when it became clear that the party "had no worthwhile ideas about the regulation and control of the atomic bomb, which after the war became my main political concern." Clearly, Furry was a harmless fellow. Bundy was so pleased with the *Crimsom* interview that he had several thousand offprints mailed to alumni.[21]

Furry, however, did not quite escape the personal consequences of waiving his Fifth Amendment rights. After testifying but refusing to name names, he was indicted and tried for contempt of Congress. Only after several years of stressful and expensive litigation was he finally acquitted.

Bundy's belief that party membership brought with it an abdication of intellectual integrity was not unusual. But he was wrong to ignore the circumstances that often made concealment of party membership a prudent course of action. Ever since the Palmer raids of 1919, when some five thousand suspected leftists were arrested without warrants, radicals had been frequently targeted

for harassment and surveillance by the FBI. In these circumstances, concealment of party membership was evidence less of conspiracy than simple caution.[22]

One former Harvard communist who testified and named names before
a congressional committee was Daniel Boorstin, later a friend of Bundy's
and a popular historian who became librarian of Congress. Boorstin testified,
". . . my feeling is that no one should be employed to teach in a university
who was not free intellectually, and in my opinion, membership in the Communist Party would be virtually conclusive evidence that a person was not
intellectually free."[23] Like Bundy, Boorstin thought Harvard communists
could not be trusted to think (and teach) independently. Many students agreed.
The leader of the Liberal Union, Chris Niebuhr—son of the theologian—told
a reporter in 1955 that he and other campus liberals "backed the university
administration when it said that it would discharge faculty members who are
proved to belong now to the Communist Party."[24]

With such campus liberals supporting his position, Bundy had every
reason to think he had staked out a sound and reasonable policy. Harvard
would defend academic freedom, but in young Niebuhr's words, the university
would take a "realistic" position. As Bundy put it in testimony before the U.S.
Senate in 1955, ". . . in our search for excellence, once we are satisfied that a
man is not a rascal (a standard which in Harvard's view excludes Americans
who still surrender to Communist discipline), we do not worry much about
his politics. . . ."[25]

To the world at large, Harvard seemed to be standing on principle, defending the academic freedom of all scholars, regardless of their politics. Harvard said it would not investigate the political credentials of any scholar except
for *acknowledged* members of the Communist Party. Only years later would
it emerge that what Harvard said was not necessarily the same as what Harvard did.

IN the summer of 1953, Sigmund Diamond earned his doctorate in history
from Harvard and was subsequently employed in an untenured administrative
post. In the spring of 1954, however, Dean Bundy offered Diamond a five-year
appointment as a counsellor for foreign students and dean of special students.
In addition, Bundy promised that Diamond would have some teaching responsibilities. The offer had been authorized by the Harvard Corporation.

Very soon afterwards, on April 21, two FBI agents visited Diamond and
asked him to talk with them on tape about his political associations. The agents
wanted him to name names. Diamond refused the interview.

Subsequently, Bundy told President Pusey that at noon on Monday,
May 3, "it was brought to my attention that there might be a question with
regard to Dr. Diamond's possible connection with the Communist Party."
Bundy did not say who passed him this information, but there is circumstan-
tial evidence that it came from the FBI. In any case, Bundy immediately called

Diamond into his office to find out if the young scholar had engaged in any political activity which "might be embarrassing to the University." Diamond forthrightly admitted in a "frank and cooperative manner" that he had been a member of the Communist Party from 1942 until mid-1950.

Diamond had been a communist, but he had never engaged in espionage or any other illegal acts, and now "had nothing whatever to do with Communism."

Evidently, this confession was not sufficient; Bundy went on to ask Diamond if he was prepared to discuss his former party membership with the "duly authorized agencies of the Federal Government." Diamond said he might be willing to talk about his own political activity, but he was "against giving the names of others who had been associated with him in the Party, on the ground that their activities were in no sense illegal. . . ."

To this, Bundy replied that it was his view that the university would now have to withdraw his appointment. He gave two reasons: first, that Diamond had not volunteered this information at the time he had been offered an appointment; and second, that he was still unwilling "to cooperate fully" with the FBI. Diamond left, shaken and depressed, feeling certain that the dean was determined to withdraw his job offer.

Just a few days later Bundy called him back for a second meeting. In the interim he had checked up on Diamond with senior members of the history department. It was their "recollection and judgement" that Diamond was indeed no longer politically active. Moreover, Bundy believed that Diamond had "performed extremely well" in his previous administrative post and that his work as a research fellow had been "wholly satisfactory." Thus, Bundy had no cause for withdrawing Diamond's appointment other than that the young man was unwilling to inform on his former political colleagues to the FBI.

In their second meeting Bundy again pressed Diamond to cooperate with the "civic authorities." In response, Diamond said he had decided that he would be willing to speak with the FBI about himself but he still would not name names. Diamond also came prepared to argue his case with a precedent: reaching into his pocket, he pulled out some faded clips from the *New York Times* of April 1938 which reported on the fraud trial of Richard Whitney of the New York Stock Exchange. The *Times* reported that two Harvard overseers, Thomas W. Lamont and George Whitney, had testified that they were well aware of Richard Whitney's illegal transgressions but had not felt it necessary to inform the authorities. Harvard, Diamond pointed out, had not penalized the two overseers for their lack of "complete candor." Why, he asked, should Harvard now penalize a young scholar for being incompletely candid about a political association which was not illegal? Bundy made no attempt to rebut this argument.

Shortly afterwards Bundy informed Diamond that the offer of a five-year contract had been formally withdrawn. As Bundy spelled it out in his formal recommendation to Pusey, Diamond would not be dismissed immediately, but his one-year administrative appointment would be allowed to run out on schedule on June 14, 1954. In this manner, Bundy wrote, "we may well be able to end his connection with the University without publicity which would be unpleasant to us and extremely damaging to Mr. Diamond personally."

One extraordinary aspect of the case is the personal regrets about the decision Bundy expressed at the time. In his letter to Pusey explaining his recommendation, Bundy wrote, "I wish I could recreate for you the impression made upon me by Mr. Diamond in our long interview. I find myself quite able to understand the pressures which led him in the first instance to join the Party. . . . We then come to the question of his failure to let us know that he had a past in the Party at the time when we recommended him for administrative work. . . . I think it is clear that pressures which worked upon him as he faced this decision were of a magnitude which not many of us have to face. . . . Mr. Diamond honestly believes, I think, that there is nothing shameful in his past. Mistakes, yes, but criminal error, no. In concealing his past membership from us, he made a wrong decision, and I think that our own necessary course is clear, but I cannot find much pleasure in the result."[26]

Obviously, Bundy understood Diamond's political motivations, and even empathized with his predicament. He knew Diamond was no criminal but a victim of political circumstances. Yet those circumstances left Harvard no choice but to sever their connections to one more victim of the country's obsession with the threat of communism.

At the time Diamond left Harvard without protest. His career was only temporarily derailed and a year later he found a tenure-track position in the sociology department of Columbia University. But in 1977 he reopened the episode by writing an essay in *The New York Review of Books* highly critical of both Harvard's policy and Bundy's role. In the essay and later in a 1992 book, *Compromised Campus,* Diamond used FBI records obtained under the Freedom of Information Act and other materials to mount a serious indictment of Harvard's conduct. He also charged that both Bundy and Pusey had tape-recorded their conversations with him. Bundy was particularly aghast at this allegation. Immediately after reading an early copy of Diamond's essay, he phoned Diamond and the two men had the following exchange:

Bundy: "You are hallucinating. It didn't happen. I never made any recordings, with you or anyone. Never."

Diamond: "That's your memory, not mine."

Later, in a letter to the editor, Bundy repeated that Diamond must be "hallucinating." Diamond insisted that his conversations with Bundy and Pusey had been recorded "on a disk, which revolved on a machine in plain sight." Diamond also backed up his claim with a statement from Professor David S. Landes, who said that when he visited Bundy to discuss the case, he too had been recorded.[27] Bundy emphatically denied to Landes that he had ever recorded anyone, in Cambridge or in Washington: "I myself believe that one-sided recording is an act of unfairness, and I think a great many of our common friends would agree. I also *know* what I have never done, and I continue to think it surprising that you do not weight this point more heavily."[28] In his letter to the editor of *The New York Review of Books,* Bundy further stipulated that the machine Diamond had seen on his desk was a dictation device which required one to speak directly into a microphone and could not otherwise have recorded a conversation.

Clearly, Bundy was upset by the implication that he had routinely recorded sensitive conversations and perhaps had subsequently turned over these disks to the FBI. Regardless of whether this was true, however, a far more damaging fact now emerged from the controversy sparked by Diamond's article. Readers learned that Diamond's was not a unique case. After Diamond published his charges in *The New York Review of Books,* Robert N. Bellah, a professor of sociology at Berkeley, wrote a letter to the editor confirming Bundy's behavior. "I was summoned to the office of McGeorge Bundy," Bellah wrote of his circumstances in 1954. "Bundy told me that an 'officer of the university' had informed him of my political past and that I had an obligation of 'complete candor,' as he put it, to confess my activities and to name all of my former associates to the FBI or any other duly authorized body. . . . One week after meeting Bundy I was picked up on the street by two FBI agents and taken to the Boston office for interrogation."[29]

Like Diamond, Bellah was untenured and refused to name names, even after Bundy threatened to have his graduate fellowship canceled. Perhaps because he was a graduate student and, unlike Diamond, had not been offered an administrative post, Bellah remained at Harvard. (It also turned out that Bundy had no control over the fellowship in question.) The following year, when Bellah was recommended by the department of social relations for an instructorship, Bundy again summoned the young sociologist. This time Bundy took a slightly different position. If Bellah accepted the teaching position, Bundy warned him that it would not be renewed if at any time in the future he was asked by the government to name names and refused. According to Bellah, Bundy pressed him to name names. Bellah again refused. At this point Bundy asked him to visit the campus psychiatrist, and when Bellah complied, it became clear in the course of the interview that the psychiatrist was trying to determine if Bellah was a practicing homosexual. Bellah denied these insinuations, and after this had been reported back to Bundy, the dean formally recommended Bellah's appointment, telling President Pusey in the spring of 1955, "A negative judgment here would come very near to a judgment that no ex-Communist need apply unless he is prepared to answer all the questions anyone asks him about other Communists he has known. I should strongly deprecate such a position."[30]

Why the change in policy? Why was Bundy willing to recommend Bellah for an appointment even though the young sociologist was still refusing to name names? In Bundy's eyes, Bellah was Harvard material—"a man of high character and remarkable scholarship"—and he was being considered for an academic, not an administrative post. Bellah also seemed emotionally balanced —evidently, he was not a homosexual—and therefore, if called to testify before a congressional committee, he might make an "effective witness."[31] But it is also important to note that a year had passed since the Diamond affair, and McCarthyite political pressures on the university were very much on the wane. Even so, as it turned out, the Harvard Corporation decided to make Bellah's impending appointment strictly conditional on his agreement to name names if asked by "any legally authorized investigating body. . . ." Otherwise, the appointment would not be renewed. Bundy said he regarded this as a mistake at the time and that he worked to persuade the Harvard Corporation to make the appointment unconditional. Before Bundy's efforts could succeed, Bellah decided to pass on the offer and took a job at a Canadian university. (Two years later, with McCarthy dead, Bellah returned to Harvard, accepting an academic appointment without any of the previous conditions. This happened, Bundy later said, with his full support.)

On two other occasions, Dean Bundy interrogated graduate students about their political views. Everett Mendelsohn was a graduate student in the history of science when he was summoned by Bundy to University Hall in the spring of 1954. The dean told the young man that he had information that the student was a communist. Was this true? Mendelsohn had indeed been an organizer in the Wallace presidential campaign, but he had never joined the Communist Party. Trying to be forthcoming, Mendelsohn talked at length about his political activities and apparently convinced Bundy that he had never been a communist. But when he pressed the dean for the source of his information, Bundy coldly refused to divulge anything. The conversation ended abruptly when Mendelsohn said he was going to consult a lawyer. That was the last he heard from Bundy. Mendelsohn went on to an illustrious career at Harvard.

His roommate, however, did not escape so easily. In the spring of 1954, Bundy called in Sydney James, a graduate student in history, who had been a communist as a Harvard undergraduate in the late 1940s. The previous year James had reluctantly agreed, when confronted by the FBI, to confirm the accuracy or inaccuracy of their information, but he refused to volunteer new information or to otherwise name names. Now, Dean Bundy said he understood that James was not being fully candid with the FBI. As Ellen W. Schrecker reported in her 1986 book, No Ivory Tower: McCarthyism & the Universities, Bundy told James that unless he revealed everything he knew to the FBI, there would be "no job as teaching fellow; no possibility of academic employment—ever."[32] James decided to comply with Bundy's wishes and answered the FBI's further questions.

Clearly, the difference between Bundy's treatment of Mendelsohn and James lay in the fact that one had been a communist and one had not. Bundy forced the communist to name names. At least two other unnamed individuals left Harvard rather than name names to the FBI.[33]

The harm done to the academic careers of these individuals was bad enough. But worse, in a sense, was the strong inference that Harvard had routinely exchanged information with the FBI about the political views of students and faculty members. This Bundy has always denied. "The FBI never came to me," Bundy later said, "for information about individuals other than for purposes of a standard security clearance. And I never provided them with any information about Harvard individuals."[34] Yet, the evidence suggests that *someone* in the Harvard administration was doing this, and that it was done with the tacit understanding of university authorities.

As both Schrecker and Diamond have documented in their respective books, beginning in 1951 the FBI disseminated confidential information on "Communists or subversive elements" in universities and other public organizations. Under the "Responsibilities Program," FBI agents regularly visited academic administrators and orally briefed them on area communists. Rarely was this sensitive information transmitted on paper, and there is no documentary evidence that Bundy was one of the "appropriate authorities" briefed by the FBI.[35] On the other hand, Bundy did participate as Harvard's representative in a December 8, 1954, meeting of administrators from six other universities with staff members of a congressional committee in which this kind of information was discussed. According to the minutes of this meeting, Bundy and the other administrators acknowledged relying on "Government investigating agencies" for such "derogatory" information. At the same time they complained that the Justice Department and the FBI "are not today following up and prosecuting cases which the universities have already handed over to them under existing law."[36]

Other FBI documents make it clear that at Yale and other universities the bureau had formal relationships with provosts and deans. The bureau took "every precaution" to protect the identity of these "Confidential National Defense Informants." A October 26, 1950, FBI document obtained by Diamond states that an unnamed Harvard official ". . . was assured that any contact for the purpose of obtaining such confidential information from Harvard University files, would be on a selective basis. . . ."

Was part of Bundy's responsibilities as dean to maintain some informal or formal relationship with the FBI? The evidence on this question is murky. Certainly, in one sense it would have been in Harvard's interest to have one officer of the university serve as an informal liaison with the FBI. This way, theoretically, the university would then have some control or at least knowledge about the bureau's information-gathering activities on campus. Bundy may well have played such an informal role and still be able to deny any formal collaboration with the FBI. On the other hand, the FBI's own records make it clear that the bureau felt it had a "most cooperative and understanding association with Harvard."[37] Could this have been the case without Dean Bundy's tacit cooperation?

For its part, the FBI knew exactly what Bundy was doing about specific cases. Soon after Bundy withdrew his job offer to Diamond, the Boston FBI office wrote J. Edgar Hoover, ". . . it appears that Dean Bundy is insisting that former Communist Party members who now have Harvard Corporation appointments shall provide the Federal Bureau of Investigation a full and complete account of their activities in the Communist Party and shall at the same time [name names]. . . ."[38]

This information came not from Bundy but from unnamed Harvard faculty members. By 1954, the FBI had some forty-two separate case files on various Harvard institutions and presumably many more informants. (We now know from FBI records that among many such informants were Professor William Yandell Elliott and teaching fellow Henry A. Kissinger, who on one occasion opened the mail of his students and passed the contents—ban-the-bomb publicity—on to the FBI.) The *New York Times's* Herbert Mitgang later called these academic informants of the FBI "subagents in place."[39]

BUNDY's official papers as Harvard's dean are closed to scholars for a period of fifty years—until the year 2003. Without access to these papers, it is difficult to judge Harvard's record on McCarthyism. But from the evidence released to date, it seems clear that the university had two policies. In public, Harvard stood simply for academic freedom. In private, however, Harvard negotiated with the FBI a much more complicated and compromised policy. Under the Pusey-Bundy regime, Harvard would not knowingly hire a communist to teach; Harvard would not spend any of its own money to provide a legal defense for faculty accused of security violations*; Harvard would not fire tenured professors who took the Fifth Amendment so long as they were wholly candid with the university about their political associations; Harvard would discourage anyone from taking the Fifth Amendment; Harvard would terminate the contracts of any untenured scholars like Sigmund Diamond or Robert Bellah who refused to name names; and finally, Harvard would share information, sometimes from its own confidential personnel files, with the FBI and use confidential information from the FBI to screen its employees.

Bundy always insisted that Harvard had acted honorably in difficult circumstances. These ex-communists were, in his view, troubled individuals, and few of them, in any case, had any "real grievances" against Harvard. "I myself," he wrote David Landes in 1977, "know of only one, and until recently I thought he had long since forgiven the University for what was indeed, in my

---

* Dean Bundy refused to pay the legal expenses of any Harvard scholars. In 1953–54, Professor Samuel A. Stouffer, a Republican and frequent consultant for the U.S. military, had his security clearance suddenly revoked while writing a study on McCarthyism and civil liberties for the Ford Foundation's Fund for the Republic. Stouffer appealed and eventually had his clearance restored, but Dean Bundy and the Harvard Corporation adamantly refused to defray any of the legal costs associated with the case.

view, a brief failure of nerve." (Here Bundy was referring to Bellah, who at the time, he thought, still wanted to remain anonymous.)[40]

"I will defend Harvard in general," he continued, "against the charge that it was wanting in courage, but I think I can understand why you would feel that it was ungenerous. I think perhaps you would have liked Harvard to spread its shelter over people like Sig Diamond precisely because of the pickle they were in, even at the price of bending its own standards of appointment, whether administrative or academic. By this standard, I will agree that the University fell short, but it is not a standard that anyone who knew the Governing Boards of that period could sensibly urge on administrators. Harvard saw its obligation then in terms of the defense of those to whom it had made academic commitments, and the institution as a whole did not see its duty as that of providing special refuge for persons not in themselves the best available."[41]

This was as best a defense as could be mounted in the aftermath of the Diamond-Bellah revelations.* Harvard did defend its tenured faculty. But if excellence was the only litmus test, why had Bundy pressured ex-communist graduate students to name names to the FBI? And why had Bundy offered to keep Diamond only if he would name names? Again, Bundy argued that different standards applied to "administrative" appointments. With the passage of time, this argument seemed more than a little ungenerous. As Robert N. Bellah put it in 1977, "The notion of Harvard as a 'bulwark against McCarthyism' was deserved only on the narrowest of grounds. No one with tenure was fired. But privately Harvard's efforts were all in the direction of cooperation, not resistance."[42] Dean Bundy had sometimes urged his people to name names, and when they refused he required them to suffer the consequences, quietly and alone. And for that, many would never forgive him.

To be sure, only a handful of such people like Sigmund Diamond, Robert Bellah, Leon Kamin and Helen Deane Markham—were forced to leave Harvard. Wendell Furry survived, but only after fighting a costly legal case. Many others were forced to endure the humiliation of naming names. No one went to prison, and most made their way in the world and otherwise created new lives for themselves. So did Harvard's conduct during the trial of McCarthyism bring with it any larger costs? We cannot know, but if Harvard had adopted a policy of forthright resistance, and not quiet cooperation, this might reasonably have created a different political atmosphere.

McCarthyism and the academic community's muddled response to it may also explain why such ignorance existed in the 1960s over the nature of

---

* Fifteen of his friends—and even a few of his intellectual adversaries over the years —came to Bundy's defense during the Diamond–Bellah controversy. In a letter to *The New York Review of Books,* J. Kenneth Galbraith, Stanley Hoffmann, Carl Kaysen, Arthur Schlesinger, Jr., Zeph Stewart and others defended Bundy as "a very remarkable Dean . . . remarkable in his hospitality to new ideas, in his recruitment of new talent and in his devotion to academic freedom."

Vietnamese and other Asian nationalisms. How many bright Harvard students decided against a career as a scholar of East Asia after reading in the *Crimson* about the treatment accorded a China scholar like John King Fairbank? As Ellen W. Schrecker has argued, "Naturally, greater access to better scholarship would not by itself have prevented the Vietnam war, but there is no doubt that the legacy of McCarthyism in the academy and elsewhere did make it difficult for the government to act wisely in Asia." If so, Dean Bundy paid dearly for what seemed at the time a perfectly reasonable policy in defense of Harvard.[43]

McCarthyism was certainly the most controversial of the issues Bundy dealt with as dean. And at the time most members of the faculty thought he handled this and many other issues with good judgment.

As dean, he presided over a staff of more than one thousand, including 288 full professors. His responsibilities included the supervision of some 5,500 undergraduates (at both Harvard and Radcliffe) and some 1,800 graduate students. He monitored the budgets for more than twenty laboratories, six museums, two forests, an arboretum and several observatories. It was a job that required a peculiar combination of qualities: tact, a willingness to circumnavigate large egos, an ability to judge the intellectual merits of scholars from a wide variety of disciplines, a capacity for detail and a ruthless decisiveness. Bundy displayed all these qualities, but particularly the decisiveness. And though, inevitably, some of his decisions had to rankle, most faculty members were at least grateful that this was a dean who could make decisions with dispatch. When Harry Murray, the eminent Harvard psychologist, one day asked him if he didn't sometimes wake up at 3 A.M. and worry that he had made the wrong decision, Bundy replied coolly, "Only when I'm soft."[44]

"Youthful," "brash," "opinionated" and even "arrogant" were words his friends used to describe him. Not everyone appreciated his wit, but he was well liked by a wide variety of faculty. "When Bundy was here," one professor later waxed nostalgically, "Harvard was like a glass of champagne and he knew every bubble by its first name."[45] Some may have thought of him as coldly intellectual, but Bundy was very much the social animal. He could talk to physicists about nuclear weapons and to playwrights about the theater. He was a blue-blood Boston Brahmin, but he socialized with Irish Catholics and Jews. "Mac may have been a Yankee swell," recalled Carl Kaysen, "but he went out of his way to surround himself with other kinds of people." Kaysen remembered Mac taking him one New Year's Eve to a party at the Bundy family home on Commonwealth Avenue, where he met Kay and Harvey Bundy. "We had a nice meal and drank some flat champagne. What struck me about the evening, however, was that Mac had invited a Jewish couple [the Kaysens] and two Irish Catholic couples. These were all people who his mother I am sure considered to be out-bounders. He seemed to be saying to his mother and father, 'Here are some of the people I like at Harvard.' "[46]

■

BUNDY had many differences of opinion but few real disagreements with President Pusey. One was over religion. Pusey complained about the "present low estate of religion at Harvard" and spent much of his time raising money for the Divinity School. Bundy was indifferent to religion. When asked one day at an Adams House seminar about his religious beliefs, Mac quipped, "I am a confirmed but unconvinced Episcopalian." [47]

Religion, however, was not a joking matter for Pusey. In the spring of 1957 he sparked a major uproar on campus when he announced that because the university's Memorial Church, built in Harvard Yard in 1927, "had always been a Christian institution," it could not be used for non-Christian weddings or funerals. In reaction, a petition quickly circulated among faculty and students protesting this blatant discrimination against, most obviously, Jews. Bundy was appalled and quietly worked behind the scenes to diffuse the issue. By late April, Pusey backed down, conceding that "Harvard had become a secular university . . . with a tradition of worship." [48]

Twenty-year-old David Halberstam, a newly elected member of the 1954 *Crimson* executive board, thought Bundy relished the idea of toppling the social barriers that divided Cambridge society. "He's smarter than most WASPs," Halberstam said. "At Harvard, he had six cards when everyone else was playing poker with five cards; he had this extra advantage. He not only was smarter than most WASPs, but in a world that was then becoming a meritocracy, where the young and upcoming instructors had names like Kissinger and Brzezinski, he had this blue-blood background. Bundy is actually quite a Semitophile; for him, Jews are brains and brains are good by any definition. These smart Jews in turn knew that he was smarter than the average blue-blood WASP. This made for a mutual attraction."

The editors at the *Crimson* instinctively liked him. "He was open," Halberstam said. "He was quick, and he seemed to dominate Pusey, who seemed in contrast to be intellectually pitted, unsure of himself in that environment. Mac could speak for both the old Harvard and the new Harvard. There was a struggle going on between these two worlds, and here was this enormously facile, quick, almost glib figure who could move in both worlds." [49]

By tradition, the editors of the *Crimson* had an opportunity to meet with the president of the university on a weekly basis. But during the early years of the Pusey-Bundy administration these press conferences were dominated by Bundy. One *Crimson* editor, Richard Ullman, vividly recalled the scene. Together with his *Crimson* colleagues, which in those years included A. J. "Jack" Langguth, David Halberstam and J. Anthony Lukas—all three of whom later became renowned reporters for the *New York Times*—Ullman would appear in Bundy's office. It was odd, Ullman thought, that the meetings were held in Bundy's office and not Pusey's. Odder still was that Pusey would choose to sit ramrod in a hard-back chair, off in a corner of the room. "Pinched into his three-piece suit," Lukas remembered, "Pusey looked for all the world like a pink-faced rabbit, while Bundy, crouched behind his desk, seemed a lion in his jungle lair, hugely enjoying the give-and-take with the student press."

Mac was usually sprawled in a brass-studded, rich brown leather armchair, the kind that could swivel and rock. With his tie loosened and his shirtsleeves rolled up, he would lean way back and sometimes prop his feet against the desk. Clearly, this was his territory and he was in charge. "We would direct questions to Pusey," recalled Ullman, "and Mac would answer." Typically, without Pusey saying a word, Mac would say something like, "The president doesn't think he should answer that." Ullman thought these performances were more than a little bit peculiar. "We were outraged by it," he said. "Halberstam really thought what Mac was doing to Pusey was outrageous."[50]

Halberstam may have grown to dislike Bundy, but many students thought he was terrific. And some discovered that one-on-one Dean Bundy could be positively human. Leslie Gelb—later to become a primary author of the Pentagon Papers, an editor of the *New York Times* and president of the Council on Foreign Relations—was a graduate student at Harvard in the late 1950s. He remembered Bundy as "a man of utter self-confidence and precision of expression." Gelb, who even then thought of himself as "virtually unintimidatable," regarded Bundy as "a personality to intimidate." He expected as much when one day he went to talk to Bundy about a paper he was writing. "But he wasn't that way at all," Gelb recalled. "He was almost gentle. We just chatted for forty-five minutes or something. He was really quite shockingly nice. It kind of surprised me." A. J. Langguth, later a *New York Times* reporter in Vietnam, had a similar experience with Bundy. Langguth recalled Bundy yelling at him about his reporting in the *Crimson*, "Damn it, Langguth, this is a lie, this is a lie." But later Dean Bundy hired him as one of his assistants.[51]

AT thirty-four, Mac Bundy looked ten years younger. Though his hairline was rapidly receding into a wispy widow's peak, his face was positively cherubic. He wore stylish, clear-plastic frame glasses and favored subdued knit ties, starched-white shirts and smart two-piece suits. Students often saw him bicycling in this attire from his home at 21 Berkeley Street, just a few blocks from Harvard Square, to his office in University Hall. He cut a dashing figure: here was the dean of the college, bicycling about Cambridge, looking all of twenty-five, brimming with energy. His blue-gray eyes nevertheless betrayed a steely competency. He also had enough confidence to bend the rules.

When John Kenneth Galbraith wanted a second, unscheduled sabbatical to finish another book, Bundy gave it to him, saying, "If you have another book in you as good as *The Affluent Society*, I will certainly help you get it out."[52] The result, many years later, was *The New Industrial State*, and Galbraith was forever grateful. "This was a very big thing for me in my life," Galbraith later said. "It was the most important book I ever wrote." A Keynesian and ardent defender of the New Deal, Galbraith was always a controversial presence on the campus. In 1949 he had barely survived a nasty tenure battle, and throughout the 1950s the Board of Overseers repeatedly tried to engineer the appointment of economists more sympathetic to the business community than the maddeningly liberal Galbraith. It was, Bundy later wrote, "an intellectually dreary affair." In his eyes, the overseers' concern for "balance" was irrelevant. What mattered was "the personal intellectual excellence of the individual proposed." He would be the first to admit that "most members of the Harvard Economics Department were liberals. . . ." And sure, a wide variety of political and social beliefs in any department was probably a "healthy" thing. But for Bundy, there "was no appeal beyond the test of excellence."

The logic of excellence was certainly compelling. But who was to define excellence? Bundy insisted that "what is important about this trivial matter is that it is all there was. . . . Generous rich men could and did build towers of special delight, but they could forbid nothing."[53] This was too glib. Political judgments were an intrinsic part of any tenure decision. Harvard's economics department had a long history of denying tenure to scholars on the left. And both before and after Bundy's deanship, the issue was always framed as one of competency. But as Galbraith himself observed in the midst of one of these tenure battles, "Competency is always a disguise for something else."[54]

Galbraith may have been a Keynesian, but he was still within the pale of free market economists. In Bundy's world, Galbraith was the left. As such, he defended it. But a real Marxist need not even be considered. As Bundy wrote in the midst of the student upheavals of the late 1960s, "Marx was not unknown in the university of the fifties, only out of date. . . ."[55]

Bundy's defense of Galbraith was in any case motivated by sheer friendship rather than politics. He admired Galbraith's wit and counted him as a friend. But it was also true that as the years passed Bundy was becoming less of a Republican. "A group of us," recalled Carl Kaysen, "used to meet on a monthly basis to discuss foreign policy issues." Members of this informal group included Bundy, Galbraith, the physicist Jerome Wiesner, Arthur Schlesinger, Jr., and the economist James Tobin. "Mac began to sound more and more like the rest of us," Kaysen said. "He stopped, for instance, being an Eisenhower fan."[56]

Bundy tolerated and perhaps even incited mischief-making on the part of faculty members like Galbraith and Schlesinger. In 1959 these two "verbally minded" Democrats circulated a petition—obviously designed to discomfit Pusey—protesting the fact that fully 85 percent of Harvard's honorary degrees in recent years had been awarded to Republicans. Bundy was much amused and quipped, "Well, I thought that was a cheap way to buy out the overseers."[57]

Galbraith remembered Bundy in these years as only a "nominal Republican." Naturally, much of the group's discussion focused on the Cold War. "We were already trying to minimize the Cold War commitment," Galbraith said, "and talk about problems of mutual survival, while living under the cloud of the hydrogen bomb. . . . Our general perception of the Soviet threat was that it had been overinflated, and that [Nikita] Khrushchev, with all his eccentricities, was nevertheless a figure with whom you could do business."[58]

If Bundy was exposed intellectually to such dissenting views, the university he managed during these years was nevertheless enmeshed in the business of the Cold War. Pusey would boast in 1959 that what "goes on in the classrooms and laboratories of Cambridge is contributing vastly to the immense national efforts we are making . . . to compete effectively in this life and death struggle in which it seems that we are to be engaged for a long time with our alien rival, the USSR."[59]

By any measure, the Pusey-Bundy administration accelerated Harvard's interlocking relationship with the federal government. The university was quickly becoming one of the nation's foremost research laboratories, with fully three-quarters of its research budget coming from the federal government. In the first decade of Pusey's tenure, Harvard's share of federal monies rose from $8 million to more than $30 million. Because only 3 percent of this federal aid was earmarked for the social sciences, the university's agenda quickly began to tilt toward the hard sciences. Particularly after the 1957 Soviet launching of the *Sputnik* satellite, defense dollars fueled most of Harvard's growth.[60]

By the end of the 1950s, federal subsidies of one sort or another exceeded Harvard's tuition revenue, and Pusey became concerned. He had been selected president, after all, in part to restore some balance between Harvard's graduate schools, with their emphasis on the hard sciences, and the university's basic business of educating undergraduates. Indeed, Pusey and Bundy did much to strengthen the undergraduate school. But they were bucking a national trend, and could pour additional resources into the School of Liberal Arts only because the overall budgetary pie was itself growing. As Bundy put it, he "could allow Widener Library to flourish because the chemists were not starving."[61] And when faculty in the social sciences complained about how little they were paid at Harvard, Bundy's response was always to point them in the direction of Washington. One evening at a reception for junior faculty and their wives, Bundy gave a short speech in which he referred to the fact that perhaps only one-fifth of junior faculty members would ever receive tenure at Harvard. "But your résumé will always have Harvard on it, and that will stand you well throughout your career." Afterwards, the wife of a young untenured psychologist cornered Bundy and began asking him how he thought she could raise a family on her husband's meager salary. Bundy politely mentioned that Washington was handing out all sorts of federal grants to scholars in the humanities, and then, staring intently at this woman's ample bosom, he said, "Lady, all he's got to do is pick a tit and hold on."[62]

Still, if the humanities were not starving, the scientists were gorging. Pusey was so alarmed that he warned against a "frenetic, concentrated effort to produce . . . hundreds of thousands of scientists and engineers." And while he admitted that the university could not withdraw from the world, "it will serve society well only as it remains true to its essential nature—a university, not an agency of government."[63] Pusey's predecessor, James B. Conant, had placed a ban on classified research, and Pusey maintained it. But he did little else to keep the government at arm's length. Like most college administrators, he wanted Washington's money without its strings.

As for Bundy, he was easily disposed to accept, as he later wrote, the "connections which now bind the world of power and the world of learning. . . ." The advances of science, foremost of which he meant the invention of weapons of mass destruction, made inevitable the "constantly expanding process of connection between the university and government." Why? Because Washington had a need now to know as much as possible about the world.

It was "a curious fact of academic history," he wrote in 1964, that the area study programs developed in American universities in the years after the war were a direct outgrowth of the Office of Strategic Services (OSS). "It is still true today, and I hope it always will be, that there is a high measure of interpenetration between universities with area programs and the information gathering agencies of the government of the United States." * [64]

The interlocking relationship between academia and government intelligence agencies was not an abstract issue for Bundy. As Harvard dean, he was a willing and eager facilitator of this sensitive partnership. On occasion, he even helped the CIA to recruit Harvard students for careers in intelligence.† Years later, when asked about Harvard's relationship to the intelligence community, retired president Nathan Pusey pleaded ignorance. But he was willing to speculate: "I always had the suspicion that Mac was dealing with the CIA. I thought they might have been approaching him as dean in the first instance, and he may have been giving information about various people they wanted to hire or use in some way. I had the faint feeling that Mac had some kind of understanding with them."[65] With his wide-ranging connections, Bundy was an ideal intelligence resource.

One of the most controversial aspects of Harvard's relationship with the CIA began in 1950 when a number of Cambridge academics were brought together in a consulting group code-named Project Troy. Initially, they were

---

* Victor Marchetti and John D. Marks wrote in their book, *The CIA and the Cult of Intelligence* (New York: Dell, 1974), that CIA director Richard Helms was handed a CIA report in 1967 that listed hundreds of university professors and administrators at over a hundred campuses who were in one way or another under contract to the CIA (pp. 76, 226).

† In 1949, Lawrence Devlin and three other Harvard undergraduates met with one of their professors to discuss the possibility of careers in the CIA. "McGeorge Bundy showed up," Devlin recalled, "Giving each of us a pep talk. He offered me a job, and negotiated the level of entry." Devlin went on to become a CIA station chief in the Congo. (Seymour Hersh, *The Dark Side of Camelot* [Boston: Little Brown, 1997], p. 191.)

asked to solve a specific problem: how could the Agency's propaganda radio broadcasts beamed into Eastern Europe circumvent Soviet jamming? This narrow technical problem led to broader discussions about how the CIA could tap into the intellectual resources of the university community. Within a year Project Troy had given birth to a think tank dubbed the Center for International Studies (CENIS). According to a Senate Select Committee on Intelligence report in 1976, the CIA donated $300,000 in 1951 to establish CENIS "to research worldwide political, economic and social change . . . in the interest of the entire intelligence community."[66]

Though CENIS drew on scholars throughout Cambridge, it had to be housed at the Massachusetts Institute of Technology because of Harvard's ban on classified research. From the beginning CENIS was a campus anomaly. Armed guards stood on continuous duty at the door and no one was admitted without displaying a security badge. An MIT economics professor, Walt W. Rostow, became the first director, but he was quickly succeeded by Max F. Millikan, who had spent 1951 and 1952 organizing the economic research unit of the CIA's Office of Research and Reports.

Bundy was well aware that the CIA's role behind Project Troy and CENIS raised difficult questions about academic integrity. He met regularly with Millikan, Rostow and others associated with CENIS to review the think tank's work. A transcript from one such meeting in the mid-1950s has survived and provides an extraordinary insight into the thinking of Bundy and his colleagues.* In response to a question from Bundy about the CIA's role, Millikan explained, "Over the five years that this relationship has been maintained there has been some continuing ambiguity as to whether we were the creatures of the CIA or whether CIA was acting as an administrative office for other agencies."

By this time, CENIS was deep into several major studies on the Soviet Union, China and nuclear weapons strategy. Monographs or books had been produced on such topics as a study of the Soviet officer corps, the evolution of the Pentagon since World War II and an analysis of America's postwar economy. Millikan confessed that at times he had been compelled by the CIA to undertake projects "under pressure."

Similarly, the public was being told that those CENIS publications which contained policy recommendations were not being financed from government funds. This was, of course, disingenuous. As Rostow admitted, "We have skirted the edges of trouble on this." He pointed out that one of his own books, *An American Policy in Asia*, was "done on private funds and time,

---

* This May 18, 1957, meeting was attended by Mac Bundy, Max Millikan, Walt Rostow, MIT president James Killian, MIT provost Julius Stratton, Professor Francis Bator, Robert Lovett and Time-Life magazine executive C. D. Jackson, who had worked in the Eisenhower White House as special assistant for psychological warfare and continued to serve the president informally as a catalyst for various intelligence operations.

nonetheless, a lot of research which made the book possible was done on government supported research." Similarly, when MIT published *The Dynamics of Society* in 1953, which contained essays by Rostow and others, no mention was made of the CIA's funding of the book.[67]

No one was ignoring the ambiguity of their position. As Millikan put it, "On the other side of the case, in an academic institution it is corrosive to have people who are supposed to be pursuing knowledge and teaching people under limitations as to whom they can talk to and what they can talk about." But it was very hard to pass up on the opportunity, as he put it, to establish "a real sense of exchange with people in operational positions."

Characteristically, Bundy summarized the sense of the meeting: "The value of classified work," he said, "is in its existence and not in its magnitude. The channel is more important than that a lot of water should be running through it." For Bundy the question was, "Is a classified facility here necessary to keep the channels open?" The answer was not in doubt. As C. D. Jackson put it, "The work has got to be done. . . . You have mentioned the corrosive effect of this thing. I have known a few of you over a number of years. I have not noticed any visible corrosion. It is all a question of the human beings involved. . . . You have worked out [an] effective operation with the government."[68]

Still, the potential for embarrassment was worrisome enough that Lovett, a former deputy secretary of defense, suggested that they should explore setting up a "fire wall" against awkward publicity. MIT president Killian agreed, saying, "I have a strange animal instinct that this is a good time to get ourselves tidied up. We shouldn't take the risk on this." Bator suggested that the "CIA may not be the only possible device for this," and Lovett agreed: "It is the least desirable and not the only organization." Bundy pointed out that it was just a "tactical decision," to which Jackson responded, "It was a wonderful cover at the time."

By the end of the meeting everyone seemed to be in agreement that a "new umbrella" should be found for CENIS which would preserve its academic integrity and yet retain what Bundy had called the "channel" to Washington. Nothing changed; CENIS continued to receive heavy funding from the CIA through the 1960s when revelations published by David Wise's *The Invisible Government* (1964) and *Ramparts* magazine (1967) compelled MIT to sever its links with the think tank.

In addition to Harvard's arms-length relationship with the MIT-based CENIS, the CIA persuaded Harvard's Center for International Affairs to host an annual summer seminar for selected foreign leaders and scholars. From 1951 to 1967, Harvard received $400,000 from the CIA, a large sum of which went to run this summer program, directed by Henry Kissinger.[69]

WHILE Pusey and Bundy formally maintained the ban on classified research, they did not prevent Harvard professors from entering into a revolving door relationship with the CIA. Bundy, for instance, thought it only natural that the historian William L. Langer, a veteran of the Office of Strategic Services, had taken a leave from Harvard to organize the CIA's Office of National Estimates (ONE). Likewise, he thought it only natural that Langer returned to Harvard in 1954 to become director of the Russian Research Center.

Bundy had many reasons to admire Langer. Perhaps Harvard's most public historian, Langer had gone to Washington at the call of the CIA and promptly hired Mac's brother Bill as one of his top aides. They were old friends and political allies. Recently, Mac had published a review in *The Reporter* of a massive two volume study of America's entry into World War II written by Langer and S. Everett Gleason.* Langer had finished the project while at the CIA, and Gleason was a high-ranking official in the National Security Council. Bundy called it a "magnificent achievement . . . so thorough that it will not have to be done again."[70] It was not hard to understand why Bundy liked a work which consciously attacked American isolationism. Langer and Gleason made no effort to hide their agenda: they had produced a history, they wrote, "calculated to offset any debunking of War aims . . ." and which would depict the "tortured emergence of the United States of America as leader of the forces of light in a world struggle which even today has scarcely abated and is still undecided."[71] Funded by the Rockefeller Foundation and the Council on Foreign Relations to the tune of $139,000—an extraordinary sum in those years—and written with privileged access to classified documents, the Langer-Gleason volumes were official history parading as independent scholarship.

Needless to say, Bundy did not bother to mention the official character of Langer's work. But other reviewers did. The prominent revisionist historian Charles Beard attacked Langer for participating in the kind of relationship with Washington that gave him access to documents which other scholars could not inspect. Another scholar bluntly labeled him a "court historian," and Langer later complained that he had been accused of "having sold my skills for vile pelf."[72]

Langer certainly wasn't the only historian in the postwar period who lent his narrative skills to a defense of Washington's interventionist policies in the Cold War. But a Harvard professor of his stature was particularly influential in persuading Americans not to revert to prewar isolationism and to shoulder their new global responsibilities as leader of the free world.[73]

Under Dean Bundy, scholars like Langer were coddled, promoted and celebrated. This was a Harvard where men like William Y. Elliott, Henry Kissinger, Robert Bowie, Samuel Huntington, Zbigniew Brzezinski and Richard Pipes floated, as Langer titled his memoir, *In and Out of the Ivory Tower.*

---

* William L. Langer and S. Everett Gleason, *The Challenge to Isolation, 1937–1940,* (New York: Harper & Bros., 1952), and *The Undeclared War, 1940–1941* (New York: Harper & Bros., 1953).

All of these men shared an expansive view of America's global responsibilities, and all of them were willing to lend their expertise to the State Department, the CIA and other branches of the foreign policy bureaucracy.

Years later, when ticklish questions were raised about Harvard's cozy relationship with Washington, Bundy characteristically sat down at his typewriter to write an essay which would place everything in a comfortable context. "There can be no denying that there were contacts between our centers [at Harvard] and the government," he wrote. But this did not mean that the university was a "tool of the military industrial complex, or the CIA, or a foreign policy establishment." Why? Well, that was easy to explain. Harvard's research centers were "run by men with minds of their own. . . ." The integrity of these scholars could not be bought. "Our business with the government was the product of choices by our faculty, not the other way around. I remember no contracts or grants that did not arise from a professor's own interest . . . neither the federal dollar nor the seductions of political power had Harvard in thrall."[74] Trust me, Bundy was saying, and trust Harvard.

WHEN Henry Kissinger first encountered William Yandell Elliott as his tutor and mentor in the government department, this already legendary Harvard figure was spending two or three days a week in Washington working as a consultant to the House Committee on Foreign Affairs. A few years earlier "Wild Bill" Elliott, of course, had promoted Bundy's own career in the government department. Now, in 1954–55, Elliott was lauding the merits of Kissinger to Dean Bundy.

In the years before he became a public figure, Kissinger could be ingratiating to those in authority, and Bundy found him ambitious but unobjectionable. When Kissinger one day brazenly requested that he be placed on a fast track for tenure, Bundy nodded his head, smiled and did nothing. Other members of the faculty might refer to Kissinger as Henry "Ass" Kissinger for his arrogance, but Bundy thought he saw someone who was not merely a self-promoter but a bright intellect. He willingly served on the original editorial board for Kissinger's magazine, *Confluence*, a publication whose sole purpose seemed to be to introduce influential men to its editor. Bundy also wrote for the magazine.[75] Neither did he mind occasionally speaking at Kissinger's summer International Seminars.

And when Kissinger decided in 1955 that he wanted to go after a job at the Council on Foreign Relations, Bundy wrote him a strong letter of recommendation. The job was to direct a study group on nuclear weapons, from which emerged Kissinger's 1957 best-selling book, *Nuclear Weapons and Foreign Policy*. On one memorable occasion, Bundy came down to New York as a favor to Kissinger and led one of the study group's discussions. Even after this, when the book had established Kissinger as a policy analyst with a popular following, he returned to Harvard to find that his tenure was by no means a foregone conclusion. As Henry Rosovsky later told a Kissinger biographer, "Henry did not have an easy time getting tenure."[76] Some faculty thought both his arrogance and his best-selling book counted against him.

Not Bundy. In 1957 he did Kissinger the great favor of finessing what could have turned into an ugly tenure battle by awarding him a half-time lectureship in the government department. Though this was not a standard tenure-track position, Bundy made it clear that the ill-defined job held the promise of short-circuiting the usual eight-year grind to achieve tenure. Simultaneously, he persuaded a reluctant colleague, Robert Bowie, to take Kissinger on as his associate director of the newly organized Center for International Affairs. In a letter to Bowie, Bundy acknowledged that Kissinger was "just a little uncertain as to whether he wanted to come back to a department which had not been unanimously friendly to him a year ago, but I tried to cheer him up on that point. . . . I am confident that he is the man we want." Bowie gave Kissinger the job and quickly regretted it: "That's the worst mistake I ever made." Soon, the two men were not even on speaking terms. Although their feud became grist for Harvard's rumor mill, Bundy did not alter his estimation of Kissinger. When Kissinger on several occasions threw one of his then already legendary temper tantrums and threatened to resign from the center, Bundy counseled him against it. And then in July 1959, Dean Bundy used a special Ford Foundation grant to endow a half-chair in the government department, which he gave to Kissinger. Henry Kissinger now had the status he so coveted, Harvard tenure.[77]

Despite everything Bundy had done for Kissinger, there was always an underlying dissonance between the two men. The dean was practiced at feeding hungry egos, but Kissinger's tiresome scheming sometimes provoked Bundy to tease his insecure colleague. One day, on the eve of taking a sabbatical, Kissinger came by Bundy's office to bid him goodbye. "I hope, in spite of our troubles and disagreements," Kissinger said, "you will not think bad of me while I'm gone."

"When you're gone," said Bundy with a gleam in his eye, "I hardly think of you at all."[78]

Kissinger was not the kind of man to forget such needling, even when spoken in jest. He later repaid Bundy by going out of his way to insult him in his memoirs: "Bundy and I had had an ambivalent relationship over the years. I admired his brilliance even when he put it, too frequently, at the service of ideas that were more fashionable than substantial. I thought him more sensitive and gentle than his occasionally brusque manner suggested. He tended to treat me with the combination of politeness and subconscious condescension that upper-class Bostonians reserve for people of, by New England standards, exotic backgrounds and excessively intense personal style."[79]

By 1979, when Kissinger's memoirs on his years in the Nixon White House were published, Bundy had for some time regretted his role in advancing the career of someone he now regarded as neither a liberal nor a pragmatist, but merely an unpleasant opportunist. He told friends, "Kissinger doesn't lie because it's in his interest; he lies because it's in his nature."[80] When *Time* magazine journalist Walter Isaacson published a devastating biography of Kissinger, Bundy praised it, saying, "Even Henry Kissinger may not think Henry Kissinger is a very nice man."[81]

DEAN BUNDY rarely had second thoughts about Harvard's relationship with Washington, but sometimes, when directly challenged, he could be forced to reconsider his position. At a faculty meeting in 1957, Bundy found himself having to defend the university's tacit approval of loyalty oaths required of students receiving National Defense Education Act grants. The university, he said by way of rationalization, was only mailing the oaths to Washington. "We're simply licking the stamps," Bundy said. At this point, Renato Poggioli, a well-known Italian scholar, responded in his thick accent, "Mr. Dean, I have spent much of my life in Fascista Italy. And in Fascista Italy, you learna one thing. First you licka the stamps. Then you licka something else."[82]

About the same time, Michael Maccoby, a young doctoral student who worked part-time as Bundy's deputy on the Educational Policy Committee, told him that he, too, was troubled by the loyalty oaths.

"OK," Bundy snapped, "be in my office at seven-thirty tomorrow morning and I will give you a half hour to make your case."

The next morning Maccoby came prepared with a sheaf of notes. "Number one, I said, Harvard is a model for the country. What we do here could be looked at as legitimizing something which is perpetuating paranoia and questioning people's loyalty at a time when this country needs a different attitude. Number two, Senator Kennedy, who is your friend, has come out against this and you are undermining him."

That was all it took. "You've made your case," Bundy said. "We won't take the money."

Maccoby later remembered thinking that this was a man who liked to have a good argument: "Bundy was very much open to intellectual debate and ideas. He listened, and he was a quick study. On the other hand, he could be overly quick and jump to conclusions. He was interested in getting things done." Maccoby liked Bundy and thought he was good for Harvard. But he also felt uneasy with the dean's glibness. He knew Bundy was popular around Harvard Square for the same reason that Pusey was unpopular. Pusey's moral rectitude, his Christianity worn on a sleeve, was something that "bright" Cambridge society scorned.

"I remember arguing with Mac about that all the time," Maccoby said. "I told him, 'The only thing you say about somebody is that they're bright or that they're not bright. It's like that's your only category.' His response was, 'Well, you're bright enough, what are you complaining about?' "

This banter between the dean and his young assistant reflected a philosophical disagreement. Maccoby thought Harvard could do much more to become a teaching university, and not just for the "best and the brightest." "I would say things to him like, 'We have people at Harvard who get lost and are not bright and flashy and brilliant, but if they were taught well and somebody cared about them even as much as at Princeton, they would do very well.' I showed him, I had a tutorial group in which I took a student who was failing, a football star, and by the end of the tutorial he had a B average. I said, 'Look, if you pay attention . . .' And he replied, 'Oh, it's just your reflected brilliance. That's all it is.' He simply believed that the 'best will triumph.' I thought it was kind of Darwinian."

Maccoby thought Harvard provided a "terrible" undergraduate education. "If you were really brilliant and entrepreneurial," he said, "you did extremely well. But otherwise, you were just lost. Most of the faculty were off doing other things, the good faculty, and they would only pay attention to a student who was very aggressive and dazzling. I think that's still probably true." [83]

Bundy constantly talked of excellence, and if the country thought Harvard was an elitist institution at the beginning of the 1950s, by the end of the decade it was by every measure even more so. Yet, in some ways the dean's rigorous adherence to excellence also accelerated the trend toward democratizing the student body. Under Bundy's regime, many of the more complacent aspects of Harvard's WASPy elitism were sacrificed on the altar of meritocracy. In 1952, 63 percent of all applicants were admitted to Harvard; by 1960, only 30 percent were. The proportion from New England steadily dropped in favor of a wider geographical distribution. More students were accepted from public schools, and fewer from the ranks of Groton, Exeter and other private prep schools. (Even so, by 1960 a hefty 44 percent still came from private schools.) [84] Diversity was sought in all forms; Harvard's admissions director, Wilbur J. Bender, actively began to recruit African-American students, albeit in small numbers. Gone was the time when the sons of alumni could count on admission.

Bundy had a similar attitude toward his faculty. He relentlessly sought out scholars he thought brilliant and cultivated them. It was this agenda in his deanship that in retrospect many would cite as both his strength and weakness. If a department was perceived as lackluster, Bundy would not hesitate to overrule department chairs in order to bring in new blood. The list of his faculty acquisitions in these years is impressive. It took several years and more than one trip to Chicago, but in 1957, Bundy managed to recruit David Riesman, the celebrated author of *The Lonely Crowd*, to be a member of Harvard's uniquely interdisciplinary department of social relations.

Erik Erikson, the author of a landmark 1950 book, *Childhood and Society*, came soon afterwards. At Harvard, Erikson would break new ground with his psycho-historical studies of Mahatma Gandhi and Martin Luther. Partly because neither scholar had a doctorate (Riesman had a law degree), Bundy had to force these controversial appointments through over the objections of the department committees. He was successful, in part, because he was able to tap Ford Foundation funds to hire these outsiders.

Riesman later wrote about Bundy's deanship, suggesting that Mac had brought to Harvard a style of governance that he called "aristocratic meritocracy." Bundy was willing to be decisive in the extreme, Riesman observed. "He'd seek advice, but not necessarily in regular channels." [85]

Bundy was attracted to Riesman's essentially nonideological, optimistic assessment of the American condition. His books seemed to confirm the "liberal (anti-communist) consensus" that Bundy wanted to believe in; moreover, Riesman seemed to have resolved the doubts Bundy and Lippmann had expressed just a few years earlier when they had tried to rewrite Lippmann's *The Good Society*. "American ingenuity and apparently unlimited planetary resources," Riesman later said of the atmosphere in which he had written *The Lonely Crowd*, "appeared to offer a continuing geographical and upward mobility for millions." Liberalism, in short, was capable of bringing with it a civil society in which economic disparities, racism and regional nationalisms would wither away. Riesman later confessed that he had been guilty of "intrepid innocence" in expounding such a "utopian" assessment of the American Dream. [86]

Predictably, *Time* magazine embraced this new voice of postwar optimism in the autumn of 1954 by putting Riesman on its cover. Riesman was actually a fairly iconoclastic intellectual who subsequently displayed an instinct for gentlemanly dissent against the nuclear arms race and the Vietnam War. But for a time he symbolized the liberal establishment's love affair with social tinkering. Suddenly sociology was hot. Ironically, in another decade critics like Mary McCarthy would charge that the "gross stupidities and overconfidence of the Kennedy-Johnson advisers, not to mention their moral insensitivity, issued from a sectarian faith in the factuality of the social sciences. . . ." Sociology and political science, McCarthy thought, were among the most pernicious "pseudo-disciplines" that thrived in the time of the Cold War. [87] For better or worse, Bundy's term as dean would be marked by the luster and prestige he brought to Harvard's department of social relations.

Many of Bundy's recruits were strong-willed men who would later become marked in the 1960s as prominent left-of-center intellectuals. Stanley Hoffmann first came to Harvard as a graduate student from his native France in 1951 and wound up taking Bundy's course on American foreign policy. By the second semester, Bundy singled out Hoffmann to be his teaching assistant. When Hoffmann went back to France, they kept in touch, and in 1954, Bundy persuaded *Foreign Affairs* to publish an essay by Hoffmann on contemporary French politics. In 1955, Dean Bundy engineered Hoffmann's return to Harvard as an assistant professor, telling U.S. immigration authorities that the Frenchman was "indispensable" to the university. Hoffmann later became a leading intellectual critic of the Vietnam War, writing frequently in *The New York Review of Books*. In the 1950s he greatly admired Bundy. With Harvard rolling in money in those years, Hoffmann saw Dean Bundy in the role of a "Medici prince," who used the money to appoint people who interested him without regard to faculty politics. "Once he had appointed them," Hoffmann recalled, "he found a niche for them in whatever department.[88]

Bundy's friendships were also eclectic. Sometime in the early 1950s he had been introduced to Lillian Hellman, probably by his close friend, the theater critic, John Mason Brown. Bundy immediately recognized a soul mate.* They were both social creatures. The playwright had the same dry, acerbic wit and valued bright conversation. They gossiped about everything except politics, or at least knew each other well enough not to take their political differences seriously.[89] One day while dining with Hellman in Cambridge, Bundy casually suggested, "Why don't you come up here and teach?"

When Hellman protested that the English department wouldn't have her, Bundy snapped, "We'll see about that." Off he went and an hour later he phoned to say it was all arranged.

"But I don't know how to teach," Hellman said.

"But you know something about writing," Bundy replied. "Give them some real work. Teach them how to take from what's really around them and how to use it."†[90]

Bundy chose as his friends people with strong, prickly personalities. Hellman, Galbraith, Schlesinger, Kaysen and the particularly eccentric Robert Lowell were all of a kind. So, too, was J. Robert Oppenheimer. Bundy had been shocked by the outcome of Oppenheimer's 1954 security trial and called it a "travesty." Here was a man who was so obviously brilliant, so cerebral, that it should have been clear to all that he was really above so tawdry an inconvenience as a security review. Oppenheimer's trial offended Bundy's pugnacious morality, and for years afterwards he made a point of publicly standing by his friend. When numerous Harvard alumni threatened in the spring of 1957 to withhold donations if Oppenheimer was allowed to give the William James Guest Lecture, Bundy first ignored the protests, then made a show of attending the lecture himself.[91]

NOT everyone had a favorable opinion of Dean Bundy. Oscar Handlin, an eminent American historian, recalled, "He was clever, he had the tone of a man who always succeeds. . . . But I don't think he was terribly successful as a Dean of the Faculty."[92]

Handlin's antipathy to Bundy, however, was exceptional. All sorts of people sought Bundy out and included him in their social set. Early in the 1950s, Elting Morison, an historian at MIT (and the nephew of the famous

---

* Later, even in the midst of the Vietnam War, Bundy was a regular guest of Hellman's, both in New York and at her home on Martha's Vineyard.

† Hellman didn't accept Bundy's invitation until after her longtime companion, Dashiell Hammett, died in January 1961. She spent that year teaching writing to Harvard undergraduates and rented an apartment from Mac's mother, Kay.

Harvard American historian Samuel Eliot Morison), recruited a dozen Cambridge intellectuals into what came to be known as the Friday Night Supper Club. This elite supper club included Mac Bundy, MIT provost Julius Stratton, Harvard economist Vassily Leontieff, the historian Robert Lee Wolff, the art historian Myron Gilmore, the sociologist George Homans, physicists Edward Purcell and Victor Weisskopf, Polaroid founder Edwin Land, the economist George Millikan and the engineer William Hawthorne.[93] They met the first Friday of each month at the St. Botolph's Club in Boston's Back Bay, and discussed everything from university gossip and national politics to the latest breakthroughs in physics.*

Bundy came to regard many of these men as good, trustworthy friends. Outside the supper club meetings, he and Mary often dined at home with Bob Wolff and his wife, Mary Lee. (Wolff was an historian of the Byzantine Empire.) And when Colonel Stimson's widow pressed him to find an historian to write a full biography of her late husband, Bundy turned to Morison. As executor of Stimson's literary estate, Bundy gave Morison exclusive access to the Stimson diary and subsidized the project with grants from the Stimson estate. The result was a 1960 volume, *Turmoil and Tradition: A Study of the Life and Times of Henry L. Stimson*, which treated Bundy's mentor in an entirely friendly and respectful manner.

DEAN BUNDY could charm all sorts. Harvard provided him a stage upon which he could perform and be seen in the company of literary figures, scholars and the occasional out-of-town celebrity. In April 1959, Premier Fidel Castro created a stir in Cambridge when he spoke to a packed audience at Soldier's Field. Because President Pusey thought it prudent to keep his distance from the Cuban revolutionary, it fell to Dean Bundy to introduce Castro to Harvard. A few days earlier Castro had barnstormed New York City, garnering publicity with visits to the Bronx Zoo, the United Nations and Harlem (where he met Malcolm X). Twenty thousand New Yorkers cheered him in the course of an hour-long speech in Central Park. On this day in Cambridge eight thousand people turned out to see Dean Bundy arrive for the event sitting next to Castro in an open convertible. Bundy opened the event with a brief introduction. Over dinner at the Faculty Club, Bundy said, Castro had just confided to him that he had once applied to Harvard and been rejected. Making the most of the story—which was probably apocryphal—Bundy joked that Harvard was now prepared to make amends and admit Castro to the Harvard class of 1963! Castro then spoke for thirty minutes and fielded some questions.

Afterwards, Bundy's attempt to talk informally with Castro was rebuffed:

---

* Victor Weisskof reports that this supper club continued to meet regularly until 1970, when it fell apart over bitter arguments about the Vietnam War. By that time, Bundy was president of the Ford Foundation, and he invited his supper club colleagues to New York to discuss their differences. The reunion, however, only proved that their views were irreconcilable and the club disbanded. (Victor Weisskopf, *The Joy of Insight: Passions of a Physicist* [New York: Basic Books, 1991], p. 161.)

"I couldn't get anywhere with him. He wouldn't talk Spanish. My Spanish is a lot better than his English, which isn't saying a whole hell of a lot. . . . He struck me as interested in public gain and not interested in private conversation."[94] Ironically, within three years, Bundy would preside at meetings in the White House where the elimination of Castro—by invasion or assassination —was high on the agenda.

HARVARD in the 1950s was not a university in intellectual ferment. Neither was it a place of mediocrity. But in retrospect, Bundy could craft a long list of what he termed "serious failures."

Politically, Harvard had been slow to acknowledge its responsibilities as a "corporate citizen in Cambridge and Boston." With regard to race, Harvard had "believed too easily that steadily expanding legal rights would lead to equal opportunity." And it had been naive to think that "the standard remedies of liberalism would meet the national problem of poverty." It had also been shortsighted and complacent to ignore the gap between appearances and reality on a host of issues. "We were not troubled by the fact that much research was supported by money from the Department of Defense; we knew the research was uncontaminated, and we knew we were not limiting but expanding our real freedom by accepting the money we did on the terms we did. . . . And so, it now appears, we stored up trouble for the future."

Neither, in retrospect, did he think Harvard was as devoted to scholarship as it could have been. "The gravest of our academic failures," Bundy wrote, "were quite simply academic . . . we were not as good as we thought we were —none of us, faculty, students, administration. The fame of Harvard covered us all with its radiance, and we all too easily assumed that the honor paid us because of Harvard was no more than our personal due. The really ruthless critics among us were too few, and the self-critics fewer still."

Ironically, it seemed to Bundy in looking back that his Harvard had an overabundance of cleverness and a shortage of sound judgment, the very quality he valued most. "Competition in cleverness is not the single best basis for a happy human community, and there was too much sharpness and not enough kindness, too much pride and not enough generosity, too much striving and not enough helping in the Harvard of the fifties. . . . There were not enough whole men among us at any rank, and there was not enough modesty. . . . We may well have been the best in the country—but we foolishly supposed that made us good enough."[95]

BY 1959, Dean Bundy's enthusiasm for his job was wearing thin. "I kept telling Mac," Pusey said, " 'This is the greatest university in the world, and you, Mac, have got to keep it that way. Keep the faculty happy.' But by the end, his heart wasn't in it. He didn't just want to be offered a position in the new administration. No, he was actively seeking a position, and that bothered me."[96]

At any time during the 1950s, Bundy could have left Harvard for a prominent appointment in the Eisenhower administration. But he was not inclined to ask for it. Indeed, for some time now his political affiliations seemed to be adrift. This became particularly apparent late in John Foster Dulles's tenure as secretary of state when Dulles agreed to field questions at a small, off-the-record meeting at the Center for International Affairs. No more than twenty faculty members attended, including Bundy, Stanley Hoffmann and Arthur Schlesinger, Jr. Bundy had made it known on many occasions that Dulles was one person he cordially disliked, and he now took the opportunity to interrogate the secretary. The chief topic was Dulles's handling of the 1958 Quemoy-Matsu crisis, an affair which Bundy believed had been much ado about nothing.

"Bundy just needled him," Hoffmann recalled. "Schlesinger was his usual rather voluble self, and Dulles, who was rather formidable, essentially treated the affair like a medieval tournament. He just threw off people one after another as they came at him with criticisms. But he couldn't get rid of Bundy. The general tone—Bundy was, of course, too polite to say so—'Why do you keep lying?' One could see that Dulles was exasperated."

Bundy disliked such superciliousness. But he also had intellectual bones to pick with Dulles and made these very clear to students in his class on U.S. foreign policy. Dulles portrayed himself as a "realist," a word much in vogue in these years due to the works of Hans Morgenthau, a renowned political scientist at the University of Chicago. Bundy thought this school of foreign policy thinking was too crude. "God knows, Bundy was aware of power, like Morgenthau," recalled Hoffmann. "But he talked about blending power with idealism. The Eisenhower approach, which was how much does it cost, the bigger bang for the buck, using nuclear weapons as a solution to political problems, these were all things he didn't like much. He was an Acheson Republican and I think that facilitated his transition into the Kennedy camp." [97]

As it became clear that Richard Nixon would be the Republican Party's nominee in 1960, Bundy's disaffection from the Republican Party intensified. "If Nelson Rockefeller had won the nomination in 1960," he recalled, "I don't know what I would have done. But Nixon had been a real four-letter word for me ever since his Senate race against Helen Gahagan Douglas." Most of his closest friends were liberal Democrats and many of them were openly promoting the unannounced presidential campaign of Harvard's own Senator John F. Kennedy. Archibald Cox, a Harvard Law professor and a friend of Bundy's, was leading the Kennedy campaign in Cambridge. Schlesinger, Galbraith and numerous other friends were already writing position papers for the senator.

Bundy, however, had not either switched his party registration or made known his preferences. He had, of course, known Kennedy since their days together in the Dexter Lower School. And they had occasionally socialized in Boston—most often at Arthur Schlesinger's home—when Kennedy was a congressman and Bundy was still just a lecturer in the government department. Bundy had advised Kennedy not to run for a Senate seat. "I thought [Henry] Cabot Lodge was a hell of a vote-getter," Bundy recalled. "I told him he would be better off staying in the House, and perhaps aim to become Speaker. Well, he proved me wrong."[98] By the late 1950s, Senator Kennedy was also a Harvard overseer and consequently was seeing Bundy rather frequently on campus.

They knew and liked each other far more than they would later let on to the national press. In a speech to the Harvard Club of Boston, Kennedy humorously referred to "Harvard's own Lyndon Johnson, Mac Bundy," and told a joke: "I dreamt that the Lord came into my bedroom and anointed my head, and said, 'John Kennedy, I hereby appoint you President of Harvard University.' Nate Pusey said, 'That's strange, Jack, because I too had a similar dream last night, in which the Lord anointed me and declared me President of the Ivy League.' And McGeorge Bundy said, 'That's very interesting, Gentlemen, because I too had a similar dream last night—and I don't remember anointing either one of you!' "[99]

On commencement evening, June 1959, Arthur Schlesinger, Jr., invited Bundy to attend one of his regular dinners with Kennedy. At Kennedy's request, these dinners were invariably held in the dark-paneled, upstairs rooms of the Locke-Ober, an old restaurant located adjacent to Boston's Common. Bundy came with Mary and found the senator sitting with the Galbraiths, Schlesinger and Thomas Finletter, a Wall Street lawyer and former secretary of the air force in the Truman administration who was then a prominent fund-raiser in the Democratic Party. Politics was obviously on the agenda so understandably the conversation turned to that week's nasty confirmation battle over Lewis Strauss's nomination as commerce secretary.

Bundy was appalled by Eisenhower's nomination of Strauss. As chairman of the Atomic Energy Commission, Strauss had orchestrated J. Robert Oppenheimer's security trial. Bundy had been convinced by Joe and Stewart Alsop's columns that Strauss had ruined an honorable man's career out of personal and political pique. That Eisenhower would try to elevate such a man to cabinet rank was the last straw in Bundy's growing irritation with the Republican Party.

That night at the Locke-Ober, Schlesinger made it clear that he felt Kennedy had to vote against Strauss if he was to succeed in his rapprochement with the liberal wing of the Democratic Party. But he also knew that Kennedy's father, an old friend of Strauss's, wanted his son to vote for confirmation. And now the senator himself expressed the opinion that a president ought to be given considerable latitude in selecting his cabinet members. "It would require," said Kennedy, "an extreme case to vote against the President." To which Bundy responded, "Well, this is an extreme case." He then laid out the case against Strauss, citing his betrayal of Oppenheimer in particular. Kennedy was impressed, perhaps more by what Schlesinger called Bundy's "audacious mind" and "contempt for orthodoxy" than by the merits of the case. But a few days later he voted against Strauss's confirmation, which went down to defeat by the narrow margin of 49–46.[100]

Later, during the 1960 presidential season, Bundy lent no formal assistance to the Kennedy campaign. But that summer he sat next to Kennedy on the podium during Harvard's commencement ceremonies and they were seen deep in conversation. Later, Bundy announced his endorsement of Kennedy. Soon afterwards, he was introduced to Kennedy's speechwriter, Theodore C. Sorensen, and then Sargent Shriver, the candidate's brother-in-law, invited Bundy for drinks at the Ritz bar. "He asked if I would be interested in a post," recalled Bundy. "I replied, yes, but I didn't say what position. The next I heard from the Kennedy people was after the election when I was asked to see Kennedy himself at the Carlyle Hotel." [101]

Kennedy had toyed with the idea of making Bundy secretary of state, telling Ted Sorensen that a "forty-one-year-old Secretary of State" might be a good idea. [102] Early in December, Walter Lippmann had an hour-long meeting with Kennedy. At the time, Kennedy was leaning toward making Senator J. William Fulbright his secretary of state, but his two other candidates were Dean Rusk and Bundy. A few days after his meeting with the president-elect, Lippmann wrote a friend that he had "advocated his appointing Bundy and taking a chance on the fact that he was so young and not well known. Now I am beginning to hope it will be Fulbright. . . ." [103] Kennedy's advisers warned him against the appointment of a Republican, particularly one so young. (Kennedy was later heard to say, "Two baby faces like mine and his are just too much.") [104] So when they met at the Carlyle that December evening Kennedy asked Bundy if he would be "interested" in the job of under secretary of state for political affairs, the number three slot in the department. "I said," recalled Bundy, " 'sure.' He then said he couldn't offer it to me since he wasn't sure who would be secretary."

Days went by until Kennedy finally phoned and Bundy recalled him saying, "Sorry, but the job I mentioned doesn't exist any more." Kennedy explained that Dean Rusk was to be secretary of state and that Chester Bowles had been promised the slot as under secretary of state for political affairs. That left the position of under secretary of state for economic affairs, and Kennedy told Mac, "I can't get away with nominating you for that job and you couldn't get away with accepting it." Beneath this easy-going banter, however, it was clear that Kennedy felt comfortable with Bundy and was going to place him somewhere in close proximity to the White House. At one point Kennedy offered him the slot of under secretary for administrative affairs. Bundy said he would think about it: "I talked to Mary about it, and Henry Kissinger, and Mary Louise Brewster [Kingman Brewster's wife]. I asked them all what I should do. Kissinger, I remember, said, 'No you don't want that.' He said I should tell the president-elect that I really couldn't do that job. So I called JFK and turned it down."

For an agonizing amount of time Bundy thought his rejection of Kennedy's offer had ended his chances of joining the new administration. He heard nothing for nearly three weeks. Then, in late December, "Kennedy called again to say, 'There's this job at the White House as the president's Special Assistant for National Security Affairs.' " On December 30, Bundy accepted and then flew off to Antigua in the British West Indies for a brief vacation.[105]

Reaction to the appointment was mixed. The major media emphasized Bundy's youth, intellect and vigor, the last a noun which was quickly becoming a catchphrase for the new administration. As the *New York Times* reported, "Mr. Kennedy went to considerable pains to fit Mr. Bundy into his Administration."[106]

David Riesman, the Harvard sociologist whom Bundy had recruited and counted as a friend, felt an uneasy premonition about the prospects of a Bundy in the White House. "He was so good," Riesman later told David Halberstam, "that when he left I grieved for Harvard and grieved for the nation; for Harvard because he was the perfect dean, for the nation because I thought that very same arrogance and hubris might be very dangerous."[107]

8

William Bundy and the CIA, 1951–1960

> *Hasn't everything turned out well? The attack on Bill has become a real turning point, I think, and to hell with Walter Lippmann, if I may be coarse about it.*
>
> JOSEPH ALSOP
> letter to Katharine Bundy
> July 1953

WHEN BILL BUNDY was finally discharged from the army in September 1945, he returned home to a very sick wife. Earlier that year Mary had contracted tuberculosis and she would remain in a sanatorium at Saranac Lake, New York, until the autumn of 1947. This was to be a difficult time in their marriage. Bill had been gone for two and a half years, and in his absence Mary had grown up. She was no longer the teenager he had married, and Bundy himself—at the age of twenty-eight—seemed much older. Like many veterans who had put their lives on hold, he was intent on going someplace. To Mary, he seemed aloof and just not much fun. Her illness made it that much more difficult for these two strangers to get to know each other again. Bill would visit Saranac Lake during the short holiday breaks from Harvard, but intent on finishing law school, he attended the summer session in 1946 and graduated in June 1947.

Though he lacked any strong passion for the law, he had done the Bundy thing and excelled; he made the law review, and served as case editor under Elliot Richardson, who was law review editor that year. Upon graduation, he received an offer to clerk with Judge Augustus Hand of the Second Circuit in New York. But Bill wanted to go back to Washington, D.C., and when the influential law firm of Covington & Burling made him an offer, Bill accepted.

At the last minute, Justice Frankfurter phoned to ask if he would serve as the second of his clerks. Though he was not aware that his brother Mac had just turned Frankfurter down for the same position, Bill still hesitated. No justice had ever had more than one clerk, and he thought being number two might not be a good experience: "I thought about it, but declined; it was probably a stupid decision . . . but I was pretty punchy in those days."[1]

So in the autumn of 1947, Bill and Mary moved into a rented house at the bottom of Foxhall Road in Georgetown. Bill immediately joined the Metropolitan Club, by far the most exclusive of Washington's clubs. Located just two blocks from the White House, Bundy found it a pleasant place to lunch. At Covington that first year, he worked under the supervision of one of the firm's junior partners, Donald Hiss. The two men quickly became friends. Hiss had also gone to Harvard Law, and was a protégé of Covington's senior partner and Bill's father-in-law, Dean Acheson, who was then serving as under secretary of state.

Acheson was also a friend of Donald Hiss's brother Alger, who had been a high-ranking State Department official until 1947, when he became president of the Carnegie Endowment for International Peace. In August 1948 a *Time* magazine reporter named Whittaker Chambers accused Alger Hiss of being a long-standing Soviet spy. Hiss denied the allegation under oath and was subsequently indicted for perjury in December 1948.

At the time, Harvey Bundy was vice chairman of the Carnegie Endowment, and when its trustees met to decide how they should respond to this indictment of their executive officer, a debate erupted. Some favored firing Hiss forthwith. But a junior trustee, David Rockefeller, protested that they should not convict a man on the basis of an indictment. Harvey Bundy, who happened to be chairing the meeting in the absence of John Foster Dulles, decided the right thing to do was to put Hiss on a paid leave of absence while he fought his legal battle. Afterwards, Harvey—who had known Hiss ever since he was a young associate at the Boston law firm of Choate, Hall & Stewart in the 1920s—sat down and interrogated him about the allegations. "I spent hours with Hiss on the whole problem," Harvey Bundy recalled, "and was completely convinced of his innocence." Not only did he staunchly defended Hiss to all his friends, but he also contributed to Hiss's defense fund.[2]

Bill Bundy had never met Alger, but he was sympathetic when the hat was passed around Covington & Burling one day for the Hiss defense fund; after consulting Mary about it, he wrote out a check for $200 and mailed it off with a supportive letter to Hiss's lawyers. He had followed the controversy with great interest and believed that "first-rate counsel in such a case was vital both for the person and for history." What he had in mind was the Sacco-Vanzetti case, in which his great-uncle A. Lawrence Lowell and that perennial Bundy family friend, Felix Frankfurter, had been adversaries. (Lowell had chaired the Massachusetts governor's advisory committee that reviewed the case and confirmed the guilt of both defendants, Italian immigrant anarchists who allegedly killed a paymaster in 1920. Despite Frankfurter's best efforts to document their innocence, Nicola Sacco and Bartolomeo Vanzetti were executed in 1927.) Bill had once read the entire record of the Sacco-Vanzetti proceedings and emerged undecided on the question of guilt. He believed "things were royally mucked up by an incompetent defense lawyer at the very first trial." Sometime in 1949 he found himself in the offices of Edward C. McLean, one of Hiss's lawyers, and Alger happened to walk in and they were introduced.[3]

By the time Hiss was finally convicted of perjury during a second trial in 1950, Bundy—like his father, Harvey—still thought it likely that justice had miscarried. As late as 1952, Bill told a friend over dinner that "he'd gone through the whole record in great detail and he simply could not see that there was evidence to conclude that Hiss was a Soviet agent."[4] Regardless of whether Hiss was guilty or not, Bill admired his father-in-law's defiance. On the day Hiss was convicted of perjury, Acheson told reporters, "I do not intend to turn my back on Alger Hiss."[5] By then, Acheson was Harry Truman's embattled secretary of state, and his political enemies would use the remark to hound him for the rest of his tenure.

BILL and Mary were frequent visitors on weekends to the Acheson farm in Maryland, where Bill would assist his father-in-law in the vigorous chores of brush clearing and wood chopping. Mary's health was still precarious. She had gone back to the Saranac Lake sanatorium for a short stay in 1948, and then in the autumn of 1949 she gave birth to a son, Michael, and promptly suffered a serious relapse. This time she remained at Saranac Lake through the spring of 1950, when she was finally released, tired but her lungs at last clear of tuberculosis after two chest operations.[6]

Through these difficult times Bill patiently applied himself to the practice of corporate law. The work was not without interest, but he was rarely captivated. One of Covington's clients was the government of Iran. Another client was a Washington State apple growers association which hired the firm to help increase its exports to Europe. Working with Senator Warren Magnuson, Bundy negotiated a deal whereby Western Europe paid for imported Washington apples with Marshall Plan funds. "It gave me good exposure to Capitol Hill," Bundy said. "I suppose you could call it lobbying."[7]

By 1950, after less than three years with Covington & Burling, Bundy knew he hated practicing law. He was desperately bored and began thinking of returning to his only real passion, history. But then a long-simmering civil war on the Korean peninsula erupted into a bloody ground war when thousands of communist North Korean troops poured across the armistice line into South Korea.[8] Truman responded by ordering American troops to intervene. When in October a massive Communist Chinese intervention put the Americans on the defensive once again, Bundy considered rejoining the army: "There was a hell of a war going on and my father-in-law was in the front lines, so to speak." Late that year, however, William Langer, one of his history professors at Harvard, called with a special invitation.

Langer had just been asked by Walter Bedell Smith, the director of the Central Intelligence Agency, to take over its Office of National Estimates (ONE). Smith told Langer that ONE was supposed to provide Washington's decision-makers with intelligence estimates of political, military and economic trends around the globe. The Korean War, he said, had demonstrated that "we haven't been doing it very well." When Smith offered Langer a staff of hundreds to do the job, Langer replied in his high-pitched Dorchester-Boston twang, "Well, I can't possibly do the job with more than twenty-five people." Now Langer was calling to ask if Bundy would be one of those twenty-five.[9]

After persuading Covington & Burling to give him a two-year leave, Bundy told Langer he would come aboard. He knew he would have to pass a security clearance, and in the era of McCarthyism it was not unusual for the process to take six months. In May 1951, at the tail end of the security review, Bundy told Allen Dulles, who was then deputy director of the CIA, of his contributions to the Hiss defense fund. (By then, Bill had contributed a total of $400 to the defense fund.) Though Dulles was a friend of his father's—and had been Mac Bundy's boss in the 1948 Dewey campaign—Bill had never met this legendary Sullivan & Cromwell lawyer and veteran of the OSS. Dulles said he would have to look into the matter, but a few days later he told Langer that he did not think the Hiss contribution was an impediment. Bundy was told to proceed to a formal interview by an internal loyalty board, which queried him closely about the Hiss contribution. At one point Bundy produced his checkbooks to demonstrate that his contributions to other charitable activities were also in the $200 range, a not inconsiderable sum in 1949–50. Shortly thereafter, he was hooked up to a "lie-detector" machine and asked numerous questions, including the standard ones about his sexual practices: "I hated it," he recalled later, "but apparently passed clear."[10] In June 1951 he went to work in the CIA's temporary headquarters, an old former Navy Department hospital at Twenty-third and E Streets, overlooking the Potomac River.

AFTER only three months of learning the ropes, Bundy became chief of the estimates staff, reporting directly to the eight-member Board of National Estimates. His job was to supervise a staff of eighteen to twenty analysts. Most of these men had advanced degrees and were experts in their field.

The relationship between the board members and the usually younger staff analysts was often contentious. The board members included senior scholars like Raymond Sontag, a conservative, rather imperious historian of German affairs from Princeton; Sherman "Buffalo" Kent, an OSS veteran and Yale historian; Bill Langer of Harvard, and a rotating number of army generals, admirals and Wall Street lawyers. The analysts were not the kind of men who easily deferred to higher authority. Ray Cline was a hefty, blond young man with an enormous ego and a Harvard doctorate. James Billington was a

Harvard- and Oxford-trained expert on Russia. Harold Ford, thirty, had a doctorate on the Far East from the University of Chicago, and had recently transferred from Frank Wisner's Office of Policy Coordination (OPC) at the CIA because he thought Wisner's laundry list of covert operations was "foolish and ill-conceived."[11] Chester Cooper, a veteran of the OSS in China, had been in the CIA since its founding in 1947. Willard Mathias was a political scientist from Harvard who had spent the war years in army intelligence and then joined the Central Intelligence Group, the CIA's predecessor in 1946. Russell Jack Smith, another OSS veteran, had a PhD in English from Cornell and had been with the CIA since 1947, as had Robert W. Komer. They were all strong personalities with formidable intellectual credentials.

Bundy was their editor, and many who had the same job later considered it a thankless one. "Despite its title," complained Russell Jack Smith, "you were chief of nothing, merely a straw boss among your peers."[12] Yet Bundy loved it. "I could comment on the papers, the estimates," he recalled, "but I did not write them myself."

He enjoyed the intellectual combat that was part of every estimate; it reminded him of his college debating and the dinner conversations at home where everyone was encouraged to interrupt. The topics were both abstract and concrete: Were the Chinese ready to settle for a stalemate in Korea? How many and what kind of nuclear weapons would the Soviet Union have by 1955? What were the electoral prospects of the Communist Parties of Italy and France? What was the future of King Farouk's regime in Egypt? What would happen in Russia after Stalin died? Could the French retain Vietnam against the Viet Minh insurgency? They were being asked to make educated guesses about things that could not be known, and Langer set the tone by making it clear that no one would be allowed to pull rank. One day, when Ray Sontag sought to prevail in an argument with Ray Cline by citing his seniority, Langer said in his nasal whine, "But Ra-a-a-a-y, a young fellow can have a good idea too, don'tcha kno-o-o-w."[13]

What counted was whether your argument could marshall a preponderance of facts. As Smith later explained, "There is almost never enough firm intelligence to support a solid, definitive statement. If there were, there would be no need for an estimate. . . . So, writing an estimate required some risk-taking, some chasm-jumping, and this was part of the challenge."[14]

Stylistically, the reports were often filled with deadly prose. Bundy much preferred the papers produced by his British counterparts. "Ours were crude and had no flowing style in the literary sense," he later observed.[15]

It was not as if men like Bill Langer, Sherman Kent and Bill Bundy lacked the ability to write an interesting sentence. Kent once described the efforts of a coup-ridden country in Southeast Asia to bring some semblance of order to "gathering piss with a rake."[16] His scatological humor was notorious. He explained the importance of semantic differences with the following story: "Husband: 'Darling, I've got my semi-annual hard-on.' Wife: 'George, you always get mixed up in your English. You mean that you've got your annual semi-hard-on.' "[17] Such language rarely made it into the estimates, but Kent's freewheeling attitude nevertheless encouraged people to ask hard questions.

When at the end of 1951, Langer returned to Harvard, Kent took charge of ONE. His administrative style was highly eccentric. "Sherman seemed almost to avoid telling anyone what to do," wrote one analyst later. "He spouted suggestions like a fountain but always with an accompanying argument that invited rebuttal. Sherman's manner—his exaggerated vehemence, the rollicking obscenity, the tugging at his suspenders, and jerking at his tie—seemed to invite a playful response, and we were sometimes surprised to find him deadly serious about a position he had stated comically."[18] Bundy loved him.

As the years passed, and ONE estimates acquired a certain cachet among Washington decision-makers, the political pressures grew to tailor the estimates to conventional wisdom. In the mid-1950s, ONE produced an estimate which concluded that Chiang Kai-shek's Nationalist forces on Taiwan had a "negligible" likelihood of recapturing the Chinese mainland. One day at a National Security Council (NSC) meeting, Secretary of State John Foster Dulles entered the room, his face flushed with anger, and said to his brother, now director of the CIA, "I can only imagine, Allen, that the men who wrote this estimate are dyspeptic!" To which Allen replied, "They are not dyspeptic. They are intelligent, knowledgeable people." His brother insisted it was a "dangerous paper," which could greatly alarm U.S. allies in Asia. At this, President Eisenhower observed, "The idea was to start a discussion, and it seems to have done that."[19] The ONE estimate was not rewritten, but neither did the Eisenhower administration alter its assumption that Chiang Kai-shek represented a realistic alternative to Mao Zedong's communist regime.

IN March 1952, Bundy became principal assistant to Robert Amory, the CIA's deputy director of intelligence and its representative to the National Security Council. Amory and Bundy clicked upon first meeting. A former Harvard Law professor, Amory was an odd combination of a Boston Brahmin and an extrovert, the kind of person who couldn't stop telling stories that most listeners suspected were overdramatized. A tall, lean man with the profile of a hawk, Amory sputtered with nervous energy. On first encounter, he seemed anything but the right kind of man to be in charge of an operation that was supposed to produce dispassionate, reasoned intelligence. But according to one CIA veteran, Amory routinely "terrorized" his colleagues with his grasp of arcane details of foreign affairs.[20] For Amory, intelligence was a vast game of trivia, and he was the master. Bundy was remarkably adept at absorbing massive amounts of information, but he marveled at Amory's faculties.

Under Amory, Bundy continued to stay on top of the flow of ONE estimates, but he no longer had the administrative duties of its chief. Instead, he became the CIA's working liaison to the NSC. It was a job without any special title, but one which brought him to the very heart of the intelligence process. He saw Allen Dulles at least weekly. Sitting in at NSC Planning Board meetings, he learned what the president and his closest foreign policy advisers needed and expected from the intelligence analysts. His job was to keep his analysts at the ONE out of the ivory tower of abstraction and grounded in the reality of what the decision-makers needed to know. He was good at it. He was privy to just about everything, including some, but not all, of what was going on in the covert wing of the CIA. "I was well aware of what was being done by people like Tom Braden and Cord Meyer. . . . They were doing things that had to be done through covert channels. They had to be covert because right-wingers in Congress would have opposed funding European social democrats and that's what Braden and Meyer were doing. It was a damn good show." * [21]

Bundy finally felt in his element. His colleagues respected his quick mind and efficiency. It was obvious to them that he had unique ties and connections in Washington. "He was very good at the cocktail circuit in Washington," recalled an ONE colleague, "meeting people, and picking up the gossip." [22] Initially, Chet Cooper, an ONE analyst, had looked "askance" at people with backgrounds like Bundy's. Dulles had recruited a great many graduates of Princeton (his alma mater), Harvard and Yale, and Cooper thought many of these men were pretty mediocre. (One-quarter of the CIA's top officers came from Harvard.) [23] Bundy was perceived by many of his colleagues as part of an elite "Grottie" clique that included such other high-ranking CIA officers as Richard Bissell, Tracy Barnes, John Bross, Kermit Roosevelt and Archibald Roosevelt. Stewart Alsop once called them the "Bold Easterners." [24]

"I knew exactly where Bundy came from," said Cooper, who was from a middle-class family in Boston. "I didn't even give him a chance." But he soon changed his mind. "It was quite clear that this was a very smart guy. And in his way, he became one of the guys." [25]

One summer day when Washington's heat was particularly brutal, Bundy came to his non-air-conditioned office wearing the outfit of a British officer in the tropics—khaki shirt and baggy shorts with white hose socks reaching almost to his knees. Hal Ford, Russell Jack Smith and some of his other colleagues were joking with him about this attire when Dulles suddenly walked into the room. The director of the Central Intelligence Agency took one look at Bundy, pushed his glasses up on his forehead and ordered him back home "to put his pants on." Bill blushed, said "Yes, sir!" and went home. [26]

Often his colleagues could hear him walking the halls, whistling a popular tune. In meetings he would chain-smoke cigarettes and take copious notes on

---

* Bundy learned only after the fact about the two major covert actions to unseat governments in Iran in 1953 and in Guatemala the following year. "The Iran operation struck me as worthwhile," he said, "but I wondered about Guatemala, whether it was necessary" (Apr. 3, 1993, interview).

yellow legal pads. He was always in a hurry. "Bill's knack for giving orders as he was rushing out of the office," said Hal Ford, "earned him the name Hoppity Skippity, after a big bunny that was then featured on a children's television show."[27] He was something of a nerd, but he was at home in a place that attracted such people. "One of the interesting things about this establishment," Cooper related, "was that it was very small and the pressures were very great. We worked very long hours, we worked very intimately. It was like one long Ph.D. examination."

By 1952, Cooper felt like a basket case. In his short career in the CIA he had dealt with one crisis after another. "I had presided over the fall of China," he said. "I had dealt with coups in Burma and Thailand, and rebellion in the Philippines, the beginning of the Korean War, the guerrilla operations in Malaya and the French Indochina business. By mid-1952, I was on my hands and knees." Cooper was rewarded with a sabbatical to the National War College.[28]

Bundy thrived on the combination of intellectual wordplay and crisis atmosphere. After two years within the CIA, he found himself so intrigued with his work that he couldn't imagine going back to the law. He did, however, begin to speculate about perhaps returning to Harvard. With the Korean War grinding into a stalemate, the national crisis that had brought him into the CIA seemed to be receding. Many of the analysts he most admired were academics; the thought occurred to him that it was time he return to his first passion, history. To that end, he wrote a letter to Bill Langer, who was now back at Harvard, and inquired about enrolling in a history doctoral program. Langer encouraged him.[29]

Events soon intervened, however, to make this a road not taken, a missed opportunity which Bundy always regretted. In the spring of 1953, Allen Dulles decided that Bundy's new work as liaison to the NSC required a "Q" clearance, which would allow him formal access to nuclear secrets. It should have been a pro forma process. But until then, Bundy's security file had remained within the CIA. Now it would be passed to Lewis Strauss, chairman of the Atomic Energy Commission (AEC). As it happened, Strauss had a long-standing dislike for Bill's father, Harvey. (Back in 1916–19, both young men had worked for Herbert Hoover's Food Administration.) During World War II, as an aide to Navy secretary James Forrestal, Strauss had been incensed when Harvey Bundy stonewalled him about the Manhattan Project.[30] Because the AEC used the FBI for its security clearances, Bundy's file was passed to J. Edgar Hoover in late June or early July 1953. Three or four days later, information from that file found its way to the offices of Senator Joseph McCarthy.

By the summer of 1953, Republican senator Joseph McCarthy's witch-hunt had destroyed the careers of hundreds of civil servants, particularly those working in the State Department. Not even the inauguration of a Republican president seemed likely to abort the endless round of accusations, investigations, dismissals and, inevitably, ritualistic naming of names. Later that year Mac Bundy would be named dean at Harvard, where he would, as we have seen, encourage Harvard's ex-communists to name names. His brother Bill, however, felt none of these political pressures in his job at the CIA. A different atmosphere existed inside Allen Dulles's fiefdom. This was the CIA; its very purpose cloaked it from public scrutiny, let alone boorish senatorial investigations. Bill was a liberal Democrat, the son-in-law of "Red" Dean Acheson, and he had on his security file the fact of his contributions to the Hiss defense fund. But even so, he had no particular fear of being targeted. The very thought was ridiculous. He was not blind, however, to what was going on around him. McCarthy had recently charged that more than one hundred communists were ensconced in the CIA; no evidence of this was forthcoming, but then no one disputed the allegation either.* [31]

Earlier in 1953, McCarthy's chief investigator, a young lawyer named Roy Cohn, was hounding the Voice of America. "Cohn went after a dear friend of mine at VOA," Bundy recalled. "This man was well known to [Senator] Mike Mansfield, so I went to Mike and he put in a very strong representation on his behalf. My friend's position nevertheless became untenable and he left within a year. Anyone who didn't have friends could easily come under attack." [32]

Was Bundy's appeal on behalf of his friend a mark of political courage? Or a combination of arrogance and naiveté? Or simply the decent thing to do for a friend? In normal times, what he did was a small thing, and he seemed to have done it almost unthinkingly. But then, these were not normal times, even for a Bundy.

THURSDAY, July 9, 1953, began like many of Bill's days. He was up early and arrived at work by 7:30 A.M. Chet Cooper wandered into his office about an hour later and queried him about an estimate they had to sort out. Bill then had to run to an ONE board meeting, but he and Chet agreed to check in with each other again in half an hour. But when Cooper tried to phone Bundy thirty minutes later, Bill's secretary, Anna Lee Haslett, curtly told him, "I'm sorry, Mr. Bundy hasn't come in today." Cooper said, "You must be mistaken, I saw him half an hour ago." Haslett replied stonily, "He's not here and he's not coming in today." [33]

Cooper knew then that something was up. When Bundy had returned from his ONE board meeting, he found his bright and very loyal secretary in a state of high tension. Haslett worriedly said that Senator McCarthy's infa-

---

* Indeed, in September 1952 the New York Times reported that Bedell Smith himself had conceded, in a libel trial between McCarthy and Senator William Benton of Connecticut: "The [communists] are so adroit and adept that they have infiltrated practically every security agency in the government."

mous investigator, Roy Cohn, had just phoned Walter L. Pforzheimer, the CIA's legislative counsel, to say that they wanted Bundy to testify before McCarthy's committee that very morning at 10:45 A.M. Haslett said Pforzheimer was now meeting with Bob Amory and that Bundy was expected in Amory's office "forthwith."[34]

When Bundy walked into Amory's office down the hall, he was briefed on what Cohn had said. It had been part of Pforzheimer's job to get to know Senator McCarthy and his staff, and he had a grudging admiration for Cohn. "I remember telling Amory that I thought Cohn was a brilliant lawyer," Pforzheimer recalled.

Pforzheimer now related his conversation with Cohn: "Walter," Cohn had said, "we trust you and we want you to understand that McCarthy wants Bundy to testify because he is up for a top security clearance and we wonder whether that should be approved." Bundy's appearance, Cohn said, "was purely personal and did not involve CIA in any way." Pforzheimer had listened and politely said, "Roy, I'll have to check; I'll be back to you."[35]

At this point Allen Dulles, who had been at an NSC meeting over at the White House, joined the discussion in Amory's office about how they should respond. Everyone understood that if Bundy was forced to testify, the fact of his $400 contribution to the Hiss defense fund would probably emerge and this would give McCarthy enormous political capital to go after the CIA. Bundy remembered Dulles saying that it was "tricky," that of course the CIA would stand by him, "but that in the meantime if Cohn reached me with a subpoena that could make it much harder." They needed to stall Cohn. A phone call was placed to the White House, and after consulting with Eisenhower's national security adviser, Robert Cutler, Dulles bluntly ordered Bundy to "get out of town."

Bundy suggested that he might visit his parents at their summer house in Manchester. Dulles agreed, and as Bundy left the room, the director said, "Be out of touch."[36]

Bundy quickly drove home to Foxhall Road and told Mary what had happened. She was shaken but stoically helped him pack a bag and saw him off to the airport, where he got on a plane for Boston. Bill had called his father and suggested it might be a good idea if they both disappeared on a golf course for the afternoon.

After Bundy had left the building, Pforzheimer called Cohn and informed him that Bundy "was on leave and would not be available." Cohn, however, who had plenty of experience in cornering reluctant witnesses, and had taken the precaution of finding out for himself whether Bundy had come to work that morning. Now he called Pforzheimer on his lie. He told him that he had phoned Bundy's office just prior to their conversation, and, without identifying himself, had inquired about Bundy. One of Bundy's secretaries, Virginia Long, had told him that Bundy had merely stepped away from his desk. Cohn now accused Pforzheimer of having sent Bundy away.

When Pforzheimer denied this, Cohn warned him that Bundy was "a serious security case; that he had 'contributed heavily' to the Hiss defense fund; that he belonged to a couple of front organizations; and had made many 'outrageous' statements about town which indicated his security unreliability." Cohn angrily demanded that Pforzheimer find Bundy and call him back.[37]

Pforzheimer was not happy to have been caught lying and he now warned his colleagues that "there might be a blast in the press" from McCarthy. Later, while eating lunch in the CIA cafeteria, Pforzheimer's secretary came running to say that Cohn had called again and now wanted Pforzheimer himself—and Bundy's secretary—to appear in an executive session of McCarthy's committee at 2 P.M. Pforzheimer went straight to Dulles' office where a group of senior CIA officials discussed what they should do in the event that a subpoena was served on any of its officials. Clearly, Dulles couldn't keep ordering his employees to disappear. On the other hand, neither did he want to open his doors to McCarthy's investigators. A wide-ranging discussion took place between Dulles, Lawrence Houston (the CIA's general counsel), Bob Amory and Pforzheimer. At one point, though, Pforzheimer took Dulles aside privately and said that he would not commit perjury to save Bill Bundy from his own mistakes. "I would not do that," he later insisted. "Dulles was shocked. He realized that he was going to have to do something about that [impending] subpoena. You know, if it had been a national security issue, if it had been a Bay of Pigs operation, I would have ducked it somehow, but not for Bill Bundy."[38]

Pforzheimer had always disliked Bundy. "Bill Bundy is a snot, not a snob," Pforzheimer recalled four decades later. "I don't mind a snob; I'm a snob." Pforzheimer came from Standard Oil wealth; his uncle had once owned the Gutenberg Bible and eventually sold his private library for millions of dollars. He was a product of Horace Mann, an elite prep school in New York, and then Yale, where he had first met the Bundys. Even at Yale, Pforzheimer liked Mac and harbored a deep resentment of Bill. "He was a shit then and he's a shit now," Pforzheimer said. "He was much more unsure of himself than Mac. Very aloof, very cold. . . . After Yale, the next time I saw him was in early 1942. I had flunked algebra, but ended up at Fort Monmouth anyway. One day I was sitting around and out popped Bill Bundy out of an adjacent room. We talked and he advised me not to work on signal intelligence."[39] Pforzheimer took Bundy's advice for condescension and remembered the incident all his life. He was a proud, earthy man whose humor after a few drinks often turned scatological, and whose prejudices he liked to parade. Though Bundy was hardly aware of it, Pforzheimer was not a friend.

As for Dulles, his first concern was to avoid the precedent of any kind of regular congressional oversight of his bailiwick. That, he believed, could severely hamper the CIA's ability to run covert operations and keep secrets. As to Bundy, Dulles was certainly inclined to protect a family friend. Initially, he was just not certain whether this required a public confrontation with McCarthy. To be sure, if a confrontation was necessary, Dulles knew Bundy was a good case. Earlier, he had asked his internal security chief, Sheffield Edwards, to check out Bundy's personal life: Edwards had told him, "I've never had a case before where someone didn't at least say, 'Well, he drinks too much.' "[40] Bundy was superclean. On the other hand, no one in the Eisenhower administration had yet taken a stand against McCarthy. It was not, in any case, Dulles's style to be decisive. He was a man who, to put it kindly, deliberated with the caution of a lawyer. "Dulles was a ditherer," Chet Cooper said. "He was not a crisp decision-maker."[41]

Pforzheimer's private insistence that he would not perjure himself if called to testify forced Dulles to dig in his heels. He could not have his own legislative counsel testify under oath that Dulles was directly defying a congressional committee. At the end of this crucial meeting it was agreed that if Pforzheimer was served a subpoena, he would refer it to Dulles, "who would in all probability take the matter up with the White House."[42]

Dulles's back may also have been stiffened by a sharp letter written by Chet Cooper and delivered to Amory that morning. Upon learning that Bundy had been ordered out of town, Cooper jumped to the conclusion that Dulles did not mean to protect Bundy. Outraged, he sat down and wrote out a stinging letter of resignation, to be effective the moment that Bundy appeared before any investigating committee. He then delivered it to Bob Amory, who tried to reassure Cooper that the CIA was taking the matter very seriously. Amory presumably either showed Dulles the letter or told him about it.[43]

Cooper's strong views were not a rarity within the CIA. "McCarthy had been a gross obscenity for several years," Cooper recalled. "I saw what he had done to the State Department; some people I knew had been hounded by him, and I felt that if the Agency were to go through a similar hounding it would be the beginning of the end. . . . I didn't know anything about Bill's connection to the Hiss case, but by then I had gotten to know Bill, and if he was going to be subpoenaed, well, Bundy to me was the essence of righteousness."[44]

Meanwhile, Roy Cohn called and left word that Pforzheimer was expected to testify in executive session at 2 P.M; Pforzheimer called back to leave word that he could not make it. Cohn called again, saying Senator McCarthy now expected him to come at 3 P.M. Finally, at 2:20 P.M., Cohn got through to Pforzheimer, who calmly said, "I can't come and the director is not coming either." Cohn was livid and sputtered, "You're flouting the Senate." He again asked where Bundy was and Pforzheimer said he did not know, but that he was probably not gone for any protracted period. "But you know," teased Pforzheimer, "if you look at our statutory regulations, we are barred from tailing any of our own people domestically. This prevents us from following Bill Bundy around the country." Cohn didn't think this was funny.[45]

By the end of the day, Pforzheimer was formally served with a subpoena, which he brought to Dulles. The real negotiations were about to begin.

■

LATE Sunday night, after a long and suspenseful weekend, Bundy finally received a phone call in Manchester informing him that the negotiations had been concluded and he could come out of hiding. He flew home that same night to a deeply alarmed wife. Mary was convinced that the CIA was abandoning her husband. Henry Brandon, a British reporter and frequent dinner guest, had come by Friday evening with rumors to the effect that the Agency was caving in to McCarthy. The newspapers over the weekend were filled with stories on the case as leaked by Roy Cohn. The *New York Times* front-page headline read, "McCarthy Strikes at Allen Dulles: Says Intelligence Agency Head Balks Inquiry into Aide, Who, He Charges, Helped Hiss." The *Washington Post* had published a widely distributed wire story that featured a mug shot of Bill in a bow tie with the caption, "William P. Bundy—Unavailable for Hearing." The wire story reported that Senator McCarthy wanted to question Bundy about his $400 contribution to the Hiss defense fund. Even worse, the story quoted McCarthy paraphrasing from a written statement allegedly prepared by Bundy which gave three reasons for his contributions: "1—That it would help out his father-in-law. 2—That it was 'imperative,' in McCarthy's words, to 'exonerate' Hiss. 3—That the trial was 'important' to the Democratic Party."[46] Obviously, McCarthy had access to at least a portion of Bundy's security file, documents which probably had come from the FBI, and he was now leaking them with politically damaging embellishments. McCarthy also incorrectly stated that Bundy had written a book defending Dean Acheson and said the book was being distributed by the Overseas Library Program of the State Department. Obviously, he had confused Bill with his brother Mac, but the implication was that Bill Bundy was not only a son-in-law of the "Red" Dean Acheson, but also a key figure in the Acheson-Hiss cabal that was subverting U.S. foreign policy. McCarthy clearly thought that in Bill Bundy he had discovered the security case that would do for him what the Hiss case had done for Richard Nixon's political career.

Mary had no doubt that her husband was all but convicted in the court of public opinion. She had seen how the press and Congress had turned on her father just a few years earlier; she was certain the same thing was happening all over again. Bill's stoic faith that Allen Dulles would do the right thing only further irritated Mary. Bill himself was still not sure what kind of deal had been struck, so he really had little to offer her by way of reassurance.

The next day, Monday, he returned to work and was greeted by his colleagues as if nothing had happened. On Tuesday he attended a meeting of the NSC Planning Board where Bobby Cutler made a show of making him welcome. The ordeal was over, or so he hoped.

Dulles had brought him back in out of the cold, but beyond that, Bundy knew little of what had transpired over the weekend. Over the next few days, and then weeks, it became clear that there was nothing clear-cut about the deal. Bundy's ordeal would last more than a year, during which time he was left hanging, uncertain of his career. Only decades later did he learn the full details of what had happened.

Now we know that after Bill was ordered by Dulles to make himself disappear, Dulles, Lawrence Houston, Deputy Attorney General William Rogers, Bobby Cutler, Treasury secretary George Humphrey, Vice President Richard M. Nixon and probably Eisenhower himself discussed how they should respond to McCarthy's threatened subpoenas of CIA personnel. As things stood now, the Eisenhower administration faced a potential constitutional crisis if the CIA refused, as Pforzheimer had told Roy Cohn, "to allow any employee to appear before any Congressional committee."[47] Eisenhower did not want either to set a precedent which might destroy the CIA, or to sacrifice Bill Bundy.*[48]

In the end, with Eisenhower's approval, they decided to make a political deal with McCarthy, with Nixon as their instrument. Nixon made some phone calls to his former colleagues in the Senate, and after cashing in some political chits, he received the promise of enough Senate Republican votes to block a full-scale investigation of the CIA if it came to that. Nixon then paid a visit to McCarthy and told him he didn't have the votes to pursue Bundy. "I told McCarthy that I had seen Bundy's performance in several National Security Council meetings and he seemed to me a loyal American who was rendering vital service to the country."[49] To win McCarthy's acquiescence, and to avoid a vote on the Senate floor, Nixon then promised that if McCarthy would henceforth refrain from summoning any CIA people, Dulles would order Bundy's case to be reviewed internally. Security standards would be tightened, and Dulles promised he would take into account McCarthy's information about security risks and deal with them "administratively."[50]

At one point in the negotiations, McCarthy turned to Nixon and asked plaintively, "But what about his [Bundy's] contribution to Hiss?" Nixon replied, "Joe, you have to understand how those people up in Cambridge think. Bundy graduated from the Harvard Law School, and Hiss was one of its most famous graduates. I think he probably just got on the bandwagon without giving any thought to where the bandwagon was heading."[51] So it was that Richard Nixon made the crucial assist in saving Bundy's CIA career.

As it turned out, neither Senator McCarthy nor Bundy was pleased with the outcome. The senator thought there would be an investigation of Bundy, and according to the explicit wording of the latest executive order on loyalty hearings, that meant Bundy should have been suspended pending the outcome of the security review. McCarthy thought he had won the battle in this sense. And when he learned that Bundy was still on the job, he was outraged. Throughout the summer he badgered Dulles with letters threatening dire consequences unless his continuing questions about Bundy were answered.

On July 16, McCarthy wrote Dulles to remind him that they had agreed

---

* Eisenhower, recalled Bundy, "had known my father in Pentagon days." George Humphrey knew Bundy as a member of the Yale hockey team captained by his son. Bobby Cutler was a friend of Harvey Bundy's during the war, and knew Kay Bundy from their work together on what became the United Way of Boston.

that their respective staffs would "attempt to work out a formula whereby our Committee could get the information to which Congress is entitled without in any way endangering the security operations of your organization." McCarthy again raised the issue of Bundy's contributions to Hiss and specifically charged that he had been "active in at least one" communist front organization. He warned Dulles that if the allegations against Bundy proved to be accurate, then he ought to be dismissed. Dulles replied on July 22 that McCarthy had some of his facts wrong: yes, Bundy had contributed to the Hiss defense fund, but not for the reasons McCarthy had stated. And as to the front organization, he conceded that in the summer of 1940, while working for Archie MacLeish at the Library of Congress, Bundy had joined the United Public Workers of America, a labor union which had since been accused of being under the influence of communists. Dulles said Bundy had attended one meeting of this union and quit after two months.

McCarthy replied by demanding further information, and when Dulles demurred, on the grounds that a loyalty board was investigating the case, McCarthy accused the CIA director of a "cover-up of Bundy."

"Your insistence," McCarthy wrote, "that the Congress is not entitled to obtain information about improper conduct on the part of your top officers is extremely revealing. . . . That the matter cannot and will not rest here is, of course, obvious."[52] Bundy himself was unaware of these threatening missives from the senator.

Only gradually did Bundy realize that he was being kept in limbo. Initially, the press had interpreted Nixon's deal as yet another concession to McCarthy, another defeat for the administration which in due course would result in further investigations of the CIA. But when it became clear that Bundy was still on the job, Allen Dulles was credited both within the CIA and in most of the media for having faced down McCarthy. That old Bundy family friend and scribe Joe Alsop proclaimed that the Bundy affair "may well be remembered as the turning of the tide . . . the main thing is that the White House has at last found courage to meet a McCarthy challenge head on."[53] On the other hand, the right-wing *Chicago Tribune* complained that Bundy's defenders were "New Deal Democrats" who had "an appalling record of bringing Communists into the public service and protecting them there."[54]

At one point that summer Dulles reportedly assembled a large group of CIA officers in an auditorium and bluntly promised he would protect any employee singled out by McCarthy. He also suggested he would fire any employee who leaked information to McCarthy. And he made it known that he had assigned Richard Helms (a future CIA director) to monitor McCarthy's efforts to cultivate sources from within the Agency, and, in effect, to reassure anyone who felt he might be blackmailed by McCarthy's investigators. The CIA was a fortress not to be infiltrated.[55]

By this time, Bundy's colleagues perceived him as a hero merely because he had not been fired. Many CIA officers realized they had similar skeletons in the closet. Few were aware that Bundy was still in the docket. They saw him back on the job and that was all that mattered.

There were signs, however, that Bundy's job was still on the line. Early in August, when Roy Cohn learned that Bundy and his family were about to board the *Queen Mary* for a European vacation, McCarthy thought it would be a splendid idea to have Bundy arrested at dockside. Independently, the State Department had sat on Bundy's request for a passport so long that he now wondered whether he would be permitted to leave the country. Learning of this, McCarthy publicly urged the State Department to deny Bundy his passport. Allen Dulles had to sort out the matter by writing a stiff letter to the State Department, pointing out that "no subpoena has been served on Mr. Bundy." But he also promised that Bundy would be back in the country by October 1. Bundy got his passport and left with Mary and the kids for a much-needed vacation.

Bundy himself initially thought little of another security review; this should have been a routine matter. As he later put it, he thought the promise of another loyalty board hearing was the "only concession to McCarthy." But it was, he later wrote, "less trivial than it may have seemed since the panel that was convened was a bunch of scared dunderheads."

The loyalty board had its first meeting on September 14, 1953, but it was not until February 1954 that Bundy was finally called in to defend himself. All the loyalty board members were civil servants, but according to Bundy, none of them knew "anything about intelligence or what a commie spy would look like. . . ." To his surprise and dismay, they "went after me, not for the Alger Hiss contributions, but for the fact that I admitted I still saw Donald Hiss socially." When they pressed Bundy to break with the younger Hiss, he replied, "I'm not going to do that unless the Director tells me to do it, because he knows more about Donald Hiss than I do. But from what I know I'm not going to do that." Bundy's defiance was instinctive and immediate. He had no doubts about either the right thing to do or with whom he was dealing: "They were obviously a bunch of second-rate hacks, scared out of their wits about McCarthy getting after them."

After "a most painful day" of interrogation (and the indignity of being hooked up to a lie-detector machine again), the panel adjourned to render its opinion. Weeks passed and Bundy heard nothing. Ever the stoic, in February 1954 he confided to Bill Langer back at Harvard, "It has been a somewhat worrisome business, but I have no doubt it will turn out all right. Everyone at the office has been superb and the work goes on as ever." [56] He had good reason to worry. After much delay the panel issued a report which concluded that while there was no evidence of treason, Bundy should be dismissed on the grounds that his character was not "suitable" for intelligence work. Bundy was outraged: "I despised them all, as I had at the hearing, but I suppose they had wives and kids and needed their jobs."

Allen Dulles called him into his office to convey the news personally. After allowing him to read the panel's report, Dulles said he had decided to refer the panel's recommendations to yet another panel, this time a CIA group empowered to determine the narrow issue of "suitability." Chaired by an army general, this panel quickly reviewed the evidence and reversed the previous panel's recommendation. That summer Dulles again called Bundy into his office and without any further postmortems told him the news and ordered him back to work. Only then did Bundy finally get his "Q" clearance. "I did not thank him at the time," Bundy later recalled, "but made my gratitude and respect amply clear over the years."[57]

Bundy was exonerated, but other CIA employees were not so fortunate. A wave of "reinvestigations" which relied heavily on polygraph evidence led to the quiet dismissal of numerous gray-area security risks, particularly suspected homosexuals. And there is some evidence that even after the Bundy affair, Senator McCarthy still had four or five "penetration agents" within the CIA who systematically attempted to purge it of presumed leftists. Not surprisingly, the tightened security had a chilling effect on the work of those who remained. How many other unproven "security risks" lost their jobs in the Agency during the 1950s will perhaps never be known.[58]

SOME of Bundy's closest friends thought he was profoundly shaken by the whole experience. "I think it probably made him more cautious," recalled Chet Cooper. "The whole period was traumatic, and if it didn't influence him I'd be pretty surprised. People were influenced who were never anywhere near McCarthy. If it could happen to him, it could happen to me."[59]

Bundy himself always denied that the experience made him more cautious than he had been before being targeted by McCarthy. The stiff-upper-lip demeanor, however, was sometimes betrayed by the words he used to describe what he had gone through: "There were a few hours of pain involved . . . it was a painful morning's questioning. . . . My wife, having suffered through that day and having suffered various people telling her that the CIA had caved in, never quite got over that initial feeling that they'd sold out."[60]

And though it seemed to some that Dulles had unnecessarily prolonged Bundy's ordeal, Bundy always defended his boss's conduct. Bill later told Dulles biographer Peter Grose, ". . . there were those who thought that Dulles or someone should have outrightly defied McCarthy in a public statement. I think that could have backfired; at any rate, it would not have fitted with the way Ike handled McCarthy." Yet, a moment later Bundy would concede, "I think Ike could have been much tougher. . . . As it was, McCarthy was henceforth out of the business with the Agency. . . . At the same time, they did put me through the wringer again."[61]

Was Bundy less of a liberal after his brush with McCarthyism? Later, during the Vietnam period, some of his colleagues thought the whole episode might explain the outward appearance of rigidity, his seemingly stubborn dedication to the hard line against "losing" to Vietnamese communists. But who could really say? He did not act like a frightened man. In 1957 he defended Raymond Garthoff, a Soviet expert, when this young Yale graduate's security clearance was inordinately delayed because of a fleeting acquaintance with a Syrian suspected of working for the Soviets. Bundy encouraged Garthoff to travel on his own to the Soviet Union for two months and promised to intervene with the CIA's internal security people if this further delayed his security clearance. When Garthoff returned from his trip, Bundy found him a temporary job until he was finally cleared as an ONE analyst. Even in 1957—the year Joe McCarthy had drunk himself to death—this demonstrated considerable self-confidence, if not courage, on Bundy's part.

Politically, Bill Bundy remained a moderate Democrat; indeed, he was one of those rare people whose political views became more liberal with age. Bundy knew who he was, and in the end he survived an experience that was probably more traumatic than he would ever admit.

One cannot say the same for Cord Meyer, the only other major target of a McCarthyite probe within the CIA. Meyer's political trajectory took a sharp turn to the right after McCarthy forced the Agency in September 1953 to put him through a security review similar to Bundy's. Meyer had been far to the left of Bundy; in his youth he had been an ardent New Dealer and an active member of the World Federalists. Subsequently, however, author Godfrey Hodgson reports that "friends say that he was irremediably scarred by the experience . . . he seems to have decided that never again would he leave room for the slightest doubt about the totality of his commitment to the hardest of hard anticommunist lines."[62] Bundy may understandably have become more cautious, but he did not, like Meyer, become an anti-communist ideologue.

As for the institution, the CIA survived McCarthy—perhaps too well. Dulles discovered that after turning back McCarthy's investigation of his turf, he could use this precedent to fend off other, more legitimate, demands by Congress for oversight of the CIA. After the Bundy affair Senator Mike Mansfield, a liberal Democrat and a friend of Bundy's, introduced legislation to create a permanent Senate oversight committee on intelligence. Dulles lobbied hard against the proposal, and eventually killed it. He also upbraided Walter Lippmann, who had warned in print against the Agency's heretofore de facto exemption from congressional scrutiny. "Secrecy," wrote Lippmann, "is not a criterion for immunity. . . . The argument that the CIA is something apart, that it is so secret that it differs in kind from the State Department or for that matter . . . the Department of Agriculture, is untenable."[63] Lippmann was practically alone in taking this position. With the exception of Hanson Baldwin of the *New York Times*, the nation's media supported the notion that the CIA should be sacrosanct. Joe Alsop was incensed by Lippmann's column and wrote Bill Bundy's mother, "Hasn't everything turned out well? The attack on Bill has become a real turning point, I think, and to hell with Walter Lippmann, if I may be coarse about it."[64]

Lippmann was prescient. Dulles's victory over McCarthy had at least two unintended consequences. First, in the long term the CIA paid dearly for its lack of congressional oversight. As one scholar has argued, "The final legacy of McCarthyism, though, was that it discredited the notion of congressional oversight. . . ."[65]

And second, despite having defended Bill Bundy and Cord Meyer, Dulles subsequently tightened the Agency's internal security reviews. The result was to reinforce "group-think." The CIA may have started out in the late 1940s with a good number of OSS veterans, some of whom had liberal or even left-wing political instincts, but during the 1950s it would recruit only the most orthodox thinkers. As the Church Committee investigations of the CIA concluded in its 1976 report, ". . . the effects of the new security standards were profound . . . in brief, individuals who had been involved in any type of leftist ideological cause would find it difficult to obtain employment with the CIA . . . [a] like-minded manner of thinking began to evolve within the agency."[66]

BILL BUNDY'S political instincts remained vaguely liberal, and it was only natural that many of the assumptions he shared with his colleagues about the Cold War colored his intelligence estimates. In a peculiar, even contradictory fashion, many of the basic ONE estimates in the 1950s rhetorically bought into Cold War assumptions about the Soviet military threat, yet sometimes managed to adopt a measured, even dovish assessment of Soviet intentions. Some estimates inflated Soviet military capabilities while others downplayed the popular notion that Soviet conventional strength posed a credible invasion threat to Western Europe.

In retrospect, we know America was facing not a monolithic, powerful enemy, but an economically inefficient system that over the next four decades would gradually collapse from within. Militarily, the Soviets were always playing catch-up to America's lead in the arms race. Marxism still carried some appeal in a romantic, ideological sense to some, particularly in the newly decolonized nations, but the Soviet Union had few resources to back this political currency. Strategically, even by the mid-1950s, the Sino-Soviet bloc was fractured. Internally, the Soviet system was politically corrupt and the only question was whether Stalin's successors could reform the system and liberalize it without either stumbling into a war or sparking an internal violent revolution. The question American leaders should have been asking was whether this trend toward internal collapse or gradual liberalization of the Soviet system could best be accelerated by a U.S. policy of military confrontation or by a policy of political, economic and cultural engagement, otherwise known a few decades later as détente.

In the aftermath of the Korean War—and the hysteria generated by McCarthyism—few Americans were willing to entertain the notion that the Soviet system might be both militarily and economically on the defensive. Bundy himself bought into the prevailing assumptions, but at the end of the Cold War, unlike many conservatives, he was prepared to admit how wrong he had been. Addressing a symposium at Princeton University in 1990, Bundy said, "the picture of a thrusting Soviet policy and acute threat entered into virtually every assessment, not only of military factors but of the political situation in countries all over the world. . . . The blunt fact was that almost everything about Soviet capabilities and, even more, Soviet intentions, as well as the economic and social condition of Soviet society, had to be a judgment extracted from frail or nonexistent evidence." [67]

Unfortunately, the CIA often allowed itself in the 1950s to be buffaloed into accepting the Pentagon's greatly inflated estimates of Soviet military strength. Year after year the official estimates asserted that the Soviets were maintaining an enormous army of 175 divisions. Robert Amory later conceded the figure was "sort of a sacred number, when sometimes they hadn't heard of a division since 1952 or 1950 or something like that." Many of these divisions turned out to exist only on paper. Not until the early 1960s, Amory recalled, did the official estimate decline to 121 divisions, and fifty of these were thought to be in various stages of incompleteness. This essentially meant the CIA had cut the estimate by half. And realistically, Amory said there were only twenty active Soviet divisions in place, ready to be thrown into action against West Germany. Throughout the Cold War, ". . . there's no question they [these twenty divisions] could take Hamburg and be on the Rhine. But there'd be nothing behind them. This would be like the Battle of the Bulge. . . . It would look lousy for the first two or three weeks, but then the obvious atomic bombing behind them would keep the reinforcements in the Soviet Union from coming up." In hindsight, the Soviet troops facing NATO were never as large or as threatening as the American people were led to believe by their leaders. [68]

Recently declassified archival materials from both sides of the Iron Curtain should completely destroy the traditional assumption that the Soviet army at the end of World War II posed a credible offensive threat to Western Europe. In 1945 roughly half the Soviet army's transport was horse-drawn, and would remain so until 1950. Moreover, Soviet troop demobilization was massive and dramatic in the early postwar period. Declassified Soviet documents report that Stalin's army rapidly shrank from 11.4 million in May 1945 to 2.9 million in June 1947. Further, a U.S. Joint Chiefs of Staff report at the end of 1948 estimated the Soviets might be able to marshal only some 800,000 troops for an attack force. Two years later the CIA used the same figure in its official intelligence estimate. [69]

George F. Kennan, the veteran diplomat and author of the influential 1947 "Mr. X" *Foreign Affairs* article on "containment policy," "never believed that they [the Soviets] have seen it as in their interests to overrun Western Europe militarily, or that they would have launched an attack on that region generally even if the so-called nuclear deterrent had not existed." [70] But by 1953, Kennan's views were regarded as unsound in Washington and he had retreated to Princeton in virtual exile.

Perhaps understandably, the CIA's estimates after the outbreak of the Korean War had to begin with the worst-case assumptions about the U.S.-Soviet relationship. It is not surprising, therefore, that Bundy and his colleagues officially shared America's prevailing notions about the Soviet menace. But it is also rather remarkable that Bundy and at least some of his colleagues harbored private doubts. "I remember," Bundy said, "reading our early estimates on the number of Soviet divisions, and like others, I had the uneasy feeling that the figures were exaggerated."[71] He was not alone.

In the summer of 1951, just as Bundy had arrived in the CIA, members of the ONE board were arguing heatedly over a draft of an estimate on Soviet military capabilities and intentions. After reaching an impasse, the board assigned a young analyst who had never written a Soviet estimate, Willard Mathias, to write a new draft in the hope that he would bring a fresh, unvarnished assessment of the evidence. "The general mood around town," Mathias recalled, "was that the Soviets are out to dominate the world by subversion if possible, but by force if necessary, and they will stop at nothing." Mathias, however, thought it was illogical to assume that the Soviets were willing to risk nuclear annihilation. Even if they did have the conventional strength to overrun Western Europe, they should be deterred from doing this by the U.S. nuclear threat. "What we had," Mathias said, "was a mutual deterrence from the very start." So in writing his estimate, Mathias proceeded to argue that "considerations of practicality" would prevent the Soviets from initiating war: "We had to pay our respects to what, by early 1951, had become a working myth in Washington, namely, that the Soviets were trying to forge a communist world." So the carefully crafted language in the Mathias draft estimate acknowledged that as Marxists, the Soviets considered themselves instruments of an inevitable historical trend which over time would lead to a communist world. But they would not invade Western Europe, nor would any of their East European satellites invade the Balkans. Indeed, Mathias's landmark estimate —National Intelligence Estimate (NIE) 25 of August 2, 1951—cautiously concluded that the Soviets would not knowingly take any actions that might provoke the United States to general war. The only danger lay in the possibility that the Soviets might "miscalculate" and war could develop from "an action or series of actions not intended to produce that result."[72]

Although Mathias's argument was bucking the conventional wisdom— and that in the midst of the Korean War—it was nevertheless endorsed by the ONE board and passed around Washington as the CIA's official estimate.

This was not the last ONE estimate to downplay the Soviet threat. Throughout the 1950s most ONE estimates doggedly attempted to reassure policy-makers that war was unlikely. In 1954, for instance, a Special National Intelligence Estimate [SNIE 11–54] flatly stated that the Soviets considered war a "hazardous gamble, involving at a minimum the certainty of widespread destruction in the USSR and at the same time carrying with it the risk that the Soviet system itself would be destroyed."[73] While the tone and language might seem to endorse the bedrock Cold War assumption that the United States faced a strong and implacable enemy—a totalitarian regime like the Third Reich—incapable of liberalization, the substance of these estimates said otherwise. Remarkably, in 1958, Mathias wrote another "world estimate" which accurately predicted how the Cold War would end: "More widespread and better education, the growth of a professional and managerial class, greater personal freedom, expectations of higher living standards and more contact with other countries are indications of significant changes within Soviet society. These changes might in the long run profoundly alter the content and structure of Soviet political life, possibly through dissipation of the Communist Party's unchecked monopoly of power, more likely through a change in the political climate within the ruling party itself."[74]

This was prescient. Yet, even Mathias's estimates invariably buried such critical observations in Cold War boilerplate language. The effect was merely to reassure policy-makers that they need not worry too seriously about plunging the country into general war.[75] But then, neither did they take their analysis a step further and point out that the Cold War emperor was in fact naked. Neither Bundy nor any of his colleagues were inspired to ask the obvious next question: if the Soviets were deterred from initiating war, and if Soviet society was headed irreversibly toward liberalization, then why were we locked into a highly charged and militarized cold war? The political atmosphere of the 1950s simply precluded asking such a question. Once, after the presentation of one of his world estimates, Mathias was bluntly told by an army general that he was "suspected of being a communist agent because I had not been tough enough on the Russians."[76] Given the times, ONE's estimates were often a courageous intellectual achievement.

BUNDY's shop, so to speak, was more often right than wrong. ONE consistently predicted that Communist China had neither the capability nor intention to invade Taiwan. Similarly, when the Chinese communists shelled the island of Quemoy in 1958, precipitating a major crisis, ONE argued that Beijing's actions did not presage war. Contrary to official orthodoxy, ONE rejected the notion that Third World nationalism or neutralist movements were initiated or controlled by Moscow. And at a time when the rest of the defense and foreign policy establishment was inflating Soviet weapons estimates, ONE at least tried to water down the highly exaggerated estimates pushed by the U.S. Air Force and other military intelligence services. Ray Garthoff, who joined ONE in 1957, remembered that Bundy was largely responsible for a major estimate on Soviet nuclear weapons and energy. "It was realistic and definitely cautionary," recalled Garthoff. "Bill was ready to listen, consider and to think about things and change his mind if it seemed necessary." Unlike some analysts, Bundy did not fall into the trap of inflating the number of weapons built just because in theory the Soviets had the ability to produce many more weapons than the hard information would suggest.[77]

Still, there were failures. "I fell for the bomber gap," Bundy recalled, "and I was slow also to recognize the real situation regarding missiles. Our problem was that we didn't start to get U-2 pictures until the fall of 1956."[78] When the U-2 high-altitude spy-plane overflights of the Soviet Union failed to find any evidence of a major Soviet deployment of long-range bombers, the CIA slashed its estimates in the spring of 1957. But the analysts then compounded their initial error by concluding that the Soviets had merely decided to leap-frog from a limited bomber capability to the production of intercontinental missiles. Garthoff argued strongly that the numbers were far too high, while Bundy opted for the comfortable middle-range estimates—which were lower than the air force's number, but still way too high. This became the source of the CIA's "missile gap" estimates, which again had to be slashed in 1961 when new photo intelligence became available through satellites.* Later, Bob Amory would realize that the mistake stemmed from a basic misunderstanding: the Soviets had built medium-range bombers and missiles—instead of the technically more difficult and expensive intercontinental weapons—because their defense strategy focused on Western Europe. "If they held Western Europe hostage," Amory said, "it was just as good in restraining us, as a deterrent to our deterrent, as if they'd had Chicago. . . . I think it was a very sophisticated analysis on the part of the Soviets, and we were very unsophisticated in not realizing it for so long."[79]

The CIA was also too cautious in its assessment of the consequences of Stalin's death in the spring of 1953, and failed to pick up on what in retrospect were several failed opportunities to come to an accommodation with the Soviets over the unification and demilitarization of Germany.[80] (Bundy later regretted that he was so skeptical of George Kennan's arguments in favor of such an accommodation.)

Bundy also admitted to being slow to recognize the Sino-Soviet split. He did not begin to suspect a rift in the communist monolith until 1958, when he was briefly assigned to the United Nations to help the U.S. Mission defend Washington's recent military intervention in Lebanon. "I remember being struck," Bundy recalled, "when the Soviets insisted that India, not China, be assigned to the U.N. committee that was to sort out the Lebanese crisis."[81] This was very late in the game. Evidence had existed almost as soon as the Chinese revolution had triumphed in 1949 that Mao Zedong and his colleagues were not happy with their Soviet comrades. But these signals had been ignored, as had the analysis of most China hands in the State Department, largely because of McCarthyism.[82]

■

* In 1961 the U.S. Air Force insisted the Soviets had 200 ICBMs, while the CIA's National Intelligence Estimate was only 50 such missiles. Actually, the Soviets probably had only 24–44 ICBMs by the time of the October 1962 missile crisis; the United States had 172 ICBM launchers.

AND then there was Indochina. After the French colonial army was defeated by Ho Chi Minh's Viet Minh forces at Dien Bien Phu in May 1954, a cease-fire was negotiated at a conference in Geneva. In July, representatives from Great Britain, the Soviet Union, France, China and the Vietnamese communists agreed to temporarily divide Vietnam into north and south sectors at the seventeenth parallel, and elections were promised to determine the future government of a unified Vietnam within two years. The United States did not sign the Geneva Agreements, but the Eisenhower administration pledged not to use force to upset them.[83]

By 1955, however, Bill Bundy found himself immersed in a terrific battle within the intelligence community over an estimate on Vietnam. In the aftermath of the Geneva peace accords, Washington policy-makers wanted to know if the anti-communist regime of Prime Minister Ngo Dinh Diem in South Vietnam was a viable entity. Specifically, they wanted to know whether Diem was an authentic political force in South Vietnam, and if so, should the United States discourage him from holding the all-Vietnam elections agreed to at Geneva?

"In the spring of 1955," Bundy recalled, "there was a colossal row about whether we should stick to Diem in Vietnam." Chet Cooper vividly recalled how heated those debates became. "There was a lot of controversy about Diem in that early period," Cooper said, "both with his legitimacy and to whom was he really going to be answerable. He had a lot of patrons in this country, primarily in the Catholic hierarchy. But there were many people who felt that his connections with the true Vietnamese society were kind of thin over the years. After all, he hadn't been there for a long time. There was also this concern that this guy was something of a neophyte in the hard world of politics. He wasn't a real politician."

By contrast, Ho Chi Minh was regarded by most observers as a formidable political leader, a dedicated communist, but also a man who had spent decades winning what many of his countrymen regarded as a just nationalist revolution against French and Japanese colonialists. The CIA reported in August 1954 that if the elections were held in two years, "the Viet Minh will almost certainly win." President Eisenhower himself later wrote in his memoirs, "I have never talked or corresponded with a person knowledgeable in Indochinese affairs who did not agree that had elections been held as of the time of the fighting, possibly 80 per cent of the population would have voted for the Communist Ho Chi Minh as their leader. . . ."[84]

Even so, as early as the autumn of 1954, Eisenhower pledged to support Diem's regime in the South. Obviously, this presidential commitment placed considerable pressure on the intelligence community to generate an estimate that justified prolonging the temporary partition promised at Geneva. So the question became, could Diem refuse to hold the elections and still create a legitimate regime in the South?

Cooper thought many of his colleagues were genuinely committed to the idea of democracy. "In those days," he recalled, "we were called liberals." If the Geneva accords called for elections, then those elections should be held, even if Ho Chi Minh won them. The liberals in the CIA made the argument that "this was a test of our commitment to democracy, our integrity with regard to agreements that were reached. On the other hand, there were others who said, 'Well look, first of all we didn't sign that agreement. We were just observers. And so whatever else you want to say as to whether he [Diem] should or he shouldn't hold those elections, it is not necessarily our responsibility because we didn't sign it [the Geneva accords].' "

According to Cooper, Bundy reluctantly sided with those against forcing Diem to hold the elections: "My sense is that Bundy obviously came to this with a more legal approach. He is a lawyer, and that's what he brings to it." He and Bundy didn't argue about the issue; they just had different instincts.[85]

In the end, Bundy recalled, "The ONE estimate concluded that Diem could hold out against his opponents." The 1956 elections would never happen. Instead, Diem hung on tenaciously in the South, jailing his communist and non-communist political enemies, and by 1957–58, even skeptics inside the CIA were talking about the "Diem miracle."[86]

Bundy's view of Diem's Vietnam was perhaps influenced by what he was seeing in the Philippines, where a U.S.-funded anti-insurgency campaign was making great progress. In the autumn of 1956, after being promoted to serve under Bob Amory as deputy assistant director of intelligence, Bundy visited the Philippines. On the same trip Bundy paid his first visit to South Vietnam. His impressions were fleeting, but he remembered meeting the already legendary Colonel Edward Lansdale on the airport tarmac. Lansdale, who had made his reputation with the CIA by directing the defeat of the Huk communist insurgency in the Philippines, was on his way out of Vietnam after spending two years helping the Diem regime find its feet.

While Lansdale's dash and general optimism impressed him, Bundy was well aware that most of his colleagues in the CIA were decidedly pessimistic about Vietnam. As early as 1952, two years before the French surrender at Dien Bien Phu, Hal Ford had written an estimate which predicted that the French were doomed. Later, as the Viet Cong communist-led insurgency in the South began to pick up in the late 1950s, the ONE estimates again proved to be accurate. As Ford recalled, the estimates "cautioned policymakers that the basic causes of Viet Cong strength within South Vietnam were indigenous; that the war there was heavily political in nature and would have to be won in the south. . . ."[87] By then, Bundy was himself serving on the Board of National Estimates and thus was in a position to challenge these judgments. He never did.

Why, then, did the recipients of these accurately pessimistic estimates nevertheless ignore these views? Why did the Eisenhower administration gradually climb deeper into bed with the Diem regime in Saigon, even as its own intelligence estimates were warning that the regime had little political viability? Ironically, one answer may be found in the legacy of McCarthyism. After Allen Dulles successfully fended off McCarthy's attacks in 1953–54—and saved Bill Bundy's career—the CIA began to be perceived as a bastion of liberalism. This perception was further assisted by its near heretical estimates downplaying the Soviet military menace. By the end of the 1950s, policymakers so inclined could discount the Vietnam estimates as the product of mushy liberal thinking.

In 1958, Bill Bundy moved his family from Georgetown to a larger house in Cleveland Park, not far from Washington's National Cathedral. By simple coincidence, this rambling old colonial home stood on the corner of a street named Lowell. Mary loved its English garden and the fact that nine-year-old Michael could walk to St. Albans, the city's premier prep school. That year she gave birth to a second child, a daughter named Carol. A third child, Christopher, arrived a few years later. While Mary spent most of her time taking care of the children, she occasionally painted and volunteered in a local conservation group. Their best friends were James and Elizabeth Rowe, who lived in the neighborhood and had a daughter the same age as Michael. They became best friends and this connection naturally brought the Bundys and Rowes together.

Raised in Montana, Jim Rowe was by then a highly connected Washington corporate lawyer; his partner was another legendary New Deal–era lawyer, Tommy "The Cork" Corcoran. As a young man, Rowe had served Franklin Roosevelt in the White House as a presidential assistant and, later, as an assistant attorney general. He introduced the Bundys to another neighbor, William S. White, a Pulitzer Prize–winning *New York Times* reporter and syndicated columnist. Bill and June White also had children the same age as the Bundys' and Rowes'. The three families often socialized, and because both Rowe and White were old friends of Lyndon B. Johnson, they all had dinner two or three times a year with the Texas senator, who was then majority leader of the U.S. Senate. These dinners usually took place at the Whites, fellow Texans, and Bundy enjoyed them thoroughly. "I was fascinated by him [Johnson]," he recalled, "interested in him, of course, as a person and as a man who also held great power, but primarily as a person." Johnson could be very hard to take; he was sometimes overbearing and even, Bundy thought, "crude" and "boorish." But this was part of his magnetism and Bundy was drawn to it. He also respected Johnson's "populist" political instincts.[88]

Bill liked Rowe and White for the same reason he was intrigued by Johnson. They were country-smart, hard-nosed liberals who knew the political lay of the land in a way Bill never would.[89]

During these years Bundy was also close friends with the Alsop brothers. "Our mothers had been great friends," Bundy recalled. "We were what Joe and that horrible world called 'tribal,' we were 'tribal' together." Unlike Mac, however, Bill was closer to Stewart than the mercurial Joe. To those who knew them both, this seemed only natural. Lyndon Johnson once said of Stewart Alsop, "[he] cares a lot about appearing to be an intellectual and a historian—he strives to match his brother's intellectual attainments. . . ."[90] Much the same could be said of Bill and Mac. Like Stewart, Bill was the thoughtful gentleman, and like Joe, Mac was the pundit, the man with the sometimes savagely entertaining wit.

While Joe Alsop might visit Bill Bundy's household a half dozen times a year, and the Bundys usually attended Joe's autumn ball, Stewart saw Bill Bundy almost daily. He and Bundy were both members of the Alley Club, so named because this old squash court could be found in an alley behind Massachusetts Avenue. Bill would play squash two or three times a week with Stewart and other members of the club, who included old friends like Marshall Hornblower from Groton days, Charlie Glover and Norman Paul from Yale, Herbert "Pete" Scoville, Jr., and David Acheson, Mary's older brother. Once a year there would be a noisy party where Bill remembered, "You cut up and danced and did things, and it was very genial indeed."[91]

On rare occasions the Bundys socialized with Allen and Clover Dulles. Every New Year's Day, Bundy was invited to a dinner Dulles hosted for the Washington staff of CBS News at the exclusive Alibi Club. Two dozen men from the CIA and CBS, including such well-known correspondents as Eric Sevareid and David Schoenbrun, were invited. "We had a CIA man next to each CBS [man]," Bundy recalled, "and there was general table conversation, very useful in giving the feeling of Allen's thinking without giving them secret material, and at the same time extracting their views and thoughts—he was particularly good at this . . . it was a very warm and relaxed occasion."[92] Even so, Bundy still called Dulles, "Sir," and thought of him as his elder.

On the weekends Bundy sometimes drove out with his family to visit Stewart and Tish Alsop at Polecat Park, their rustic Maryland farm. Bundy so enjoyed these weekend retreats that sometime in the mid-1950s he bought his own little farm, not far from Harwood, Dean Acheson's place in the Maryland countryside. Like Stewart Alsop's farm, it was very bare-bones: an old stone house surrounded by fifty acres of brushland. Bill named it Brookville. Bill had a small swimming pond carved out of the land, and on weekends the family would invite friends out for picnics.

It was during these years that Bundy first met David Rockefeller. The occasion was a cocktail party in 1953 hosted by Charles Cremeans, the number two analyst on Near Eastern affairs for the CIA. An Arabist, Cremeans had befriended Rockefeller in North Africa during the war, and when Rockefeller expressed an interest in meeting some CIA analysts Cremeans invited him to the party. When Bundy and the thirty-eight-year-old Rockefeller were introduced, something clicked. Rockefeller, who had just become a vice president of Chase Bank, had become very interested in foreign affairs because of his new job and Bundy impressed him as a most knowledgeable professional. The two men were uncommonly serious, intense and studious. Their natural reserve could sometimes be taken for aloofness. And both men had brothers whose public brilliance somehow placed their own achievements in the shadows. Bill Bundy was exactly the kind of solid character David Rockefeller could easily come to trust. Over the years they saw each other regularly, and in 1971 David would present his friend with the gift of a new career—the editorship of *Foreign Affairs*.[93]

By 1959, Bill Bundy had spent seven and a half years in the CIA and he was tiring of the routine. He knew that if he stayed, there was only one other step up for him and that would have been to replace his boss, Bob Amory, as deputy director of intelligence. "I would have found that interesting, but I frankly felt that the Agency was a bit cramping."[94] So when in February 1960 he was offered a leave of absence to serve as staff director of President Eisenhower's Commission on National Goals, Bundy immediately accepted. The idea of bringing together a group of wise men to study what the country's goals ought to be for the coming decade was a notion particularly pleasing to Eisenhower's orderly military mind. In due course eleven commission members were named.* With a budget of $1 million, Bundy spent the next ten months meeting with the commission and recruiting authors for the commission book, including Harvard's Bill Langer, John J. McCloy (then chairman of Chase Manhattan Bank), John W. Gardner (president of the Carnegie Corporation) and Clinton Rossiter (a Cornell University scholar known for his works on the American presidency).

For Bundy, the goals commission was "my coming in from the cold, so to speak." It gave him a chance to get out from under the CIA's culture of "extreme secrecy," to get out in the world and talk freely with all sorts of people. For the first time in years he would be writing something for publication. He suddenly realized how "blinkered" was the life of a CIA analyst. The corporate chiefs, labor union officials and scholars he encountered on the commission looked at the world in a very different way from many of his colleagues inside the CIA. As a rule, they were far more conservative than Bundy.[95]

Even so, the commission's final report was on the whole a remarkably liberal manifesto. Equality was a major theme. As the country "approached a

---

* The commission members included Henry M. Wriston (president of the American Assembly), Frank Pace, Jr. (chairman of the board, General Dynamics Corporation), Erwin D. Canham (editor in chief, *Christian Science Monitor*), James B. Conant (former president of Harvard University and ambassador to Germany), Colgate W. Darden, Jr. (former governor of Virginia and president of the University of Virginia), Crawford H. Greenwalt (president of Du Pont Company), General Alfred M. Gruenther (Supreme Allied Commander in Europe, 1953–56), Judge Learned Hand (U.S. Court of Appeals for the Second Circuit), Clark Kerr (president of the University of California), James R. Killian, Jr. (chairman of the corporation, Massachusetts Institute of Technology) and George Meany (president, AFL-CIO).

classless society," the commission argued that in the 1960s, "Every man and woman must have equal rights before the law. . . ." The report boldly proclaimed, "Vestiges of religious prejudice, handicaps to women, and, most important, discrimination on the basis of race must be recognized as morally wrong, economically wasteful, and in many respects dangerous." Most controversially, the commission called on the federal government to deny funds to any employers who discriminate on the basis of race. (The Du Pont president dissented from this recommendation.) It urged a dramatic increase in the salaries of public servants, and a doubling of federal expenditures on public education. Astonishing many budget-conscious conservatives, the commission also supported a broad increase in federal funding of the arts, worker retraining, unemployment insurance, medical insurance, the training of doctors and urban renewal. It called for government intervention to "reverse the process of decay in the larger cities." On questions of foreign policy, the commission advocated increases in foreign aid, and flatly stated that because nuclear war would be a "catastrophe, the limitation and control of nuclear armament is imperative. Disarmament should be our ultimate goal." The United Nations should be vigorously supported and the idea of international law should be expanded by "further development of the International Court of Justice." The commission argued that the country had to be prepared militarily to meet the Soviet military threat, but implied that the Cold War was essentially a political contest in which Washington should be "prepared to negotiate" and seek a "basis for mutual tolerance."[96]

In sum, the President's Commission on National Goals had produced a planning document edited by Bill Bundy for what would become Lyndon Johnson's Great Society. It anticipated the Civil Rights Act, the War on Poverty and the revolution in the status of women in the American work force. It did not, of course, anticipate the Vietnam War, nor the countercultural upheavals of the 1960s. Indeed, its near self-congratulatory tone later would seem wildly optimistic. It was, however, liberalism at its most hopeful.

When the report was released in a smartly packaged book just after the November 1960 election, some commentators regarded it as an implied indictment of Eisenhower's passive leadership style. The activist role the commission report assigned to the federal government seemed tailor-made for the incoming Kennedy administration. The *Washington Post* commented that the report's "conclusions reflect many of Mr. Kennedy's campaign promises." In June 1960, well before the election, Bundy gave Kennedy an advance briefing on the commission's work. "I had a very brief two-minute session with him [Kennedy]; in and out quickly to tell him where we stood." After the election he forwarded the final report to the president-elect with a handwritten note: "A really great campaign, Jack, and I am sure a great Administration!"[97]

Bundy knew Kennedy, of course, since childhood, when they had played football at the Dexter school. But since then they had had only fleeting encounters. Sometime in 1947–48 they ran into each other at a dinner party thrown by Phil and Katharine Graham of the *Washington Post*. Bundy remembered the occasion because Kennedy, seated next to Mary, had surprised everyone by speaking so warmly about a new congressman from California named Richard M. Nixon. Bundy had thought that an odd sentiment coming from a Democrat about a Republican who had won considerable national notoriety by red-baiting his Democratic opponent in the 1946 election. But that was ancient history. Now, Kennedy had been the only man standing between Nixon and the White House, and Bundy had fervently hoped for a Democratic victory. Indeed, that autumn he was contemplating whether he should quit the CIA if Nixon won and accept an offer from A. Whitney Griswold, the president of Yale University, to become a college master and lecturer on international relations. Academic life was tempting.

"And if Nixon had won, I think I would have taken that offer very seriously." But he told Griswold, "Let's wait and see how the election comes out." After Kennedy's narrow victory Bundy sent word to Griswold that he was prepared to gamble on getting a position in the new administration.

He knew a lot of Democrats and thought his chances of being offered a fairly high position were good. His credentials for a foreign policy job were pretty obvious, more so certainly than his brother Mac's. After all, Bill had been a solid Democrat since the age of eighteen; he had a Harvard law degree and nine years of experience as a top-ranking CIA official. His father-in-law was the last Democratic secretary of state, and now Bill had shepherded to publication a presidential report on national goals that should have broadcast his credentials as a thoughtful, establishment liberal. But Bill was not Mac, and he was not courted by Kennedy's people in the same way.

Sometime prior to the election Bill recalled having lunch with "a funny little guy named Max Freedman, a Canadian newspaperman but very buddy with the Kennedy crowd. I've forgotten what we talked about, but in retrospect, he may have been sizing me up." If so, Bundy may have been found wanting because weeks went by and he heard nothing from the Kennedy camp. (As a Washington correspondent for the *Manchester Guardian*, Freedman had written a speech for Kennedy early that summer which contained the memorable phrase "New Frontier.")[98]

Finally, late in December, Bill received a call from Paul Nitze, a close friend of Dean Acheson's. As director of the State Department's Policy Planning Staff in 1950, Nitze had authored a seminal document on U.S. strategy in the early Cold War, NSC-68, which had called for a massive U.S. defense buildup against the Soviets. Nitze was very much a hard-line Cold Warrior, and he had expected a better posting from Kennedy. But it was already Christmas, late in the transition game, so when he was offered the job of assistant secretary of defense for international security affairs, he promptly accepted. Nitze now asked Bundy to serve as his deputy.

"I think he tried a couple of people first," Bundy recalled, "but he turned to me, and I snapped it up. I just grabbed it quickly."[99] Bundy too had expected more, but he would settle for what was his only offer. Bill had seen Nitze on occasion at Acheson's home, but they were not close. Nitze's decision to hire Bundy probably came about at Acheson's insistence. The feisty old man did not like the idea that Mac Bundy had just won a plum job in the administration. Acheson thought his son-in-law the more solid of the two Bundy brothers, and Mac's elevation above his older and, in Acheson's eyes, more qualified brother only confirmed his suspicion of the immaturity of the very young president-elect.[100] What neither Acheson nor Nitze—or for that matter, Bill Bundy—understood was that Kennedy was about to change all the rules. Prior to 1960 those recruited for assistant secretaryships, jobs which require Senate confirmation, were generally men of affairs. It helped to have an establishment education or cultural background, but one at least had to have had practical experience as a corporate lawyer—like Harvey Bundy—or to have worked one's way up the bureaucratic ladder in the Foreign Service or some other government agency—like a George Kennan. Now all that was to change. John Kennedy would inaugurate a new era in which men with no experience other than that found in the groves of the academy were elevated to power. Bill Bundy had all the conventional qualifications of his father's generation, but he did not have the cachet of a policy intellectual like his brother Mac.

9

The Kennedy Years

> *If every question in the world becomes an intellectual exercise on a totally pragmatic basis, with no reference to moral considerations, it may be that we can escape disaster, but it will certainly be putting the White House group to a test.*
>
> UNDER SECRETARY OF STATE CHESTER BOWLES
> April 22, 1961

MAC BUNDY RETURNED from his Caribbean vacation in early January 1961 to a bitterly cold New England winter. A few days later, President-elect John F. Kennedy was escorted inside Arthur Schlesinger, Jr.'s Cambridge home to meet with a select group of his Harvard-based advisers. As a team of Secret Service men stood guard outside, Bundy rode his bicycle past a crowd of onlookers, dismounted and, after leaning his bicycle against the gate, strode in to meet with his new boss.[1] Inside were some of the well-known scholars who would be joining Bundy in Washington. Schlesinger himself was already slated to work as one of the president's assistants; Jerome B. Wiesner became White House science adviser, and John Kenneth Galbraith was named ambassador to India.

When Kennedy announced Bundy's appointment on January 1, the president-elect said that his national security adviser would be "helping me to strengthen and to simplify the operations of the National Security Council."[2] What he really meant was that Bundy was going to dismantle much of the NSC's bureaucratic paraphernalia created during the Eisenhower years. Both Kennedy and Bundy had read Richard Neustadt's 1960 book, *Presidential Power*, which contrasted the freewheeling presidential style of Franklin Roosevelt with the rigid, military chain-of-command system Dwight Eisenhower had brought to the White House. A trendy political scientist at Columbia University, Neustadt argued that Roosevelt's disorderly style actually exposed him to more information from a wider range of sources and gave him the flexibility that was the genius of his administration. Neustadt's book gave Kennedy and Bundy the intellectual rationale to do what they were going to do anyway—run the White House as if it were Harvard, with Bundy as dean and Kennedy as president.

They would promote disorder. There would be fewer people, reports and formal meetings of the National Security Council. Bundy himself would take the jobs of five of Ike's NSC aides. The NSC would become more of a mini–State Department and less of a debating society. Within a month the NSC's staff was cut from seventy-one to forty-eight. In place of weighty policy papers, produced at regular intervals, Bundy's staff would produce crisp and timely National Security Action Memoranda (NSAMs). The new name signified the premium that would be placed on "action" over "planning." In effect, foreign policy would no longer be made at cabinet-level meetings. In theory, the men who came to advise the president in these smaller, freewheeling NSC meetings would represent no bureaucratic constituency other than the president, and they would argue the merits of each policy course based on substance. This was how intellectuals, not bureaucrats, would make foreign policy.[3]

Bundy immediately began recruiting his own staff, and many of them were also Cambridge men. Kennedy himself hired Walt W. Rostow to fill one slot in the NSC. Temperamentally, Bundy's old MIT friend was hardly the kind of man to serve as a deputy. Rostow was voluble, exuberant and full of good and sometimes foolish ideas. Bundy didn't mind. The former Harvard dean would give Rostow all the flexibility of a tenured member of the faculty.

Just ten days after the inauguration Bundy phoned another Cambridge friend, Carl Kaysen, forty, and said, "I need help. I'm having a lot of fun. Come work with me." Kaysen replied, "Mac, have you already forgotten Harvard? I have two courses I am committed to teaching this semester."

"Oh, just come and we'll talk about it," Bundy insisted. Kaysen came, was introduced to Kennedy in the Oval Office and agreed to start work in May.[4]

Bundy was not as eager to recruit Henry Kissinger; he knew from personal experience that Henry was hardly a team player. At Kennedy's invitation Kissinger visited the White House in early February. It is unclear whether Bundy ever offered Kissinger a full-time position; Kissinger later suggested that Bundy did not seem to share "the President's sense of urgency to add to the White House staff another professor of comparable academic competence."[5] Kissinger wanted to be a player in the new administration, but he also wanted to retain his tenured position at Harvard. Bundy was annoyed, but nevertheless arranged a part-time consultancy in which Kissinger would fly down four or five days a month. The arrangement did not last, and when Kissinger created a diplomatic gaffe during a trip to India in early 1962, Bundy quietly dismissed him.[6]

Having recruited quite a few outsiders, Mac called his brother Bill for the names of a few veterans of government service who knew the drill in Washington. Bill gave him the names of two colleagues from the CIA, Bob Komer and Chet Cooper. Cooper would soon spend half his time in the White House under Bundy. Komer soon went to work as Bundy's man on the Middle East and South Asia. (Blunt and abrasive, Komer would later earn the sobriquet "Blowtorch Bob" for his tough stance on the Vietnam War.)[7]

Despite his qualms about Bundy's move to the White House, or perhaps because of them, David Riesman began lobbying his old dean early that year to hire a young man whom he promised would be the "conscience" of his staff. At twenty-six, Marcus Raskin came to Washington with hardly any of the usual establishment credentials expected of an NSC staffer. A concert-level pianist (he once taught the composer Philip Glass), Raskin had abandoned a career in music to study law at the University of Chicago. In 1959, two years after earning a law degree, he became a staff assistant to Congressman Robert W. Kastenmeier (D.-Wis.). Kastenmeier put Raskin to work coordinating an informal caucus that included nine other congressmen interested in developing a new liberal agenda. They called themselves the Liberal Project, and by 1960, Raskin was editing a collection of essays for publication. Together with another Kastenmeier aide, Arthur Waskow, Raskin had drafted for inclusion in the book an essay critical of nuclear deterrence theory called "The Theory and Practice of Deterrence." Riesman was greatly impressed with the essay and the work of the Liberal Project.

Soon after the inauguration, Riesman persuaded Bundy to talk to Raskin about a White House job. The interview took place in Bundy's office, Room 374A of the Old Executive Office Building next door to the White House. "We had a good talk," Raskin recalled. "He was funny and witty; I was also at my best. I remember him asking me, 'Well, Mr. Raskin, do you have a liberal theory of deterrence?' I was all of twenty-six, and I handed him this essay."[8] Bundy was not altogether unfamiliar with the arguments contained in the Raskin-Waskow essay; he had, after all, picked up a healthy skepticism of deterrence theory from his work with Oppenheimer nine years earlier.

Later, as Raskin was about to come on board, Bundy asked him some difficult questions that clearly stemmed from the FBI's security check. Didn't he have a cousin, he asked, who was a communist? Raskin said he really didn't know, and hadn't seen her in years.

"You were on a program with I. F. Stone," the radical journalist, Bundy said. "We know that he is a communist."

"I don't know that," Raskin replied hotly. At this sign of vehemence, Bundy turned crimson, and Raskin later recalled being struck that Bundy was clearly embarrassed. Despite this exchange Raskin was hired.

Bundy knew he was getting a free spirit, a left-of-center, Jewish intellectual who might be troublesome. Curiously, at one point he asked Raskin, "Would you mind being the Oppenheimer of this administration?"

A few weeks later Bundy wrote Riesman, thanking him for his referral of Raskin: "With any luck, he should be at work here in another few days. In my few conversations with him, I have found just the qualities you describe.

... He has a remarkably powerful and lively mind, and it is flanked by both moral and physical energy. I think we shall probably have some disagreements, but I shall feel a lot better for knowing that certain problems have passed by his critical eye on their way to resolution."[9]

INFORMALITY was the rule in Bundy's shop, which he likened to a think tank. Mac had pulled together a staff of very independent-minded men: Kaysen, Rostow, Komer, Raskin, Bromley K. Smith, Dave Klein, Ralph Dungan and, on occasion, Kissinger. These were all "very high-powered, strong-minded people" and Bundy generally made no attempt to block their access to the president. He and his principal deputy, Kaysen, made a point of taking staff members into the Oval Office and allowing them to brief Kennedy on their area of expertise. "We were few enough," Kaysen recalled, "so that the president had some idea of who we were and what we were doing."[10]

Bundy's daily routine was hectic. Each morning at 7:45 A.M. a government-chauffeured Mercury sedan picked him up at his spacious, white-bricked home in the Spring Valley section of Washington and ferried him down to the White House. Along the way, he dropped off his sons at St. Albans, Washington's elite prep school. After glancing at the early-morning cable traffic—some seven pounds of paper each day—Bundy would preside over a 9 A.M. staff meeting where he peppered his aides with questions. "Mac is brilliant at 9 o'clock in the morning, as very few other people can be," recalled one staffer. Afterwards, Bundy would go up to the president's quarters and brief Kennedy on the overnight intelligence developments from around the globe.[11]

Most evenings he did not return home until eight o'clock at night. Over a bourbon-on-the-rocks or a martini, he would spend a little time in horseplay with his sons before their bedtime. He enjoyed good food and vintage wines, and was known to consume large quantities of ice cream. He and Mary rarely entertained in their home, but not infrequently attended dinner parties on the diplomatic circuit or with such old friends as Joe Alsop, Walter Lippmann and Felix Frankfurter. Mary found the change of pace from Cambridge "a little frightening. All those parties—I wasn't used to it, you know. It took a lot out of me."[12]

KENNEDY's foreign policy team was ostensibly headed by Secretary of State Dean Rusk (formerly president of the Rockefeller Foundation) and Robert S. McNamara, who had left his new job as president of the Ford Motor Company after only thirty-four days to become secretary of defense. Bundy immediately recognized a soul mate in McNamara, whose persona as a "whiz kid" meshed nicely with his own peppery personality. By contrast, Mac quickly decided that Rusk's bland demeanor masked neither wit nor intelligence. Very early in the new administration it became clear that Bundy's shop was running circles around Rusk's State Department. Bundy had daily access to the president; Rusk did not. With calculated modesty, Bundy would tell the press that his job was only that of a "traffic cop—to see what gets forwarded to the President." It was that and much more. One day, the president told his wife, Jacqueline, "Damn it, Bundy and I get more done in one day in the White House than they do in six months at the State Department." Soon, the *Washington Post* labeled Bundy a "shadow secretary of state." Asked what he would have done if Bundy had been at the NSC when he was secretary of state, Dean Acheson replied, "Resign."[13]

After two months on the job Bundy quipped to a *New York Times* reporter, "Yes, at this point we are like the Harlem Globetrotters, passing forward, behind, side-wise and underneath. But nobody has made a basket yet."[14] About the same time he wrote Stanley Hoffmann, then attending a seminar in Geneva, "Your description of Geneva makes it sound like the opposite of Washington. There you have serious discussions in an atmosphere of unconcern, and here . . ." But then he confided, "I think perhaps we are moving toward a period in which we shall be able to take serious decisions, some of them even based on thought."[15]

KENNEDY had a special rapport with his national security adviser. "They think alike," said one colleague. "He knows what the President wants. The President's intensity is perfectly complemented by Bundy's ability to move things."[16] Kennedy hated small talk and quickly cut off those who bored him. Bundy, of course, never bored anyone. It was not long before the *New York Times* was quoting an anonymous official as saying that Bundy was the president's "alter-ego . . . another Harry Hopkins—with hand grenades."[17] The analogy was both apt and inept. Franklin Roosevelt's friend and confidant was a gentle soul, an intensely introspective man who arrived at his judgments after exhaustive consultations. There was nothing abrupt about Hopkins. But perhaps just as Hopkins came to symbolize an archetype for the action-oriented intellectual of the Roosevelt era, so too Mac Bundy would soon become a model for the liberal policy intellectual of the 1960s. He knew he was serving a man impatient with the language of bureaucrats. So he took to summarizing tedious State Department cables with one-liners that amused the president. He once said of a visiting foreign diplomat that the man possessed a "very tactical sense of the truth."[18]

Bundy didn't hesitate to push Kennedy if he thought the president was wrong. When Kennedy kept interrupting Bundy's early-morning intelligence briefing with complaints about press leaks, Bundy calmly cut the president off. "Goddammit, Mac," Kennedy was once overheard exclaiming, "I've been arguing with you about this all week long."[19]

There was no mistaking that they liked each other immensely. Kennedy jokingly told his (and Bundy's) childhood friend, *Newsweek* bureau chief Ben Bradlee, "I only hope he [Bundy] leaves a few residual functions to me. . . . You can't beat brains. . . . He does a tremendous amount of work. And he doesn't fold or get rattled when they're sniping at him."[20] Temperamentally,

Bundy and Kennedy were cast from the same impatient mold. A Harvard professor who knew both men said of Bundy, "He pays no attention to what the other fellow may think. He's as cold as ice and snippy about everything. He and Jack Kennedy are two of a kind."[21]

Yet, Bundy sometimes could surprise people with unexpected warmth. Once, after hearing Kennedy give a State Department official a tongue-lashing on the phone that "made the wires sizzle," Bundy called the official fifteen minutes later and said, "I was in the room when the President was . . . er, talking to you, and I just wanted to say that it has happened to all of us. This little hot spot will quickly cool, and you should realize that the President would not have permitted himself that kind of blow-off if you were not one of those he regards highly and fully trusts." The official in question, Roger Hilsman, would have his differences with Bundy, but he always thought of him as a "man of warmth and thoughtfulness."[22]

Kennedy also found it convenient that his national security adviser was a Republican. When Bundy suggested that he now "felt like a Democrat" and that perhaps he ought to change his party registration in time for the 1962 congressional elections, Kennedy told him that it was "marginally more useful to me to be able to say that you're a Republican."[23]

Jack Kennedy was also a man who felt compelled to complicate his sexual life with a large cast of women—both inside and outside the White House. It helped that Bundy was the kind of Boston Brahmin who was not a prude. Evidently, Kennedy trusted him enough that he felt no need to hide all of his sexual dalliances from his friend. Still, it could be awkward, particularly when the president arranged for one of his lovers—a Radcliffe graduate he had met in 1959—to work on Bundy's staff. "It was very embarrassing," the woman later told Seymour Hersh. "It put McGeorge in a very creepy situation."[24] In any case, Bundy was a paragon of discreetness.

What for some was Bundy's arrogance appeared to Kennedy as simple "balls." Kennedy respected balls. When the president's brother Bobby, the attorney general, resigned his membership in the Metropolitan Club over the club's refusal to admit a black guest, Bundy astonished all of Washington by joining the club just a month later. When reporters queried him about it, Bundy responded, "This is a question each man must decide for himself. . . . If I were Attorney General I might come to a different conclusion. I have no quarrel with those who reached a decision to resign." He did not say so, but among those who had resigned was his own brother Bill, then deputy assistant secretary of defense. "There'd been a recurrent question of blacks coming to the club," Bill Bundy recalled. When the club made it clear that blacks weren't welcome even as guests, "this raised it to the level of outrage," he said, "and I resigned. It wasn't a very great sacrifice. . . ." It was not an issue between the brothers, but the incident spoke volumes about their respective political sensibilities.[25]

■

PEOPLE who worked with both Bundy brothers were struck by how different they were. "Mac had a mathematical mind," recalled Chet Cooper, who first met the younger brother in 1961. "Very clipped. Almost surgical. And then there's Bill with the legal thing, who was able, I think, to argue for either the plaintiff or the defendant. They were two brothers, very different mind-sets, although in many respects, very much the same. A staff meeting with Bill and a staff meeting with Mac are really two very different kinds of sessions." [26]

Friends naturally wondered about sibling rivalry. That chemistry had to be there, people thought, but the Bundys rarely gave evidence of it. Mac confessed to at least one friend that he had "twitches of conscience because his brother had so much more governmental experience than he had." But there was no time to dwell on the ironies of life. By his own testimony, Mac was a man "genuinely in a hurry." [27]

At the age of forty-four, Bill seemed on first impression more easygoing than Mac. Walt Rostow—who knew both Bundys from Yale and now was working for Mac in the White House—thought Bill "rather straitlaced in appearance, but he could turn around and suddenly dance the Charleston. He sometimes did imitations of people; he could be quite fun. I've never seen Mac Bundy do anything like that." Bill's secretary, Blanche Moore, always pictured him arriving each morning at his office humming Broadway tunes or whistling. But he was also very demanding, expecting her dictation to be letter perfect. "He dictated like a lawyer," Moore recalled. "He never had to back up; his sentences were always full, grammatical sentences. You didn't change anything. It was such a pleasure to see his mind work." When he once discovered that Moore had not returned a classified document to the vault, he made her go down to the security office and confess the transgression. "He told me," Moore said, " 'I have given my word, and if I don't keep it, how can they trust me?' I felt so ashamed. But after that incident, he never checked up on me." Moore would loyally serve Bundy as his secretary for more than a dozen years. [28]

At the end of a long day Bundy typically invited a reporter into his Pentagon office—just down the hall from where his father had worked under Stimson—for a drink, something Mac never did except with senior journalists like Joe Alsop or James Reston. Bill saw working reporters like Henry Brandon, Meg Greenfield and Joe Kraft. He would stretch his six-foot four-inch frame out on his office couch, sip his drink and smoke short, nonfilter cigarettes. Off the record, he "chewed" over the day's events and quizzed reporters about what they thought. He laced his speech with quaint, "hasty-pudding" expressions which his friends came to call Bundyisms. "No strain," he would say to his secretary when she couldn't find a book he wanted. "I must have pinched it." He used phrases like "whiff of grapeshot," "cannonball on the deck," and when an unsatisfactory memo landed on his desk, he would say, "We need to bring this up to concert pitch." To voice his disapproval of an idea, he would say, "Well, we can't suck eggs on that one." [29]

There was nothing archaic about Mac in these years. Where Bill could be disarmingly polite, Mac was brisk to the point of brusque. Bill could be harshly self-critical, while Mac—though not oblivious of his mistakes—had no time for introspection. "Most men have too much ego," said one of Bill's colleagues years later. "But Bill has just the right amount. He doesn't feel like he has to convince people of his worth. But then he also thinks people will naturally be interested in hearing what he has to say."[30]

Bill was the kind of man who was generally liked by just about anyone he got to know. Mac, however, could arouse extreme passions. People either liked him immensely or feared him. After dining with Mac one evening, the Oxford historian Isaiah Berlin wrote Joe Alsop, "I have never admired anyone so much, so intensely, for so long as I did him during those four hours . . . his character emerged in such exquisite form that I am now his devoted and dedicated slave. I like him very much indeed, and I think he likes me, now, which was not always the case."[31] On the other hand, an anonymous colleague told the New York Times in 1962, "I would not like to have him as my enemy." And another half-admirer said, "McGeorge Bundy is the iron priest of an iron faith in the definitiveness of his yes or no, and he has such a marvelous storehouse of language to make everything he says sound plausible that he scares the hell out of me."[32]

Mac scared people, but some learned that if you stood your ground he would listen. "Sure he's sharp; at times even nasty," said a State Department official, "if he thinks you're off base. But often, suddenly, halfway through the conversation, he'll turn and tell you, 'You're right.' The important thing is that he is there and he listens." Mac once told Max Frankel of the New York Times that he understood that "where feelings become strong and differences of opinion become evident, there is some truth on every side and also some danger of error."[33]

Some people loved Mac Bundy even when they disagreed with him. James C. Thomson, Jr., worked for both Bundy brothers during the early 1960s and would clash repeatedly with them over Vietnam policy. But Thomson relished in Mac what so many people found dangerous. "Mac loved taking risks," Thomson said. "He loved irreverence and humor. He loved hearing dissent. He loved all the things that troubled his older brother. Bill was prim about irreverence, humor and all the things that made Mac so earthy, funny and wise."[34]

Mac always got good press during these years, while Bill labored in relative obscurity. Reporters found Mac colorful and unusually spontaneous for a White House official. They were astonished, for instance, that he rarely spoke from a prepared text. One day a reporter called and learned that Bundy was just beginning to think about what to say an hour before he was scheduled to give a formal address. When the reporter expressed some surprise at this, Bundy explained, "I'm used to the university lecture platform." Then he added what the reporter dubbed Bundy's Law: "Never write it out unless you have to get it cleared for security reasons."[35] This was good copy and endeared him to members of the press.

When Bobby Kennedy decided he wanted to host a monthly seminar at his Hickory Hill estate, Mac was the Bundy brother he thought to invite, not Bill. Organized by Schlesinger, Bobby's seminars brought together no more than twenty-five or thirty people—husbands and wives—and served to remind them, in Schlesinger's words, that "a world of ideas existed beyond government." Scholars like Isaiah Berlin, Ken Galbraith, George Kennan and Eric Goldman would give a short lecture and then the audience—which included such leading lights of the Kennedy administration as Bob McNamara, Assistant Attorney General Nicholas Katzenbach, Secretary of the Interior Stewart Udall and Ambassador-at-Large Averell Harriman—would pepper them with questions. "They sound rather precious," Alice Roosevelt Longworth later said, "but there was nothing precious about these lectures. It was all sorts of fun." At Hickory Hill, Mac got to know Bobby Kennedy as an eager interrogator, "a terrier of a man" who like himself could sometimes seem abrasive to people, particularly upon a first meeting. Mac didn't often say a great deal; the seminar topics—though not the surroundings—must have seemed old hat to a former Harvard dean. The seminars continued throughout the Kennedy presidency, and Mac would be there for most of them.[36]

At forty-two, Mac looked ten years younger. He wore the same clear-plastic frame glasses that he had sported as a Cambridge dean. He dressed his five-foot ten-inch, 160-pound frame in casual suits cut with the narrow lapels fashionable in the early 1960s. His cheeks were perpetually rosy, and his thinning sandy brown hair was brushed straight back—and disheveled just enough to suggest a man in a hurry.

WHILE Mac Bundy was busy pulling together his team, the new president was weighing what to do about Fidel Castro's Cuba. Ever since Castro's guerrilla insurgency toppled the corrupt dictatorship of Fulgencio Batista in January 1959, Cuban-American relations had soured. By the autumn of 1960, Dean Bundy was telling the Harvard *Crimson* that it would be "difficult for us not to support a movement on the part of true Latin American liberals to depose the current regime."[37] Just eight days after the inauguration, CIA director Allen Dulles told Kennedy and Bundy, "Cuba is now for practical purposes a Communist-controlled state." Ten months earlier President Eisenhower had authorized the CIA to train Cuban exiles for an invasion of the island, and in the meantime the Agency organized a series of hit-and-run attacks along the Cuban coastline. The CIA also began hatching assassination plots against Castro. On January 3, 1961, the Eisenhower administration broke diplomatic relations with Castro's regime. In effect, Ike was handing his successor an undeclared war.[38]

Now CIA chief Dulles urged the Kennedy White House to approve a plan to topple Castro with an invasion force of some 1,500 Cuban exiles trained by the CIA in Guatemala. Kennedy was noncommittal. By February 8, Bundy was telling him, "Defense and CIA now feel quite enthusiastic about the invasion. . . . At the worst, they think the invaders would get into the mountains, and at the best, they think they might get a full-fledged civil war in which we could then back the anti-Castro forces openly." [39] Kennedy's cautious response came just a few days later. After reading a *New York Times* story which went into considerable detail about the planning behind what was supposed to be a covert operation, Kennedy dictated a memo to Bundy: "Has the policy for Cuba been coordinated between Defense, CIA [and State]? . . . If there is a difference of opinion between the agencies I think they should be brought to my attention." [40]

Bundy replied with a "road map" to these differences. Defense and CIA were "quite enthusiastic," while the State Department "takes a much cooler view. . . ." He reported that he and Dick Goodwin "join in believing that there should certainly not be an invasion adventure without careful diplomatic soundings. We also think it almost certain that such soundings would confirm the judgment you are likely to hear from State." In other words, Bundy was skeptical of an "invasion adventure." [41] Skeptical, but not opposed.

Throughout February, Kennedy refused to make a decision about the operation, and indeed, he kept asking for "alternatives to a full-fledged invasion." Could not, the president asked, "such a force be landed gradually and quietly and make its first major military efforts from the mountains—then taking shape as a Cuban force within Cuba, not as an invasion force sent by the Yankees?" The notes Bundy took of this particular conversation make it clear that the CIA's deputy director for plans, Richard Bissell, just didn't think there were "other really satisfactory uses of the troops in Guatemala. . . ." Bissell and Kennedy were talking right past each other. [42]

Over the next two months Bundy thought he was doing his job, playing gatekeeper to the Oval Office. On February 18, Bundy handed Kennedy two memos, one from the CIA's Bissell and another from Thomas C. Mann, assistant secretary of state for Latin America. "Bissell and Mann are the real antagonists at the staff level," Bundy wrote in a cover note to the president. "Since I think you lean to Mann's view, I have put Bissell on top." Bundy then told the president that he thought the "gloomier parts of both papers are right. . . . The one hope I see is in an early—even if thin—recognition of a rival regime." Bundy wanted to stall for time, recognize a government-in-exile, impose a "full trade embargo against Castro," and then, "conceivably, we could hold back Bissell's battalion for about three months and even build it up somewhat. And when it did go in, the color of civil war would be quite a lot stronger."

The Bissell-Mann debate came down to the fact that Mann thought it highly unlikely that the invasion would spark a popular uprising, and without such a rebellion, Mann thought the invasion force would be doomed. Bissell responded that in the absence of a general revolt, the invasion force could be sustained almost indefinitely as a guerrilla force. Kennedy read the Mann and Bissell memos, but he again decided to postpone a decision on whether to authorize the invasion. In retrospect, Bundy clearly should have used Mann's dissent memo to press for a full-dress debate. Bissell later told the historian Piero Gleijeses that he had never seen the Mann memo. Mann later said of his memo, "It was like a stone falling in water." Eventually, even Mann would decide that his dissent had gone far enough, and he voted to proceed with the operation.[43]

By March 11, when Bissell gave another briefing to the president, Kennedy persuaded himself that he had to approve some kind of operation involving the landing of "an appropriate number of patriotic Cubans to return to their homeland."[44] The CIA-backed force of Cuban exiles was a fact which would not go away, Allen Dulles told him. As Bundy later put it in a post-mortem, the president was being told that the Cuban force had to leave Guatemala in the near future. Politics was a major factor. If the operation was canceled, Republicans would have blamed "this antsy-pantsy bunch of liberals. . . . Saying no would have brought all the hawks out of the woodwork."[45]

So for domestic political reasons, Kennedy allowed the CIA to refine its covert plan to ease the exile army into Cuba. As designed by Bissell, Operation Zapata would be executed without any overt involvement of U.S. military forces. The brigade of Cuban exiles would seize a beachhead at the Bay of Pigs on Cuba's southern coast and establish a defensive perimeter that would include control of a local airstrip. A CIA-run air strike from planes based in Guatemala could then be attributed to defectors from the Cuban air force. Within days the exiles would be launching air strikes all over Cuba from the Bay of Pigs airstrip, creating chaos throughout the island. A new government would be proclaimed, which would immediately be recognized by Washington.

Bissell—the "Great Expositor"—convinced Bundy that Operation Zapata had a "fighting chance."[46] On March 15, Bundy told Kennedy that he thought the CIA had done "a remarkable job of reframing the landing plan so as to make it unspectacular and quiet, and plausibly Cuban in its essentials. I have been a skeptic about Bissell's operation, but now I think we are on the edge of a good answer."[47] So concerned was Bundy to disguise the American hand, he failed to grill Bissell about whether such a small invasion force could defend itself on the ground against Castro's militia. He knew Bissell better than to have been so unquestioning: on February 25, Bundy had written the president that "if Dick [Bissell] has a fault, it is that he does not look at all sides of the question. . . ."[48]

In the weeks leading up to the April invasion, no one inside the administration would question the military feasibility of the plan. And only Senator William Fulbright (D.-Ark.), the powerful chairman of the Senate Foreign Relations Committee, would question whether it was the right thing to do. On March 30, Fulbright gave Kennedy a memo urging him to pursue a policy of isolating Castro, not overthrowing him: "The Castro regime is a thorn in the flesh," argued Fulbright, "but it is not a dagger in the heart." Five days later Kennedy invited the chairman of the Senate Foreign Relations Committee to a full-dress review of the CIA operation. In the presence of Mac Bundy, Bill Bundy, Arthur Schlesinger, Defense Secretary Robert McNamara, Paul Nitze and three members of the Joint Chiefs of Staff, Fulbright listened as Dulles and Bissell outlined the operation. Finally, Kennedy turned to Fulbright and asked him what he thought. As Schlesinger later recalled, "Fulbright, speaking in an emphatic and incredulous way, denounced the whole idea. The operation, he said, was wildly out of proportion to the threat."[49] Far from being moved by Fulbright's eloquence, the president's advisers closed ranks against the outsider.

Bill Bundy remembered being annoyed that Fulbright was even there; to his mind the senator's presence turned the meeting into a "charade." Instead of debating whether the invasion could succeed, Fulbright's pitch forced everyone to defend the morality of the intervention. "Damn it to hell," Bundy thought to himself, "these are bridges we crossed long ago."[50] Though Bill had been swamped with other work on Laos, the Congo and Berlin, he had been assigned by his boss, Nitze, to monitor the Cuban operation. And that had entailed several rather pessimistic briefings from Colonel Edward Lansdale. This veteran counterinsurgency expert questioned the basic assumption behind the venture: that the exile force would be welcomed by the Cuban masses. Nitze later wrote that Lansdale "had caused me to doubt the practicality" of the operation. But in the meeting with Fulbright and the president, Nitze did not pass along his reservations, partly because he did not want to appear to be buttressing what he regarded as Fulbright's moralistic arguments against intervention. But Nitze also knew that Bundy disagreed with Lansdale; based on intelligence estimates from his former colleagues at the CIA, Bundy thought there was a reasonable expectation that the Cuban people would respond to the invasion with an uprising. But he had not, as Nitze thought, carefully analyzed the military aspects of the operation. In fact, Bundy was just passing along what the Joint Chiefs were saying about the operation. As Bill later put it, "The ball was dropped between the two of us. . . . It would have been clear in a five-minute conversation that I had not dug deeply on it, and he [Nitze] would then have said, 'For God's sake, dig, really come up with something.' "[51]

He later felt some personal responsibility: "We were one of the 'joints' of the policy-making process, where you ought to be very critical of the political assumptions, very critical of the military assumptions. . . . And between us, we really weren't doing that. And McNamara wasn't doing what he invariably did after this, that is, to impose himself—some would say to excess —between the Joint Chiefs and the President." When Kennedy asked for a vote at the critical April 4 meeting with Fulbright, Bill Bundy thought, "This is not the right way to do it." But then he, Mac and everyone else in the room voted "yes."[52] Planning for the invasion proceeded.

Once the decision was made, Mac Bundy made sure that no further dissents reached the president. Richard Goodwin, a close aide to the president, remembered how one morning shortly before the invasion, he met Bundy, Walt Rostow and Arthur Schlesinger in the White House mess for breakfast. Clearly overwrought, Goodwin pressed Bundy, saying, "Even if the landings are successful and a revolutionary government is set up, they'll have to ask for our help. And if we agree, it'll be a massacre. . . . We'll have to fight house-to-house in Havana." Bundy responded, "Listen, Dick, I have an idea. Why don't you go over to see Rusk. . . ." Only afterwards did Goodwin realize that Bundy had shunted him out of the way, knowing that the secretary of state had no inclination to change the president's mind. Bundy was also unpersuaded by two memos from Schlesinger, who voiced his blunt opposition to the whole scheme: "I am against it." In the end, vigorous dissents from Schlesinger, Mann, Fulbright and Goodwin did not persuade Bundy to come out against the operation.[53]

EARLY on the morning of Monday, April 17, some 1,300 members of Cuban Exile Brigade 2506 landed on the beaches of the Bay of Pigs and fought until they ran out of ammunition. Only hours before, on Sunday evening, Mac Bundy had phoned Bissell and the CIA's deputy director, General Charles P. Cabell, to say that Kennedy had decided to cancel the D-day air strikes, which would have been flown by American pilots. Bundy explained that the president believed the air mission would reveal too much of the American hand in the operation.[54] Bissell was stunned. Even with air cover, the brigade at best could hold its beachhead for days or maybe even a week or two. If they lasted that long, Bissell thought, anything could happen. Without air cover, the game could be up within hours. Indeed, within a day the force, with its back to the ocean, was surrounded by 20,000 Cuban troops and militia. By Tuesday morning, Bundy was writing the president, ". . . the situation in Cuba is not a bit good."[55] Even then, Bundy still thought that at worst the exile force could melt into the mountains. In fact, by Thursday the battle was all over: 114 exiles were dead and 1,189 captured. Air strikes or not, the Bay of Pigs was a military and public relations fiasco that could not have turned out otherwise.

Mac immediately sent Kennedy a handwritten resignation note: "You know that I wish I had served you better in the Cuban episode, and I hope you know that I admire your own gallantry under fire in that case. If my departure can assist you in any way, I hope you will send me off."[56] Resignation was not a real option. Instead, Kennedy rewarded Bundy with an office closer to the Oval Office, moving his whole operation from the Old Executive Office Building to the basement of the West Wing of the White House.

Mac felt the Bay of Pigs had been a mistake, but not one that really belonged on his ledger. Indeed, when General Maxwell Taylor, who had been appointed by the president to investigate what had happened, circulated his critical report on the fiasco in early May, Bundy wrote a vigorous rebuttal defending his staff and making it clear that crucial information had been withheld from the president by the Joint Chiefs. Taylor's report suggested the fiasco occurred because the operation was "run from the White House." This Bundy vigorously denied. The president had repeatedly stated that he did not want any overt use of U.S. military forces. "I recall no word of opposition," Bundy wrote, "to this decision. . . ." [57] Bundy was angry, and like Kennedy, he felt he had been misled by the Joint Chiefs, the CIA and his old economics professor at Yale, Dick Bissell.

Bissell knew he was through and did not even try to defend the operation. A few days after the fiasco Mac gently told Bissell, "The president thinks you should swing your axe elsewhere for a while." [58] Some months later Bissell was given a medal and then prematurely retired.

Historians remain puzzled by many aspects of the Bay of Pigs operation. Why, for instance, did such smart men think that so few troops could land and defend themselves against Castro's army? As Dean Acheson chided Bill Bundy afterwards, it didn't take "Price Waterhouse to discover that 1,500 Cubans weren't as good as 25,000 Cubans." [59] Mac Bundy insisted that Bissell and Dulles "never really believed Kennedy when he said he wasn't going to put American forces in, so they didn't worry about whether the landing force would succeed because they believed whatever Kennedy said he would reinforce them once the game was joined. . . . We told them as flatly as we knew how that it was never going to be an American venture. And they heard all that, but they didn't believe it. . . . It's incredible, but it's the fact." [60]

As Mac put it later, the Bay of Pigs entailed a "very big failure in communication." He told one of Ben Bradlee's reporters from Newsweek, "We were just freshmen, and as freshmen you don't go in and say, 'Dammit, Mr. President, you're not getting the right kind of information.'" [61] The Bay of Pigs was not that important. Bundy called it just "a brick through the window." This was clever spin control, both self-deprecating and protective of Kennedy. [62]

But later, even Bundy would sometimes wonder if Bissell and his boys in the CIA had told him and the president the whole plan. Some evidence has emerged from unverifiable Cuban sources that there was another piece to this puzzling episode. One of Castro's veteran counterintelligence officers, General Fabian Escalante, claimed that years after the failed invasion Cuban intelligence learned that one of the decoy ships had a far more important mission: to approach the U.S. base at Guantánamo, three hundred miles to the southeast, and land a force of troops dressed in uniforms of Castro's army, who would then stage an "attack" on the U.S. base. This staged attack would then provide the provocation for a full-scale U.S. military intervention in support of the landing force at the Bay of Pigs. In the event, the decoy ship, Santa Ana, with a force of some 164 men, did arrive at the mouth of the Macambo River, near Guantánamo. According to one member of the force, his men were dressed in the kind of khaki uniforms that could easily have been mistaken for those of the Cuban army. As it turned out, the landing was aborted when a small surveillance unit from La Playa happened to encounter a Cuban patrol.

The staged attack on the U.S. base was thus aborted, leaving Bissell without the pretext he needed to push Kennedy into authorizing further air strikes over the Bay of Pigs, and perhaps even a full-scale invasion.[63]

When asked years later about this scenario, Mac Bundy responded, "I don't remember it, but it is not out of bounds. Somebody might have thought this up."[64] Bissell died before he could be asked about Escalante's information, but in his posthumously published memoirs, he reported that just a week before Kennedy was inaugurated, President Eisenhower said he was "prepared to 'move against Castro' before Kennedy's inauguration if a 'really good excuse' was provided by Castro." According to Bissell, Secretary of State Christian Herter then "suggested we stage an attack on Guantánamo."[65] Perhaps this was Bissell's backhanded way of signaling to his readers that there was more to the invasion plan than could be revealed. If true, the failure of the decoy ship to carry out the covert attack on Guantánamo was part of what Bundy called "this dunces performance."[66]

RECRIMINATIONS about the Bay of Pigs would reverberate throughout the remaining years of the Kennedy administration. The defeat turned Cuba into an obsession. "We were hysterical about Castro," McNamara said later.[67] Even two years later a reporter noticed that together with the usual in- and out-boxes on Bundy's cluttered walnut desk were two other boxes, one marked "President's box" and the other "Cuba."[68]

Publicly, Kennedy made a dignified show of taking full responsibility for the disaster. But among themselves, the Kennedy men blamed Eisenhower. "Ike left Kennedy an impossible situation," Bill Bundy said. "A grenade with the pin pulled."[69]

They also blamed the military; the Joint Chiefs would never be trusted again. "We were all very disillusioned with the Joint Chiefs," recalled Bill. "It was unforgivable that they should operate on the assumption that the president would order" U.S. forces to intervene "in a pinch."[70]

Not surprisingly, Kennedy was annoyed by a Walter Lippmann column on May 2 that reported how right Senator Fulbright had been in his opposition to the operation. "He [Fulbright] foresaw what would happen. . . . Senator Fulbright was the only wise man in the lot." Bundy promptly wrote Lippmann, ". . . your column this morning seemed to me hard but fair. . . ."[71]

An even harsher judgment came from Under Secretary of State Chester Bowles. "The Cuban fiasco," Bowles wrote in his diary, "demonstrates how far astray a man as brilliant and well intentioned as Kennedy can go who lacks a basic moral reference point." Bowles would soon be dismissed, partly because Kennedy thought he had leaked to the press his early opposition to the operation, and partly because in one of the NSC meetings following the fiasco Bowles had argued that it would be a great mistake "to create additional sympathy for Castro in his David and Goliath struggle against the United States." According to the minutes of the meeting, Bowles's "comments were brushed aside brutally and abruptly by the various fire eaters who were present." Needless to say, Bundy was one of the fire-eaters.

Bowles wrote that he left this meeting "with a feeling of intense alarm. . . . If every question in the world becomes an intellectual exercise on a totally pragmatic basis, with no reference to moral considerations, it may be that we can escape disaster, but it will certainly be putting the White House group to a test when . . . the minds that are attempting to do this are tired, uneasy, and unsure, the values and the arithmetic are unlikely to reflect wise courses." [72] These were bitter words, written by a prophet who knew he was being banished from Camelot.

A crisis was no time, thought Bundy, to be pressed with cloying "moral considerations." As it happened, Marcus Raskin, the young man David Riesman thought could serve as Bundy's moral conscience in the White House, did not receive his security clearance until mid-April. So when Raskin showed up on Monday, April 17, for his first day of work, everyone was talking about an isolated swamp in Cuba called the Bay of Pigs. By Wednesday morning, when Bundy held a staff meeting it was painfully clear that the CIA's operation was an unmitigated disaster. The meeting took place across from Bundy's office on the third floor of the Old Executive Office Building. Raskin thought it a surrealistic atmosphere: "There was this enormous bowl of fruit on the table in this very ornate, high-ceiling room; you have to remember, there were people dead on the beach that day and I'm eating fruit." As they discussed what was happening, Bundy flippantly said, "Well, Che learned more from Guatemala than we did." (Castro's fellow revolutionary, Che Guevara, had been in Guatemala during the CIA's 1954 coup, which had succeeded in part due to the operation's air superiority.) To which Raskin interjected, "And what have we learned?" Bundy stared at him stony-faced, and another aide quickly suggested that there should be no recriminations: "We must show a unified front within the administration." The next day Raskin was told, "Mac would prefer you not to come to the meetings—he'll have you report to him at the end of the day." Raskin later heard that Bundy had explained, "I can't take Marc anywhere without worrying that he won't pee on the floor." [73]

Still, Bundy didn't get rid of Raskin. He liked having difficult men like Raskin, Komer and Kaysen hanging about. So long as they didn't lecture him about morality he could tolerate a great deal of intellectual debate. If anything, the Stimsonian in Bundy thought the real lesson of the Bay of Pigs was that they had not been pragmatic enough. On May 16 he tried to reassure Kennedy: "Cuba was a bad mistake. But it was not a disgrace and there were reasons for it. If we set our critics on the left and right against each other they would eat each other up, and we already know more about what went wrong and why than any of them. . . . Against our hopes and our responsibilities, Cuba is a nitpick—it must not throw us off-balance."

Bundy warned the president that his true friends "now fear that because of Cuba we may turn back to cautious inactivity." [74] Far from heeding Fulbright's or Bowles's warnings, the White House would now redouble its efforts to overthrow Castro by covert means. In the summer of 1961 the CIA was ordered to come up with a plan to oust Castro. Thus was born Operation Mongoose, an escalation of the sabotage and hit-and-run attacks Eisenhower had authorized against Cuba in 1960.

For the next eighteen months the Kennedy administration waged an undeclared war on Cuba. Bundy specifically rejected Fulbright's alternative policy of merely isolating Castro's regime. And only four months after the Bay of Pigs, he and Kennedy scorned an olive branch offered by Castro's closest associate, Che Guevara. In an extraordinary meeting in Uruguay initiated by the Cubans, Guevara told White House aide Richard Goodwin that he and Castro wanted a modus vivendi with the United States. Without giving up their socialist agenda inside Cuba, Guevara said they nevertheless were willing to accept some limits on their foreign policy. Specifically, he said they "could agree not to make any political alliance with the East [the Soviets] . . . [and] they could also discuss the activities of the Cuban revolution in other countries." Guevara also volunteered that Cuba could pay for American property confiscated by the Cuban revolution. Goodwin passed a detailed memo of his three-hour conversation with Guevara to Bundy and Kennedy, and recommended that they "seek some way of continuing the below ground dialogue which Che has begun." The president and his national security adviser never bothered to respond to this offer of détente. Without a modus vivendi, Guevara ended up in Moscow the following summer to negotiate the delivery of nuclear-tipped missiles to deter the expected American invasion of Cuba. The missile crisis of October 1962—the most dangerous nuclear confrontation between the United States and the Soviet Union of the entire Cold War—was a direct consequence of the Bay of Pigs.[75]

SOME of the fallout from the Bay of Pigs would land in Laos, a sliver of a peasant nation unknown to most Americans. The Kennedy style of flexibility had its costs, and one of them was that White House task forces tended to personalize each crisis. Bundy and his colleagues had a tendency to apply lessons learned from the handling of one crisis to the next in a very different part of the world. So it was that the failure in Cuba had consequences in faraway Southeast Asia.

In March 1961, Kennedy had focused the nation's attention on a crisis in Laos, where a local communist insurgency appeared to be on the verge of seizing power. Kennedy initially turned this obscure local conflict into a Soviet-American confrontation with a televised speech in which he was seen by millions of Americans brandishing a wooden pointer at large maps of Laos depicting the communist aggression. His performance led many Americans to believe that U.S. troops would soon be dispatched there. But then came the disaster in Cuba in April, and the Kennedy White House became highly skeptical of advice from the Joint Chiefs. In one meeting Bundy so exasperated

Army General Lyman Lemnitzer with icy, baiting questions that the chairman of the Joint Chiefs abruptly conceded that any intervention in Laos was likely to lead to a full-scale ground war. This persuaded Kennedy to accept a Soviet offer to negotiate a neutral, coalition government in Laos. Bobby Kennedy later confirmed, "if it hadn't been for the Bay of Pigs, we would have sent troops into Laos."[76] Instead, the crisis in Laos quickly receded with a "neutralist" solution. Anyone who knew anything about Laotian affairs thought this was a pretty good solution; it made no sense for America to go to war in Laos. Kennedy's right-wing critics, nevertheless, could claim that the administration had compromised with communists, and that, of course, meant the president had incurred some domestic political costs by doing the sensible thing in far-off Laos. Moreover, if the Cuban fiasco led to caution in Laos, the muddied nature of Laotian neutralism persuaded some Kennedy men, particularly Mac Bundy, that they might have to draw a line in neighboring Vietnam.

Just one day after the collapse of the Bay of Pigs operation, Kennedy ordered a review of U.S. options in South Vietnam. In the aftermath of the 1954 Geneva Agreements that had ended the French Indochina War, South Vietnam's anti-communist leader, Ngo Dinh Diem, had consolidated his power. With American support, Diem had refused to hold the 1956 elections specified under the Geneva Agreements that would have reunified North and South Vietnam. In 1959 communist and nationalist forces indigenous to South Vietnam began to take up arms against Diem's regime. By the spring of 1961, Viet Cong guerrilla bands, with some logistical support from the North, were challenging Diem's control of much of the countryside.

April 29, 1961, was later described in the classified official history of the war known as the Pentagon Papers as a day of "prolonged crisis meetings at the White House." On that spring day President Kennedy made a series of fateful decisions on Vietnam. With Bundy's support, he ordered the deployment of four hundred Special Forces anti-guerrilla troops to South Vietnam. American advisers would now train South Vietnamese troops to conduct "ranger raids and similar military actions in North Vietnam as might prove necessary or appropriate." Because these actions constituted what the Pentagon Papers described as "the first formal breach of the Geneva agreements," no publicity was given to the decisions. Within weeks the government of North Vietnam was lodging formal protests that its airspace and territory were being violated by foreign aircraft and South Vietnamese combat teams. An Indochina war that had begun in 1945 was about to enter a new phase.[77]

Not coincidentally, Bundy himself began boning up on a country about which he knew practically nothing by reading Bernard Fall's new and very pessimistic book, *Street Without Joy*.[78] A French journalist who first went to Indochina in 1953 on a Fulbright fellowship, Fall brought a distinctly European perspective to his reporting on the Vietnamese conflict. An anti-communist, he nevertheless was a critic of the French colonial experience and the subsequent American intervention. He described the full extent of the French defeat at the hands of powerful nationalist forces, led by an indigenous communist movement determined to reunite the country. No one who read *Street Without Joy* in 1961 could later claim to have been innocent about the prospects for keeping Vietnam divided.

THE Cuban fiasco also placed enormous pressure on Kennedy to show his mettle with the Soviets in Germany. That spring Soviet premier Nikita Khrushchev was again making threats about ending the postwar agreement that established four-power control over a divided Germany and its former capital, Berlin. Early in the Cold War, Washington had decided to keep Germany divided, and consequently the American, French and British occupation zones had been forged into a sovereign West German state allied to the North Atlantic Treaty Organization (NATO).[79] In reaction, the Soviets forged their own communist-dominated East German state. Berlin, though located deep inside East Germany, remained divided into four sectors governed, respectively, by the Soviet Union, the United States, Great Britain and France. The allure of West Berlin's free market economy and open democratic society was a constant irritant to East Germany's communist rulers. Hundreds of East Germans were leaving daily by simply walking into West Berlin. This population drain threatened the very existence of the East German state. It seemed obvious to Khrushchev in 1961 that he could stabilize the status quo by simply abrogating the four-power status of Berlin and absorbing West Berlin into East Germany. To his mind, if the Americans wanted to keep Germany divided, then the anomaly of West Berlin had to end. Khrushchev's threats, therefore, were very much on Kennedy's mind as he prepared for a summit meeting in Vienna with Khrushchev in June 1961.

Khrushchev's reputation for bombast posed a dilemma for Kennedy. The narrowly elected young president felt that he could not ever appear to be cowed by the man who had once pounded his shoe at the U.N. General Assembly. Yet, many of Kennedy's advisers who knew Khrushchev best believed that this earthy Soviet communist was someone with whom Washington could quite possibly negotiate an armistice to the Cold War.

Khrushchev had risen to power in Joseph Stalin's shadow, and as such he had been a witness and collaborator to some of the tyrant's worst crimes. But he was not Stalin, and he had repeatedly taken steps toward liberalization, including dramatic cuts in the Soviet defense budget, that encouraged some in Washington to believe that an early détente was possible. Averell Harriman, who had served as Franklin Roosevelt's ambassador to Moscow during World War II, was now one of Kennedy's most important advisers on Soviet affairs. Significantly, Harriman believed the key to détente was a resolution of the German question. The Soviets still feared Germany, even as it remained divided and virtually occupied by a handful of foreign armies.

Harriman had visited Khrushchev in the Kremlin in the summer of 1959 and came away impressed with the Russian premier's fierce intelligence and basic sincerity. "We want to disarm and cease the Cold War," Khrushchev had said. As a start, the Soviet Union was prepared to negotiate an end to all testing of nuclear weapons. He was also prepared to end the division of Europe. What he had in mind was the proposal floated by Polish foreign minister Adam Rapacki which envisioned a vast demilitarized zone composed of the two Germanys, Poland and Czechoslovakia. In his controversial 1957 Reith Lectures on the BBC, George Kennan, the father of containment policy, had advocated a similar solution: a unified, but neutral and demilitarized Germany. "Many of Mr. Kennan's ideas," Khrushchev told Harriman, "would be acceptable to us, and should be to the advantage of the U.S. as well."

As to Germany, Khrushchev gave Harriman a vivid demonstration of his ribald humor. "There is a current joke in Russia," Khrushchev said, "that if you look at [West German Chancellor Konrad] Adenauer naked from behind, he shows Germany divided. If you look at him from the front, he demonstrates that Germany cannot stand." The joke said it all. Germany was divided and no one wished to see it rise up once again.

"We will not agree to your taking over Eastern Germany, and I know you will not agree to a united Germany that does not have your system. In fact, no one wants a united Germany. [French president Charles] De Gaulle told us so; the British have told us so; and Adenauer himself when he was here said he was not interested in unification. Why, then, do you persist in talking about it?"

As to Berlin, Khrushchev reasoned, "You state you want to defend the two million people in West Berlin. We are prepared to give any guarantees you desire to perpetuate the present social structure, either under the supervision of neutral countries or under the U.N. However, we are absolutely determined to liquidate the state of war with Germany. It is an anachronism."

And then, as he often did when pressed about Berlin, Khrushchev began to threaten war. "What good does it do you to have eleven thousand troops in Berlin? If it came to war, we would swallow them in one gulp . . . you have surrounded us with bases but our rockets can destroy them. If you start a war, we may die but the rockets will fly automatically."

This was the Soviet leader's bluster, and Harriman took it with a grain of salt. Harriman, too, feared the Germans, and did not wish to see an economically vibrant Germany reunited under any circumstances. He disliked Kennan's notion of a unified, demilitarized Germany. Like many other members of the American foreign policy establishment, Harriman preferred to keep Germany divided as long as possible. There were, however, unspoken costs to this policy. One was that the West Germans had to be cajoled into accepting the situation. They had been given "sovereignty" even as American, French and British troops continued to be stationed on West German territory. Washington's recognition of West German sovereignty in 1952 had been one more violation of the Yalta accords. As Khrushchev had just told him, "You recognized West Germany on conditions contrary to those agreed upon during the war." So from Khrushchev's perspective, it was only fair that the Soviets accord recognition to East Germany as a sovereign state with full control over its territory. This would help to ease Russian fears about Germany, but it would also, as Kennan had pointed out, condemn the East Germans—and much of Eastern Europe—to living within the communist sphere.[80]

Viewed in this light, Khrushchev's talk of normalizing the abnormal division of Germany was not threatening to the West in any military sense. He was attempting only to cloak the de facto division of Germany with a reassuring legality. He was attempting to place the status quo in concrete. From the Soviet perspective, this was a purely defensive policy. But from the perspective of the Kennedy administration, recognition of the East German state, even by just Moscow, threatened political embarrassment because it suggested that Washington's commitment to Germany's freedom and democracy was laced with hypocrisy. Some members of the new administration understood this conundrum and wished to stabilize the status quo in Central Europe, which was defined first and foremost as a divided Germany. But they could not be seen to do this while giving way to Khrushchev's threats.

A few days before Bundy accompanied the president to Vienna, he tried to summarize the administration's dilemma: "At one extreme are those who feel that the central Soviet purpose is to drive us out of Berlin and destroy the European Alliance as a consequence. On the other extreme are those who feel that if we think in terms of accommodation, we should be able to avoid a real crisis. . . . The one thing which must be avoided . . . is any conclusion that the United States is feeble on Berlin itself. . . . We ourselves might indeed have new proposals at a later time."[81]

Bundy didn't have to name names: that spring Dean Acheson had been "a man with a mission," as Bundy later put it in his 1988 book, *Danger and Survival*. Convinced that the Soviets were determined to take over West Berlin and thereby destroy NATO's credibility, Acheson was using all his prestige to persuade the young president to confront the Soviet challenge in Germany with a show of force. Acheson was ready for war. At the other extreme, men like Walter Lippmann, George Kennan and many of Bundy's friends at Harvard (Riesman, Hoffmann and others) were convinced that it was in America's interest to come to a realistic accommodation with Khrushchev over Germany's postwar status. If Berlin was an artificial construct, then Khrushchev's insistence that there should be an end to its peculiar status was not entirely unreasonable.

Unfortunately, at Vienna Khrushchev acted the boor. In his meetings with Kennedy he employed much the same blend of earthy realpolitik and bluster that he had with Harriman two years earlier. Worse, in his public statements Khrushchev made it clear that he was making demands on Berlin. Afterwards, on June 15, he imposed a deadline, insisting that a peace treaty formally ending World War II and recognizing the division of Germany must be signed by the end of the year.

It seems clear in retrospect that the Soviet leader neither expected nor wanted a military confrontation, let alone a war, over Berlin. We now know from East German and Soviet archives that Khrushchev was being pushed by his own hard-liners and most particularly, by the communist leader of East Germany, Walter Ulbricht.[82] Both the Soviet and East German leaders feared a collapse of the East German state if the exodus of Germans from east to west was not halted through the West Berlin window. Khrushchev also had wholly reasonable fears that a resurgent West Germany would soon be given de facto control over the NATO nuclear weapons stationed on its soil. West German defense minister Franz-Josef Strauss was publicly advocating that the West German Bundeswehr should be given independent access to nuclear weapons. Adenauer himself had stated that West Germany had "renounced the right of production, but not that of possession" of nuclear weapons.[83] The prospect of a unified, nuclear-armed German state in alliance with the West alarmed many West Europeans, let alone Russians. Men like Kennan and Lippmann thought it a legitimate goal of Soviet policy to prevent this prospect. Kennedy returned from Vienna unnerved by his meeting with the voluble Khrushchev and determined to reverse the public's perception that he was on the defensive.

Bundy, too, was badly shaken by the harsh words exchanged at Vienna. At the end of one long day Bundy took out his frustrations on Marc Raskin, who had been trying to push Bundy into reading a long memo by David Riesman on rethinking German policy. Both Riesman and Raskin thought the administration was taking Khrushchev's threats far too seriously. Behind the bravado, they thought, was good evidence that the Soviets wanted to defuse the Berlin issue. Bundy had heard this argument before, and intellectually he understood its merits. But today he wanted none of it. Suddenly, he got red in the face and began screaming at Raskin, "Khrushchev is a pig, he's just a pig!" Raskin was shocked. "It had become a very, very personal thing," he recalled.[84]

As the Berlin crisis continued to dominate headlines that summer, Kennedy ordered Bundy to have the NSC draw up contingency plans for what to do if Khrushchev seized West Berlin. Raskin subsequently learned that Kaysen and Henry Rowen, one of Paul Nitze's deputies in the Pentagon, had been working on a contingency first-strike war plan. Kaysen characterized it as a "back-of-the-envelope" effort "to show that we could have a successful, clean first strike." Theoretically, according to Kaysen, the United States had a 90 percent chance of wiping out all Soviet strategic nuclear weapons, making any retaliation by the Soviets against American cities or military targets impossible. Millions of Russians would still die.[85]

Because there was still a 10 percent chance that even one Soviet bomber or missile might get through to bomb an American city in retaliation, civil defense became a part of the plan. Even if the United States did not intend to launch a first strike, in order to make nuclear deterrence credible, Kaysen argued that Washington had to convince the Soviets that the United States was willing to fight a nuclear war. One way to do that was to demonstrate a heavy investment in a civil defense program that would protect Americans from the few Soviet missiles that might survive a first strike or preemptive attack on Soviet nuclear forces.

As a contingency, Kaysen bought into the logic of this argument. Raskin, however, was appalled when he saw Kaysen's memo.* He asked Kaysen, "How does this make us any better than those who measured the gas ovens or the engineers who built the tracks for the death trains in Nazi Germany?"

"It was unbelievable," Raskin later said. "Kaysen was going into all these details on how many millions would be killed. We argued for hours, we screamed, and at one point we found ourselves crying. I cried, he cried; we had been great friends and I guess we knew this would end our friendship."[86] Raskin's relationship with Kaysen would never be the same. "Raskin thought it wicked of me to even discuss that we had a first-strike capability against the Soviets," Kaysen recalled. "I just thought it was a good idea to have a plan since we were, after all, relying on these weapons for deterrence. Having a plan is different from recommending its use. Marc was sort of a pacifist at heart, while I had been in a war before and therefore had a different attitude."[87]

Bundy was well aware of Raskin's argument with Kaysen, but from his perspective Kaysen was only attempting to introduce some flexibility into what Bundy knew to be the Pentagon's dangerously rigid contingency plan for nuclear warfare. He later said it would have been "irresponsible for the administration not to have considered the possibility of using nuclear weapons in the [Berlin] crisis, but even more irresponsible to have actually used them." The line, however, between a mere "contingency" and concrete "planning" for a first strike was extremely thin.[88]

Kennedy himself was compelled to discuss such nuclear contingencies. In a meeting with the Joint Chiefs, Kennedy was told that the U.S. Senate Foreign Relations Committee, meeting in executive session, "wanted to know how long we could fight a conventional war prior to employing nuclear weapons with the build-up now anticipated and asked for. It was the sense of the Committee that we must prove our willingness and agree to use nuclear weapons if this crisis continues." Kennedy then talked about the difficulty of waging a conventional war in Central Europe and "stated that he felt that the critical point is to be able to use nuclear weapons at a crucial moment before they [the Soviets] use them. He inquired as to our capabilities of making such a decision without letting the enemy know that we are about to do it."[89] Clearly, a first-strike attack on the Soviets with nuclear weapons was being discussed. In this sense, the "back-of-the-envelope" first-strike plan developed by Kaysen out of Bundy's shop was something more than an abstract contingency plan.

Bundy vividly remembered one meeting that summer which seemed to

---

* Ted Sorensen told Kaysen after he saw the first-strike plan, "You're crazy! We shouldn't let guys like you around here" (Michael Beschloss, *The Crisis Years: Kennedy and Khrushchev, 1960–1963* [New York: HarperCollins, 1991], p. 256).

crystallize for him the contradictory logic of having to rely on weapons which ultimately should never be unleashed. Alone with Kennedy and Acheson in the Cabinet Room, Bundy heard the president ask the former secretary of state just when he thought nuclear weapons should be used. Acheson sat in silence for a moment, and then quietly said he thought Kennedy should give this question the "most careful and private consideration, well before the time when the choice might present itself," and that "he should tell no one at all what that conclusion was." Years later Bundy thought Acheson was telling the president that "the right final choice might be to accept defeat, and the loss of West Berlin, if the only remaining alternative were to start a nuclear war." Bundy's evidence was an article Acheson himself had written in 1959 in the *Saturday Evening Post* in which he had concluded that West Berlin was worth a conventional fight, but that it would be a mark of "wisdom and restraint" if Washington nevertheless had to accept defeat in order to avoid a nuclear war.[90]

The incident underscored for Bundy that if even an original Cold Warrior like Acheson was ultimately unwilling to fight a nuclear war over such a critical issue as Berlin, then nuclear deterrence was mere bluff. Bundy had grappled with these notions about weapons of mass destruction at least as early as his conversations with Oppenheimer in 1952. His problem now as the president's national security adviser was to keep control over these weapons and make certain that they were never used. On this score, he had to worry about the brass in the Pentagon as much as the Soviets.

BACK in late January 1961, Bundy had been given an extraordinary briefing by Daniel Ellsberg, a twenty-nine-year-old analyst working for the RAND Corporation, a think tank that did classified studies for the federal government. A junior fellow at Harvard, and an expert in game theory, Ellsberg was one of only a handful of civilians who had seen the Joint Chiefs' operating war plans, known as the Joint Strategic Capabilities Plan (JSCP). What he saw sickened his stomach. The war plans called for the swift destruction of every city of any consequence in the Soviet Union, China and Eastern Europe. "It was just a trucking plan," Ellsberg said, "for moving thermonuclear explosives as fast as possible to every urban center in the Eastern bloc." Moscow alone was to receive 170 atomic and hydrogen bombs.[91] There were no intermediate steps, no flexibility and no warnings. He called it a first-strike plan because it was the Joint Chiefs' planned response to any level of "armed conflict with the Soviet Union." The chiefs' planned response to a division-level Soviet attack on West Berlin, for instance, would be the annihilation of hundreds of millions of civilians. Ellsberg thought there were few safeguards against an accidental triggering of the JSCP. Worse, he had been told that Eisenhower had given individual commanders written authorization to use their nuclear weapons if in their best judgments they were under attack and out of communication with the White House. Ellsberg knew that the commander of the Seventh Fleet in the Pacific, for instance, was out of communications with

Washington on average a few hours each day. So it was entirely possible that a nuclear war could be initiated by an isolated admiral without the president's knowledge.*

Ellsberg was worried. Within days of Kennedy's inauguration, he had convinced Assistant Secretary of Defense Paul Nitze that he ought to see the JSCP. Nitze authorized his deputy, Harry Rowen, and Ellsberg, working under him, to study the whole problem.

Almost immediately, Ellsberg and Rowen were stymied; after requesting a copy of the war plan for Nitze's reading, Ellsberg was told by a two-star army general working for Nitze, "No, he can't see it. He has no need to know." Nitze was not the kind of man who liked to be told no, and when he learned of this rebuff, Rowen arranged for Ellsberg to see Mac Bundy in the White House. When Ellsberg arrived, he began by trying to explain how he had received access to a document as sensitive as the general war plan. Bundy interrupted and said coldly, "Is this a briefing or a confessional?"

Ellsberg pulled himself together and replied, "There is a plan which no president has read, and which no secretary of defense has read, and it has the following characteristics." He then reeled off the bare facts of the plan, emphasizing how small of an armed conflict could initiate full-scale nuclear war. Within thirty seconds Bundy took out a pad of paper and began scribbling notes.

A briefing that was scheduled to last ten minutes stretched to an hour and a half. Mac was particularly astonished by Ellsberg's assertion that Eisenhower had issued presidential authorization in writing that would allow individual commanders to launch nuclear weapons.

Soon after Ellsberg left, Bundy picked up the phone and called the staff director of the Joint Chiefs. When he got a deputy, he said, "This is Mac Bundy; the president wants to see the JSCP." There was a long silence at the other end of the line until the general replied, "Oh, we never release that." Bundy responded, "No, I don't think you understand. I'm calling for the president and he wants to see the JSCP." Again the general said, "But we don't release that." Dumbfounded, Bundy shouted, "I don't think I'm making myself clear." At this point the general offered a compromise, "Well, we could give the president a briefing on the JSCP." Bundy snapped, "The president is a great reader; he wants to read the JSCP."[92]

Bundy never did see the full war plan, but he wrote a memo to Kennedy describing a summary of the plan he had been given by the Joint Chiefs. He called it "dangerously rigid and, if continued without amendment, may leave

---

* Documents declassified in 1998 confirm that President Eisenhower gave U.S. military commanders written authorization in 1957 to use nuclear weapons "when the urgency of time and circumstances clearly does not permit a specific decision by the president. . . ." (Walter Pincus, "Military Got Authority to Use Nuclear Arms in 1957," *Washington Post*, March 21, 1998.)

you with very little choice as to how you face the moment of thermonuclear truth." [93] Sometime that summer the president was given a formal briefing on the strategic war plan, and afterwards he turned to Dean Rusk and muttered, "And we call ourselves the human race." But if Kennedy recognized that the war plan was irrational, he nevertheless decided to sidestep the issue. Why confront the Joint Chiefs over an abstraction? As Carl Kaysen told Ellsberg, "This is not a good time for *Lieutenant* Kennedy to reverse the orders of the great general [Eisenhower]." Later in the autumn of 1961, Bundy helped to draft an "action memorandum" that signaled the adoption of what would later be called the strategic doctrine of flexible response. [94] In the future, if armed conflict was initiated, the United States would first respond with conventional forces, and only later, if necessary, with nuclear weapons.

THE summer of 1961 was a gloomy time for anyone working in the Kennedy White House. Khrushchev's year-end deadline to "normalize" Berlin's status had not been withdrawn and some observers thought this might mean war. Bundy later remembered it as "a time of sustained and draining anxiety," and thought his old Cambridge neighbor Robert Lowell had it right when he wrote,

> All autumn, the chafe and jar
> of nuclear war;
> we have talked our extinction to death. [95]

At a June 28 NSC meeting to discuss the Berlin crisis, a feisty Acheson urged Kennedy to respond to Khrushchev's threats by sending an army division (15,000 troops) down the Autobahn to West Berlin. Any effort, he said, "to solve the Berlin issue by negotiations is worse than a waste of time and energy. It is dangerous." Because Khrushchev obviously didn't believe Kennedy was willing to use nuclear weapons over Berlin, Acheson insisted the president must devise a military response that "will change the present apparent Russian disbelief that the United States would go to nuclear war over Berlin, rather than submit." The danger, Acheson believed, was that Berlin would prove the whole idea of deterrence was an empty threat. [96]

Afterwards, a shocked Averell Harriman complained to Arthur Schlesinger that Acheson, a "frustrated and rigid man," was "leading us down the road to war." [97] Bundy took Acheson's bellicosity with a grain of salt. "Dean loved popping off," Bundy would explain later. Privately, the former secretary of state was astounded that White House aides were making foreign policy instead of the State Department. Acheson had always been rankled by Bundy's brashness, and his performance in the Bay of Pigs, Laos and now Berlin had done nothing to elevate his opinion of the younger man's judgment. [98] He thought Mac was soft, and Bundy, for his part, thought Acheson was posturing.

In the following month more than 30,000 refugees crossed into West

Berlin, draining the East German state of many of its best-educated workers. It was clear that either the Soviets would have to do something to end the exodus or the East German state would collapse, creating the prospect of either a major war or the reunification of Germany under NATO's banner. And no one but the Germans welcomed the idea of a reunified Germany. Kennedy himself understood the macabre irony of the West's dilemma over Berlin. Flying home from the disastrous Vienna summit with Khrushchev, he had turned to his old friend and aide Kenneth O'Donnell and remarked, "all of us know that Germany will probably never be reunited. . . . God knows, I'm not an isolationist, but it seems particularly stupid to risk killing a million Americans over an argument about access rights on an Autobahn . . . or because the Germans want Germany reunified. If I'm going to threaten Russia with a nuclear war, it will have to be for much bigger and more important reasons than that."[99]

Kennedy decided not to send additional troops to West Berlin, but he and Bundy did conclude that they had to make it clear to Khrushchev where the United States would fight. So on July 25, Kennedy gave a televised speech in which he announced the calling up of 150,000 reservists and a $3.25 billion increase in the defense budget. These signs of bellicosity prompted Khrushchev to complain that the speech was "a preliminary declaration of war."[100] But there were also signals in the speech of Kennedy's willingness to negotiate. At Bundy's urging, Kennedy acknowledged "the Soviet Union's historical concerns about their security in Central and Eastern Europe" and the "enormous losses . . . bravely suffered [by] the Russian people" during World War II. The president also made a subtle distinction when he emphasized the inviability of *West* Berlin's rights, suggesting that "the endangered frontier of freedom runs through divided Berlin. . . ." Years later Bundy would write that this distinction "may have given advance encouragement to Khrushchev" to resolve the crisis by building a wall through the divided city.[101]

Kennedy and Bundy knew the wall or something like it was inevitable. Early in August, Kennedy told Bundy's deputy, Walt Rostow, "Khrushchev is losing East Germany. He cannot let that happen. If East Germany goes, so will Poland and all of Eastern Europe. He will have to do something to stop the flow of refugees—perhaps a wall. And we won't be able to prevent it. I can hold the Alliance together to defend West Berlin but I cannot act to keep East Berlin open."[102]

At 2:30 A.M. Berlin time on Sunday, August 13, East German paramilitary police began throwing up barbed-wire barricades between East and West Berlin. Four days later the barbed-wire began to be replaced with a concrete wall. Kennedy was up in Hyannis Port, sailing for the weekend, and when he returned to Washington on Monday morning, Bundy had a memo prepared for the president which concluded there was nothing to be done. Bundy had already talked with both Joe Alsop and George Kennan, two men he respected who did not often agree with each other. But on what Bundy called this "border closing episode," they both agreed: "(1) this is something they [the Soviets] have always had the power to do; (2) it is something they were bound to do sooner or later, unless they could control the exits from West Berlin to the West; (3) since it was bound to happen, it is as well to have it happen early, as their doing and their responsibility."[103]

Acheson was livid. Mac knew that Acheson felt "the Wall would have come down in a day if Harry Truman had been President." Acheson later wrote a friend, "It seems to me interesting that a group of young men who regard themselves as intellectuals are capable of less coherent thought than we have had since Coolidge. They are pretty good at improvising. . . . But God help us . . . if they are given any time to think!"[104] The Berlin wall not only divided a city, it also confirmed Acheson's worst instincts about Mac Bundy.

For the next twenty-eight years the Berlin wall would stand as the defining symbol of the Cold War. To most Americans, it was a monument to Soviet tyranny, even as most Americans forgot that the real division of Germany had occurred in 1946–48. Far from inaugurating the division of Germany— and by definition, the condemnation of millions of East Germans to communist rule—the Berlin wall merely ratified the largely American initiative to divide Germany at the very beginning of the Cold War.[105] President Kennedy and his advisers fully recognized that the Berlin wall was necessary if Germany was to remain divided. They also knew that there was an alternative to what was, after all, an artificial construct.

In the midst of the crisis, Carl Kaysen sent Bundy a memo which he described as "my instinctive reactions to the Berlin situation."* Kaysen's August 22 memo is a seminal document of the Cold War. Written at a moment of great tension, it nevertheless managed to raise broad questions about the necessity for any conflict at all with the Soviets. A "cold war stance," he suggested, had "significant defects." A policy of confrontation with the Soviets forced a certain "rigidity" on Washington. "Further, its internal consequences are highly undesirable: McCarthyism was not unconnected with the fact that we were literally at war with the Soviet Union in Korea." Logically, "when we take a strongly military stance, we face a dearth of suitable objects of action. This aggravates the internal [domestic] political consequences of such a stance, and we seek enemies within when we cannot come to grips with the enemies without." This was an extraordinary admission, particularly coming from the president's number two deputy on the NSC. Because the Cold War could never become "hot," or, in Kaysen's words, because we cannot "come to grips" with the enemy, "radical right-wing elements" in the United States are natu-

---

* Kaysen's memo shows the influence of David Riesman and Erich Fromm, who had lobbied him in July to change U.S. policy on Germany. For a detailed summary of their views, see their unpublished letter to the *New York Times*, July 19, 1961. Kaysen was no doubt also influenced by Marcus Raskin's July 6 memo to Bundy on the same subject.

rally empowered. Kaysen thought this an unacceptable cost and he now told Bundy that he was convinced that the "only one of our past aims which we must continue to pursue is the freedom of West Berlin."

In return for a Soviet accommodation in which the freedom of West Berlin is guaranteed, Kaysen argued that the United States should be prepared to offer "(1) acceptance of the Oder-Neisse line as the final boundary of West Germany"; (2) recognition of East Germany; (3) negotiations between the two Germanys on unification; (4) mutual security guarantees for both German states and, most significantly, "the creation of a nuclear-free zone in Germany." These steps would, Kaysen argued, create an accommodation that would transform the Cold War from a militarized confrontation into a relationship of "peaceful coexistence." With the settlement of the "German question"—which had always been at the heart of the Cold War—the two ideological systems would henceforth compete on strictly economic and political playing fields.

Having proposed a radical reversal of U.S. policy, Kaysen went on to lay out all the reasons such an accommodation would be in Washington's interest. Recognition of East Germany would naturally lead to increased contacts between East and West Germany, and the contrasts in the quality of life between the two would naturally enhance the attractiveness of the West. Likewise, acceptance of the Oder-Neisse line [the river dividing Poland from Germany] would bury forever any future German claims to additional territory to the East. This, in turn, would ease fears of German revanchism in East Europe and allow the Soviets to consider loosening their tight control over Poland, Hungary, Czechoslovakia and East Germany itself.

Kaysen's memo ended with an acknowledgment that the most important political obstacle to such a policy change was undoubtedly domestic: "As the crisis grows tenser, the ability of the administration to espouse any policy which involves 'concessions' to the Soviets diminishes, for fear that the opposition will attack it for appeasement. The whole argument of this essay is the error of such a view, and there is no way of dealing with it other than by meeting it head-on." There was nothing to be done, Kaysen concluded, than to call for negotiations.* [106]

Kaysen's was no lone voice. George Kennan had been making the same argument for years. Averell Harriman said much the same thing in a secret letter to Kennedy on September 1: "Since Potsdam, I have been satisfied that Germany would be divided for a long time. I am sure Khrushchev means what he says when he told me as well as others that 'We [the West] would never agree to a united Germany under socialism (as he calls it) and I will never

---

* Kaysen's argument was soon echoed by the West German Social Democratic Party (SPD) politician Egon Bahr, who in 1963 urged a policy of *Wandel durch Annäherung* (change through rapprochement). The SPD's Chancellor Willy Brandt would later win the Nobel Peace Prize for carrying out this rapprochement, which he called Ostpolitik.

agree to a united Germany under your system.' . . . In addition, I believe Khrushchev is sincerely concerned with the remilitarization of Germany, particularly with the prospect of her eventually getting independent nuclear capability. . . . He feels Adenauer is safe enough, but he said to me, 'What will happen if Strauss or someone else gets control?' . . . She [Germany] will have the strongest army in Europe, and who can stop her if some leader determines that she shall produce her own nuclear weapons?" Harriman urged Kennedy to negotiate a "denuclearized control zone of West Germany and East Germany. . . ." Finally, the veteran diplomat with the Secret Service code name of Crocodile told Kennedy, "He [Khrushchev] obviously does not want nuclear war. . . ."[107]

A reasonable argument can be made that if the policy shift advocated by Kaysen and Harriman had been accepted by the Kennedy administration, the Cold War might have ended much earlier than 1989. If there had been a settlement in Germany that ended the division of Europe, most of the tensions that fueled the militarization of the Cold War would have quickly receded. Certainly, the ideological contest between the Soviets and the Americans, particularly in the developing world, would have continued, but this rivalry was always peripheral to the high stakes that existed in Europe. If a European détente had been achieved in the early 1960s, the evolutionary forces of economic and cultural liberalization that ultimately brought about the collapse of the Soviet system in 1989–91 would have become powerfully evident much earlier in the Cold War's trajectory. We now understand from the very manner in which the Cold War ended that there was nothing inevitable about the conflict.[108] It was not, as two of Bundy's successors in the NSC job—Henry Kissinger and Zbigniew Brzezinski—later argued, a permanent confrontation. Kaysen didn't think this, and neither did Averell Harriman nor George Kennan. Nor did Mac Bundy.

Six days after receiving Kaysen's memo, Bundy wrote Kennedy that there was a growing belief among his advisers "that we can and should shift substantially toward acceptance of the GDR [East Germany], the Oder-Neisse line, a non-aggression pact, and even the idea of two peace treaties."[109] Far from disagreeing with Kaysen, Bundy accepted the logic of his argument and was willing to endorse the policy change to his president.

Kennedy did not reject this advice outright, but as the weeks and months rolled by American policy did not change. Right-wing domestic political opinion, combined with Adenauer's insistence on the status quo, persuaded Kennedy to drop the matter. In doing so, President Kennedy missed a major opportunity to demilitarize the Cold War. Throughout his short presidency, Kennedy's political instincts persuaded him to avoid the political risks of accommodation and to accept the risks of military confrontation. After the Bay of Pigs he could not afford to look feeble.

In his own history of the period Bundy later acknowledged his advice to Kennedy, but blamed Khrushchev for the missed opportunity. "Clearly if we had heard proposals of this sort from Moscow," he writes, "coupled with a prospect of reassurances on West Berlin, we would have had powerful reasons to press Bonn for concessions that did not come for another decade." [110] But this was turning the argument upside down. As Bundy knew from Kaysen's memo, and from Khrushchev's own public statements, the Soviet leader was on record as favoring most of the steps delineated in Kaysen's proposal. The ball was in Washington's court, not Moscow's. Moreover, Washington, not Moscow, would be negotiating from a position of strength.

BUNDY had learned "within weeks" of taking office that "there was no discernible missile gap." But again, for political reasons, Kennedy would not yet admit publicly that a major theme of his presidential campaign had been based on myth. The truth was that America possessed a vastly superior nuclear strike force. In 1961 the United States had roughly 1,685 nuclear warheads and some 1,000 delivery systems (mostly long-range bombers and over a hundred intercontinental ballistic missiles). By contrast, the Soviet Union had fewer than 250 nuclear warheads and around three hundred delivery systems. (These included only four intercontinental missiles, some two hundred bombers capable of hitting the United States and a small fleet of submarines equipped with short-range nuclear-tipped missiles.) Even so, Kennedy proceeded with his determination to rectify what he had claimed was Eisenhower's neglect of both conventional and strategic defense forces. [111]

The defense budget in the Kennedy years would climb rapidly. Conventional forces were modernized and the country's "triad" of strategic nuclear delivery systems—ICBMs, submarine-launched Polaris missiles and long-range bombers—was vastly expanded.

There was nothing secret about this defense buildup. What was Khrushchev to think? He knew how weak his own strategic forces were and now he knew that Kennedy was building what Soviet generals considered a first-strike nuclear arsenal. Khrushchev's own military establishment demanded a response. The Kennedy arms buildup led in the short term to the Cuban missile crisis and in the long term to a dangerous and costly arms race. As the historian Michael Beschloss later wrote, ". . . throughout his term, Kennedy rarely showed the magnanimity that should have been expected of a superior power. Instead he aroused the Western world to an hour of imminent danger that did not exist, provoked the adversary by exposing Soviet nuclear weakness to the world, and unwittingly caused the Soviets to fear that he was on the verge of exploiting American nuclear strength to settle the Cold War on American terms, perhaps even in a preemptive strike." [112]

Bundy knew there were alternatives. In the autumn of 1961, just as the missile buildup was getting under way, a classified study group operating within the new Arms Control and Disarmament Agency (ACDA) came up with a plan to place a cap on the missile race. The Foster Panel—so named after William Foster, the president's new disarmament adviser—first tried to determine how many delivery vehicles would be necessary to maintain deterrence. Assuming that any enemy would be deterred from major war by the certainty that half of its citizenry would be annihilated, the Foster Panel concluded that no more than two hundred to five hundred strategic delivery vehicles were necessary. Just to be sure, the panel doubled its higher estimate and recommended that the president propose to the Soviets that a ceiling of one thousand delivery vehicles be placed on each country's strategic nuclear arsenal.

If Kennedy had accepted this recommendation—and if the Soviets had agreed to it—the arms race might have been capped at a relatively low level. Kennedy made his decision at a meeting in Hyannis Port the day after Thanksgiving. The air force was asking for 2,400 ICBMs. McNamara knew from quizzing his own whiz kids from the RAND Corporation that no more than four hundred such missiles were necessary to destroy half the Soviet population. But he nevertheless told Kennedy that he would be "politically murdered" if he built less than a thousand missiles. Kennedy agreed, even though Ted Sorensen warned him that such a dramatic missile buildup was sure to accelerate the arms race.[113]

As to the Foster Panel's proposal to negotiate a formal cap of one thousand land- and sea-based missiles and bombers, Bundy labeled the proposal "too radical" and the president rejected it. Jerome Wiesner, the president's science adviser, thought Bundy was being "much too cautious." Years later one of the ACDA officials who had supported the Foster Panel recommendations confronted Bundy about this missed opportunity. Bundy conceded that his decision might have been a mistake.[114]

IN the autumn of 1961, Bundy was distressed to hear his friend and mentor Walter Lippmann publicly complain that Kennedy's policies were no different from Ike's: "It's like the Eisenhower administration thirty years younger." Lippmann had severely criticized the Bay of Pigs invasion, called for negotiations with Khrushchev over Berlin and questioned the necessity for any military intervention in Southeast Asia. But the nation's premier pundit had not given up on Kennedy's men. He had been in nearly constant touch with Bundy, Schlesinger and the president himself, and in private he gave them specific ideas and even tried his hand at a draft speech. Lippmann thought the president should stand up to his right-wing critics and forcefully rebut the charges of appeasement to which he was being subjected over Cuba, Berlin and Vietnam. He told the president's speechwriter, Theodore Sorensen, that Kennedy was the first president in history to have to deal with the fact of "nuclear parity." The president, Lippmann wrote, should make "our people realize how primitive and romantic are men like [Republican Senator Barry] Goldwater, who talk as if war today would be like the Alamo. . . ." There was a difference, Lippmann argued, between appeasement and compromise, and the president should explain to the American people that merely negotiating with the Soviets did not mean another Munich.[115] Bundy, who was appalled by the jingoism and blustering of Kennedy's right-wing opponents, agreed with much of this criticism. Well aware of the dangers of nuclear war, he recognized the reality of nuclear parity. He understood Khrushchev's fears of a nuclear-armed Germany and the need for some kind of coexistence with the Soviet Union. He was painfully skeptical of those who urged Kennedy to mount military adventures in places like Cuba, Laos and Vietnam.* But as a liberal, he also thought Lippmann underestimated the power of the right wing, and failed to understand that Kennedy had to look tough if he was ever going to be allowed to change the direction of the Cold War.

One year into the new administration, a growing number of Bundy's Harvard friends found themselves questioning his good judgment. David Riesman thought the new administration was "almost out of control." During the Berlin crisis Riesman and Erich Fromm had visited Bundy's deputy, Carl Kaysen, to plead that the president's tough rhetoric was inflating the crisis and undermining the very real possibilities for negotiating a U.S.-Soviet settlement of the German question. Kaysen and Schlesinger firmly rebuffed them, and afterwards Riesman told a friend he found the atmosphere in Washington "frightening."[116]

Riesman in particular was appalled by Kennedy's endorsement of a national civil defense program that encouraged citizens to dig nuclear fallout shelters in their backyards. He and many other Harvard colleagues—including Stanley Hoffmann, Robert Paul Wolff, Michael Walzer and Martin Peretz—were also critical of the administration's decision to renew U.S. atmospheric nuclear tests in response to Khrushchev's decision to do the same. (A voluntary moratorium on such tests had been observed by the United States, the Soviet Union and Great Britain since 1958.)

In mid-February 1962 two Harvard students active in the Cambridge peace group Tocsin, Peter C. Goldmark, Jr., and Todd Gitlin, organized a march on Washington that brought, by varying accounts, four thousand to eight thousand demonstrators to stand outside the White House in a blinding snowstorm. The protestors distributed a document calling for an end to nuclear testing, an end to the civil defense program and the unilateral removal of American intermediate-range ballistic missiles (IRBMs) from Turkey. Kennedy sent out a White House butler with an urn of coffee for the freezing demonstrators and allowed Mac Bundy to meet with a few of their leaders in his White House basement office. Gitlin felt the meeting degenerated into "a dialogue of the moral with the deaf." Bundy came off as condescending, telling

---

* On May 10, 1962, President Eisenhower told Mac Bundy and CIA director John McCone that if troops were sent to Laos, "he would follow them up with whatever support was necessary to achieve the objectives of the mission, including—if necessary—the use of tactical nuclear weapons" (Michael Forrestal, SECRET EYES ONLY Memo, May 11, 1962).

his earnest young visitors that while he applauded the demonstrators for providing a "counterweight" to the "cold warriors" in Washington, they had to understand that "politics is the art of the possible." On the issues at hand, he defended Kennedy's policies, including the civil defense program. Goldmark, who would become president of the Rockefeller Foundation in 1988, later grumbled that Bundy hadn't even bothered to read their policy statement.[117]

In private, Bundy had a healthy skepticism for civil defense. He once sardonically told the syndicated columnist Joseph Kraft, "There are many who appear to think that the way to win the Cold War is to move it underground."[118] But he had not put up a fight when Kennedy decided to ask Congress for $207 million for a national civil defense program.* Similarly, he could quip, "The law of diminishing returns applies to strategic missiles as to all other commodities"—and then turn around and support Kennedy's decision to build one thousand missiles, double the number he considered necessary to achieve deterrence.[119] It was easy to see why such a man could prove to be so infuriating to left-of-center intellectuals in the early 1960s. He knew and understood, and sometimes even accepted, the intellectual integrity of their arguments, but on grounds of pragmatism—or simple political expediency—he supported the status quo.

ALTHOUGH Mac had surrounded himself with lively, opinionated men, he could not tolerate having their views made public. In the spring of 1962 the volume of essays Marc Raskin had edited for Congressman Kastenmeier's Liberal Project was published under the title *The Liberal Papers*. The book rapidly became a minor best-seller, selling 30,000 copies, and created a furor on Capitol Hill. Conservative politicians like Republican Senators Barry Goldwater of Arizona and Everett Dirksen of Illinois charged that the book's agenda was appeasement and unilateral disarmament. The Republican Party prepared a campaign brochure with damaging quotations from the book. It quickly became apparent that anyone associated with the book would be tarred as a radical.

Bundy, of course, knew many of the authors quite well. He liked and respected David Riesman, and felt much the same regard for Michael Maccoby, his former assistant from his years as Harvard dean. These and other authors Bundy knew by reputation as serious scholars outlined some provocative ideas; the goal of disarmament was taken seriously, deterrence theory was questioned, an argument was made for admitting Communist China to the United

---

* Bundy the historian would later write in *Danger and Survival* (New York: Random House, 1988), p. 355, that Kennedy's civil defense program was "unwisely" announced "with inadequate preparation" in the president's July 1961 speech on the Berlin crisis. This, he concludes, needlessly alarmed Americans and made it seem as if the program was a response to imminent danger. "Civil defense," he writes, "is not a reinforcement of deterrence," but merely an insurance policy.

Nations, and policies for strengthening the United Nations were outlined. One author predicted that the Cold War "will henceforth be waged on economic and ideological, rather than military, battlegrounds . . ." and therefore it would be in Washington's interest to "de-emphasize military aid" to countries like Laos and South Vietnam. Bundy did not think any of these arguments were illegitimate per se, but after previewing the book prior to its publication he told Carl Kaysen, "Either Marc takes his name off the book or he has to leave the staff." Raskin took his name off the book. Still, as the controversy brewed, word leaked around town that one of Bundy's own NSC staffers had edited the book.

In a memo to the president in late April, Bundy reported, "That young menace, Marcus Raskin, has returned from Geneva [where he had been attending disarmament talks with the Soviets] . . . you may be curious about Raskin, who has been a good staff officer in spite of—and perhaps partly because of—his insistent effort to find ways of making progress in this most unpromising field [disarmament]." Based on his private conversations with members of the Russian delegation, Raskin was then bucking the conventional wisdom by reporting that a deal could be cut on a test ban treaty. (An atmospheric test ban treaty would be agreed to a little more than a year later.) Bundy then advised Kennedy that "critics of the *Liberal Papers* may be trying to focus attention on Raskin, and in that event we may have a small fuss. If he comes under that kind of fire, I would much rather keep him and ride it out than try to move him on a basis that would be misunderstood . . . we will probably know better in a week or two which way the wind is likely to blow." [120]

The wind blew against Raskin. Late that spring Raskin noticed that his end-of-the-day chats with Bundy had ceased abruptly. Weeks went by, then Bundy called him into his office and said, "It just isn't working out." Though his firing was not unexpected, Raskin was saddened and yet also as ambivalent as Bundy was about their relationship. "He liked me very much," Raskin later said, "and I liked him. He was funny and smart. We had a good thing, but the differences were profound. We weren't singing from the same hymnbooks." [121]

By the summer, Raskin had been quietly shunted over to the Bureau of the Budget (though still on the NSC's payroll), where he worked on education policy. By the end of the year, he had left government altogether to co-found the Institute for Policy Studies, a left-of-center think tank. Initially, Bundy's liberalism was inclusive enough to tolerate someone with Raskin's political views. Intellectually, he was both entertained and intrigued by someone who could question some of the holy grails of the Cold War. But as a pragmatist, Bundy practiced a liberalism that was all about what was politically possible in a conservative era. For the remainder of the 1960s, men like Raskin would drift into what became known as the New Left; in a few years, as America's involvement in the Vietnam War deepened, Raskin would stand trial for abetting draft evasion. For Bundy, it may well have been a tragedy that this troublesome twenty-six-year-old was no longer by his side to serve as his "conscience."

By the autumn of 1961, with the Berlin crisis receding, Vietnam suddenly became a priority in Mac Bundy's in-box. Never very stable, the regime of Ngo Dinh Diem seemed to be falling apart from within just as the Viet Cong insurgency was growing to battalion-strength operations. That September, President Kennedy sent his White House military adviser, General Maxwell Taylor, and Walt Rostow, by then chairman of the Policy Planning Council at the State Department, to Saigon for an overview of the situation. They came back with a report filled with disturbing facts about Diem's political and military incompetency, but they nevertheless recommended a limited military commitment of some eight thousand American troops. McNamara and the Joint Chiefs responded that if military intervention was contemplated, the administration should be willing to do whatever was necessary to defend South Vietnam. In their estimate, this might mean 205,000 ground troops. A debate ensued within the administration.

Kennedy was very skeptical. "It will be just like Berlin," he told Schlesinger. "The troops will march in, the bands will play, the crowds will cheer, and in four days everyone will have forgotten. Then we will be told we have to send in more troops. It's like taking a drink. The effect wears off, and you have to take another." [122]

At one point, Bill Bundy weighed into the debate with a one-page memo addressed to McNamara: "For what one man's feel is worth, mine—based on very close touch with Indochina in the 1954 war and civil war afterwards till Diem took hold—is that it is really now or never if we are to arrest the gains being made by the Viet Cong." Bill knew far more about the French defeat in Indochina than his brother Mac; he understood that Vietnam was one nation, if not one country, and he also knew that "*all* depends on Diem's effectiveness, which is very problematical." Yet, he found a way of talking himself into a recommendation for intervention: "An early and hard-hitting operation has a good chance (70% would be my guess) of *arresting* things and giving Diem a chance to do better and clean up. . . . The 30% chance is that we would wind up like the French in 1954; white men can't win this kind of fight." Still, "On a 70–30 basis, I would myself favor going in." But if a month goes by, he warned, the odds would slip sharply down to 50 percent.

This was peculiar advice. Bill was profoundly pessimistic. Intervention with U.S. combat troops would probably only "arrest" the deterioration of Diem's regime, and even then these "white men" might well wind up like the French. But he was nevertheless willing to risk it.[123]

The debate within the administration stretched into November. John Kenneth Galbraith, who happened to be back briefly from his post as ambassador to India, derided Walt Rostow's proposal to send U.S. troops under the guise of a flood control program as "half-baked intervention." Galbraith subsequently noted in his diary, "Mac thinks there is no occasion when I would urge the use of force. I have to admit that my enthusiasm for it is always very low." [124] On his way back to New Delhi in late November, Galbraith dropped into Saigon and sent Bundy and Kennedy a blistering nine-page cable. Galbraith agreed that the Viet Cong were strengthening their hold on the countryside. But he cautioned, "We must not forever be guided by those who misunderstand the dynamics of revolution and imagine that because the communists do not appeal to us they are abhorrent to everyone." The United States had "unquestionably exaggerated" the role of external support to the guerrillas: ". . . the amount of ammunition and weaponry that a man can carry on his back for several hundred kilometers over jungle trails was not increased appreciably by [Karl] Marx." (Indeed, the CIA later concluded that at this stage of the war most of the Viet Cong's weapons were captured from their adversaries.) The "key and inescapable point," Galbraith wrote, was "the ineffectuality (abetted debatedly by the unpopularity) of the Diem government." Diem was not going to reform ". . . because he cannot. It is politically naive to expect it. He senses that he cannot let power go because he would be thrown out." The only solution in this "hopeless game" was "to drop Diem." Though not ideal, Galbraith wrote, "We should not be alarmed by the army as an alternative. . . ." A military regime might "buy time and get a fresh dynamic." In any case, the time would inevitably come when it would be clear to all in Washington that Diem has not carried out the promised reforms and American "troops will be urged to back up Diem." Needless to say, Galbraith observed, "It will be sufficiently clear that I think this must be resisted. Our soldiers would not deal with the vital weakness. They could perpetuate it . . . there can't be enough of them to give security to countryside. . . ."

Well aware that such advice would be falling on unsympathetic ears, Galbraith added this strikingly emotional appeal: ". . . it is those of us who have worked in the political vineyard and who have committed our hearts most strongly to the political fortunes of the New Frontier who worry most about its bright promise being sunk under the rice fields." And knowing of Bundy's predilections for an Achesonian toughness, Galbraith went on to observe that in similar circumstances, "[John Foster] Dulles in 1954 saw the dangers in this area. Dean Acheson knew he could not invest men in Chiang [Kai-shek]." [125]

Bundy was unmoved. When he finally got around to responding to Galbraith with a personal letter in December, he reprimanded him for using "Acheson's techniques on an anti-Acheson position." He pleaded with him to moderate his mood. Galbraith noted in his diary that he had received "a rather sharp letter from McGeorge Bundy complaining that I have been insufficiently pleasant to some of the more pompous people in Washington. He says that both Rusk and Alexis Johnson have come to suspect that I do not have a very high regard for them. This does credit to their perception." [126] Galbraith did not care if he was burning his bridges within the bureaucracy. He had a direct line to the president and Bundy.

Shortly before receiving Galbraith's dissent on Vietnam, Mac was swimming with the president in the White House indoor pool when Kennedy bluntly asked him what they ought to do about Vietnam. Bundy replied that he would compose an answer on paper, and a day or two later a carefully worded memo appeared on Kennedy's desk. "I believe," wrote Bundy, "we should commit *limited* U.S. combat units, if necessary for *military* purposes (not for morale), to help save South Vietnam." Bundy's reasoning was complicated. He argued that sending combat troops had "become a sort of touchstone of our will." Why not, therefore, pledge one division? After all, "the odds are almost even that the commitment will not have to be carried out." He saw the danger of committing combat troops for something as nefarious as morale boosting. Yet he felt the more limited actions proposed so far—an increase in the number and training of South Vietnamese troops and the adoption of different tactics—might not succeed without the prior U.S. commitment to send its own combat troops. "A victory here," argued Bundy, "would produce great effects all over the world. A defeat would hurt, but not much more than a loss of South Vietnam with the levels of U.S. help now committed or planned." Since the U.S. Army commander on the ground was not now urging the use of American combat troops, a mere pledge for their use in the future, if necessary, was not a hard decision.

But why South Vietnam? Why should a line be drawn in the sand here? Why not in Laos? Bundy had an answer: South Vietnam, he argued, stands "on a footing wholly different from Laos. Laos was never really ours after 1954. South Vietnam is and wants to be. Laotians have fought very little. South Vietnam troops are not U.S. Marines, but they are usable." [127]

The logic was seductive, yet, in the end, Kennedy managed to resist. That autumn he refused to send combat troops. But in the months ahead he quietly authorized the gradual introduction of many more military advisers. This suggests that he accepted Bundy's argument with one major exception: he did not want to publicize his decision.

This fall 1961 debate on Vietnam was revisited in the spring of 1962 when Galbraith sent Kennedy yet another missive on the subject. Even from the distance of his ambassadorial perch in India, Galbraith was alarmed by the trend of events. "We have a growing military commitment," Galbraith warned. "This could expand step by step into a major, long-drawn out indecisive military involvement. We are backing a weak and, on the record, ineffectual government and a leader who as a politician may be beyond the point of no return. There is a consequent danger we shall replace the French as the colonial force in the area and bleed as the French did."

Galbraith's prescription was "to keep the door open for [a] political solution." He proposed several negotiating tactics which might induce Hanoi to agree to a standstill in Viet Cong activity in return for a phased American withdrawal and an agreement "to talk about reunification after some period of tranquillity." The Indian government, he wrote, could be asked to make that approach to Hanoi. "In the meantime policy should *continue* to be guided by the following: (1) We should resist all steps which commit American troops to combat action. . . . (2) We should disassociate ourselves from action, however necessary, which seems to be directed at the villagers, such as the new concentration program [a reference to the U.S.-sponsored strategic hamlets program]. . . . Americans in their various roles should be as invisible as the situation permits." [128]

Two days later President Kennedy discussed Galbraith's memo in a meeting with Averell Harriman and Michael V. Forrestal, Mac Bundy's new deputy for Far Eastern affairs. According to Forrestal's classified notes of the meeting, the president and Harriman agreed that "it was important that the overt association of the U.S. with military operations in Vietnam be reduced to absolute minimum." On the other hand, Harriman said he was not in favor of reconvening the Geneva Conference and disagreed with Galbraith's implied notion of seeking a "neutral solution" in Vietnam. Kennedy nevertheless expressed interest in exploring Galbraith's suggestion that the Indian government might serve as a conduit to negotiations with Hanoi. The meeting ended with Forrestal noting, "The President observed generally that he wished us to be prepared to seize upon any favorable moment to reduce our involvement, recognizing that the moment might yet be some time away." [129] Clearly—at least at this moment in early 1962—Kennedy was seeking an escape route out of Vietnam.*

By the end of 1961, Bundy's characteristic self-confidence had taken a battering. One crisis had followed another and none seemed to have a decisive ending. Fidel Castro was still a problem, and the situations in Berlin, Laos and Vietnam were filled with more ambiguity than Bundy liked. None of these festering issues were likely to disappear, and absent military intervention—which he realized the president shunned—Bundy increasingly looked to the CIA to provide him with alternatives.

As the president's national security adviser, Bundy's duties included chairing the meetings of the 5412 Committee, or Special Group, which supervised all covert operations for the president. Bundy approved literally dozens of such operations, including Operation Mongoose, the effort to dislodge Castro's regime. Bundy recruited Brigadier General Edward G. Lansdale, the legendary counterinsurgency veteran, to run the operation. Mongoose quickly ballooned into a $50 million a year project.

In the course of five years in the White House, Bundy learned that accountability was an elusive quality in the intelligence business. "It can happen," he later testified, "and I think it has happened that an operation is presented in one way to a committee [the 5412 Committee] and executed in a

---

* Forrestal's classified notes—heretofore unpublished—represent the only contemporaneous documentary evidence that Kennedy "wished . . . to reduce our involvement" in Vietnam.

way that is different from what the committee thought it had authorized." But at the time, there was an inclination—despite the Bay of Pigs—to turn to the CIA when someone wanted something done. Early on, Kennedy told him, "I don't care what it is, but if I need something fast, the C.I.A. is the place I go. . . ." Many covert operations spun out of control in Laos, Cuba, the Congo, the Dominican Republic, Tibet and a half-dozen other hot spots in the Cold War. Bundy was involved in all of them.

Some of these operations included contingency planning for assassinating foreign adversaries. In 1975 the U.S. Senate heard testimony from William Harvey, a legendary CIA operative, that Richard Bissell had told him that "the White House" had twice urged the creation of an "Executive Action Project." Subsequently, a project code-named ZR/RIFLE was established, and one agent with the cryptonym QJ/WIN was assigned to work under Harvey's supervision. ZR/RIFLE was later described in a CIA inspector general's report as a project to research means for overthrowing foreign leaders, including the "capability to perform assassinations."

In 1975, Mac Bundy confirmed to the Senate Select Committee to Study Government Operations with Respect to Intelligence Activities chaired by Democratic Senator Frank Church that Richard Bissell had briefed him sometime in early 1961 on the CIA's assassination capabilities, but because no target was mentioned, he did not "discourage or dissuade" Bissell. Though they were talking about "killing the individual," Bundy told congressional investigators that he thought the Agency was merely "testing my reaction," not "seeking authority." "I am sure I gave no instruction. But it is only fair to add that I do not recall that I offered any impediment either." So far as he could recall, Bundy testified, he had not informed President Kennedy about his conversation with Bissell. He felt he did not need to "pursue the matter at all" because "this was not an operational activity, and would not become such without two conditions: first, that there be a desire or a request or a guidance that there should be planning against a specific individual; and second, that there should be a decision to move against the individual." [130]

Bundy was ready to discuss the CIA's assassination capabilities in the abstract, but he always claimed ignorance of its attempts to assassinate Fidel Castro. Bissell testified that he never briefed Bundy on the Castro operation. On the other hand, Bundy admitted that he had a "very vague, essentially refreshed, recollection that I heard the word 'poison' at some point in connection with a possibility of action in Cuba. But that is as far as I have been able to take it in my own memory." The proposal to use poison had seemed "impractical" to him because it would involve killing "a large group of people in a headquarters mess, or something of that sort." [131]

None of the CIA's many schemes to assassinate Castro came to fruition, but on May 30, 1961, the right-wing dictator of the Dominican Republic, Rafael Trujillo, was gunned down by the "action" arm of a group of Dominican dissidents who had been in close contact with the CIA. Bundy and the Special

WILLIAM PUTNAM BUNDY
September 24, 1917

Form Secretary '32
Form Councillor '30
Hockey Squad '31, '33, '34, '35
Soccer Team '32, '33; Co-Captain '34
Second Form Chronicle
Editor-in-Chief *Third Form Weekly*
Grotonian
YEAR BOOK
Debating Team '35
Missionary Society '34; Secretary-Treasurer '35
Secretary Civics Club
Librarian

Boston, Mass.   Yale

Groton School Year Book, 1935

McGEORGE BUNDY

School Prefect
Tennis Team '35, '36
Soccer Team '34, '35
School Wall-Scaling Team '35, '36
Dramatic Association, '35, President, '36
Sixth Form Players
Grotonian, Editor-in-Chief
Third Form Weekly
Choir '32, '33
Bell-Ringer
Debating Team '35; Captain '36
Secretary-Treasurer Athletic Association
Assistant Treasurer Athletic Store
Missionary Society
Junior Debating Society, Captain of Ciceros
Civics Club

Boston, Mass.   Yale

Groton School Year Book, 1936

Family and Groton

Above: Katharine Bundy and children *(left to right, top)* Harvey Jr., McGeorge, William, and *(front)* Laurie and Harriet, circa 1935. *(Courtesy of Bundy family)*

Left: Dr. Endicott Peabody, headmaster of the Groton School from 1884 to 1940, educated his boys with a stringent program of "muscular Christianity." *(Groton School Archives)*

Below left: William Bundy, twenty-one, Yale Class of 1939.

Below right: McGeorge Bundy, twenty-one, Yale Class of 1940. *(Both, Yale University)*

Katharine and Harvey Bundy, circa 1940s. *(Courtesy of Bundy family)*

Harvey Bundy, Secretary of War Henry L. Stimson and an American general in France in July 1944. *(National Archives)*

1940s

Lieutenant William Bundy at Bletchley Park, England, where he led a team of American cryptologists in helping to break the German cipher Ultra, the war's most closely guarded secret. *(Courtesy of Bundy family)*

Admiral Alan Kirk decorates Captain McGeorge Bundy for his service as Kirk's intelligence officer aboard the heavy cruiser *Augusta* during the Allied invasion of Normandy in June 1944. *(National Archives)*

In 1953, at the age of thirty-four, McGeorge Bundy was appointed dean of Harvard College, where he diversified the faculty and student body. While he defended the university from McCarthyism, he also fired some untenured faculty who refused to "name names" to the FBI. *(AP/Wide World Photos)*

In 1953, at the age of thirty-six, William Bundy was already a high-ranking officer in the CIA. A year later, his career was briefly put on hold when Senator Joseph McCarthy learned that Bundy had contributed $400 to the Alger Hiss defense fund. *(UPI/Corbis-Bettmann)*

1950s

In April 1959, Cuba's premier, Fidel Castro, was introduced to a Harvard audience by Dean McGeorge Bundy (seated to the right). "I couldn't get anywhere with him," Bundy said. Within three years, he would preside in White House meetings where the elimination of Castro—by invasion or assassination—was high on the agenda. *(AP/Wide WorldPhotos)*

Left: Soviet Premier Nikita Khrushchev greets President Kennedy at the beginning of their stormy summit meeting in Vienna in June 1961. Afterward, Kennedy told an aide, "all of us know that Germany will probably never be reunited." *(Stanley Tretick/Look)*

Left below: McGeorge and Mary Bundy inspect the Berlin Wall in September 1962. *(AP/Wide World Photos)*

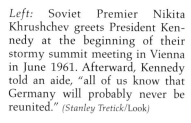

Kennedy Years

Right: President John F. Kennedy and his national security adviser, McGeorge Bundy, consulted daily on foreign policy issues ranging from the Cuban missile crisis to the Vietnam War. *(JFK Library)*

Below: South Vietnam's President Ngo Dinh Diem was assassinated on November 2, 1963, during a military coup approved by President Kennedy and his national security adviser, McGeorge Bundy.

Bottom: On November 29, 1963, just a week after President Kennedy's assassination, William Bundy *(left)* was sworn into office as assistant secretary of defense by Defense Secretary Robert McNamara *(right)*. Bundy's former boss, Paul Nitze *(center)*, became secretary of the navy. *(Two photos: UPI/Corbis-Bettmann)*

Mentors

OPPOSITE:

Top: Dean Acheson *(left)* and soon-to-be-confirmed Supreme Court Justice Felix Frankfurter were two of the Bundy brothers' most powerful mentors.

Center: J. Robert Oppenheimer, the brilliant physicist who directed the Manhattan Project during World War II, convinced McGeorge Bundy that the riven atom was in the long run a "growing menace to us all."

Bottom: Walter Lippmann, America's most influential columnist, once urged John F. Kennedy to appoint McGeorge Bundy as his secretary of state. Lippmann later was disturbed to learn that Bundy was "much more pro-war than I knew." *(Five photos: AP/Wide World Photos)*

Right top: Pulitzer Prize–winning poet Archibald MacLeish was a long-time family friend and mentor to both Bundy brothers.

Right bottom: Syndicated columnist Joseph Alsop—shown here waiting for a plane in Laos—was one of McGeorge Bundy's closest friends, but they disagreed about Vietnam. Bundy complained to President Lyndon Johnson: "I think he [Alsop] really wants to have a little old war out there."

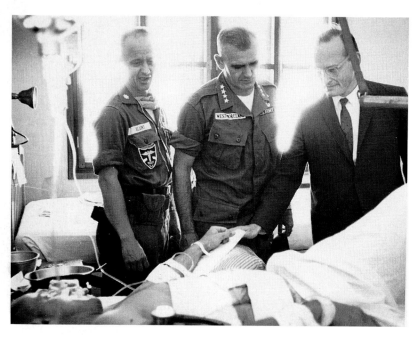

Vietnam

Above: McGeorge Bundy with General William Westmoreland at a field hospital in South Vietnam after the February 1965 Viet Cong attack on U.S. military installations at Pleiku. Bundy recommended a program of sustained bombing of North Vietnam and later told a reporter, "Pleikus are like streetcars." *(AP/Wide World Photos)*

Left: McGeorge Bundy and South Vietnam's Premier General Nguyen Khanh in South Vietnam, February 1965, shortly before the start of Operation Rolling Thunder, the sustained bombing of North Vietnam. *(UPI/Corbis-Bettmann)*

Right: President Lyndon Johnson consults with his press aide, Bill Moyers, and McGeorge Bundy, who recommended that Moyers succeed him as national security adviser.

Below: Guy J. Pauker, Zbigniew Brzezinski and McGeorge Bundy (with Eric Sevareid moderating in the middle) debate the Vietnam War with Hans Morgenthau, O. Edmund Clubb and John D. Donoghue on national television, June 21, 1965. Afterward, LBJ threatened to fire Bundy: "I'm not going in the liberal direction," Johnson yelled. "There's no future with them. They're just out to get me." *(Two photos: AP/Wide World Photos)*

With Mary at his side, McGeorge Bundy makes a point to LBJ at his farewell party in February 1966. Bundy left the White House supporting the war: "If the basic questions of interest, right and power are answered, the casualties and costs are to be accepted." *(Yoichi R. Okamoto, LBJ Library Collection)*

Vietnam

Left top: U.S. Ambassador Henry Cabot Lodge, South Vietnam's Premier Nguyen Cao Ky and Assistant Secretary of State William Bundy conferring in Saigon in March 1967. Bundy thought the Ky-Thieu regime was "absolutely the bottom of the barrel." *(AP/Wide World Photos)*

Center: The October 1967 March on the Pentagon. Although William Bundy tried to ignore the anti-war protestors, "They caused you personal pain because many of them were your friends." *(UPI/Corbis-Bettmann)*

Below: A November 2, 1967, meeting of the Wise Men: LBJ, Walt Rostow, Robert McNamara, McGeorge Bundy, John McCloy and others. Bundy told the president, "Getting out of Vietnam is as impossible as it is undesirable." *(Yoichi R. Okamoto, LBJ Library Collection)*

As president of the Ford Foundation from 1966 to 1979, McGeorge Bundy handed out millions of dollars to fund the most liberal and innovative programs he could find in the fields of civil rights, public television, the environment and public interest law. *(Bruce Davidson, Magnum Photos)*

McGeorge Bundy's plan for decentralization of New York City's public schools sparked a teachers' strike in September 1968. Joseph Alsop warned him that decentralization "opened the whole Pandora's box of race hatred in New York." *(AP/Wide World Photos)*

Mary and McGeorge Bundy at their Massachusetts summer home, circa 1995. *(Courtesy of Bundy family)*

In 1988, McGeorge Bundy published *Danger and Survival: Choices About the Bomb in the First Fifty Years.* He was working on a Vietnam memoir—"I had a part in a great failure"—when he died in September 1996. *(David Olds, UPI/Corbis-Bettmann)*

In 1998, William Bundy published *Tangled Web: The Making of Foreign Policy in the Nixon Presidency,* in which he wrote that Nixon and Kissinger "deceived" the "public, and especially Congress, far too often." *(©Jim Kalett, Council on Foreign Relations Archives)*

Group had been briefed on the planned coup attempt. And late in the game they learned that the Eisenhower administration had authorized the passing of a small number of carbines to the dissidents. Some of these carbines were in the possession of the assassination team, but it seems that Trujillo was killed with the use of handguns and shotguns. A decade later Bundy said with hindsight, "I had that serene confidence that we knew what was going on until the assassination stories began to appear years later." [132]

Mac brought a heavy dose of pragmatism to his supervision of covert operations. Whatever worked was fine. And even those operations that aides like Michael V. Forrestal advised him were dubious—like the cross-border raids into Tibet from Nepal by thousands of Tibetan guerrilla troops trained by the CIA in a secret army base in Colorado—were allowed to putter along so long as they didn't get out of hand. [133] Throughout 1962, Bundy approved covert counterinsurgency operations in Laos and Cambodia, the introduction of intelligence-gathering teams into mainland China and the insertion of sabotage teams into North Vietnam. But none of these paramilitary operations matched the scale of Operation Mongoose. By the summer of 1962, the Kennedy administration's covert efforts to eliminate Castro's regime were a secret only to the American people. In response, Khrushchev would soon decide to so increase the stakes that the Americans would find themselves on the brink of thermonuclear war.

10

The Cuban Missile Crisis

> ROBERT MCNAMARA: "I don't think there is a military problem here. This is my answer to Mac's question—"
>
> MCGEORGE BUNDY: "That's my honest judgment."
>
> MCNAMARA: "—and therefore, I've gone through this today, and I asked myself, Well, what is it then if it isn't a military problem? Well, it's just exactly this problem, that if Cuba should possess a capacity to carry out offensive actions against the U.S., the U.S. would act. . . . This is a domestic, political problem . . . we said we'd act. Well, how will we act?"
>
> BUNDY: "Yeah."
>
> ExComm Meeting, October 16, 1962

AT 8:30 P.M. ON MONDAY, October 15, 1962, Mac Bundy was hosting a dinner party at his home when he received a phone call from Ray Cline. The deputy director of intelligence at the CIA cryptically informed Bundy, "Those things we've been worrying about in Cuba are there." Bundy asked, "You're sure?" Cline was sure. A U-2 spy plane had just returned photographic evidence of Soviet medium-range missile sites in Cuba. Only the previous day Mac had told a nationwide TV audience that there was "no present evidence" and "no present likelihood" that the Soviets would install offensive weapons in Cuba. Yes, there were MiG fighters, and there may be additional military aircraft arriving on the island, but Bundy emphasized, "The United States is not going to be placed in any position of major danger to its own security by Cuba."[1] Now he had to tell Kennedy that he had been wrong, that the Soviets were indeed building missile bases on the Caribbean island.

Bundy knew right away that the news was political dynamite. In less than three weeks voters would be casting their ballots in a midterm congressional election in which Republicans had portrayed Kennedy as a weak Cold Warrior, a president standing by as communists made dramatic gains in Cuba,

Laos, Vietnam and Berlin. Only a week earlier the Republican senator from New York, Kenneth Keating, had charged that his own secret sources indicated that the Soviets were building six medium-range missile sites in Cuba. This had prompted Bundy's firm denial on Sunday. Obviously, the Republicans were going to have a field day if, come November, voters knew that a battery of Soviet nuclear-tipped missiles were dug in only ninety miles off the Florida coast.

Despite the momentous nature of "this very big news," Bundy calmly decided to return to his dinner guests without calling the president. He told Cline to prepare a briefing for Kennedy on the photographic evidence for the next morning. "It was a hell of a secret," Bundy later explained in a memo to Kennedy, "and it must remain one until you had a chance to deal with it . . . there should be no hastily summoned meeting Monday night." Mac also knew Kennedy was tired, having just returned from campaign appearances in Niagara Falls and New York City. "So I decided that a quiet evening and a night of sleep were the best preparation you could have in the light of what would face you in the next days."[2]

It was eight o'clock on Tuesday morning, October 16, when Bundy walked out of his basement office in the White House and took the elevator to the presidential living quarters. He found the president still wearing his pajamas and dressing gown, sitting in bed and reading the morning papers. Kennedy looked up and immediately launched into a familiar patter of wry commentary on the day's headlines. He was particularly annoyed that morning by a page-one story in the New York Times headlined "Eisenhower Calls President Weak on Foreign Policy."

"Mr. President," Bundy interrupted, "there is now hard photographic evidence, which you will see later, that the Russians have offensive missiles in Cuba." Kennedy's first reaction was to sputter, "He [Khrushchev] can't do that to me!"[3] An hour later Attorney General Robert Kennedy stormed into Bundy's office and asked to see the photo evidence. After a CIA analyst showed him the briefing boards and pointed out fourteen missiles, Bobby began pacing back and forth in Bundy's cramped office, pounding a fist into the palm of his hand and muttering, "Oh shit! Shit! Shit! Those sons a bitches Russians."[4] The president's campaign manager knew that these missiles posed a formidable political threat to the Kennedy presidency.

IN strict military terms Bundy and other senior Kennedy administration officials understood that in sheer numbers the United States possessed substantial strategic superiority over the Soviet Union. In October 1962, President Kennedy had at his command around 18,000 nuclear weapons of all kinds, including many thousands of nuclear-tipped artillery and mortar shells. About three thousand of these weapons could be counted as nontactical, strategic warheads. The United States had about 172 ICBM launchers and 1,450 long-range bombers to deliver these nuclear warheads on targets in the Soviet Union. In contrast, the Soviets had roughly twenty-four to forty-four ICBM launchers, about 250 strategic warheads and perhaps 200 long-range bombers. (The Soviets also had a substantial number of low-yield tactical nuclear weapons and a small number of intermediate-range ballistic missiles and submarine-launched ballistic missiles.) The exact figures in U.S. intelligence estimates were highly classified, but the fact of overwhelming American superiority had been explicitly advertised the previous year in a speech by Deputy Secretary of Defense Roswell L. Gilpatric, which Mac Bundy had helped to draft. McNamara had also publicly boasted in June 1962 that the American missile force was so large and so accurate that if it came to war the United States could afford to target only Soviet military installations, sparing the civilian population direct nuclear attacks. This implied that U.S. leaders thought they could pull off a successful first-strike attack. Such talk must have worried Soviet military planners. As the missile crisis began, Kennedy believed that the strategic gap was more than five to two against the Russians. Actually, it was more like nine to one.[5]

But did this mean that Kennedy could with any confidence order a first-strike nuclear attack on the Soviets? Hardly. Only a madman could have ordered such an attack, knowing for a certainty that it would have killed in excess of tens of millions of Soviet citizens—and in all probability, in retaliation, a few million Americans. However overwhelming the American first-strike attack capability was, any rational person would have to assume that at least a few Soviet missiles or bombers would survive to drop their deadly cargo on New York City or Washington, D.C., or Miami. Could any American president initiate such a holocaust knowing that a million—or even a half million—Americans would probably also die? As Robert McNamara later wrote, "No responsible political leader would expose his nation to such a catastrophe." Bundy later wrote much the same thing: ". . . if even one Soviet weapon landed on an American target, we would be the losers."[6]

In October 1962, John Kennedy engaged in a cautious but firm policy of nuclear brinkmanship, confident that the United States possessed both conventional and strategic superiority over the Soviets. We know from the most reliable of historical documents—verbatim transcripts of their deliberations—that the president repeatedly rejected any advice which he thought might lead to a nuclear exchange.[7] Kennedy and his advisers thought that if a full-scale war happened, it would be the result of either an accident or a terrible miscalculation. They counted on Nikita Khrushchev's basic rationality, believing that he understood neither side could resort to nuclear weapons. Only much later would Bundy realize that the game they had played had come much closer to an accidental nuclear exchange than they had thought possible.

ON that first day of the missile crisis, Tuesday, October 16, Kennedy chaired the first meeting of an executive committee, or ExComm, specially created to handle the crisis. The meeting began at 11:50 A.M. Present, among other officials, were Mac Bundy, Defense Secretary McNamara, General Maxwell Taylor (chairman of the Joint Chiefs of Staff), Treasury Secretary Douglas

Dillon, Vice President Lyndon Johnson, Attorney General Robert Kennedy and two CIA officials, Arthur C. Lundahl and Sidney Graybeal. The group met again that evening at 6:30 P.M. for an hour and a half. It is clear from these first two meetings that Bundy, McNamara and President Kennedy himself realized that the presence of Soviet missiles in Cuba did not substantially alter the strategic equation. But it is also clear that from the very beginning everyone assumed that the missiles had to be removed, either through a surprise air attack or by some combination of military and diplomatic pressure.

They speculated about why Khrushchev had surreptitiously placed missiles in Cuba, knowing that they would eventually be discovered.

Rusk: "I would not think that they would use a nuclear weapon unless they're prepared to (join?) a nuclear war. I don't think. I just don't . . . see that possibility."

Bundy interjected, "I agree." Then Mac got to the heart of the issue by asking, "What is the strategic impact on the position of the United States of MRBMs [medium-range ballistic missiles] in Cuba? How gravely does this change the strategic balance?"

McNamara: "Mac, I asked the chiefs [Joint Chiefs] that this afternoon, in effect. And they said, substantially. My own personal view is, not at all."

Bundy: "Not so much."

General Maxwell Taylor then said, ". . . Mr. President. You're quite right in saying that these, these are just a few more missiles targeted on the United States. However, they can become a very, a rather important adjunct and reinforcement to the strike capability of the Soviet Union. . . ."

Kennedy observed that ". . . you may say it doesn't make any difference if you get blown up by an ICBM flying from the Soviet Union or one that was ninety miles away. Geography doesn't mean that much." He then paused and said something astounding: "Last month I should have said, we're—that we don't care. But when we said we're not going to and then they go ahead and do it, and then we do nothing, then. . . ." What he meant was that he now wished he had not made a public statement about not tolerating offensive weapons in Cuba. The president now felt boxed in: "What difference does it make? They've got enough to blow us up now anyway. I think it's just a question of—after all this is a political struggle as much as military." The real problem was one of appearances, or as Kennedy put it, "It makes them [the Soviets] look like they're co-equal with us. . . ."[8]

LATER in that same evening discussion, after the group had discussed in great detail when and how to launch air strikes against the missile sites, McNamara insisted that his colleagues consider what he called a "political approach."

McNamara: ". . . I'll be quite frank. I don't think there is a military problem here. This is my answer to Mac's question—"

Bundy: "That's my honest judgment."

McNamara: "—and therefore, I've gone through this today, and I asked myself, Well, what is it then if it isn't a military problem? Well, it's just exactly this problem, that if Cuba should possess a capacity to carry out offensive actions against the U.S., the U.S. would act. . . . This is a domestic political problem . . . we said we'd act. . . . Well, how will we act?"

Bundy said, "Yeah," meaning he agreed with McNamara.

McNamara then suggested a solution: "Well, first place, we carry our open surveillance, so we know what they're doing. All times. Twenty-four hours a day from now and forever. . . . What else do we do? We prevent any further offensive weapons coming in. In other words, we blockade offensive weapons."

Bundy: "How do we do that?"

McNamara: "We search every ship."

Thus was born the strategy that Kennedy ultimately adopted. It would prove to be messy, but as McNamara said a few moments later, "Now this alternative doesn't seem to be a very acceptable one, but wait until you work on the others."

Thus, two of the president's most influential advisers—McNamara and Bundy—agreed that the missile crisis was essentially a domestic political problem and not a wholly new military threat. Certainly, the missiles were not worth risking a nuclear war over, but at the same time the political threat was such that one way or another the missiles had to come out.

Off and on throughout the next few days, Bundy repeatedly raised the possibility of a limited air strike, one that would try to take out the Soviet missiles without going on to bomb Cuban airfields and other military installations. He argued on the evening of October 16 that the "political advantages are very strong, it seems to me, of the small strike . . . the punishment fits the crime in political terms . . . we are doing only what we warned repeatedly and publicly we would have to do."[9] Kennedy agreed.

Speculating about why Khrushchev had done something so provocative, Rusk recalled that CIA director John McCone had suggested some weeks ago that the Soviet leader "knows that we have a substantial nuclear superiority, but he also knows that we don't really live under the fear of his nuclear weapons to the extent that he has to live under fear of ours. Also we have nuclear weapons nearby, in Turkey and places like that."*

This was not the last time anyone mentioned the obvious similarity between the missiles in Cuba and the medium-range ballistic missiles the United States had stationed in Turkey. Later that same evening, in the second ExComm meeting, Kennedy said of the Cuban missiles, "It's just as if we

---

* In Moscow on October 24, Khrushchev told a visiting American businessman an old Russian fable: Falling on hard times, an old peasant had been forced to live in a stable with his goat. Try as he might the peasant never liked the stench of the goat. But he learned to tolerate it. We Russians, Khrushchev said, have learned to tolerate the stench of the American nuclear goat, and now you Americans will have to do the same.

suddenly began to put a major number of MRBMs in Turkey. Now that'd be goddamn dangerous, I would think."

"Well, we did, Mr. President," responded Bundy.[10] Kennedy seemed to have momentarily forgotten about the Turkish deployment. While President Eisenhower had authorized the shipment of Jupiter medium-range ballistic missiles to Turkey, Kennedy had actually approved their installation. The Jupiters became operational in March or April 1962. Ironically, April was the same month in which Khrushchev, brooding about the Jupiters in Turkey, had decided to explore the option of deploying his own medium range missiles to Cuba.[11]

THE next morning, Wednesday, October 17, Bundy sat in on CIA director John McCone's briefing of the president. A conservative Republican who had replaced Allen Dulles in the aftermath of the Bay of Pigs fiasco, McCone had blunt advice for Kennedy: "Take Cuba away from Castro."[12]

Later that morning Dean Acheson began attending the ExComm meetings. He favored an air strike, but to his annoyance he found himself being challenged by Bobby Kennedy, a young man he thought both foolish and inexperienced. Bombing Cuba would be a "Pearl Harbor in reverse," said the attorney general. Acheson thought that was nonsense. He had in mind another defining metaphor of his generation—Munich and appeasement. This generational clash between Acheson and Bobby Kennedy would become a recurrent theme in the ExComm discussions. Acheson spewed fire and brimstone, while Bobby Kennedy increasingly dominated the discussions. Acheson quickly made himself irrelevant, while Bobby would soon begin secretly negotiating the deal—behind the backs of Acheson, McCone, Johnson and others—that would end the confrontation.

Interestingly, the Bundy brothers found themselves in the middle of this generational clash: they were certainly closer in age to the thirty-seven-year-old Bobby, but their instincts were Achesonian.

When Acheson pressed his case for an air strike in another meeting that Wednesday with the president, McNamara told the president that an effective air strike could not be surgical and would in all probability lead to a full-scale American invasion. President Kennedy listened and gave no hint of his own inclinations. But when he repeated his brother Bobby's remark that bombing Cuba would be a "Pearl Harbor in reverse," Acheson interrupted to say that Pearl Harbor was an absurd analogy.[13] Obviously, it was going to be difficult to achieve any consensus among men as different as Dean Acheson and the Kennedys.

By Thursday, the third day of deliberation, the ExComm members were leaning toward a blockade, which was seen as the middle course between a limited air strike and an outright invasion. Bundy was uneasy and said he thought it was too soon to settle on any one response. That evening, as he was having a cocktail with his wife before returning to the White House for another ExComm session, Mary told him, "I hope you all will choose the least violent course you can." Bundy took this admonition to heart. Later that evening, according to Ted Sorensen, "somewhat to everyone's surprise, Mac Bundy urged that we not overlook the justification of no action at all." Mary's comment had reminded Bundy that there really was no military threat that would require the use of force, so why go to the brink? Why not explore a simple, low-key diplomatic response? His colleagues were unimpressed. "Everybody jumped down my throat," Bundy recalled.[14] Everyone agreed the missiles had to come out—for domestic political reasons—and no one was convinced that the missiles could be brought out by negotiations alone. By the end of the meeting, Bundy was even skeptical that a blockade would succeed. Nevertheless, when a vote was taken, he voted with the majority, eleven to six, for a blockade over an air strike.

Pushed largely by Bobby Kennedy, the ExComm members were moving toward a blockade, but there was still not the consensus the president wanted. And now Bundy would appear to change his mind. The next morning, Friday, October 19, John Kennedy entered the Oval Office where Bundy, Acheson, General Taylor and the Joint Chiefs were waiting. The military brass wanted approval for a large air strike—with a total of eight hundred individual sorties —to take out the missiles. And they wanted it now. Time was running out, the secret would soon leak, and they argued that even if he ordered the air strike immediately, it could not be launched until Monday, the twenty-second. Bundy indicated his support for the plan, even though the previous evening he had voted for a naval blockade. According to Sorensen, Kennedy was "a bit disgusted" and impatient that Bundy had changed his mind. Before opting for a blockade, however, Kennedy felt he needed to establish a record that the Joint Chiefs had been fully consulted and approved his decision. He needed a consensus and he expected Bundy to guide the ExComm meetings toward that consensus. Instead, here was Bundy prolonging the debate, giving the hawks a chance to revive their arguments on behalf of an air strike. As Sorensen later recalled, "it was not one of Bundy's best weeks" and the president "didn't like it."[15]

With the country still unaware of the crisis, Kennedy left Washington to keep to his public campaign schedule, while the ExComm met again that Friday morning. In this meeting Bobby Kennedy pressed for a "quarantine" while Acheson, Taylor, McCone, Nitze and Dillon pushed for the air strike. Acheson argued that the missiles were not just Soviet missiles aimed at the United States: "Here they were in the hands of a madman [Castro] whose actions would be perfectly irresponsible. . . ."

To the surprise of his fellow ExComm members—at least those who had not attended the meeting with the Joint Chiefs earlier that morning—Bundy explained that he had changed his mind. Unable to sleep, he said he had thought all night about the blockade option and now felt that it was inadequate. He favored "decisive action," specifically, an air strike that would quickly and "surgically" take out the missiles. "An airstrike would be quick," Bundy said. He favored "confronting the world with a fait accompli." [16]

Thus, in a period of less than twenty-four hours, Bundy managed to make the argument for all three options: diplomacy, blockade and bombing. Obviously, his mind was not made up. To put it generously, he was still exploring all options; to put it less generously, Bundy was confused and deeply conflicted. Mac Bundy "did some strange flipflops," Bobby Kennedy later observed. "First he was for a strike, then a blockade, then for doing nothing because it would upset the situation in Berlin, and then, finally, he led the group which was in favor of a strike—and a strike without prior notification, along the lines of Pearl Harbor." Bobby scrawled these lines in some handwritten notes on October 31, 1962, soon after the crisis had receded, and at a time when he was still obviously annoyed with Bundy's behavior.[17]

At the very least, Bobby Kennedy and some of the other ExComm members were impatient with Bundy for dragging out their discussions with excursions on arguments they thought had already been settled. Emotions were high, and everyone was tired. Bundy felt Bobby was trying to impose a consensus where there was none, and then was implying that dissenters from this nonexistent consensus were somehow "deserters." Even years later Bundy bristled at the notion that he was breaking ranks with the president: "I thought I was getting paid to keep the argument going and make sure we got it right." He thought Bobby Kennedy "wasn't as good as somebody who took longer to make up his mind." [18]

At one point that morning, as tempers flared, Bobby again suggested that an air strike on Cuba would be reminiscent of Pearl Harbor: "A sneak attack was not in our traditions." Bundy instinctively distrusted moral arguments and he now responded rather testily that "this was very well but a blockade would not eliminate the bases; an air strike would." [19] With the meeting threatening to degenerate into open animosity, Rusk suggested the ExComm members break into two working groups, one headed by Vice President Johnson that would work out the details of a blockade scenario, the other to be chaired by Bundy to do the same for an air-strike scenario. After three hours the two groups reconvened and first took up the blockade scenario, which was dissected in detail for a full two hours. Only then did they turn to Bundy's air-strike option. Trying to lighten the atmosphere, Bundy joked that it had been "much more fun . . . to poke holes in the blockade plan. . . ." Significantly, they spent only thirty minutes discussing his air-strike scenario. Dillon, Acheson, Taylor and Bundy still favored an air strike without warning, but their arguments left everyone else unconvinced.[20]

In the years to come Bundy would tell friends he had only been playing devil's advocate, that he wanted to be sure the president heard all the arguments. "I was trying to keep the air strike alive," he recalled, "not so much because I was sure it was good, but because I wasn't a bit sure the blockade was good. . . ." His colleagues were certainly perplexed by his show of stubbornness. "I think he [Bundy] just grasped at this initial concept of an air strike," Roswell Gilpatric recalled, "and then he formulated arguments in support of it." Gilpatric was one of those who was annoyed by Bundy's behavior: "He tends to light initially on an absolute proposition . . . he's very intolerant of obfuscation and ambiguity and uncertainty."[21] Had Bundy's instincts made him side with the "hawks" against the "doves" led by Bobby Kennedy?* Perhaps.

But it was also true, as Bundy insisted, that the president had instructed him to keep the air-strike option open. A new document, never before published, makes this clear. In a memorandum written for his private files in March 1964, Bundy recorded,

> President Kennedy gave up the notion of a limited air strike against the Soviet missiles in Cuba only on the Sunday morning before his speech, very late in the game, and after specifically instructing me when he went away on his campaign trip West—on Friday, I think it was—to keep that option open as best I could. I didn't succeed in keeping it very open because the only allies I got for an air strike were people who wanted to strike everything that could fly in Cuba, and that wasn't exactly what the President had in mind. . . . he shared, in some degree at least, my fear that a quarantine would lead to a Berlin quarantine. In fact, we talked that over Thursday night because when he reached the first decision that he would buy the quarantine track—which had very powerful backing from all the people you could hear—I didn't sleep a bit well that Thursday night, and went up and saw him while he was dressing Friday morning and told him that I really thought this was very dangerous and uncertain and I wasn't sure it would bring an answer. He said, "Well, I'm having some of those same worries, and you know how my first reaction was the air strike. Have another look at that and keep it alive." Well, I mention this in this context because the more you thought about an air strike the more you could ask yourself what the natural counter to that was. And you were going to be in a very difficult position if the Soviets took out an equivalent number of European-based soft first-generation missiles. Were you going to make that a trigger for a NATO war? Not bloody likely. Then what had you done? You had put something in to defend somebody and all you had done was get them shot up."

This suggests that Bundy was quite aware of the drawbacks to both a quarantine and an air strike. But in the end, he realized that an air strike was

---

* The CIA's Ray Cline coined the terms "warhawks" and "Picasso doves" in a conversation with Bundy at this time. Bundy later passed these labels along to the columnists Stewart Aslop and Charles Bartlett, who popularized them.

the option that was most likely to cause the Soviets to respond in Europe. Was the Unites States eager to go to a nuclear war in Europe over Cuba? "Not bloody likely."*

It was clear that the president was inclined to cast his fortunes with the doves. Influenced by his brother Bobby, and by McNamara's argument that even the most surgical of air strikes could not guarantee the elimination of all the missiles, the president eventually settled on the blockade option. Even as he made the decision, John Kennedy was thinking about how it would affect the upcoming election. At the very end of the ExComm meeting on Sunday, October 21, he quietly said, "Well we've made our decision now. Quite frankly, I think it'll be an unpopular decision. I think we will lose votes. . . . But we've made the decision, and the thing to do is to stick with it and try to carry it through." Michael Forrestal, one of Bundy's aides, remembered Kennedy quoting the Chinese proverb "success has many fathers, but failure is an orphan." This was Jack Kennedy at his most fatalistic. The president's words, Forrestal said, "produced quite an emotional effect that made everybody in the room feel—Well, let there be an end to the debate." 22

WHILE Mac was totally absorbed with the crisis, his brother Bill found himself in the outer loop, getting his information secondhand from his boss, Paul Nitze. Throughout that first week of decision-making, Bill knew what was happening but had to act as if he didn't. He didn't even tell his wife: "It would only have perturbed her, so I didn't." By Saturday, October 20, he was in charge of procuring the military aircraft that would fly the president's emissaries to Paris and Bonn where De Gaulle and Adenauer would be briefed on the crisis. Bill was at a dinner party that evening in honor of his old friend Jim Rowe's twenty-fifth wedding anniversary. Bill spent the evening "jumping up and down like a jack-in-the-box through most of dinner . . . the lid was starting to come off, there were a lot of other dinner parties in Washington that night where people were behaving strangely." 23

On Monday evening, October 22, President Kennedy went on national television to inform the American people of the presence of Soviet missiles in Cuba and his intention to impose a naval quarantine around the island. It was a tough speech. Bundy recalled that he and his NSC staff "sure didn't feel as good as that speech sounded." For the next six days, many Americans—Bundy included—went home every night wondering if they would see another day.24

Khrushchev's initial response came in a letter to Kennedy dated October 24. He called the U.S. quarantine a "serious threat to peace" and stated that the weapons he had sent to Cuba were purely "defensive" and were intended to deter an American invasion. Kennedy replied with a terse note demanding

---

* This document was found among Bundy's papers after his death. An excerpt of the document was provided to the author by Professor Francis M. Bator on March 27, 1998.

that Khrushchev "issue immediately the necessary instructions to your ships to observe the terms of the quarantine. . . ." Khrushchev replied the next day with an extraordinarily personal letter. "Just imagine, Mr. President, that we had presented you with the conditions of an ultimatum which you have presented us by your action? How would you have reacted to this? I think that you would have been indignant. . . ." The Russian premier pointed out quite correctly that Kennedy's quarantine was "violating the universally accepted norms" of international sea law, and that he was doing so "not only out of hatred for the Cuban people and its government, but also because of considerations of the election campaign in the United States." Khrushchev ended by warning Kennedy that the Soviets would protect their rights against any "piratical acts by American ships. . . ." [25]

Yet, even as Khrushchev protested the unilateral character of Kennedy's actions, Soviet ships plowing their way toward Cuba on the high seas began to slow down or alter their course. Khrushchev was not a madman and did not intend to risk nuclear war. When the ExComm members heard an intelligence report that on Thursday morning, October 25, some of the Russian ships had stopped dead in the water, Rusk turned to Mac Bundy and said, "We are eyeball to eyeball, and the other fellow just blinked." [26] In fact, the crisis was far from over. Construction on the missile sites in Cuba continued at a frantic pace, and Bundy was told that some of the Soviet missiles already on the island would be fully operational within thirty-six hours.

Late that same week Bill Bundy sat down at his typewriter and pounded out a short memo for Nitze on a scrap of yellow legal pad paper. It was his "feeling," Bill wrote, that the Soviets were "nearer to finishing these installations than some people are saying, and we may have to think very hard about a preemptive air strike." *[27] Though Bill didn't know it, Mac was thinking along the same lines.

At the morning ExComm meeting on Friday, October 26, Kennedy had mused that he doubted the quarantine alone could produce a withdrawal of the missiles. The missiles would come out, he said, "only by invading Cuba or by trading." Perennial presidential adviser John McCloy, who had been invited by Kennedy to attend this particular ExComm meeting, echoed this view: the United States would have to "get them [the missiles] out or trade them out." (Private citizen McCloy had been assigned by Kennedy to assist Ambassador Adlai Stevenson in the negotiations with the Soviets at the United Nations.) [28]

By that Friday, Kennedy was worried that events were slipping from his control. He knew his generals were itching to get into a fight. And he feared someone lower down in the chain of command would do something that would push the crisis beyond the brink. Earlier that week, on Wednesday evening, McNamara and his deputy, Roswell Gilpatric, had gone down to Flag

* Of the forty-two medium-range missiles in Cuba, half would be ready to be fueled and mated with their warheads by October 28.

Plot, the navy's command center, to question Admiral George W. Anderson, Jr., the navy's chief of operations. How exactly, McNamara asked, did the navy propose to stop a ship if it violated the quarantine? Did each ship have aboard a Russian-speaking officer? Did the admiral understand that the point was not to inflict casualties or to humiliate Khrushchev?

Fighting to contain his anger at what he regarded as civilian interference, the red-faced Admiral Anderson picked up a copy of the navy regulations manual and said, "It's all in there."

"I don't give a damn what John Paul Jones would have done," McNamara retorted. "I want to know what you are going to do, now."

Anderson replied coldly, "Now, Mr. Secretary, if you and your deputy will go back to your offices, the Navy will run the blockade."

McNamara wheeled about and left the room, muttering to Gilpatric, "That's the end of Anderson. . . . As far as I'm concerned, he's lost my confidence." Bill Bundy and many others around Washington heard this story within hours, and presumably the president heard it, too.[29]

Late on Friday evening, October 26, Forrestal knocked on the door of the president's study, adjacent to his bedroom, and walked in to show Kennedy a message from the Situation Room. Forrestal later remembered the message saying something like, "Status Zebra has been ordered. All units have assembled to cobra area. Sixteen circuits have been activated." When Kennedy asked him what he thought it meant, Forrestal replied, "I think from what I've been told, it means we have done certain things, taken certain defensive measures, that the Soviets will know about very quickly and it will frighten them."

Kennedy replied, "That's right." And then he paused a moment before asking, "You think we're right—doing this?"

"Mr. President," Forrestal replied, "I don't know whether we're right or not."

"Well," Kennedy said, "I'm not sure I do either."[30]

Forrestal returned to the Situation Room deeply shaken by his conversation with the president.

That evening Khrushchev cabled a long rambling letter, proposing that in return for a U.S. pledge not to invade Cuba, the Soviets would declare that the "necessity of the presence of our military specialists in Cuba will disappear." In other words, a no-invasion pledge would remove the missiles. That same evening at 10 P.M. the ExComm met to consider this proposal, noting with satisfaction that Khrushchev had made no mention of the American missiles stationed in Turkey. Bundy and his colleagues retired thinking that the crisis would end the next day with an American acceptance of this deal.

The next morning, Saturday, October 27, Radio Moscow began broadcasting a second Khrushchev letter. In contrast to Khrushchev's personal message of the day before, this second letter was cold and formal, reflecting the collective voice of the Kremlin's apparatchiks. Now, Khrushchev was stating an additional condition for ending the crisis: a *public* trade of the Turkish and

Cuban missiles. To most of the hawks on the ExComm, a public trade was unacceptable.

The president turned to his advisers and said, "That wasn't in the [Friday] letter we received, was it?"

"It's very odd, Mr. President," Bundy replied. "If he's changed his terms from a long letter to you . . . only last night, set in a purely Cuban context, it seems to me . . . there's nothing wrong with our posture in sticking to that line. . . . I would answer back saying, 'I would prefer to deal with your . . . interesting proposals of last night.' "[31] After much discussion this was the tactic adopted in Kennedy's reply: he would ignore Khrushchev's Saturday letter and simply accept the proposal contained in the Friday letter.*

In the midst of this already tense Saturday meeting, word was received that a U-2 spy plane had strayed into Soviet airspace over Siberia. McNamara blanched white, and President Kennedy shook his head and said, "There is always some son of a bitch who doesn't get the word." An hour later, another U-2—piloted by Air Force Major Rudolf Anderson, Jr.—was shot down over Cuba. Clearly, things were getting out of hand. Kennedy's men assumed that the decision to fire on the U-2 had been made in Moscow. (In fact, the decision was made unilaterally by two Soviet commanders in Cuba who were later reprimanded.)[32]

In this tense atmosphere, with the crisis rapidly deteriorating, President Kennedy convened a rump meeting of his ExComm members to discuss the idea of having his brother Bobby go to Soviet ambassador Anatoly Dobrynin and offer him a private assurance on the Jupiters. According to Bundy in Danger and Survival, Bobby would be instructed to say that "while there could be no deal over the Turkish missiles, the president was determined to get them out and would do so once the Cuban crisis was resolved."

Bundy reported that "the proposal was quickly supported by the rest of us and approved by the president. It was also agreed that knowledge of this . . . would be held among those present and no one else . . . we agreed without hesitation that no one not in the room was to be informed of this additional message."[33] (Only Bobby Kennedy, Bundy, Rusk, McNamara, Sorensen, Under Secretary of State George Ball, veteran diplomat Llewellyn Thompson and Deputy Secretary of Defense Roswell Gilpatric were present.)

After Bundy's Danger and Survival was published in 1988, Dobrynin complained at a 1989 conference that Robert Kennedy's Thirteen Days and accounts by other American officials were disingenuous, that in fact there had been an explicit deal to trade the Turkish missiles. In response, Ted Sorensen said he had a confession to make to his colleagues: "I was the editor of Robert

---

* Kennedy's reply later became known as the Trollope ploy, named after the plot in an Anthony Trollope novel in which the heroine interprets a mere flirtation as a full-fledged offer of marriage. Though Bobby Kennedy claimed credit for the strategy in his book Thirteen Days, it was actually Bundy's idea.

Kennedy's book. It was, in fact, a diary of those thirteen days. And his diary was very explicit that this was part of the deal; but at the time it was still a secret even on the American side, except for the six [sic] of us who had been present at that meeting. So I took it upon myself to edit that out of the diaries...."[34]

It was not until 1994 that Dobrynin's top-secret memorandum of his conversation with Bobby Kennedy on Saturday, October 27, surfaced in a Moscow archive. It sheds even more light on what was the single most important meeting of the crisis. " 'I want,' R. Kennedy stressed, 'to lay out the current alarming situation the way the president sees it.' " Referring to the U-2 surveillance plane that had just been shot down, Bobby told Dobrynin that President Kennedy was under "strong pressure . . . to respond with fire. . . . But if we start to fire in response—a chain reaction will quickly start that will be very hard to stop. . . . A real war will begin, in which millions of Americans and Russians will die. We want to avoid that any way we can. . . ."

In an extraordinary admission—or in an effort to frighten the Soviets—Bobby then suggested that his brother might not be able to control his own generals: "(here R. Kennedy mentioned as if in passing that there are many unreasonable heads among the generals, and not only among the generals, who are 'itching for a fight'). The situation might get out of control, with irreversible consequences."

Bobby then outlined the deal: in return for eliminating the missiles from Cuba, the U.S. government would end the quarantine and promise not to invade Cuba.

"And what about Turkey?" Dobrynin asked Kennedy.

Bobby replied that "the president doesn't see any unsurmountable difficulties in resolving this issue." The only problem was that because the U.S. missiles in Turkey had been deployed by a decision of the NATO Council, the president couldn't unilaterally withdraw them without damaging "the entire structure of NATO."

"I think that in order to withdraw these bases from Turkey," Bobby said, "we need 4–5 months." In addition, President Kennedy could not say anything about the Turkish missiles in public. Bobby then warned Dobrynin that "his comments about Turkey are extremely confidential; besides him and his brother, only 2–3 people know about it in Washington."

Bobby left Dobrynin the number of a direct telephone line to the White House, and urged him to persuade Khrushchev to reply the next day. Dobrynin ended his report to Moscow with the observation that Bobby Kennedy "was very upset; in any case, I've never seen him like this before. . . . He didn't even try to get into fights on various subjects, as he usually does, and only persistently returned to one topic: time is of the essence and we shouldn't miss the chance."[35]

Khrushchev later wrote in his memoirs that Dobrynin's report of his conversation with Bobby Kennedy was the "culminating point of the crisis."

Khrushchev was convinced that if he didn't end the crisis right away, the Americans might just be crazy enough to invade Cuba. He believed the Kennedy brothers were under tremendous pressure to authorize what the Joint Chiefs wanted: an air strike and invasion on Monday.

Years later Ted Sorensen recalled the atmosphere in the ExComm meeting later that Saturday night: "The only word to describe the meeting that night is 'rancorous.' " Everyone, including Bundy, was showing the effects of fatigue and stress. As the hours passed, Sorensen said, the proponents of an air strike became insistent: "The president was under tremendous pressure at that point for military action." McNamara later said he "wasn't sure I would ever see another Saturday night." Bundy spent the night in his office, while the president stayed up and watched a movie, *Roman Holiday*, starring Audrey Hepburn and Gregory Peck.[36]

THE next day, Sunday, October 28, Foreign Minister Andrei Gromyko cabled Dobrynin, "Get in touch with Robert Kennedy at once and tell him . . . the president's message of October 27 will be answered on the radio today, and the answer will be highly positive." Dobrynin breathed a sigh of relief and immediately called Bobby. Within an hour Bobby met with Dobrynin and heard Khrushchev's reply. "At last," he told Dobrynin with a smile, "I'm going to see the kids. Why, I've almost forgotten my way home." * On his way out, he again underlined the importance of maintaining the strictest secrecy about the accord on the Turkish missiles.[37]

Mac Bundy heard the news while having breakfast in the White House mess. He rushed to a phone and immediately called the president. "It was a very beautiful morning, and it had suddenly become many times more beautiful. And I am sure the President felt the same way from the feeling between us as we talked about it. . . . We all felt that the world had changed for the better."[38]

Bobby Kennedy had ended the crisis with an explicit deal on the Turkish missiles. They would be gone within "four to five months." Mac Bundy, Ted Sorensen and seven other men (including the president and Bobby Kennedy) would be party to the secret. The American people—and Vice President Lyndon Johnson, CIA director John McCone and other ExComm advisers—would think there had not been a deal. (Neither was Fidel Castro aware of the deal.)

Over the next several decades Bundy would repeatedly lie in order to keep his promise to his president. Eventually, he acknowledged that there was a cost to this deceit. "Secrecy of this sort has its costs," he wrote. "By keeping

---

* Not everyone was relieved. At the White House, Admiral Anderson complained, "We have been had." General Curtis LeMay pounded the table and cried, "It's the greatest defeat in our history, Mr. President. . . . We should invade today!" According to McNamara, Kennedy was so shocked at this display that he sat there "stuttering in reply." (Michael Beschloss, *The Crisis Years: Kennedy and Khrushchev, 1960–1963* [New York: HarperCollins, 1991], p. 544.)

to ourselves the assurance on the Jupiters, we misled our colleagues, our countrymen, our successors, and our allies. We allowed them all to believe that nothing responsive had been offered. . . ." In effect, people were allowed to think that the great lesson of the missile crisis was that "unwavering firmness" had carried the day. The appearance of uncompromising toughness in facing down a Soviet threat may have aided Kennedy politically, but it also sent a message to the American people that a confrontational policy against communists was necessary at all times. This, in turn, would make it harder for Kennedy and his successors to have any flexibility in dealing with the Soviets, or for that matter, such other communist adversaries as the North Vietnamese. Bundy nevertheless concluded that for "all its costs, secrecy prevented a serious political division both within the United States and in the Atlantic alliance." In Bundy's history, the revelation years later that there had been a "private assurance" merely underscored Kennedy's statesmanship. The president's critics on the left were wrong to condemn Kennedy's "unforgivable risk taking," Bundy argued, precisely because he had been flexible and had quietly ended the crisis in part by giving Khrushchev something he needed in the way of a face-saving out.

Actually, in the event that the Soviets refused a private deal on the Jupiter missiles in Turkey, there is some evidence that Kennedy was willing to accept, as a fallback position, a *public* trade of the Turkish missiles.

At some point on Saturday, October 27, Kennedy pulled Dean Rusk aside and instructed him to call Andrew Cordier, a dean at Columbia University who had recently left the United Nations where he had served for fifteen years as executive assistant to the secretary-general. According to Rusk, who only revealed this information to his fellow ExComm members in 1987, Kennedy told him to dictate a statement to Cordier proposing the removal of both the Jupiters and the missiles in Cuba. "Mr. Cordier was to put that statement," Rusk said, "in the hands of [Secretary-General] U Thant only after a further signal from us."[39] According to Rusk, Kennedy was not going to allow the Jupiters to become an obstacle to reaching a settlement short of war. This was Kennedy's final way out; if at the last moment all else failed, the president could make it appear that he was accepting a U.N. proposal to defuse the crisis. Rusk never had to activate the U.N. option because by Saturday evening Khrushchev was so thoroughly frightened that he was willing to accept the much more politically palatable—for Kennedy—private assurances on the Jupiters.

Bundy was party to Kennedy's earlier decision to give Khrushchev a secret assurance on the Jupiters, but he was unaware at the time about the Cordier option. He had warned Kennedy during the ExComm meeting on Saturday morning, October 27, that a public trade of the Turkish missiles would be seen by America's allies as a betrayal: "That would be the view in all of NATO," he told Kennedy. "It's irrational, and it's crazy, but it's a terribly powerful fact." But in retrospect, Bundy admitted in *Danger and Survival* that

he was "less impressed by my own insistence on the reality of NATO sentiment than I am by the president's unwavering recognition that the basic
interest of all concerned was to find a peaceful end to the crisis, and that the
Turkish missiles, whatever the opinions of allies, did not justify bloodshed in
Cuba." Once again, the missile crisis was portrayed as a problem of appearances—or even mere public relations. [40]

In the end, Kennedy made sure that one way or another a deal could be
struck that exchanged the Cuban missiles for the Turkish missiles. It would
either be a private deal as reflected by Bobby Kennedy's secret pledge to
Ambassador Dobrynin, or, if necessary, a public deal brokered by the U.N.
secretary-general. Also included in the deal was the promise of a pledge by
Kennedy that the United States would not invade Cuba. Taken together, these
two elements of the deal addressed Khrushchev's two primary reasons for
deploying missiles in Cuba in the first place: his worry about Turkish Jupiters
and his fear that the United States was about to invade Cuba.

KHRUSHCHEV's fears of an invasion, we now know, were eminently reasonable.
Bundy, McNamara and other members of ExComm have always denied that
the Kennedy administration intended to invade Cuba in the autumn of 1962.
"Nothing of the sort was in our heads," Bundy insisted at a conference twenty-
five years after the crisis. The Soviets, however, had every reason to think an
invasion probable. Some $50 million was being spent on Operation Mongoose
in 1962, and the result was an escalating campaign of covert operations in
which Cuban sugarcane fields, harbor facilities and the occasional power station were being destroyed in hit-and-run attacks. Bundy later admitted in his
1988 book, *Danger and Survival*, "Khrushchev certainly knew of our program
of covert action against Cuba, and he could hardly be expected to understand
that to us this program was not a prelude to stronger action but a substitute
for it." [41]

Operation Mongoose may have been a "substitute" for, and not a prelude
to "stronger action," but Bundy in his role as de facto chair of the highly
secret Special Group Augmented (SGA) was spending an inordinate amount
of his time in the spring and summer of 1962 on plans for the overthrow of
Castro. An interagency group of CIA, State and Defense Department aides,
the SGA (previously known as the 5412 Committee) met frequently that
year with Attorney General Robert F. Kennedy. Mongoose's operational chief,
Brigadier General Edward G. Lansdale, reported directly to Bundy and the
SGA, and by February 1962, Lansdale had submitted a detailed, six-phase plan
for the removal of the Castro regime by that October. While the immediate
goal was to foment a "popular revolution" against Castro, guidelines for Mongoose approved by Bundy and the president made it clear that "final success
will require decisive U.S. military intervention." [42]

Defense Department documents, moreover, show that Operation Mongoose had an initial timetable which culminated in an October 20, 1962,

deadline. By that date, the U.S. military were supposed to have finalized preparations for a full-scale invasion of the island. In April and May the U.S. military held widely publicized military exercises in the Caribbean in which 40,000 marines and navy personnel staged a mock assault on an island off the coast of Puerto Rico. On July 25, 1962, Lansdale reported to Bundy and the SGA that the Joint Chiefs of Staff had "fully met its responsibility, under the March guidelines," for "planning and undertaking preliminary actions for a decisive U.S. capability for intervention in Cuba."

In fact, Lansdale's schedule was slipping as it became clear that popular unrest inside Cuba was less than expected. Even so, by August, Bundy was receiving such alarming information about Soviet military shipments to Cuba that a new track for direct military intervention—separate from Mongoose— was initiated. Bundy still told CIA director John McCone that any U.S. actions against Cuba must be covert because "overt actions would involve serious consequences all over the world. . . ." He was thinking of Berlin. Nevertheless, just two days later, on August 23, McCone succeeded in winning President Kennedy's approval to develop options "to deliberately seek to provoke a full-scale revolt against Castro that might require U.S. intervention to suc- ceed." Such a plan would provide for "the instantaneous commitment of suffi- cient [U.S.] armed forces to occupy the country [Cuba], destroy the regime, free the people, and establish in Cuba a peaceful country. . . ."[43]

A few days later, after reading intelligence reports describing the invasion plans, Arthur Schlesinger wrote a memo to the president warning that "Cuba would become our Algeria [where the French had recently been forced to withdraw after a bloody and debilitating colonial war]."[44] Young Marc Raskin —by now shunted over to the Bureau of the Budget—had also heard rumors of another intervention in Cuba. Dismayed, he wrote a note to Carl Kaysen in late September 1962, reminding him that Franklin Roosevelt had also once been urged to restore order in Cuba by military intervention. Roosevelt called his vice president, Jack Garner, a crusty Texan who hated everything about the New Deal: "What do you think we ought to do, Jack?" Roosevelt inquired.

"I'd stay out of Cuba if I could," replied Garner.

"But suppose an American citizen is shot?" Roosevelt countered.

"I think I'd wait and see which American it is," said Garner.[45]

Raskin thought this light anecdote might help to put the Cuban threat in perspective. Kaysen didn't even bother to reply. Bundy was well aware that men like Schlesinger and Raskin disapproved of the administration's Cuban policies, and that was one of the reasons they had been consigned to the periphery.

The same week Raskin was writing to Kaysen, Bundy passed on to Lans- dale a memo written by a friendly congressman suggesting yet another mili- tary operation: the invasion by Free Cuba forces [with U.S. logistical support] of the Isle of Pines, a sparsely populated 1,100-square-mile island located thirty-five miles off the southwest coast of Cuba. Having "liberated" a piece of Cuban territory, the émigré force would declare itself the rightful government of all Cuba. Washington could extend recognition to a new Cuban government. This, in turn, would give the Kennedy administration the legal cover to defend this piece of "free" Cuba by imposing a blockade against Castro's regime on the main island. Bundy liked the idea, at least as a fallback position. On September 19 he sent a short note to Lansdale saying, "I think the attached is one of the military contingencies that ought to be worked out carefully in the light of its obvious political possibilities."[46]

Clearly, military intervention was the game to be playing. On September 14, Kennedy discussed a detailed plan for an aerial attack against Cuba with McNamara and the Joint Chiefs.[47] Finally, on October 1—more than two weeks before the Soviet missile sites in Cuba were discovered—Admiral Robert Lee Dennison, commander in chief of the Atlantic Fleet, was ordered by McNamara "to be prepared to institute a blockade of Cuba." That evening Admiral Dennison ordered his fleet commanders to "take all feasible measures necessary to assure maximum readiness to execute CINCLANT OPLAN 312 [an air strike] by October 20." Simultaneously, U.S. Army commanders were informed of the "imminence of a possible implementation of CINCLANT OPLAN 316–62," a full-scale invasion of Cuba. Furthermore, Admiral Dennison took steps to mask all these preparations with the public announcement of a "large-scale amphibious assault exercise [to provide] a cover for our Caribbean preparations."[48] Reporters were told that the reputed target of this amphibious exercise—scheduled to begin on October 15—was code-named Ortsac: Castro spelled backwards. An obvious message was being sent to the Soviets and to Castro.

Far from being *routine* contingency planning, these and other documents uncovered by historian James G. Hershberg make clear that the Pentagon was taking extraordinary measures to preposition all the supplies, weapons and troops necessary for carrying out an invasion of Cuba. This suggests the Kennedy administration was hatching an "October surprise," an invasion of Cuba just weeks before a hard-fought midterm congressional election. If so, the invasion was preempted by the discovery of Soviet missiles in Cuba on October 15. Bundy himself seemed to have been torn. As late as October 5, he admitted to McCone that the administration's policy "was not clear." The alternatives came down to either "we would have to go in militarily (which seemed to him intolerable)," McCone noted, or "we would have to learn to live with Castro, and his Cuba and adjust our policies accordingly."[49] It is possible, as Bundy later insisted—even after being shown the CINCLANT documents uncovered by Hershberg—that the CINCLANT invasion plan was "pure contingency planning."[50] But if so, this particular contingency plan goes far to explain why Khrushchev took the risk to place ballistic missiles in Cuba.

IN the aftermath of Khrushchev's humiliating withdrawal of the missiles from Cuba, Robert McNamara exulted, "There is no such thing as strategy, only crisis management." A quarter century later, when confronted with new evidence about what transpired during those thirteen days, a chastened McNamara conceded, "You can't manage crises." Far from a triumph of crisis management, the missile crisis is a story of human fallibility, misinformation and simple misjudgment. At the time Bundy and his colleagues believed that while the Soviets probably had not had the time to ship and mount nuclear warheads atop their missiles, they nevertheless had to assume that some warheads were present. Not until 1989–91 did scholars learn the facts: according to Soviet General of the Army Anatoli I. Gribkov, who helped to plan the 1962 Cuban operation, thirty-six nuclear warheads for medium-range missiles—and 158 tactical nuclear warheads—had made it to Cuba prior to the blockade.* Gribkov also revealed that the Soviet commander in Cuba had been given discretionary authority to use the tactical nuclear weapons against any U.S. invasion force. This authorization was not withdrawn until October 22, 1962—the day President Kennedy revealed the existence of the missiles. And even then, according to Gribkov, a few days later the warheads for these tactical weapons were moved from storage and dispersed to Soviet combat units in preparation for the expected U.S. invasion. Obviously, in the heat of battle, they might well have been used even without direct authorization from Moscow.

Bundy and McNamara were shocked at these revelations. They had also assumed that there were no more than 20,000 Soviet troops on the island; in fact, there were over 41,000. If Kennedy had ordered an air strike—which in all probability would have led to an invasion—U.S. troops might have been met on the beaches with tactical nuclear weapons.[51] In this event, the odds that the crisis would have escalated to a full strategic nuclear exchange rise dramatically. Humanity should be extremely grateful that Kennedy did not accept the advice of Acheson, Nitze, the Joint Chiefs and Bundy to take the missiles out with an air strike.

Bundy had an instinctive sense of just how close they had come to an apocalypse. Just two days after the end of the crisis, Mac scribbled in longhand a note to one of his old mentors, Archie MacLeish: "I daren't hope that all we have done in the last two weeks will have seemed right to you, but I do want to tell you that on Sunday evening, after it was clear that a decent outcome could be reached (with fingers still crossed, of course), I read 'At the Lincoln Memorial' [a MacLeish poem] for the first time carefully. It seemed written for us all and for that moment of the worst avoided and the hope renewed."[52]

BUNDY was not only a key adviser in this most dangerous of the Cold War's nuclear confrontations, but he also later became an influential historian of the

---

* Most of these tactical warheads were loaded on short-range cruise missiles that could have been fired from patrol boats. A half dozen atomic bombs were outfitted for IL-28 bombers.

crisis. His treatment of the crisis in *Danger and Survival,* like his history of the Hiroshima decision in Stimson's memoirs, was serious and even at times moderately self-critical. *Danger and Survival* is a very good book. Yet, it is also a skillful defense of his president. His narrative acknowledged but down-played five critical issues: the secret Turkish trade, the impending threat of a U.S. invasion of Cuba prior to the crisis, the implicit no-invasion pledge, the defensive nature of the Soviet missiles and the fact that domestic politics was driving Kennedy's response throughout the crisis. Indeed, Bundy raised to the level of statesmanship Kennedy's vulnerability to domestic political attacks. The assumption was that given the expectations of the American people and Kennedy's right-wing critics, the president had no choice but to engage in brinkmanship. As Bobby Kennedy told his brother in the midst of the crisis, "if you hadn't acted, you would have been impeached."[53] But was brinkman-ship really inevitable?

As the historian Barton J. Bernstein has suggested, "a different president than Kennedy might well have chosen not to launch the Bay of Pigs venture, not to pursue clandestine activities against Cuba and Castro, not to build up the American nuclear arsenal well beyond the size of the Soviets', and not to place the Jupiters in Turkey."[54] All these actions led Khrushchev to respond with a clandestine shipment of missiles to Cuba, a gambit which turned out to be a glaring political miscalculation. He had not understood how weak Kennedy felt in the face of a deeply conservative Cold War political culture. This miscalculation would lead to Khrushchev's own political humiliation in the eyes of his politburo colleagues. In the end, Kennedy was not impeached, but in 1964 Khrushchev would be unseated by a cabal within the Kremlin that was determined to achieve, among other purposes, nuclear weapons parity with the United States. In effect, Kennedy's "victory" in the missile crisis closed the door on Khrushchev's experiments with internal reform of the Soviet system and prolonged the Cold War. In retrospect, this was a heavy price to pay for an ephemeral victory.

As Bundy himself later put it in *Danger and Survival,* the missiles had to come out of Cuba "because we found them politically intolerable, and not because we must somehow remove a usable Soviet asset."[55]

Once again, domestic politics had driven Kennedy's foreign policy, even to the point of nuclear confrontation. The president's approval rating in the Gallup polls jumped twelve points in late October. In this sense his handling of the crisis was very much a personal victory, and one which tended to wipe the slate clean. He and Bundy could put the Bay of Pigs, the Berlin wall and the messy Laotian crisis behind them. For a long time to come all presidents would be judged by the standard Kennedy set in October 1962. Kennedy's resident historian, Arthur Schlesinger, Jr., would later write glowingly of the president's "combination of toughness and restraint, of will, nerve, and wis-dom, so brilliantly controlled, so matchlessly calibrated."[56]

Naturally, Mac Bundy's reputation was enhanced as much as Kennedy's.

The *Washington Post* columnist Chalmer Roberts wrote in early November 1962 that "the one-time dean rates an A" for his handling of foreign policy. "Today Bundy is the linchpin of a tight little White House foreign policy shop of inestimable value to Mr. Kennedy."[57]

IN June 1963, Kennedy was scheduled to visit West Berlin. Though the trip had been planned for months, the president kept complaining to Bundy that he really didn't want to go, saying, "Oh, this trip's got nothing in it but bad news, I think I'll cancel it."

"You can't do that, Mr. President," Bundy quipped. "You've committed to six governments and five popes and four secretaries of state, and of course you're going to go and it's going to be a triumph." Bundy knew Kennedy knew he had to go: "He just wanted to bitch about it."[58]

On their flight across the Atlantic, Kennedy began polishing the speech he intended to deliver in West Berlin when he glanced over at Kenny O'Donnell and asked, "What was the proud boast of the Romans? . . . Send Bundy up here. He'll know how to translate it into German." When Mac walked into the president's cabin, he mustered whatever German he had learned years ago at Yale to translate the Latin phrase *Civis Romanus sum* into "Ich bin ein Berliner!" Kennedy stammered to pronounce the guttural German with his thick Boston accent. The president, Bundy recalled, "had no feeling for any foreign language. So there we were on the goddamn airplane coming down on Berlin while he repeated the phrase over and over again . . . and it worked. God, how it worked!"[59]

Bundy stood on the balcony behind Kennedy as he gave the speech of his lifetime. Nearly a million Berliners roared their approval at Kennedy's words. "What I remember about it," Bundy recalled, "was what an extraordinary and fantastic, I've-never-seen-anything-like-this-before kind of day. . . . It went on all day long." Leaving Berlin, Kennedy slumped into his seat aboard *Air Force One* and said to Sorensen, "We'll never have another day like this one as long as we live."[60]

NOTWITHSTANDING Kennedy's pounding rhetoric in Berlin, earlier in the month Bundy had encouraged the president to deliver a quite different speech at American University in Washington, D.C. Bundy always regarded this "peace speech," as it later became known, as the rhetorical high mark of the Kennedy years. As usual, Sorensen was the primary oarsman in drafting the speech, but Bundy, Norman Cousins, Kaysen, Bowles and Schlesinger also contributed suggestions. Bundy made it clear that no one should talk about the speech outside this narrow circle. This was a speech that could happen only if it was not cleared by the Joint Chiefs, the State Department and the CIA. This was to be a speech where Kennedy, finally, would step out of his role as the tough Cold Warrior and speak from the heart about the central issue of his time: nuclear weapons.

"Let us reexamine our attitude toward the Cold War," the president said on June 10. War is not inevitable, mankind is not doomed. "Our problems are manmade. Therefore, they can be solved by man." Communism may be repugnant to the American people. "But we can still hail the Russian people for their many achievements. . . . Almost unique among the major world powers, we have never been at war with each other." Kennedy tried to humanize the Soviets for his American audience: they were a people, he explained, who had lost twenty million in the last world war, and their country had been "turned into a wasteland, a loss equivalent to the devastation of this country east of Chicago."

What kind of peace did we seek? the president asked. "Not a Pax Americana enforced on the world by American weapons of war. Not the peace of the grave or the security of the slave." A fresh start was needed, and he proposed a test ban treaty which would address "one of the greatest hazards which man faces in 1963, the further spread of nuclear arms. It would increase our security. It would decrease the prospects of war."

Khrushchev told a visiting foreign dignitary that it was "the best speech by any President since Roosevelt."[61] Bundy agreed. He knew that a nuclear war in 1963 would have utterly destroyed American and Russian civilizations. There was, moreover, something unreal, even false, about a confrontation rooted in ideological differences—and little else. Détente had always been one element in the complex reality of the Soviet-American relationship. As another devoted Stimsonian, John J. McCloy, had said at the beginning of the Cold War, Russia and America would naturally "walk stiff-legged around the ring a bit," but they had no interest in a real fight. Their respective visions—individual freedom and economic egalitarianism—were certainly in conflict. But this need not lead to war, particularly nuclear war. The Soviet system was cruel and repressive. But unlike the Nazi fascists, the Soviet empire was turned inward, and particularly since Stalin's death, it had proved itself capable of liberalization. Indeed, Bundy, Kaysen and the other men who contributed to Kennedy's speech thought that further diplomacy could lead to greater liberalization. Bundy was relieved that Kennedy now felt politically strong enough, particularly in the wake of the missile crisis, to prepare the country for an open détente.[62]

A test ban treaty would be the first concrete step to this kind of détente. Both Kennedy and Bundy knew it was a long overdue step, and they now had to select a negotiator who could win Khrushchev's agreement. When Kennedy's first choice, John McCloy, turned down the assignment, Bundy urged the president to send Averell Harriman, accompanied by Carl Kaysen.[63] The seventy-two-year-old multimillionaire and veteran diplomat was instructed to explore the possibility of a comprehensive treaty banning all nuclear tests. On July 25, after two weeks of intensive bargaining, he and Khrushchev initialed a partial test ban treaty, one which permitted further underground testing, but banned tests in the atmosphere, in the oceans and in outer space. As

Bundy later wrote, the partial test ban treaty was "well worth having, a first good step."[64] But it was only a good first step if it were quickly followed by other steps toward a comprehensive ban on underground tests, and eventually, a steady decline in the number of all nuclear weapons.

Upon returning from Moscow, Harriman sat down and wrote a "Secret" memo for Bundy and the White House analyzing Khrushchev's position. The Soviet leader, wrote Harriman, was seeking a "palpable relaxation of tensions, presumably of some duration." Economics was his motivation. Khrushchev wanted to cut his defense budget and use the savings to modernize Soviet agriculture. He had "quite enough missiles." But he also told Harriman that his generals were "willing to 'go on and on with their demands unless someone curbed their appetite.' " He claimed to have rebuffed a request to use the savings from missile expenditures for conventional armaments. "Khrushchev also implied," Harriman reported, "a limitation if not reduction in military spending." Production of fissionable material had "stopped expanding" and "very possibly" would be terminated altogether in the "near future."[65]

Obviously, if what Khrushchev told Harriman about his military budget was true—and subsequent evidence from the Moscow archives suggests that Soviet defense spending was indeed on hold—then a significant opportunity existed for further progress on arms control. Harriman also urged the administration to negotiate seriously on a nonaggression treaty, a Soviet proposal that Kennedy and Bundy had been resisting. Though his argument was reminiscent of Carl Kaysen's 1961 memo to Bundy—in which Kaysen proposed normalizing relations with East Germany—the Kennedy White House ignored Harriman's advice.[66]

Despite such reports Bundy and Kennedy made no further efforts in 1963 to build on the achievement of the test ban treaty.[67] To the contrary, U.S. defense spending in 1963 continued to increase sharply at a time when the consensus within the intelligence community was that the Soviet system was economically deteriorating. One highly classified CIA report concluded that Khrushchev was facing agricultural stagnation, a restless intelligentsia, and mounting economic and political difficulties in Eastern Europe.[68] Clearly, this was not the adversary that right-wing Cold Warriors portrayed in the media; but liberal Cold Warriors like Bundy and Kennedy nevertheless thought it politically prudent not to challenge the notion of a strong and vibrant Soviet threat. Kennedy had his campaign for reelection in 1964 in mind, and he thought his Republican challenger would be the ultra-conservative Republican senator from Arizona, Barry Goldwater. A partial test ban treaty, Kennedy concluded, was about as much as he could expect to get through Congress, regardless of how much more Khrushchev was willing to offer.

11

Autumn Assassinations

Friday and Saturday I cried at home—after that not.

McGEORGE BUNDY,
December 4, 1963

ARLY IN 1963, Mac Bundy sent one of his aides, Michael V. Forrestal, on a four-week tour to South Vietnam, accompanied by Roger Hilsman, the State Department's assistant secretary of state for the Far East. By then, there were more than 10,000 U.S. military advisers in the country, and President Kennedy wanted to know whether they were making any difference. Forrestal and Hilsman returned with mixed conclusions. "Despite the fact that the land reform program had been a complete failure," Forrestal later said, "despite the fact that Diem had not introduced any of the fiscal reforms that we had asked him to; despite a certain amount of rumbling about Diem—on balance, you had to say it looked as though the government forces were doing better than the Viet Cong."[1]

Kennedy was pleased, even though the Forrestal-Hilsman report also suggested that there were some very big problem areas. As Forrestal bluntly explained it to the syndicated columnist Joseph Kraft in a series of off-the-record interviews in 1964, ". . . both our army and the Vietnamese Army tended to want to fight the Viet Cong by whatever mechanical means they had at their disposal (artillery, air power, napalm—anything that you could get) and without much attention being paid to the populace." American pilots were flying "unofficial" combat missions. "They bombed the hell out of the villages . . . certainly without the Americans checking on what kind of villages these were," Forrestal said. The Viet Cong invariably knew well in advance when the planes were going to arrive, so "of course, we and the Vietnamese ended up bombing peasants."

Forrestal also reported that similar tactics were being used on the ground. "They had these classic military sweep-up operations, where you get one or two battalions and a lot of American-supplied equipment and advisors clanking out over the countryside in pursuit of Viet Cong. They hardly ever made contact with any Viet Cong, but they almost always ran over a village and left that in flames and burning behind. This simply wasn't calculated to win the people . . . these kinds of operations were very unproductive." When Forrestal complained to American officers, they would admit this was probably a "bad thing to do," but nobody seemed able to prevent it. Forrestal reported to Bundy, "Admiral [Harry D.] Felt's own justification for this is hair-raising." The admiral "defended it on the grounds that the enemy is the enemy, and if you have to kill a few innocent people to get him, better kill innocent people."[2]

Forrestal was one of Mac Bundy's closest friends, and certainly, together with Carl Kaysen, one of his most trusted aides.* If such reports came from Forrestal, Bundy would not doubt their veracity.

Michael Vincent Forrestal was a complicated man. Born in 1927, his father was James V. Forrestal, a Wall Street lawyer who later served as secretary of the navy and then as the nation's first defense secretary under Harry Truman. Michael was schooled at Phillips Exeter Academy (class of 1945), Princeton (1949) and Harvard Law School (1953). In 1946, at the age of nineteen, he managed through his father's connections to land a job as an assistant to the U.S. naval attaché in Moscow, where his father's good friend Averell Harriman was ambassador. Harriman so liked the younger Forrestal that he made Michael his special assistant when he took charge of the Marshall Plan in 1948. When Michael's father committed suicide in 1949, Harriman virtually adopted him, serving as his mentor and guardian. In the 1950s, Forrestal practiced corporate law with the firm of Shearman & Sterling, where he was made a partner in 1960. By then, Forrestal had acquired numerous foreign clients, including some in the oil business.

A large, handsome man, Michael Forrestal possessed a gluttonous appetite for just about everything in life. He relished good wine, food and chocolates. An avid deep-water sailor, he found time to sail the Caribbean. He loved opera, and later served for many years as the chairman of the Metropolitan Opera Guild. He traveled extensively, and seemed to know an unusually wide variety of all the most interesting people in New York, Washington, London and other cities around the globe. He was, in short, a cosmopolitan.[3]

Recruited by President Kennedy himself to work with Bundy in early 1962, Forrestal obviously had all the right establishment credentials. By 1963, he was seeing the president on a daily basis. Kennedy himself once referred to Forrestal as part of his "inner club."[4] Both Kennedy and Bundy appreciated Michael's irreverent smarts. He could and did tell them exactly what he thought. Bundy trusted him unequivocally and soon put him in charge of

---

* When Forrestal died suddenly in 1989 of an aneurysm, Mac Bundy eulogized his friend, saying with notable understatement, "The courses that he advocated would be ones to consider if one could replay the tragic history of our connection to Southeast Asia. He was a good companion."

keeping tabs on covert operations. And when there was trouble abroad, Bundy would send Forrestal as his eyes and ears.

Unlike some of his counterparts in Dean Rusk's State Department, Forrestal was not the kind of man who shut himself off from critical sources of information. By the summer of 1963, journalists David Halberstam and Neil Sheehan had filed such pessimistic accounts of the war that they were practically personae non gratae among U.S. embassy officials in Saigon. Forrestal made a point of seeking out their friendship. Few U.S. officials wanted to be seen talking to someone like Halberstam. "I mean," Halberstam said, "we would go out to the airport, and there would be the ambassador, various generals and forty people on one side of the room, and Neil Sheehan and me standing alone on the other side of the room." Forrestal didn't observe such invisible barriers. "He was the first person in government who was really ever nice to me," Halberstam recalled. "I was the enemy to them."

Forrestal not only listened, he voiced his own complex doubts about the war. Halberstam was astonished. Here was a White House aide who "didn't believe all this stuff, someone who had a dark vision of what was happening." Forrestal became an unnamed source for Halberstam's *New York Times* dispatches, which would soon earn him a Pulitzer Prize. When Halberstam left Vietnam at the end of 1963 to write a book, *The Making of a Quagmire*, one of his first dinners back in the United States was with Forrestal. It was, of course, a two-way street. In his own way, Forrestal was just as much a reporter as Halberstam, and he passed what he gleaned from their conversations on to Assistant Secretary of State for the Far East Averell Harriman, Mac Bundy and the president himself.[5]

In the summer of 1963, Diem's regime began to unravel. Initially, the political crisis was sparked by a dispute over whether the Buddhist community could display their distinctive five-color banner. During the course of an anti-Diem demonstration in early May 1963, a woman and seven children were killed in a mysterious explosion in Hue. In the ensuing melee, Diem's troops fired into the crowd and more people were injured. Civil disturbances then escalated across the country. On June 11 an elderly Buddhist monk doused himself with gasoline and lit a match. Malcolm Browne of the Associated Press was on the scene and his photograph of the grisly suicide was published in newspapers around the world.

Diem responded by allowing his military chiefs to crack down on the dissident Buddhist community, which made up about 30 percent of the population. Diem, of course, was a Catholic, and many of his co-religionists had come from the North as refugees in 1954. By the 1960s, South Vietnam's two million Roman Catholics were certainly the most cohesive political grouping in the South. But the majority of South Vietnamese came from a fluid mosaic of Buddhist, Confucian, Taoist and animist sects. Diem's own cabinet was by no means dominated by Catholics (five Catholics, five Confucians and eight

Buddhists). But in the summer of 1963, Diem nevertheless set himself on a collision course with a politically active faction of the Buddhist community.[6]

The Buddhist crisis took Bundy by surprise. Until then, as Forrestal explained just a year later, "no American, that is no American whose report was read in Washington, was aware that there was an incipient problem between Buddhists and Catholics . . . we didn't have any contact with the Buddhists. We didn't even know who they were. . . . We knew who the Catholics were because the government was Catholic."[7]

In July, Bundy again sent Forrestal out to Saigon to be his eyes and ears. By then, Diem had arrested some three thousand people, but not just any three thousand people. Fearing a coup, Diem had targeted for arrest the elite: students, the French-speaking elite, and even the relatives of his own cabinet ministers and army officer corps. Forrestal found Saigon a "city of terror . . . a city sick with fear." Diem, he thought, was "losing touch with what was going on in his own country."

To his consternation Forrestal also picked up on rumors that Diem's brother and confidant Ngo Dinh Nhu was conducting secret negotiations with Hanoi. This set off alarm bells in Washington, where it was believed that any negotiations would undermine the war effort and inevitably lead to a communist triumph. Forrestal thought Nhu was "probably the evil genius" behind all of the regime's problems. Three months earlier President Kennedy himself had drawn Forrestal's attention to an article Nhu had written on the war's prospects. Nhu claimed that the war was drawing to a close, and that soon the American presence would no longer be necessary. Forrestal's interpretation of the article was that Nhu thought "he might be strong enough to bargain with Hanoi on this basis, using the withdrawal of the Americans as the basis of his argument."[8]

For their part, Diem and Nhu were increasingly unhappy with their American allies. Diem was particularly annoyed that the Americans had assigned two thousand U.S. advisers to provinces where they could control the distribution of foreign aid—and otherwise monitor the regime's activities. "All these soldiers I never asked to come here," Diem complained to the French ambassador. "They don't even have passports." Earlier that spring Diem had requested the removal of these officers from the countryside, which in Washington was read as further evidence of his unwillingness to fight the war efficiently.[9]

In the end, Nhu's secret negotiations with Hanoi and Diem's inept handling of the Buddhist crisis prompted Forrestal and Bundy to question whether there were alternatives to Diem.

The crisis came to a head in the third week of August, just as the Kennedy administration's leading officials scattered to their respective vacation retreats. Kennedy left for Hyannis Port, Bundy went to Manchester-on-the-Sea, McNamara was climbing the Grand Tetons in Wyoming, Rusk was watching a ball game at Yankee Stadium, and the CIA's John McCone was on a yacht in the Puget Sound. A few days earlier, on August 21, Diem's police had burst into four of Saigon's largest pagodas, beating hundreds of Buddhist priests and possibly killing some. Intelligence reports flooded Washington with information that the Saigon regime was grinding to a halt. Civil servants were not showing up at their offices and troops in the field were not moving. The CIA was also reporting that a collection of Saigon generals wanted to know what Washington's reaction would be to a coup directed against Nhu—and possibly Diem.

On Saturday, August 24, Averell Harriman asked Forrestal whether in the wake of the latest attacks on the pagodas Diem could any longer be supported. Forrestal replied that he thought Diem should be given notice. The same day Roger Hilsman prepared a draft cable to newly arrived Ambassador Henry Cabot Lodge which later became known as the "green light" cable. The cable instructed Lodge, "You may also tell appropriate [South Vietnamese] military commanders we will give them direct support in any interim period of breakdown central government mechanism." The embassy staff should in the meantime make "detailed plans as to how we might bring about Diem replacement if this should become necessary." [10]

Though Harriman and Hilsman had received clearances from the president himself and numerous other officials, by Monday morning everyone was having second thoughts. Within hours Lodge was receiving instructions not to back off, but to proceed with extreme caution. Diem's plotting generals were themselves not quite ready to act, so nothing happened.

Kennedy was furious, not with the policy, but with the dissension within his own ranks. He blamed Forrestal for the weekend mix-up and exploded, "This shit has got to stop!" When Forrestal offered to resign, the president shot back, "You're not worth firing." The president's brother Bobby thought others were just as much to blame: "Mac Bundy wasn't particularly helpful." Mac had been too much the "gatekeeper" and not enough of an adviser. Bundy himself quipped that the lesson to be learned was: "Never do business on the weekend." [11]

The president was also annoyed by the perception that the administration's policy was being driven by David Halberstam's tough reporting in the New York Times on the Diem regime's abuses. "Gaddammit, I don't want you reading those stories in The Times," Kennedy told his aides. "We're not going to let our policy be run by some twenty-eight-year-old kid." [12]

Vietnam was becoming more than a mere annoyance. Careers such as Halberstam's were being put on the line. Tempers were flaring. Powerful men like Rusk, McNamara and Bundy began venting their frustrations in meetings that never produced the clear-cut answers they sought.

At an NSC meeting on August 31, the consensus around the table was that Diem should be pressured to dismiss his brother Nhu, but Washington would not actively promote a coup. The bottom line, nearly everyone agreed, was that the United States had no intention of withdrawing from the Vietnamese contest. Vice President Lyndon Johnson was particularly vocal in his support for Diem and the war.*

Only one person at this NSC meeting disagreed, but he was the only official present who had any deep experience with Vietnam. Paul Kattenburg, forty-one, had spent the 1950s in Vietnam as a young Foreign Service officer. A day earlier he had returned from a short visit to Saigon, where he had gone to inspect the situation in his job as chairman of the State Department's Vietnam Task Force. What he had seen made him realize that Diem was finished. Most Vietnamese both in the cities and the countryside were disaffected and desired an end to the war. The army was corrupt, and the U.S. counterinsurgency effort to build "strategic hamlets"—where villagers had been forcibly moved into armed stockades—had succeeded only in antagonizing the peasantry. The whole U.S. policy, he decided, was just "nonsense." After listening in silence as his superiors voiced the prevailing consensus, Kattenburg finally interrupted. Diem, he said flatly, was not about to introduce political reforms and he certainly was not going to fire his brother Nhu. Believing the situation in South Vietnam would continue to deteriorate, Kattenburg urged that "it would be better for us to make the decision to withdraw honorably." Rusk responded by calling Kattenburg's comments "speculative." General Taylor, chairman of the Joint Chiefs, challenged Kattenburg's assessment of the military situation in the countryside. Former ambassador Frederick E. Nolting, Jr., harshly disagreed with Kattenburg. Bundy sat in silence, neither coming to Kattenburg's defense nor joining in the attack on his heresy.[13]

Kattenburg later recalled with considerable bitterness, "There was not a single person there that knew what he was talking about. . . . They didn't know Vietnam. They didn't know the past. They had forgotten the history. They simply didn't understand the identification of nationalism and Communism. . . . I thought, 'God, we're walking into a major disaster.' "[14]

Honorable withdrawal was a viable option to Kattenburg only because he sensed that if South Vietnam was to maintain its separate status from the North, the regime would have to seem as nationalist as the communists. Ultimately, that meant no dependence on a foreign power. But if Diem was incompetent and politically inept, the war was lost anyway. And if the war was lost, then the United States would be foolish not to take advantage of Diem's secret flirtations with the communists to ease itself out of any military commitment, leaving behind an ostensibly neutral regime. (Kattenburg was dismissed from the Vietnam Task Force in January 1964, largely at the insistence of Bill Bundy, who charged that his pessimism was a "disservice.")[15]

Mac was not blind to Kattenburg's arguments. He just thought they were irrelevant. Obviously, Diem was in trouble. And perhaps, Bundy thought,

---

* Mac Bundy noted the next day in a memo to the president that so far forty-six Americans had been killed in Vietnam due to "hostile action."

Diem had turned himself into a Catholic dictator in a Buddhist/animist society. And perhaps he did not project any credible claim as a nationalist. That autumn Bundy heard the same arguments from his Harvard friend and colleague Stanley Hoffmann, who wrote him a letter arguing that the heart of the matter was that the Saigon regime lacked any legitimacy. Drawing on his French background, Hoffmann suggested it was naive to expect that the Americans could succeed where the French had failed in turning puppet regimes into legitimate governments. "I got a very interesting letter back," Hoffmann recalled, "typical Bundy, the tone of which was, 'You're quite right; I agree that the crux of the matter is the South. . . . And it is true that for the time being the government we have there is pretty shaky. But we can concoct one, if we only try.' " [16]

Bundy thought any policy prescription, like Kattenburg's, which tolerated neutralism was a dead issue. Vietnam was a mess, an annoyance. But he had heard all the same arguments about Diem's ineffectiveness back in the autumn of 1961. The Kennedy administration had stabilized the situation then by sending more advisers and more hardware. Perhaps the same formula would work again; just a little more military commitment and Diem—or his successors—could stay the course. In any event, a neutralist outcome would be viewed as a defeat for America. Once again, domestic political factors—and Bundy's Cold War liberalism—were driving foreign policy. As Kattenburg put it later, an opportunity was missed in 1963 for an honorable withdrawal merely because of "the fear of our top leadership that it might look weak—to Congress and the U.S. public even more than to the Soviets." [17]

Neutralism was very much an option. On August 29—in the midst of the coup planning—France's President Charles de Gaulle issued an invitation to all parties in North and South Vietnam to meet in Paris and negotiate the reunification of Vietnam on the basis of a government of national unity and neutralism. If Kennedy had wanted it, the French president was offering the perfect vehicle for a graceful and honorable withdrawal. But Mac Bundy regarded De Gaulle's proposal as an interference, a bald attempt by the French president to reinsinuate French influence over a former colony. In a memo to the president, Mac observed ". . . that we do best when we ignore Nosey Charlie." Bill Bundy called the proposal "impractical if not mischievous." [18]

But the fear that Diem, or more likely his brother Nhu, might use the French overture to open public negotiations with Hanoi intensified the drift in Washington toward a coup. Mac Bundy still wondered whether Diem could be redeemed, and if not, whether the generals could be counted on to launch a successful coup without plunging the regime into civil war. But there were still many players at State and the Pentagon—not to mention the vice president—who strongly opposed any further green lights for a coup.

IN mid-September 1963, President Kennedy ordered McNamara and General Taylor to fly to Saigon with a team to resolve the policy impasse. On the

Sunday before their departure, Mike Forrestal, who was slated to go on the trip, showed up at Bill Bundy's home. Bill had just returned the previous day from a three-week vacation in Europe. Forrestal explained that McNamara wanted Bill to serve as his chief of staff for the mission: "This town is just split down the middle over what to do with Diem; feelings are running very high. . . . You're the only guy around who wasn't in any way involved [in the August coup cables]." Bill Bundy would be the disinterested, objective drafts- man of the mission's report. He had, of course, been working on Vietnam off and on for two years. But this trip was to be his baptismal experience; Vietnam would consume his professional life for the next six years. The trip was, he later wrote, "perhaps the most intense ten days of work in my whole experience."[19]

On the plane out to Saigon, Bundy and the others were given large binders which contained a draft of the report they were supposed to write at the conclusion of the trip. The conclusions, as Forrestal recalled, were already "carefully spelled out, [with] all the statistics to back them up."

Forrestal thought it a "dreadful visit," by which he meant that people kept trying to lie to them with "phony statistical" stories. But the lies were too transparent. Finally, a briefing was arranged with a group of junior U.S. Army officers in Can Tho. In the presence of McNamara and Bill Bundy, Max Taylor asked a young major who was a provincial adviser how the war was going. "Lousy, General," the major replied.

"What do you mean by that?" Taylor asked. Whereupon the officer poured out the gruesome details, "very convincingly," according to Forrestal. This gave courage to the other officers, and "all hell broke loose." The team boarded their helicopter out of Can Tho with an extremely pessimistic assess- ment. This encounter, and two other confidential interviews McNamara had with Nguyen Dinh Thuan, Diem's minister of defense, and British journalist Patrick Honey, a longtime expatriate resident in Saigon, gave the defense secretary a distinctly "bearish" view of the war.

Bill Bundy himself talked to a broad range of sources, including reporters like Neil Sheehan and David Halberstam. He had been reading their critical dispatches for some time, and unlike some back in Washington, he "wasn't on the ceiling about them."[20]

By the end of the trip, after talking to literally dozens of people, Bundy "became aware for the first time of how immensely diverse the war was in itself. . . ." He was stunned to learn, for instance, that just outside Saigon, in the populous province of Long An, the Viet Cong ruled with impunity. Sud- denly, there were no certainties. "I was left, as I think McNamara was, with a lasting skepticism of the ability of any man, however honest, to interpret accurately what was going on. It was just too diffuse, and too much that was critical took place below the surface." Leaving Saigon, Bill and most of his colleagues had concluded that "an unchanged Diem regime stood only a small chance of holding South Vietnam together and carrying the conflict with the

Viet Cong and Hanoi to a successful conclusion. What Diem and Nhu were doing was not merely repugnant, but seemed calculated to end in chaos."[21]

The McNamara-Taylor report—hastily rewritten on the plane back to Washington—was a "mishmash of everything," according to Forrestal. Though they knew otherwise, the authors (with Bundy as chief draftsman) asserted that the "military campaign has made great progress." Yet, the Diem-Nhu regime was becoming "increasingly unpopular." Accordingly, the report recommended actions to impress upon Diem "our disapproval of his political program." Specifically, food aid—which the Saigon regime sold on the local market, generating cash to pay its civil servants—should be suspended. In addition, a special $200,000 a month cash payment used by Diem to supplement the salaries of his Special Forces unit—stationed in Saigon as his personal protection force—was to be cut off unless the Special Forces were deployed to the countryside. This was a pointed inducement to the generals plotting a coup. As Forrestal later explained, "It was the first sign the generals had . . . that maybe the United States was serious about this. . . ."[22]

Bill Bundy later admitted that the McNamara-Taylor report contained a "clear internal inconsistency" between its military assumptions—that the war could be won on the ground if the political reforms were made—and its political analysis that Diem was unlikely to make the necessary political reforms. Bill had slept only two hours during the twenty-seven-hour flight from Saigon to Washington and emerged exhausted. He later commented with characteristic understatement, "Neither draftsmanship nor judgment is likely to be at its best under such working conditions."[23] Flawed as it was, the document became Washington's script in the coming crisis.

BACK in the White House, Mac Bundy fully approved the McNamara-Taylor recommendations. He and his brother Bill were of the same mind: the Diem regime's internal repression of its Buddhist political opponents jeopardized the military effort against the Viet Cong. Mac had probably encouraged Joe Alsop to write a column highly critical of the Diem regime on September 18, aptly called "Very Ugly Stuff." Alsop highlighted the reports of Ngo Dinh Nhu's secret negotiations with Hanoi's representatives. Mac's only concern was that the fiscal sanctions against Diem should remain out of the newspapers and to this end he sent an "eyes only" cable on October 5 urging Ambassador Lodge to keep the sanctions secret.[24]

Mac Bundy had tried to change only one aspect of the report drafted by his brother, the assertion that U.S. counterinsurgency programs in Vietnam could be phased out by the end of 1965. Mac thought it unwise to set a date, particularly one which seemed so unrealistic given military realities. Bill understood his brother's objections, but when pressed, he said, "Look, I'm under instructions!" Mac then phoned McNamara, who refused to change the language, indicating that this was something the president wanted.[25]

The report also recommended the withdrawal of one thousand U.S. mili-

tary personnel by the end of December 1963, an action which was later interpreted by some historians as evidence that President Kennedy intended to
phase out the entire Vietnam intervention. This notion is not supported by
any hard archival evidence, though McNamara, Hilsman, Gilpatric and a few
others said years later that Kennedy personally told them that this was his
intention.[26] In fact, Kennedy himself on October 2 told Bundy and McNamara
that he "objected to the phrase 'by the end of the year' in the sentence"
announcing the withdrawal of one thousand military personnel. Why? Because he "believed that if we were not able to take this action by the end of
this year, we would be accused of being over optimistic." McNamara pressed
the president, however, to retain the language "in order to meet the view of
Senator Fulbright and others that we are bogged down forever in Vietnam."
McNamara even went so far as to say that the end-of-the-year deadline "reveals that we have a withdrawal plan."[27] Clearly, the only withdrawal plan
McNamara had in mind was contingent on getting the South Vietnamese
army to fight. Viewed in the context of what was taking place in the autumn
of 1963 in Vietnam, the scheduled withdrawal of one thousand U.S. personnel
meshed perfectly with President Kennedy's campaign to exert pressure on the
Diem regime for internal reforms. The fact that this withdrawal was publicly
announced on October 2 is particularly telling. Perhaps even more compelling
is a cable to Bundy on October 8 in which the U.S. Pacific Command confirmed
that in drawing up plans for the limited withdrawal, its "objective is to withdraw units rather than individuals to the extent practicable to gain maximum
psychological impact rather than reach a predetermined in-country
strength . . ." by the end of 1963. In addition, Bundy was informed that the
"withdrawal, if decreed, should take place with minimum impact on the combined US-RVN capabilities to bring counter-insurgency campaign to successful
conclusion in shortest possible time."[28] Clearly, the White House wanted a
noisy, public—but cosmetic—withdrawal that would not harm the military
effort.

In retrospect, Bill Bundy flatly asserted that "up to his death JFK had not
changed his mind on US policy in South Vietnam."[29] This is not to say
that Kennedy had made a decision to introduce combat troops. As Hilsman,
Schlesinger and others have related anecdotally, Kennedy had a strong aversion to Americanizing the war. He had, after all, repeatedly resisted sending
combat troops, as opposed to "advisers." Recall that in the spring of 1962,
Michael Forrestal had noted in his memorandum of conversation with Kennedy and Harriman, "The President observed generally that he wished us to
be prepared to seize upon any favorable moment to reduce our involvement,
recognizing that the moment might yet be some time away."[30]

When Kenneth O'Donnell once asked Kennedy how he could withdraw
the American forces, Kennedy said, "Easy, put a government in there that will
ask us to leave." Robert Kennedy told Daniel Ellsberg in October 1967, "Of
course no one can know what my brother would have done in 1964 or 1965,

but I do know he was determined not to send ground troops. He would rather do anything than that." When Ellsberg pressed him, "But was he prepared to see Saigon go Communist?" Bobby replied, "We would have fuzzed it up, the way we did in Laos." When Ellsberg asked, "What made your brother so smart?" Bobby suddenly flared and shouted, "Because we were there! We were there. We saw what happened to the French." Indeed, the Kennedy brothers had visited Vietnam together back in 1951 and had come away disillusioned with the French effort in Indochina.*[31]

Senator Mike Mansfield also insisted that Kennedy once told him of his intention to withdraw from Vietnam. In December 1962, Mansfield returned from Vietnam with a highly pessimistic assessment of the Diem regime. "President Kennedy was not pleased with the report I gave him," Mansfield recalled. But a few months later, Mansfield said, "President Kennedy did inform me in early 1963 that he did plan to begin the withdrawal of some troops from Vietnam following the next election."[32] Though no contemporary record of the exchange exists, Mansfield recalled that Kenny O'Donnell witnessed the conversation. Was Kennedy the politician simply telling Mansfield what he wanted to hear? Perhaps.

Michael Forrestal later recalled a conversation he had with Kennedy which, if true, suggests that the president was indeed struggling in his own thinking toward a neutralist-withdrawal solution for Vietnam. Forrestal saw Kennedy for the last time on Thursday, November 21, 1963, in the Oval Office. Forrestal was about to fly to Phnom Penh, where he had instructions to reassure Cambodia's ruler, Prince Norodom Sihanouk, that the United States still strongly supported his country's neutrality. "During the course of this conversation," Forrestal said, "he [Kennedy] did what he sometimes did at the end of the day, or when he was a little tired. He asked me to stay a bit and he said, 'You know, when you come back, I want you to come and see me because we have to start to plan for what we are going to do now in South Vietnam.' He said, 'I want to start a complete and very profound review of how we got into this country, and what we thought we were doing, and what we now think we can do.' He said, 'I even want to think about whether or not we should be there.' He said, because this was, of course, in the context of an election campaign also, that he didn't think that we could consider drastic changes of policy, quickly." Forrestal claimed that Kennedy wanted to think about "how some kind of a gradual shift in our presence in South Vietnam [could] occur." Forrestal emphasized that he had "a very clear recollection of it [the conversation] and, of course, the following morning when I arrived in

---

* In October 1951, Bobby Kennedy wrote his father from Vietnam that the French were "greatly hated. . . . As it stands now, we are becoming more & more involved in the war to the point where we can't back out. It doesn't seem to be a picture with a very bright future" (Arthur Schlesinger, Jr., *Robert Kennedy and His Times* [New York: Ballantine, 1978], p. 99).

Saigon, actually it was night out there, or two o'clock in the morning, he was killed."[33]

If President Kennedy was thinking about a "gradual shift" in policy, clearly it was only going to happen, if at all, after the election. In 1963 he had one overarching concern when it came to the "commitment" in Vietnam, and that was campaign politics. He told O'Donnell, "If I tried to pull out completely now from Vietnam, we would have another Joe McCarthy scare on our hands, but I can do it after I'm re-elected."[34] Thus, for domestic political reasons, Kennedy was far from ready to walk away from Vietnam. What he would have done in 1965 will remain unknown. But we do know that in the autumn of 1963 he was encouraging the Bundy brothers and other advisers to do everything they could to create a viable political regime in Saigon, one capable of winning the war against the Viet Cong in the countryside.

It should also be noted that the president's closest adviser, his brother Robert, also seemed to have been skeptical of the American commitment. At a September 6 meeting of the NSC, according to Hilsman, Bobby Kennedy even echoed the fundamental question raised by Kattenburg a week earlier: could any Saigon government successfully resist a communist takeover? "If it could not," Bobby said, "now was the time to get out of Vietnam entirely, rather than waiting. If the answer was that it could, but not with a Diem-Nhu government as it was now constituted, we owed it to the people resisting Communism in Vietnam to give Lodge enough sanctions to bring changes that would permit successful resistance."[35] Bobby Kennedy could ask whether it was time to get out of Vietnam, but his question was predicated on such an imponderable—no one had enough facts to know whether any Saigon government could resist the Viet Cong—that the answer was clear: they would have to get rid of Diem if they wanted to find out.

BACK in Saigon, Ambassador Lodge pressed ahead with his own private campaign for a change in government. Knowing of the Kennedy White House's preoccupation with Castro's Cuba, Lodge cabled, "We do not want to substitute a Castro for a Batista. . . ." In other words, if Washington waited too long, Diem's successor might be someone to the left of Diem. This was an argument which resonated with Mac Bundy.

Not surprisingly, the unannounced economic sanctions and Lodge's public posture of "silence and correctness" toward Diem soon provoked the regime's internal critics. October became a month of coup plotting. On October 5 the generals who had first approached the CIA in August again signaled their intention to organize a coup. By the end of the month, Mac Bundy was receiving almost daily cables from Saigon reporting on the coup plans of a group of generals led by General Duong Van Minh, otherwise known as Big Minh. Bundy's major concern was that any coup attempt might degenerate into civil war. He did not want to be in a position of "thwarting" a coup, but he and Kennedy "would like to have the option of judging and warning on any plan with poor prospects of success." This was, Bundy cabled Lodge, a "large order." (The final sentence of this cable was prudently cut before it went out to Lodge, but it shows Bundy's mind at work: "The difficulty is of course that we want to be able to judge these plans without accepting responsibility for them; the impossible takes a little longer.") Mac was wrestling with considerable doubts. He worried about "plausible deniability" and the possibility that Diem's brother Nhu might have "masterminded a provocation" and was merely waiting to crush the generals. Late in October he scrawled in his tiny handwriting a question to himself, "Should we cool off the whole enterprise?"[36]

Lodge, however, did everything he could to win Bundy's acquiescence. He bluntly warned, ". . . [we] do not think we have the power to delay or discourage a coup." To stop a coup now, Lodge argued, he would have to pass information to Diem and that "would make traitors out of us." Bundy disagreed. He thought, ". . . what we say to coup group can produce delay of coup and betrayal of coup plans to Diem is not rept [repeat] not our only way of stopping coup." Bundy was trying to manage the details of a coup from nine thousand miles away; he wanted to know everything: the exact lineup of troops on each side, the names of the generals party to the coup plans and how far over the horizon U.S. Marines were to be stationed in the event American lives became endangered. He wanted a coup, but only if he could "have assurance [that] balance of forces clearly favorable."

Despite all the hedging, on October 30, Bundy cabled Lodge a final green light: "Once a coup under responsible leadership has begun . . . it is in the interest of the U.S. Government that it should succeed."[37] By then, he knew that a coup was scheduled to occur sometime prior to November 2. On the morning of November 1, Lodge had a short meeting with Diem in which the Vietnamese dictator signaled his willingness to implement whatever reforms Washington thought necessary. Afterwards, Lodge reported to Washington, "In effect he [Diem] said: tell us what you want and we'll do it."[38]

Diem had capitulated, but it was too late. That afternoon at 4:30 P.M., Diem phoned Lodge at the U.S. embassy and said, "Some units have made a rebellion and I want to know, what is the attitude of the U.S.?"

"I do not feel well enough informed to tell you," replied Lodge. "I have heard the shooting, but I am not well enough acquainted with all the facts. Also it is 4:30 A.M. in Washington and the U.S. government cannot possibly have a view."

"But you must have some general ideas. After all, I am a Chief of State. I have tried to do my duty. I want to do now what duty and good sense require. . . ."[39]

After offering in a perfunctory manner to provide Diem a safe passage out of the country, Lodge hung up. That evening Lodge went to bed at nine-thirty, as was his habit, even as artillery fire echoed throughout the city.

Meanwhile, back in the White House, Bundy had gone to the Situation

Room, where he began receiving detailed accounts of the coup from the CIA's Lou Conein, who was sitting in the rebel generals' headquarters. At one point early that morning (Washington time) Bundy and Roger Hilsman cabled the embassy in Saigon that if the coup succeeded, the rebel generals should publicly declare that one of their chief motivations had been that "Nhu was dickering with Communists to betray the anti-Communist cause. High value of this argument should be emphasized to them at earliest opportunity." The embassy quickly replied, "Point has been made to the generals." [40]

At 8 A.M. Washington time Bundy chaired a meeting of his staff and coolly reported that he and Forrestal had "spent a quiet night watching the cables from Vietnam." Almost laconically, he observed that "Diem was still holding out at the palace, adding that no one wanted to go in for the kill." [41]

Actually, that night Diem and his brother Nhu had slipped out of the palace and fled to the home of Ma Tuyen, an influential businessman in Saigon's Chinese quarter. The next morning they sought refuge in St. Francis Xavier Church and gave themselves up to an army unit loyal to General Minh. Hours earlier Minh had reportedly asked U.S. authorities for a plane to ferry Diem out of the country. Though Lodge and Bundy's people in the White House had known for days that this moment might soon arrive, no contingency plan had been made for whisking Diem to safety. Lou Conein told Big Minh that no plane would be available for at least twenty-four hours. This sealed Diem's fate. Rebel troops soon appeared outside the church and forced Diem and Minh into an armored personnel carrier. When the door was opened at the end of their short trip to the Vietnamese Joint General Staff headquarters, the two men were dead, their hands bound behind their backs. Both had been shot and Nhu had been knifed as well. The assassinations had been carried out on the orders of General Minh. [42]

Back in Washington, when President Kennedy learned of the deaths, he turned ashen and rushed from the Situation Room with what Max Taylor called "a look of shock and dismay on his face which I had never seen before." Mac Bundy was equally appalled, but quickly moved to limit the political damage. He cabled Lodge that the deaths had "caused shock here . . . simple assertion of suicide obviously will not end the matter." When Lodge replied that the assassinations were the "kind of thing that will happen in a coup d'etat," Bundy insisted that the coup leaders had to issue a statement emphasizing the ". . . extensive efforts we understand they made to prevent this result." When the generals lamely suggested that perhaps it could be said that the deaths had been an "accidental suicide," Bundy firmly instructed Lodge that this explanation too had to be quashed. [43]

Diem was murdered by his own generals. Though Bundy and others denied it, their complicity in the assassination was palpable. Marguerite Higgins, the reporter whom Bundy derisively called the firebug (he thought she was capable of arson if it would get her a story), called Roger Hilsman as soon as she heard the news and said, "Congratulations, Roger, how does it feel to have blood on your hands?"

"Oh, come on now, Maggie," replied Hilsman. "Revolutions are rough. People get hurt."[44]

DIEM was gone and with him a regime that had been closely allied to Washington for nine long years. After his death in a coup intimately promoted by an American president it would be much harder for Washington to avoid responsibility for a war that would not end. As Bill Bundy put it later, "In an intangible way, Americans in both public and policy circles were bound henceforth to feel more responsible for what happened in Vietnam."[45]

Indeed, with Diem gone, the attitude in Washington was that now the business of winning the war could proceed. On November 21—one day before President Kennedy boarded a plane for a campaign swing through Texas—Mac Bundy sent his brother Bill a short memo referring him to a draft National Security Action Memorandum on Vietnam.[46] The NSAM gave lip service to the October 2 decision to withdraw one thousand U.S. military personnel, but the bulk of the document outlined further steps "to assist the people and Government of that country [Vietnam] to win their contest against the externally directed and supported Communist conspiracy." The military campaign would focus anew on the populous Mekong Delta region in South Vietnam, and a "detailed plan" would be developed for "sea-going" missions against North Vietnam. In the same vein, military operations would be stepped up against the North Vietnamese supply lines, requiring deep incursions into neighboring Laos. In other words, the war was about to expand beyond the South.

Diem's murder closed the door on what was regarded at the time—and not merely in retrospect—as an opportunity to end the American adventure in Vietnam. The coup achieved what the Kennedy White House wanted, which was to build a dam against the incipient political currents in Saigon toward the reunification of Vietnam under the guise of a negotiated neutralism.

Writing in 1971, Bill Bundy claimed that no one in Washington truly feared "that any of the possible contestants for power in Saigon were really likely to call off the war or seek peace on North Vietnamese terms." That Nhu had been talking about a "neutral" Vietnam—and about sending the American advisers home—was evidence of what Bill Bundy thought was Nhu's "irrational behavior"—or worse, it was merely another of Nhu's "ploys, an attempt to scare us."[47] But this ignored the fact that Nhu was not the only South Vietnamese figure who essentially thought of the war with the Viet Cong as a political contest, one which could be lost if the American military presence became too visible. His successors had similar instincts.

Mac Bundy was soon disturbed to hear reports that General Minh himself was inclined to open negotiations with Hanoi, and that like the men he had assassinated, Big Minh was reluctant to accept an increase in American military advisers. Only five weeks after Diem's assassination, Ambassador Lodge received a harsh assessment from Colonel F. P. Serong, the commander of Australian forces in Vietnam. The new government, Colonel Serong claimed, had shown itself incapable: "Meanwhile the war and the nation is disintegrating—You must take control of GVN [Government of Vietnam]. Force it to accept policy and executive direction at all levels . . . tell [General] Minh that the government of Vietnam should accept an American commander for their Army as no one in Vietnam is up to it." When Lodge passed this report to the White House, Forrestal brought it to Bundy's attention with a cover note that said, "Mac: The diagnosis is alarmist and the cure too drastic; but the direction is right."[48]

Forrestal's mind-set was very much Bundy's. Both men believed the communist insurgency could not be defeated unless a competent government in Saigon reformed itself and its army. Liberal reform would win the war by creating a government responsive to the people. U.S. policy-makers had been compelled to remove Diem from the scene because he had become an obstacle to both reform and progress on the battlefield. If his successors proved to be incompetent, then perhaps they, too, would have to make way for a government that could win the war.

HARVEY BUNDY died at his home in Boston on October 7, 1963. Four years earlier he had undergone surgery for prostate cancer. When the cancer recurred Harvey was still working out of his law office. "He fought like a tiger to live," recalled his wife. He suffered every possible operation and numerous cobalt treatments. He seemed in such pain that in the end his children were saying to their mother, "Oh, don't let him have another operation, don't let him, Dolie." Kay Bundy thought it "ghastly" to see her husband suffer so, but she told the children, "Let him? If there is anything anybody can do, he's going to do it."[49]

The Bundy clan, including Bill and Mac, visited him in Manchester several times that summer. "I didn't see him as much as I should have," recalled Bill. "We were pretty damn busy." The funeral took place at a time when both brothers were "intensely preoccupied with the question of Diem."[50]

Ironically, Harvey had died just as his son Bill was being nominated to be an assistant secretary, a title Harvey had once held. Bill's boss, Paul Nitze, left that autumn to become secretary of the navy, and McNamara had immediately recommended Bill's promotion. (Kennedy had already heard Bill praised by Ken Galbraith: "Bill is also intelligent, and willing to act. He shoots from the hip on occasion but usually in the right direction.")[51] After a perfunctory Senate hearing, Bundy's nomination as assistant secretary of defense for international security affairs was confirmed by voice vote at 1 P.M. on November 22. Precisely thirty-four minutes later a wire service flashed the first report that President Kennedy had been shot in Dallas. Bill was sitting in his Pentagon office, waiting to hear about his Senate confirmation, when an aide rushed in with the news.

At that same moment Mac Bundy and Carl Kaysen also happened to be at the Pentagon, sitting in Bob McNamara's office, when an aide walked in and handed the defense secretary a note. McNamara looked stunned for a moment, then handed to Bundy and the three or four other men in the room a brief news wire report that Kennedy had been hit with gunfire. Bundy immediately took McNamara's limousine back to the White House and went directly to the Oval Office. A few minutes later Ted Sorensen came in and said, "It's all over, he's dead." With uncharacteristic emotion, Mac put his arm around the man whose words had made Jack Kennedy's speeches soar with eloquence.

The phone began ringing incessantly. Bobby Kennedy called Bundy to ask about the status of his brother's papers. Bundy called the State Department, and upon being reassured that the presidential papers belonged to the Kennedy family, he ordered the combinations on all the dead president's locked files changed. Not long afterwards he received several phone calls from *Air Force One*, which was about to fly back to Washington with Kennedy's body. "I talked briefly" with Lyndon Johnson, Bundy wrote in his notes twelve days later, "to say that he must get back to Washington where we were all shaky." [52] Another caller from *Air Force One* phoned to say that Johnson wanted him to be at Andrews Air Force Base to meet him upon arrival.

It was dark when the plane landed before a crowd of numbed diplomats, generals and other dignitaries, including Bill Bundy. Mac stood alone, off to one side, clutching a small briefcase under his arm, and watched in stunned silence as Jacqueline Kennedy emerged from the plane, her clothes stained with the blood of her husband. Soon afterwards John Kennedy's coffin was carried off the plane and placed in a truck. Standing in the glare of television lights, the new president read a short statement and then walked toward a waiting helicopter. Motioning to McNamara, Johnson said he wanted the defense secretary, Bundy, George Ball and several other familiar aides to accompany him to the White House. On the ten-minute flight to Washington, Bundy sat next to Mrs. Johnson. As they were landing, he heard Lyndon Johnson praising John Kennedy: "Kennedy did something I couldn't have done. He gathered around him the ablest people I've seen—not his friends, not even the best in public service, but the best anywhere. I want you to stay. I need you. I want you to stand with me." No other words could have better appealed to Bundy's sense of himself and his duty to the presidency. [53]

FOR Mac Bundy, the next few days were a blur of tears and the mundane. He now was serving two masters, but one was waiting to be buried. He thought of himself as a "maid of all work," who "fussed around" attending to the details of the transition. On Saturday—the first full day of Johnson's presidency—he escorted the new president into his office, where CIA director John McCone gave Johnson his first global intelligence briefing. Chet Cooper was struck by how ashen Mac looked. "He looked awful, just terrible," Cooper recalled. "But he sensed what he had to do and he did it." Cooper went home that night and told his wife how impressed he was with Bundy's "control of himself." [54]

That same Saturday Johnson convened an awkward cabinet meeting which Bobby Kennedy would not have attended unless Bundy had told him he had to be there. Bobby arrived late and sat in brooding silence. Mac told a colleague later that afternoon that he was worried, that Bobby "was reluctant to face the new reality." Some thought Bundy was too quick to face reality, and specifically, too quick to urge Johnson to occupy the Oval Office. He had also annoyed Bobby by conveying Johnson's desire to address the nation the day after the funeral. This had led to angry words. Bobby told Mac, "Well, the hell with it." Bundy just thought he was doing his job, and that it didn't make sense to leave the "command post empty because the commander has fallen." [55]

Mac described his grief as "deep and general." Less than a month earlier he had lost his father, and now his president. But he was the kind of man who dealt with his grief in private. His good friend Arthur Schlesinger noted at the time, "for some people, personal emotion is very difficult. . . . Bundy has everything under iron control. I do not think that this means that they feel things less than the rest of us." Bundy did have his emotions under control, but as he later wrote, "Friday and Saturday I cried at home—after that not." After learning of Lee Harvey Oswald's arrest and subsequent murder, Bundy decided that the assassination was not part of a broader conspiracy. All that weekend the German word *Unsinn* ("absurdity") kept popping into his mind, and a few days later he wrote, "the dominant meaning of the tragedy is that it was senseless. . . ." To his mind, Kennedy had been martyred for nothing.[56]

On Sunday afternoon, November 24, the day before the hastily organized state funeral, Mac went over to the White House mansion and in the president's living quarters sat down with Bobby Kennedy and Jacqueline to discuss what should be read at the funeral. Bundy and Sorensen had marked numerous passages from the late president's speeches. Sorensen picked up a Bible and selected the somber passage, "To every thing there is a season, and a time to every purpose under the heaven: A time to be born, and a time to die . . ." Jackie immediately agreed. And then she suddenly announced, "And there's going to be an eternal flame." Bundy wrote a few days later of the funeral, "it came out right—as did just about everything that Jackie touched those days —and she touched nearly everything." [57]

Later that Sunday, Mac brought two of his sons, Stephen and Andrew, to view the coffin lying in state in the East Room. "By some accident we had him to ourselves for the few moments that we had the strength to linger." Bundy was exhausted, and the exhaustion brought some relief. "Sunday night was less terrible," he later wrote. He slept and the next morning rose to bury the president.

Together with French president Charles de Gaulle, Ethiopian emperor Haile Selassie, the entire Supreme Court, the cabinet and most of his White House colleagues, Bundy marched in Kennedy's funeral procession down

Pennsylvania Avenue. "What friends he had, and how much they cared," he wrote. "Even in our grief we were . . . proud of his confidence and proud of each other. . . . The end of the service at Arlington was like the fall of a curtain, or the snapping of taut strings."[58] It was done.

ONE of the new president's first official acts was to accept the Senate's confirmation of Bill Bundy as assistant secretary of defense. In early December, Johnson called Mac at his home to say that he had heard that Bundy's mother was in town visiting. Could he talk to her? Mac laughed and went to find her. Kay was on the other phone, talking to a Lowell, when he told her that "the president would like to speak with you." Thinking this was one of Mac's "silly jokes," Kay paid no attention to her son. After fidgeting for a minute Mac finally said, "Mother, how long are you going to keep the president of the United States waiting?" When she finally picked up the other phone, she heard Johnson's booming Texas drawl, "I want to see you, Mrs. Bundy. I want to see you tomorrow morning." The very next day Mac ushered her into the Cabinet Room. "She was one-on-one with Johnson," Bill Bundy recalled, "and he poured himself out about how his mother had meant more to him than anything in the world, he just really laid it on. The LBJ trowel treatment."[59] Kay, of course, was never at a loss for words and told Johnson at great length about her previous visits to the White House during the Hoover administration, and once as a debutante when Theodore Roosevelt was president. Johnson's efforts were somewhat superfluous. To the surprise of some in the Kennedy family, particularly Bobby, Mac had already decided to remain in the White House as long as the new president wanted him.

Although he had cried in the dark for his president, Mac felt that his loyalties should be to the office of the presidency. Later, when some would whisper that he had been too quick to transfer his loyalties, Bundy observed that "in different ways each circle of hurt found it easy to forget that others were also in grief. In particular it was easy to forget that the new President and his circle were hurt, too."[60] Arthur Schlesinger knew instantly that he would be leaving, and he assumed that "the whole crowd of us should clear out—that is, those of us in the White House." The only exception, he thought, was Bundy, who "has created his own job."[61]

Mac's willingness to serve the new president could be interpreted as further evidence of his ambition, but this would be far too simple an explanation. Bundy always had other attractive career options. Indeed, in the weeks before Kennedy's death, Mac had been seriously weighing a discreet but quite firm invitation to become president of Yale University. Ironically, one of the last pieces of paper handed to Jack Kennedy on his way out of the Oval Office on November 21 was a brief note from Mac saying that he had finally decided to reject the Yale overture.[62] Bundy knew the Yale job seemed rightfully destined for his old friend Kingman Brewster, but still, it had been difficult to turn down Eli. Having made the decision so recently to remain in the White

House, Mac was not the kind of person to have second doubts—even after the assassination.

In any case, Johnson was courting the Bundy brothers and all of the slain president's other close aides. A veteran legislator and instinctive arm-twister, Lyndon Johnson was nevertheless feeling very insecure as president. "I needed that White House staff," Johnson later told biographer Doris Kearns. "Without them I would have lost my link to John Kennedy, and without that I would have had absolutely no chance of gaining the support of the media or the Easterners or the intellectuals. And without that support I would have had absolutely no chance of governing the country." [63] To reassure himself—and a nation in mourning—he was determined to surround himself with the slain president's advisers and make it clear that John Kennedy's agenda was his. "It's a mistake," Senator Richard Russell of Georgia, LBJ's old Senate mentor, told Johnson's secretary one day after emerging from a White House meeting. "He ought not to keep them. It's a mistake and I've told him so." [64]

At home, the new president would soon steer into law an astonishing array of social welfare and civil rights legislation. At home, Lyndon Johnson would quickly personify a triumphant liberalism. But on the foreign policy ledger, Johnson's holdovers from the Kennedy years would prove incapable of controlling the president's latent compulsions to resolve troublesome foreign problems with military intervention. Mac and Bill Bundy had more often than not pushed President Kennedy—a cautious Cold Warrior—to persevere in the wars against communism. But with President Lyndon Johnson they would sometimes find themselves dragging their heels and holding onto his coattails.

The Bundys and Lyndon Johnson would over time prove to be an unfortunate mix. They were too confident, and he was too insecure about his Texan roots and too enamored of Cold War shibboleths. They were loyal to a fault when they should have deserted him. But though the personal chemistry was all wrong, this would not become evident for many months. The Bundy brothers were the quintessential Stimsonians: tough-minded realists who nevertheless had liberal sensibilities about America's role in a world dominated by the Cold War. Such men, thought Johnson, were invaluable—even if they did reek of Harvard and Yale.

12

LBJ and Vietnam, 1964

What we are dealing with then is social revolution by illegal means, infected by the cancer of Communism. I have been told by people in our Government that there is no time to reform South Vietnam. We must win the war first, and then we can get on with the problem of social reform. . . . I believed this too, until after the third or fourth trip to Vietnam. But the problems are not separable. The Viet Cong know this. It is why they are winning.

Michael Forrestal
SECRET Memorandum to
John McNaughton and McGeorge Bundy
May 1, 1964

SOON AFTER THE NEW YEAR Mac Bundy boarded a plane for Antigua, his favorite winter resort, much in need of a rest. He brought with him only one assignment, a request from Hamilton Fish Armstrong, the editor of *Foreign Affairs,* to write an essay that would reassure the journal's elite readership around the world that despite the assassination, Kennedy's spirit lived on in the new administration.

"It was not just the loss of the intellectual Kennedy and the Kennedy in action that has been so deplored," Armstrong had written Bundy. "It was the loss of what I can't describe better than by calling it the Kennedy style. . . . Let us take this moment to tell them that the Kennedy style lives on, that we are as sensible, as helpful, as imaginative as ever about the things that concern us all. The very fact that it was you who wrote an article of the sort I have in mind would be the assurance that this was so."

The assignment appealed to Bundy, partly, as he told McNamara, because it "should be useful to the President we have, as well as a tribute to the one we have lost. . . ." Published in the April 1964 issue, Bundy's "The Presidency and the Peace" acknowledged Kennedy's grace and wit—qualities, of course, which everyone knew Johnson lacked. But for Bundy the real meaning of Kennedy's years in office was that "the American Presidency, for better, not for worse, has now become the world's best hope of preventing the unexampled catastrophe of general nuclear war." The defining moment of the Kennedy years—his astute management of the Cuban missile crisis—demonstrated that this American president understood that in the face of the communist threat to liberty, the United States had to insist on a decidedly unequal nuclear balance: "In that balance there is American superiority . . . but it is a superiority that does not permit any lack of respect for the strength of the Soviet Union."

If the missile crisis proved America's "resolution," the test ban treaty demonstrated America's readiness to work for humanity's survival in the nuclear age. Kennedy had "shown his spreading grasp of his duty to mankind as Chief Executive for Peace." Lyndon Johnson's four short months in office had already demonstrated that "the pursuit of peace remains his central concern." In a pointed admonishment to those who would restore "Camelot," Bundy concluded that "loyalty to President Kennedy and loyalty to President Johnson are not merely naturally compatible, but logically necessary as a part of a larger loyalty to their common purpose."

Finally, in a portentous aside, Bundy commented, "The new kinds of strength deployed to South Vietnam have not finished that hard job, but they have prevented an otherwise certain defeat and kept the door open for a victory in which the end can be won only by the Vietnamese themselves."[1]

WAITING in his in-box when he returned from Antigua was a top-secret, thirteen-page interdepartmental report entitled "Operations Against North Vietnam." Dated January 3, 1964, it outlined a year-long program of covert operations: phase one, to begin on February 1, would include "about 20 destructive undertakings," such as the destruction of a bridge, a radar station, road ambushes and other such targets inside North Vietnam. The attacks would be carried out by South Vietnamese commandos trained and financed by the CIA and the U.S. military. Bundy passed the document to Michael Forrestal, who was becoming more skeptical of, and yet more resigned to, such covert operations. Forrestal dryly replied to Bundy that such operations were "difficult" and usually "ill-fated. . . . In short, we will be sending men to their deaths." Even so, Forrestal didn't bother to make an argument for stopping the operations. Instead, he tinkered with the planning document: "Can we justify the road-cutting operations in terms of the cost of human life? We should be able to find economically more important targets whose sabotage would have a significant and longer lasting effect." He noted that any such covert operations would have "a minimal influence on Hanoi's policies toward the South." Bundy agreed, but his attitude was that anything not too expensive that could be done should be. On January 7 he recommended the program to the president. Isolated covert operations against the North had occurred earlier, but now there would be a methodical campaign.[2]

On January 6, Senator Mike Mansfield had warned President Johnson, "We are close to the point of no return in Viet Nam." In an earlier telephone conversation Johnson had observed that he didn't want to see "another China in Vietnam." The president was thinking politically about the wounds Democrats had taken during the debate of 1949–50 over "who lost China." Mansfield "respectfully" demurred. "Neither," he wrote the president, "do we want another Korea." Americans had a tendency in both situations to "bite off more than we were prepared in the end to chew." American interests in Vietnam, Mansfield contended, were not worth the "blood and treasure" that would accompany armed intervention. The time had come to avoid another Korea by seeking a peaceful solution, perhaps through neutralization.[3]

Lyndon Johnson had a high regard for Mansfield, but his instinctive political fear of being labeled soft on communism led him to distrust the senator's advice. Bundy reinforced Johnson's instincts with his own comments "as an ex-historian." According to Bundy, Mansfield was using the wrong analogy and misinterpreting the lessons of both China and Korea: "The political damage to Truman and Acheson from the fall of China arose because most Americans came to believe that we could and should have done more than we did to prevent it. This is exactly what would happen now if we should seem to be the first to quit in Saigon."[*]

Such advice to the president, coming from the "ex-historian," the former Harvard dean and, even more tellingly, the young man whose book *The Pattern of Responsibility* had defended Acheson from such right-wing attacks in 1951, must have seemed irrefutable to Johnson. The president had to avoid becoming the Dean Acheson of the 1960s. In Vietnam, Bundy argued, that meant supporting the war effort and rejecting neutralization. "*When* we are stronger," he concluded, "*then* we can face negotiation" [Bundy's emphasis]. This was a political judgment, not an analysis of foreign policy. Bundy was well aware that such close friends as Ken Galbraith and Walter Lippmann disagreed with him and favored Mansfield's position.[4]

Mac had been not only a friend but a political compatriot of Lippmann's. By 1964, however, Bundy believed his onetime mentor was too enamored of unrealistic "Gaullist" notions about the Cold War. While they still had lunch on occasion, and Lippmann continued to use Bundy as an unnamed source in his columns, the two men found they no longer agreed on many issues.

One day later that spring, Lippmann dropped in on Bundy at his office in the White House basement. The columnist had just come back from Paris, and when the subject of Vietnam came up, Bundy flatly said that De Gaulle's

* Later that year Bundy wrote Johnson, "I myself believe that before we let this country go, we should have a hard look at this grim alternative [sending "substantial armed forces"], and I do not at all think that it is a repetition of Korea" (Michael Beschloss, *Taking Charge: The Johnson White House Tapes, 1963–1964* [New York: Simon & Schuster, 1997], p. 546).

neutralization proposal was merely a disguised prescription for a communist takeover. "Mac, please don't talk in such clichés," Lippmann said. "We both know better than that." A neutralist, communist regime like Tito's Yugoslavia, he said, was probably the best Washington could hope for in South Vietnam. Bundy responded that it would be a shame if Americans had died in Vietnam only to see communists seize power. Lippmann was stunned by the exchange. When he returned to his home on Woodley Road, he told his researcher, Elizabeth Farmer, that Bundy's years in the White House had coarsened his mind. The next day Lippmann wrote an unusually blunt column endorsing De Gaulle's neutralization proposal and charging that the Johnson administration had "no credible policy for winning the war or for ending it."

Bundy's response was to make sure that a week later Lippmann was invited to the White House. When Lippmann walked into the Oval Office, he found Bundy, McNamara and Under Secretary of State George Ball waiting to hear him debate the issue with Johnson. Fingering a sheaf of top-secret cables, the president assured him that the door to negotiations was still open. "Unless I have been grossly and continuously misled," Lippmann told his readers afterwards, "our objective is to create a balance of forces which favors and supports a negotiated settlement in Southeast Asia."[5] Lippmann was still on board.

WHILE Bundy steadied Johnson's hand against the advocates of neutralization on Capitol Hill and elsewhere, he was soon discomfited to hear renewed reports that Diem's successors in Saigon were moving very much in that direction. Ambassador Lodge reported on January 21 that the junta led by General Duong Van Minh was distinctly unenthusiastic about the plan to launch a campaign of covert attacks against the North. When informed that the Americans were considering using U.S. aircraft with South Vietnamese markings to bomb the North, Minh told McNamara that bombing "would not produce good military results" and would merely harm "innocent Vietnamese." The junta leaders stressed the "extreme undesirability of Americans going into districts and villages" because this would lend a "colonial flavor to the whole pacification effort." Worse, it soon became clear that the junta wished to draw the political arm of the Viet Cong, the National Liberation Front (NLF), out of the jungles and into a government of national reconciliation. That prospect set off alarm bells in Washington.[6]

But before anyone in Washington could formulate a strategy for dealing with the direction the junta was taking, General Nguyen Khanh seized control of Saigon in a bloodless coup, imprisoning Minh and his colleagues. Khanh appeared to have acted independently, though he had guardedly signaled his intentions two days earlier in conversations with the CIA station chief and Ambassador Lodge. According to Bill Bundy, the coup of January 30, 1964, "was most definitely not anticipated or stimulated by any American." But it was nevertheless welcomed. "Both Lodge and [General Paul] Harkins [commander of the U.S. military assistance program in Saigon since 1962]," Forrestal reported that day to Bundy and the president, "think that Khanh is a tough, able military leader." Upon assuming power, General Khanh quickly indicated his disapproval for any steps toward neutralization. He vigorously supported the planned covert sabotage campaign against the North and reversed Minh's objection to sending American advisers into the countryside.[7]

A week after the Khanh coup, Mac Bundy had a revealing phone conversation with the president. Ever sensitive to press criticism, Johnson was troubled by intimations he read in the *New York Times* and elsewhere that the sensible solution in Vietnam was neutralization. Bundy found himself once again trying to reassure Johnson: "Well, the *Times* editorial page is a soft page, Mr. President. It makes Walter Lippmann look like a warmonger. They're clever, but they don't have a whole lot of judgment. . . . They're tempted by neutralization in Vietnam, which doesn't make any sense at this stage."

When Johnson asked, "What do we say about neutralization of Vietnam?" Bundy replied, "If the U.S. forces were withdrawn, that thing [the Saigon regime] would collapse like a pack of cards. Maybe when we have a stronger position, maybe when we've pressed through with this and maybe if they can get a government that'll move . . . there'll come a time when there'll be a balanced force in South Vietnam that can survive. But anyone who thinks that exists now is crazy and anybody who says it exists is undermining the essential first effort. And that is the hazard of what de Gaulle is doing and it's the hazard in what some other people are suggesting."[8]

It was Bundy's persistence that kept that "essential first effort" on track. The goal was to maintain the status quo without escalating the conflict and without withdrawing. It was a difficult balancing act for everyone. Walter Lippmann attacked the policy from the left, while Joe Alsop charged the administration was being far too timid. In early March, Mac Bundy mentioned to Johnson that he had to have lunch with Alsop. "I think," Bundy told the president, "he really wants to have a little old war out there."

When Johnson confided he just wanted to "maintain the status quo for six months," Bundy replied, "The only thing that scares me is that the government would up and quit on us, or that there would be a coup and we'd be invited out."

The question, Bundy said, was whether a little "stiffener" in the form of another couple of thousand advisers might demonstrate "that we think this damn thing can be done."[9]

By the spring of 1964, both Bundy brothers were spending a lot of time on Vietnam. Bill Bundy was spending all his waking hours on the war. The previous December, President Johnson had sent McNamara and Bill Bundy to Saigon for another look. There, they found the military situation once again critical in at least thirteen of the forty-six provinces. Bill thought that much of what had been reported to Washington was superficial at best and certainly "misleading." McNamara was profoundly shaken by what he heard.[10]

Even after the Khanh coup, Bill was persuaded that the situation was nearly hopeless. Early in February he and other top officials, including the president, received a CIA report based on a field investigation by ten intelligence officers with long experience in Southeast Asia. The report was decidedly pessimistic and convinced many readers that a Viet Cong takeover of Saigon was probable within months.

In this atmosphere, the Johnson administration announced on February 29 that Bill Bundy would replace Roger Hilsman as assistant secretary of state for the Far East. Joe Alsop was heartened by the change, believing that Hilsman had been a weak reed. Mac Bundy told Johnson that Alsop was "all cheered up because he was very wary of [Roger] Hilsman and thinks that is, that Bill [Bundy] going in there is in itself sort of a solution to the problem. It's not. No one man is going to solve a headache like this one."[11]

Bill himself was not particularly uplifted by the appointment. "It was a change," he later wrote, "I had not sought or desired." At defense, he had had ample responsibility in supervising a 360-person shop. So wide-ranging were his powers that *Time* magazine had recently called him "in effect, the Pentagon's 'Secretary of State.' " He had been happy working with McNamara, who in turn was "very reluctant" to let him go. Nor was Bill certain that he would have the same rapport with Dean Rusk. His father-in-law had such a low opinion of Rusk that when he heard people complain that it was hard to decipher the secretary's thinking, Acheson snapped, "Did it ever occur to you that he wasn't thinking?"

Acheson went so far as to try to persuade the president to let his son-in-law stay with McNamara, but Johnson thought Bundy had exactly the kind of toughness he wanted in a State Department known for its procrastination. Johnson blamed Hilsman for pushing through the coup that killed Diem; by contrast, he thought of Bundy as a man who would "run it through to the hilt." Bundy, in any case, felt obligated to accept the job.[12] In a brief profile of the new assistant secretary, *U.S. News & World Report* observed that Bundy "has not been strongly identified with either the 'tough line' or the 'soft approach' in meeting Red pressures around the world."[13]

On March 5, even before he was sworn into his new office, Bill once again found himself clambering aboard a windowless air force plane, bound for Saigon on yet another mission with McNamara. The defense secretary had firm oral instructions from Johnson that he should make it clear to all that General Khanh was "our man." There could be no more coups.

Even then, Bill realized that any effort to expand the war to the North would be "complex, costly, and unpredictable." By then, covert teams of South Vietnamese commandos had been operating against the North for at least a month. Bill noted that these operations reflected a "general picture of failure and discouragement." After four days of whirlwind briefings in South Vietnam, McNamara held a joint press conference with General Khanh and dramatically endorsed him as "our man." Bill disapproved of this public spectacle, but recalled, "I remember crossing my fingers, no more."

The resulting McNamara Report was, as usual, by and large Bundy's handiwork. The report bluntly warned that either a Viet Cong takeover or a negotiated neutralist solution would lead to communist control of South Vietnam—and probably all of Southeast Asia, including Indonesia. "Thus, purely in terms of foreign policy, the stakes are high. They are increased by domestic factors." What Bundy meant, of course, was the prospect of igniting a "who lost Vietnam" debate, a political fistfight that liberal Democrats could not win.

Soon after coming back from Vietnam, Bill and an aide, James C. Thomson, Jr., were told to draft a speech for McNamara which would clearly blame the conflict on external aggression from the North. Thomson annoyed Bundy by musing, "But in some ways, of course, it is a civil war." Bill snapped, "Don't mince words with me." Of course, Bill knew it was a civil war, and the speech as much as admitted that point by speaking of the Viet Cong's "large indigenous support" as well as Hanoi's support for the guerrillas. But in 1964, Bundy also understood that the defense secretary could not label the conflict a civil war without undermining U.S. domestic political support for intervening in Vietnam.[14]

The Joint Chiefs, for their part, were disappointed that the president had not decided in March to carry the war to the North with overt U.S. attacks. As one general told Forrestal after a "rather wet working dinner," he felt that if "we couldn't make the high jumps in South Vietnam, that we should pole-vault into the North." Forrestal reported to Mac Bundy that the generals thought President Johnson was avoiding the "correct decision" in Vietnam because he did not wish to face a domestic political crisis before the November election.* This sentiment suggested a risk that the military brass might begin leaking their views to the press and make the president look weak. Forrestal reassured Bundy that if a public debate was to emerge, the administration could handle it: "Prudence and caution are really more popular stances, I believe, than loud demands for war." To protect themselves, responsible officials in the government should emphasize that the situation was being constantly reviewed. Indeed, the door was open to further military action.[15]

THAT spring both Bill and Mac Bundy participated in the first of two major war games on Vietnam. SIGMA I-64 was played in April at the Pentagon. Players were divided into Red and Blue teams. The game focused on a tit-for-tat scenario in which the United States (the Blue Team) responded to guerrilla attacks in South Vietnam with gradually escalating air attacks (by U.S. aircraft with South Vietnamese markings) on North Vietnam. A declassified summary

---

* Johnson told Mac Bundy on March 4 that the Joint Chiefs "say get in or get out." Johnson then explained to them that he was only a "trustee" president: "I got to win an election . . . and then, uh, you can make a decision. But in the meantime let's see if we can't find enough things to do to keep them off base and stop these shipments that are coming in from Laos, and take a few selective targets to upset them a bit without getting another Korea operation started" (Beschloss, *Taking Charge*, p. 267).

report of the game eerily predicted that if the cover for the U.S. bombing was "so thin as to resemble cynical aggression, we may encounter severe problems in the UN and before the bar of world opinion . . . a significant vocal proportion of US opinion may join in the hue and cry." In both this game and the second one, SIGMA II-64, played during September, the Blue Team launched major bombing campaigns that failed to break the will of the Red Team. Indeed, in the war game the Red Team responded to each escalation in the bombing by sending larger numbers of ground troops to the South.

The Bundys, according to one participant, "brushed off the result of the war games."[16] And perhaps for good reason. They were all too surrealistic. Mac Bundy thought the games brought out the worst instincts in the military brass. One day, during an intermission, General Curtis LeMay, air force chief of staff, complained that his air power was being misused, that if the United States was going to bomb, there should be nothing limited about the bombing. American bombers should flatten not only North Vietnam's oil depots, but its ports and fragile dikes as well. "We should bomb them into the Stone Age," LeMay said.

"Maybe," Bundy shot back, "they're already there."

"I don't understand it," LeMay insisted. "Here we are at the height of our power. The most powerful nation in the world. And yet we're afraid to use that power, we lack the will. In the last thirty years we've lost Estonia. Latvia. Lithuania. Poland. Czechoslovakia. Hungary. Bulgaria. China . . ."

"Some people," Bundy interrupted, "don't think we ever had them."[17]

Bundy came away from the encounter convinced that he had to watch out for fools who happened to have stars on their shoulders. He knew from Ken Galbraith, who had worked on the U.S. Strategic Bombing Survey, that air force brass like LeMay had greatly exaggerated the effects of strategic bombing during World War II. If anything, the war games confirmed Bundy's judgment that if the administration ever decided to take the war north by bombing, careful limits would have to be set.

THE real war was another matter. On June 1, Mac Bundy reported to President Johnson that 140 Americans had been killed in Vietnam since the beginning of 1961 due to "hostile forces." (Eighty-seven more had died for noncombat reasons.) But thirty-six of those combat deaths had occurred in the first five months of 1964, an indication that the war was beginning to exact a higher toll.[18]

Such casualties worried both Bundy brothers, who had already begun to seek out expert opinion on Southeast Asia. That spring Bill Bundy met Bernard Fall, a French-born combat reporter and author of several books on Vietnam. He and Bundy were introduced at a small gathering of liberal Democratic senators. Fall had recently written an article in *The Reporter* in which he opposed the U.S. counterinsurgency strategy, the introduction of U.S. combat troops and direct strikes at North Vietnam. Instead, his preferred policy was to "negotiate from strength." In his exchange with Bundy, Fall seemed to be suggesting that the threat of bombing Hanoi's factories—built at great cost since the French had left—might prove to be an effective diplomatic tactic. Ironically, Bundy responded that the United States could hardly afford to make threats it was not prepared to carry out. Afterwards, Bundy made an effort to keep in touch with Fall. "I valued his first-hand observations and made a real effort to see him whenever he had been on the scene." But as time went by, Bill became annoyed with Fall, whom he thought was playing to his audience by becoming more critical of the war.[19] (In February 1967, Fall was killed by a land mine in South Vietnam.)

Early that summer Mac Bundy saw his former Harvard aide and *Crimson* editor A. J. Langguth. Now a *New York Times* reporter, Jack Langguth dropped by the White House to say that he had been posted to Saigon. Though Langguth hadn't seen his old dean in nearly eight years, Bundy greeted him warmly. In preparation for his assignment, Langguth had spent days reading through the *Times*'s clip files on Vietnam, and the more he read, the more depressed he got. Inevitably, Mac raised the subject, asking, "So you're going to Vietnam, what do you think?"

"I think it looks terrible," Langguth said.

"Well," Mac replied, "my role is to get people to say it's not as bad as Langguth thinks it is, and it's not as good as Marguerite Higgins thinks it is." *[20]

On June 2, Bill Bundy flew out to Honolulu to join McNamara, Ambassador Lodge, General William Westmoreland [the newly appointed commander of U.S. military assistance in Saigon], General Maxwell Taylor [chairman of the Joint Chiefs], CIA director John McCone, Assistant Secretary of Defense for International Security Affairs John McNaughton and veteran diplomat William Sullivan for a major review of Vietnam policy. At this meeting Bill presented an "action plan" that began with a congressional resolution authorizing U.S. military action and ended with air attacks on North Vietnam.[21]

Bill later explained his drafting of the congressional resolution as a mere contingency. There was a moment in the spring of 1964, he said, when he, his brother, McNamara and others thought the military situation would compel a decision to intervene. If that happened, they realized they would have to go to Congress for some kind of authorization for the expenditure of funds and the deployment of troops in Vietnam. So a resolution was drafted, and then quickly pocketed, because the military crisis seemed to recede, and because Congress was absorbed with passing the civil rights bill and could not be diverted into a debate over Vietnam. And because the presidential campaign was looming, they also knew that nothing they did in Vietnam should inter-

---

* A Pulitzer Prize–winning reporter for *Newsday* and other papers, Higgins strongly endorsed the American war effort.

fere with the need to defeat Barry Goldwater. That summer Ray Cline recalled Mac Bundy asking him about Vietnam: "We know we're not going to do a goddamn thing while this goddamn election is going on. Can we make it that far?"[22]

The military crisis in Vietnam may have receded enough to allow Bill Bundy to shelve his draft of a congressional resolution. But Vietnam still absorbed much of his and Mac's attention that summer. Mac worried about who should replace Lodge as ambassador in Saigon—and went so far as to volunteer himself. On June 6 he dictated a memo to the president listing six candidates: Sargent Shriver (a Kennedy brother-in-law), Deputy Secretary of Defense Roswell Gilpatric, Bob McNamara, Robert Kennedy, William Gaud (deputy director of the Agency for International Development) and himself. Each of these men possessed a stature far beyond the rank of a mere ambassador. But Mac Bundy obviously thought Vietnam was crucial enough to warrant sending the defense secretary, the attorney general or even the president's national security adviser. His only reservation about sending McNamara off to the "provinces" was that he was "a little stale" on Vietnam and "in a curious way, he has rather mechanized the problem so that he misses some of its real political flavor." As to himself, Mac wrote, "I am no judge of my own skills, and it is certainly true that I have never run an embassy or a war. On the other hand, I think I do understand the issues. I know I care about them. I speak French and I have a heavy dose of the ways of thinking of all branches of the U.S. team in South Vietnam."[23] If the president's national security adviser was willing to go to Saigon, he must have known that Vietnam was not a war about to fade away.

Four days later Bundy again pushed Johnson on naming Lodge's replacement: "Until we get a new Ambassador, we cannot really mount a sound program for crash action—political, social and economic—in South Vietnam." Spurred on by Johnson himself, Bundy reported that plans were afoot for "additional steps . . . on the basic theory that Americans can and should do more."[24]

Mac understood better than most of the president's advisers that the war would be won off the battlefield, in the "hearts and minds" of the Vietnamese people. Again, Michael Forrestal was his tutor on these matters. One day that spring Bundy's young aide lost his temper as he stood in an elevator with John McNaughton. A former Harvard Law professor and one of McNamara's brightest whiz kids, the soft-spoken McNaughton had angered Forrestal with a remark on the economics of counterinsurgency. Forrestal had heard it all before and cut him off sharply. Afterwards, he went back to his White House office and wrote a four-page apology, stamped it "Secret" and sent it over to McNaughton, with a copy to Mac.

After apologizing for his "reactive logic" in the elevator, Forrestal tried to explain his frustration. The meeting with the brass that afternoon, he stated, had once again demonstrated that "we have not been able to develop a concept of the kind of war we are fighting that goes beyond the useless observation that the war is more political than it is military . . . we have spent the last two and a half years squabbling among ourselves, at great cost not only to the human beings involved, but also to our own confidence. . . ."

He questioned "whether we can learn fast enough to avoid disaster in Southeast Asia. . . . We may be facing a situation in which the classic American pragmatic approach to problem-solving breaks down because our past experience is not relevant to the current problem."

Recalling what a Frenchman had told him about France's experience in Vietnam, he said, "We are using a pile-driver to kill a fly." The problem, Forrestal believed, was economic inequality and simple social justice. It was naive to expect that reform could occur by legal means "where the social and economic structure are frozen because of the power of the mandarins. . . .

"What we are dealing with then," he wrote to McNaughton and Bundy, "is social revolution by illegal means, infected by the cancer of Communism. I have been told by people in our Government that there is no time to reform South Vietnam. We must win the war first, and then we can get on with the problem of social reform. You may have had something like this in mind yourself when you were talking about the 'time fuses' today. I believed this too, until after the third or fourth trip to Vietnam. But the problems are not separable. The Viet Cong know this. It is why they are winning. To the extent we manage our economic assistance, our military action, and our political advice so as to perpetuate a social and economic structure which gave rise to the very problem we are fighting, we will fail to solve that problem." [25]

What did Mac Bundy think of Forrestal's analysis? Did he upbraid his aide for voicing such heresies? Did he call him into his office and suggest that it was time for him to go back to Wall Street? On the contrary, Bundy would seek out Forrestal's views on Vietnam for as long as he remained national security adviser. Later the same month he even sent Forrestal back to Vietnam on yet another investigative trip. Why? Because he trusted Forrestal absolutely, and because there were no fundamental differences between them on Vietnam. Bundy agreed that the war would be won or lost in the political sphere, and that is why he was willing to put himself forward as Lodge's replacement. The generals could not win this war, but perhaps a hard-nosed intellectual like himself could go out to Saigon and create the kind of "crash action" program of political, economic and social reforms that would win the war.

BECAUSE Forrestal's secret memos to Bundy have remained classified—indeed, Forrestal and Bundy may have had the only copies—historians have not realized the extent to which the president's national security adviser understood that the war was to be won only off the battlefield. As early as the spring of 1964, Mac Bundy was exposed to the kind of critical assessments of the war that McNamara, for instance, would not begin to share in private with his closest colleagues until early 1966. This did not mean that Bundy favored withdrawal and its inevitable consequences—a neutral coalition government in the South soon to be followed by a reunified Vietnam governed by the communist regime in the North. For Bundy, that was still unthinkable, at least until a concerted effort had been made to institute social and economic reforms inside South Vietnam. This would take time, and in the meantime the war could not be abandoned.

Forrestal agreed precisely because he was so pessimistic about the Saigon regime's ability to wage the war alone. After spending two more weeks in Vietnam, he wrote Bundy on May 26 that he had brought back with him two very strong opinions: First, the United States "must take a fairly dramatic step soon against the North . . . a bit of a shock is needed." Second, "I think we have to increase significantly our penetration of the Vietnamese civilian and military bureaucracy at the corps and province levels. . . ." Americans, Forrestal wrote, must "interpose themselves much more directly in the chain of command between Saigon and the villages." Forrestal understood the dangers of Americanizing the conflict, but he also knew the war was essentially political, that it could not be won without the kind of "social revolution" in the countryside that the Saigon generals and mandarins had long resisted. If the South Vietnamese wouldn't do it, then the Americans would have to direct the pacification effort themselves.[26]

That same day Bundy passed Forrestal's "important memorandum" to President Johnson and later cited Forrestal's conclusions as he drafted talking points for the president's meeting that afternoon with a group of Republican senators. The situation was so bad that "some very serious possibilities . . . may lie ahead of us." Mac was recommending air attacks: "We should strike to hurt but not to destroy," he told Johnson, "and strike for the purpose of changing the North Vietnamese decision on intervention in the South."[27]

The very next day Johnson had a phone conversation with Bundy. As Mac came on the line, Johnson had his secretary turn a switch which activated a tape recorder. There were some conversations he wanted on tape and this was one of them. (Bundy was unaware that the presidential taping system even existed.) No doubt thinking of Bundy's Vietnam memorandum of the day before, Johnson began the conversation by saying, "I'll tell you . . . I just stayed awake last night thinking about this thing. The more I think of it, I don't know what in the hell, it looks to me like we're getting into another Korea. It just worries the hell out of me. . . . I don't think it's worth fighting for and I don't think we can get out. And it's just the biggest damn mess."

Bundy: "It is. It's an awful mess."

Johnson later commented, "Of course, if you start running from the communists, they may just chase you right into your own kitchen."

"Yeah," Bundy replied, "that's the trouble. And that is what the rest of that half of the world is going to think if this thing comes apart on us. . . . That's exactly the dilemma."

LBJ: "But everybody I talk to that's got any sense in there nearly says, 'Oh my God, please, give this thought.' . . . But this is a terrible thing we're getting ready to do."

Johnson then asked, "What does Bill [Bundy] think we ought to do?"

"He's in favor of touching things up," Mac replied vaguely, "but you ought to talk to him about it."

When Johnson pressed him as to what concrete action should be taken, Bundy replied, "I think that we *really* need to do you some target folder work, Mr. President, that shows precisely what we do and don't mean here . . . the main object is to kill as few people as possible."

Johnson and Bundy were well aware that most Americans had no idea why the United States was involved in Vietnam. Bundy suggested "it's ninety percent of the people who don't want any part of this."

Johnson agreed, and said, ". . . it's damned easy to get into a war, but it's going to be awfully hard to ever extricate yourself if you get in." [28]

Clearly, Johnson was at war with himself, tormented and feeling trapped by the issue. Politically, Johnson couldn't bear the idea that he might be accused of losing Vietnam to communism. A couple of weeks later he told Senator Russell, "I'm confronted. I don't believe the American people ever want me to run [abandon Vietnam]. If I lose it, I think they'll say I've lost it. . . . At the same time, I don't want to commit us to a war. And I'm in a hell of a shape."

Russell then warned him, prophetically, that a full-scale effort to save South Vietnam would "take a half million men. They'd be bogged down in there for ten years." [29]

Bundy too felt trapped by the dilemma. That's why he kept saying to Johnson that there were only "some marginal things that we can do." He didn't want to escalate the war, but he did want to find "some means of stiffening" the war effort by the South Vietnamese.

Everyone kept saying the war had to be won in the South, but Northern intervention might first have to be ended. A couple of weeks later Forrestal restated the position he and Bundy basically shared: "As in most insurgency situations, South Vietnam is undergoing a kind of social revolution. At the same time, she is being attacked from the North. Therefore, we have had to learn not only how to defend against armed terrorism, but also how to effect fundamental changes in the political and economic structure of the country. This is a tall order, but the British experience in Malaya and the Philippine experience with the Huk rebellion has proven that it can be done, *if* outside intervention is controlled." [30]

This two-pronged strategy—interdicting the terrorism exported from the North while waging a social revolution in the South—would become Washington's policy in Vietnam for the remainder of Mac Bundy's tenure in the White House. The logic required additional Americans on the ground, ostensibly not in combat roles, but to wage the pacification effort that the

South Vietnamese generals seemed incapable of winning. Accordingly, late in July, Bundy and Forrestal drafted the presidential announcement that American troop strength in Vietnam would rise to 22,000 men. The statement flatly asserted that "no combat units are included" in the increase in personnel, and that there would be "no change" in their purely "advisory relationship."[31]

THAT summer Bill Bundy began to feel the pressures of his new job. The *New York Times* was reporting that he had "become more visible [than Mac] as a central figure in the United States policy-planning on critical security developments. . . ." The *Times* even reported that "there is good-natured speculation in Washington about which brother will get to be Secretary of State, as if success for one were a foregone conclusion." During the Kennedy years the odds favored Mac, but now "the long-striding William seems to have forged ahead."[32]

But the reality was very different. Increasingly, Bill found himself having to defend the distasteful, even ugly aspects of the war. In July he was asked to brief the British embassy "on the military effectiveness of napalm"—an anti-personnel weapon that indiscriminately incinerated anyone within reach.[33] In private, he was filled with doubts, some of which he recorded in personal memos to his files or in private notes to John McNaughton, a kindred spirit. But on the surface he projected confidence and toughness.

Some colleagues, like Forrestal, thought Bill was adopting a rigid line on Vietnam. That spring Forrestal wrote his close friend, the sculptor Alexandra Whitney, "There is a new Assistant Secretary for the Far East, Bill Bundy. They say that whom the Gods wish to destroy, they first make Asst. Secretary for the Far East. Be that as it may, it's been a little difficult breaking in the new man."[34]

"Another point that bothers me," Forrestal wrote to Mac, "is the tendency toward a 'hard line' that is developing in the Department. . . . In his backgrounder on Wednesday, Bill apparently left the impression that we were determined to 'roll back' PL [Pathet Lao] gains. . . . Since we are not willing to use U.S. ground forces in Laos, we condemn ourselves in advance to a political defeat if we insist on Communist concessions we know we can't get. We have found as much mushiness as possible is the best posture in Laos."

Forrestal also complained that Bill was not consulting enough with "some of us who have been working a long time on Far Eastern problems." Instead of reaching out beyond his relatively inexperienced staff, Bill "leaves the distinct impression that he prefers not to have outsiders interfere with his affairs." Forrestal warned Mac that "in view of the weakness" of Bill's staff "and the hidden traps lying all over his area, I think he could get some useful help, primarily from Averell [Harriman] and to a lesser extent from [William] Sullivan and myself, if he would encourage us."[35]

Mac let it ride. Bill was, after all, the elder brother, and Mac knew better than to try to tell him how to run his shop.

Perhaps because of the tensions associated with the war, around this time some of Bill's colleagues in the State department became aware of his strong temper. Allen Whiting, a China expert in the Department, recalled one incident: "He threw papers at an associate of mine, someone I knew. He threw papers the full length of the room; I mean just screamed. And that doesn't happen when people have themselves together."[36]

Bill Bundy's Groton and Yale classmate Marshall Green was now his deputy. "I had the office next door to him," Green remembered. "So I could hear him very plainly when he began screaming at people. He wasn't an easy person to work with. He was extremely tense. He always took upon himself more than he should have, and this alone set many people against him. People felt uneasy in his presence, precisely because he was so exacting. Bill could do the dirty work. He wouldn't hesitate to knife you in the chest." He could be very hard on himself as well. "He'd lie there on his office sofa late at night," Green said, "haggard as hell, dictating."[37]

James Thomson, Jr., was also taking heat from Bundy in 1964. "Bill Bundy's tantrums were notorious," recalled Thomson. Gregarious and bright, Thomson had grown up in China, the son of missionaries. He had excelled at Yale, where he had been editor of the *Yale Daily News*, and in 1961 had earned a Harvard doctorate. His mentor at Harvard had been John K. Fairbank, the same professor of Chinese history whom Dean Mac Bundy had shielded from McCarthyite attacks. Thomson was a liberal's liberal.

When Bill Bundy replaced Roger Hilsman as assistant secretary of state, he inherited Thomson as one of his top aides. But the personal chemistry was all wrong. Thomson was too flippant for Bill's taste. Like Fairbank, Thomson thought the United States should initiate talks with Communist China. "Bill knew that I knew a lot about China, and he really couldn't tolerate anything I would say on this subject. . . ."

Thomson's views were an anomaly. For a decade Far Eastern affairs had been the most ideologically rigid of the department's bureaus. "It was a bureau," Thomson later wrote, "that had been purged of its best China expertise, and of farsighted, dispassionate men, as a result of McCarthyism. Its members were generally committed to one policy line: the close containment and isolation of mainland China. . . ." The bureau had loosened up a little under Bill Bundy's predecessor, but Bill himself often seemed under the sway of Rusk and Acheson when it came to matters Chinese. And that went far to explain, in Thomson's eyes, why Bill Bundy could inflate the importance of making a stand against communism in South Vietnam.[38]

ON July 31, Bill Bundy wrote a memo to Mac that summed up his views just days before the fateful Gulf of Tonkin incidents. The loss of South Vietnam, he argued, "would have extremely serious consequences for the preservation of non-Communist governments in the rest of Southeast Asia. . . ." On the other hand, he was not ready to escalate U.S. involvement in the war. That would be a "grave" matter and "should not be impatiently undertaken." As he later characterized his position, "We were muddling through with our fingers crossed." [39]

Bill could sometimes give credence to the domino theory even though Sherman Kent, his old friend and colleague from the CIA's Board of National Estimates, had written an official estimate disparaging the whole notion. By the summer of 1964, Kent's paper was known throughout the intelligence community as the "Death of the Domino Theory Memo." Kent flatly concluded, "We do not believe that the loss of South Vietnam and Laos would be followed by the rapid, successive communization of the other states of the Far East. . . . With the possible exception of Cambodia, it is likely that no nation in the area would quickly succumb to Communism as a result of the fall of Laos and South Vietnam." [40]

When Kent's critique arrived at the White House, Mike Forrestal passed it on to Mac with a note attached: "Mac: This is obvious but good. Might help answer one of the Pres's questions." But like his brother, Mac failed to use Kent's conclusions to force a debate on the issue. [41]

That summer everyone was coasting until the election had passed. Bill Bundy was watching "with fascination and a little horror" as Barry Goldwater captured the Republican presidential nomination in July. Goldwater seemed a dangerous anachronism, a throwback to the isolationist instincts of the 1930s. Bundy also realized that Goldwater presented the Johnson administration with a delicate problem in explaining its Vietnam policy. In the looming campaign, Johnson, the "peace candidate," clearly intended to portray Goldwater's advocacy of bombing North Vietnam as bellicose. At the same time, as Bill wrote Mac on the last day of July, the bombing option should not appear "so unattractive that we are tying our hands if we should ever decide to do it." [42]

The next day, August 1, Bill took his family up to Martha's Vineyard for a much-anticipated ten-day vacation. "Trouble was the last thing we expected," Bill later wrote. [43]

Early on the morning of Sunday, August 2, reports reached Washington that a U.S. Navy destroyer, the USS *Maddox*, had been attacked by North Vietnamese patrol boats while in international waters in the Gulf of Tonkin. At least three torpedoes had been fired at the American ship. In response, planes from a U.S. aircraft carrier attacked the North Vietnamese patrol boats and left one damaged and burning in the water. Bill was called off the tennis court and informed of the incident, but he was told not to return to Washington. Tonkin Gulf was not yet a crisis.

Mac, however, who had gone to Manchester for the weekend, was called back to Washington. On Monday morning he sat listening to the intelligence briefings and doodling in his microscopic handwriting. He filled a page with his usual motif, a series of tiny rectangles, finely drawn in black ink. They were the doodles of a mathematical mind, creating a delicate maze of geometric patches. At one point in the briefing, he interrupted his doodling to write, "34-A?"

This was the code name for the pinprick covert operations against the

North that had begun earlier that year.* Three nights before, on July 30, the first serious naval operations of this covert campaign had taken place when two North Vietnamese islands, Hon Me and Hon Ngu, were attacked by four high-speed motorboats manned by South Vietnamese commandos trained and armed by the CIA. The islands were a mere three and four miles off the North Vietnamese coast. Simultaneously, the U.S. destroyer *Maddox* received orders to patrol just eight miles off the coast of North Vietnam, well within the territorial waters claimed by Hanoi. The *Maddox's* mission was to collect electronic intelligence by provoking the North Vietnamese to turn on their shoreline radar defenses. As it happened, the *Maddox* was attacked thirty miles from one of the islands that had been the target of the 34-A operation less than sixty hours earlier.

Mac Bundy quickly realized that the North Vietnamese attack on the *Maddox* was a direct response to the 34-A operation. Indeed, Mike Forrestal reported to Mac on August 3, "It seems likely that the North Vietnamese and perhaps the Chicoms [Chinese Communists] have assumed that the destroyer was part of this operation. . . . It is also possible that Hanoi deliberately ordered the attack in retaliation for the harassment of the islands." [44]

For the moment, President Johnson decided merely to file a formal protest with Hanoi. He also announced that the U.S. destroyer patrols in the Gulf of Tonkin were legal and would continue. Bill Bundy thought the administration's statement would be the end of it, that "this had been a one-shot event most unlikely to be repeated. . . ." [45]

The next morning, Tuesday, August 4, at 9:40 A.M. (Washington time) the White House received a message from the *Maddox* that its radio operators had just intercepted a North Vietnamese radio transmission indicating enemy patrol boats were preparing to attack. A few minutes later the *Maddox* and another destroyer, the *C. Turner Joy*, radioed that they were under attack from enemy gunboats. It was a stormy and moonless night in the Gulf of Tonkin, "darker than the hubs of hell," as one sailor said later. Soon, even though their lookouts couldn't see anything, both destroyers were firing in all directions as they zigzagged through the water to avoid any torpedoes.

All morning Mac Bundy and his aides monitored the cable traffic in the White House Situation Room. Later, over lunch at the White House, President Johnson told his assembled advisers that he had decided to bomb the naval facilities from which the North Vietnamese had launched their attacks. He had also decided that the time had come to submit a formal resolution to Congress authorizing the use of military force in Vietnam. A meeting was scheduled that evening to brief congressional leaders.

* Just a week earlier, on July 24, Bundy had reported to LBJ that since April 1964 there had been eight airdrops into North Vietnam of 34-A commando teams: "These efforts have been only very moderately successful, and the casualty rates are high, but we still have radio contact with about half of these people."

When McNamara returned to the Pentagon at three that afternoon, however, he was informed that the commander of the *Maddox* now had doubts about whether the second attack had actually taken place. A review of the "engagement," Navy Captain John J. Herrick cabled, "makes many reported contacts and torpedoes fired appear very doubtful. . . . Freak weather effects and overeager sonarmen may have accounted for many reports. No actual sightings by *Maddox*." This information should have put on hold any plans for retaliation, but McNamara pressed for a review of the intercept intelligence. By the end of the afternoon, he concluded that the intercepts of North Vietnamese radio traffic were definitive: the attack had taken place. Accordingly, Johnson met with congressional leaders that evening and told them he had ordered retaliatory air strikes against North Vietnam. Barely seven hours later, jets from the aircraft carrier *Ticonderoga* bombed a naval base and oil storage facilities in North Vietnam.

The next day Johnson submitted a resolution to Congress supporting the "determination of the President, as Commander in Chief, to take all necessary measures to repel any armed attack against the forces of the United States and to prevent further aggression." During the ensuing debate Senator Wayne Morse (D-Ore.), who would vote against the resolution, charged that the *Maddox*'s mission was part of South Vietnamese patrol boat raids on the North. (Morse had received his information from an informant with access to classified information.) Fully relying on Johnson administration briefings, Senator Fulbright denied Morse's accusation. On August 7, after barely eight hours of debate, the Senate passed the resolution by a vote of 88–2. Ten absent senators publicly endorsed the measure. The House of Representatives adopted the resolution by a vote of 416–0.[46]

Three days later, on August 10, Clark Clifford, chairman of the President's Foreign Intelligence Advisory Board, called President Johnson. CIA deputy director Ray Cline had recently told Clifford that after a close inspection of the intercept intelligence, he was "rather negative" about whether there had been a second attack. Clifford no doubt conveyed this information to Johnson during their phone conversation because soon afterwards the president began expressing his own doubts—privately—that the attack had taken place. By then, however, he had his congressional mandate—and he was not about to give it up. Consequently, in the days ahead, Johnson allowed his aides to sustain the fiction that the second attack had occurred.[47]

THIRTY-ONE years later, in 1995, Robert McNamara finally conceded after meeting with Vietnam's General Vo Nguyen Giap in Hanoi that the second attack on August 4 had never happened. Bill Bundy, for his part, always insisted that no one "had any doubt that day that the second attack had taken place." But Bill had not been called back from his vacation in New England until the afternoon of Tuesday, August 4, hours after the alleged second attack that morning. When he arrived in Washington he was quickly briefed on the intercept intelligence. At the time, it seemed to him absolutely conclusive. Even as late as 1993, he still insisted that "no one can be categorical that a second attack did or did not take place on August 4. . . ." By then, however, Bill was also aware of an alternative explanation: that the intercepted North Vietnamese messages were, as he later wrote, "misinterpreted—that they in fact referred to the undoubted August 2 attack." This is exactly what happened.[48]

In essence, the Gulf of Tonkin affair had begun with an honest mistake. As Bill Bundy insisted, "There was definitely not any fabrication that day. What was said was what was believed." Yet, it quickly became apparent that what had been said was not factual. As Edwin Moise, the leading historian of the affair, has written, once the Johnson administration obtained a congressional resolution based on a "phantom" battle, these same officials "had to conceal or obfuscate any evidence that turned up casting doubt on the reality of the August 4 attack."[49]

At the time, however, the second attack constituted, in Bill Bundy's words, "dramatic proof" of Hanoi's aggression and therefore justified the kind of congressional resolution on Vietnam that only the previous spring had seemed out of reach politically. The draft resolution written by Bill Bundy was retrieved and substantially rewritten. (George Ball recalled that Bundy's draft was "too long and wordy.") But the intended effect was the same: to authorize whatever military force the president thought necessary to defend U.S. interests in Vietnam.[50]

In obtaining the congressional resolution, McNamara flatly told Congress that the U.S. Navy "played absolutely no part in, was not associated with, was not aware of, any South Vietnamese action, if there were any. I want to make that very clear to you. The Maddox was operating in international waters, was carrying out a routine patrol of the type we carry out all over the world at all times. It was not informed of . . . any possible South Vietnamese actions. . . ."

All of this was less than the full truth. The CIA's John McCone himself had bluntly told the president on August 4, "The North Vietnamese are reacting defensively to our attacks on their off-shore islands." If McNamara had somehow convinced himself that the phantom battle of August 4 had actually taken place, he nevertheless blatantly deceived Congress when he claimed that the Maddox and Turner Joy had no relationship to the 34-A operations that had so clearly provoked the North Vietnamese.[51]

On August 15, Bill Bundy was asked on a worldwide Voice of America (VOA) radio broadcast about the relationship between the August 2 attack on the Maddox and the "reported presence and attack earlier by a South Vietnamese gunboat on some North Vietnamese islands." Bundy replied, "The point I would like to make perfectly clear is that at that time, assuming such an attack took place, the Maddox was at least 100 miles distant. . . . She did proceed into the Gulf of Tonkin and was attacked approximately two days after this alleged South Vietnamese attack . . . the Maddox—had no connection whatever with whatever may have been going on in connection with these islands." [52] In fact, one mission of the 34-A patrol boat attacks was to provoke the North Vietnamese to turn on their shore radar units, allowing the *Maddox* to use its sophisticated electronic gear to pinpoint the location of these radar units. The intelligence derived by the *Maddox* was therefore directly related to the 34-A patrol boat attacks. The intelligence mission of the *Maddox* in the Gulf of Tonkin was, of course, highly classified information, which Bundy was bound to protect. By withholding the information from his VOA listeners, Bundy was only doing his job. But doing his job required him to be less than candid. [53]

Ultimately, the escalation in the war that resulted from the Gulf of Tonkin incident was Lyndon Johnson's responsibility. He had decided to act, and once he made the decision he also made it clear to Mac Bundy that he didn't want any contrary advice. On the morning of the second Tonkin "attack," Johnson had come storming over to Bundy's office in the west basement and announced that he had decided to retaliate, that he was going to give a nationally televised speech and that he wanted a congressional resolution prepared. "I interrupted," Bundy recalled, "and said I thought we ought to think it over." Johnson snapped back, "I didn't ask you that. I told you to help me get organized." Later, Bundy realized that Johnson had first learned of the August 4 incident while attending a breakfast meeting with congressional leaders. The sentiment among the legislators was, "We've gotta do something." According to Bundy, this explained why the crucial Tonkin decision was made without Johnson consulting any of his foreign policy advisers. "I was just a messenger boy," Bundy said. "And he made sure I stayed that way." [54]

NOT surprisingly, the North Vietnamese interpreted the events of that week in August quite differently. Officials in Hanoi knew that the second attack had not taken place because they knew where their gunboats were that night—in dock. They couldn't understand what the Americans were shooting at in the darkness. According to archival records in Hanoi inspected by historian William Duiker, a Vietnamese-speaking former U.S. Foreign Service officer, the subsequent U.S. bombing raids and the Gulf of Tonkin resolution convinced Hanoi that Washington had crossed a major threshold and would now commit its military might, as the French had done, to block the reunification of the country. "Up until this point," Duiker concluded, "party strategists in Hanoi had consistently hoped to avoid actions that might incite the United States to escalate its role in the conflict in South Vietnam." Now, from Hanoi's perspective, Washington had concocted the August 4 "attack" in order to justify an escalation of the war. According to Duiker, the Gulf of Tonkin incident persuaded the politburo in Hanoi that it would now have to commit organized units of regular North Vietnamese army troops to support the Viet Cong in the South.

Contrary to what some Pentagon officials believed, Hanoi had not yet sent substantial numbers of regular army troops to the war in the South.

Until the end of 1964, that struggle had been fought almost wholly by Viet Cong irregulars indigenous to the South. But after the Tonkin Gulf events, because the United States seemed about to intervene in force, Hanoi's leaders believed the time had come for them to intervene in force and "achieve a decisive victory in the next one or two years." The first regular North Vietnamese forces departed in September and October, arriving in the South at the end of 1964.[55] The war in the South had entered a new dimension.

MEANWHILE, Lyndon Johnson was desperately trying to dodge both a larger war or the alternative of withdrawal. Campaigning in Oklahoma on September 25, he declared, "There are those that say you ought to go north and drop bombs. . . . We don't want our boys to do the fighting for Asian boys. We don't want to get involved in a nation with 700 million people [China] and get tied down in a land war in Asia. There are some that say we ought to go south and get out and come home, but we don't like to break our treaties. . . . We are not about to start another war and we're not about to run away from where we are."[56] Johnson wasn't prepared to go to war, but neither was he willing to be tarred as weak on communism.

Several weeks later Bill Bundy's former colleagues at the CIA were telling him that the war was already virtually lost. On October 1 a Special National Intelligence Estimate predicted "increasing defeatism, paralysis of leadership, friction with Americans, exploration of possible lines of political accommodation with the other side, and a general petering out of the war effort."[57] On the same day Mac Bundy, recognizing how badly the war was going, told the president that when speaking of Vietnam on the campaign trail, "I think you may wish to give a hint of firmness. It is a better than even chance that we will be undertaking some aid and land action in the Laotian corridor and even in North Vietnam within the next two months, and we do not want the record to suggest even remotely that we campaigned on peace in order to start a war in November."[58]

Sensing the drift toward intervention, Under Secretary of State George Ball now weighed in with an extraordinary sixty-seven-page paper entitled "How Valid Are the Assumptions Underlying Our Viet-Nam Policy?" Written with the assistance of Allen Whiting and Michael Forrestal, Ball's October 5 report questioned the notion that "we can take offensive action while controlling the risks." To the contrary, he warned, "once on the tiger's back we cannot be sure of picking the place to dismount." He complained that his colleagues had given almost no attention to finding a political way out of the war and that the time had come to undertake a "searching study of this question without further delay." Ball sent his paper to Rusk, McNamara and Mac Bundy, but President Johnson would not see the document for months. Ball later said that McNamara, for one, was "absolutely horrified" by the paper and handled his copy "like a poisonous snake."[59]

Bill Bundy, however, saw it and found himself in agreement with many of its assumptions. Bill regarded Ball as a man on a par with his father-in-law. While he thought Ball's papers were sometimes written "at white heat," he shared some of Ball's fundamental doubts about the nature of the war. Ball always emphasized the notion that the Americans were doomed to repeat the French experience in Vietnam. Bundy well understood the power of this historical argument, but he could also be annoyed by the French analogy. "Every now and then," Bill later told the historian David DiLeo, "he [Ball] overdid the comparison in a setting when we were so cross with the French for so many other reasons. Sometimes it was quite irritating to hear that argument." [60]

That autumn, however, Bill Bundy harbored many doubts about the war. For a few days in October he came very close to casting his lot with George Ball. On October 19 he responded to Ball's "poisonous snake" with his own forty-two-page paper, "The Choices We Face in Southeast Asia," which explored Ball's argument for a political solution. The document contained, in his words, "all the apparent heresies" he could think of and even posited a plan for initiating a negotiated withdrawal: "Continue present programs, but add actions to convey a believable threat of force, then negotiate." [61] This was a veiled prescription for "fighting one's way to the negotiating table." Bill was not happy about the prospect of a neutral South Vietnam. But he was willing to concede that such a result might be tolerable: "Let us accept that the domino theory is much too pat." He believed a coalition government in Saigon would lead inevitably to reunification with the communist north. But he pointed out that such a " 'solution' reached in this way would be a *Vietnamese* solution without Chinese participation, and almost certainly Hanoi would bend every effort to have it this way and to keep it this way." Beijing "would not have re-entered Southeast Asia in any concrete sense, and there is at least some hope that Communist Vietnam . . . would be to some extent a buffer against further spread of Chinese influence." If South Vietnam went communist, world opinion would blame the South Vietnamese, not the Americans: "The basic point, of course, is that we have never thought we could defend a government or a people that had ceased to care strongly about defending themselves." The loss of South Vietnam, therefore, "could be made bearable."

He had no illusions: America's allies in Europe and Asia "would in the main be very unsympathetic to wider action." The American people were on the whole "looking for a way out with honor. . . ." In short, it was time to "take a really hard look . . . at the courses of action open to us, including the frank consideration of negotiating avenues that we have hitherto excluded. . . ."

Astonishingly, Bundy even disabused his readers of the official line that South Vietnam was a separate, sovereign nation. "A bad colonial heritage of long standing, totally inadequate preparation for self-government by the colonial power, a colonialist war fought in half-baked fashion and lost, a nationalist movement taken over by Communism ruling in the other half of an ethnically and historically united country, the Communist side inheriting much the better military force and far more than its share of the talent—these are the facts that dog us today." In this one long-winded sentence, Bundy managed to touch just about all the points I. F. Stone, Bernard Fall or other early critics of the war would make within a year.

Still, before making the case for negotiations, Bundy carefully explained why further military actions appeared to be so futile. Military plans existed for "systematic air attacks on North Vietnam," aerial mining of key harbors and the deployment of limited ground troops—"perhaps a division"—in South Vietnam. Bundy noted that the "essentials of this course of action have been worked out with some refinement." (This, of course, would have been news to the American people, who in October were being told by Lyndon Johnson that he was the peace candidate in the upcoming presidential election.) Bundy pointed out that in recent September war games, all the players had agreed that none of these actions would have compelled Hanoi to pull out of the war. To the contrary, he said, the war game "reached a point where major ground forces on our side, and/or the use of tactical nuclear weapons, were required to counter a ground reaction estimated as likely from North Vietnam alone." In other words, even without Chinese intervention, the war was likely to escalate to the point where U.S. military leaders would want to use tactical nuclear weapons.

Clearly, this was a gloomy prognosis. In lieu of military action, Bundy said there were three negotiating strategies: (1) "Continue Present Programs, but Wink at Intra-Viet-Nam Negotiations"; (2) "Continue Present Programs, but Take a Negotiating Initiative Ourselves"; and (3) "Continue Present Programs but Add Actions to Convey a Believable Threat of Force, then Negotiate."

Bundy favored the last of these, which he characterized with an old baseball adage: "Swing wildly at the first one, then bunt." * Swinging wildly meant provoking "another Gulf of Tonkin incident, followed by a harder strike than last time." Bombing the hell out of North Vietnam for a short time—presumably a week or even a few days—would create an international crisis. At this point, Washington could respond to "overwhelming pressures" from the international community to reconvene the Geneva Conference of 1954. The bombing would stop and negotiations would begin. Bundy warned that "we would find ourselves being driven in the direction" of a neutralist, coalition government. South Vietnam would probably become communist in a year or two, but in the meantime Washington would "gain time to shore up the next line of defense in Thailand. . . ." [62]

---

* Jim Thomson said much the same thing to Mac Bundy just a week before the election: "I assume that we will have to choose roughly between escalation towards negotiation on the one hand, and a muddle-through towards negotiation on the other." Thomson favored muddling through. (Thomson to Mac Bundy, Oct. 23, 1964, Thomson Papers, Box 11, JFK.)

Bill sent his memorandum to Rusk, Forrestal, McNamara, McNaughton, Ball and his brother. But perhaps because everyone knew that no decisions would be made until after the election, he received no formal response from any of the principals. President Johnson himself was busy on the campaign trail and apparently did not see the memo.

Both Bundy brothers knew that the war could not be allowed to drift much longer without major decisions being made. Just days before LBJ won election in a landslide as the peace candidate, Viet Cong guerrillas destroyed more than a dozen aircraft at Bien Hoa airfield near Saigon, killing four Americans and wounding seventy-two. Senator Barry Goldwater demanded immediate air strikes against the North. President Johnson announced instead the formation of an interagency working group headed by Assistant Secretary of State William P. Bundy.

THE Bundy Vietnam Working Group held its first meeting on election day, November 3. Even as voters were going to the polls, Bill Bundy and his colleagues were trying to rethink the war. The issue was so sensitive that the entry in Bill's desk calendar for that day noted cryptically, "9:30—Topic A." [63]

The Bundy working group met every day and through the weekends for the next two weeks. Bill later called it the "most comprehensive" review of Vietnam policy during either the Kennedy or Johnson administrations. [64] Many members of the working group were skeptics: Michael Forrestal, Robert Johnson (an NSC aide), Jonathan Moore (an aide to Bill Bundy), Allen Whiting, Thomas Hughes (assistant secretary of state for intelligence and research), George Ball, Averell Harriman, Harold Ford (a high-ranking CIA analyst), John McNaughton and Daniel Ellsberg would all become prominent doves on the war.

Mac Bundy, Rusk and McNamara sat in on all the key meetings, as did Mac's two NSC assistants responsible for Asian matters, Chet Cooper and James C. Thomson, Jr.* All in all, as Bill Bundy later wrote, "this was a full-scale mobilization of the relevant men in Washington." Never again would such a large group study the problem of Vietnam with such intensity and openness. After November, President Johnson, fearing press leaks, kept such internal policy reviews to a minimum.

Initially, the Bundy group outlined three basic policy options. Option A consisted of more of the same with the expectation that eventually the Saigon regime would give way to a government dominated by North Vietnam. Option B called for massive bombing of the North. Option C called for a slow and gradual bombing program calibrated to open up negotiations with the North. From the start Bill Bundy was inclined toward Option C, as were Forrestal

---

* Cooper had only just formally joined Mac Bundy's NSC staff. Bundy told him he would focus on Vietnam issues, and he warned him that it would be a "difficult, thankless task." (Chester Cooper, *The Lost Crusade: America in Vietnam* [New York: Dodd, Mead, 1970], p. 249.)

and McNaughton, who, along with Bundy, were the major drafters of the group's papers.

By the third week of November, the working group found itself divided. The Joint Chiefs' representative, Admiral Lloyd M. Mustin, flatly embraced the domino theory, arguing that the collapse of all of Southeast Asia was as good as inevitable if South Vietnam went communist. Others believed that "the harm would be mild and bearable." Bill Bundy tried to craft a compromise of these two views. He thought the domino theory was "too pat," that the fall of South Vietnam would probably mean the collapse of Laos and a "high degree of accommodation" to communist forces in Cambodia. But he thought it at least possible that Thailand, Malaysia and the rest of Southeast Asia "would somehow stand, if the U.S. carried on strongly, even after a Communist takeover in South Vietnam."[65] A gradual escalation, Option C, therefore seemed the most reasonable and flexible strategy. At one point, when the working group was discussing just how heavy the bombing should be, Bill Bundy was heard to say, "It seems to me that our orchestration should be mainly violins, but with periodic touches of brass." Heads nodded and some smiled at this perfect "Bundyism."[66]

Most of the other civilians on the working group accepted Bill's judgment, characterizing it as just the right tone of "dark gray." Bill thought this was the "best that I could do," but he still wasn't comfortable. There were too many "ifs" in the paper for it to work as a policy prescription for the president. "It did not seem good enough," he later wrote, "to me or to the others." So a few days before the working group was scheduled to present its findings to the president, Bill began to reconsider his position. Perhaps greater clarity could be reached by a reasoned argument that the United States could simply live with a communist outcome in Vietnam. Perhaps, Bundy thought, Washington should just negotiate a clean-cut withdrawal.

He spent a long weekend trying to make the case for a "mild" view: "The result was long and much rewritten, relying on no theory but on as many facts and as precisely stated subordinate judgments as could be turned up. . . . It was as strong a brief for a mild view as I knew how to write, and honest in a mind that truly was not made up."

On Monday morning, November 23, Bill went into his office with his long memo, talked it over with one or two colleagues, and then sent it to McNamara and Rusk. "If they had bought what I had written," he later wrote in his understated fashion, "that would almost certainly be decisive." Bundy's memo landed on McNamara's desk like a bombshell. After reading it, McNamara left immediately to talk with Rusk at the State Department. Bundy was summoned to Secretary Rusk's seventh-floor office, where he found Rusk alone with McNamara. If the subsequent war could ever be said to have turned on a single meeting, this was for Bundy the defining moment. "It was not a long meeting," he later wrote, "nor was much said—though it was clear that they had had some time together before. At any rate, the verdict was clear and succinct: 'It won't wash.'"

Bill argued with them only briefly. A different man might have resigned or gone about the arduous process of privately building a coalition within the bureaucracy for his views. But Bill was not the kind of person to go public. Neither was he one to go behind the backs of his superiors. Seven years later he would write, by way of explanation, that a "day of reflection had brought me to the same conclusion in my inner mind and heart." He still could not accept the domino theory's extreme conclusion of an "inevitable collapse" of Southeast Asia, but McNamara and Rusk persuaded him that "the problems of carrying on" in the event that South Vietnam did go communist seemed "nearly insuperable."

Never again would Bill Bundy attempt to make the case that the Americans should walk away from Vietnam. And neither would many people in Washington ever learn of Bill's doubts. His "private paper" to McNamara and Rusk has never surfaced in the archives. When, three decades later, McNamara wrote his Vietnam memoirs, he had either forgotten or studiously avoided any mention of Bundy's memo.⁶⁷

A few people who did see the memo, however, would always remember it. Dan Ellsberg, who was working for McNaughton at the time, recalled being astonished: "I remember discussing it with McNaughton and saying, 'Wow. This is a get-out-of-Vietnam memo.' McNaughton replied, 'Yeah, this is Ball's line.' "

Ellsberg said that the memo not only questioned the domino theory but also proposed a rather precise strategy on how the United States could withdraw. Bundy was suggesting that the next time the Viet Cong carried out a major attack on a U.S. installation, Washington should respond with a major attack on the North. This would be a replay of the Gulf of Tonkin scenario, but this time, behind the scenes, Washington would signal that the door was open for the United Nations to reopen Geneva-style negotiations for a broad Indochina settlement. Ellsberg called it "shooting your way out of the saloon."

McNaughton and Ellsberg thought it extremely important that someone like Bundy was now taking Ball's line. "It was also very clear," Ellsberg said, "that no one would put such a thing on paper without having given it very heavy thought and without knowing that he was taking a real bureaucratic risk." Within hours of Bundy's meeting with McNamara and Rusk, Jonathan Moore, Bundy's assistant, walked into Ellsberg's office at the Pentagon and said, "I've got to collect every copy of that memo."

"Uh-oh," Ellsberg said, "Admiral Mustin didn't like it, right?"

Indeed, Admiral Mustin had already written a blistering response in which he all but accused Bundy of treason. From the perspective of the Joint Chiefs, the people who "lost China" were now busy working to lose Indochina. "This was not a minor little episode," Ellsberg later said. "This was a little tight wire act that Bundy did in full view of the Joint Chiefs. . . . Bill almost lost his career on that afternoon."⁶⁸ Ellsberg was well aware that Bundy had almost lost his job once before, when Joe McCarthy had singled him out at the CIA. The political dynamics for liberals had not changed that much from the McCarthy period of a decade earlier. Lyndon Johnson didn't know what he was going to do about Vietnam, but he certainly didn't want it on the record that an assistant secretary in his administration was proposing that the United States could live with a communist Southeast Asia. That would be throwing red meat to the right wing.

Fortunately for Bill Bundy, his stealthy dissent had been made privately and with considerable secrecy. He had put the unthinkable on paper, but he had been careful to keep the dissemination of this "private paper" to a very small number of players. And when he was told, "It won't wash," he had been able to take it back.

AFTER all the meetings and arguments, the Bundy working group reached no consensus. By the end of 1964, the president's closest advisers remained divided. Rusk, General Westmoreland, Mac Bundy and Walt Rostow argued that a bombing campaign against the North would significantly alter the dynamics of the war in the South. Bill Bundy, McNamara and McNaughton also favored some bombing of the North, but they were not under the illusion that such attacks would win the war in the South. They believed the war in the South could be won only with a stable and viable government in Saigon.

Without really arguing the merits of withdrawal, the Bundy working group finally settled on Option C: gradually escalating the military pressure while at the same time preparing to negotiate. Bill favored a "soft" version of Option C while Mac, according to his brother's notes, spoke up in favor of "a firmer way of conducting Option C," which presumably meant a more intense bombing program. As to negotiations, Mac Bundy scribbled in the margins of one late November document, "No hurry." Time, he hoped, was on their side. With a little patience, perhaps the military facts on the ground would change, and then they could negotiate.[69]

Both Bundy brothers had arrived at Option C—gradual escalation—despite having heard warnings from numerous quarters that such a strategy was unwise. Ball had said it in his October 5 sixty-seven-page memorandum. Bill Bundy himself had said it. Senator Fulbright had publicly warned on December 4 that escalating the war would be "senseless." The French had said it by urging neutralization.[70] And Mac was hearing similar warnings from his own staff.

In early December, Mac called Jim Thomson over to his basement office. Mac had recruited the thirty-three-year-old China expert from his brother's staff at the State Department the previous July. Marc Raskin was long gone, but in Mac's mind, if Thomson had not exactly taken Raskin's place as his thorny "conscience," he nevertheless knew Thomson as a skeptic on Vietnam. Just a week earlier Thomson had written him, "What I fear most of all in this juncture would be our move onto a policy track in Vietnam that could cripple the new Administration and tarnish its bright promise. . . ."[71] When Thomson walked in, Mac told him, "I want you to read something. Sit right here, and read it carefully, and tell me what you think." He then handed him a thick sheaf of papers, the conclusions of Bill Bundy's working group. Thomson sat down on a sofa in Bundy's office and read.

"It was all about a fantastic, escalatory multiple-bombing track to force the North Vietnamese to their knees," Thomson recalled. When he finished reading, Mac asked, "What do you think?"

Thomson took a deep breath and said, "Look, sir, I don't know anything about firepower. But this document is trying to tell us that we can bomb them into submission, and my fear, since I know China, and I have learned something about Indo-China, is that those people we're bombing will survive our taking out everything they've built over these past many years, their infrastructure and so forth. [Then] they will go back into the jungles, and why? Because they know they have no place to go. And eventually, we will go home. And so, I'm not sure this is going to work. . . . They know that we know that we will have to go home, someday, quite soon."

Mac sat in silence for a long moment, staring at Thomson, and then said, "Well, James, that's a good point. You may well be right. Thank you so much."

That was it. Thomson would never forget the moment. He sensed that Bundy had rejected his advice, but he respected him for listening to what must have been an unsettling opinion.[72]

LYNDON JOHNSON possessed none of Mac Bundy's self-assurance; indeed, Mac's mere presence seemed to feed the president's basic insecurity. Johnson routinely referred to Bundy as his "Harvard man" or "my intellectual" but he said this in a tone that suggested not only pride of ownership but a bit of sarcasm as well.[73] In the first few months after Kennedy's assassination, both men had tried hard to accommodate each other, muting their cultural and personal styles. Uncharacteristically, Johnson tried to listen more and to give orders that sounded like suggestions. For his part, Bundy went out of his way to prove his loyalty to the man as well as the office. During that first year it seemed as if they had succeeded in establishing an uneasy working relationship.

Johnson often had good reason to marvel at Bundy's abilities. When Mac went off to the Caribbean in early 1964, Johnson had noticed that the normal flow of official papers through the White House had suddenly stalled. Bundy was a workhorse and that earned Johnson's respect. But, at times, the president used Bundy unmercifully, asking him to perform political missions that were bound to humiliate him. In the summer of 1964, when a groundswell of political support was building to have Johnson name Bobby Kennedy as his vice-presidential running mate, the president asked Bundy to persuade Bobby to publicly take himself out of the running. Bundy dutifully placed a phone call to Kennedy and made the pitch. Bobby brusquely responded that any public statement would have to come from Johnson. Kennedy was astonished that Bundy had agreed to such an "obnoxious chore." Clearly, Kennedy's regard for Mac was now tainted by his contempt for Johnson. About this time he told a friend that LBJ was "able to eat people up, even people who are considered rather strong figures. I mean . . . Mac Bundy or Bob McNamara: There's nothing left of them."[74]

A few weeks later Bundy encouraged Johnson to think of bringing the liberal wing of the Republican Party into his electoral campaign. Mac was unashamedly buttering up his president. In a memorandum entitled "Backing from the Establishment," written only slightly tongue in cheek, he said he was hearing "mutterings" that "we may not be doing as well as we should with the very first team of businessmen, bankers et al. . . . I think the key to these people is [John] McCloy. He is for us, but is under very heavy pressure from Eisenhower and others to keep quiet. I have told him that this is no posture for a man trained by Stimson, and I think he agrees in his heart, but I also think that in the end the person to whom he will want to say 'yes' is you. He belongs to the class of people who take their orders from Presidents and no one else."[75]

It must have seemed at times to Lyndon Johnson that Mac Bundy was capable of anything. One day Mac could advise him on how to win favor from the establishment, and the next day he could preside over a meeting on nuclear weapons or the Congo crisis or the latest covert action against Castro. Vietnam was only one among dozens of issues Mac dealt with each week.

After the November election Bundy decided to sink one of George Ball's more dubious schemes, a long-standing and much fought-over proposal to assuage West German desires to have a finger on the nuclear button by building a multilateral force (MLF) within NATO. (In an MLF, troops from different countries would serve in integrated units.) "George insists on being the piano player," Bundy told a colleague. "Well, it's time to bring this concert to an end."[76] In a pithy, two-page memorandum stamped "Literally Eyes Only," Bundy quickly demolished the arguments on behalf of an MLF, listed the formidable political hurdles to be run if the president was to build such a controversial nuclear-armed multilateral force and concluded that Washington should "now arrange to let the MLF sink out of sight." Almost as soon as the memorandum had been delivered to Rusk and McNamara, the debate was over, the bureaucracy folded and the MLF was dead. Bundy's memo became part of his legend.[77]

At times Bundy regarded Vietnam as a persistent nuisance compared to what Henry Stimson would have called the imponderables of his office. For instance, on September 15, Bundy met with Rusk, McNamara and McCone to brief the president on the impending Chinese acquisition of nuclear weapons. Mac led a discussion of several options, including whether the United States should launch an "unprovoked unilateral U.S. military action against Chinese nuclear installations. . . ." Every one agreed that while this was not a good idea "at this time," if someday "we should find ourselves in military hostilities at any level with the Chinese Communists, we would expect to give close attention to the possibility . . ." of targeting such facilities. Alternatively, Bundy and his colleagues told Johnson that they thought there were "many possibilities for joint action with the Soviet Government . . . even a possible agreement to cooperate in preventive military action." With Johnson's approval, Rusk was instructed to explore the matter "very privately" with Ambassador Anatoly Dobrynin.[78] There is no record of whether Rusk and Dobrynin discussed the issue, but just a month later the Chinese tested their first nuclear device.

Bundy's ability to deal with such heady issues was reassuring to a president who often felt insecure. But as time went by, and particularly after he won the presidency in his own right, and by a landslide at that, Johnson's relationship with his national security adviser began to wear thin. Bundy had hoped that after the election Dean Rusk would resign and Johnson would appoint him secretary of state. As recently as July, Rusk had signaled his intention to leave, and Bundy was disappointed when he changed his mind. "Mac is a bit blue," Joe Alsop confided to a mutual friend right after the election, "(I suspect, for he says nothing) about indefinitely prolonged White House duty, but will certainly carry on."[79]

Over time Johnson's manner with Bundy became more informal, earthy and abrupt. Johnson became more Johnson. He routinely carried on conversations with Bundy and other aides while he sat on the toilet. He took delight in embarrassing Bundy and later told the historian Doris Kearns about "one of the delicate Kennedyites who came into the bathroom with me and then found it utterly impossible to look at me while I sat there on the toilet. You'd think he had never seen those parts of the body before. For there he was, standing as far away from me as he possibly could, keeping his back toward me the whole time, trying to carry on a conversation. I could barely hear a word he said. I kept straining my ears and then finally I asked him to come a little closer to me. Then began the most ludicrous scene I had ever witnessed. Instead of simply turning around and walking over to me, he kept his face away from me and walked backward, one rickety step at a time. For a moment there I thought he was going to run right into me. It certainly made me wonder how that man had made it so far in the world."[80]

Johnson clearly relished telling this story, and it seemed of a piece with Bundy's Brahmin image. Mac, of course, had a slightly different take on the story. He told his old Groton friend Louis Auchincloss that, yes, the president sometimes asked people to talk to him while he was sitting on the toilet. "I remember Mac saying," recalled Auchincloss, "that the difference between Kennedy and Johnson was that with Kennedy you would go into the bathroom and both pee, and you didn't think that that was the president and you'd just go on with what you were saying. With Johnson, there was this visceral sense of the man and what he was doing." Auchincloss confirmed that Mac "had a certain distaste for the man."[81]

Johnson repeatedly demanded demonstrations of Bundy's loyalty. Among other things he required that Mac report in writing on every meeting or phone call he had with any member of the press. When in early December 1964, Bundy asked Johnson's permission to go on Lawrence Spivak's television program, *Meet the Press*, confiding, "I admit that I enjoy this kind of thing," the president bluntly told him, "Not now." The same day Bundy had to apologize for his friendship with Ben Bradlee—"Ben and I have known each other all our lives"—because Johnson was angry about a story *Newsweek* had published. "I used to find him a bit slick and cynical," Bundy wrote LBJ, "but in the last year or two Mary and I have thought he was maturing remarkably. . . . Knowing your own reservations, I have been extraordinarily careful about discussing your business with him. . . ." That he had to cater to Johnson's insecurities with such obsequiousness must surely have rankled Bundy; Jack Kennedy had never worried about his contacts with the press.[82]

Bundy nevertheless tried to satisfy this president's peculiar needs, even as he knew how fully distrustful the man could be. "Johnson was worried about the unknown," Bundy would say later. "He knew how many unknowns there were; he knew how complicated and uncertain life was. He knew that the way to avoid failure was to put yourself on guard against it, and he was, in that sense, the wariest man about whom to trust that I have ever encountered."[83] Mac knew he would always be regarded with suspicion by Lyndon Johnson. Yet, he remained at his side.

13

Vietnam: The Decision, 1965

[The] danger to one man's life, as such, is not a worthy guide. . . . If the basic questions of interest, right, and power are answered, the casualties and costs are to be accepted.

McGeorge Bundy
February 15, 1966

Oᴺᴇ ᴅᴀʏ in early 1965, Lyndon Johnson casually asked Mac Bundy if he had any notions about who should someday succeed him as national security adviser. Mac quickly replied that he had indeed thought about it and said he would get back to him with some concrete suggestions. A few weeks later Mac placed a one-page memorandum on Johnson's desk entitled "A Deputy or Potential Successor in My Office." He made it clear that he had "no present intention of quitting," but assuming that Johnson would run and win a second full term in office, "I doubt very much that it would be in your interest for me to go on here until 1973."

Bundy then listed the names of three men he would like to see "come in as a Deputy in this office with a prospect of succession as and when a vacancy occurs." His "first preference," indeed, "the ideal man for this job," he said, would be Bill Moyers, the thirty-year-old special assistant to the president. Moyers was an obvious and yet peculiar choice. Obvious, because Bundy knew Johnson liked this young Oklahoma-born graduate of the University of Texas and the Southwestern Baptist Theological Seminary. (Moyers was sometimes called, behind his back, the "deacon" or "Bishop Moyers.") It was peculiar, however, because Moyers was not known outside the White House for his interest, let alone expertise, in foreign affairs. Bundy knew otherwise. As a Harvard dean Bundy had a knack for picking out talent, and he recognized that Moyers was not only someone who could handle Lyndon Johnson, but that he was also an intellectual in the best sense of the word. "I do know," he told Johnson, "that he has an abiding interest and talent for foreign affairs.

I believe that he would be extremely good at this job, and I think he would like it."

If not Moyers, Bundy had two other candidates: Abram Chayes, forty-two, legal adviser to the secretary of state, and Thomas Hughes, thirty-nine, assistant secretary of state for intelligence and research. Any of these men, Bundy said, possessed "an instinctive understanding for the requirement that the man in this job must protect the President's right to hear both sides of hard cases."[1] Perhaps the most striking thing about Bundy's memo was what he left unsaid. All three of these young men were liberals; indeed, they were probably liberal enough even in 1965 to be regarded as to the left of Mac Bundy. Chayes and Hughes had both worked for Chester Bowles, and like Bowles, their political sensibilities sprang from the New Deal, populist wing of the Democratic Party. As to Moyers, his stint as associate director of Kennedy's Peace Corps had done nothing to dilute his own prairie populism.

Within a year Moyers, Chayes and Hughes would be regarded within the circles of government as dovish on the war. Even in early 1965, Hughes was already known by the White House to be a leading critic on Vietnam. Though his intelligence operation had little influence over the White House policymakers, Hughes's estimates were known to be consistently pessimistic.[2] Why then, did Bundy promote the idea that three such liberal critics of the war should be groomed as his eventual successor? Bundy cared less that these three men had a particular view of the war than that they were smart and possessed a liberal sensibility. Moreover, he understood and even agreed with much of their analysis of the Vietnam quandary. To his thinking, if the president decided to persist in the American commitment to Vietnam, he should do so with men who were not blind to the war's pitfalls.

Johnson, needless to say, did not act on Bundy's recommendations. No deputy was appointed and the president made it clear that he expected Bundy to remain on his team.

Bill Bundy, meanwhile, was warning of another crisis in Saigon. The man who had written two papers in the autumn of 1964 exploring how the United States could ease itself out of Vietnam was now warning that "key groups" in Saigon might soon undercut Washington's commitment by initiating negotiations with the National Liberation Front (NLF) or Hanoi itself. Since November, Bill noted, events had "moved quite markedly in the direction of seeking a negotiated outcome."[3] If negotiations commenced, Bill realized that it would be hard to turn them off, and at the same time he thought nothing good could come from negotiations when the United States had such a weak hand in Saigon.

So shortly after the New Year, Bill spent two days drafting a memorandum with Mike Forrestal and Leonard Unger. After three years of being the key staff aide on Vietnam, first at the NSC under Mac and then as a special assistant to Rusk in the State Department, Forrestal felt burnt-out. When he announced that he would return to Wall Street early in 1965, Unger—a regular Foreign Service officer and, most recently, ambassador to Laos—was brought in to replace him. On January 6, Bundy sent the results of their collective thinking to Secretary Rusk:

> The situation in Vietnam is now likely to come apart more rapidly than we had anticipated in November . . . the most likely form of coming apart would be a government of key groups starting to negotiate covertly with the Liberation Front or Hanoi, perhaps not asking in the first instance that we get out, but with that necessarily following at a fairly early stage. In one sense, this would be a "Vietnam solution," with some hope that it would produce a Communist Vietnam that would assert its own degree of independence from Peiping and that would produce a pause in Communist pressure in Southeast Asia. . . . [But] the outcome would be regarded in Asia, and particularly among our friends, as just as humiliating a defeat as any other. . . .[4]

Bill and his colleagues were rejecting a "Vietnam solution" in order to avoid the appearance of a humiliating defeat in the Cold War. The time was past for "insisting on perfectionism in the Saigon Government. . . ." Even stiff action could only promise "some faint hope" of staving off defeat in the South. But if the South still went communist, Bundy argued that at least "we would still have appeared to Asians to have done a lot more about it." Appearances mattered.[5]

Bundy recommended a bombing campaign against the North, but he also noted that the "introduction of limited U.S. ground forces into the northern area of South Vietnam still has great appeal to many of us. . . ." Why? Because it would have a "real stiffening effect in Saigon, and a strong signal effect to Hanoi." The drawback, he noted, was that such forces could become "attrition targets for the Vietcong." The intention here was not to get the United States involved in a major ground war, but only to "signal" American resolve in the faint hope that this would persuade North Vietnam's Ho Chi Minh to negotiate. In other words, the recommendation for escalating the war was motivated by deep pessimism. Forrestal had been writing the gloomiest of estimates on Vietnam for more than a year. So, too, in his own long-winded fashion, had Bill Bundy. But now their pessimism had perversely led them to endorse a deeper intervention.

George Ball would later comment in his memoirs that he had always "marveled at the way ingenious men can, when they wish, turn logic upside down, and I was not surprised when my colleagues interpreted the crumbling of the South Vietnamese government, the Viet Cong's increasing success, and a series of defeats for South Vietnamese units not as proving that we should cut our losses and get out, but rather that we must promptly begin bombing to stiffen the resolve of the corrupt South Vietnamese government. It was classic bureaucratic casuistry."[6]

■

If Bundy was deluding himself, he had plenty of company. Most observers were betting that neutralists would soon dominate the Saigon regime. McNamara, McNaughton, Rostow and both Bundy brothers consequently were telling the president that it was too late to see if the Saigon regime could clean up its act. Now was the time to intervene with a program of retaliatory bombing or to give up the cause as lost. Still, not all the president's advisers were persuaded by this logic. At the height of the January debate, Mac's Vietnam assistant, Jim Thomson, ran into Hubert Humphrey at a dinner party. When Thomson confided to him his worries about the bombing option, Humphrey said, "I'm convinced that we don't have to worry about this because, before this bombing can be undertaken, there will be a neutralist government in Saigon and we will be invited out."[7]

To Mac Bundy's mind, this was a defeatist attitude. On January 27, he and McNamara had a "very private discussion" with Johnson on the war. In preparation for this critical meeting, Mac drafted a long memorandum in which he flatly stated that he and McNamara were both "now pretty well convinced that our current policy can lead only to disastrous defeat." Washington, he argued, could no longer wait for a stable Saigon government. "Bob [McNamara] and I believe that the worst course of action is to continue in this essentially passive role which can only lead to eventual defeat and an invitation to get out in humiliating circumstances."

Temperamentally, Lyndon Johnson hated not to be in control. To have his national security adviser describe his Vietnam policy as "passive" must have rankled.

The United States faced only two alternatives, Bundy wrote: "The first is to use our military power in the Far East and to force a change of Communist policy. The second is to deploy all our resources along a track of negotiation, aimed at salvaging what little can be preserved with no major addition to our present military risks." While acknowledging that Secretary Rusk still favored more of the same—the "middle course"—Bundy reported that he and McNamara "tend to favor the first course, but we believe that both should be carefully studied and that alternative programs should be argued out before you." The time had come for "harder choices." Then Mac added an unmistakable warning: "A topic of this magnitude can only be opened for initial discussion this morning, but McNamara and I have reached the point where our obligations to you simply do not permit us to administer our present directives in silence and let you think we see real hope in them." Surely, such language must have alarmed a president so insecure in his reputation for handling foreign policy. Was he being told that his two top foreign policy aides were threatening to abandon his administration? If Vietnam policy went unchanged, would Bundy and McNamara leave, or worse, go public with their views? Would they say that their president was not doing enough to save Vietnam from the communists? Clearly, Mac was pushing his president, albeit in a very private manner. No one besides Johnson, Rusk and McNamara saw this memo, not even Bundy's two assistants whose responsibilities at this time focused almost exclusively on Vietnam—Chet Cooper and Jim Thomson.[8]

Johnson reacted predictably to Bundy's memo. That same day he fired off a cable to his ambassador in Saigon, General Maxwell Taylor, declaring, "I am determined to make it clear to all the world that the U.S. will spare no effort and no sacrifice in doing its full part to turn back the Communists in Vietnam." No one was going to accuse Lyndon Johnson of being weak in the face of a communist threat.[9]

Still, the president was reluctant to order an escalation of American military involvement. Instead, he asked Mac Bundy to go to Saigon for a personal inspection. The die might be cast, but Johnson seemed painfully determined to delay the hard decisions. "The sense in the White House," Bill Bundy later wrote, "was that the President did not want to do this, and this was one reason for the McGeorge Bundy mission—his felt need for a final determination shows his reluctance."[10]

Mac quickly arranged to arrive in Saigon on February 4, the last day of the Vietnamese Tet holiday. Unlike "that other Bundy," as Johnson referred to Bill, Mac had never been to Vietnam. Accompanied by John McNaughton from Defense, Leonard Unger from State and Chet Cooper from his NSC staff, he scheduled three days for talks in Saigon, with a fourth day left open for a trip to the countryside. The idea was for the group to split up in Saigon and for each to see as many people as possible: Buddhists, students and politicians both inside and outside the regime. Fire-brigade missions of this sort rarely uncover facts not already known and reported by seasoned diplomats on the scene. And Bundy's trip was no exception to the rule.

When they arrived they were greeted with the news that just an hour earlier a senior embassy official had been kidnapped by the Viet Cong. That was just the beginning. Bundy was not impressed by the South Vietnamese officials he met; they seemed "gray and tired." And after a two-hour meeting with a group of Buddhist leaders, Chet Cooper recalled Mac emerging with his mind "reeling." Bundy's "razor-sharp mind," wrote Cooper, "just couldn't cut through the ooze of generalities. Two cultures and two educational backgrounds did not directly conflict but rather slid past one another."[11]

By the end of his first day in Saigon, Mac was reporting back to the White House that "the current situation among non-communist forces gives all the appearance of a civil war within a civil war." He had heard much the same thing from Mike Forrestal after his trips in 1963–64. But perhaps simply being there in person finally brought it home and made him understand how utterly hopeless was the notion that this or any other Saigon regime would ever win the war on its own. Because the Buddhists remained committed to a neutralist, coalition government that would include representation from the National Liberation Front, Bundy concluded that any government acceptable to the Buddhist leadership would be unacceptable to Washington. No matter,

Bundy said, a government of national unity could be constructed by engaging in "sharp confrontation" with the Buddhists.[12]

Bundy was still sure that there had to be something that would turn things around. The next day Bundy's team met with the U.S. embassy's Country Team to discuss a "graduated reprisal program." The agenda was entitled "Extension of the War Beyond SVN [South Vietnam]." What they contemplated was a carefully calibrated bombing campaign—a "measured, controlled sequence of actions"—designed to persuade Hanoi "to stop its intervention in the south." No decisions were being made because everyone knew the president had not yet given the green light to a bombing campaign. On the other hand, Bundy's team was not crafting any alternatives other than those that involved bombing.

And then, at 2 A.M. on February 7, a company of Viet Cong soldiers attacked an isolated U.S. helicopter base and barracks at Pleiku, killing eight Americans and wounding 126 men. Ten U.S. planes were destroyed. Using captured U.S. mortars, the Viet Cong had simply rocketed a loosely guarded airstrip that happened to have some inviting high-profile targets. The enemy often launched major operations at the end of the Tet holidays. One State Department official, China expert Allen S. Whiting, had forecast that the Viet Cong would attempt to hit an American target during Bundy's visit.* Other Americans had been killed in other incidents in December and January. Pleiku was in some respects entirely predictable.

When Mac awoke that morning in Saigon, he went immediately to the U.S. Military Assistance Command, Vietnam (MACV) operations room, where the entire Country Team had gathered, including Ambassador Taylor, General Westmoreland and Deputy Ambassador U. Alexis Johnson, among others. Bundy took charge, peppering everyone with a litany of questions. General Westmoreland thought Bundy was on edge, showing signs of "field marshal psychosis." Others in the room saw Bundy at his coolest—lucid, sharp and utterly in control of the chaos around him. He kept being interrupted by phone calls from the White House, where a meeting of the NSC had convened. The men in the White House wanted information, and they wanted it now. After taking the fourth such phone call, Bundy muttered to Chet Cooper, "If those guys would only leave us alone for an hour, perhaps we could work things out." Finally, he called the White House Situation Room and spoke with Deputy Secretary of Defense Cyrus Vance. He told him the time for debate was over. It seemed utterly clear that the Viet Cong challenge had to be met with instant retaliation. Talking into a secure phone, Bundy advised a quick retaliatory bombing raid, even though the Soviet Union's Premier Aleksei N. Kosygin was then in Hanoi on an official visit. President Johnson

---

* In 1997 the North Vietnamese told a group of American historians that the Viet Cong commander had no knowledge that Bundy was in the country (A. J. Langguth interview Mar. 25, 1998).

was meeting upstairs in the Cabinet Room with Bill Bundy, McNamara, George Ball and others to discuss the crisis. After Vance conveyed Mac Bundy's recommendation, Johnson went around the table and asked each man whether he agreed. Everyone concurred with the exception of Senator Mike Mansfield, who startled Johnson by saying, "I think you should negotiate, Mr. President." Johnson brushed this dissent aside and quickly approved a list of targets in North Vietnam, including four army barracks. If the raids went according to plan, casualties would run as high as 4,500 North Vietnamese military personnel.[13]

Less than fourteen hours after the Pleiku attack, 132 carrier-based jets were dropping their bombs over North Vietnam. In the meantime Bundy had hopped aboard a helicopter and flown up to Pleiku, where he walked among the wounded and saw with his own eyes the devastation wrought by the Viet Cong mortar attack. He was moved. David Halberstam reported that those with him were "surprised by the intensity of his feeling . . . a rare emotional response." Richard Critchfield of the *Washington Star* reported that Bundy "looked stricken" as he talked quietly with a wounded teenage enlisted man. From these reports a myth arose that it had been a distraught Bundy, unnerved by the sight of blood, who had advised the president to bomb the North. "That's nonsense," Bundy later told veteran reporter Stanley Karnow. "I had already recommended retaliation beforehand." Even so, Lyndon Johnson helped to perpetuate the legend that Bundy had returned from Pleiku a new man, hardened to the realities of the war. "Well, they made a believer out of you, didn't they," he teased Bundy. "A little fire will do that."[14]

Bundy returned from Vietnam on February 7, convinced that retaliatory bombing for specific incidents was not enough. The message would not get through to Hanoi unless Washington engaged in a sustained bombing program. On the plane back to Washington, he and McNaughton crafted a thirteen-page memorandum for the president. Upon landing, Mac was driven straight to the White House, where at about 11 P.M he handed the report to Johnson. The president read it that night before going to sleep.

Bundy's report began on what must have seemed a depressingly familiar note: "The situation in Vietnam is deteriorating and without new U.S. action defeat appears inevitable—probably not in a matter of weeks or perhaps even months, but within the next year or so. There is still time to turn it around, but not much."

Bundy told the president, "The American investment is very large. . . . There is no way of unloading the burden on the Vietnamese themselves, and there is no way of negotiating ourselves out of Vietnam which offers any serious promise at present. It is possible that at some future time a neutral non-Communist force may emerge, perhaps under Buddhist leadership, but no such force currently exists, and any negotiated U.S. withdrawal today would mean surrender on the installment plan."

Bundy was wrong in his assumptions but right in his conclusion. Even in early 1965 the U.S. "investment" was not very large, and only the "expert" foreign policy professionals sitting in Washington truly believed that Vietnam was an American "responsibility." Such establishment voices as the *New York Times* and syndicated columnist Walter Lippmann did not share Bundy's assumptions, and they were still urging a neutralist settlement. But Bundy was probably right that if Saigon was turned over to a neutralist government, South Vietnam would quickly find itself taken over by the revolutionary forces of the Viet Cong. This would have been "surrender on the installment plan" only if South Vietnam was America's to surrender. Mac Bundy had always prided himself on the pragmatic bent of his Cold War liberalism; he was no ideologue in the mold of John Foster Dulles. He was a realist who should not have been blinded by talk of "international prestige." But he just could not face the prospect of "surrender on the installment plan." So, though the situation in Saigon looked utterly hopeless, and his closest aides had been telling him for several years that the South Vietnamese were not willing to fight, Mac Bundy lost what was liberal and flexible about his pragmatism and was left with only his Cold War liberalism.

Johnson sat in bed as he read Mac's prescription for a "policy of sustained reprisal." Isolated bombing raids in response to Viet Cong attacks on U.S. facilities such as the Pleiku air base were not sufficient. Bundy did not believe sustained bombing would change the North's commitment to reunification. Rather, he wrote, "our primary target in advocating a reprisal policy is the improvement of the situation in South Vietnam." Bombing the North, in other words, might help to win the hearts and minds of a demoralized constituency in South Vietnam. "We cannot assert that a policy of sustained reprisal will succeed in changing the course of the contest in Vietnam. It may fail, and we cannot estimate the odds of success with any accuracy—they may be somewhere between 25 percent and 75 percent. What we can say is that even if it fails, the policy will be worth it. At a minimum it will dampen down the charge that we did not do all that we could have done, and this charge will be important in many countries, including our own." [15]

Ultimately, the decisive factor was once again domestic politics. The Cold War liberal did not want to be accused of not doing everything that could be done to defeat the communists. Predictably, Johnson accepted Bundy's recommendation. Operation Rolling Thunder, a program of sustained bombing of North Vietnam, would begin on March 2.

Once the decision had been made, Johnson's advisers assumed the president would announce the change in policy in a major address to the nation, and that Johnson would personally make his case to the American people and the Congress in a forthright manner. Accordingly, both Bundy brothers and George Ball drafted material which they thought could be used in a major presidential speech. All three men were stunned when Johnson rejected the idea of a major speech. Instead, he chose to announce his decision in a few paragraphs at the end of a routine speech on February 17. Regular, sustained bombing raids against North Vietnam were presented as merely an extension of present policy.[16] Thus the credibility gap was born.

"PLEIKUS are like streetcars," Mac later told a reporter, meaning one comes along every few minutes. The quip would haunt him in the years to come. It cut too close to the truth. It made it seem as if the decision to escalate America's involvement in the war through a program of sustained bombing had been taken beforehand, and that Johnson had merely waited for some Americans to be killed. In one sense this was true. But the comment made Bundy seem cold and calculating, and the decision somehow Machiavellian. He had not meant to give that impression. All he meant to convey was his irritation with the reporter's naiveté. To him, it seemed so obvious. The decision to escalate had not been taken lightly. There had been, after all, literally months of painstaking deliberations. Mac himself had listened to all sides of the debate, and while he now favored bombing, he still thought of himself as a moderate. On the right, there were "wild men waiting in the wings" who wanted to invade North Vietnam, even at the risk of a war with China. And on the left, there were some who would let Vietnam and much of Southeast Asia go communist, a step Mac viewed as akin to stepping onto the slippery slope of isolationism. America was waging a cold war with Moscow and Beijing, so in the larger scheme of things Pleiku was merely a streetcar. If you didn't mount this streetcar, it could head straight to Munich, appeasement and world war. So you had to get on and at least try to alter its course.[17]

Bundy's China specialist, Jim Thomson, thought South Vietnam was the wrong place to make a stand against communist aggression. Deeply troubled by the direction of U.S. policy, on February 19, Thomson wrote Bundy a strongly worded memorandum entitled "The Vietnam Crisis—One Dove's Lament." Thomson warned that a policy of sustained reprisals risked a ground war with China—"a war in which we do not have the wherewithal to achieve any meaningful 'victory.' . . ." The only rational alternative, Thomson argued, was negotiation. But even the door on this option was quickly closing. "If we have many more speeches like those of [Thomas J.] Dodd [D-Conn.] and [Everett] Dirksen [R-Ill.] yesterday, the option of negotiation will become far more difficult—through its repeated equation with appeasement and sell-out (and ultimately, treason.)"[18] Again, the danger was another round of McCarthyism.

BUNDY's old mentor Walter Lippmann also disagreed with the new policy. The columnist had supported the initial retaliatory raids on North Vietnam in the wake of Pleiku. But he assumed—because he thought Bundy agreed with him on this—that the administration's act of military toughness would be followed by negotiations. Lippmann spent the morning of February 17 writing a column in which he said it would be "supreme folly" to become involved in a land war in Asia. "While the warhawks would rejoice when it began, the people would weep before it ended. There is no tolerable alternative except a negotiated truce. . . ." *

Having filed his column for publication the next day, Lippmann then went to the White House for an appointment with Bundy. Mac was in an awkward position. He could not tell his old friend and mentor that the post-Pleiku bombings were only a prelude to Operation Rolling Thunder. Johnson did not want to announce the escalation to a sustained bombing campaign. So as the columnist's biographer, Ronald Steel, related, Bundy "told Lippmann what he wanted to hear: that the President truly sought a negotiated settlement." [19]

The next day Lippmann taped one of his annual CBS television interviews hosted by veteran broadcaster Eric Sevareid. Vietnam dominated the hour-long interview. Lippmann made it clear that he sympathized with the men in the White House, whom he said were facing a terrible dilemma between widening the war or negotiating an "embarrassing and humiliating" truce that would lead inevitably to the collapse of the Saigon regime. There were "war hawks," Lippmann said, who wished to "knock out the whole industrial system of North Vietnam," and if necessary, even bomb China. The war hawks were contemplating sending in "hundreds of thousands of American troops to hold the line." Lippmann assured Sevareid that the war hawks were not to be found in the White House. "That I feel sure of," he added, no doubt thinking of his conversation with Bundy the previous day. [20]

If Bundy had advocated a different course, if he had sided with George Ball, Jim Thomson, Ken Galbraith, Walter Lippmann, Joseph Kraft and congressional leaders like Senator Mike Mansfield, his opposition to escalation might well have been decisive. Arguably, Bundy's opposition could have trumped McNamara's forceful arguments on behalf of bombing. Johnson himself was torn. Chatting in an off-the-record session with some reporters, Johnson compared his situation to a man standing on a newspaper in the middle of the ocean. "If I go this way," he said, tilting his hand to the right, "I'll topple over, and if I go this way," whereupon he tilted his hand to the left, "I'll topple over, and if I stay where I am, the paper will be soaked up and I'll sink slowly to the bottom of the sea." The reporters watched, mesmerized, as Johnson lowered his hand slowly to the floor. [21]

The president obviously felt trapped. But even as he sensed the potential disaster in Vietnam, he felt he could not ignore the advice of his two most influential foreign policy advisers. Johnson said the war would be over in a

---

* Lippmann's fellow columnist Joseph Kraft was making much the same argument. In the December 1964 issue of *Harper's*, Kraft had published an essay entitled "A Way Out in Viet-Nam." Based on his secret briefings from Michael Forrestal over the previous year, Kraft called it an "impossible war" and urged that the Viet Cong be invited to join a coalition government. Washington could live with any outcome, "even if Hanoi does come to dominate Saigon. . . ."

year or eighteen months; it would be like a "filibuster—enormous resistance at first, then a steady whittling away, then Ho hurrying to get it over with."[22]

PLEIKU had come along, and no sooner had Johnson boarded that "streetcar" than he was persuaded by Bundy and McNamara to authorize sustained bombing. Then as the "streetcars" came along at a regular clip, Johnson found it necessary to board every one. If the United States was going to bomb the North on a regular basis, why not do it from air bases in the South? Johnson authorized that. But if U.S. aircraft were stationed on the ground, the brass said the planes needed to be protected by anti-aircraft defense systems. Johnson authorized them. And if you were going to have that many men and equipment on the ground, you would need, as General Westmoreland recommended, a contingent of U.S. Marines to protect the air base's perimeter. On March 6, the marines waded ashore at Danang.

Having crossed this Rubicon, Johnson soon decided to send in more troops. On March 10, he met at Camp David with Mac Bundy, Rusk and McNamara. According to Bundy's notes, Rusk pointedly said they would soon have to decide whether to escalate or negotiate. Johnson replied that he was interested in any "honorable" settlement, but that he doubted the North Vietnamese were ready because "We've not done anything yet." As to an escalation, Johnson said, "I did cross [that] bridge in my own mind in December [1964]." Even so, "If you show me any reasonable out I'll grab it." Bundy's abbreviated notes then reflect the president saying, "To give in = another Munich. If not here—then Thailand. Come hell or high water, we're gonna stay there. Beg, borrow or steal to get a government."

That same day McNaughton sent Bundy a memo weighing the motivations behind the new U.S. policy: fully 70 percent was simply to avoid a "humiliating U.S. defeat." Allowing the South Vietnamese to live in a free society was assigned merely 10 percent, while keeping South Vietnam from Chinese influence was assigned 20 percent. Both Bundy brothers agreed with McNaughton. Vietnam itself was less important than the idea of maintaining America's Cold War credibility as the guarantor of freedom.[23]

Convinced that he couldn't abandon Vietnam, President Johnson had no faith that bombing alone would persuade Hanoi to end the war. Earlier in the year he had told Max Taylor that "this guerrilla war cannot be won from the air." Combat troops would be necessary—but he didn't want to publicize the fact.* On April 1 the president told Bundy he had authorized the sending of 18,000 to 20,000 more troops to Vietnam. Moreover, these troops would

* On March 15, 1965, President Johnson met with General Harold K. Johnson and General Earle C. Wheeler of the Joint Chiefs. Bundy was apparently not in the room, but according to Wheeler's assistant, General Andrew J. Goodpaster, General Johnson told the president that to win the war it could take "500,000 U.S. troops and five years." (William Conrad Gibbons, The U.S. Goverment and the Vietnam War, part III [Princeton: Princeton University Press, 1989], p. 166.)

have a new mission. In a memorandum for the files, Bundy noted that Johnson had approved "a change of mission for all Marine Battalions deployed to Vietnam to permit their more active use." No longer would the marines be used for mere "static defense." For the first time, American soldiers were to engage in "ground combat." Another American land war in Asia had begun. Significantly, Bundy noted, "The President desires that . . . premature publicity be avoided by all possible precautions. The actions themselves should be taken as rapidly as practicable, but in ways that should minimize any appearance of sudden changes in policy. . . . The President's desire is that these movements and changes should be understood as being gradual and wholly consistent with existing policy."[24]

Bundy knew otherwise. The introduction of ground combat troops constituted a new policy. Politically, he thought this should be publicly acknowledged and explained. But if his president had decided to send in the troops without any fanfare, he felt he had no choice but to go along. When asked, Bundy would now tell the press that the additional marines meant no change in "existing policy." Already, the *Washington Post* had complained in one editorial of "McGeorge Bundy's repeated attempts to sidetrack reporters' questions," and of the "many recent examples in which the Administration, sometimes explicitly, has deliberately sought to misinform the public. . . ."[25] The reporters' questions would become only more critical in the months to come.

Even Bundy's closest friends were no longer sure where he really stood on the war. A siege mentality was beginning to take hold of the Johnson White House. Doors were closing that used to be open. Arthur Schlesinger told Averell Harriman about this time that the president was allowing himself to become a "prisoner" in his own home; he said Bill Moyers had described the White House as a "closed shop." Certain people were in and some were definitely on the out. "Humphrey's out," Schlesinger told Harriman. "You're out. Moyers is in and out." Both Schlesinger and Harriman were alarmed by the drift toward escalation in Vietnam. Harriman plaintively told Schlesinger, "We have got to have a settlement. Why don't we try to do something? . . . We are applying the stick without the carrot."

As to Mac, they still believed their friend had an "open mind," particularly in contrast to Rusk, who seemed to be such a hawk. "Mac is in an uneasy position," Schlesinger told Harriman. "[He has] less authority. Open-minded in the beginning; went along with Rusk and his brother Bill." But then Schlesinger confessed, "I don't know where he is now."[26] Obviously, Schlesinger himself was on the out in the Johnson White House, so much so that Mac was no longer confiding in his old friend.

BILL BUNDY, meanwhile, had been busy creating his own credibility gap. On February 27 the State Department had released a White Paper on Vietnam which Bill had been working on intermittently since the autumn. It was, Bill later admitted, a "serious failure." For months he had painstakingly gathered evidence of North Vietnamese intervention in the South from raw intelligence reports and the testimony of captured North Vietnamese soldiers. The purpose was to justify the bombing of the North under international law and reassure "the newly aroused intellectuals" that their government was acting rationally. Characteristically, Bill poured his heart and soul into the effort and the resulting document was chock-full of dates, lists of captured armaments and names of North Vietnamese infiltrators. The document ran to sixty-four pages.

Unfortunately for the administration's case, Bill's effort attracted the attention of I. F. Stone, the indefatigable editor of *I. F. Stone's Weekly*. On March 8, two days after the first U.S. ground forces landed in Vietnam, Izzie Stone published his "Reply to the White Paper." Using Pentagon statistics and material from Bundy's own appendix, Stone demolished the White Paper. "A good way to read a government document," Stone told his biographer, "is backward." While the *New York Times* regurgitated the White Paper's conclusion that "incontrovertible evidence" had been found of Hanoi's weapons supply program, Stone reported that Appendix D told a very different story. The sum total of communist East bloc–produced weapons captured from the Viet Cong came to 179 items, including 72 rifles, 64 submachine guns and the odd pistol and mortar. Stone reported that some 7,500 comparable weapons of U.S. manufacture had been captured from the enemy during the same period.

As Bill himself later explained, any attempt to highlight North Vietnamese arms supplies to the South "was bound to run into the fact, embarrassing to explain, that most VC [Viet Cong] arms all along had been of American types supplied during the 1950–54 period, or more recently, and then captured from government forces." Put another way, the Viet Cong—the rebel forces indigenous to the South—were obtaining virtually 95 percent of their arms from the South. True, the White Paper's argument was slightly buttressed by the February 17 interception of a ship carrying 4,000 arms bearing Hanoi shipping labels. But as Bundy conceded, "this one swallow hardly made a summer." * To Bundy's further embarrassment, Stone's report was reprinted in the *New York Times* as an advertisement by an anti-war group. Intended to rally support for the war, Bundy's White Paper convinced many Americans that the administration was lying.

While the White Paper's evidence seemed pathetic, Bundy was actually quite right that since the Gulf of Tonkin incidents in August 1964, the North Vietnamese had dramatically increased their support for the Viet Cong, and indeed, had begun infiltrating regular North Vietnamese army troops into the South. To his regret, Bundy had been forced to withhold the most compelling

---

* On March 20, 1982, the *Washington Post* reported the allegation of a former CIA officer that this shipload of arms was actually a CIA fabrication. See George McT. Kahin, *Intervention: How America Became Involved in Vietnam* (New York: Knopf, 1986), p. 290.

evidence of Hanoi's role, namely, classified intercepts of the North's radio communications with its units in the South. But in a larger sense, this evidence was irrelevant. Critics of the war were not really disputing the North's involvement. The very first sentence of Izzie Stone's rebuttal to the White Paper had stated, "That North Vietnam supports the guerrillas in South Vietnam is no more secret than that the United States supports the South Vietnamese government against them." Critics like Stone argued that Vietnam had always been one nation, and that the conflict in the South was a civil war in which nationalist revolutionary forces (to be sure, led by communists) were pitted against the remnants of French colonial interests. Bundy's White Paper began with a quite different proposition: that South Vietnam was indeed a sovereign country with no political ties at all to the North. Few "newly aroused intellectuals" were likely to accept at face value a notion so factually at odds with the history of Indochina. Bundy's White Paper didn't have a chance.[27]

Izzie Stone wasn't the only critic to lash into Bundy's work that spring. Marc Raskin published his own "Citizen's White Paper" and had it inserted in the *Congressional Record.* In response, Mac sent Raskin a cold note telling him to stop identifying himself as a former NSC staff member. Raskin also received a sharp-tongued note from Bill Bundy, who found particularly objectionable Raskin's charge that South Vietnamese troops were torturing Viet Cong prisoners "with either American participation or acquiescence." After denying that any American had assisted in torture, Bill observed, "Unquestionably, war is ugly, and Asian standards in its conduct are not always our own." Furthermore, why had not Raskin addressed himself to Hanoi's conduct, which included assassinations and atrocities, not to mention a deliberate course of subversion and aggression over many years? "Your whole handling of this aspect," Bill wrote, "reminded me all too painfully of attitudes in Europe in the 1930's that equated every police measure by Benes against the Sudetens morally to the whole course of Hitler's conduct. Some day I shall write a piece on what might be called the 'extreme liberal syndrome' and its usefulness, or otherwise, in foreign affairs." Raskin was astonished by the anger in Bundy's letter. "Pardon me," he replied, "but your tone suggests misguided passion which obscures, rather than illuminates our interest in Southeast Asia."[28]

CRITICS like Stone and Raskin were a serious annoyance. But Walter Lippmann was a threat. Already, Lippmann was asking irritating questions in his columns. At Mac Bundy's urging, Johnson had Lippmann into the White House for lunch on March 15. After showing him a sheaf of classified cables containing a rosy assessment of the latest military encounters with the Viet Cong, Johnson complained, "I don't understand why those people in Hanoi won't negotiate with me." Lippmann replied, "Your policy is all stick and no carrot, Mr. President." When Lippmann argued the merits of a "peace offensive," the president grabbed a phone and called Bundy: "Mac, I've got Walter Lippmann over here and he says we're not doing the right thing. Maybe he's right." This was presidential blarney; Johnson had a war program and he was trying to get the influential columnist on board.

Two days later, Bundy met Lippmann for lunch at the Metropolitan Club, just around the corner from Lafayette Square. Once again Lippmann presented his views and left thinking that the president would soon be making a major speech that would lay out a plan for a comprehensive peace settlement.

In principle, Mac didn't disagree. Ever since Pleiku he had been trying to persuade Johnson to explain the war, and that included the peace terms. Already, a nascent anti-war movement was showing signs of increasing activism. Teach-ins had been organized on several major university campuses where speakers had criticized the bombing. This caused Bundy to cast about for some "dramatic packaging" of the administration's Vietnam policy, something that would help to sell the idea of a limited war in Vietnam to Johnson's liberal constituency. To Bundy's mind, the answer lay in Johnson's newly formulated Great Society. On March 30 he sent Johnson a memorandum proposing the formation of a Southeast Asia Development Corporation which would pump billions of dollars into the development of the region. Once the war was settled, North Vietnam would be invited to participate in this extension of the Great Society to Vietnam. He specifically proposed funding a major dam project for the Mekong Valley—"bigger and more imaginative than TVA; and a lot tougher to do."[29]

Bundy calculated that such a proposal would be warmly received by the New Dealer in Johnson. It still took, he recalled, a lot of work to persuade Johnson to give the speech, but after much prodding, the president finally incorporated the idea into a major address he delivered in Baltimore at Johns Hopkins University on April 7. As the historian Lloyd Gardner has observed, Johnson thought he had finally discovered a way out of the Vietnam dilemma. He would bring the New Deal to Vietnam, just as Franklin Roosevelt had helped a young congressman named Lyndon Johnson electrify the Hill Country of East Texas. He would win the war by exporting the Great Society, just as he would defend the Great Society programs from its domestic enemies by winning a crusade against communists in South Vietnam. Taking his cue from Bundy's memorandum, Johnson and his speechwriters crafted a text which proposed the formation of a Mekong Valley Authority and promised billions in development aid. Here was the carrot Lippmann wanted. Johnson would promise Ho Chi Minh more bombing of the North if the war did not end in the South—and billions of dollars if it did.

When the speech was ready, Bundy sent Johnson a memo suggesting that Lippmann be shown an advance copy. "A part of our purpose, after all," Bundy said, "is to plug his guns, and he can tell us better than anyone to what degree we have done so." It would be tricky, however, because the columnist was wedded to the idea of immediate negotiations. So Bundy urged Johnson to "make it clear to Lippmann that when we say we are ready to talk, we do not at all mean that we are ready for a cease-fire. The fact is that we expect our own military action to continue unless we see a prospect of a better situation in the South than we have now. Walter needs to understand this, and if he gets it straight from you, he is less likely to be objectionable about it."

Early that evening Lippmann walked into the anteroom off the Oval Office and heard Johnson say, "Walter, I'm going up to Baltimore tomorrow to give a speech, and I'm going to hold out that carrot you keep talking to me about. Now Mac here is going to show you the speech, and I want to know what you think of it."

But then for the next hour Johnson harangued Lippmann. "I'm not just going to pull up my pants and run out on Vietnam," he bellowed. "Curtis LeMay wants to bomb Hanoi and Haiphong. You know how much he likes to go around bombing. Now I'm not going to do that. . . . Then there's the Wayne Morse way, which amounts to turning the place over to the communists. I'm sure as hell not going to do that. You say to negotiate, but there's nobody over there to negotiate with. So the only thing there is to do is to hang on. And that's what I'm going to do."

When Johnson finished his monologue, Lippmann was finally allowed to go off to another room with Bundy. After going through the text of the speech, the columnist couldn't find the carrot. Looking to Bundy, he said, "This isn't going to work, Mac. It's just a disguised demand for capitulation. You've got to give the communists some incentive to negotiate."

"Like what?" Mac said.

"Like an unconditional cease-fire," Lippmann replied.

For an hour the two old friends argued over whether a cease-fire could be arranged. Bundy seemed to be seriously considering the proposition, and Lippmann went home hopeful that he had persuaded him that a cease-fire was essential if negotiations were to begin. He was wrong. Johnson gave the speech as it had been written—and there was no mention of a cease-fire, only a vague call for "unconditional discussions." Moreover, Johnson insisted, "We will not be defeated." Afterwards, when Lippmann again went to the White House for a postmortem, Bundy told him that Johnson had firmly decided not to negotiate until the military situation in the South had stabilized. This meant continued war.[30]

If Johnson's Baltimore speech failed to persuade Lippmann, it did nevertheless achieve the purpose of convincing many liberals that the president's rationale for the war was credible. It did not, however, derail a long-planned March on Washington on April 17, sponsored by the Students for a Democratic Society (SDS). Three days earlier Bundy advised Johnson that "a strong peaceloving statement tomorrow or Friday might help cool them off ahead of time."[31] Johnson ignored the advice. That weekend some 25,000 protestors descended on the city to picket the White House and hear speeches by I. F. Stone, Senator Ernest Gruening and other critics of the war. The largest peace march in American history, the demonstration marked the real beginning of the anti-war movement. The march ended at the foot of the Washington Monument, where SDS president Paul Potter gave a spellbinding speech that evoked the heart of the New Left's message: "We must accept the consequences that calling for an end of the war in Vietnam is in fact allowing for the likelihood that a Vietnam without war will be a self-styled Communist Vietnam. . . . I must say to you that I would rather see Vietnam Communist than see it under continuous subjugation or the ruin that American domination has brought."

In Potter's view, the war was not a mistake made by unwise or evil men. It was the result of a "system" and therefore "the war has its roots deep in the institutions of American society."

"I do not believe," Potter told the crowd, "that the president or Mr. Rusk or Mr. McNamara or even McGeorge Bundy are particularly evil men. If asked to throw napalm on the back of a ten-year-old child they would shrink in horror—but their decisions have led to mutilation and death of thousands and thousands of people. What kind of system is it that allows good men to make those kinds of decisions?"[32]

Such language was incomprehensible to Bundy. At Harvard, he was familiar with liberals like H. Stuart Hughes, whose political sensibilities Bundy recognized came from Henry Wallace and the Progressive Party. But the New Left was something wholly different. He was rankled by such personal attacks, particularly when they came from Harvard Square. In February, Harvard's *Crimson* had bluntly editorialized that the United States should "get out of Vietnam." On April 20, Bundy wrote an eleven-page letter to one of the editors of the *Crimson*, who just happened to be Donald Graham, the son of his good friend Katharine Graham, the publisher of the *Washington Post*. (Upon his graduation in 1966, Donald Graham would join the U.S. Army and serve in Vietnam.) Mac wanted to defend himself against his Harvard critics and explain the war to the younger Graham. "Both individual advisers and individual actions are fair targets for critical judgment," he wrote, "but no useful purpose is served by assuming that Dr. Strangelove is in charge down here."

He insisted that the aggressors in Vietnam resided in Hanoi and that it would be wrong to appease them. Mac had in mind the lessons he had learned as a young Stimsonian from the appeasement of Hitler at Munich in 1938. "The way to peace," he wrote, "lies over the hard road of determination. It has been so since 1940 for us all."[33] The lessons of Munich, he thought, fully explained why the United States had to stand fast in Vietnam in 1965. It seemed so obvious, but then he knew the young men out in the streets that spring disagreed.[34]

One such angry young man, Eli S. Zaretsky, a graduate assistant in the history department at the University of Maryland, wrote Bundy a passionate and eloquent letter that weekend in which he spelled out many of the anti-war movement's arguments. Vietnam, Zaretsky wrote, was not in "my interest, or the interest of Negroes in Harlem, or miners in Kentucky. . . ." He presumed that Bundy must believe that the national interest could be defined by "a small group of men." And if, indeed, Bundy was right, was he prepared to have America's crusade for freedom in South Vietnam followed by similar efforts against other tyrannies? "After we clear up the 'mess' in Vietnam are we planning to invade South Africa?"

After receiving this broadside, Bundy insisted that Zaretsky come to his White House office, where they talked about their differences for thirty minutes. "I wasn't telling him anything he didn't know," Zaretsky recalled. "But he wasn't in the least condescending." Mac could not say that he had not heard an intelligent articulation of the early New Left's critique. He had listened and it had been spelled out quite clearly.[35]

THE first of the spring teach-ins against the war was organized by a group of professors at the University of Michigan who had publicly supported Lyndon Johnson against Barry Goldwater. They now felt betrayed. By early April, faculty from an ad hoc group, the Inter-University Committee for a Public Hearing on Vietnam, were planning a national teach-in. Sensitive to charges that the earlier events had been one-sided, the organizers decided to invite a prominent government official to make the case for the war. As a former Harvard dean, the president's national security adviser was thought to be a natural choice to debate the issue. On April 16, Bundy declined the invitation with a positively insulting letter. After dismissing the organizers' letter of invitation as "a piece of propaganda," Bundy smugly noted, "I have written enough to suggest that if your letter came to me for grading as a professor of government, I would not be able to give it high marks."

Not surprisingly, this insult spurred the professors to redouble their efforts to stage a confrontation with Bundy. After four hundred University of Michigan faculty members signed another letter of invitation, Bundy tentatively agreed to participate in a public debate. Citing personal reasons, he declined to appear with Professor Hans Morgenthau, a prominent scholar at the University of Chicago who had recently said that Bundy and McNamara were "devoid of sound judgment and understanding of foreign policy."[36] He also refused to debate the administration's most vehement critic in the U.S. Senate, Senator Wayne Morse. Finally, the organizers put forward the name of Professor George McT. Kahin, a scholar of Asian affairs at Cornell University, and Bundy agreed. A date was set for Saturday, May 15, in Washington, D.C.

"An unprecedented battle of eggheads is shaping up here," wrote columnist Peter Lisagor, "threatening to leave the administration's already frayed links with the intellectual community in rubble." The morning of the scheduled debate, the Washington Post reported, "Combative emotions on both sides have been honed to razor edge." In anticipation of Bundy's appearance, more than seven hundred advance tickets had already been sold and 130 radio stations had lined up to broadcast the debate. But then, just three hours before Bundy was scheduled to speak, Professor Ernest Nagel of Columbia University, the designated moderator, was summoned to the White House, where he was told that Bundy would not appear.[37]

The teach-in nevertheless proceeded, and over the course of the next fifteen hours some three thousand people attended and nearly 100,000 students listened via phone lines connecting the Washington event to a hundred campuses around the country. The centerpiece of the teach-in, the Bundy-Kahin debate, was televised as planned with Berkeley political scientist Robert Scalapino standing in for the national security adviser. The television cameras focused on an empty chair behind Bundy's nameplate.

Unknown to those participating in the teach-in, Mac Bundy wasn't there because the president had suddenly ordered him to get on a plane with Cy Vance and fly to the Dominican Republic, where U.S. Marines had recently invaded the island to quell an allegedly communist-inspired uprising. The Dominican negotiations, in fact, were merely a convenient pretext for getting Bundy off the debating platform. Johnson simply didn't like the idea of seeing his national security adviser provide his critics with a televised platform from which to voice their opposition to the war. Some of the country's leading intellectuals—scholars like Hans Morgenthau, China expert Mary Wright, Marxist historian Isaac Deutscher and diplomatic historian William Appleman Williams—were seen on television by a national audience for the first time. An early revisionist historian of the Cold War, D. F. Fleming, debated Harvard's conservative political scientist Samuel Huntington. Bernard Fall, Seymour Melman, Robert Scheer, Staughton Lynd, Eric Wolf and other prominent writers participated.

A few lower-level administration officials put in appearances, including Walt Rostow, who debated Morgenthau, Harvard's Stanley Hoffmann and Bundy's former aide Marc Raskin. Rostow reported back to Dean Rusk that these critics of the war were not only sanctimonious, but represented "in American academic life a minority of no great distinction."[38]

Arthur Schlesinger, Jr., gave a speech in which he voiced support for the Johnson administration's war aims but criticized the U.S. bombing of North Vietnam. Citing the conclusions of the Strategic Bombing Survey following World War II, Schlesinger argued that such bombing would only strengthen the enemy's will. What was needed in Vietnam, Schlesinger said, was more troops, not bombs. "Indeed," he said, "if we took the Marines now in the Dominican Republic and sent them to South Vietnam, we would be a good deal better off in both countries." When these remarks were greeted with hissing and long-winded questions from angry students, Schlesinger snapped, "When I hear questions like that, I begin to wonder whether Mac Bundy might not be right."[39]

At one point Professor Nagel read a letter from Bundy that began by apologizing for his sudden absence. But Mac conceded nothing: "All of us want a decent settlement. None of us wants other men to be forced under a totalitarian political authority. All of us seek a solution in which American troops can be honorably withdrawn." [40]

Needless to say, the statement did nothing to mollify his critics. Washington University biologist Barry Commoner stood up late in the day and complained that Bundy, "who gave professors bad marks, has turned in a terrible record on attendance . . . we have to give him a makeup exam." Afterwards, leaders of the teach-in cabled Bundy, challenging him to "an alternative confrontation which will allow you to fulfill your commitment to us. . . ." They proposed that he meet with them on national television to debate the war.[41] Obviously, McGeorge Bundy—the intellectual, the former Harvard dean, a man who seemed to symbolize reason in power—had become the issue. His intellectual peers were determined to hold him accountable.

When it was all over, the *New York Times* praised the "academic community" for giving the American people and its government the "most comprehensive and civilized public debate on the Vietnamese war in all the decade since the United States became involved in the conflict there." [42] It would also turn out to be the last time the war was debated in a civil fashion before any kind of national audience. The teach-in accomplished what President Johnson feared—it legitimized the notion that fundamental questions could be asked about the war. Establishment reporters like Max Frankel of the *New York Times* and Lawrence Stern of the *Washington Post* began writing about the war with a new perspective. Radical intellectuals like Isaac Deutscher, Staughton Lynd and Marc Raskin were suddenly part of the debate. Izzie Stone told his readers, "The intellectuals are beginning to do their duty." [43] All in all, it was a significant event, and Bundy knew he should have been there.

ONLY in retrospect did Mac Bundy realize that Johnson had rushed him off to Santo Domingo not because there was any pressing need for his presence on the island, but "to keep me away from all those wild men." [44] He thought it unseemly that he should be seen to have ducked a debate, particularly one organized by university faculty. Robert Scalapino, the Berkeley political scientist who stood in for Bundy, now urged him to "make some attempt to counteract the feeling in some intellectual circles that the academic world is being neglected." [45] Bundy agreed. The Harvard dean in him might sometimes express exasperation with his former colleagues, but he also appreciated the potential influence intellectuals wielded in creating and maintaining a national consensus over issues as fundamental as war and peace. Neither did he lack any confidence in his ability to win such a debate.

Upon his return from the Dominican Republic, Bundy took steps to honor his previous commitment to debate the war. He would, however, make sure that he controlled the format. Instead of a teach-in filled with hostile students, Bundy wanted a studio audience and a "non-partisan" moderator. On his own initiative he approached Fred Friendly at CBS News and expressed interest in participating in a live televised debate on the war. CBS jumped at the opportunity and assigned veteran broadcaster Eric Sevareid to moderate the event. In return, Bundy agreed to debate Professor Hans Morgenthau.

The encounter was televised on June 21.[46] That morning Mac walked into his office and, with a glint in his eye and a tight little smile, told his colleagues, "Well, my wife said to me last night, 'Try to be tonight the man I married and not the man I almost didn't marry.' " Everyone laughed. Mary, of course, wanted her husband to display a little of the warmth and humor his friends knew so well. But Mac could not help himself: Long ago, over the Bundy dinner table and later at Groton and Yale, he had been taught to win debates. He would be absolutely ruthless.[47]

That evening Sevareid opened the exchange by posing four questions central to the administration's justification for the war. So cued, Bundy crisply made the administration's case, citing heavily from official papers: Washington was fulfilling its treaty obligations and repelling aggression from the North. He concluded that there were only two alternatives: intervention or withdrawal. When Morgenthau responded, it quickly became clear that Bundy would win the debate. Morgenthau could not bring himself to make the case for withdrawal, and merely confined himself to the much weaker argument that the war was going badly and that the administration should seek some "face-saving" negotiations. In his rebuttal, Bundy charged the professor with "giving vent to his congenital pessimism." He then proceeded to ridicule Morgenthau by quoting the professor's previous predictions, to wit, that the postwar Marshall Plan was doomed to failure, and that "Communist domination of Laos is virtually a foregone conclusion."

Morgenthau was reduced to pleading, "I may have been dead wrong on Laos, but it doesn't prove that I am dead wrong on Vietnam."[48]

Clearly, Bundy had won the debate on points. To a few viewers, Bundy's treatment of Morgenthau came across as mean-spirited, shallow and arrogant. But there was no doubt about its political effect. Bundy had won. Morgenthau lamented his own naiveté. He had debated Bundy "in the naive assumption that if power were only made to see the truth, it would follow that lead." University of Michigan professor Stanley Diamond agreed: "After viewing the program," he wrote his fellow teach-in organizers, "I am forced to conclude that we pursued McGeorge Bundy until he caught us."[49]

Lyndon Johnson, however, was not happy. Bundy had defied him. Prior to the debate, Bill Moyers had walked into the Oval Office to find Johnson angrily waving a wire service report: "Did you see this? Bundy is going on television—on national television—with five professors. I never gave him permission. That's an act of disloyalty. He didn't tell me because he knew I didn't want him to do it. Bill, I want you to go to Bundy and tell him the president would be pleased, mighty pleased, to accept his resignation." Johnson paused a moment and then said, "On second thought, maybe I should talk to him myself." When Moyers, rather stunned at this outburst, didn't respond,

Johnson said, "No, you go do it." Breaking the awkward silence that followed, Johnson grumbled, "That's the trouble with all you fellows. You're in bed with the Kennedys."

Moyers was a Johnson man, of course, not a Kennedy man, and he was shocked by his boss's behavior. That night he called Richard Goodwin, who later jotted in his diary, "He [Moyers] said he was extremely worried, that as he listened to Johnson he felt weird, almost as if he wasn't really talking to a human being at all."

The next morning Johnson asked Moyers, "Did you speak to Bundy?" When Moyers said no, the president grunted and returned to his reading.

Moyers had, however, warned Bundy that the president wanted him to back out of the debate. Bundy felt he had made a commitment and had gone ahead anyway.

Afterwards, despite Bundy's trouncing of Morgenthau, Johnson said nothing to him about his performance—a sign Bundy took to mean disapproval. In fact, Johnson still had thoughts of firing him. The morning after the debate, Moyers and Goodwin were standing in the Oval Office when Johnson suddenly snapped. "I am not going to have anything more to do with the liberals," Johnson said. "They won't have anything to do with me. They all just follow the communist line—liberals, intellectuals, communists. They're all the same. . . . I can't trust anybody anymore. I tell you what I'm going to do. I'm going to get rid of everybody who doesn't agree with my policies. I'll take a tough line—put Abe Fortas or Clark Clifford in the Bundy job. I'm not going in the liberal direction. There's no future with them. They're just out to get me, always have been." Goodwin and Moyers wondered whether the president was becoming unhinged with paranoia.[50]

They didn't confide their fears to Bundy, but he nevertheless understood that a line had been crossed with Johnson. "He didn't want me to do it [the debate]," Bundy recalled. "And he knew that I knew he didn't want me to do it—and I did it anyway." Mac later acknowledged that he had been angry with Johnson about the whole affair, and knew that the president was himself "angry about getting pushed around into explaining things he didn't want to explain. . . . But I just thought that not defending the damn war, or any policy, well, that was not the way to deal with these characters. They were a bunch of undergraduates and that was a breed I knew—the worst thing you could do to them was ignore them. . . . [Besides] they were entitled to hear what the hell the government thought it was doing."[51]

That week Time magazine put Bundy on its cover under the headline "The Crucial Choice: U.S. Foreign Policy in Action." Johnson was not the kind of man who liked his aides getting credit, and here was Bundy's face plastered across Time with a presidential eagle hovering in the background. The accompanying story depicted Bundy as the president's "Ambassador to the Academe," a man with "solid gold credentials." Johnson was described as depending heavily on Bundy's every word, consulting him no less than eighty-six times during the first days of the Dominican crisis. The story portrayed Bundy as a man of eloquence—in obvious contrast to Lyndon Johnson—a man who could speak without a text before an audience of a thousand Harvard students and stand his ground. Earlier in June, Bundy had gone back to Harvard's Lowell Lecture Hall, and *Time's* reporters described how for two hours he stood and argued the case for the administration's Vietnam policy. His old friend and former aide Carl Kaysen had moderated the event while outside on the sidewalk students marched with pickets that read "When Will Bundy Pay for His War Crimes?"

The newsweekly also reported that Bundy had told friends that he had only "marginal differences" with either Kennedy or Johnson, and that he was now "in strong general agreement" with Lyndon's views. He would have quit a long time ago if this was not the case.[52]

Actually, even as *Time* was celebrating Bundy's brilliance, Mac was indeed thinking about quitting. His differences with Johnson were subtle and complicated, but hardly marginal. The two men increasingly found themselves annoyed by each other. In retrospect, Bundy thought his debate with Morgenthau marked a turning point in his relationship with Johnson. "Obviously, I'm not going to quit overnight," he recalled. "I can endure it. It's just that I don't think it is working very well, or is going to work very well. And I think he'll do better with someone that he's more comfortable with. Nonetheless, there we are working. . . . You know, I was fond of the old bastard. You couldn't help it. He was a marvelous guy, except that he's such a bitch." Johnson felt the same mix of feelings for his closest foreign policy adviser: he could admire him, even envy his intelligence—but increasingly he snidely referred to Bundy behind his back as "my debater." To Johnson, this was no compliment.[53]

THE April intervention in the Dominican Republic only exacerbated the Johnson administration's credibility problems—and further complicated Bundy's relationship with the president.

On the afternoon of April 28, Bundy was meeting with Johnson, Rusk, McNamara, Moyers and Ball to discuss Vietnam when the president was handed an urgent cable from his ambassador in the Dominican Republic. The ambassador reported that the Dominican army had split into two factions and the island was collapsing into civil disorder. When Johnson was told that the CIA believed that three leaders of the rebel forces were Castro-trained agents, he quickly decided to send four hundred U.S. Marines to the Dominican capital of Santo Domingo with thousands of additional troops to follow. In the larger scheme of things, the Dominican Republic was merely a blip on Bundy's foreign policy radar screen. On the other hand, if it was true that the rebels were Cuban-style communists, then this fact alone warranted intervention. Even Richard Goodwin, who had helped to fashion President Kennedy's Alliance for Progress policy for Latin America, told Johnson on April 29 that "anything, including military intervention, should be done if essential to prevent another Castro-type takeover in the Caribbean."[54] Goodwin, however, did not think intervention was necessary, and he was appalled to hear the news from Bundy. When he asked if anything could be done to stop it, Bundy replied, "They're already in the air."

"But why the marines?" Goodwin said, knowing what a symbol of Yankee imperialism the U.S. Marines were in the eyes of most Latin Americans. "Why not the army?"

Walking into the Cabinet Room with Goodwin trailing behind him, Bundy couldn't resist laughing and telling the assembled advisers, "You know what Goodwin says? He wants to know if we can send someone else besides the marines." Goodwin didn't think it was a laughing matter.[55]

To Johnson, sending in the marines was an easy decision. He was preventing not only another Castro, but also another Vietnam by acting decisively and in force. "What can we do in Vietnam if we can't clean up the Dominican Republic?" Soon, however, it became clear to the reporters covering the story that there was no substance to the American embassy's claim that fifty-eight card-carrying communists were behind the rebellion. The reality was a little more complicated: the Dominican army had split into two factions, a minority supporting the return of Juan Bosch, a liberal intellectual who had been elected president in 1962 and then deposed in an army coup ten months later. The army's majority faction, however, regarded Bosch as a dangerous leftist.

When the media and congressional figures began questioning the necessity of rushing 24,000 U.S. troops to settle an arcane political dispute, the president began to embellish the story as only Lyndon Johnson could. He told a press conference that "some 1,500 innocent people were murdered and shot, and their heads cut off." The U.S. ambassador, Johnson claimed, "was talking to us from under a desk while bullets were going through his windows and he had a thousand American men, women and children . . . pleading with their President for help to preserve their lives." None of this happened, of course, and Bundy knew it.

"Those weren't lies," Bundy later told Randall Bennett Woods, an historian and biographer of Senator Fulbright. "He was building up, 'argufying'; he was certainly going beyond the truth, but that's not the same as lying. In his mind, he was 'trying to make the whole situation totally clear.' " Bundy admitted that he had a terrible time trying to control Johnson's flair for "unfettered exposition." He knew Johnson had lied to him when he said it was necessary for him to skip the May 15 debate on Vietnam and fly to Santo Domingo. Mac had dutifully tried to negotiate a political settlement between the Bosch and army factions. He failed, but later in the summer an agreement was finally reached to hold elections in 1966. A conservative politician, Joaquin Balaguer, won that election. But in the end, the American intervention did not prevent Bosch from eventually winning the presidency in subsequent elections; he would rule the island for many years to come. More importantly, the Dominican affair convinced Senator Fulbright that Lyndon Johnson was not to be trusted. By contrast, Mac Bundy knew that in dealing with Johnson he was dealing with a man who easily embellished the truth: "If I could get used to it in my cold-roast New England way, why couldn't Fulbright?"[56]

ALL that spring and early summer, Mac felt as if he was pouring his energies into "trying to concert a position" on Vietnam that could be sold to the American people. But Johnson wasn't selling, at least to the public. The president was acting like the Senate majority leader he once was, concentrating on manipulating the Senate. "I had no clout with him on the money matter, going to Congress and getting the money to finance the war," Bundy later recalled. "Bob [McNamara] tried to persuade him of that as well." The president, however, was adamant; he would do nothing to jeopardize congressional appropriations for his Great Society programs. Explaining the war—and specifically how much it would cost—was just not a priority. That became, Bundy said, "a basic, real disagreement" between the two of them: "I had reached the conclusion in the summer of 1965 that I really wasn't doing much good with Johnson. I wasn't able to communicate with him; he needed somebody he trusted more . . . somebody like Moyers."

Early that summer Mac picked up the phone and called Nate Pusey. When the Harvard president came on the line, Mac asked, "If I needed a job, could you take me back?" He was thinking of a professorship, and Pusey quickly assured him that something could be arranged.[57] Bundy wasn't yet ready to quit, but he felt the time had come to explore his options.

ON the surface, both Bundy brothers still seemed to have it all. Just a few months before the spring teach-ins, their approach to Vietnam had seemed so cool, so measured that most reporters could not peg them as either hawks or doves. Columnist Joseph Kraft quipped that Mac was the "iron knight of the soft line." Even as late as that summer, Kraft wrote in a magazine essay that Mac Bundy "is the leading candidate, perhaps the only candidate, for the statesman's mantle to emerge in the generation that is coming to power. . . ."[58] This was the last time Bundy would be praised so unreservedly.

Mac himself felt the atmosphere in Washington was growing colder. Not only was his relationship with Johnson becoming strained, but so too were many of his long-standing friendships from Cambridge. Henry Kissinger—not one of his favorite Harvard figures—wrote him that spring to endorse the administration's Vietnam policies as "just right: the proper mixture of firmness and flexibility." Kissinger explained, "I say this because the carping of some of your former colleagues at Harvard may create a misleading impression of unanimity." Mac thanked him, adding, "I fear you may be somewhat lonely among all our friends at Harvard."[59]

Early that summer the poet Robert Lowell decided to protest the war by sending a letter to the *New York Times* announcing his refusal to attend an arts festival at the White House. Within days twenty other prominent writers —including Lillian Hellman, Mary McCarthy, William Styron, Hannah Arendt, Alfred Kazin, Robert Penn Warren, Philip Roth and Dwight Macdonald —had signed a telegram in support of Lowell's action. The arts festival went forward, but it was an unmitigated public relations disaster. Author John Hersey decided to attend and to make an anti-war statement by reading passages from his book *Hiroshima*. Lady Bird Johnson tried repeatedly to dissuade Hersey: "The President and I," Mrs. Johnson told an aide, "do not want this man to come here and read this." Hersey read the passage anyway, and a mortified Lady Bird sat with her hands folded in her lap as the rest of the audience loudly applauded. Johnson was furious and later complained, "I don't think I will ever get credit for anything I do in foreign policy because I didn't go to Harvard." In Johnson's mind, these were Bundy's friends turning on their president.[60] He was right.

Even one of Bundy's oldest and dearest Cambridge mentors, Archibald MacLeish, was reluctantly asking troubling questions about the administration's interventions in both Vietnam and the Dominican Republic. When Mac decided to use MacLeish as a foil to answer the administration's intellectual critics, Archie cooperated. In an exchange published on July 3 in the *Saturday Review*, MacLeish asked Bundy if the show of military force meant "that we are no longer that idealistic nation of the First World War . . .? Have our ways of thinking and of feeling altered? Are we 'realistic' now? 'Hardheaded'? "

Bundy's reply was gentle and deferential. The exchange between the old poet and his younger friend captured the generational differences between those liberal Wilsonian internationalists of the World War I era and those liberal Cold Warriors like Bundy who believed that America had become a global power with hegemonic responsibilities.

MacLeish was asking a fundamental question: had the character of America changed? Bundy's answer was essentially yes. He pointed out that the "structure of our contemporary role in the world rises upon rocks that were put in place in the time of Franklin Roosevelt, in the time that followed the fall of France in that terrible spring of 1940. For it is from that moment that one must date the inescapable place of the United States . . . as one of those nations inescapably drawn to difficulty and to responsibility all over the world."

Bundy did not expect unanimous approval "when we move, as we have had to move, in difficult and dangerous areas like Vietnam and the Dominican Republic." In both countries, communist conquest "would not only be deeply against our interests but also against their own." But here Mac strained to differentiate himself from the simple-minded anti-communism of the right wing. "We run a constant risk, it seems to me, of two alternate errors. . . ." One was to dismiss the dangers of communism. The other was to become obsessively anti-communist: "anti-Communism alone is almost never a sufficient guide to policy."[61] MacLeish could hardly disagree with this classic re-statement of the liberal anti-communist position. Bundy had once again positioned himself in Arthur Schlesinger's vital center, a reasonable liberal who could distinguish—unlike the McCarthyites of the 1950s—between recognizing the communist danger and obsessing about it. He did not realize, however, that his formulation had nothing to do with the realities of Vietnam. In responding to MacLeish, Bundy was addressing himself to a domestic political audience, a liberal political constituency still scarred by McCarthyism. When he thought of Vietnam, his concern was to fashion a policy that avoided the domestic political pitfalls of McCarthyism and yet could still be described as dealing realistically, even hardheadedly, with the dangers of communism. Politically reasonable, Mac's argument had nothing to say about the hard reality of Ho Chi Minh's decades-long nationalist revolution.

Mac's relations with Archie MacLeish remained warm, despite the older man's growing skepticism about the war.* But Vietnam was straining his old friendship with Walter Lippmann. A few days after the April March on Washington, Lippmann had written a particularly troubling column, asserting that Ho Chi Minh surely would have won the elections in 1956 if Washington had allowed them to take place.[62] He cited Dwight Eisenhower's memoirs to support this opinion. He also questioned the Johnson administration's claim that the 1954 "demarcation" line constituted a legally recognized boundary between two independent states.

Bundy was taken aback. Lippmann was questioning the very legitimacy of the South Vietnamese state, echoing arguments made in the recent teach-ins. Yet Mac could only muster a weak response: "I have questions about those basic propositions, but I have not had a chance to do the necessary historical checking. In particular, I am inclined to think that it is quite wrong to assert that the notion of independence in South Vietnam is something new." He then added that it was his "strong impression" that the United States and many other countries had recognized that South Vietnam "has had the essentials of an independent nation for many years." He was quite wrong, and Lippmann knew it. To the elderly columnist, it appeared that America was going to war to defend the sovereignty of a country which existed only because Washington had unilaterally declared that it existed.

Painfully, Lippmann concluded this exchange of correspondence with his protégé on a note of sympathy: "These are trying times for all of us, and I am very conscious of the heavy burden which you bear."[63] He and Bundy would remain on friendly terms and continue to socialize occasionally. But this was

---

* By 1968, Archie would be supporting Eugene McCarthy's anti-war campaign for the presidency and saying, "It's a war we never meant to get into and don't know how to get out of and the country has been increasingly sick of it for months" (Scott Donaldson, *Archibald MacLeish: An American Life* [Boston: Houghton Mifflin, 1992], p. 485).

the last serious exchange they had on the war. Lippmann later told his biographer, Ronald Steel, "I had assumed that we were in agreement, but I discovered that we weren't. It came as a great surprise to me to learn—and it slipped out only gradually—that he was much more pro-war than I knew." Mac was "very cagey, a person who, I now feel, was not in the open, not clear about where he stood." [64]

LIPPMANN would have been even more alarmed had he known that the Bundy brothers were blocking an effort by George Ball, Dean Acheson and Lloyd Cutler (another powerful Washington corporate lawyer) to ease Johnson off the escalation track. Late in April, Ball persuaded the president to have Acheson and Cutler prepare a negotiating proposal. According to minutes of the meeting taken by State Intelligence Director Thomas L. Hughes, "Ball has been given carte blanche by LBJ to prepare the political track." By early May, Acheson and Cutler had crafted a recommendation which Ball "thought was damn good." It proposed a halt to the bombing and a program for peace talks based on the significant concession that the National Liberation Front could be invited to participate in "peaceful politics" within South Vietnam and join a Committee of Reconstruction. The Saigon government would pledge to hold elections and later hold a referendum on reunification of North and South Vietnam. According to Hughes, Bill Bundy "immediately fretted." Bill argued that they shouldn't "seem to backtrack on our firmly held positions . . . can't go in the direction, for instance, of admitting that this is a civil war." Bill was so certain that it was the wrong time for a serious negotiation that he now scuttled his father-in-law's report. On May 12, 1965, Ball told Hughes that he was "stunned" to learn that LBJ had instead adopted an unenticing proposal directed toward Moscow with "no carrots or concessions at all." The bombing pause—code-named Operation Mayflower—would last less than a week. Hughes wrote in his notes that this "Torpedoes the Ball-Acheson ploy. Bundys did it with full knowledge that it would . . . Ball is sick: cuckolded. Bill to Mac to LBJ apparently. Acheson undermined in the family."

Mac Bundy didn't think of himself as pro-war. Pressed from the left by Lippmann and just as hard from the right by Joe Alsop, Mac thought of himself as occupying the reasonable center. Indeed, relations with the mercurial Alsop were almost as tattered as his friendship with Lippmann. Alsop was telling friends like Richard Rovere that a defeat in Vietnam would "poison our national life for a generation." In his column he even went so far as to ask whether Lyndon Johnson was "man enough" to stand up to the communists. [65]

One day Alsop and Bundy—two old Grotonians—were standing outside National Airport when they began arguing furiously. Joe was relentless, pressing Mac ruthlessly about how little was being done to win the war. Bundy tolerated this kind of treatment from only one man—Joe Alsop. But finally, his patience at an end, he turned to Joe and announced that he was not going to discuss Vietnam with him. Then he stomped away, leaving Alsop fuming with anger. Afterwards, Mac wrote Joe a handwritten note, trying to make amends. "I think you'll agree that the North Terminal on Wednesday evening was a poor place for a serious talk. I was trying only to say that for the present I would prefer not to discuss one tough matter of business with you, and I am quite willing to agree that my way of saying it was infelicitous. . . . I think you'll also agree that any one in my place has an obligation to decide whom when and what in his dealings with reporters, even when they are very close friends." Joe had a right to "holler bloody murder," Mac wrote, but "what I won't and can't admit is that such a good business quarrel has anything to do with our friendship—because if I admit that, then our friendship depends on my talking to you only on your terms—and that won't do."

"So I love you—and I meant no offense—and I still prefer not to talk about South East Asia right now—but I'm perfectly willing to have a fight about why if you think it worthwhile." [66]

LATER that spring Mac relented and began listening once again to Alsop's sermons on Vietnam. After one such talk Mac reported to Johnson, "I told him also that any difference between us on bombing was a matter of pace and judgment—that he could be quite confident of your firmness. I did *not* tell him about the problem of keeping our liberal friends on board because he has no sympathy with that part of your job and would simply denounce us for neglecting a fire while seeking an unreal consensus. He obviously believes we can never keep the *Times* with us and might as well ignore it." [67]

For some time now Mac had been playing a delicate balancing game between defending Johnson to elite critics like Lippmann, James Reston and Alsop, and nudging the president to respond to their criticisms. At times, Bundy's notes to the president bordered on the obsequious, so intent was he to soothe the man's insecurities. "From Lyndon Johnson's point of view," Bundy would later say, "anything less than 100% support was rank desertion." [68]

MEANWHILE, back in Saigon yet another bloodless coup in June removed the civilian veneer of the government that had ostensibly ruled since February. Prime Minister Phan Huy Quat was forced to step down and General Nguyen Cao Ky, the flamboyant chief of South Vietnam's air force, became prime minister. Major General Nguyen Van Thieu was elevated to head of state. Ky was described by one U.S. diplomat as an "unguided missile," and in hindsight, Bill Bundy characterized the Ky-Thieu regime as "absolutely the bottom of the barrel!" [69] On June 14, General Westmoreland told Johnson that the war was lost "without substantial US combat support on the ground." U.S. combat strength already stood at nearly 75,000 men, and Westmoreland now asked for an additional 90,000, and even then, the general made it clear that this would be only the beginning. Four days later George Ball submitted his own assessment to the president, ominously beginning by quoting Ralph Waldo

Emerson's line, "Things are in the saddle and ride mankind." Ball's advice was explicit and unwavering. If the president wanted to retain control over events, he had to set some limits to the U.S. commitment. "Before we commit an endless flow of forces to South Vietnam we must have more evidence than we now have that our troops will not bog down in the jungles and rice paddies— while we slowly blow the country to pieces." Ball suggested the president could raise the U.S. commitment to 100,000 troops—but no more—and that he should make it clear to the Joint Chiefs that this was a "controlled commitment for a trial period of three months . . ." In the meantime, he argued, the bureaucracy should be instructed to come up with a plan for a political settlement. "The last should be regarded," Ball said, "as plans for cutting losses and eventually disengaging from an untenable situation."[70]

Ball understood that what he was proposing was unpalatable to both the president and his advisers. But by explicitly stating the obvious—that no one had studied the option of disengagement, Ball hoped to persuade Johnson to order his people to rethink their assumptions. His appeal was addressed to Mac Bundy as much as to the president. He hoped that if he could convince Mac, the national security adviser would convince the president.

Johnson read the Ball memo at Camp David and was impressed enough to order both McNamara and Ball to produce a paper with specific policy recommendations. He gave them each a week to make their case. This was not just an intellectual exercise; Johnson had serious doubts. Yet, at the same time, events really were in the saddle. The Viet Cong had launched another offensive, American boys were dying in Vietnam, and the Saigon generals were pleading for more American troops.

McNamara weighed in on June 26 with a memo entitled "Program of Expanded Military and Political Moves with Respect to Vietnam." It recommended that U.S. forces should be raised to whatever force levels would persuade the Viet Cong that they "cannot win" the war.[71] For now, that meant 200,000 troops, a tripling of bombing sorties against North Vietnam and a naval blockade of northern ports.

Bundy was appalled. On June 30 he sent McNamara a strongly worded memo questioning his entire program. It was Mac at his most incisive. He told the secretary of defense that his memo to the president had "grave limitations."

McNamara's proposal required "a new land commitment at a time when our troops are entirely untested in the kind of warfare projected." The secretary was recommending an escalation of the bombing campaign "when the value of the air action we have taken is sharply disputed." McNamara was contemplating mining North Vietnam's harbors "when nearly everyone agrees the real question is not in Hanoi, but in South Vietnam."

And then, in an extraordinary statement, Bundy wrote: "My first reaction is that this program is rash to the point of folly." Bristling with ironic understatement, Mac then said, "I see no reason to suppose that the Viet Cong will accommodate us by fighting the kind of war we desire. Fragmentary evidence so far suggests that they intend to avoid direct contact with US forces and concentrate their efforts against the Vietnamese Army. I think the odds are that if we put in 40–50 battalions with the missions here proposed, we shall find them only lightly engaged and ineffective in hot pursuit."

Even worse, to Mac's thinking, was the notion of making this kind of commitment without extracting the political reforms from Saigon which might make the war winnable. "This is a slippery slope toward total US responsibility and corresponding fecklessness on the Vietnamese side." And what were the upper limits of so Americanizing the war? "If we need 200 thousand men now for these quite limited missions, may we not need 400 thousand later? Is this a rational course of action?" And if U.S. casualties go up sharply, what further actions would McNamara recommend?

Alternatively, if escalation was the game, why not give Hanoi a "much more drastic warning"? "If General Eisenhower is right in his belief that it was the prospect of nuclear attack which brought an armistice in Korea, we should at least consider what realistic threat of larger action is available to us for communication to Hanoi." Bundy was not advocating the use of nuclear weapons in Vietnam.* Instead, what he had in mind was "a full interdiction of supplies to North Vietnam. . . ." McNamara had proposed only a naval blockade. Bundy was contemplating both a naval and air blockade. Even then, he was hopeful that an ultimatum threatening such a full blockade might be enough to persuade Hanoi to change course.

Finally, Bundy faulted McNamara for not addressing the fundamental goal of the U.S. effort in Vietnam. Sounding very much like George Ball, Mac asked, "If it [the goal] is to get to the conference table, what results do we seek there? Still more brutally, do we want to invest 200 thousand men to cover an eventual retreat? Can we not do that just as well where we are?"[72]

For its time—and even more so in retrospect—Bundy's June 30 memo was an extremely astute document. Clearly, the president's national security adviser understood the grave risks associated with any attempt to wage a ground war in Southeast Asia. Indeed, his instinct was against such a venture. If his public persona during the debate with Morgenthau left the impression of a man who felt intellectual contempt for critics of the war, his most private counsel to the secretary of defense would seem to indicate otherwise.[73]

This is not to say that Bundy was a closet dove. That would be too simple. Years later he suggested: "I think Kennedy was more a dove than Johnson, and my surest judgment for that is that I was more of a hawk than Kennedy, and Johnson was more of a hawk than I. . . . In the Johnson years, you know your guy is not going to say 'to hell with it.' He is going to want to find the

---

* In his 1995 book McNamara mistakenly states that Bundy was suggesting that "we should consider threatening" the use of nuclear weapons (Robert McNamara, *In Retrospect: The Tragedy and Lessons of Vietnam* [New York: Times Books], p. 194).

least sin to commit or the best sin to commit. He is going to stay with it, and there's no point in telling him not to."[74] This was how Mac Bundy remembered it.

Even so, in early 1965 it was Mac who had urged Johnson to begin the sustained program of bombing against the North. And there is nothing in the record to suggest that Bundy counseled against the landing of marines at Danang or the gradual escalation in troop landings throughout that spring. At the same time Mac always seemed respectful of the counsel he was receiving from men such as Mike Forrestal and Jim Thomson. From them, he knew the real war would be decided in Saigon, and it would hinge on the political viability of a Saigon regime that was a government in name only. Agreeing with Ball's basic assumption, Bundy told the president on June 27, "My own view is that if and when we wish to shift our course and cut our losses in Vietnam we should do so because of a finding that the Vietnamese themselves are not meeting their obligations to themselves or to us."[75]

Indeed, up until that summer, all of Bundy's advice to the president had been aimed at buying time for the Saigon regime to get its political house in order. Years later it was Bundy's memory that "we didn't want to have a large ground war . . . that we really were talking about the limited use of mainly air power, and then suddenly it switches in the spring. . . . He [Johnson] wants to fight the war and win it, because that's what Texas boys do."

By June, with American combat troops pouring into Vietnam, Bundy later recalled that he saw himself digging in his heels, "holding onto the president's coattails." He felt "essentially weary" about the whole notion of ground combat troops. When he saw McNamara's escalation memorandum, Bundy wrote McNamara, not the president, because he thought Johnson's mind was already made up. In Bundy's memory, his memo to McNamara was an effort to say "don't do what the president's telling you to do."[76]

AFTER the decisions of that fateful summer, a myth arose that Lyndon Johnson's advisers were virtually unanimous in recommending the escalation to a ground war. Only George Ball dissented, according to the popular perception, and his was a ritualistic dissent. In fact, Johnson's national security adviser asked some of the same questions as Ball, and challenged the primary advocate of escalation, Bob McNamara, to consider the consequences of a major ground war. To this extent, Ball's was hardly a lone voice.*[77] Not only that, but Bundy was also willing to consider the idea of withdrawal. He had asked McNamara,

---

* Ball probably did not know it, but his position was also shared at the time by Clark Clifford, who had written the president on May 17, urging him to keep U.S. ground forces to a minimum: "This could be a quagmire. It could turn into an open ended commitment on our part that would take more and more ground troops, without a realistic hope of ultimate victory." Johnson never replied. (Clark Clifford, with Richard Holbrooke, *Counsel to the President* [New York: Random House, 1991], p. 410.)

"... do we want to invest 200 thousand men to cover an eventual retreat? Can we not do that just as well where we are?"

On June 28, Ball bluntly urged the president to "cut our losses" and withdraw. Mac Bundy himself had raised this option as a question, but he was not sure of the answer. The imponderable for him was whether the time had come when it could be said that the South Vietnamese had no will to defend themselves. Had time run out or not? The implied assumption behind McNamara's proposal to Americanize the war was that the Saigon regime was hopeless and the war was lost. Ball agreed with the analysis and disagreed with the prescription. Unlike Bundy, he was willing to argue the merits of complete withdrawal as the only logical course of action.

Bill Bundy vividly remembered what he called the critical turning point in the debate. It took place during an "intense meeting" on the morning of June 28 between Ball and a group of other State Department officials. Ball read a draft of yet another memorandum to the president. The language was passionate—too passionate for Bill Bundy's taste.[78]

"The decision you face now ... is crucial," Ball had written. Large numbers of American troops would soon mean "heavy casualties in a war they are ill-equipped to fight in a non-cooperative if not downright hostile countryside." The outcome, Ball predicted, would be "national humiliation."

Ball then pleaded with the president to "seek a compromise settlement which achieves less than our stated objectives and thus cut our losses while we still have the freedom to maneuver to do so. ..."[79]

Ball understood that if he was to convince his colleagues he would have to reassure them that abandoning South Vietnam was not also a betrayal of their Cold War principles. "The position taken in this memorandum," Ball wrote, "does not suggest that the United States should abdicate its leadership in the cold war. But any prudent military commander carefully selects the terrain on which to stand and fight, and no great captain has ever been blamed for a successful tactical withdrawal. ... Politically, South Vietnam is a lost cause. The country is bled white from twenty years of war and the people are sick of it. The Viet Cong—as is shown by the Rand Corporation Motivation and Morale Study—are deeply committed. Hanoi has a government and a purpose and a discipline. The 'government' in Saigon is a travesty. In a very real sense, South Vietnam is a country with an army and no government. In my view a deep commitment of United States forces in a land war in South Vietnam would be a catastrophic error. If ever there was an occasion for a tactical withdrawal, this is it."[80]

After Ball finished reading his draft memorandum to his colleagues, he rose and wandered back to his office to finish polishing the document. Bill Bundy followed him, feeling oddly unsettled, a mood which he later described as "a small state of personal crisis." Sensing that he might have found an ally, Ball asked Bundy if he would join him in his memorandum and make it a Ball-Bundy argument. Bill said he agreed with much of Ball's description of the difficulties, but he "still could not accept the idea of early American withdrawal." He told Ball that he was torn and had decided he would try his hand at his own paper.

Two weeks earlier, on June 19, Bill had sent a "Top Secret, Personal and Confidential" letter to a handful of key U.S. ambassadors serving in East Asia. He told them that the situation in South Vietnam was "very gloomy indeed," and that there now seemed to be three possible courses of action: (a) broadening the air strikes; (b) mining the Haiphong harbor and/or blockading all of North Vietnam, and (c) increasing U.S. ground combat forces.

Bill told the ambassadors that he disliked all three options. He said further air strikes might easily stir latent feelings in Japan, Korea and elsewhere in Asia that "white men were beating up on Asians. . . ." A naval blockade or mining Haiphong harbor might just push the North Vietnamese into a deeper dependency on the Chinese. And increased U.S. combat troops could quickly backfire. Already, there were 20,000 U.S. ground combat troops within an overall total of 70,000 American military personnel in the country. The Pentagon was asking for additional troops to bring the total up to 100,000 or perhaps 150,000 to hold the Viet Cong in check through the monsoon season. "The key point, to me," Bill wrote, "is we may be approaching the point at which the South Vietnamese themselves might conclude we were taking over the war, and that this might result in a slackening of their own effort. . . ."

Worse, Bill suggested that as U.S. combat troops pushed into the countryside, "we would be regarded by the local population, as we destroyed their villages in pursuit of the VC, as acting for all practical purposes like the French." From a strictly military point of view, there was probably a case to be made for sending "whatever is necessary, up to even 300,000 men" if that is required. "But the underlying worry must be whether . . . we would not end up fighting the whole war in a country that would be at best submissive and at worst downright hostile."

Neither was he optimistic that any combination of these three options seemed likely to turn the situation around. Being a Bundy, he could not resist quantifying the odds: "15 percent without such actions to 25–30 percent with them." Perhaps the odds of victory were greater with a massive commitment of ground forces, but that, he warned, "involves the imponderable and possibly truly disastrous case of the South Vietnamese themselves turning against us."[81]

This was a truly gloomy assessment. But instead of concluding, like Ball, that perhaps Washington should cut its losses and withdraw altogether from Vietnam, Bill preferred to take almost any kind of measured action. By the end of June, he had talked himself into thinking that things weren't as bad in the South as General Westmoreland and others had painted. Perhaps the South Vietnamese were "tougher than we gave them credit for." If so, then perhaps there was no need for either a massive escalation or a precipitous withdrawal. His new paper, drafted on June 30, would make the argument for a "middle way" of holding on through the summer at roughly the present level of 85,000 troops.[82]

For Bundy, the French experience in Indochina had always been critical. At some undefined point, he wrote, the presence of U.S. combat troops would begin to turn "the conflict into a white man's war with the U.S. in the shoes of the French." He thought of this imponderable in terms of a nautical expression—the "Plimsoll line"—which refers to a sailing vessel's load line in the water, the line at which a ship is so clearly overloaded with cargo that its seaworthiness becomes questionable.* "This was a Bundyism," recalled Allen Whiting, the State Department's China expert. "Bundyisms were marvelous. Bundy could fuzz up anything. . . . We'd be sitting there, and he'd turn to me and say, 'Al, when do you think we'll reach the Plimsoll line in Vietnam?' I didn't know what the hell it was."[83]

Bundy knew: "We should have enough ground combat forces to give the reserve/reaction concept a fair test, but at the same time not to exceed significantly whatever the current Plimsoll line may be." He guessed that the Plimsoll line in Vietnam probably lay somewhere between 70,000 and 100,000 U.S. forces in total. As he wrote in his unpublished history of the war, "I took very seriously indeed Ball's arguments about the dubious military effectiveness of American forces and their negative political and psychological effects, having myself soaked in the earlier Indochina war and its literature." But he was still willing to run a test for two months to see how well the troops performed. In the meantime, Washington would galvanize the Ky regime to implement "maximum revolution and reform, but minimum repression" in an effort to create a political constituency in the South. Bureaucratically speaking, Bill's was a clever memorandum precisely because he had seized the vital center and carved out a position that was all things to all parties.[84]

By July 2, the president had three policy papers on his desk, each proposing a different strategy: (1) McNamara's June 26 proposal for a major military buildup; (2) Ball's June 28 argument on behalf of a negotiated withdrawal; and (3) Bill Bundy's June 30 case for "holding on" at present force levels, but using slightly more of these troops in ground combat to see how well they could operate in the jungles of Vietnam.

Johnson did not make an immediate decision, but it quickly became clear that for political reasons the president wanted to postpone for as long as possible any radical change in policy. Not surprisingly, a consensus began to develop around Bill Bundy's approach which simply bought time. Under Bill's plan, Westmoreland would be allowed to send the forces at hand into aggressive "search and destroy" missions throughout the remainder of the summer.

---

* The term comes from S. Plimsoll, M.P. from Derby, whose agitation for the Merchant Shipping Act of 1876 resulted in a law requiring that a load line be painted on the hulls of all British ships.

If these combat missions went well, then more troops could be sent to secure the military victory that had so far eluded South Vietnamese troops. But if American combat troops began to sustain serious casualties, well then, Washington could still fall back on Ball's plan for a negotiated withdrawal. As Bill himself put it a few years later, the United States could then seek a "method of extrication that would do as much as possible to sustain the remaining key areas of Southeast Asia, especially Thailand." To be sure, Bundy wrote the president, "There may come a time when the South Vietnamese really have shown they have abandoned the struggle, [but] that time is by no means here now." [85]

Mac Bundy's position at this point in the internal debate was complicated. He agreed with much of Ball's assessment. But like his brother, he couldn't bring himself to "pull the plug." Chet Cooper felt the same way. After reading Ball's memorandum, Cooper wrote Mac, "God help us, [it is] perhaps a realistic account of what we confront in Vietnam. A more ebullient artist might have cast the situation in somewhat less somber tones, but there is not much point here in determining how dark a grey or how deep a black to use." Still, he offered the glimmer of hope that if the Saigon regime could just survive the summer, "we may be over the hump." [86]

Mac felt the same way. The next day, July 1, Bundy wrote a memorandum to President Johnson which was to seal the decision to continue the war at a higher level of intervention. "McNamara and Ball honestly believe in their own recommendations," Bundy wrote, "though Bob would readily accept advice to tone down those of his recommendations which move rapidly against Hanoi by bombing and blockade. Dean Rusk leans toward the McNamara program, adjusted downward in the same way. The second level men in both State and Defense are not optimistic about the future prospects in Vietnam and are therefore very reluctant to see us move to a forty-four battalion force [about 200,000 men] with a call up of reserves. So they would tend to cluster around the middle course suggested by my brother. They would like to see what happens this summer before getting much deeper in. The Joint Chiefs are strongly in favor of going in even further than McNamara. Specifically, they want to take out the SAM sites, the IL-28s [bombers], and the MIGs in the Hanoi area."

Mac then offered his own advice: "My hunch is that you will want to listen hard to George Ball and then reject his proposal. Discussion could then move to the narrow choice between my brother's course and McNamara's. The decision between them should be made in about ten days. . . . I think you may want to have pretty tight and hard analyses of some disputed questions like the following:

1. What are the chances of our getting into a white man's war with all the brown men against us or apathetic?
2. How much of the McNamara planning would be on a contingency basis with no decision until August or September?

3. What would a really full political and public relations campaign look like in both the Bundy option and the McNamara option?

4. What is the upper limit of our liability if we now go to 44 battalions?

5. Can we frame this program in such a way as to keep very clear our own determination to keep the war limited? (This is another way of stating question 4.)

6. Can we get a cold, hard look at the question whether the current economic and political situation in Vietnam is so very bad that it may come apart even before this program gets into action? (I don't believe it is that bad, but no one seems to be really sure of the facts today.) [87]

In his role as gatekeeper, Bundy was suggesting that the president should hear a debate on some of the most critical questions, most notably, "What are the chances of our getting into a white man's war with all the brown men against us . . .?" But in the end, his "hunch" was to reject Ball's advice and make what he thought was merely a decision to seek more time by choosing his brother's "middle way." In the weeks ahead, however, Mac failed to insist that studied answers be given to the hard questions he and Ball had asked. In the meantime, Lyndon Johnson's own powerful instincts were driving him toward a major escalation. He had always been skeptical of McNamara's faith in bombing; if the job really needed to be done, he always thought ground troops would be needed to do it right.

In retrospect, it seems clear that the president's mind was already made up. Lyndon Johnson was not going to allow South Vietnam to be lost to a communist insurgency. Such a loss would be used to discredit him and his Great Society programs in the same way that the Republicans had used the loss of China to smear Harry Truman's presidency. Lyndon Johnson feared an American land war in Vietnam—but he feared even more the prospect of reigniting the ugly political passions of McCarthyism. Nicholas Katzenbach, Johnson's attorney general and a future under secretary of state, believed Johnson to be a man of "enormous insecurity, enormous paranoia." "It's my view," Katzenbach later said, "that it would not have made any difference what anybody advised him—he would have done what he did. . . . It was fear of the right wing." [88]

What followed in the ensuing weeks was not careful deliberation but a charade. On July 8–9 the president convened his Wise Men—a group of senior former government officials—in Washington to consider Vietnam policy. Dean Acheson, John McCloy, Eugene Black (former president of the World Bank), General Omar Bradley, Robert Lovett and eleven other "gray-hairs" thought they were being consulted for their gravitas. All of these men were members in good standing of the Stimsonian foreign policy establishment, and as such, they were all firmly Eurocentric in outlook. They understood little about Vietnam, its history or culture, and did not care to for the simple reason that by and large they did not think Vietnam itself was particularly important. McCloy had serious doubts that merely "blunting the monsoon offensive" would put Hanoi in a "negotiating mood." But because an American commitment had been made, McCloy told Rusk and McNamara, "You've got to do it. You've got to go in."

Bill Bundy's notes from one of the meetings summed up the consensus. If Vietnam was lost to the communists, "De Gaulle would find many takers for his argument that the US could not now be counted on to defend Europe." The war in Vietnam, in other words, was all about NATO's credibility in Europe. Such was the Cold War logic that permeated the room. Much later an acerbic Lovett would say, "Getting into Vietnam was one of the stupidest things we ever did. We didn't know what the hell we were doing there."

At the end of the first day of their deliberations, a select group of the Wise Men were invited to have a drink with the president in the Cabinet Room. After they were served cocktails, Johnson began a monologue long on self-pity. "We were all disturbed," Acheson later wrote in describing the session to Harry Truman, "by a long complaint about how mean everything and everybody was to him—Fate, the Press, the Congress, the Intellectuals and so on. For a long time he fought the problem of Vietnam (every course of action was wrong; he had no support from anyone at home or abroad; it interfered with all his programs etc., etc.)."

Finally, Acheson told Truman, he couldn't stand it any more. "I blew my top and told him he [Johnson] was wholly right on Vietnam, that he had no choice except to press on, that explanations were not as important as successful action." This scolding emboldened the others in the room to join in. "With this lead my colleagues came thundering in like the charge of the Scots Greys at Waterloo. They were fine; old Bob Lovett, usually cautious, was all out. . . . I think . . . we scored." Indeed, the next day, Mac Bundy reported to his aides, "The mustache was voluble."[89] It was all terribly misinformed advice, but by playing the role of a beleaguered president, Johnson had manipulated, indeed, provoked these gray hairs into throwing their caution to the winds.

Bill Bundy later came to believe that in July 1965 there had been no searching examination of the problem. Instead, "the men who met with the President on July 8th were bound to give him and his advisers every benefit of acceptance. . . . It was a poor way to proceed."[90]

After the Wise Men deliberations, McNamara was ordered to Saigon to conduct another review of the situation and to size up the newly installed government led by Generals Ky and Thieu. Soon after his arrival, he received a cable from Johnson saying that he had decided to approve Westmoreland's request for forty-four battalions and that he should return home immediately. The "review" was over.[91] To be sure, there would be still more meetings and more arguments. But both Bill and Mac knew the president had decided to make a stand.

When McNamara returned from Saigon he submitted a report which forcefully argued against any more "incrementalism." The time had come to weigh in with decisive force—perhaps 375,000 troops over the next year. Essentially, McNamara believed that Bill Bundy's "middle way" of holding on for a test period of a few months was no longer practicable. The South Vietnamese army would collapse without a decisive intervention. In his discussions with McNamara and his staff, Bill Bundy found himself wavering. Perhaps they had been setting their sights too low, perhaps the time had come to break the trend. "I was forced to agree," Bill wrote later, "even though it meant accepting the chance that the war would be increasingly Americanized."

The day of decision came on July 21. In the afternoon Johnson met with all his major advisers, and Ball once again was allowed to make the case for withdrawal. Bill Bundy remembered it as "George Ball's last stand."

Ball told the president the "least harmful way to cut our losses is to let the GVN [Government of Vietnam] decide it doesn't want us." The way to do this, he said, was to propose the kind of negotiated settlement of the war that the Ky-Thieu regime in Saigon was certain to reject, and then Washington could declare it favored neutralization. "I have no illusions [but] that after we were asked to leave, SVN [South Vietnam] would be under Hanoi control."

Johnson interrupted to ask, "Wouldn't all these countries say Uncle Sam is a paper tiger?" To which Ball replied, "The worst blow would be that the mightiest power in the world is unable to defeat guerrillas. . . . If we were actively helping a country with a stable, viable government it would be a vastly different story." If either of the Bundy brothers had come to Ball's support perhaps the president would have seriously considered a withdrawal strategy.

"Looking back on it," Tom Hughes later said, "if Bill had decided in 1965 to join Ball and oppose the war, it might have made all the difference. . . . Bill's opposition would have caused a problem with many people, including Mac Bundy. It would have been very difficult for Mac to take the line that he did if his brother had sided with Ball." [92]

Instead, Mac Bundy, McNamara and Rusk each said they disagreed with Ball's analysis. A withdrawal in Vietnam would be too costly to U.S. interests in Asia and elsewhere in the world. Cold War logic required making a stand in Vietnam. In any case, Mac argued, there would always be time later to reconsider "after we have given it a good try." He meant that if the ground war wasn't going well in a few months they could always come back to Ball's strategy of disengagement. Ball objected, pointing out that the larger the U.S. commitment of combat forces, the harder it would be to change course. According to the minutes of this meeting, Bundy flatly disagreed: ". . . the kind of shift in U.S. policy suggested by Mr. Ball would be 'disastrous.' " Mac said he "would rather maintain our present commitment and 'waffle through' than withdraw. The country [United States] is in the mood to accept grim news." [93]

This sharp exchange captured the essence of the entire month's debate over the war. Both Bundy brothers had been exposed repeatedly to the arguments against a deeper involvement; they understood those arguments, but in large measure because their president could not abide a defeat in Vietnam —"that's not what Texas boys do"—they had talked themselves into thinking that there was still time to "waffle through." And if it turned out badly, well then, they could always come back to Ball's prescription.

Using one of his favorite poker expressions, Johnson said he had decided "to put in his stack." The only decision remaining was how to implement the escalation. Specifically, should the National Guard be mobilized? Should Congress be asked to appropriate additional funds for the defense budget? Mac Bundy assumed that both steps were a foregone conclusion if 200,000 troops were being sent to Vietnam. In a phone conversation on July 14, McNamara had told Johnson, "Almost surely, if we called up reserves, you would want to go to the Congress to get additional authority." Johnson seemed to agree by saying, "Well, that makes sense."[94]

But when on July 28 the president announced the decision, he did not call up the reserves or ask Congress for additional funding. "We did not choose to be the guardians at the gate," Johnson intoned, "but there is no one else. . . . We will stand in Vietnam."[95] He made the announcement at the end of a seemingly routine press conference, and even then he mentioned only that an additional 50,000 troops were being sent to Vietnam. (By then, there were already 90,000 Americans in Vietnam.)

It was not the way Bill Bundy had planned it. He had assumed that Johnson would announce the full deployment, and that he would go to Congress for authorization. Some years later, when Bill was asked by a BBC reporter if he thought Johnson had been honest, he replied, "Well, it depends on your view. It was certainly in my judgment at least as honest as many things that Franklin Roosevelt did in 1941. The trouble was that this turned out badly, and therefore looks much worse in history."[96]

By September, General Westmoreland had asked for 35,000 more troops and advised the president that he expected to have a total of 325,000 troops on the ground by July 1966. In November, Westmoreland revised this estimate upward to 410,000 troops by the following July. On November 7, McNamara warned the president that U.S. combat deaths could rise to 500–800 per month: "And the odds are even that the DRV/VC [North Vietnamese and Viet Cong] will hang on doggedly, effectively matching us man-for-man . . . and that, despite our efforts, we will be faced in early 1967 with stagnation at a higher level." Stagnation was certainly not the road to victory. Remarkably, only four months after he had led the charge for a major escalation with ground troops, McNamara later wrote that he felt the war was not winnable "short of genocidal destruction."

At the time, he told the president that he thought the prospects for ending the war were bleak: the question of a "'compromise solution' . . . may have to be faced soon." The North Vietnamese leaders showed no signs of being ready to negotiate even when U.S. bombers were pounding their people with tons of ordnance every day. McNamara's prescription was a two-pronged strategy: (1) increase U.S. troop commitments to 350,000 by the end of 1966; and (2) implement a month-long bombing pause. Sending more troops would demonstrate to the enemy that they could not win the war, while a bombing pause might set the stage for negotiations sometime in 1966 which could lead to a compromise political settlement. This was a truly grim assessment. But McNamara saw no other way, and in order to avoid a "costly national political defeat," he urged the president to stay the course.[97]

McNamara wrote these words two weeks prior to the bloody battle of Ia Drang, where some 305 American men and 3,561 North Vietnamese were killed in fierce close-hand combat. The enemy had stood its ground and fought the best troops in the U.S. Army, units of the elite First Cavalry heliborne division. General Westmoreland looked at the ten-to-one 'body count' and declared the battle a victory. The war, he argued, could be won by attrition.

McNamara went to South Vietnam for a personal review in the wake of the battle, and by the time he left Saigon he was telling reporters, "It will be a long war." On the flight back to Washington, he wrote a memorandum in which he said the North Vietnamese were more than matching the U.S. build-up. The president had two choices: he could opt for withdrawal, or he would have to approve General Westmoreland's most recent request to more than double the number of U.S. troops serving in Vietnam. Even then, such a deployment "will not guarantee success. U.S. killed-in-action can be expected to reach 1,000 a month, and the odds are even that we will be faced in early 1967 with a no-decision at an even higher level." Perhaps with 600,000 U.S. troops on the ground, the Americans could prevent the North Vietnamese from "sustaining the conflict at a significant level." But at that point, McNamara said, he thought the Chinese could be expected to intervene. Clearly, in these terms the war was unwinnable.[98]

Public opinion polls still showed that most Americans thought the war was just and that progress was being made against the communist enemy. Yet, by the autumn of 1965, a significant minority of citizens were regularly being exposed to information that told them that the war was not going well. Intellectuals inside and outside the academy were likely to be highly critical of the war. Most of the men and women whom the Bundy brothers counted as their friends—even the brothers' own wives—were critics. Establishment figures like George Kennan had testified against the war, and mainstream pundits like Walter Lippmann and Joseph Kraft were consistently arguing against the notion that Vietnam was worth American blood. By the end of 1965, serious periodicals like *The New Republic, The Nation, Commentary, The Reporter* and the hottest new intellectual periodical, *The New York Review of Books*, were regularly publishing essays highly critical of the war. The Bundys read these journals. They knew that they stood in lonely isolation against a growing body of informed opinion. In mid-October as many as

100,000 anti-war demonstrators turned out in over ninety cities across the country. On November 27 somewhere between 20,000 and 40,000 demonstrators marched on Washington. To their discomfort, the Bundy brothers were becoming household names, singled out on anti-war placards as war criminals. It was not pleasant. Bill made a point of trying to ignore the demonstrators: "I wasn't paying attention to demonstrators; they were something I tuned out by habit."[99]

By the autumn of 1965, Mac Bundy was actively looking for a way to bail out of the White House. He was tired. His relationship with the president was strained. And McNamara had convinced him that this was going to be a bloody, protracted war. He did not, however, want to leave the White House in a manner that would suggest any policy differences with Johnson over the war. He really didn't disagree with Johnson about Vietnam. They had some tactical differences, but Bundy supported the idea of at least trying to make a stand in Vietnam. He supported a bombing pause not because he thought it would lead to negotiations, but because it would prove "our own good faith as peace lovers."[100] If it was going to take a protracted war to defend South Vietnam against a communist "war of national liberation," well, perhaps that was a necessary chapter in the Cold War. If it had been Jack Kennedy's war, he would have remained, but he didn't want to fight Lyndon Johnson's war. In the end, his motivation for leaving was personal. Johnson's overweening ego —not to mention his petty insecurities—grated on Bundy.

It was also true that Mac's wife disapproved of the war. This was not something they fought over at the dinner table, but Mary was the kind of woman who quietly, but firmly, made it clear that she had a different view of the war from her husband's. In fact, both "Mary Mac" and "Mary Bill" were regarded as doves by all their friends. "The women involved with the men involved with Jack Kennedy were all against Vietnam," recalled Ben Bradlee. The brothers' sister Hattie Bundy Belin and her husband were also early critics of the war. (Don Belin later helped to organize the Boston Lawyer's Committee Against Vietnam.) Hattie never discussed the war with her brothers, but they knew her views. "I knew," recalled Hattie, "that Mary [Mac's wife] had a different point of view [from Mac]." Mac would never have admitted it at the time, but the fact that his wife, his sister, his brother's wife and so many of his Cambridge friends all opposed the war must have made it easier to make the decision to leave.[101]

Early that autumn Mac was sounded out from several quarters about whether he was interested in a new job. Katharine Graham, the publisher of the *Washington Post*, called to offer him the job of editorial page editor. He had socialized with the Grahams until Katharine's husband, Phil, committed suicide in August 1963. To the surprise of many Washingtonians, Katharine was asserting her control over the *Post-Newsweek* publications. She thought Bundy would be a prize catch. Mac's interest was piqued, but ultimately he just could not think of himself as a journalist.[102]

THE most intriguing offer came from John J. McCloy, the seventy-year-old chairman of the Ford Foundation's board of trustees and a perennial figure in the foreign policy establishment. An old friend of Harvey Bundy's, Jack McCloy had known Mac since he was a boy, and they had seen each other frequently in recent years. McCloy had served as President Kennedy's disarmament adviser and had sat on the Warren Commission to investigate Kennedy's assassination. More recently, McCloy had participated in the Wise Men meeting in July which ratified Johnson's decision to escalate the war. McCloy suspected that Bundy was ready for a change, and he also knew that Bundy had an interest in the Ford Foundation. In the spring of 1962, McCloy had solicited Bundy's opinions about the foundation's policies and had been surprised to receive several lengthy memorandums outlining Bundy's critique of the foundation's administrative expenses and suggesting several new initiatives. Bundy had obviously given some thought to what it would be like to run the largest philanthropical institution in the world—a whale among a school of tuna fish, as Dwight Macdonald had described it in *The New Yorker*.[103]

On November 7, McCloy phoned Bundy and asked if he had any interest in the presidency of the foundation. Bundy said yes, he might indeed be interested. Shortly thereafter, McCloy sent a fellow Ford trustee, Judge Charles E. Wyzanski, Jr., down to Washington to make a personal pitch.

Wyzanski, Harvard '27, had known Bundy since the 1940s, first as a senior fellow of the Society of Fellows and then as a member and president of the Harvard Board of Overseers. An ebullient, gregarious conversationalist, Charlie Wyzanski quickly had become a Mac Bundy mentor—one of a long line of older, powerful men who promoted Mac's career. Charlie and his engaging wife, Gisela Warburg, had remained the closest of friends with Mac and Mary. Wyzanski had unsuccessfully lobbied his Harvard colleagues to make Bundy president of Harvard in 1953, and twelve years later he was determined to woo him into the Ford Foundation. Not only did the judge think Mac was perfect for the job, but he thought it was time for his old friend to leave the Texan occupying the White House.

On November 13, the three old friends—Charlie, Gisela and Mac—met for breakfast in Washington's Sheraton Carlton Hotel. Charlie said he came as a friend, not a Ford Foundation trustee. He admitted that after the White House, Mac might not find "any private post exciting at first." But the Ford presidency could easily become a stepping-stone; after seven or eight years he might "have a chance to be Secretary of State, or president of Harvard. . . ."

Wyzanski suggested that Mac should look upon the Ford presidency as a bully pulpit, "a sort of ministry not only of education, but whatever may be important in the country," such as urban community development or race relations. Because of the foundation's business abroad, the presidency was also an "ambassadorship" and Charlie confided that he thought the job should come with an official residence, "say a Sutton Place house with room to entertain simultaneously all the trustees." The job also paid $75,000—a sizable increase over Mac's $30,000 annual salary in the White House.[104]

Bundy responded to Wyzanski's pitch by volunteering that "five years [in the White House] seemed enough to justify leaving." He then asked Charlie how much support he had among the trustees. Charlie said it was unanimous. He confided that the trustees had considered McNamara for the job, but had concluded that "McNamara's dominating personality presented problems absent in Bundy's case." Taking up this thread, Mac bluntly asked if he had "too abrasive" a personality?

Charlie responded, "Who knows better than I that abrasiveness is a danger?" At this point Gisela laughed and chimed in that Mac and Charlie were "alike in this fault." Mac agreed that he had not always suffered fools gladly, but that truly, he "never got credit for all the fools he did suffer."

Clearly, Bundy was strongly inclined to take the job. As they parted, Charlie told Mac what he had said to Gisela when he proposed to her: "Don't answer now—but do say yes!"[105]

Vietnam was not even mentioned by the two men, but it was most definitely on Bundy's mind. "Three things were apparent," Bundy later recalled. "Mary wanted to come to New York. That's not the first reason, but that's a decisive one. I wanted to do that job [at the Ford Foundation]. And the world would not catch on that I was in any disagreement with Johnson."[106]

The next morning, November 14, James Reston reported on page one of the *New York Times* that Bundy had been offered the Ford presidency. Johnson was furious. At the time, the president was convalescing from a gall bladder operation at his Texas ranch. Bundy had sent him a handwritten note informing him of the Ford offer on November 8, the day after McCloy had broached the subject. But Johnson had pointedly put off talking about it. On November 19 they finally had a real conversation. Bundy told him he had decided to accept the Ford job and the next day they agreed that Mac would leave the White House by the end of February 1966. "He was really mad," Bundy recalled. Typically, Johnson made a point of deprecating anyone who left his ship of state, and he did the same with Bundy, telling people that Mac was "a smart kid, period."[107]

McNamara truly regretted Bundy's impending departure. They had not always agreed, but in most matters they had been allies and even soul mates. Though Bundy never said as much to him, McNamara suspected that his friend was leaving because of Vietnam: "He could have left the administration," McNamara later wrote, "because of the attractiveness of the Ford Foundation job alone, but I doubt that was the case. I speculate the true reason was his deep frustration with the war. I believe he was frustrated not only with the president's behavior but also with the decision-making process throughout the top echelons. . . ."[108]

By December 1965, McNamara's own views on the war were in turmoil.

For a month he had been trying to persuade Johnson to order a bombing pause with the hope that it would open the door to negotiations with Hanoi. The Joint Chiefs, Clark Clifford and many other advisers opposed the idea. But when Mac Bundy made it clear that he supported McNamara, a skeptical president finally agreed on December 18 to order a pause. It would run through the end of January 1966.

McNamara had fought for a pause because he no longer believed the bombing could interdict supplies to the Viet Cong from the North. Worse, he thought the bombing, which was supposed to provide Hanoi with an incentive to negotiate, now seemed an obstacle in itself to negotiations. Furthermore, he had shocked Johnson by telling him, in Bundy's presence, that he now thought a military solution had only a one in three chance of being achieved. "You mean," Johnson said, "that no matter what we do in the military field, you think there is no sure victory?"

"That's right," McNamara replied. "We have been too optimistic. . . . I'm saying that we may never find a military solution. We need to explore other means. Our military approach is an unlikely route to a successful conclusion."

Still, McNamara continued to favor a huge increase in ground troops, from the current 200,000 to at least 400,000 men. He admitted this "may seem like a contradiction," and explained that because he realized this escalation might be matched by a North Vietnamese counterescalation, "I am simply suggesting that we look for other alternatives first." [109] Bundy and many others in Washington knew McNamara was deeply troubled.

On January 6, 1966, Arthur Schlesinger hosted a dinner party—at McNamara's request—where the defense secretary told Carl Kaysen, Ken Galbraith and Richard Goodwin that he no longer thought that a military solution in Vietnam was possible. His only hope now, he said, was "withdrawal with honor." Afterwards, Schlesinger noted in his journal, "He seemed deeply oppressed and concerned at the prospect of indefinite escalation. Our impression was that he feared the resumption of bombing might well put us on the slippery slide." [110]

Ben Bradlee also knew about McNamara's private agony over the war. A few months earlier Bradlee had jumped from *Newsweek* to become deputy managing editor of the *Washington Post,* and on the last day of 1965 he went to a New Year's Eve party with his wife, Toni. "We witnessed this extraordinary thing," he recalled, "McNamara sitting on a couch with Toni, and he was quite obviously upset. Tears were gushing down his cheeks. He was doing most of the talking. Toni was saying very little." They were talking about the war, a war which Toni was against. The spectacle of the secretary of defense shedding his tears was witnessed several times in Washington society over the next two years. Everyone knew Bob McNamara was dreadfully unhappy with the way the war was going. But for the television cameras he told a different story. [111]

IN January 1966, in the middle of the month-long bombing pause, Johnson ordered Mac Bundy to accompany Vice President Hubert Humphrey on a trip to Saigon. It would be Bundy's Vietnam valediction, and ironically, the occasion for Humphrey's Vietnam baptism. A year earlier Humphrey had written a strong dissent against Vietnam policy, and ever since he had been literally banished from any deliberations on Vietnam. If the Saigon trip was LBJ's way of giving his vice president a second chance, Humphrey was determined to make the most of it. Also on the delegation were Chet Cooper, Jim Thomson, Averell Harriman and Ed Lansdale—all in all, a high-powered group of Vietnam hands.

Landing in Saigon, Humphrey and his companions spent three days in whirlwind meetings with Saigon brass, Vietnamese and American. Jim Thomson, however, broke away for a day and a night foray into the Mekong Delta, accompanied by Ward Just, a *Washington Post* reporter, and Richard Holbrooke, a particularly well-informed young Foreign Service officer. "I learned things," Thomson later said, "that I knew but never had the evidence to prove." Arriving back at the U.S. embassy, Thomson walked into a cocktail reception hosted by Ambassador Lodge and was quickly pulled aside by Mac Bundy, who said, "What have you found out?" They talked for an hour. "I told him that the war was unwinnable, that we were losing it, that it would take a million or even two million American troops, and that we should get out." Mac didn't argue. He just nodded his head and said, "OK."

When Bundy returned to Washington, he essentially ignored what Thomson had told him and gave a relatively optimistic briefing on his trip to his staff. But at its conclusion Mac said, "If you want a rather different view, you must wait until Jim Thomson comes back, and listen to him."

A few weeks later, at a farewell party held in the White House mess, Mac came over and shook Thomson's hand and said, "Well, bye-bye, Mao Tse-Thomson, my favorite dove." It was done lightheartedly, and everyone laughed. Thomson was flattered to be so singled out.[112]

Bundy, however, was not himself a dove. To the contrary, in late January he was strongly urging the president to resume the bombing. "If we give up the bombing when we get nothing but a brutal 'No' from Hanoi," he told Johnson, "we will give them a wholly wrong signal . . . the people who talk about an indefinite suspension are working against peace and not in favor of it."[113] Mac was always tolerant and certainly understanding of the views of doves like Thomson, but when a critical decision had to be made he invariably favored a demonstration of force.

If anything, his views had hardened since the autumn, when he and McNamara had teamed up to advocate a bombing pause. Two weeks before he left the White House, Mac wrote a memorandum for his files in which he took issue with what he called the "Lippmann Thesis." Contrary to Lippmann's assumption that the United States didn't belong in Southeast Asia, Bundy noted that "we have been the dominant power" there for twenty years. "The truth is that in Southeast Asia we are stronger than China." The war's casualties were terrible, but the "danger to one man's life, as such, is not a worthy guide. . . . If the basic questions of interest, right, and power are answered, the casualties and costs are to be accepted."[114] Both publicly and in his private thoughts, Mac Bundy would leave Washington defending the war.

BUNDY's last day in office was February 28, 1966. A week earlier Senator Robert F. Kennedy had issued a statement suggesting that the political arm of the Viet Cong, the National Liberation Front (NLF), should be admitted to the political process in South Vietnam and perhaps even share power in a coalition government. The statement created a firestorm. The next day Bundy appeared on *Meet the Press* and said the senator's proposal was neither useful nor helpful. To Bobby's annoyance, Mac went on to quote President Kennedy in opposition to the notion of coalition governments with communists. Wounded, Kennedy phoned Bundy at the White House to complain that he should have had the courtesy to warn him before criticizing him on national television. Mac was unrepentant.[115]

His relations with the Kennedys may have been strained, but this did not prevent Bobby and Ethel Kennedy from attending Mac's farewell party in Georgetown hosted by Joe Alsop and Congressman William Moorhead. Ethel showed up in a miniskirt made of black and white vinyl squares and danced to the beat of The Decadents. Other guests included Marietta Tree (the granddaughter of Groton's Endicott Peabody), Kennedy family intimate LeMoyne Billings, Bill Moyers, Jack Valenti and dozens of Bundy's friends. "It was an evening," wrote a society columnist, "that brought down from New York various members of the Shuttle Society, that constantly commuting elite group of peripatetic party-goers who have too much power and brain power to be classed with the idle rich of the Jet Set."[116]

As Bundy was being feted in Georgetown, the city's punditocracy set in type their assessments of the Bundy era. Though frustrated and somewhat disillusioned with his erstwhile protégé, Lippmann wrote not one, but two columns about Bundy's departure. Lippmann praised Bundy's "incomparable ability to reduce complex problems to the choices which the President must make. . . . There must be someone who orders and orients the torrent of information. . . . Someone will have to step into Mr. Bundy's shoes and show whether he can fill them."[117]

Joe Kraft thought no one could fill Bundy's shoes. To his mind, Bundy's departure was not so much the end of the Kennedy era as the "death of the Establishment as the dominant force in American foreign policy." There were no establishment heirs groomed to succeed Bundy. Stewart Alsop wrote that Bundy's departure marked "the Johnsonization of Washington."[118]

Arthur Schlesinger, appropriately enough, wrote about Bundy as a living icon. President Kennedy, he explained, had come to Washington wanting to bring together the world of power and the world of ideas. "Bundy suited his theory and his needs perfectly." He described Mac as a "professional intellectual with the instinct for hard judgment. . . . He knew everybody, feared nobody, respected the President's power of decision, stated each side of an argument better than the protagonists and was always cool, swift, lucid, precise and funny." True, not everyone liked Bundy; some resented his air of invincibility. But he was, wrote Schlesinger, "a great public servant." Schlesinger's words were published in the *Washington Post,* accompanied by a David Levine caricature of Mac standing with his hands thrust in his pants pockets, scowling at his audience. All in all, it was a living obituary for a man not yet forty-seven years of age.[119]

BUNDY had hoped that Bill Moyers would replace him that spring. Indeed, he had not changed his mind since January 1965 when he had recommended to Johnson that Moyers, Tom Hughes or Abram Chayes should be groomed to replace him. As if to underscore the point, in early 1966 he passed the same memorandum to Johnson with a new date. He was later "dumbfounded" to learn that the president had chosen Walt Rostow, a man whom Bundy thought had to decide an issue "before he thought about [it]."[120]

Johnson picked Rostow because his enthusiasm for the war had never waned. Increasingly frustrated that men like McNamara and Bundy were showing signs of pessimism, the president was determined to shield himself from the bad news with a man who exuded eternal optimism. Rostow had a prophet's ability to see inevitable victory in the midst of the worst eyewitness reports from the battlefield. Most people like an optimist, and so it was with Walt Rostow. He was also a man Lyndon Johnson could own. After Rostow's appointment Johnson told one former Kennedy administration official, "I'm getting Walt Rostow as my intellectual. He's not your intellectual. He's not Bundy's intellectual. He's not Galbraith's intellectual. He's not Schlesinger's intellectual. He's going to be *my* goddamn intellectual and I'm going to have him by the short hairs." He was also reported to have muttered, "We're not going to have another Bundy around here."[121]

Mac Bundy had left the White House because he knew the chemistry wasn't right between the president and himself. The chemistry was perfectly right between Johnson and Rostow. Senator Fulbright called Rostow the president's "Rasputin." Deputy Assistant Secretary of Defense Townsend Hoopes thought he was a "fanatic in sheep's clothing." A manic optimist, Rostow was the kind of liberal who could contemplate what Bundy ultimately could not —nuclear blackmail. Three months after replacing Bundy, he told Averell Harriman, "The President is going to stick it out. The bombing will escalate." When Harriman suggested that one had to be careful that the bombing campaign didn't eventually place us in a nuclear confrontation with the Soviet Union, Rostow replied, "Oh yes, we will probably have to get there [to a nuclear confrontation] because it is only in extreme crises that some settlement will come."[122]

That Lyndon Johnson would choose such a man to be Bundy's successor underscored how much Vietnam had become his war. True, Bundy, McNamara and Rusk had pushed Johnson to bomb the North, send combat troops and otherwise do what could be done to prop up a failing regime in Saigon. Bundy in particular had told the president that an effort had to be made, even if the odds favored defeat. Rostow, however, believed in victory. Where Bundy had told Johnson that he might, just might, avoid a defeat in Vietnam, Rostow was telling the president that he could win. That was a message Johnson liked.

THE Bundy brothers were deeply aware of just how unworthy of American blood sacrifice was the cabal of generals who gave Saigon the pretense of government. In the summer of 1965, Bill Bundy had called the Ky-Thieu regime "absolutely the bottom of the barrel!" [123] Mac had called McNamara's escalation program "rash to the point of folly." And Bill had warned that at some point U.S. combat troops would begin to turn "the conflict into a white man's war with the U.S. in the shoes of the French." [124] They knew everything the intellectual critics of the war knew. They understood the risks of Americanizing the war on the ground. But they shunned the option of a negotiated withdrawal under the guise of neutralization. The lessons of Munich, the legacy of McCarthyism and, most fundamentally, their Stimsonian assumptions about America's hegemonic responsibilities in the world compelled them to gamble once more to prop up a military regime in Saigon that was a government in name only.

So, by the summer of 1965, they helped to make Vietnam Lyndon Johnson's war. Despite all their doubts they urged Johnson to make a stand in Vietnam. Their Option C—the proverbial vital center—quickly led to the introduction of 200,000 combat troops. When barely six months later it became clear that the experiment was not working, that the North Vietnamese were more than matching Washington's escalation, Mac Bundy left the White House. Mac had private qualms about the war, but these were questions he felt compelled to keep to himself. Years ago at Groton he had been taught by Endicott Peabody the importance of duty and personal loyalty. As he quietly left Washington, Mac saw it was his duty to loyally defend the president and his war. He left behind a brother who would fight the war for another three years.

14

Vietnam Quagmire,
1966–1969

This damned war really is much tougher than—and very different from—World War II and Korea, and I just don't think the country can be held together much longer by determination and patriotism alone.

McGeorge Bundy
to President Johnson
March 22, 1968

Precisely because the war was going so badly, Bill Bundy couldn't even think of leaving Washington. As assistant secretary of state for the Far East, Bill felt it was his personal duty to remain at his station. When Mac told him of his decision to resign, Bill was initially astonished. But then he thought, "Hell no, he's been through an awful lot, and at a much more acute pace than I had." Early in 1966, before Rostow was given the nod by Johnson to replace Mac, Bill Moyers approached Bill and asked him if he might be interested in the NSC job. He declined. "I think it would have been a great mistake for me to follow in his [Mac's] footsteps. I thought I'd assumed a considerable responsibility for what we were doing in Vietnam, and I ought to stick to that." [1]

Watching Bill Bundy from within the State Department, Tom Hughes recalled a man "enormously caught up in and savaged by the war." Hughes sensed that Bundy sometimes wished he could have ducked the whole issue like Rusk: "Rusk just sat there listening and nodding his head like he was above it all. But Bill was the action officer on Vietnam; he had to deal with it every day. He could have done what McNamara did—he could have been for the war by day and against it by night. But Bill Bundy wasn't like that. He was consistent." [2]

When the bombing of North Vietnam resumed at the end of January 1966, Bill Bundy understood that the war had become a "newer and tougher ball game."[3] Clearly, Hanoi was prepared for a long struggle. To make matters worse, that spring the Saigon regime was rocked by another round of political protests organized by Buddhist dissidents. The Struggle Movement threatened to bring down Marshal Ky's regime and replace it with a government which in all likelihood would have invited the National Liberation Front (NLF) into a coalition government. The Americans were aghast and perplexed by the resiliency of the protests. McNamara warned in early April that the "Struggle Movement may be too strong to throw off. . . . They obviously have strength we didn't know about." Bill Bundy remembered the crisis as "a terrific setback, a very, very negative development in every possible way."

President Johnson himself momentarily thought the time had come to call it quits. Perhaps, he said in a White House meeting on April 2, U.S. forces should get out of Vietnam and "take a stand in Thailand." Two days later, after three thousand South Vietnamese soldiers joined in the anti-government demonstrations in the northern city of Hue, Johnson suggested the "time has come when the alternative is to get out—or do what we need to do to get the government shored up." Buddhists associated with the Struggle Movement were arrested or exiled and the crisis eased. Afterwards, the irrepressibly optimistic Walt Rostow even suggested, "We may be seeing the emergence of a nation from this tripartite mess." To which Bill Bundy retorted, "Walt, are you mad?"[4]

In Bill Bundy's eyes, there was only one bright spot in the spring of 1966 and that was Indonesia, a country which McNamara had once called "the greatest prize of all."[5] One of the rationales all along for intervening in Vietnam was to draw a line against Communist Chinese influence throughout Southeast Asia. In 1964–65 it appeared to most observers that the dictator of Indonesia, President Sukarno, was drifting into an open alliance with the Communist Party of Indonesia (PKI). Even though Mac Bundy's NSC shop had been absorbed with Vietnam decision-making, at the end of June 1965, Mac took the time to send President Johnson a rare—but prophetic—memorandum on the situation in Jakarta: "As you know, our policy is cool and correct with the door open to friendly relations, but we have removed the Peace Corps and other targets of Communist agitation. We are really playing for breaks in a situation in which the Communists are gaining influence, but the prospect of a reaction by the military is strong."[6]

Relations between Washington and Jakarta had so deteriorated that in late August 1965 Bill Bundy and other State Department officials met to decide whether the U.S. embassy staff should be pulled out. Under Secretary of State George Ball opened the meeting by observing that Indonesia was at least as important as the whole of Indochina. Couldn't something be done, he asked, "to slow or counter these trends?" According to Bundy's recollection, Ball specifically asked if a covert action could be launched by the CIA. Bundy said the subject was "disposed of very quickly," with a CIA officer explaining that its Indonesian contacts were "totally frigid." Essentially, Bundy recalled, "The CIA man said there was no way they could do anything even by way of influence let alone any substantial covert operation."[7] The meeting adjourned with a decision to keep a scaled-down embassy in place with Bundy's old Groton friend Marshall Green as ambassador. To Bundy's thinking, the fact that Indonesia was drifting into the communist camp was all the more reason for the United States to make a stand in Vietnam.

On the afternoon of September 29, Bundy had one of his monthly meetings with his CIA counterpart, William Colby. Colby presented the CIA's operating plans in Indonesia for the coming month, a list which he described as thin. "We just don't have the assets," he claimed.[8]

That night Bundy, Francis Underhill, the State Department's Indonesian desk officer, and many other officials around Washington were called by the State Department's Operations Center and informed that a coup d'état was in progress in Jakarta. Gradually, it emerged that a group of junior army officers, led by Lieutenant Colonel Untung, had arrested and then killed six army generals. If they intended to seize power, their plans were inept. They had not, for instance, even bothered to target for arrest the army's number two officer, General Suharto, and within a day it was clear that Suharto had marshaled more than enough forces to seize control of Jakarta.[9]

Responsibility for the failed coup and the assassination of the six generals was quickly laid at the doorstep of the Indonesian communists. Over the years, however, most scholars have concluded that the September 30 failed coup was either planned by right-wing elements in the Indonesian army—with or without the CIA—or was a purely internal army affair. In either case, the coup served as the provocation General Suharto and his colleagues needed to launch their own attack upon the Indonesian Communist Party.[10]

Beginning in early October, General Suharto rapidly consolidated his power, arresting thousands in Jakarta and other urban centers. The army orchestrated a bloodbath. To be sure, many victims were singled out merely for their Chinese ethnicity. But ethnic and religious animosities do not account for what happened. The vast majority of the killings occurred during army sweeps through the countryside. Estimates of the massacre range from 78,000 (an Indonesian government commission) to a 1983 Amnesty International report that "many more than a million" died. The American embassy itself used a figure of 250,000, while most scholars today use the figure of a half million. (Another 750,000 individuals were imprisoned in concentration camps, where some remain more than three decades later.) Sukarno himself survived for five months as a figurehead president, but by the early spring of 1966, General Suharto was exercising complete authority.[11]

By all accounts, the Suharto coup d'état took both Bundy brothers by surprise. (When in 1967, Dan Ellsberg asked Bill whether there had been any U.S. involvement, Bundy responded, "No, we just lucked out.")[12] But they were both well informed of the organized massacres. On November 5 the U.S.

embassy's deputy chief of mission, Francis Galbraith, reported to Washington that he had told a high-ranking Indonesian army officer "that the embassy and the U.S.G[overnment] were generally sympathetic with and admiring of what the army was doing." In mid-December, George Ball commented that the army's campaign against the PKI was "moving fairly swiftly and smoothly." By the end of the year, Ambassador Green was reporting, "The elimination of the communists continues apace." A CIA assessment concluded on January 3, 1966, "The army has virtually destroyed the PKI."* And on February 10, Bob Komer, a special assistant to the president, reported to Johnson that "some 100,000 Communists have been killed." No one in the Johnson administration bothered to protest the killings.[13]

To the contrary, American officials, led by Ambassador Marshall Green, were doing what they could to assist the Indonesian army in its purge against the Indonesian Communist Party. Early in the crisis, when Green decided to hand over to General Suharto $40,000 worth of walkie-talkies, Bill Bundy sent his old friend a cable strongly endorsing his action.[14] Communications equipment was one thing. But the army was also provided with a small number of weapons, which the U.S. embassy cabled would be used to "to arm Moslem and nationalist youth in Central Java . . . [and] to eliminate the PKI." In addition, in the months prior to the coup, the United States had shipped a number of small planes which the Indonesian army now used to coordinate their assault against the PKI.[15]

In 1990 journalist Kathy Kadane revealed that U.S. embassy officials had also given an emissary from the Indonesian army a list containing five thousand names of PKI members and functionaries. Painstakingly compiled from open sources such as newspapers and PKI publications, the list—which often included photographs and detailed biographies of PKI leaders—was an intelligence bonanza for the Indonesian army officers assigned to hunt down and kill key PKI leaders.[16] Based on taped interviews with Ambassador Green, political officer Robert Martens and other embassy officials, Kadane demonstrated that the list was passed to the Indonesian army at a time when U.S. officials had unconfirmed reports that the army was forming firing squads to execute PKI prisoners.[17]

Bill Bundy was unaware at the time that such a list had been passed to the Indonesians. Years later he said no one should be ashamed of it. "It was pretty plain that they [the Indonesians] were going to do whatever they wanted to do anyway. We didn't say do this. They didn't need to be told. . . . I don't suppose that certain people would forgive what we did, but I thought that it was eminently justified."[18] His attitude was shared by most American officials who had anything to do with Indonesia in those years. If the United

---

* The CIA's December 1968 report, "Indonesia—1965: The Coup That Backfired," ranked the Indonesian purge as "one of the worst mass murders of the 20th century. . . ."

States was not the instigator of the 1965 massacres, it was, as one scholar put it, "an important and witting accomplice."[19]

Bundy also thought that what happened in Indonesia in 1965–66 was in some distant fashion a major benefit of the American decision to send combat troops to Vietnam. Just before the Tet offensive of 1968, he gave a speech in which he said, "What happened in Indonesia was, above all, the work of heroic and dedicated non-Communist nationalists. I am quite sure that had we not stood firm in Viet-Nam in 1965—and had Viet-Nam thus been rapidly on the way to a takeover by force from Hanoi, as would surely have been the case—Aidit [the PKI leader] and company would not have needed to force their luck and the morale of the non-Communists would not have been equal to the very tight struggle for power that ensued for the next six months."[20]

Mac Bundy agreed, writing Joe Alsop in early 1967, "I think more and more the truth of Vietnam is in the nearby countries. . . . I don't have the wonderful self-confidence of Isaiah [Berlin]—'I'm a terrific domino man'—but I share the feeling that's where we have done best." Alsop wrote back enthusiastically that he was quite sure "that the great change in Indonesia would have been aborted somehow, if we had shirked the Vietnamese test." Mac replied, "You are absolutely right about Vietnam. . . ."[21]

Marshall Green thought that after April 1966, when it became clear that Indonesia was not going to become a fallen domino, the "domino theory thereafter lost whatever validity it had once had. . . ." Like Bill Bundy, Green had always had misgivings about becoming enmeshed in a ground war in Indochina. But after the decimation of the Indonesian communists, Green favored bringing the Vietnam War "to a rapid conclusion, even on risky terms." Thereafter, Green became an early advocate of turning the "dirty" ground combat aspects of the war over to the South Vietnamese army. Vietnamization was a policy he later administered as Bundy's successor in the Nixon administration.[22]

THROUGHOUT most of 1966, Bill Bundy spent much of his time working on political efforts to shore up the Ky regime. Elections had been promised for a constituent assembly, and in due course a semblance of political stability was restored to Saigon. Unlike Rostow, Bill understood how fragile, indeed, how artificial, was this construct. If Rostow was always a believer, evangelizing the president and anyone else who would listen to his sermons about nation-building, Bill was the agnostic. Townsend Hoopes, who then had Bill's old job as deputy assistant secretary of defense under John McNaughton, later wrote, "Bundy's real convictions about the war remained to the end a carefully guarded enigma, but in the manner of a professional public servant he lent his considerable diplomatic and legal skills to the support and advocacy of the Rusk position."[23] Rusk was obsessed with the lessons he had learned from the last war—Korea. He saw China as the ultimate strategic enemy, and in his view American troops in Vietnam were actually containing Chinese expansionism. His single greatest fear was that the Chinese might repeat their performance in Korea and suddenly dispatch hundreds of thousands of troops to fight alongside the North Vietnamese. The State Department's leading China expert, Allen Whiting, repeatedly warned his colleagues that the Chinese were getting into the war. In fact, we now know the Chinese sent more than 320,000 troops to North Vietnam between 1965 and 1973. Though most of these military personnel served in logistical units, rebuilding roads and railroads, some 1,100 Chinese were killed by the American bombing over the years. In this sense, it was a much wider war than most Americans thought.[24]

IN public, Bill Bundy attempted to project a hard-nosed optimism. In a speech in Detroit on May 23, 1966, he told an audience of business executives, "Today the military picture is an encouraging one." He then compared the struggle in Vietnam to the Greek civil war in the late 1940s. "I was in Greece as a young lawyer during the heart of that conflict. I remember the desperate situation of late 1947 and early 1948. . . . The Greek Communists were still able to obtain aid from neighboring Albania and Bulgaria, but their morale had been weakened and finally broke. By the end of 1949 the guerrilla war was over. . . . I am not suggesting anything as rapid as that is now in prospect in Viet-Nam. I am saying that there are traces of cracks in Viet Cong morale that could at some point become critical." Obviously, Bundy knew that things could be a lot better, but his message was nevertheless one of perseverance: "I think we should go on and must go on."[25]

According to Averell Harriman, McNamara was telling him as early as May that he saw no value in any further escalation, and furthermore, that "we should agree . . . to let the South Vietnamese decide their own future even if it meant a coalition government with the Viet Cong, which might or might not take over." In another conversation that May, which Harriman reported in a memo marked "PERSONAL & SECRET—GOVERNOR HARRIMAN ONLY (ABSOLUTELY NO ONE ELSE TO SEE)," McNamara said he believed the Saigon regime "will become weaker and weaker as time goes on. . . . Under the circumstances, he feels we should get in touch direct with the NLF, also the North Vietnamese, but particularly the NLF, and begin to try to work up a deal for a coalition government." There was good reason for Harriman's discretion; had the memorandum leaked, it would have created a firestorm of controversy. McNamara no longer believed U.S. objectives in the war could be won. On the other hand, his prescription for ending the conflict was oddly naive. He kept asking Harriman why a settlement couldn't be reached "if we make it plain we are willing to take all of our troops out if the North Vietnamese do the same?" He could not understand that the North Vietnamese were not about to withdraw from their own country.[26]

Later that autumn, when Harriman and McNamara had the same conversation all over again, the elder man patiently explained that "there was little that we were offering Hanoi. . . . Ho Chi Minh had been fighting for a quarter of a century for the independence and unification of his country. He thought that he had been cheated by the [19]54 agreements, and didn't want to give up now." Five weeks later, Harriman noted in a private memorandum for his files, McNamara agreed with him that if the war was not settled, "the President would probably get beaten. He said, 'It must be settled this year.' I said, 'Well, early next year.' Then he spoke of the dangers of escalation if a settlement was not reached."[27]

ON the ground in South Vietnam, General Westmoreland deployed his troops in search and destroy missions, sweeping through the countryside in search of an elusive enemy. In this strange sea of villages, the usual distinctions between civilians and combatants quickly eroded. Free-fire zones were created and large areas of South Vietnam were stripped of vegetation by extensive use of defoliants. Over time, Westmoreland's attrition strategy drove the peasantry like frightened cattle into the slums of South Vietnam's cities. As the historian Marilyn B. Young has noted, by 1968 the urban population had increased from 15 to 40 percent of the country's total population. Normally a rice-exporting country, by 1967 South Vietnam was having to import 750,000 tons of rice. There were, however, political advantages to this "forced urbanization"—a term coined by Harvard political scientist Samuel P. Huntington, who justified the policy as a legitimate response to "Maoist inspired rural revolution." Even as large patches of the countryside became effectively controlled by the Viet Cong, a larger percentage of the country's population came under the nominal control of the Saigon regime.[28]

The war's cost quickly came to be calculated in many different currencies. By the end of 1965, 1,636 Americans had been killed in Vietnam, with another 7,655 wounded. This was only the beginning. In just the first two months of 1966, there were another 4,300 casualties. After Mac Bundy left, and while Bill persevered in his duties, another 19,255 Americans died and 120,687 were counted as casualties in the period from January 1966 through March 1968.[29]

This was a war that would end only after 14 million tons of explosives were dropped on Vietnam—compared to 2.5 million tons of explosives used by the United States during World War II. The casualties, particularly among the Vietnamese, were devastating. The journalist and historian Stanley Karnow later wrote that more than four million Vietnamese on both sides were either killed or wounded—roughly 10 percent of the population.[30]

If all wars are brutal, this one was particularly so. High-ranking American officials were well aware of the precise nature of this brutality. Averell Harriman was told in 1966 that "torture, including electric shock and other 'refined' techniques, was often employed by the South Vietnamese." Viet Cong prisoners were routinely killed or "permanently crippled."[31] In February 1967, Bob Komer, the president's special assistant, told Johnson after returning from a visit to Vietnam: "Wastefully, expensively, but nonetheless indisputably, we are winning the war in the South . . . we are grinding the enemy down by sheer weight and mass."[32] That May, Johnson ordered Komer, who was known by reporters as Blowtorch Bob, to Saigon to supervise the pacification program in Vietnam. Pacification included the Phoenix program, which systematically identified Viet Cong cadres for arrest and elimination. In 1969 alone, the Phoenix program "neutralized" 19,534 Viet Cong cadres, of whom 6,187 were killed. The CIA's William Colby later claimed that the program eliminated some 60,000 communist agents. Colby testified that perhaps as many as 20,000 of these individuals were killed while resisting capture or arrest by South Vietnamese police and military personnel.[33]

By the end of 1966, nearly 400,000 Americans were in South Vietnam. And by the end of 1967, the number was approaching half a million. Even so, sometimes even the most hardened Cold Warriors could see that nothing had changed. After a visit to South Vietnam in the summer of 1966, Henry Kissinger told Averell Harriman that "18 months after our arrival in Danang, it was still impossible to go four kilometers outside of the city without running a real risk of being shot." Despite all of America's efforts, Kissinger said, the "basic situation had not changed since October of '65."[34]

EARLY in 1967, Bill Moyers resigned as Johnson's press secretary. He had grown quite fond of Bill Bundy and wrote him, "Ours has been the best of all relationships I have had in Washington. You never close out something like that. I shall miss you, but I also intend to see you often."[35]

Moyers left just as a running battle was being fought within the administration over whether the air war should be extended to include the destruction of North Vietnam's irrigation dikes. McNamara and his chief aide, John McNaughton, fought a rear-guard action against this murderous tactic, which surely would have led to the deaths of many more tens of thousands of innocent civilians—just as strategic bombing in World War II had killed many innocents to no military effect. While McNamara argued for a de-escalation or even a suspension of the bombing, Bill Bundy treaded water in the "vital center" of this debate, opposing an extension of the bombing, but also opposing a suspension.

Bill thought the administration had given "a very jerky and impatient impression to Hanoi." What was needed was a "steady firmness." Without escalating the war, Bill nevertheless believed Washington had to persuade Hanoi that "we are prepared to stick to it if necessary."

Meanwhile, Mac Bundy still occasionally visited the White House to advise LBJ on Vietnam, Soviet relations and a variety of other issues. On May 4, 1967, Mac Bundy weighed into the debate with a private, unsolicited letter to Johnson. He said he was appalled when he learned, perhaps from his brother, of the Joint Chiefs' desire to escalate the bombing in the North and send another 100,000 troops to the South. These all too predictable recommendations "should be rejected," he bluntly told the president, "and that as a matter of high national policy there should be a publicly stated ceiling to the level of American participation in Vietnam, as long as there is no further marked escalation on the enemy side." Mac didn't oppose the current level of bombing: "To stop the bombing today would be to give the Communists something for nothing. . . ." But he argued that there was no evidence that the mining of Haiphong harbor or the bombing of additional targets in the North would have any effect on Hanoi's actions. He favored "tactical" bombing and opposed "strategic" bombing. More importantly, he argued, the "war at home" and the "uncertainty about the future size of the war is now having destructive effects on the national will." Any expansion of the war, in other words, was likely to erode support for the war in Johnson's domestic constituency.

Once again, Mac, like his brother, positioned himself in the "vital center" and disparaged both hawks and doves: "Doves and hawks are alike in their insatiable appetites. We can't really keep the hawks happy by small increases in effort—they come right back for more." Having held on so long, and "having nothing much left to lose," Bundy thought the North Vietnamese were bound to keep on fighting. "Since only atomic bombs could really knock them out (an invasion of North Vietnam would not do it in two years, and is of course ruled out on other grounds), they have it in their power to 'prove' that military escalation does not bring peace—at least over the next two years."

Consequently, Bundy advised the president that his bid for reelection would have to be fought on other grounds: ". . . what we must plan to offer as a defense of Administration policy is not victory over Hanoi, but growing success—and self-reliance—in the South."

Self-reliance on the part of the South Vietnamese was an early prescription for continuing the war through a policy of Vietnamization, a strategy Richard Nixon would pursue from 1969 onward. "The fact," Bundy wrote, "that South Vietnam has not been lost and is not going to be lost is a fact of truly massive importance in the history of Asia . . . the largest part of the job is done. This critically important achievement is obscured by seeming to act as if we have to do much more lest we fail." [36]

Mac Bundy's words must have come as cold comfort to a president feeling increasingly under siege. Here was the author of the strategy of gradual escalation telling him that the bombing was never intended to break Hanoi's will, that the war could not be won—short of nuclear weapons—prior to the 1968 elections, that his only real choice was to do more of the same. In retrospect, Bundy's logic was brutally accurate. Having come so far, Hanoi was not about to abandon its war aims a mere eighteen months before the 1968 elections. But the logic was also brutally cynical. It was the logic that would keep the war going for eight long years.

To be sure, Bundy's views were representative of not only the foreign policy establishment, but also of most Americans. Polls in the spring of 1967 indicated that only 19 percent of the American public thought the United States should simply withdraw from Vietnam. Nearly 40 percent supported the Johnson administration's policy of "limited" war, while 30 percent favored further escalation into a "major" war. Even such a knowledgeable critic of the war as *New York Times* reporter Neil Sheehan wrote in late 1966 that despite his misgivings about the war, "I do not see how we can do anything but continue to prosecute the war." Why? Because any other course "might undermine our entire position in Southeast Asia."[37]

Those who argued forthrightly for immediate withdrawal were few. They included iconoclastic politicians like Senator Wayne Morse (D-Ore.) and intellectuals on the left who were not afraid to question the liberal assumptions that underpinned the American commitment in Vietnam. Writing in publications like *Ramparts* and *The New York Review of Books*, Noam Chomsky was arguing that the war would end only when the Americans abandoned Vietnam. Chomsky was right, but his reward was to be treated as a pariah by the establishment press.

Arthur Schlesinger was another matter. Late in 1966, Mac Bundy's old friend published a thin volume, *The Bitter Heritage: Vietnam and American Democracy, 1941–1966*, which garnered favorable reviews across the country. Back in 1950, Schlesinger had stamped himself an early proponent of the domino theory, arguing that a French withdrawal from Indochina "might cause a chain reaction." Sixteen years later he was making a cautious case for de-escalation—not unilateral withdrawal. He thought the original intervention unwise, but having made the commitment, he argued that the United States should extricate itself slowly, tapering off the bombing "as prudently as we can." Proposals for an immediate cease-fire were "possibly very dangerous," and he said any cease-fire "should come at the end, not at the beginning, of negotiations." He urged a "middle course" that would "stop widening and Americanizing the war." The South Vietnamese, he argued, had an "army of some 600,000 men, which can take all the initiative it wants." Essentially, his book made a case for taking the first steps toward a strategy of Vietnamization.[38] Even such a mild program as this made Schlesinger feel embattled among some of his friends. Shortly after the book was published, Joe Alsop reported to Mac Bundy, "I saw dear Arthur last night. He spoke but did not shake hands. How wonderfully silly!"[39]

In part, Alsop himself was to blame for the increasingly harsh tenor of the debate over the war. In the spring of 1966 he wrote a column lambasting the *New York Times* for its "wholly false" reporting and an editorial line which he thought verged on the unpatriotic. The *Times*'s editorial page editor, John Oakes, complained that Alsop had accused the newspaper of "treason." Yet Joe's own brother Stewart was beginning to express strong doubts about the war. In September, Stewart wrote a column entitled "Vietnam: Great Miscalculation?" The Alsop brothers began to argue heatedly. The mood of the country had shifted dramatically, and Joe didn't like it. He complained to Sir Isaiah Berlin, "I cannot tell you how isolated and suddenly out of fashion I feel. The old way of looking at the world in this country, which was everyone's way from the defeat of Henry Wallace until about a year ago, is now increasingly outmoded among the intellectuals." Sir Isaiah responded grimly, "I see the thin red line, formed by you and Mac [Bundy], and me, and Chip [Bohlen]—four old blimps, the last defenders of a dry, and disagreeably pessimistic tough and hopelessly outmoded position—one will perish at least with one's eyes open."[40]

Mac Bundy strongly disagreed with Schlesinger. His position on the war had not changed. He was particularly annoyed with those of his liberal friends who argued that America could afford to finance either Vietnam or the War on Poverty at home, but not both. In January 1967, Bundy argued in the pages of Foreign Affairs, "Since the costs of Viet Nam are in fact quite manageable, and since they are likely to continue for years, the notion of using Viet Nam as a reason for delay at home becomes absurd. . . . It is therefore an act of folly for any true liberal to argue that we must choose between Viet Nam and social progress." In the event of defeat, Bundy saw a resurgence of the right wing at home. "Retreat in Viet Nam is not the road forward at home," he warned. "The real consequence of a pullout in Southeast Asia, for our domestic affairs, would almost surely be heavy reaction."[41]

Most liberals, in fact, still supported the war. And those who counted themselves as critics of LBJ's handling of the war—like Schlesinger—merely argued for an "honorable" de-escalation of the war. By the spring of 1967, one such liberal intimately involved in prosecuting the war had become deeply disillusioned. John McNaughton's numbers crunchers in the Pentagon's Office of International Security Affairs were producing all the data anyone needed to be convinced that the war was not being won. Privately, McNaughton was heard to say, "This war is shit." This was the same official who in January 1966 had urged the study of a proposal to bomb North Vietnam's dikes, which would flood the country's rice fields and lead, he estimated, to the "widespread starvation" of "more than a million" people. But now, in official deliberations, he urged McNamara and others to find some way to extricate U.S. troops from Vietnam with some semblance of honor. "A feeling is widely and strongly held that the 'Establishment' is out of its mind," McNaughton wrote McNamara in May 1967. "The feeling is that we are trying to impose some US image on distant peoples we cannot understand (any more than we can the younger generation here at home) and we are carrying the thing to absurd lengths. . . . [T]he increased polarization . . . [signals] the worst split in our people in more than a century."[42]

McNamara agreed and yet, like McNaughton, he could not bring himself to either resign or recommend a negotiated withdrawal. Years later he would tell his biographer Deborah Shapley, "I saw no low-cost means of withdrawal." Instead, he urged Johnson in a May 19, 1967, memorandum to persevere in the middle course, a "cool drive to settle the war" with a few more troops, but carefully avoiding the dangers of a larger war. At the same time Washington should clarify its war goals, by which McNamara meant that the United States should no longer hope to ensure a "free and independent" South Vietnam. Instead, the goal should be to prevent external interference with South Vietnam's self-determination. Such an outcome would not exclude a "role in the South for members of the VC." All in all, it was a very mixed prognosis. The war would not be won in a "military sense" but neither would it be lost completely. "More than that cannot be expected," he said.

McNamara's May 19 memorandum, drafted for him by McNaughton, was greeted with nearly universal condemnation by the select band of officials who were authorized to read it. Only Nicholas Katzenbach, the under secretary of state, agreed with it. The Joint Chiefs were outraged. Rostow was highly critical. And Bill Bundy called the memo "a fig leaf cover for withdrawal."[43]

It was a fig leaf. The trouble was that by 1967, those who knew the war was lost nevertheless felt that a fig leaf was politically required to sell any withdrawal policy. Bill could easily spot a fig leaf, but he still could not reconcile himself to defeat. He knew the war was stalemated. That spring, while visiting Saigon, he made a point of requesting a briefing from Dan Ellsberg. "I came off patrol in Danang in combat gear," Ellsberg recalled, "and took a space-available military flight to Saigon. There was no disagreement from Bill at that point as to how bad things were, how deeply stalemated we were. He never disagreed with me."[44]

On July 1, McNamara reiterated his utterly bleak views in another "confessional" with Averell Harriman, saying, ". . . it is impossible for us to win the war militarily." His real fear now was that the Joint Chiefs might persuade the president to expand the war. Harriman noted that McNamara "hoped that the pressure on the President from the hawks wouldn't be so great that the war would be expanded into confrontation with the Soviet Union or China." Saigon, he believed, had to negotiate with the NLF. He confided that Dean Rusk had asked him to "lay off" this point, and for the time being, he had agreed. But after the September elections inside South Vietnam, "we ought to come down with all our influence to force Saigon to begin to negotiate seriously with the NLF."[45]

BILL BUNDY was increasingly perceived as a hawk, and sometimes deservedly so, not so much for what he said as for what he didn't say. In 1967, Defense Department officials like Mort Halperin and Leslie Gelb who believed the war was unwinnable would come back from meetings with Bill Bundy terribly frustrated, even angry, with the way Bill kept critical information about the war out of circulation. Gelb sensed that Bundy was overintellectualizing the massive amount of information pouring into his office each day. "These are people," Gelb recalled, "who are really quite disciplined intellectually. They're trained that way. Part of being a serious thinker is to go through that discipline, looking at your own argument and making arguments against your argument. George Ball had that quality of mind. He could lick his own arguments." Bill Bundy did this every day, and as the war dragged on it never got easier.[46]

By the summer of 1967, Bill was exhausted physically and mentally. His wife, Mary, told him he ought to leave the government. Bill refused, telling himself, "You can't desert the troops in the field." Much later he would admit that he had been afflicted with the "delusion of indispensability," but at the time he just could not think of leaving. By then, Mary thought the war was "hopeless" and the fact that her husband was so intimately involved was "very painful."[47]

Bundy later admitted that some "fairly close relatives of mine were alienated from me." One relative wrote him a particularly "anguished letter." But at the time he tried to ignore the anti-war protestors: "They caused you personal pain, because many of them were your friends. But I guess I'm just stubborn and Puritan enough to say that you've got to do what you think is the right thing." His son Michael was at Harvard at a time when the name Bundy was on occasion linked with the phrase "war criminal." Michael had an artistic bent and wasn't particularly interested in politics. His father later explained, "He went off and did other things, more or less to get out of it— my firing line. It was terribly hard on him personally."[48]

The war even came home to Manchester-on-the-Sea, where Kay Bundy, now in her late seventies, still presided over the Bundy brood's summer vacations. Feisty as ever, Kay later described herself as "one of those dreadful people who think if we'd gone at it [the war] just a little bit harder . . . we could have won it." Kay was not in sympathy with the protestors. "I had one grandson who was shouting at the pool, 'Ho, Ho, Ho Chi. . . .' " She told him, "You can't cheer Mr. Ho Chi Minh at my pool. No, and not while soldier boys are being killed." Kay nevertheless knew what the war had done to her sons: "Mac got out of it, but I think Bill's ulcer is the Vietnam war."[49]

In mid-August, Bill Bundy debated former White House aide Richard N. Goodwin at a forum sponsored by the University of Maryland. Both men were politely received by the student audience, but Goodwin's anti-war stance made him the crowd-pleaser. "The dissent is getting through to the American people," Goodwin said. "The futility and horror of this war is penetrating." Bundy demurred, saying that if the United States persisted, "the prospects for a peaceful and secure Southeast Asia appear brighter than they have been at any time since" the end of the colonial era. Goodwin responded that Bundy was speaking of a "fairy tale that, like most fairy tales, is comforting and warming, but is not true."[50]

Increasingly, Bill Bundy became the administration's point man for defending the war. That autumn he and Ken Galbraith debated each other in the pages of the New York Times Magazine. Galbraith proposed de-escalating the war as a prelude to reconvening the Geneva Conference. Bundy responded, "Let no reader mistake Galbraith's proposal for anything but a thinly disguised proposal for withdrawal. . . ." He again asserted that the war was being won, that the Viet Cong controlled less than 20 percent of the population and that Washington's policies were in fact supported by most governments in Asia. Bundy was conceding nothing to his critics.[51]

While Goodwin and Galbraith were politely engaging Bundy in debate, Marc Raskin, Mac Bundy's former NSC aide, was calling for open resistance to the war. In the spring of 1967, Raskin and a colleague from the Institute for Policy Studies drafted "A Call to Resist Illegitimate Authority." Modeled after a similar petition circulated by French intellectuals who had opposed France's colonial war in Algeria, Raskin persuaded numerous scholars, including Dr. Benjamin Spock, to sign the "Call." In October, it was published in both *The New York Review of Books* and *The New Republic*. Subsequently, hundreds of young men turned in their draft cards at a public ceremony in Washington, D.C.—the day before a massive demonstration at the Pentagon. A few months later, Raskin, Dr. Spock, the Reverend William Sloane Coffin and two others were indicted on charges of conspiring to violate the Selective Service Act. After a highly publicized trial, Raskin and his colleagues were eventually acquitted. Soon after the trial, in June 1968, Raskin dropped by to see Mac Bundy at the Ford Foundation. Far from breaking with Raskin over his radical politics, Bundy had tried to recruit him to work at the Ford Foundation in 1966. On this occasion, Bundy seemed pleased that his former aide had been acquitted. By then, Raskin's petition had garnered over four thousand signatories.[52]

By the autumn of 1967, there were some 480,000 American troops in Vietnam, but because the highly mechanized and heliborne army required so many support troops, less than 100,000 were available for actual combat. Officially, these American combat troops, together with the half million combat troops fielded by their South Vietnamese allies, faced an enemy troop strength of something less than 300,000 men. This was General Westmoreland's official estimate for the enemy's "order of battle." The figure, however, was being hotly disputed that summer and fall by the CIA's top analysts. Relying on captured enemy documents, some in the intelligence community believed the true enemy order of battle was more like a half million or even 600,000 men.[53]

Bill Bundy was well aware of the dispute over the estimate of enemy forces, and when he saw a final draft of the order of battle document rammed through by Westmoreland and the Joint Chiefs, he lodged a complaint with Walt Rostow. It was not true, he said, that the Viet Cong's "self-defense forces," or militia, numbering nearly 300,000, did not pose a military threat as Westmoreland claimed. This assertion should be deleted "in light of the intelligence judgment that these forces do inflict casualties and are also included in military loss totals on a regular basis." His advice went unheeded.

We now know from a 1985 legal suit (*Westmoreland* vs. *CBS*) and from Sam Adams's 1994 book, *War of Numbers: An Intelligence Memoir*, that the military brass consciously fixed the numbers for reasons of public relations. In an eyes-only March 9, 1967, cable, General Earle Wheeler, chairman of the Joint Chiefs, bluntly warned Westmoreland that any dramatic upward revision of the enemy order-of-battle estimates would have serious political consequences: "If these figures should reach the public domain . . . [they] would, literally, blow the lid off Washington."[54] The lower estimates were used to justify the war's progress. The same numbers were also used to brief the president's Wise Men—who included Dean Acheson, John J. McCloy and now McGeorge Bundy, among others—on the evening of November 1, 1967. Two years after Mac had told Johnson that he was leaving, the president made a point of including him in these select deliberations.

During the briefing the Wise Men were shown a graph prepared by military intelligence which claimed that Viet Cong strength had fallen off from 285,000 in August 1966 to 242,000 one year later. About the same time, the *New York Times,* citing the same information, reported on page one that "US Aides Say Foe Is Weakening Fast." This was not true. Nevertheless, Mac Bundy and his fellow Wise Men concluded that the war was being won, albeit slowly, and advised Johnson to persevere.[55] As Dean Acheson told the president, "I got the impression that this is a matter we can and will win." Drawing an analogy to Korea, he suggested that the war in Vietnam would end when the communists realized that the Americans were prepared to stay for the duration. Mac Bundy agreed, saying, "Getting out of Vietnam is as impossible as it is undesirable." On the other hand, Mac was struck by McNamara's pessimistic assessment of the bombing. The defense secretary was clearly disillusioned and even distraught. Disturbed by McNamara's performance, Bundy left the meeting without giving voice to his own confused thoughts.[56]

Ten days later, however, Mac tried to summarize his views in a memo to Johnson. In the process of drafting his November 11 memo, he said, he had found "my own mind stretched to some new thoughts. . . ." He agreed with McNamara that the bombing could no longer be justified on the grounds that it was interdicting supplies to enemy forces in South Vietnam. Clearly, the enemy was able to supply its troops in the South despite the bombing. Neither would the bombing compel the North to the negotiating table. Still, Bundy could not bring himself to agree with McNamara's conclusion that the administration should opt for a bombing pause. Sustained bombing, he thought, was justified merely on the grounds that it was inflicting some damage on the enemy's military machine.

Bundy then observed that General Westmoreland's search and destroy strategy appeared to be far more costly financially and less effective militarily than had been expected. If the war was to be won by a strategy of sheer endurance, then the matter of cost was essential. "There just has to be an end to the cost of build-up at some point, and we ought not to let anyone believe that the dollar in Vietnam doesn't matter. It matters like Hell to our ability to stay the course . . . since I think the Communists have proved more stubborn than we expected at every stage, I think that sooner or later we are going to have to find a way of doing this job that is endurable in cost for a long pull."

Bundy was worried about the impact of the war at home, where he said the president faced "a contest that is more political in its character than any in our history except the Civil War." Clearly, he told Johnson, "public discontent with the war is now wide and deep. One of the few things that helps us right now is public distaste for the violent doves—but I think people are really getting fed up with the endlessness of the fighting." Without backing off his earlier recommendations not to pause the bombing, not to negotiate and not to escalate, Mac told the president, "I think some visible de-escalation, based on success and not failure, is the most promising path I can see. I can't prove this path exists, but I think we should search for it."

Despite the fog of his argument it is clear Mac was advising Johnson to consider a new strategy, one which would "enlarge the real and visible role of the South Vietnamese."[57] No doubt aware that McNamara himself was making the same pitch, Bundy was deftly advocating a de-escalation of American involvement in the war and an escalation of the role of the South Vietnamese. Vietnamization was the way out of the war.

Johnson's response to Bundy's memo was to decide three days later to nominate McNamara to become president of the World Bank. The appointment was quickly confirmed and announced at the end of November. McNamara would be leaving the Pentagon early in the new year. "To this day," McNamara later told his biographer Deborah Shapley, "I don't know whether I resigned or was fired." Shapley thought this disingenuous. McNamara, she wrote, had been asking to be fired. His November 1 performance before the Wise Men made it clear he was no longer a member of the team. If Mac Bundy had still been in the White House, he too might have been given the same treatment. This was still Lyndon Johnson's war, and he was going to fight it with or without two of the war's original architects.[58]

MEANWHILE, back in Saigon, an astute member of the CIA station, Joe Hovey, began to notice that the Viet Cong were behaving differently. On November 27, Hovey cabled a report to Washington that was read in mid-December by President Johnson himself. It predicted that the enemy were planning "a political and military offensive utilizing all VC assets" against "all major cities" in South Vietnam. The offensive would run from January through March 1968.[59] Typically, when policy-makers are given the benefit of good intelligence, they file it away. And so it was with Tet.

On the evening of January 30, 1968, Bill and Mary Bundy were celebrating their twenty-fifth wedding anniversary at a party thrown for them by friends. It was a rollicking affair with scores of people in attendance. In the midst of the festivities, Walt Rostow was called to the phone, and when he returned, he pulled Bill aside and told him that Viet Cong sappers had invaded the grounds of the U.S. embassy in Saigon. Bill and Walt quietly left the party and drove to the White House, where they scanned the early reports on the Tet offensive.[60]

The news was bad and would get worse, even though it quickly became clear that the enemy's offensive would be crushed. The Viet Cong had hoped that their urban offensive would be met with a popular uprising. This did not materialize, and the Saigon regime managed to survive and inflict horrendous losses on the Viet Cong's indigenous forces. But the Tet offensive finally destroyed whatever credibility the Johnson administration had with the American people. Bill Bundy thought it wasn't nearly as bad as the press portrayed it, but even so the "defection of Walter Cronkite," as he put it, was an "absolute landmark." On the CBS Evening News the veteran newscaster bluntly challenged the administration's claim that the war was being won. "Palpably, you were in a different ballgame," Bill recalled. "With me that was somewhat slower to sink in, but within three or so weeks after Tet, you knew, you just couldn't see the country supporting a major force increase."[61]

As the early reports on the Tet offensive filtered into Washington, Senator Fulbright tried to describe the atmosphere of quiet desperation gripping the Johnson administration. In a note to the psychoanalyst Erich Fromm, Fulbright wrote, "There is literally a miasma of madness in the city, enveloping everyone in the administration and most of those in Congress. I am at a loss for words to describe the idiocy of what we are doing."[62]

Unknown to Fulbright, there were many within the administration who shared his feelings. Bill Bundy was with McNamara the day the secretary of defense fell apart. It was February 27, 1968, and after seven years in office McNamara was leaving Washington. Bundy, Clark Clifford, Dean Rusk, Walt Rostow, Joe Califano (a special assistant to the president), Harry McPherson (special counsel to the president) and Nicholas Katzenbach had gathered in the State Department's ornate executive dining room to discuss the war. General Westmoreland had just requested an additional 205,000 troops. McNamara called the request "madness." Katzenbach and Bundy reportedly nodded in agreement. Suddenly, even before lunch had been served, McNamara rose and announced he couldn't stay. But then he began speaking passionately about the "goddamned bombing campaign, it's been worth nothing, it's done nothing, they've dropped more bombs than in all of Europe in all of World War Two and it hasn't done a fucking thing." McNamara's voice then disintegrated into "suppressed sobs." After a moment he turned to Clifford, his newly designated successor, and said, "We simply have to end this thing. I just hope you can get hold of it. It is out of control." Clifford later wrote of the moment in his memoirs, "We were all stunned, but, out of a shared pain and sense of embarrassment, we went on with the discussion as though nothing out of the ordinary had occurred."

Keeping a stiff upper lip, Bundy nevertheless endorsed McNamara's sentiments, saying, "South Vietnam is very weak. Our position may be truly untenable. Contingency planning should proceed toward the possibility that we will withdraw with the best possible face and defend the rest of Asia."

Califano later wrote of the luncheon that it was the "most depressing three hours in my years of public service." McNamara, Katzenbach and Bundy were "beyond pessimism." "They sounded a chorus of despair. Rusk appeared exhausted and worn down." [63]

Depressed as he was, Bill Bundy had not budged in his basic assumption that the administration should not end the bombing. He knew the war could not be won militarily. He essentially agreed with McNamara that Westmoreland's request for another 205,000 troops was "madness." But he still opposed a unilateral suspension of the bombing. On March 3 he wrote that negotiations were unlikely: "If we sat down at the table with them now, the odds are overwhelming that their position would be totally stiff and unyielding." Early negotiations would be "disastrous." It might be acceptable to work on opening up some channels of communication to the NLF, "but this must be done in the utmost secrecy and in full consultation with the GVN [the Saigon regime]." [64] He opposed any major escalation of the bombing or any further increase in troop deployments, but he was still prepared to see the war continue at its present level of intensity.

By contrast, Mac Bundy's views had changed, but only marginally so. Perhaps because he was outside Washington, Mac was a little more sensitive than his brother to the fact that Tet had dramatically changed the mood of the country.

On March 20, Mac joined the president and his immediate advisers to discuss a draft of what was being billed as a major presidential address on Vietnam. To the disappointment of many, by the end of the meeting Johnson had decided to cut out any references to peace initiatives. Bundy felt compelled the next day to send Johnson a memo arguing that the draft speech "will be profoundly discouraging to the American people." In the wake of the Tet offensive, most Americans were weary of the war. "I think it is a miracle, in a way, that our people have stayed with the war as long as they have, but I do not see how we can carry them with us for very much longer if all we seem to offer is more of the same, with stalemate at a higher cost as the only prospect." A day later he added a postscript: "This damned war really is much tougher than—and very different from—World War II and Korea, and I just don't think the country can be held together much longer by determination and patriotism alone." It was time, he bluntly told the president, to end the bombing. "I've been against them [advocates of a bombing halt] all up to now —but no longer . . . I think nothing less will do." [65]

Soon after receiving this gloomy message, Johnson gathered the Wise Men for another reassessment. This time, however, when Dean Acheson received the call from the White House he laid down some conditions. "Mr. President," he said, "I won't give you one word of advice until I have had a chance to go over the situation with great care, on paper and through talks with responsible officials. I am tired of these briefings by paper the night before and I will not give you any advice on that basis." He wanted personal, one-on-one briefings and complete access to whatever reports he could digest. Johnson agreed, and Bill Bundy was delegated to arrange the briefings.

Bundy selected three briefers: Army General William DePuy for the Pentagon's perspective, Philip Habib from the State Department and George A. Carver, Jr., from the CIA. Bundy knew each of them well. Habib was his own assistant, and Bill must have known he would give a sobering assessment of the political situation in Saigon. Bundy also knew that DePuy had a reputation for independent thinking within Pentagon circles. As for Carver, he had served in Bundy's old ONE shop (Office of National Estimates) within the CIA for eight years, and consequently, he had been in the thicket of the recent dispute over the enemy order of battle.* [66]

Asked later if he had stacked the deck by selecting these particular briefers, Bundy said, "No, but I had a pretty damn good idea that they certainly would not give us high hopes of drastic improvement in any short term." At Acheson's insistence, each of these men came separately to his home on P Street in Georgetown and briefed the old man for hours at length in his parlor. After he had cross-examined the experts handpicked by his son-in-law, Acheson was convinced that Johnson's war policy was utterly futile. So when the Wise Men began their deliberations in mid-March, Acheson was already primed to lead the discussion. [67]

It quickly became apparent from the Wise Men's questions that Acheson was not the only one to have changed his mind about the war. Mac Bundy and Clifford asked tough questions. When General DePuy reported that 80,000 enemy soldiers had been killed, U.N. Ambassador Arthur Goldberg asked what the ratio of wounded to killed was. DePuy said three to one. And what was the general's estimate on the number of enemy troops fighting in the South? DePuy said 230,000. "Then who the hell are we fighting?" Goldberg asked in exasperation.

Walt Rostow watched the Wise Men's performance with growing unease. "I smelled a rat," he later recalled. He suspected that the Bundy brothers, together with Clark Clifford and Acheson, had choreographed the meeting. "I thought to myself," he noted with his usual flair for the dramatic, "that what began in the spring of 1940 when Henry Stimson came to Washington ended tonight. The American Establishment is dead." [68]

The next morning Johnson was shocked when he learned what had happened. Someone, he complained, had "poisoned the well." Over lunch with

---

* Carver had encouraged his deputy, Sam Adams, to attack Westmoreland's rosy statistics, yet he had also signed off on the key estimate of the previous September in which the CIA had acquiesced to the military's numbers. In a cable to his superior, Richard Helms, Carver confessed, "We have squared the circle." (Sam Adams, *War of Numbers: An Intelligence Memoir* [South Royalton, Vt.: Steerforth, 1994], p. 117; John Prados, *The Hidden History of the Vietnam War* [Chicago: Dee, 1995], pp. 29–33, 275–81.)

the president, Mac Bundy—the youngest of the Wise Men—summarized their views: "There is a very significant shift in our position. When last we met we saw reasons for hope." Not any longer. When General Wheeler protested that America's aim was not a military victory per se, Acheson bellowed, "Then what in the name of God are five hundred thousand men out there doing—chasing girls? This is not a semantic game, General; if the deployment of all those men is not an effort to gain a military solution, then words have lost all meaning."

At this point Rostow suggested that there was something the military could do to change the equation: invade North Vietnam. Johnson flinched at the suggestion and said, "No, no, no, I don't want to talk about that."[69]

In the days following his meeting with the Wise Men, Lyndon Johnson took his own counsel. One way or the other, the president wished to find a way to do what was necessary to "end this thing."[70] He knew the country was demoralized, that his advisers were divided. Some were urging a unilateral and complete bombing halt, while others favored a partial bombing halt above the twentieth parallel in North Vietnam. Bill Bundy was convinced that an immediate total halt to the bombing would be "devastating" to the morale of the Saigon regime. He urged Johnson to wait a month or two, to give Saigon time to stabilize politically in the wake of the Tet offensive, and then announce a complete halt to the bombing in return for peace talks. Instead, Johnson opted for a partial bombing halt.

On March 31 the president gave his long-awaited address to the nation in response to the Tet events. Having had a hand in drafting the speech, Bundy thought he knew Johnson's script. As the president came to the end of the speech, Bill got up and was about to turn off his television when Johnson announced that he would "not seek, and I will not accept, the nomination of my party for another term as your president." Bundy was as stunned as anyone else by Johnson's abdication. To his mind, the fact that Johnson was now a lame-duck president only made his partial bombing halt even more ineffective. Johnson should have ordered a complete bombing halt or nothing at all. Peace talks soon began in Paris, where Averell Harriman headed an American delegation that met periodically with a North Vietnamese delegation. But they would spend the next six months arguing over the conditions for a complete end of the bombing. "It always seemed to me a pity," Bundy later said. "If he [Johnson] just did it [unilaterally ended all bombing], and said we're going to be in Paris a week from Monday, ready to talk the substance of peace, you might have gotten somewhere. I think it would have been a shock to the South Vietnamese, but I think they could have learned to live with it. Instead, we had this feckless summer. God, it was a feckless summer."[71]

MARTIN LUTHER KING was gunned down on April 4, 1968. And then on June 5, Bobby Kennedy was killed just after claiming victory in the California Democratic primary. Kennedy's assassination deprived the peace movement of its most promising presidential candidate. Both Bill and Mac were as disheartened as most Americans by these tragedies. If Robert Kennedy had lived, and had won the Democratic nomination, the Bundys would certainly have voted for him in November. Their differences with him over the war would have been of no consequence compared to the fact that he was John Kennedy's brother —and that the alternative was Richard Nixon.

By June, it was clear that Nixon, whom the Bundy brothers detested, would win the Republican nomination for president. With Kennedy dead, Humphrey was likely to receive the Democratic nomination, but most observers thought he had little chance of winning the presidency unless he either disassociated himself from Lyndon Johnson or the war was quickly ended. For that reason, Bill Bundy now wanted to persuade Johnson to end the bombing of North Vietnam unconditionally, a step which most of the president's advisers at the Paris peace talks thought was essential if a cease-fire was to be negotiated prior to the election.

In mid-July, Bundy flew to Paris, where he met with Averell Harriman, Nicholas Katzenbach, Philip Habib and Cyrus Vance. Inside the embassy's security bubble, a soundproof room where they could talk freely, these five old friends decided to appeal to the president to end the bombing unilaterally. A cable was drafted and sent to the White House, and Bundy was charged with the task of talking to Johnson about it.

Back in Washington, Bundy immediately went to see the secretary of state. He told Rusk that "this was a very seriously thought-out proposal" and that the men behind it "hope very much that the President will see it their way." The next morning Bundy was summoned to the White House. Johnson took him into a small sitting room adjoining the Oval Office and told him, "I'm just not having any part of this. I want you to know it and not to have the slightest doubt that I'm not having any part of it. I don't want you talking about this, and I don't ever want to hear about this again." Bundy didn't even try to argue. "I think I just said, 'Yes, sir.' I didn't try to fight him."

By then, Bill had experienced the best and the worst of Lyndon Johnson. He knew the man and knew enough when not to argue with him. As he later told a friend, "Unquestionably, he [LBJ] was crude, boorish and on many occasions, both professional and personal, very hard to take." Frequently, Bill said, he had to go home to "blow off steam . . . about his faults." Never had he been more exasperated with Johnson.[72]

Later, at the August Democratic convention in Chicago, Johnson stubbornly blocked a proposed platform plank that would have opened the door to a unilateral cessation of the bombing. To Bundy's mind, Johnson had "created the situation that tore the convention apart." And that, Bundy later thought, made all the difference in Humphrey's very narrow defeat at the polls in November.[73] In his view, Johnson made Richard Nixon's election possible.

Late in the autumn campaign a breakthrough occurred in the Paris talks when Hanoi signaled its willingness to allow representatives of the Saigon regime to participate in peace talks. This concession should have cleared the way for substantive negotiations to end the war. The previous June, President Thieu had assured Johnson that he would approve a bombing halt if the North Vietnamese would drop their resistance to South Vietnamese participation in the Paris peace talks. But inexplicably, President Thieu reneged on his promise and raised objections which delayed the Paris talks for a crucial ten days. Only later did Bundy learn that Johnson and his inner circle had access to cables (intercepted by a U.S. intelligence agency) from the South Vietnamese embassy in Washington, D.C., to President Thieu in Saigon making it clear that the Nixon campaign had been urging Thieu to abort or cripple the deal by refusing to participate in the peace talks. Bundy was outraged to learn of Nixon's effort to sabotage the talks—he called it a "covert operation"—and later charged that Nixon's denial that he had any knowledge of the affair was "almost certainly a lie."[74]

SHORTLY before Nixon narrowly won the presidency, Mac Bundy gave a major speech at DePauw University that called for steady troop reductions and a bombing halt even if no truce was reached with North Vietnam. A front-page headline in the *New York Times* proclaimed, "Former White House Aide Alters Stand on Vietnam Policy He Helped Make." Though a significant departure from his previous public position on the war, Bundy had not come out against it. Indeed, he made a point of defending the war policies with which he and his brother were so closely associated: "To say that the burden of this war must now be lifted is not at all to say that it should never have been fought. It is not even to say that it has been fought the wrong way. . . ." He went on to say that the "avoidance of defeat" was so important that "the basic decision in 1965, to stand and fight in South Vietnam, was right." In a veiled reference to Indonesia, he added, "I also believe that in this fundamental sense the decisions of 1965 have already been validated by events in the area."

For Mac, the American burden in the war had to be lifted because the costs in dollars and blood were too great. Short of using nuclear weapons, Bundy said, a military solution cannot be expected. And "it would be the worst kind of folly to use nuclear weapons of any sort at any time in this contest." The American people would reject the use of such weapons, and "it would be equally fruitless to seek a military victory by an escalation of conventional force. . . ."

While Bundy said he supported the Paris peace negotiations, he warned that Hanoi may prove intransigent to "any settlement that will be remotely acceptable to the people of this country." Neither did he think that a coalition government in Saigon would prove to be acceptable to all parties. A diplomatic solution, therefore, might not be possible, at least in the near term.

That left Washington with only one logical policy: a unilateral decision to de-escalate the war. The goal, Bundy said, should be to withdraw 100,000 or 150,000 U.S. troops from South Vietnam by the end of 1969. This would still leave as many as 400,000 troops in Vietnam, but Bundy suggested similar withdrawals could be scheduled for 1970–71. "This reduced level of effort is more than enough still to sustain and execute the basic purpose of our forces in Vietnam—the purpose of preventing defeat." In the absence of a negotiated "decent settlement," Bundy said Americans should be prepared to keep "at least a hundred thousand troops in place for years. . . ." In the meantime, the United States should continue to modernize the reinforcement of South Vietnamese forces.[75]

Mac Bundy was mapping out a plan for prolonging the war at a lower cost to the American treasury and American lives. It was a plan for Vietnamization of the war which Henry Kissinger and Richard Nixon would execute for five long years.

By 1968, some of Mac Bundy's friends at Harvard were hardly on speaking terms with him. To be sure, Galbraith, Riesman, Kaysen and many others simply decided, in deference to their friendship, to avoid the subject. (On April 1, Galbraith had publicly called on Bill Bundy to resign his office, on the grounds that Bundy was so closely identified with Johnson's war policy. Bill ignored Galbraith's statement.)[76] Those who chose to challenge Mac Bundy, however, quickly found themselves shunned by their old dean. When Bundy came up to Harvard in March to give a talk on Vietnam, the university cast about for someone to debate him. Stanley Hoffmann volunteered. "It was perhaps not the smartest thing I've done in my life," Hoffmann recalled. "It ruined my relations with Bundy." Prior to the debate, Mac showed up at Hoffmann's home in Cambridge and said he had a proposition: "Let's not attack each other," he said. "Let's be bland. Let's not say too much." Hoffmann was surprised. This was not like the Bundy he knew, and he rebuffed him: "I didn't buy it, so we went at each other in the debate." Mac gave his standard defense of the war and Hoffmann gave a steely rebuttal. "That was the end of our friendship," Hoffmann said. "He never forgave me. He was angry. He was very angry." Much later, Hoffmann realized that at the time Mac was about to tell the president in the course of the Wise Men meetings that the war had to be de-escalated. "Bundy didn't tell me that," Hoffmann said. "He came as the defender of the war. Well, if he had told me that he was in a difficult position, that he was defending something that he didn't believe in very much any more, that would have made me think. But that wasn't his style." Mac never again spoke about serious matters to his former protégé.[77]

Bundy would soon break with another of his former colleagues, James C. Thomson, Jr., who was sitting in the audience the day of his debate with Hoffmann. Thomson was startled to hear Bundy say, "Those who had been entrusted with responsibility by a president had been handed a pistol along with that trust, and that those who later spoke out about their period of service not merely broke the trust, but turned that pistol on the man who had trusted them and shot him in the head."

Thomson's wife, Diana, elbowed him and said, "He's talking about you." "No, no," whispered Mac's former aide, "he's talking about Arthur Schlesinger." When the next day Thomson ran into Schlesinger and related the story, Schlesinger said, "No, no, he was talking about Ken Galbraith and Dick Goodwin."[78] On reflection, Thomson thought his wife was right, and that Mac's comment had been directed at him. A year earlier Thomson had published a letter to the editor in the New York Times in which he identified himself as a former NSC aide who believed there had been constructive alternatives to escalation in the war, but that these had been repeatedly rejected since 1961. It was one thing, Bundy thought, to voice dissent in private, among your Cambridge friends or even in Washington; but it was quite another thing to speak out in public.

For a good Stimsonian like Mac Bundy, speaking out against one's president amounted to murder. Indeed, everything about Mac's life—his Brahmin upbringing, his Groton/Peabody education, his Skull and Bones comradeship, his military service as a signals intelligence officer and his tenure as Harvard dean—had taught him to value loyalty and to devalue the man who voiced his dissent in public.

Despite Bundy's strongly implied warning to keep his silence, Thomson was about to cross the line into full and open dissent. In April, just a few weeks after Bundy's Harvard debate, Thomson published a candid and confessional essay in The Atlantic entitled "How Could Vietnam Happen?: An Autopsy." While not mentioning the Bundys by name, his thinly veiled description of the men he had once worked for in the White House and the State Department was transparent. He quoted "my senior White House employer" (Mac Bundy) calling him his "favorite dove" and quoted "an assistant secretary of state" (Bill Bundy) advocating a bombing policy with the following words: "It seems to me that our orchestration should be mainly violins, but with periodic touches of brass." Thomson accused his former colleagues of an "abuse" and distortion of history. Vietnamese history, he said, had been rewritten to justify the American involvement. "Highly dubious analogies from our experience elsewhere—the 'Munich' sellout and 'containment' from Europe . . . have been imported in order to justify our actions." He also said it was "undoubtedly false" that the American effort in Vietnam had saved Indonesia from communism. "I tried to prove it, during six months of careful investigation at the White House, and had to confess to failure."

He described his former colleagues' doubts about the policy and their toleration for dissenting opinions like his own. But he also suggested that they had "warmly institutionalized" dissenters like Ball and himself, and the result had been a "domestication" of these critical views. A "humane doubter" like Chet Cooper, Thomson suggested, was kept busy in public relations, massaging "the doubting intelligentsia."

Thomson was saying that far from being foolish about Vietnam, men like the Bundys had known enough and possessed enough private misgivings about the war that they should have acted against it. He bluntly argued that his former colleagues had fallen into the trap of rationalizing their repeated decisions to stay aboard when they should have resigned in protest against policies they knew had little chance of success. Instead, they remained loyal to Cold War assumptions about America's place in the world that had nothing to do with the realities of Vietnam. "Crucial throughout the process of Vietnam decision-making was a conviction among many policy-makers: that Vietnam posed a *fundamental test of America's national will* [italics in original]. Time and again I was told by men reared in the tradition of Henry L. Stimson that all we needed was the will, and we would then prevail. . . . To put it bluntly: at the heart of the Vietnam calamity is a group of able, dedicated men who have been regularly and repeatedly wrong. . . ."

Tragically, Thomson pointed out that his colleagues were well aware that there had been an alternative. After the November 1964 election "this President could have used the largest electoral mandate in history to de-escalate in Vietnam, in the clear expectation that at the worst a neutralist government would come to power in Saigon and politely invite us out. Today, many lives and dollars later, such an alternative has become an elusive and infinitely more expensive possibility."[79]

Thomson's essay was as informed as it was insightful in its indictment of the policies and the men who had been so closely associated with their execution. The Bundys were personally offended. Mac interpreted the essay—correctly—as a personal attack. So, too, did Bill, who later referred to Thomson's *Atlantic* essay as "the voice of an inherently small man. I've never known quite why Thomson stayed in government if he felt as he now says he felt." Mac dropped a short note to Thomson rebuking him for betraying a personal trust: "I wonder what standards of personal decency can have caused a man to do what you have done."[80] The two men would not be on speaking terms for eight years.

DAVID HALBERSTAM later wrote that Mac Bundy did indeed have doubts in 1966–68 about the war, but that "his doubts were very pragmatic ones, whether Vietnam was worth the time and resources it was absorbing and the division it was creating." And Halberstam was probably right to suggest that the more doubts Mac had about the war, the more arrogant he sometimes seemed in publicly refusing to engage with his critics: "There was that quality to him—ferocious pride, belief in self, inability to admit mistakes that kept him from being able to react to the war in a human sense." Even after Tet, and after his participation in the March 'Wise Men' session in which he had taken a lead in rejecting Westmoreland's request for more troops, Bundy would not trade in public on his doubts. At Harvard that spring he astonished one audience with a particularly brazen remark that he could not bother to defend the administration's current Vietnam policy "because I have a brother who is paid to do that."[81] This was Bundy arrogance at its worst—or more charitably, Bundy's razor-sharp brand of self-deprecating humor at its worst. But in either case, Halberstam was right: Mac found it hard to deal with the human consequences of the war.

Bill was always pained by the war in ways that his brother was not. By early 1969, some of his friends thought, wrongly, that he was on the verge of a nervous breakdown. "I didn't consult a doctor," Bundy said, "and ask him if I was on the edge of a nervous breakdown. I knew damn well I was at the end of my tether. That's the way I would have put it. I just knew I was bone tired."[82] Despite his personal distaste for the new president, he was offered two jobs in the Nixon administration: ambassador to Japan or the assistant secretary slot for European affairs. He turned down both offers and instead moved to Cambridge, where he would spend two painful years trying to write a full history of the decision-making that led the United States into the war. It was not something his brother would have done. By then, Mac had spent nearly three years at the Ford Foundation.

15

The Ford Foundation

The first conclusion I offer is that the most deep-seated and destructive of all the causes of the Negro problem is still the prejudice of the white man.

McGEORGE BUNDY
February 2, 1968

$\mathbf{M}$AC AND MARY BUNDY loved their new life in New York. In the spring of 1966 they bought a spacious apartment on Fifth Avenue, facing Central Park. One of their neighbors was Jackie Kennedy, widow of the slain president. Every morning at 8:15 a limousine ferried Mac downtown to his spacious office in the Ford Foundation headquarters. Three television sets dominated the room and, somewhat incongruously, off on a side table stood a handsomely framed photograph of Henry Stimson. Mac tried to reserve half the mornings for reading and thinking. Then he spent the rest of the day on the phone to his staff and conducting committee meetings where he peppered his aides with questions. It was a busy schedule, but nothing like the White House. Judge Charles Wyzanski, his old friend and a Ford trustee, had assured him that a good foundation executive needn't spend more than half his time on the job. "It hasn't worked out that way," Bundy told the *New York Times*, "but in hours it's a lot easier here than it was in Washington."[1]

Early in Bundy's tenure, the Ford Foundation moved into new quarters on East Forty-third Street. Built at a cost of $17 million, Bundy called it "surely one of the most remarkable modern office buildings in existence." From the outside, the structure's skin of black steel and glass seemed sleek, cold and authoritative. Once inside, however, visitors suddenly found themselves viewing an enormous jungle in an atrium, eleven floors high and almost as wide. Journalist Nicholas von Hoffman once called it "the only air-conditioned forest in New York or maybe the world."[2] A brick pathway meandered past magnolia trees, azaleas and camellia bushes and across a small hill and down to a gurgling pond. Bundy and his four hundred–plus employees sat in their glass offices, attending to the business of intelligent charity, while taking inspiration from the perpetually green forest below them. Their offices were furnished with Honduran mahogany desks, white oak parquet floors and marble and brass fixtures. The walls were adorned with Belgian linen, and many offices boasted lithographs by Picasso, Miró and Chagall.

Though the building was designed by architect Kevin Roche long before Bundy came to Ford, its intimidating exterior and lush, warm interior seemed a perfect metaphor for its new president. "It's a hell of a place to invite a community organizer from Harlem," quipped one of Bundy's foundation officers.[3]

As president of the Ford Foundation, Bundy had been promised that he could be his own boss. Charlie Wyzanski, McCloy and other trustees had assured him that he would have the freedom to make mistakes. "They were eager for new ideas," Bundy said. "There was no unwillingness—as a conscious desire —to move into the hot firing line." And that's what Bundy was eager to do. "He will be," remarked one Ford trustee a bit nervously, "a *very* stimulating influence."[4]

WHEN Bundy left Washington in 1966, a colleague had said, "There goes a future secretary of state."[5] Others thought the presidency of the Ford Foundation was a step down—or at least a diversion from Bundy's true calling. Louis Auchincloss, a close friend, thought Bundy belonged back on campus. "If Kennedy hadn't picked him out of Harvard," Auchincloss said in 1966, "he'd be president of Yale today, and set there for the rest of his life."[6] But Kennedy had called, and Bundy's five years in the White House had changed his outlook. Once a Republican liberal, he was now a Bobby Kennedy liberal. Like the newly elected senator from New York, Bundy believed in the power of government. As a "vital-center" liberal, he still believed in the creation of the kind of vibrant "welfare-market society" he and Walter Lippmann had corresponded about in 1949. A pragmatist, he felt he understood both Washington's power and its limitations. And now he was determined to use Ford's $3.7 billion in assets to leverage change in America.

The pressures put upon him would be enormous. As Dwight Macdonald once put it, the Ford Foundation "is a large body of money completely surrounded by people who want some." Over the next thirteen years Bundy would have about $200 million to give away annually. He was determined not to fritter this money away. "I don't mind being a lightning rod for anger," he told a journalist. "Anyone serving that purpose is useful and important."[7]

In the 1950s and 1960s the foundation's instincts had been exceedingly cautious. Ford money had gone to universities, international development programs, large hospitals and elite cultural institutions such as philharmonic orchestras and opera companies. In 1962, when Ford board chairman John McCloy had solicited Bundy's opinion about the foundation's priorities, Mac had replied, "A machine filled with conventional wisdom in 1950 would have produced about 80% of the results Ford Foundation has produced. . . . But what really large and constructive forces has it let loose in our society?"[8] Four years later, Bundy intended to experiment in a big way.

As the Harvard dean or the president's national security adviser, Mac Bundy had never been faulted for procrastination. One foundation officer observed of Bundy's style, "What we have around here these days is a think tank in five-minute takes."[9] Mac thought foundations ought to do more than just study a problem. He wanted to try out various solutions, even those that might be considered risky for a charitable institution to touch. "Our job," Bundy later told the *New York Times*, "is to make our decisions, to defend and explain them, and then go on to the next one with serenity. Otherwise," he said with a shrug, "we might as well just throw the money up and see where it blows down."[10]

After only five months on the job, Bundy announced major initiatives on two of the most controversial subjects in American life: public television and the future of the American Negro.

For some years, the Ford Foundation had funded nearly half the bill for the country's infant educational television programming. But by 1966, it was clear that educational television was going nowhere. Bundy quickly decided that such a powerful medium as television should not be left entirely in the hands of commercial broadcasters. What the country needed, Mac thought, was not merely local educational programming, but a public broadcasting corporation modeled after the British Broadcasting Corporation (BBC) and dedicated to airing high-quality noncommercial programs. And Bundy knew just the man who could build such a system.

Early in 1966, Fred W. Friendly had resigned his post as president of CBS News after the network failed to carry live broadcasts of Senator Fulbright's Senate hearings on Vietnam. (Instead, CBS broadcast reruns of *I Love Lucy*.) Although Bundy thought ill of the Fulbright hearings, he nevertheless knew and admired Friendly from their collaboration during the Bundy-Morgenthau televised debate of 1965. "The day after I left CBS," Friendly said, "I had a phone call from a White House operator." It was Mac Bundy, who said, "You know I'm leaving here to be president of the Ford Foundation. We've put a hundred million dollars into educational television, and we haven't got our money's worth. Would you talk about it with me?" Mac flew up that day to New York and the two men talked until midnight. Shortly afterwards, Friendly joined the Ford Foundation and began crafting a proposal to fund public television programming by taxing network franchises.[11]

On August 1, 1966, Bundy unveiled his plan before the Federal Communications Commission: an ambitious proposal to create a public corporation that would own and operate a satellite system. Commercial television stations and the networks would be required to pay for use of the satellites to beam their programming to stations across the country. The satellite revenues would then be used to fund a national network of noncommercial programming. The press quickly dubbed the public satellite the "Bundy Bird." If approved by Congress, the monies generated from such a venture would finance a full-scale public television system for years to come. Not surprisingly, business interests, led by the phone monopoly AT&T, Comsat, Western Union and IT&T—which stood to lose millions in revenue from such a venture—vigorously lobbied against the idea. Though the press hailed the idea as "a historic occasion in the evolution of broadcasting," the Bundy Bird was allowed to die a slow death in the halls of Congress.[12]

Bundy and Friendly nevertheless pushed ahead with other schemes to build noncommercial television. In 1967 the foundation gave the newly established Public Broadcasting Laboratory $10 million in start-up funds, which were used to produce the country's first live Sunday-evening television newsmagazine. Friendly told its producers, "Don't be afraid to be controversial." A year later CBS copied the experiment with *60 Minutes*. Meanwhile, Congress passed the landmark Public Broadcasting Act in 1967, partly in response to Ford's push to give some coherence to the nation's fragmented system of public television stations. Two years later Bundy became a major architect for the creation of the Public Broadcasting Service (PBS). In place of a unified public television network, PBS's purpose was merely to help local public stations acquire high-quality programs from diverse sources. From 1968 to 1974 some $32 million of Ford Foundation money was spent to develop local public stations, and by the end of the 1970s, the foundation had spent hundreds of millions of dollars to create an alternative to commercial broadcasting.[13] Public television was Mac Bundy's creation.

Even Ford's pockets were not deep enough, however, to marshal the resources necessary for a high-quality public television network. If America's public television never came close to the quality and breadth of its British counterpart, Bundy and the Ford Foundation nevertheless could claim credit for much that was good about public programming. In the years ahead, millions of viewers would benefit from such programming as *Sesame Street*, the *MacNeil/Lehrer Report*, gavel-to-gavel coverage of the Watergate hearings and such free-spirited experimental talk shows as *Free Time*. When the groundbreaking *Bill Moyers' Journal* fell victim to the Nixon administration's budget attacks on PBS, Bundy revived the show in October 1973 with a timely grant.[14]

ON August 2, 1966, just a day after he had plunged the foundation into a firestorm of controversy with his proposal for a public television corporation, Bundy went to Philadelphia to give a speech at the annual convention of the National Urban League. His rhetoric fairly soared: "We believe that full equality of all American Negroes is now the most urgent domestic concern of the country. . . . If the ghetto pulls the central city down . . . if bad schools drive out good parents of all colors; if slums beget slums and hatred hate . . . then we shall know a time when the shame of Lincoln Steffens's cities will seem a tale of Pollyanna." In Bundy's judgment, white America was to blame for the condition of the Negro. "We believe that a wider and deeper and stronger effort among white leaders is needed so that the white American can see the problem as it really is, and recognize his need to face it, and to act."

White America, Bundy said, had to make a major commitment to end racism: "the level of effort—financial and political and personal—which is here required is fully comparable to the effort we now make as a nation in Vietnam." [15] The analogy would prove to be apt for reasons Bundy would regret. He still believed in the war effort. And in a similar vein, he was sure that if the nation turned its energies to the problem of racism, it too could be solved. His confidence was very Bundy, but also very American. And liberal. Race would dominate much of Bundy's thirteen years at the Ford Foundation. [16]

The historical facts of slavery and segregation have always festered at the heart of the American experiment in democracy. That Bundy thought of the problem of race as central is admirable. That he thought it could be addressed marked him as a quintessential American liberal. As with the war that was still raging in Southeast Asia, Bundy believed that if Americans could only marshal enough resources and commitment they could lick the enemy of racism. He would discover, however, that even in the 1960s—a decade of social upheaval and reform—America was fundamentally still a conservative society.

Mac had no expertise or even personal knowledge of racial questions. Indeed, as the civil right movement was beginning to make headlines in 1962–63, Bundy admitted he had rarely had time to read the newspaper reports about the Freedom Riders, the marches and sit-ins. Years earlier, however, he had read a book which had convinced him that race was America's Achilles' heel. "I have believed, ever since I read Gunnar Myrdal's An American Dilemma, that this question of bringing an end to racism . . . was the leading moral and political question, next only to the survival of the democratic process in the United States." [17]

That first summer at the Ford Foundation, Bundy studied the problem of race by reading numerous books and talking to black leaders. He invited them individually to his home for Sunday brunches and in small groups for dinner at the exclusive Century Club. Some of these dinners stretched late into the night, with Bundy provoking the assembled men to speak their minds.

By the summer of 1966, the civil rights movement was already splintering between advocates of integration and nonviolence—led by Dr. Martin Luther King, Jr.—and a younger group of black power advocates who argued that economic and political power for the black community was more important than the goal of a truly integrated society. The new chairman of the Student Non-Violent Coordinating Committee (SNCC), Stokely Carmichael, had popularized the term in an angry speech earlier that summer. Perhaps to demonstrate that he was not unaware of these trends, Bundy made a point in his August 2 speech to the National Urban League to mention black power, though he coyly looked up from his text and admitted that he didn't wholly "understand" the term. To the consternation of many of Mac's own friends, he would soon involve himself and the foundation in the thicket of black power politics.[18]

Initially, Bundy quickly approved major grants to such long-established civil rights organizations as the National Association for the Advancement of Colored People (NAACP), the Urban League and Martin Luther King's own Southern Christian Leadership Conference (SCLC). Culturally and historically middle class, all of these groups were integrationist and committed to nonviolence. Even so, Bundy fully understood the political consequences of giving Ford money to activists like King who were using civil disobedience, boycotts and mass demonstrations to achieve their aims. The press noted that even as Bundy was giving Dr. King's SCLC $230,000 to train ministers in the problems of the inner city, the civil rights leader was planning another march on Washington that was intended to cause the "massive dislocation" of the nation's capital. Bundy was unfazed. "Picketing," he said with a mild grimace, "is better than rioting." In the next two years Bundy roughly doubled Ford's spending —to $40 million—for programs that addressed the plight of the American Negro.[19]

Bundy was also funding such black power advocates as Floyd McKissick, the young national director of the Congress of Racial Equality (CORE). After taking over CORE in 1966, McKissick had led the organization to the left; he began speaking about the "revolution" to come, and in July 1967, CORE amended its constitution to delete the word "multiracial" from its social agenda. Two weeks later Bundy announced a Ford grant of $175,000 to CORE's chapter in Cleveland, where riots had erupted the previous summer. A foundation officer explained that the grant would demonstrate that "a militant organization can work within the system." CORE used the money to register black voters and to train community organizers. Cleveland's local political establishment was horrified. Bundy, however, felt vindicated at the polls that autumn when Cleveland elected Carl B. Stokes as the first black mayor of a major American city. "Motherhood, boy scouts, voter registration," he quipped, "everyone's for it, as an alternative to rocks and fire bombs. And it turned out that way in Cleveland." In August 1968, Bundy renewed CORE's Cleveland grant.[20]

A year later President Richard Nixon instructed a political aide, Tom Huston, to get the Internal Revenue Service to take a look at the "activities of left-wing organizations which are operating with tax-exempt funds." Huston reported back, "Certainly we ought to act in time to keep the Ford Foundation from again financing Carl Stokes' mayoralty campaign in Cleveland." Nixon replied, "Huston, follow up hard on this."[21]

Where Bundy saw his foundation taking courageous risks to help create a more open and democratic society, his critics on the right saw a tax-exempt entity using its funds for partisan political purposes. Bundy ignored the charge. When he had decided something he rarely looked back. "Look, I'm settled about this," he was heard to say in one staff meeting. "Let's not talk about it any more. I may be wrong but I'm not in doubt."[22]

After violent racial riots broke out in cities across the country in the summer of 1967, it became even harder for liberals to defend the trend in the civil rights movement toward black nationalism. But in a preface to the Ford Foundation's 1967 annual report, Bundy unflinchingly lectured the country on the broader lessons to be learned from the riots. "The first conclusion I offer," Bundy wrote, "is that the most deep-seated and destructive of all the causes of the Negro problem is still the prejudice of the white man." It was the "white man's fears and hates that must have first place" in explaining the condition of the American Negro.

Bundy went on at length to describe the problem of race in America. "I think we make a mistake when we attempt to compare the white/black relation with those between the Yankees and the Irish, or the WASPs and the Jews, or any other of the dozens of conflict-laden relations that have marked our social history. This one is so much deeper and bigger that it has a different order of meaning." As to the debate over black nationalism, Bundy observed that Negroes obviously have "the same rights as the rest of us to make their own decisions about what they will do and with whom they will associate. That much said, it seems to me the plainest of facts that the destiny of the Negro in America is to be both Negro and American, and that as he makes progress he is likely to do what the rest of us do: he will take pride in his particular group at the same time that he insists on full membership in the society as a whole. . . ."

Bundy was saying as explicitly as he could that there was room in America for black nationalism and indeed black power. The Ford Foundation would lend its resources to "attacking" white prejudice wherever it was found. As to black power, Bundy promised, with a note of defiance, that "the Ford Foundation will work with Negro leaders of good will and peaceful purpose without any anguished measurement of their position on the issue of a separated power of blackness as against the continuing claim to integration."

This was an extraordinary statement. Few white liberals were willing to listen to black power advocates. Bundy was willing to fund them. To be sure, only a small fraction of the foundation's money in 1967 was going to such political activists, and Bundy was also funding such moderate black leaders as Bayard Rustin, a former aide to the Reverend King and director of the A. Philip Randolph Institute in New York. Even so, the funding of any radicals at all was sure to be controversial. Late in 1967, Joe Alsop urged Bundy to "disengage, with due deliberate speed" from such projects. Alsop specifically warned Bundy against CORE's McKissick, and asserted that "all the Black Power people, including CORE, have now crossed the divide between rational political action and the kind of political action that will always be counterproductive and may often be socially or even legally impermissible." Bundy replied that he understood his old friend's concerns, and that although there might be mischief makers among the black militants, "I would claim that their bark is worse than their bite."[23]

By this time, Alsop also strongly disapproved of what Bundy was doing to the public school system in New York City. Like those of many big cities, New York's schools were still largely segregated. And by 1966, the local black community had given up hope that the city's school board, dominated by white liberals, would go beyond the tokenism of voluntary school busing to achieve integrated, quality schools. Black leaders began pushing for community control over their own schools—a form of black power on the local level. In the autumn of 1966, African-American parents in Harlem organized a boycott of the segregated and underfunded schools they felt were not effectively teaching their children.

Soon afterwards, at Mayor John Lindsay's invitation, Bundy agreed to chair a panel which quickly drafted a plan for decentralization of the school system. Bundy's plan was a concession to the black community, but it was also crafted as an alternative to an even more radical form of community control which would have given parents sweeping powers over both the schools' budgets and the hiring and firing of teachers. As a good liberal, his instinct, as in Vietnam, was to seize the vital center and carve out a middle course, this time, between a militant teachers union and an aroused black community. And as with Vietnam, Bundy managed to antagonize partisans of each camp.

The next spring he gave Ford Foundation grants to fund experimental community-control school boards in several black and Puerto Rican neighborhoods of the city. One such start-up grant for $59,000 went to a community school board dominated by radical activists in the Ocean Hill–Brownsville section of Brooklyn. (Eventually, Ford grants to the Ocean Hill district totaled $334,000.) Within weeks the largely black school board charged a dozen white (mostly Jewish) teachers with being "incompetent." The dispute came to a head in the spring of 1968 when the school board attempted to transfer or dismiss nineteen teachers. The teachers union responded with a strike. By the autumn, Ocean Hill–Brownsville schools were the scene of picketing and angry, often violent confrontations. Eventually, the teachers union declared a city-wide strike that caused more than a million students to lose more than forty days of school. The strike unleashed racial prejudices simmering between blacks and Jews, communities which heretofore had been closely allied in the struggle for civil rights. During the ensuing controversy the writer Michael Harrington observed, "no decent person on either side could be happy."[24]

The Bundy Plan for school decentralization and its author were blamed for creating a political conflict that gave vent to black anti-semitism and racial slurs against the black community.[25] *Commentary* magazine, a publication edited by Norman Podhoretz and read by many Jewish intellectuals, suggested that upper-crust WASPs were encouraging blacks to attack Jews out of their own residual anti-semitism. Podhoretz charged that Bundy's financing of black militants signaled "the formation of a new alliance between the patriciate and the underclass against the liberal center." He warned that "in the name of justice to Blacks, discriminatory measures were to be instituted once more against the Jews."[26]

Podhoretz's drift away from his somewhat left-of-liberal stance in the early 1960s probably began with the June 1967 Arab-Israeli war. But the real turning point for Podhoretz came with the teachers strikes of 1967–68. Podhoretz and several other once liberal Jewish intellectuals became neoconservatives in the 1970s and ardent defenders of Reaganism in the 1980s. Ironically, they turned down this path at least partly because of the heated controversies unleashed in 1967 by Bundy's plan for school decentralization in New York City. Soon, Podhoretz would be writing polemics against school busing, job quotas for minorities and public housing. In his view, liberalism had run amok and there was no better symbol of it than McGeorge Bundy.[27]

Bundy also managed to antagonize Albert Shanker, president of the United Federation of Teachers. With 55,000 members, the UFT was probably the single most powerful white-collar union in the country. Having supported the civil rights movement and opposed the war in Vietnam, the UFT boasted impeccable liberal credentials—until Bundy came to town. Shanker detested him. "Bundy has really given up on education in New York," he charged, "and is ready to destroy the schools and use them as a means of redistributing political power." The son of lower-middle-class Jewish immigrants, Shanker came from a different world than Mac's Boston Brahmin upbringing. Bundy had managed to bridge such cultural divides in the past, but not with Shanker. The union leader saw in Mac Bundy a political opponent easily caricatured. This critic of the public school system, after all, sent his four sons to a private school (Groton). Shanker made it personal. He accused the Ford Foundation of being a "political lobby" and called on Congress to revoke its tax-exempt status. In Shanker's view, Bundy embodied "the phenomenon of the guilty white liberal."[28]

Not all of Shanker's teachers agreed. During the strike some Jewish and other white teachers defied the union by continuing to work. They did so out of the belief that the conflict was more about class than race. Some who crossed the picket lines were called "commie bastards" and "nigger-lovers." The strike thus divided New Yorkers in many ways: white against black, Jewish against black, but also liberals against the left, and even left against left. Intellectuals who normally thought of themselves as political allies now suddenly had to make messy choices. Michael Harrington, the author of *The Other America*, a groundbreaking study of poverty published in 1963, accused Bundy of hawking "corporate liberalism." The Bundy Plan for decentralization, he argued, was "the very essence of 'Let Them Eat Cake.' " Such well-known New York intellectuals as Dwight Macdonald, Nat Hentoff and Jason Epstein disagreed. Writing in *The New York Review of Books* on October 10,

1968, Epstein argued that the "storefront schools" which Bundy was helping to fund had demonstrated "exemplary" success and ought to be copied. For these intellectuals, the strike was about job security for a few unionized teachers versus the effort of poor black parents to take some responsibility for educating their children. In their view, the anti-semitic rhetoric of a few black militants was unrepresentative of those black parents actually involved in the experimental community boards. Writing in *Ramparts,* a magazine of the New Left, Sol Stern argued, "Every incident of anti-Semitism was played up by the union chief [Shanker]. . . . Had the union fought for strong decentralization, with adequate legal safeguards for the rights of teachers, had they cooperated with the local governing board at Ocean Hill–Brownsville in making decentralization work, they would be in a better position today to protect their members in the ghetto." Sitting in his glass tower over at the Ford Foundation, Bundy couldn't have agreed more with the writer from *Ramparts.*[29]

Some thought it was Shanker, not Bundy, who polarized New York City in 1967–68. The angry union leader lashed out at Bundy's "support of extremists," and said he took a dim view of a "high-type foundation planner" who decided that because the system wasn't working, it was time to build "from the ashes." Shanker admitted that 80 to 85 percent of ghetto children were emerging from the schools after ten years as illiterate as when they started. "But the 15 percent who are making it are not a negligible number. At least it's something."

"I do believe," Bundy responded, "that the system is not working." And while he didn't believe that decentralization was a panacea, "reform is indispensable and that one element in reform must be a major increase in serious participation by local communities—particularly parents—in setting basic policy for their schools." Schools, he thought, must be accountable to parents. "Which doesn't mean," he was quick to add, "parents can treat teachers like hired hands."

Bundy would always win any debate in logic against someone like Shanker. His was the voice of reason. But invariably, that voice, with its slight Cambridge twang—evidence of all that education and privilege—incited class resentment.

Early in the strike Bundy had traveled around the city, talking and listening to citizens groups. Understandably, African Americans were initially suspicious of this emissary from the power elite. "When he first walked in," said one black, "I think the reaction was, oh boy, here comes another one, another untouchable, a big cold hawk-bird from Washington, made that war and all. But after a while they decided this one's all right, he's come to learn, he can learn, he keeps his word." Bundy made the same attempt to reach out to Shanker and his people, but they quickly came to the conclusion that he was the kind of upper-crust white liberal who could afford to brush off their fears of black militants.

"What ensued," wrote David Halberstam in *Harper's* in 1969, "was a particularly painful confrontation which saw the very poor and the moderately poor at each other's throats, a collision between a militant new union and militant blacks, each wanting finally to exercise power, a shattering experience against the backdrop of the city's traditional liberalism." Bundy didn't see the potential for arousing deep animosities. But then, who did? The remarkable thing is that he consciously decided in any such confrontation to side with the "very poor" and the "militant blacks."[30]

For this, some of his friends would judge him harshly. Daniel Patrick Moynihan, who like Podhoretz was then entering his own neoconservative phase, thought Bundy had unfairly raised the expectations of the poor. Similarly, Joe Alsop used his column in the *Washington Post* to warn that Bundy's school project had "opened the whole Pandora's box of race hatred in New York."[31]

In the face of such criticism, Bundy remained cool and un-apologetic. "It could still turn out," he said in the spring of 1969, "that New York, because its engagement is deepest, and because it is now in full-scale, open debate over fundamental questions, has actually begun to move ahead of the country." That's what he was telling the press. Inside the foundation, he and his colleagues felt the confrontation was good for Ford and good for the city.[32]

Bundy was nevertheless blamed for being naive, liberal and arrogant. He may have been all of these things, but he was probably also right to believe that given the facts of segregation—and white resistance to do anything concrete to desegregate public schools—the notion of some community control was reasonable and just. Taking responsibility for the education of their children might reasonably encourage African Americans to assert themselves politically in other arenas. Bundy thought black political empowerment at a community level might even reasonably become a step in the direction of a democratic and integrated society. This idea fit with what he had been learning intellectually about racial relations. Black Power might well be simply a way station on the road to racial harmony. Thirty years later Bundy's notion of community control and decentralization is still on the table as part of the solution to a terribly complex social condition.

If, in retrospect, Bundy's views appear more visionary than naive, at the time he angered many powerful political figures. On the floor of the House of Representatives, Congressman Wright Patman charged that "the Ford Foundation [had] a grandiose design to bring vast political, economic and social changes to the nation in the 1970s."[33] Patman was more right than wrong.

Fortune magazine editorialized, "He [Bundy] has . . . led the way in making the private foundation a significant third force in American life—a powerful engine for social change independent of the dominant power centers of business and government."[34] Bundy could have ensured that the Ford Foundation kept its distance from major social and cultural upheavals sweeping across America in the late 1960s. Instead, he sought out every opportunity to ride the wave of reform.

In 1968, Bundy arranged to give over a half million dollars to the Southwest Council of La Raza, a new organization which promised to do for Mexican Americans what the NAACP had done for African Americans. About the same time he authorized a $2.2 million, eight-year grant to the Mexican-American Legal Defense and Education Fund (MALDEF). In addition, he gave a grant to a youth group calling itself the Mexican American Youth Organization (MAYO). All three organizations attracted young, dedicated Mexican Americans eager to challenge both the gringo establishment and the complacency of their own ethnic communities. Soon, MALDEF had filed lawsuits across Texas charging various state and municipal governments and private companies with job discrimination, swimming pool segregation and police brutality. One suit charged discrimination in the funding of the public school system because schools in San Antonio slums were receiving only $246 per student annually versus $1,149 in the wealthy Houston suburbs. Naturally, Texas power brokers were unhappy that such troublesome issues were being raised by people whose salaries came from Ford Foundation grants.

BY 1969, though Bundy was clearly putting Ford money into the pockets of people who described themselves as social activists, progressives and agents of radical change, his name was still anathema to many on the left because of his association with the war in Vietnam. At the same time his battles with local establishments across the country over school decentralization, race, public interest law and community development had won him many enemies on the right. He was, to say the least, politically exposed.

In the end, however, it was a personal act of political charity that finally caused Congress to open full-fledged hearings on Bundy's running of the Ford Foundation. In the sad, chaotic days after Bobby Kennedy's assassination in June 1968, Bundy arranged fellowships totaling $131,000 for eight members of Kennedy's campaign staff. Recipients included Frank Mankiewicz ($15,692 for a study of the Peace Corps in Latin America), Adam Walinsky ($22,200 for a study of community action programs) and Peter Edelman ($19,090 for a study of community development programs around the world). When critics labeled the fellowships politically partisan, Bundy replied that the recipients were unusually talented men "who had been uniquely stricken in a moment of terrible tragedy." They ought, he said, to be encouraged to continue to use their talents in the public interest. Besides, the Ford Foundation had awarded similar grants to some two thousand individuals over the years.[35]

Bundy's defense didn't wash very well in Washington. Congressman Wilbur Mills's powerful House Ways and Means Committee opened hearings on the activities of various foundations. A star witness in the 1969 proceedings, Bundy was vigorously interrogated, both about the grants to Kennedy's aides and about Ford's efforts at social engineering. Characteristically, he defended himself with equal vigor, asserting that if they so desired, "the board of trustees of the Ford Foundation could give $3 billion tomorrow to any one of thousands of institutions . . . and individuals." He then went on to lecture the congressmen, "It is just as clear as it can be that foundations are a valuable and unique part of the American system."[36]

Congress nevertheless proceeded to punish Bundy—perhaps as much for his unapologetic demeanor as for his political activities—by enacting legislation that forced all foundations to pay a 4 percent tax on net annual investment income. In effect, Congress was penalizing Bundy to the tune of $10 million of the Ford Foundation's annual earnings. In addition, the legislation barred foundation officers from influencing "legislation through communications with government personnel. . . ." (Ford officials had helped the Johnson administration draft the legislation which created the Office of Economic Opportunity, an anti-poverty agency which many conservatives disliked because it had become a conduit for government funding of community activists.) And to prevent any reoccurrence of the CORE Cleveland episode, Congress specifically barred foundations from funding one-time, municipal voter registration drives.

While some aspects of the new legislation were clearly warranted, such as the stricture against self-dealing and some of the law's financial reporting requirements, many philanthropists understood that Congress was warning them not to follow the Ford Foundation down the path of funding social reform. Conservative foundations were pleased. Because all foundations were saddled with additional red tape and cumbersome reporting requirements, Bundy's colleagues in the world of philanthropy blamed him for the outcome, calling it his personal Bay of Pigs. "I admire greatly what Mac has achieved at Ford," said the executive director of another foundation. "But in my opinion most of the punitive aspects of this bill can be directly related to his behavior at the hearings."[37]

Mac had been arrogant—or as he had once admitted in a backhanded way, he "never got credit for all the fools he did suffer."[38] But Congressman Wilbur Mills and countless other politicians had made it known for years that they would like to clip the wings of foundations, particularly those involved in funding grass-roots activists working on civil rights or inner-city poverty. So it was probably true that there was nothing Bundy could have done to appease these congressional conservatives. They had a political agenda and he had his.

In response to this political backlash, Bundy essentially refused to back off. To be sure, he funded fewer projects with the high political profile of CORE. On the other hand, soon after the congressional hearings of 1969, he gave $3.5 million to set up the Washington, D.C.–based Center for Community Change, a group dedicated to organizing the poor to demand their rights (and resources) from the federal government. Its president was Jack Conway, a veteran labor union official, and on its board sat a group of former Bobby Kennedy aides, including Frank Mankiewicz, Burke Marshall and Fred Dutton.[39]

In the same vein, Bundy systematically poured money into nonprofit community development corporations in dozens of America's troubled inner cities. The first of these was the anti-poverty organization which Senator Robert F. Kennedy launched in Bedford-Stuyvesant. A black ghetto in central Brooklyn, Bedford-Stuyvesant was larger and more economically depressed than Harlem. With grants from the Ford Foundation and the Astor Foundation, by the end of 1966 Kennedy was able to announce the formation of the Bedford-Stuyvesant Development and Services Corporation. A young black lawyer named Franklin A. Thomas became the head of the organization's community action arm. John Doar, Kennedy's former deputy assistant attorney general for civil rights, directed the task of persuading business leaders to invest in the community. Working in the most difficult of circumstances, the Bedford-Stuyvesant project nevertheless won plaudits from the most skeptical of observers. A decade after its founding, the writer and political activist Michael Harrington called the project "a modest success—which, in the context of so many failures, is to say a remarkable success."[40]

Bundy quickly appreciated the potential such projects held for leveraging Ford Foundation funding. Using Ford's money, community development corporations could get some things done through the political system that Ford itself could not do. The theory was that these community-based organizations could attract private business investments by cleaning up neighborhoods and providing rudimentary social services. Just as importantly, they also served as a catalyst for bringing much-needed federal and state resources into neglected communities. In the next two decades, Ford would spend an estimated $200 million on some 2,000 CDCs across the country.[41]

Similarly, it was Bundy who pushed Ford into the contentious territory of public interest law. Bundy realized that by funding public interest lawyers to bring suits on behalf of the underprivileged he could force state and federal government to reorder budget priorities for education, worker safety, environmental protection and a host of other social issues. If, for instance, one was concerned about the maldistribution of public funding for school districts, most foundations would have commissioned a study. Bundy's strategy was entirely different. At a cost of $13 million he set up public-interest law operations across the country that eventually brought legal suits on behalf of citizen groups in poor, underfunded school districts.[42]

Over the years of Bundy's presidency these public-interest law groups spawned a whole new culture of public litigation. The legal suits filed by the Mexican-American Legal Defense and Educational Fund, the Environmental Defense Fund, the Sierra Club Legal Defense Fund, the Women's Law Fund, Georgetown University's Institute for Public Interest Representation and a host of other groups forced Congress to pass legislation on the environment, consumer protection, racial and sexual discrimination, zoning laws, health services, worker safety, public access to broadcasting and literally dozens of other public interest issues.

Bundy's decision to pour millions of dollars into these groups dramatically enhanced the power of the generally powerless—the poor, minorities, women and citizens groups determined to protect the environment—in a political battlefield normally dominated by private corporations. Fueled with Ford Foundation dollars, the field of regulatory law underwent a revolution.

Despite the controversy associated with family planning and abortion, organizations such as the Population Council benefited richly from Bundy's belief in the importance of birth control programs, both in the United States and abroad.

In a similar fashion Bundy used Ford money to underwrite the early environmental movement. He gave $400,000 to the Natural Resources Defense Council to sue the U.S. Environmental Protection Agency for not enforcing its own anti-smog standards. Such tactics angered the Nixon administration and auto manufacturers, who surely noted the irony that Bundy was using the money of the late Henry Ford—the country's chief auto pioneer—to attack auto polluters.[43]

Bundy understood and publicly acknowledged the class nature of such funding. A 1975 internal memo to the trustees defined the foundation's larger mission as the "redress of inequity" or seeking "a juster [sic] distribution of the material and nonmaterial things that society prizes most."[44] In a variety of ways, Bundy led the Ford Foundation to the left.

In another sharp departure from conventional practice, Bundy announced that Ford would place part of its investment portfolio in enterprises which he believed could bring a "high social yield." One million dollars was invested in a South Carolina steel mill owned and operated by its African-American employees. Similar socially "responsible" investments were made in companies committed to building integrated housing and decent shopping centers in black neighborhoods.[45]

Some liberals sat up and took notice of what Bundy was doing. Writing in the *Washington Post*, Nicholas von Hoffman observed that for most of its existence the Ford Foundation had been accused of timidity and excessive caution. Only under Bundy had the foundation finally broken "out of luxury into reality" by "attempting to do some useful things in the area of race relations." Writing only slightly tongue in cheek, Hoffman went on to say, "In doing so he [Bundy] was implementing the desire of that portion of the American ruling class that is usually called the Eastern Establishment. These are the couth, polished fellows who believe in fair play and enough social change to prevent the mobs on the street from stealing their money." Now that they're being yelled at by conservatives, Hoffman predicted that Bundy and his associates "won't fight back. They'll collapse."[46] Hoffman underestimated Bundy.

President Richard M. Nixon and his aides also took notice of Bundy's political activism. In 1972, Nixon aide Patrick J. Buchanan wrote a long memo to the president complaining about the "ideological bias" of the foundation: ". . . the Ford Foundation has become the Exchequer and Command Post for the entire American Left. Groups as diverse as [the] Brookings [Institution], the Fund for the Republic, NPACT TV* and the Southern Christian Leadership Conference—all depend for survival upon the financing of Bundy and his friends." Buchanan suggested that public exposure of Ford's record might frighten them away from " 'social activism,' and perhaps produce a cornucopia of Ford funds for Republican and Conservative causes—to spare Ford from being taken apart by the Congress at some future tax reform hearings. Despite the appearance of power and solidity and confidence, the Ford Foundation, like the American Left, is a paper tiger." Buchanan, too, underestimated Bundy's resiliency.[47]

IF Bundy's domestic priorities sometimes seemed to mark him as a man of the left, he remained a liberal Cold Warrior when it came to the foundation's international grants. He greatly admired the Congress for Cultural Freedom (CCF), an American organization which throughout the Cold War attempted to rally anti-communist intellectuals in Western Europe and elsewhere to the cause of freedom. Bundy knew, however, that the congress had been founded with CIA money and personnel, and continued to receive CIA funds in addition to Ford Foundation monies. Bundy knew the CIA funding, if it became known, spelled trouble. Francis Sutton, a career foundation officer, remembered Bundy coming to the Ford Foundation with the "idea that one of the things he would do right away would be to see if we couldn't bring it [the CCF] in from the cold." As it happened, Sutton was working on arrangements to phase out the CIA's funding of the CCF when the media broke the story in 1967. Bundy then asked Sutton to go to Europe and determine if the revelations had fatally damaged the congress's ability to function. He was pleased when Sutton reported back that the congress "still has the loyalty of a lot of high quality people, and therefore ought to continue." With Ford grants of about $1.5 million a year, the congress was kept alive—and pretty much ineffectual—for another decade. Ironically, many of the American intellectuals associated with the Congress for Cultural Freedom went on in the 1970s to become neoconservatives. In the words of Sutton, however, Mac remained "an unreconstructed liberal."[48]

BUNDY had taken many risks in his first several years at Ford. He could have played it safe. But he thought the foundation had to be the scout on the battlefield of social reform. Where Ford and other foundations pioneered projects that worked, the federal government could follow with much larger resources—and the force of law. "Philanthropy is a very hard business," Bundy told the journalist Milton Viorst in a 1969 interview. "It's easy to give away pretty buildings to a nice place. But our social system needs a lot of change, a lot of renewal, which is our problem too, and that's much harder."

He really didn't care if he made mistakes or made some people angry.

* The National Public Affairs Center for Television was a short-lived vehicle for national news programming created by the Ford Foundation.

"We're concerned about whether our society works," he told Viorst. "Tearing the whole structure down isn't the best thing to do, but we can't go back either. Foundations can't take the place of public policies, but we do have a continuing responsibility. It's terribly important for us to sort out what it is." Mistakes would be made, he said, because foundations "are, after all, merely human institutions." Referring to New York's school crisis, Bundy added, "We're not going to be frightened out because Ford has been criticized. Our problem now is where do we go from here. One way to avoid attention is to lie low. But we're too big. And, besides, it's wrong."[49]

When the stock market slide of the early 1970s forced the foundation to cut back on its funding, Bundy did what was necessary to cut the budget. But even then, his liberal priorities prevailed. Always open to being challenged, he allowed a group of junior program officers to form what was essentially an internal foundation called the Public Policy Committee. Chaired by Harold Howe, Mac's Skull and Bones friend whom he had recruited to be Ford's vice president for educational programs, this committee dispensed several million dollars a year on projects which were seen as too far afield from Ford's guidelines. Small grants were given to train people in public policy work. Offbeat playwrights and novelists were funded. "We did a few nutty things," Howe recalled. "We gave $10,000 to a guy who wanted to study the nine day week . . . we were criticized for that one."[50]

By and large, Bundy rarely clashed with his trustees. Despite his long-standing friendship with Henry Ford II, Mac had no problem saying no—at least initially—to the grandson of the foundation's founder. (Bundy had been an usher at Ford's first wedding in 1940, and Ford had given each of the ushers a Ford car.) When Ford asked about a contribution to the Henry Ford Hospital, Bundy bluntly told him that "giving to hospitals is not part of our program." Ford's wife, Cristina, then confronted Bundy, "How can you do this? Do you forget that the old man left three billion dollars to the foundation? He gave it to you instead of to his own children!" Bundy again said no, so Cristina appealed to Ford Foundation trustee Robert McNamara, who promised, "Cristina, I'll try to talk to Bundy. But you know how stubborn he is." After Henry Ford himself began canvassing the trustees, Bundy finally surrendered and agreed to a $100 million, one-time-only grant. But he made it clear that he had drawn the line against any further consideration for the Ford heirs.[51]

On occasion, Bundy gave grants to long-standing personal friends. In one of his first acts as president, Mac persuaded the trustees to approve a $4.5 million grant in 1966 to endow Wolfson College at Oxford University. Joe Alsop brokered the deal on behalf of their close mutual friend, the English philosopher Isaiah Berlin. "Isaiah was a friend," Bundy recalled. "Anybody who knew Isaiah learned and gained . . . your judgment is improved by trying to think as well as he does. . . . One of the first acts that I took as president of the Ford Foundation was to persuade the board, somewhat to its surprise—I guess they did it partly because I was just arrived; they didn't want to say no

—to build that college, and we did." Mac did it as much for his old friend Alsop as he did for Sir Isaiah.[52]

By and large, most of his colleagues thought Bundy made the most of his thirteen years at Ford (1966–79). Any executive in his position would have made some mistakes, and Bundy certainly made his share. He also shouldered blame for the foundation's shrinking assets. (Ford's portfolio shrank from some $3.7 billion in 1966 to $1.7 billion in 1974.) At the same time, he imparted a sense of excitement and of mission to his staff. To some, he even became a beloved figure.

Toward the end of his long tenure, however, some trustees felt Bundy had brought too much vision and too little hands-on management to his job. In 1976, Henry Ford II created a stir when he resigned as a Ford trustee and released a letter to the press that contained implicit criticisms of Bundy's priorities. The Ford Foundation, he reminded everyone, "is a creature of capitalism. . . . It is hard to discern recognition of this fact in anything the Foundation does."

Bundy's reply was dismissive: "He has a right to expect people to read his letter carefully but I don't think one letter from anyone is going to change the foundation's course." Besides, Bundy told reporters with his tight smile, wasn't it obvious that the Ford Foundation was "making the world safe for capitalism"?[53]

A year later Bundy formally announced, as he had planned for many years, that he would step down as president in 1979, when he turned sixty years of age.

He would leave the Ford Foundation with an enduring and impressive record. In a deeply conservative country experiencing an era of often divisive social change, Bundy had stubbornly persisted in his efforts to finance agents of liberal social change. More than any other foundation, Ford dominated funding of public policy grants, particularly in the fields of civil rights, public interest law, public broadcasting, environmental protection and community development. In his last annual report as president, Bundy reminded his constituency that as he looked back to the "troubles of 1969," the real threat posed by the congressional investigations of that year had been that "timid trustees would . . . shy away from controversial activity." At least at Ford, that had not happened. To be sure, "We have certainly taken greater pains, since 1969, to avoid the appearance of *hubris*," Bundy wrote, "and here the Trustees have gently instructed the president." But no one could say that Bundy had subsequently steered clear of the difficult and controversial. Not even the fact that Ford Foundation officials had made it onto Richard Nixon's "enemies list" had dissuaded them from funding projects they knew would earn the animosity of the Nixon administration.[54]

To the end, however, the question of race remained Bundy's primary concern. Despite all the setbacks and the sobering realization that racial prejudice often seemed to be an immutable fact of American life, Bundy never altered his fundamental convictions. For him, the hurdles faced by African Americans were unique and therefore required unique answers. He believed that affirmative action as a remedy was not only legitimate, but was "in some fundamental sense required by our Constitution, our history, and our intent as a nation to get past our terrible inheritance of racism." When in 1977 the *Bakke* case came before the Supreme Court to challenge the constitutionality of affirmative action, Bundy wrote a long essay on the case for *The Atlantic.*

"Precisely because it is not yet 'racially neutral' to be black in America," he wrote, "a racially neutral standard will not lead to equal opportunity." Any racially neutral criteria for admissions will result in the exclusion of African-Americans as a group; the Harvards and Yales of America would once again become a reservation of white males. Through most of our history, Bundy wrote, "most institutions of higher learning, like the rest of America, have been blatantly racist. . . . For only about ten years out of our two centuries as a nation has there been a serious nationwide attempt to make room in the higher reaches of this world for those who have been held back for so long." It would, he wrote, "seem genuinely tragic to block this great new effort at racial fairness just as it begins." If society's goal was to open such institutions to blacks, then race had to be taken into account, not for all time, but surely for more than a decade.

As it happened, Supreme Court Justice Harry Blackmun read Bundy's essay and, persuaded by its arguments, cast the fifth and determining vote in favor of upholding the constitutionality of affirmative action. In an extraordinary acknowledgment of the force of Bundy's reasoning, Justice Blackmun borrowed the language of Bundy's fundamental argument almost word for word: "To get past racism," Bundy had written, "we must here take account of race." If Justice Felix Frankfurter had been alive, he would have felt vindicated in his belief that young Mac Bundy's true calling had always been the law.[55]

African Americans would remember him as a white liberal who did more than talk. Together with Harold Howe, Bundy persuaded the Ford trustees to allocate $50 million over the years for black colleges and another $50 million to help African Americans obtain doctoral degrees at major universities across the country. When Bundy retired from the Ford Foundation (he was succeeded by Franklin Thomas), much of the country's black leadership turned out for a party hosted by Urban League president Vernon Jordan.* "I remember," Howe said, "a wonderful evening where we all sat around and drank too much and admired each other."[56]

At the end of his Ford years, Bundy gave a speech before an audience

---

* A good friend of both Bundy brothers, Vernon Jordan was recruited by Bill Bundy in the late 1980s to join the Bilderberg Group, an elite annual gathering of corporate and political leaders from both sides of the Atlantic.

largely of African Americans in which he spoke of the naiveté of the 1960s: "We were, and I don't think I was entirely out of tune . . . believers in an early solution. We thought commitment and resources would be enough. That, if you will, was a false high, a short-term reaction. The question is, do we give up. No, we believe there is still a place to attack; there are still moves you can make. If you take the longer view, you can see we have come a distance."[57] Such was the journey of a liberal philanthropist in a conservative age.

16

Vietnam Aftermath

I was never able to convince myself that there was a cost-free alternate course, as from 1961, or that any of the different strategies since proposed, especially those involving stronger military action, would have made sense. In a nutshell, my present feeling is that it was a tragedy waiting to happen, but one made much worse by countless errors along the way, in many of which I had a part.

WILLIAM P. BUNDY
June 1989

IT WAS APRIL 1971. Two thousand angry veterans of the war had descended on Washington for a five-day demonstration organized by a ragtag group called the Vietnam Veterans Against the War (VVAW). The organizers called it "a limited incursion into the country of Congress." Only soldiers who had fought in Vietnam were invited to participate. They came wearing fatigues adorned with medals and ribbons, and in the course of that weekend they threw their Bronze Stars and Purple Hearts across a high fence erected by the police to keep the demonstrators off the Capitol steps. And then they wept. One of their leaders, John Kerry, was given the opportunity to testify before the Senate Foreign Relations Committee.

Five years earlier Kerry had been a senior at Yale when Bill Bundy came to campus and gave a speech defending the war. Bundy knew Kerry—both as a Skull and Bones man and as the roommate of his nephew—and after his speech he and the young man had "quite a heart-to-heart talk about the war." Despite having vague qualms about the war, Kerry had decided to enlist in the U.S. Navy, and soon he would be on his way to the South China Sea. Bundy remembered being impressed by the young man.[1]

Kerry returned from Vietnam with a Silver Star, a Bronze Star and three Purple Hearts. But now, in 1971, Kerry wanted to know where the men were who had sent him off to war. In a scene televised to the nation, the handsome, tousled-haired Kerry—a future United States senator—spoke in measured, angry tones.

"We are also here to ask," Kerry said, "and we are here to ask vehemently, where are the leaders of our country? Where is the leadership? We are here to ask where are McNamara, Rostow, Bundy, Johnson and so many others? Where are they now that we, the men whom they sent off to war, have returned?" By their silence, the men who had planned the war were now "attempting to disown us." In response, Kerry said, the veterans were determined "to undertake one last mission—to search out and destroy the last vestige of this barbaric war, to pacify our own hearts, to conquer the hate and the fear that have driven this country these last ten years and more, so when thirty years from now our brothers go down the street without a leg, without an arm, or a face, and small boys ask why, we will be able to say 'Vietnam' and not mean a desert, not a filthy obscene memory, but mean instead the place where America finally turned and where soldiers like us helped in the turning."[2]

A month after Kerry's anguished testimony, Mac Bundy was invited by the Council on Foreign Relations to give three invitation-only, off-the-record talks on "Vietnam Revisited." The council's membership turned out in droves to hear Mac reflect on what had happened and to learn whether he had undergone a change of heart. Many were disappointed. David Halberstam stormed out of the council after one of the talks, saying at the top of his voice, "That lying son-of-a-bitch."[3]

Daniel Ellsberg flew up to New York from Washington to attend the first of Mac's lectures on May 3. That morning he had been maced by Washington police during one of the largest anti-war protests ever staged. Seven thousand demonstrators were arrested that day and penned up in RFK Stadium. Having just showered the tear gas out of his hair, Ellsberg was in an angry mood, and what he heard from Bundy's talk made him seethe. Only in a backhanded fashion did Bundy admit that the United States had been defeated. "Extrication from Vietnam," he said, "is now the necessary precondition of the renewal of the U.S. Army as an institution."[4] Worse, Bundy refused to take any questions from the audience. Afterwards, Ellsberg bumped into Bill Bundy in Cambridge and complained about his brother's performance. "He was sore at Mac," recalled Bill, who was then sharing adjacent offices with Ellsberg at MIT. "He felt he hadn't recanted. He wasn't wearing sackcloth and ashes. Dan had that Old Testament thing about him."[5] Ellsberg was at MIT that summer in part because Bill had recommended him for a university fellowship. Unbeknownst to Bill, Ellsberg was at that moment anxiously awaiting to see what the *New York Times* would do with the Pentagon Papers, a classified study of the war which he had recently handed over to the newspaper.

By June 1971, Bill Bundy had spent two years in Cambridge trying to write a book about how Vietnam had happened. MIT provided him with a senior fellowship and an office. One evening a homemade bomb exploded in a bathroom adjacent to his offices, causing $35,000 in property damage. Fortunately, no one was injured. A women's faction of the radical Weatherman's group calling itself the Proud Eagle Tribe claimed credit for the attack. No arrests were made. At the height of the anti-war demonstrations, in 1970–71, Bill's home on Brattle Street was picketed by protestors bearing placards that accused him of being a war criminal. On another occasion, Bill attended a MIT panel discussion on the war in which members of the audience stood up and accused him of being a "murderer" and "liar." The protestors became so disruptive that Bundy had to be escorted by police out of the room. Americans were still dying on the battlefields of Vietnam while Bill labored to explain how such a divisive war had begun. In such angry, passionate times, he characteristically persevered in his work, and by June 1971, he had in hand a 1,100-page manuscript that was still unfinished.[6]

On June 13 the Pentagon Papers were published by the New York Times. Ellsberg's revelations made Bill's lengthy manuscript virtually unpublishable. Bill had carefully and selectively paraphrased from the classified Pentagon Papers in his possession. The New York Times edition of the Pentagon Papers quickly became a best-seller. Bill tried that summer to rewrite the manuscript to take into account everything that Ellsberg had put into the public record. But his heart wasn't in it. The writing had been a therapeutic, almost cathartic experience: ". . . it did help to work the pain out. . . ." But he could not bear to finish it.[7]

Bill thought what Ellsberg had done was wrong; leaking government documents was a violation of his duty as a government official. He also thought the materials had been presented out of context and remarked bitterly that Neil Sheehan, who had written the lead story in the New York Times, had "much to answer for at the bar of history." On July 8, in the midst of the controversy, Bill wrote the Alsop brothers, "What a wallowing in self-righteousness is this. . . . Ellsberg is just the Whittaker Chambers of the New Left, but those who exploit him deserve less charity."[8]

Mac thought the Times's reporting on the documents was one-sided, and that the documents themselves were "just internal memoranda on things that had long since been made public." But when Ellsberg was indicted on twelve counts of conspiracy and violations of the Federal Espionage Act, Mac, to the surprise of many of his friends, nevertheless appeared for the defense at Ellsberg's trial, testifying that the release of the papers had not damaged national security.[9]

The brothers naturally disliked the retrospective judgments occasioned by the Pentagon Papers controversy. But this did not mean that they had not drawn lessons of their own. Hardly anyone noticed, but in 1971, just prior to the release of the Pentagon Papers, Mac Bundy gave congressional testimony in favor of legislation limiting presidential power to fight wars without the consent of Congress. Mac thought Johnson was wrong to have gone to war in 1965 without clear congressional authorization and he wished to prevent it from happening again.[10]

Mac would not talk about the war in public. But with the release of the Pentagon Papers, he told his colleagues at the Ford Foundation that he would meet in the auditorium with anyone who had questions about his role in the war. Not once, but at least twice, he subjected himself to these polite, but pointed exchanges. "People would go down to the auditorium," recalled his old Skull and Bones friend Harold Howe, "and chew on him, and he'd chew back."[11]

Some of Mac's friends wanted him to do much more to defend himself. But everything he had been taught at Groton and Yale (and Skull and Bones) compelled him to pay homage to that old Yankee creed: "You don't explain yourself, and you don't defend yourself." He wouldn't even allow his friends to defend his record. After the Pentagon Papers were released, Carl Kaysen and Francis Bator heard that some Bundy memorandums to the president that still remained classified recorded Mac's early doubts about the war. After Mac himself brushed their inquiry off, they went to Mary Bundy and told her, "You've got to get Mac to publicize these memos." Mary listened and asked her husband about it, but he would have nothing to do with any effort to defend his record.[12]

SHORTLY before the Pentagon Papers became public, Bill Bundy was invited by David Rockefeller to attend a Harvard-Yale football game. Bill had known Rockefeller ever since his CIA years and had always liked him.

As it happened, Rockefeller had some business to conduct with Bundy that afternoon. In his capacity as chairman of the board of trustees of the Council on Foreign Relations, Rockefeller had been authorized to sound out his friend about whether he had any interest in serving as president of the council. Rockefeller casually broached the subject to Bundy as they sat in the bleachers. Bill hesitated. The presidency was an administrative and fund-raising job, and what he wanted was intellectual work. Soon he confessed that his real aspiration was to edit the council's flagship publication, *Foreign Affairs.* Upon hearing this, Rockefeller offered him the job on the spot. Bill accepted.

When news of the decision leaked to the press, a firestorm erupted within the council. A substantial and vocal minority of its members argued that Bundy's record as one of the chief architects of the Vietnam War made him morally and politically unfit to edit the journal. Richard Ullman, Richard J. Barnet and Richard Falk were among Bundy's critics. Ullman, who had helped to compile the Pentagon Papers and hence was familiar with Bundy's role in the war, wrote a letter to Rockefeller protesting Bundy's selection, but he was also careful to disassociate himself from some of the language being used by Bundy's critics.

Barnet, who received anti-semitic mail from other council members, explained his position to a reporter from the *Washington Post:* "This was a man [Bundy] who was willing consistently—despite evidence of some private doubts . . . who was willing to service this policy . . . to put great effort and energy into deceiving the Congress, into deceiving the public. . . . He displayed a pattern of conduct which is criminal." Professor Falk's memo to the council asserted, "Mr. Bundy's role in planning and executing illegal and criminal war policies in Indochina should disqualify him from holding an editorial position of this kind." David Rockefeller dismissed the tempest, saying, "Why, I know all the Bundys, and they're a fine, upright family." [13]

Bundy was pained by the personal attacks but refused to withdraw his candidacy. He complained to reporters of the "demagoguery" and charged that some of the criticisms were "McCarthyite in flavor." Referring to Vietnam, he said, "We were probably quite wrong in all this, but certainly we were honest." When it was over, he won the editorship by a two-thirds vote of the council's board of directors. Ken Galbraith, who had earlier resigned from the council "out of sheer boredom," remarked that *Foreign Affairs* "is already so unreadable that I don't see how Bill Bundy can do it any damage." [14]

To the surprise of many readers of *Foreign Affairs*, Bill Bundy opened its pages to critics of the war. Soon after he became editor, Bill made a point of inviting Richard Barnet to lunch. Barnet had just published *Roots of War*, a book which accused Bundy and other national security managers of "bureaucratic homicide." In the course of their luncheon conversation, Bundy demonstrated that he had indeed read the book and took its critical thesis seriously. A few years later Bundy published one of Barnet's essays in the journal. Bundy also reached out to another critic, Richard Ullman, who soon began to write frequently for *Foreign Affairs*. They eventually became good friends and neighbors in Princeton, New Jersey.

Throughout much of the 1970s, both Bundys had a running feud with President Nixon's national security adviser, Henry Kissinger, much of which was reflected in the pages of *Foreign Affairs*, where they criticized Kissinger's handling of the Vietnam War, his support for right-wing dictatorships and his flip-flops on various arms-control issues. Bill remained editor of *Foreign Affairs* until 1984, when he retired to work on a book critical of the Nixon-Kissinger foreign policy. [15]

AFTER their children left home for college and careers, both Bundy wives had careers of their own. Mary "Mac" Lothrop Bundy surprised her husband in the late 1970s by announcing that she was going back to school. In 1980, she earned a masters degree in social work and then went to work for the Jewish Board of Family and Children's Services in Brooklyn. Mary "Bill" Acheson Bundy also acquired a career late in life as a serious painter, holding numerous exhibitions in the 1980s and 1990s.

By all accounts, both Bill and Mac were good, even beloved fathers. Their children coped with the burden of having fathers who led such contentious public lives. Bill's two sons (Michael and Christopher) and daughter (Carol) went to Harvard and Yale and pursued careers in the arts. Mac sent all four of his sons to Groton, and all of them finished college and grew into stable, interesting young men with careers and wives and children.

At times, however, in the late sixties and early seventies, the younger Bundys were reminded that their surname was inextricably linked to the Vietnam War. One day at Harvard, Mac's eldest son, Stephen McGeorge Bundy, walked into the offices of the *Crimson* and found the editors throwing darts at a photograph of his father pinned to the dartboard. Later, as a by-stander to one of the confrontations between police and anti-war demonstra-tors in Cambridge, Stephen was roughed up by the police and had to be taken to the emergency room for a few stitches. After law school, he practiced corporate law but eventually left a lucrative job with Cravath, Swaine & Moore to teach law.[16] Mac's other sons also fared well. James became a theater director, William went into real estate, and Andrew became a community organizer and fund-raiser on the West Coast. Eventually, Andrew moved back to Boston where he went to work for the public school system. Andrew is the most political of Mac's sons. "Yelling 'war criminal' at someone like my father may feel good," Andrew once told *Mother Jones,* "but it cuts off the dialogue that could have happened." Andrew is very much a Bundy in his father's image. "It sounds a little strange, but the values I learned around the dinner table and at my grandmother's in the summer are the values that inform my feminism and my socialism. You have a responsibility to others. You must serve. It's very Puritan; it's very noblesse oblige, very much a part of my class ethos, and it can make for good radicals."[17]

In 1976, Mac flew up to Cambridge at the invitation of Jim Thomson, Jr., who was then running Harvard's prestigious Nieman fellowships for journalists. After eight years of not being on speaking terms, they had reconciled, and Thomson was delighted to have the Ford Foundation president lecture his Nieman class. In the question-and-answer session, however, one young jour-nalist, Ron Javers—whom Thomson remembered as a Leon Trotsky look-alike —needled Mac with questions about the war. Mac finally ended the exchange by saying, "Your problem, young man, is not your intellect but your ideol-ogy."

Not to be put off, Javers later cornered Mac at a cocktail reception and said, "What about Vietnam?"

"I don't understand your question," Mac replied.

"Mac, what about you and Vietnam?"

"I still don't understand," Mac said.

"But Mac, you fucked it up, didn't you?"

The glacial silence that followed was broken only when Bundy smiled and said, "Yes, I did. But I'm not going to waste the rest of my life feeling guilty about it."

Later that evening Thomson drove Mac to the Harvard Square subway station (Bundy said he loved to ride Boston's "T"). During the short drive

Bundy spoke with some melancholy about the encounter. With a note of resignation he told Jim, "I'll never be appointed secretary of state—or even a university president." But then he allowed as he had decided that someday he wanted to work on the overriding problem of nuclear weapons, and perhaps write a book. He sounded upbeat about it. He sounded, Thomson remembered, as if he truly wasn't going to waste the rest of his life because of Vietnam.[18]

Few people, however, particularly in academia, would let him forget the war. In 1979, upon leaving the Ford Foundation, he was appointed to the history department at New York University. But no sooner had it been announced than twenty-four professors who were soon to be his colleagues protested the appointment. Later, many of these faculty members were pleasantly surprised to find that Bundy invariably supported them on tenure decisions and other issues attending to university governance. In the faculty lounge, he was their liberal ally, while down the hallway in the classroom they lectured their students about his responsibility for the war. To some of these colleagues, it was all slightly unnerving.

In 1988, Mac Bundy published *Danger and Survival: Choices About the Bomb in the First Fifty Years.* The book deservedly won favorable reviews from a wide range of critics. In 1998, after fourteen years of painstaking labor, Bill published a major history of his own, *A Tangled Web: The Making of Foreign Policy in the Nixon Presidency.* The book is both a serious history and a severe indictment of the policies executed by his successors. Nixon and Kissinger, Bill writes, "deceived" the American "public, and especially Congress, far too often." Their judgment was "erratic and often subjective, and their vision too narrow." Bundy conceded that American policy in Indochina from the early 1950s right through the end of the war in 1975 was a "disaster." But he argued that what happened during Nixon's years in power was particularly blameworthy. "The price that was paid to sustain Nixon's Indochina policy—especially in Asian lives, in destruction in Indochina, and in continued disunion and demoralization of the American people—was even more out of proportion to results achieved than in earlier periods."[19]

Throughout the 1980s the brothers wrote numerous articles and opinion pieces, and otherwise participated in public debates over a host of issues. Mac was particularly active, defending the notion of affirmative action and criticizing the Reagan administration's profligate defense spending policies in the 1980s. In 1982, together with George Kennan, Gerard Smith and Robert McNamara, Mac wrote a major essay in *Foreign Affairs* arguing that the United States should abandon its policy of "first use" of nuclear weapons in the event of a Soviet invasion of Western Europe. The essay made headlines around the world. In subsequent years, he became a leading arms-control advocate, urging dramatic cuts in the world's nuclear arsenal.

In 1984, Mac Bundy told a writer from *Mother Jones* (after a couple of tall scotches), "The Vietnam War is not a black-and-white issue. If you want to know how I feel about it now, my answer would depend on what year of the war you're talking about." If he had regrets, he suggested, it was about the decisions in 1965. "I did have reservations about that and it can be argued that I didn't press hard enough. But I didn't see any way of leaving Vietnam alone and simply getting out in 1965. Oh yes, I worry about that all the time, but I'm not prepared to sort it out yet. That's going to have to happen some years from now."[20] Only in the 1990s, in the years before he died, did Bundy try to confront what had happened. He left an unfinished manuscript in which he confessed, "I had a part in a great failure." But the thesis he was trying to develop when he died would nevertheless have emphasized the "centrality of presidential leadership." In effect, he was blaming the war on Lyndon Johnson's determination to send in combat troops—a decision Bundy in retrospect thought John Kennedy would have avoided. At the same time, he knew he shared some real responsibility for the decisions made in that fateful July. In his own reckoning, he concluded, "Since on balance I am in favor of trying harder, not heading for the exit, I am ready to help the president do it his way; he's the boss. I am for more explanation, and more congressional participation . . . more emphasis on [Saigon's] contribution . . . a less open-ended commitment. The president knows all that and prefers his course. I help him. That's an indispensable part of what the White House staff is for."[21]

At first glance, this is a plausible summary of what happened. As Mac told an audience at the Cosmos Club in 1967, "Gray is the color of truth."[22] But it is not very satisfying to those who fought for or against the war to be told that one of its chief architects was actually terribly ambivalent about both the initial decision to go to war and the less than candid way in which it was prosecuted. Worse, there is something diminishing—not merely self-deprecating—in the portrayal of an intellectual like Mac Bundy merely carrying out the president's orders. And in any case, if both brothers had private doubts about Lyndon Johnson's course of actions in 1964–65, neither of them forcefully brought those doubts to the attention of the president in a fashion which would have compelled Johnson to reconsider his inclination to intervene with large numbers of ground troops. Indeed, far from voicing dissent, the brothers often encouraged Johnson to think that he could not easily walk away from Vietnam. The Bundys lacked the courage to insist on their doubts and instead consistently chose the easier path of steering the president toward what they thought was a middle course. That is their personal tragedy and the nation's.

Why did presidential loyalty require Bundy to continue to defend the war long after he left government in 1966? And why, when in 1969–70 it was clear that Kissinger and Nixon were prolonging the war, did both brothers fail to come out forcefully against the war and the Vietnamization policies that were prolonging it? The Bundys never answered these hard questions.

THERE was always a quality in the character of both brothers that was somwhat remote and reserved. In the case of Mac this distant demeanor vanished with familiarity. To his friends, he was a source of warmth, wit and sheer fun. As the years passed, both brothers loosened up. But Bill was always far more reserved, though certainly always the more gracious brother with strangers.

Bill dealt with the personal burden of Vietnam in a far more forthright fashion than his brother. Because he had little patience for dredging up the past, Mac only grudgingly talked about the war with a number of serious historians. But Bill seemed willing to talk to almost any scholar, exposing himself to the same endless questions. For him, this was an intellectual duty. He prepared for the interviews, studied the documents shown him by scholars and honestly tried to engage their arguments. When a number of military figures—most notably, General William Westmoreland—published "revisionist" accounts suggesting that the war could have been won if only the civilians had not forced the military to fight with "one hand tied behind their back," Bill quietly demurred. Even in hindsight, he always believed "there was no military way to win the war that the American public would have supported for the time it would have taken to make it effective."[23] Blaming the war on Halberstam's "best and brightest," he would argue, ignored the centrality of Lyndon Johnson's role, and failed to appreciate the "depth of the dilemmas he [Johnson] confronted at every stage." For Bill, the system worked. The deliberations over the war constituted "a rational and careful process that still produced disastrous decisions."[24]

Within his own circle of friends and colleagues in the Council on Foreign Relations he could be far more reticent. "The only time Bill ever talked to me about Vietnam," recalled his deputy editor, James Chace, "he said it all went wrong 'when the means used far exceeded the ends sought.' "[25]

In 1989, on the occasion of the fiftieth Yale class of '39 reunion, Bill waxed philosophical about his life. He felt "terribly fortunate," he wrote for a Yale reunion publication, "to find life happy and rewarding." His career in international affairs had been "extraordinarily fortunate both in opportunities and colleagues." Abruptly changing tone, he went on to acknowledge that there had been a blight in his life: "The blight was, of course, my deep involvement in a key phase of the Vietnam War. Its personal impact remains trivial alongside what the war did to young men and our country, but it was especially hard on Mary and the children. . . . I was never able to convince myself that there was a cost-free alternate course, as from 1961, or that any of the different strategies since proposed, especially those involving stronger military action, would have made sense. In a nutshell, my present feeling is that it was a tragedy waiting to happen, but one made much worse by countless errors along the way, in many of which I had a part."[26]

This was a confession of sorts, certainly more heartfelt than his brother would ever make. But was it true that because there were no "cost-free" alternatives, Vietnam was inevitable, a "tragedy waiting to happen"? Did it have to happen? Or to put it another way, were the Bundy brothers aware at the time of all the arguments for not sending combat troops to Vietnam? Yes. Were they ignorant of the dangers of Americanizing the war effort? No. Were they naive about the nature of the Saigon regime? Not at all. Did they understand the history of the Vietnamese struggle? Did they realize that

Americans were gambling that they could win in Indochina what the French colonialists had lost? Absolutely. Were they aware of how risky this gamble was? Yes. They knew these things, but they failed to pass on their doubts to President Johnson. In June 1965, Mac warned Johnson's defense secretary, Robert McNamara, that his program was "rash to the point of folly." But he failed to use the same strong words with the president. Similarly, the previous November, Bill had crafted a memorandum for McNamara and Rusk filled with "all the heresies," making the argument for walking away from Vietnam. But when McNamara said it wouldn't "wash" Bill folded. He never sent this memorandum to the president. In the end, both brothers argued with themselves, wrestled with the long odds against success and still found it possible, even necessary, to take the gamble.

The gamble was not a requirement of the Cold War. George Ball, Clark Clifford and many of Mac Bundy's own deputies were also Cold War liberals, yet they did not think it was necessary to draw the line in Vietnam. The Bundys talked themselves into thinking that the line had to be drawn against wars of national liberation somewhere in Southeast Asia and that it might as well be in Vietnam. If you bought into the assumptions about America's stake in the Cold War, then a war somewhere like the one that was fought in Vietnam was probably inevitable. As such, the Cold War was a necessary precondition for the Vietnam War, but it was not by itself sufficient to explain Lyndon Johnson's decisions in the summer of 1965.

Domestic politics had something to do with the compulsion to intervene in the Vietnamese civil war. As liberals serving two liberal Democratic presidents the Bundy brothers were particularly afraid of being tarred by the right wing with having "lost" Vietnam to the global communist menace. As intellectuals, they knew such a charge was ridiculous. They were not ideologues. They understood that the notion of a monolithic communist movement directed from Moscow was mythical. They were aware of the Sino-Soviet split and its geopolitical implications for U.S. foreign policy. They thought the so-called domino theory simplistic and even dangerous as a guide to policy. They always emphasized that the most important factor in the outcome of the war was the internal political dynamics of the entity called South Vietnam. They knew that society was not a nation. And they knew the war could be won only if the Saigon regime acquired the genuine characteristics of nationhood. They knew all this, and still felt compelled to help Lyndon Johnson Americanize the war.

Tragically, when it became clear that their doubts were being realized, they did not even consider the possibility of speaking out publicly. Neither did Bill nor Mac consider a public resignation. Far from protesting the carnage, Mac quietly left the White House and continued to support the war in public, while Bill loyally stayed the course, trying to make the best of a war that would not end until America withdrew its shattered men. This was their worst and most personal mistake, a failure of imagination and courage.

■

On Wednesday, September 11, 1996, Mac Bundy spent five hours working with his research assistant, Gordon Goldstein, a Columbia University doctoral student. By then Mac had pieces of a small manuscript, an intellectual memoir on the Vietnam War. Goldstein recalled that Mac was in his usual good form that day, full of energy and stamina, eager to read more of the archival documents, insatiable in his appetite for more questions. He was having fun with the project, and was telling friends that unlike McNamara, he was not writing a book which "pointed fingers at others." His would not be a defensive book.

Late that afternoon Mac ran off to keep an appointment for a routine physical. His doctor gave him a clean bill of health. Later that week, he flew up to his summer home—his parents' old home—in the Bundy compound at Manchester-on-the-Sea. He intended to spend the long weekend relaxing, staying up late as was his habit, perhaps playing with his mother's old jigsaw puzzles, some of them now sixty or seventy years old and as large as the dining room table. The old house hadn't really changed much since his childhood days when he and Bill and Harvey and the girls had played with the same jigsaw puzzles, gone swimming and played softball with his mother as umpire. Manchester would always be home.²⁷

Saturday evening he was stricken with a heart attack. He was rushed in an ambulance to Massachusetts General Hospital in Boston, where he died Monday afternoon, September 16. He was seventy-seven years old.

He was buried the following Saturday, September 21. The service was held in St. John's Church, the same church in Beverly Farms, Massachusetts —just a few miles down the road from Manchester—where he and Mary had been married forty-six years before. Mary insisted on a small service attended by family members and a few of Mac's closest friends. A hundred and fifty people came. Bill was there, of course, and his sisters, Harriet Belin and Laurie Auchincloss, along with his eldest brother, Harvey. Also present were all four of Mac's sons and daughters-in-law. A few of his Skull and Bones mates, led by Gordon Grayson, also came. Arthur Schlesinger, Jr., came, and so too did Fred Friendly from Mac's Ford Foundation years. Ken Galbraith couldn't make it, but the widow of Kingman Brewster flew all the way from England to attend the funeral. The family managed to keep the press away, in part by announcing that there would be a public memorial service later in New York City. But just to be sure, a young man was stationed at the entrance to the church, armed with a list of those invited, who checked the names of everyone attending.

Harold Howe II, a Skull and Bones man from the Yale class of 1940, and a godfather to one of Mac's sons, gave the eulogy. He began by making everyone laugh by telling a story about the young man he had known so long ago. "In the more than fifty years of my friendship with McGeorge Bundy," Howe said, "I noticed only one shortcoming in his character, and that was his lack of affection for the outdoors." He then related how he had once visited his friend at Henry Stimson's Highhold estate when the young Harvard junior fellow was working on the Colonel's memoirs. Over a fine dinner, Stimson had regaled Howe with tales of his hunting expeditions at the turn of the century. "Mac was bored," Howe recalled, "and to prove it he went to sleep and snored while the secretary was talking."

Without naming the war, Howe gently touched on the painful history that weighed so heavily on everyone in attendance: "The major crosscurrent in Mac's life, created by five years as the adviser of two presidents on international affairs, brought a mixture of great achievements, deep frustration, self-examination and a long-term commitment to a peaceful world. A hundred years from now, these matters will still be debated. . . . It must be said, however, that many people with varied viewpoints hold positive views supporting Mac's integrity, even as they question some of his judgments." Howe went on to praise Bundy's work at the Ford Foundation and his "great contribution" to the world in thinking and writing about how to live with "that dreadful weapon"—the atomic bomb. He ended on another wry note of affection, saying, "In my sixty years of friendship with him, I can't recall his mentioning the hereafter, but wherever his spirit is now, it is a better place for his presence."

The service followed the spare Episcopal ritual for the funeral mass. Bundy's name wasn't even mentioned until halfway through the service. The last hymn sung was the nation's unofficial anthem, "America the Beautiful." It brought tears to the eyes of his family and friends. Afterwards, Mary held a reception in the Manchester house.[28]

Six weeks later, another memorial service was held in New York at St. James Church. Hundreds were invited and hundreds came, including Cyrus Vance, Bill Moyers, Carl Kaysen, Nathan Pusey, Louis Auchincloss, Theodore Sorensen and Nicholas Katzenbach. Curiously, not a few of Bundy's critics attended the event, including such old adversaries as Henry Kissinger, Marcus Raskin and Robert Silvers, the editor of The New York Review of Books.* Mac's Cambridge friend and former White House colleague Francis Bator gave a spirited eulogy in which he noted that a lot of good things had happened on Bundy's watch in the White House. And then he asserted, "With the one very bad thing that happened he had much less to do than the common version of the Vietnam story would have it." Bator then quoted from Mac's June 30, 1965, note to McNamara "that this program is rash to the point of folly." It was as good a defense as could be mounted by a loyal friend.

In death as in life, McGeorge Bundy was certain to provoke strong opinion. His death gave partisans on all sides occasion to reargue all the passions of the

---

* Upon receiving his invitation to the memorial service, Kissinger phoned to ask if there would be reserved seating for "VIPs." When Mary Bundy heard of his inquiry, she expressed the hope that Kissinger would not attend.

war that had torn the country apart. The *Washington Post*—whose publisher, Katharine Graham, had once offered Mac the job of supervising the editorial page of her newspaper—now labored to defend the man and his legacy. If his name was "inextricably linked to the costly and bitter defeat" of Vietnam, the *Post* reminded Americans that this was not the full measure of the man. Bundy had shared in "making explicit and operative the national moral and political purposes of foreign policy." His intentions—and by implication, the intentions of Cold War America—had been laudable and honorable. "The American role in the Vietnam War, for all its stumbles, was no accident. It arose from the deepest sources—the deepest and most legitimate sources—of the American desire to affirm freedom in the world." Besides, according to the *Post*, Bundy had criticized the war two years after leaving office when the count of American dead "exceeded any reasonable expectations of gain. Or, in the parlance of the day, he came out 'against the war.' And so he did. Many did, including President Nixon, to whom it fell to end the direct American involvement." By such a standard, Bundy looked good. Knowing this to be overly generous, the newspaper's editorial writers were quick to add without further comment, "Mr. Bundy was criticized for the relative tardiness and modesty of his turn." Still, in the view of the *Post*, this was a man who went on "to make other contributions to his country."[29]

The *New York Times* was decidedly more caustic, highlighting Bundy as a man who "was the very personification of what the journalist David Halberstam . . . labeled 'The Best and the Brightest': the well-born, confident intellectuals who led the nation into the quagmire of Vietnam." The *Times* pointedly reminded readers of Bundy's role as a war hawk by quoting at length from his February 7, 1965, memorandum to President Johnson, urging a policy of "sustained reprisal" against North Vietnam. The obituary mentioned only briefly Mac's thirteen-year tenure as president of the Ford Foundation.[30]

Time magazine's managing editor, Walter Isaacson, wrote that Bundy had come "to personify the hubris of an intellectual elite that marched America with a cool and confident brilliance into the quagmire of Vietnam."[31]

Writing in *George*, a new political magazine edited by John F. Kennedy, Jr., son of the slain president Mac had served, Arthur Schlesinger, Jr., wistfully noted that Bundy represented "the last hurrah of the Northeast Establishment. He was the final executor of the grand tradition of Henry Stimson, Dean Acheson, Averell Harriman, Robert Lovett, John J. McCloy—patricians who, combining commitment to international responsibility with instinct for command and relish in power, served the republic pretty well in the global crises of the twentieth century." On a personal level, Schlesinger remembered his friend as a man of "sparkling personality, witty and elegant." Bundy, he said, had displayed the courage to "transcend the politics and the complaisancies of his class." Born a privileged Republican, he had become a liberal Democrat. "A single tragic error," Schlesinger concluded, "prevented him from achieving his full promise as a statesman."[32]

James C. Thomson, Jr., whose dovish counsel Bundy had simultaneously tolerated and ignored, wrote an op-ed piece in the *New York Times* defending his old boss. "In my view, the obit writers got it wrong," Thomson said. "The man, and the circumstances, were a lot more complex." [33]

The obituary writers, the devoted friends, the hardened, bitter critics all possessed pieces of the man. Mac Bundy was all these things. He and his brother Bill were complex men. As high-ranking officials of the American establishment they exercised considerable power and influence at the height of the Cold War. As intellectuals they wrote about the atomic bombing of Hiroshima, the quandary of nuclear weaponry, the ethical and political dilemmas posed by McCarthyism, the problem of racism in America, the Cold War and the Vietnam War. Their books and other writings thus helped to shape the historical record that they had lived. They were remarkably intelligent and thoughtful men who had the capacity to write critically about what they had done as mandarins in power. Ultimately, they were liberals of the "vital center" whose ambitions for themselves and their country were shattered by the Cold War compulsion to wage an unjust and unwinnable war far from home. Theirs was indeed a peculiarly American tragedy.

Notes

THIS BOOK was written largely from the documentary record found in the presidential libraries of John F. Kennedy and Lyndon Baines Johnson. From 1992 to 1996, I had eight interviews with McGeorge Bundy and ten interviews with William P. Bundy. Each of these interviews averaged two hours in length and most of them were taped. Altogether, I interviewed eighty individuals. I was fortunate to be able to take advantage of thousands of pages of newly declassified documents, particularly those presidential tape recordings related to the 1962 Cuban missile crisis and the Vietnam War. In response to a Freedom of Information Act request, the State Department released in 1997 some five hundred pages of previously classified documents from William Bundy's papers as assistant secretary of state.

This book also contains critical material from the private and official papers of Averell Harriman and Michael V. Forrestal, an aide to McGeorge Bundy from 1962 to 1965. I was given access to these papers by Harriman prior to his death in 1986. Many of Harriman's memorandums of conversations and particularly Forrestal's memos to McGeorge Bundy contain previously unpublished information about the early decisions on the Vietnam war.

ABBREVIATIONS

AH	Averell Harriman Papers, Library of Congress and author's archives
CFR	Council on Foreign Relations Archives, New York, NY
CUOH	Columbia University Oral History Collection, New York, NY
DDE	Dwight D. Eisenhower Presidential Library, Abilene, KS
FF	Ford Foundation Archives, New York, NY
FOIA	Freedom of Information Act
FRUS	Foreign Relations of the United States
GCM	George C. Marshall Library, Lexington, VA
GS	Groton School Archives, Groton, MA
HH	Herbert Hoover Presidential Library, West Branch, IA
HL	Houghton Library, Harvard University, Cambridge, MA
HST	Harry S Truman Presidential Library, Independence, MO
HU	Harvard University Archives, Cambridge, MA

JFK	John F. Kennedy Presidential Library, Boston, MA
JJM	John J. McCloy Papers, Amherst College, Amherst, MA
LBJ	Lyndon B. Johnson Presidential Library, Austin, TX
LOC	Library of Congress Manuscript Collection, Washington, D.C.
MB	McGeorge Bundy interview by the author
MF	Michael V. Forrestal papers, author's archives
NA	National Archives
NS	National Security Archive, Washington, D.C.
NYT	*New York Times*
PU	Princeton University Seeley Mudd Manuscript Library, Princeton, NJ
SL	Schlesinger Library, Harvard University, Cambridge, MA.
WP	*Washington Post*
WPB	William P. Bundy interview by the author
WPB Vietnam Manuscript	William P. Bundy manuscript on file at the John F. Kennedy and Lyndon B. Johnson Presidential Libraries
Yale	Yale University Archives, New Haven, CT

INTRODUCTION

1. Donald Woutat, "89 Jailed in City Sit-In: Northfield Group Blocked Federal Building Doors," *Minneapolis Star,* May 7, 1970. Among those arrested with us were two Carleton College faculty members, one of whom, a twenty-five-year-old untenured professor of government, Paul Wellstone, would be elected a U.S. senator from Minnesota in 1990.

2. Neil Sheehan, *A Bright Shining Lie: John Paul Vann and America in Vietnam* (New York: Random House, 1988), p. 592.

3. MB interview, Sept. 19, 1995.

4. James C. Thomson, Jr., "How Could Vietnam Happen?: An Autopsy," *The Atlantic,* April 1968, pp. 47–53.

5. Neil Sheehan et al., *The Pentagon Papers as Published by The New York Times* (New York: Bantam, 1971), pp. 423–27; George Kahin, *Intervention: How America Became Involved in Vietnam* (New York: Knopf, 1986), pp. 281–83; Lyndon Johnson, *The Vantage Point: Perspectives of the Presidency, 1963–1969* (New York: Holt, Rinehart and Winston, 1971), pp. 126–27. Bundy also came back from Vietnam with a new respect for the enemy: "They can appear anywhere—and at almost any time. They have accepted extraordinary losses and they have come back for more. They show skill in the sneak attacks and ferocity when cornered." Even so, he forced himself to conclude, "[T]he weary country does not want them to win." (Michael H. Hunt, *Lyndon Johnson's War: America's Cold War Crusade in Vietnam, 1945–1968* [New York: Hill & Wang, 1996], pp. 90–91.)

6. Larry Berman, *Planning a Tragedy: The Americanization of the War in Vietnam* (New York: Norton, 1982), pp. 187–89.

7. William Conrad Gibbons, *The U.S. Government and the Vietnam War,* part II (Princeton: Princeton University Press, 1989), pp. 330–42; WPB Vietnam Manuscript, ch. 27, p. 8.

8. WPB memo, June 25, 1965, "Ideas and Possible Outline for Project," TOP SECRET, FOIA document declassified Jan. 14, 1997.

9. Lloyd C. Gardner, *Pay Any Price: Lyndon Johnson and the Wars for Vietnam*

(Chicago: Dee, 1995), pp. 291–92; Untitled Notes, Feb. 15, 1966, Bundy Papers, Box 2, LBJ.

10. *NYT,* Apr. 30, 1950; Bruce Cumings, *The Origins of the Korean War: The Roaring of the Cataract, 1947–1950* (Princeton: Princeton University Press, 1990), p. 387.

11. *Annual Report, Ford Foundation, 1967.*

12. Richard H. Pells, *The Liberal Mind in a Conservative Age: American Intellectuals in the 1940s and 1950s* (Middletown, Conn.: Wesleyan University Press, 1989).

1: HARVEY HOLLISTER BUNDY: THE PATRIARCH

1. Drew Pearson and Robert Allen (published anonymously), *Washington Merry-Go-Round* (New York: Liveright, 1931), pp. 107, 109. Godfrey Hodgson, *The Colonel* (New York: Knopf, 1990), p. 390.

2. Henry Stimson and McGeorge Bundy, *On Active Service in Peace and War* (New York: Harper and Bros., 1948), pp. 108–109; Richard N. Current, *Secretary Stimson: A Study in Statecraft* (New Brunswick, N.J.: Rutgers University Press, 1954), pp. 7, 12.

3. Kai Bird, *The Chairman: John J. McCloy/The Making of the American Establishment* (New York: Simon & Schuster, 1992), p. 19.

4. Charles A. Beard, *President Roosevelt and the Coming of the War, 1941* (New Haven: Yale University Press, 1948), p. 239.

5. Current, *Secretary Stimson,* p. 120.

6. Ibid., p. 248.

7. David Halberstam, *The Best and the Brightest* (New York: Random House, 1972), p. 49.

8. "Family Matters: Conversations with Katharine Lawrence Putnam Bundy, 1978," taped and edited by Jessica D. Warren, SL (hereafter cited as KLPB Oral History), p. 48.

9. Harvey H. Bundy Oral History, CUOH (hereafter cited as HB Oral History), pp. 5, 10, 19, 22.

10. KLPB Oral History, p. 3.

11. Ibid., pp. 14, 35–36, 39–40, 44.

12. David Halberstam, "The Very Expensive Education of McGeorge Bundy," *Harper's,* July 1969, p. 24.

13. HB Oral History, p. 61.

14. Ibid., p. 70.

15. Katharine L. Bundy interview by John S. Monagan, July 10, 1980, p. 10, courtesy of Monagan.

16. Liva Baker, *Felix Frankfurter* (New York: Coward-McCann, 1969), p. 35; Ronald Steel, *Walter Lippmann and the American Century* (Boston: Little, Brown, 1980), p. 121.

17. HB Oral History, p. 66.

18. KLPB Oral History, p. 45; John S. Monagan, *The Grand Panjandrum: The Mellow Years of Justice Holmes* (Lanham, Md.: University Press of America, 1988), p. 66.

19. KLPB Oral History, pp. 47–49.

20. Katharine Bundy interview by Monagan, p. 37.

21. HB Oral History, pp. 76–80.

22. Harriet Bundy Belin interview, June 20, 1993, and KLPB Oral History, pp. 51–52.

23. Scott Donaldson, *Archibald MacLeish: An American Life* (Boston: Houghton Mifflin, 1992), pp. 102, 122.

24. KLPB Oral History, p. 55; ibid., p. 103.

25. MB interview, Apr. 21, 1992.

26. KLPB Oral History, p. 61.

27. WPB interview, Aug. 19–20, 1992; Harriet Bundy Belin interview, June 20, 1993; Milton MacKaye, "Bundy of the White House," *Saturday Evening Post*, Mar. 10, 1962, p. 82.

28. Harriet Bundy Belin interview, June 20, 1993.

29. Harvey Bundy, Jr., interview, June 20, 1993; ibid.

30. MB interview, Apr. 21, 1992.

31. Milton Viorst, *Hustlers and Heroes: An American Political Panorama* (New York: Simon & Schuster, 1971), p. 273.

32. KLPB Oral History, p. 60; WPB interview, Aug. 19–20, 1992; Benjamin C. Bradlee interview, Dec. 17, 1993.

33. HB Oral History, p. 87.

34. In 1924, Bundy published a magazine article defending "tax evaders" like William G. Rockefeller who had sheltered millions of dollars from the federal income tax by investing in tax-exempt securities. Harvey H. Bundy, "Hit or Miss Tax Enforcement," *The Independent*, Nov. 22, 1924, p. 425.

35. KLPB Oral History, p. 49.

36. HB Oral History, pp. 97–99.

37. Ibid., p. 112.

38. Henry L. Stimson diary, May 10–11, 1931, LOC.

39. Henry L. Stimson diary, June 1, 1931, LOC.

40. KLPB Oral History, p. 54; Stimson diary, Jan. 2, 1933, LOC; WPB interview, Aug. 19–20, 1992.

41. Harriet Bundy Belin interview, June 20, 1993.

42. WPB interview, Aug. 19–20, 1992.

43. KLPB Oral History, pp. 54, 69.

44. HB Oral History, pp. 306–307.

45. WPB interview, Aug. 19–20, 1992.

46. HB Oral History, p. 106; Henry L. Stimson diary, Sept. 11, 1931, LOC; Current, *Secretary Stimson*, p. 44.

47. HB Oral History, pp. 113–18.

48. Current, *Secretary Stimson*, pp. 97, 107–108.

49. Harriet Bundy Belin interview, June 20, 1993.

50. KLPB Oral History, p. 53; Stimson diary, Mar. 4, 1933, LOC.

51. WPB interview, Aug. 19–20, 1992.

2: GROTON: A VERY EXPENSIVE EDUCATION

1. Al Laney, *Prep Schools* (Garden City, N.Y.: Doubleday, 1961), p. 53.

2. E. Digby Baltzell, *The Protestant Establishment: Aristocracy & Caste in America* (New York: Random House, 1964), p. 113.

3. Frank D. Ashburn, *Peabody of Groton: A Portrait* (Cambridge: Riverside, 1967), p. 218.

4. Archie Roosevelt, *For Lust of Knowing: Memoirs of an Intelligence Officer* (Boston: Little, Brown, 1988), p. 23; Marshall Green interview, Oct. 16, 1992.

5. WPB interview, Aug. 19–20, 1992; *Views from the Circle: Seventy-five Years of Groton School* (Groton, Mass.: The Trustees of Groton School, 1960), p. 35.

6. James MacGregor Burns, *Roosevelt: The Lion and the Fox* (New York: Harcourt, Brace & World, 1956), p. 12.

7. WPB interview, Aug. 19–20, 1992.

8. MB interview, Apr. 21, 1992; Marshall Hornblower interview, Mar. 18, 1993.

9. Roosevelt, *For Lust of Knowing*, p. 25.

10. Louis Auchincloss, *A Writer's Capital* (Minneapolis: University of Minnesota Press, 1974), p. 38.

11. Ashburn, *Peabody of Groton*, pp. 96–97.

12. *Views from the Circle*, p. 243; Auchincloss, *A Writer's Capital*, p. 69.

13. Roosevelt, *For Lust of Knowing*, p. 24; David C. Acheson, *Acheson Country: A Memoir* (New York: Norton, 1993), p. 40; John Gunther, *Roosevelt in Retrospect*, (New York: Pyramid, 1962), p. 184.

14. WPB interview, Aug. 19–20, 1992.

15. Marshall Green interview, Oct. 16, 1962; Marshall Hornblower interview, Mar. 18, 1993.

16. Cleveland Amory, *The Proper Bostonians* (New York: Dutton, 1947), pp. 88–89.

17. Auchincloss, *A Writer's Capital*, p. 38.

18. Marshall Hornblower interview, Mar. 18, 1993.

19. Louis Auchincloss interview, Feb. 15, 1994.

20. WPB interview, Aug. 19–20, 1992; MB interview, Apr. 21, 1992.

21. Richard K. Irons interview, July 14, 1992.

22. William McCormick Blair, Jr., interview, Nov. 30, 1992.

23. MB interview, Apr. 21, 1992; WPB interview, Aug. 19–20, 1992.

24. Baltzell, *The Protestant Establishment*, p. 249.

25. Burns, *Roosevelt*, p. 15.

26. Amory, *The Proper Bostonians*, p. 323.

27. George Biddle, *An American Artist's Story* (Boston: Little, Brown, 1939), p. 67.

28. McGeorge Bundy to Scott Buchanan, Aug. 26, 1935, Miriam T. Buchanan Papers, HL.

29. MB interviews, Apr. 21 and Dec. 2–3, 1992; McGeorge Bundy, "Reform," *The Grotonian*, May 1935, pp. 185–88.

30. Auchincloss, *A Writer's Capital*, pp. 53–61.

31. Louis Auchincloss interview, Feb. 15, 1994.

32. WPB interview, Aug. 19–20, 1992; Richard K. Irons interview, July 17, 1992.

33. Richard K. Irons interview, July 14, 1992; David Halberstam, *The Best and the Brightest* (New York: Random House, 1972), p. 52.

34. Stanley Resor interview, Apr. 5, 1993; Marshall Hornblower interview, Mar. 18, 1993.

35. Harriet Bundy Belin interview, June 20, 1993; MB interview, Apr. 21, 1992.

36. Harvey H. Bundy, Jr., interview, June 20, 1993; John S. Monagan, *The Grand Panjandrum: The Mellow Years of Justice Holmes* (Lanham, Md.: University Press of America, 1988), p. 29.

37. Stanley Resor interview, Apr. 5, 1993.

38. KLPB Oral History, p. 112.

39. Richard K. Irons interview, July 14, 1992.

40. MB interview, Dec. 2–3, 1992.

41. *The Grotonian*, vol. 51, no. 8 and vol. 52, no. 4.

42. By the time of his death in 1944, Peabody had married over one-third of Groton's graduates (Amory, *The Proper Bostonians*, p. 315).

43. Groton alumni include Frank L. Polk (1890); Joseph C. Grew (1898); Franklin Delano Roosevelt (1900); Francis Biddle (1905); Theodore Roosevelt, Jr. (1906);

W. Averell Harriman (1909); Junius Spencer Morgan, Jr. (1910); B. Sumner Welles (1910); Dean Acheson (1911); J. Pierrepont Moffat (1913); F. Trubee Davison (1914); John Jay Pierpont (1919); Samuel Reber (1921); James Roosevelt (1926); C. Douglas Dillon (1927); Joseph W. Alsop, Jr. (1928); Richard M. Bissell, Jr. (1928); C. Tracy Barnes (1929); John A. Bross (1929); Stewart Alsop (1932); Jonathan B. Bingham (1932); W. Osborn Webb (1932); Franklin D. Roosevelt, Jr. (1933); Kermit Roosevelt (1934); William McCormick Blair, Jr. (1935); William P. Bundy (1935); Marshall Green (1935); Stanley Resor (1935); McGeorge Bundy (1936); Archibald B. Roosevelt, Jr. (1936); and Francis M. Bator (1943).

44. Halberstam, *The Best and the Brightest*, p. 51; Marshall Hornblower interview, Mar. 18, 1993; Richard K. Irons interview, July 14, 1992.

45. Joseph W. Alsop, with Adam Platt, *"I've Seen the Best of It": Memoirs* (New York: Norton, 1992), p. 59; Marshall Green interview, Oct. 16, 1992.

3: YALE: THE "GREAT BLUE MOTHER"

1. MB interview, Apr. 21, 1992.

2. Marshall Green unpublished diary, June 26, 1935, courtesy of Green.

3. Marshall Green unpublished diary, June 25–27, 1935.

4. Marshall Green unpublished diary, July 10, 1935; Marshall Green interview, Oct. 16, 1992.

5. WPB interview, Aug. 19–20, 1992.

6. Marshall Green unpublished diary, July 31, 1935.

7. Marshall Green interview, Oct. 16, 1992; MB interview, April 21, 1992.

8. Brooks Mather Kelley, *Yale: A History* (New Haven: Yale University Press, 1974), pp. 371, 376, 389.

9. George Wilson Pierson, *Yale: The University College, 1921–1937* (New Haven: Yale University Press, 1955), p. 423.

10. Dan A. Oren, *Joining the Club: A History of Jews and Yale* (New Haven: Yale University Press, 1985), p. 66; WPB interview, Aug. 19–20, 1992.

11. *Yale Class Yearbook: 1939*, p. 188.

12. WPB interview, Aug. 19–20, 1992.

13. William P. Bundy letter to Stanley Resor, April 1992, courtesy of Resor.

14. *A History of the Class of 1940, Yale University.*

15. Stanley Resor letter to Bill Bundy, April 2, 1993, courtesy of Resor, and Stanley Resor interview, Apr. 5, 1993.

16. WPB interview, Aug. 19–20, 1992.

17. Oren, *Joining the Club*, p. 66.

18. Gordon Grayson interview, July 28, 1993; MB interview, Apr. 21, 1992; *A History of the Class of 1940, Yale University*, p. 89

19. Oren, *Joining the Club*, pp. 24, 67; Gordon Grayson interview, July 28, 1993.

20. Oren, *Joining the Club*, p. 23.

21. WPB interview, Aug. 19–20, 1992.

22. McGeorge Bundy, *Yale Daily News*, May 6, 11, 1938. Two boys tapped by Skull and Bones that week declined the invitation.

23. MB interview, Dec. 2–3, 1992.

24. Marshall Green interview, Oct. 16, 1992.

25. Kelley, *Yale*, p. 224.

26. Richard Bissell interview, July 13, 1992; Ron Rosenbaum, "An Elegy for Mumbo Jumbo," *Esquire*, September 1977, p. 148.

27. *NYT*, Nov. 4, 1988.

28. Mark Singer, "La Cabeza de Villa," *The New Yorker*, Nov. 27, 1989; Rosenbaum, "An Elegy for Mumbo Jumbo."

29. WPB interview, Aug. 19–20, 1992.

30. MB interview, Dec. 2–3, 1992.

31. *NYT*, May 12, 1991, p. 23; MB interview, Dec. 2–3, 1992.

32. WPB interview, Aug. 19–20, 1992; MB interview, Dec. 2–3, 1992.

33. Gordon Grayson interview, July 28, 1993. Grayson was Mac Bundy's closest friend in Skull and Bones.

34. Ibid.

35. WPB interview, Aug. 19–20, 1992.

36. Kingman Brewster, "Pre-War Uncertainty," *Seventy-five: A Study of a Generation in Transition* (New Haven: Yale Daily News, 1953), p. 66.

37. Milton MacKaye, "Bundy of the White House," *Saturday Evening Post*, Mar. 10, 1962; *Yale Daily News*, May 13, Oct. 10, 12, Nov. 4, Dec. 14, 1938.

38. William Kunstler interview, July 29, 1994.

39. David Dellinger, *From Yale to Jail: The Life of a Moral Dissenter* (New York: Pantheon, 1993), p. 25; Walt Rostow interview, Dec. 16, 1992.

40. Dellinger, *From Yale to Jail*, p. 192.

41. Brewster, "Pre-War Uncertainty," p. 65; Gordon Grayson interview, July 28, 1993.

42. WPB interview, Aug. 19–20, 1992.

43. MacKaye, "Bundy of the White House."

44. *Yale Daily News*, Oct. 3, 1938.

45. William Kunstler interview, July 29, 1994.

46. WPB interviews, Aug. 19–20, 1992; Mar. 11, 1993.

47. William Bundy letters to Dean Acheson, Dec. 15, 1937; Feb. 3, 1938, Acheson Papers, Yale.

48. WPB interviews, Aug. 19–20, 1992; Mar. 11, 1993.

49. McGeorge Bundy, et al., *Zero Hour: A Summons to the Free* (New York: Farrar & Rinehart, 1940), pp. 81–83, 87–88, 92, 110.

50. MB interview, Apr. 21, 1992.

51. Archibald MacLeish letter to MB, Jan. 3, 1940, Box 4, MacLeish Papers, LOC.

52. Gordon Grayson interview, July 28, 1993; MB to Archie MacLeish, Sept. 26, 1940, Box 4, MacLeish Papers, LOC.

53. Richard Norton Smith, *The Harvard Century: The Making of a University to a Nation* (New York: Simon & Schuster, 1986), p. 97.

54. Seymour Martin Lipset and David Riesman, *Education and Politics at Harvard* (New York: McGraw-Hill, 1975), p. 316.

55. Harvard, *Crimson*, May 13, 1954, p. 2.

56. Archie MacLeish wrote the society, "Mac seems to me as attractive as a human being as he is promising as a young scholar. He has a warm and keenly perceptive mind and a degree of maturity which is, in my experience, quite unusual in a boy of his age. If I may say so, I think it would be a grand thing all around." (MacLeish to Professor Lawrence Henderson, Jan. 28, 1941, Box 4, MacLeish Papers, LOC.)

57. Carl Kaysen interview, June 18, 1993; Francis X. Sutton interview, Dec. 1, 1994.

58. MB interview, Dec. 2–3, 1992. Bundy lost to Democrat Frank Foster by a margin of thirty-five votes.

4: THE WAR YEARS, 1941–1945

1. KLPB Oral History, p. 91.

2. HB Oral History; Henry L. Stimson and McGeorge Bundy, *On Active Service in Peace and War* (New York: Harper & Bros., 1948), p. 343.

3. KLPB Oral History, pp. 91–93.

4. WPB interview, Mar. 11, 1993.

5. David McCullough, *Truman* (New York: Simon & Schuster, 1992), p. 951.

6. Zeph Stewart interview, June 16, 1993.

7. *Boston Globe,* Jan. 31, 1943; WPB interview, Mar. 11, 1993.

8. Zeph Stewart interview, June 16, 1993.

9. WPB interview, Mar. 11, 1993.

10. WPB interview, Mar. 11, 1993; Thomas Parrish, *The Ultra Americans: The U.S. Role in Breaking the Nazi Codes* (New York: Stein & Day, 1986), p. 100.

11. Arthur J. Levenson interview, Apr. 8, 1992.

12. Alfred Friendly, "Confessions of a Code-Breaker," *WP,* Oct. 27, 1974.

13. Parrish, *The Ultra Americans,* p. 108; Gordon Welchman, *The Hut Six Story: Breaking the Enigma Codes* (New York: McGraw-Hill, 1982), p. 135.

14. Arthur Levenson interview, Apr. 8, 1992.

15. Peter Calvocoressi, *Top Secret Ultra* (New York: Pantheon, 1980), p. 13.

16. Parrish, *The Ultra Americans,* p. 121.

17. Calvocoressi, *Top Secret Ultra,* p. 96.

18. William P. Bundy, "Some of My Wartime Experiences," *Cryptologia,* April 1987, p. 73.

19. Parrish, *The Ultra Americans,* pp. 118, 121.

20. W. P. Bundy, "Some of My Wartime Experiences," p. 68.

21. Malcolm Muggeridge, *Chronicles of Wasted Time: The Infernal Grove* (New York: Quill, 1982), p. 129.

22. Parrish, *The Ultra Americans,* pp. 165–67; Friendly, "Confessions of a Code-Breaker."

23. WPB interview, Mar. 11, 1993; Friendly, "Confessions of a Code Breaker."

24. WPB interview, Mar. 11, 1993.

25. MB–Archibald MacLeish letters, June 19, 25, 1942, Box 4, MacLeish Papers, LOC.

26. Milton MacKaye, "Bundy of the White House," *Saturday Evening Post,* Mar. 10, 1962.

27. MB interview, Dec. 2–3, 1992.

28. McGeorge Bundy, "Ultra Warnings," in Paul Stillwell, ed., *Assault on Normandy: First-Person Accounts from the Sea Services* (Annapolis: Naval Institute Press, 1994).

29. Isaac Kramnick and Barry Sheerman, *Harold Laski: A Life on the Left* (New York: Allen Lane/Penguin, 1993), p. 335. See also McGeorge Bundy correspondence, Frankfurter Papers, LOC.

30. MB interview, Dec. 2–3, 1992. In April 1944, Mac spent an afternoon with the playwright George Bernard Shaw.

31. John Mason Brown, *Many a Watchful Night* (New York: Whittlesay House, 1944), p. 148.

32. MB interview, Dec. 2–3, 1992; McGeorge Bundy, "Ultra Warnings"; Milton Viorst, *Hustlers and Heroes: An American Political Panorama* (New York: Simon & Schuster, 1971), p. 276. Captain McGeorge Bundy was awarded a Bronze Star medal for "meritorious service . . . during the assault on Normandy" (U.S. Navy Naval Command Press Release, Dec. 8, 1944, *Washington Post* Library).

33. MB to John Mason Brown, Jan. 29, 1945, Brown Papers, HL.

34. Calvocoressi, *Top Secret Ultra*, p. 110.

35. W. P. Bundy, "Some of My Wartime Experiences," p. 76.

36. HB Oral History, p. 211.

37. James B. Conant, *My Several Lives: Memoirs of a Social Inventor* (New York: Harper & Row, 1970), pp. 280–81; HB Oral History, pp. 176–77; James Hershberg, *James B. Conant: Harvard to Hiroshima and the Making of the Nuclear Age* (New York: Knopf, 1993), p. 155; Harvey H. Bundy, "Remembered Words," *Atlantic Monthly*, March 1957, p. 57.

38. HB Oral History, pp. 177, 229, 235, 262–74, 243–46.

39. Kai Bird and Lawrence Lifschultz, eds., *Hiroshima's Shadow: Writings on the Denial of History and the Smithsonian Controversy* (Stony Creek, Conn.: Pamphleteer's Press, 1998), pp. 90–98.

40. Harvey Bundy memo, unsigned, undated, "Do We Need Russia in the Japanese War?" Harvey Bundy War Department papers, courtesy of Sanho Tree.

41. Kai Bird, *The Chairman: John J. McCloy/The Making of the American Establishment* (New York: Simon & Schuster, 1992), p. 248.

42. WPB interview, Mar. 11, 1993.

43. MB interview, Dec. 2–3, 1992; Archie MacLeish to MB, Mar. 16, 1945, Box 4, MacLeish Papers, LOC.

44. Harvey Bundy letter to Katharine Bundy, July 21, 1945, courtesy of G. d'Andelot Belin and Harriet Bundy Belin. After receiving yet another Japanese peace feeler—this time through Allen Dulles in Switzerland—McCloy noted in his diary, "Maybe the Secretary's big bomb may not be dropped—the Japs had better hurry if they are to avoid it" (John J. McCloy diary, July 27, 1945; DY Box 1, Folder 18, JJM).

45. KLPB Oral History, pp. 100–101.

46. Bird and Lifschultz, eds., *Hiroshima's Shadow*, pp. li–liv.

47. Godfrey Hodgson, *The Colonel: Henry Stimson's Life and Wars, 1867–1950* (New York: Knopf, 1990), p. 350; Stimson to Colonel John Spencer Muirhead, Dec. 12, 1947, Stimson Papers, LOC; Bird, *The Chairman*, p. 261.

48. Hodgson, *The Colonel*, p. 355.

49. Stimson and Bundy, *On Active Service*, pp. 642–45.

5: STIMSON'S SCRIBE

1. MB to John Mason Brown, Oct. 6, 1943, Brown Papers, HL.

2. Stimson diary, Sept. 4, 1945, LOC.

3. Godfrey Hodgson, *The Colonel: Henry Stimson's Life and Wars, 1867–1950* (New York: Knopf, 1990), p. 367.

4. Cass Canfield to Arthur Page, June 10, 1946, Stimson Papers, LOC.

5. James Hershberg, *James B. Conant: Nuclear Weapons and the Cold War, 1945–1950*, thesis for Tufts University, May 1989, p. 140.

6. James Hershberg, *James B. Conant: Harvard to Hiroshima and the Making of the Nuclear Age* (New York: Knopf, 1993), p. 284.

7. Kai Bird, "The Curators Cave In," *NYT*, Oct. 9, 1994.

8. Hershberg, *James B. Conant*, p. 292.

9. Kai Bird and Lawrence Lifschultz, eds., *Hiroshima's Shadow: Writings on the Denial of History and the Smithsonian Controversy* (Stony Creek, Conn.: Pamphleteer's Press, 1998), pp. 305–306.

10. Hershberg, *James B. Conant*, p. 285.

11. Hershberg thesis, p. 167; Hershberg is citing Conant to H. Bundy, Sept. 23, 1946.

12. Hershberg, *James B. Conant*, pp. 293–94.

13. Ibid., p. 294.

14. Ibid., pp. 294–95; Stimson to Frankfurter, Dec. 12, 1946, Frankfurter Papers, LOC.

15. Hershberg thesis, p. 172; Rudolph Winnacker, the army historian, wrote Bundy his own analysis, which he published in *Military Affairs* (Spring 1947).

16. Barton J. Bernstein, "Seizing the Contested Terrain," *Diplomatic History* (Winter 1993), pp. 46–47.

17. Ibid., p. 47.

18. Hershberg, *James B. Conant*, p. 297.

19. Ibid., p. 298.

20. Ibid., p. 833.

21. McGeorge Bundy to Henry Stimson, Feb. 18, 1947, Stimson Papers, LOC. In the same letter, Bundy describes Truman as "the little man in the White House. . . ."

22. Hershberg thesis, pp. 180, 183.

23. Bundy acknowledged that he could not recall any documentary source for the million casualty figure (MB interview, Dec. 2–3, 1992). In June and July 1945 the Joint Chiefs reasoned that if the Kyushu invasion took place in November, American forces could expect 132,000 casualties (25,000 fatalities) and a total of 220,000 casualties if the invasion of Honshu took place in the spring of 1946 (Bernstein, "Seizing the Contested Terrain," p. 48). See also "Memorandum of Comments on Ending the Japanese War," GAL—14 June 1945; Memorandum for the Secretary of War from Gen. Marshall, 15 June 1945, both contained in Folder 29, Box 84, Marshall Papers, GCM. Bird and Lifschultz, eds., *Hiroshima's Shadow*, pp. 130–40.

24. William R. Castle diary, Feb. 9, 1947, HH.

25. Grew to Stimson, Feb. 12, 1947, Eugene H. Dooman Papers, Atomic Bomb file, Box 2, Hoover Institution on War, Revolution and Peace. Excerpts of this letter are reproduced in Joseph C. Grew, *Turbulent Era: A Diplomatic Era of Forty Years*, vol. II (Boston: Houghton Mifflin, 1952), p. 1428.

26. Stimson to Joseph Grew, June 19, 1947, Stimson Papers, LOC.

27. William R. Castle diary, Jan. 26, 1947, p. 19; Feb. 9, 1947, p. 28, HU, courtesy of Sanho Tree. Castle later wrote Herbert Hoover, "It was simply a lie to say he [Stimson] had no idea Japan was ready to surrender and this vitiates all the rest of what he said" (June 6, 1948, HH).

28. Stimson statements to Mac Bundy, "Atomic Energy," pp. 176–77, Stimson Papers, LOC. (Note that this particular transcript is dated "HLS 7/9/46" but discusses the *Harper's* piece and therefore must have been misdated as 1946 instead of 1947.)

29. Stimson statements to Mac Bundy, pp. 176–77, Stimson Papers, LOC.

30. George Kennan to MB, Dec. 2, 1947, Marshall Papers, GCM

31. MB to George Kennan, Dec. 4, 1947, Marshall Papers, GCM.

32. MB to George Kennan, Dec. 22, 1947, Stimson Papers, LOC.

33. Henry Stimson and McGeorge Bundy, *On Active Service in Peace and War* (New York: Harper & Bros., 1948), p. 629.

34. *Foreign Affairs*, July 1948; *The New Republic*, May 10, 1948; *Saturday Review of Literature*, Apr. 17, 1948; *Survey G*, May 1948.

35. J. Samuel Walker, "The Decision to Use the Bomb: A Historiographical Update," *Diplomatic History* (Winter 1990), p. 110; Gar Alperovitz, *The Decision to Use the Atomic Bomb and the Architecture of an American Myth* (New York: Knopf, 1995); Martin Sherwin, *A World Destroyed: Hiroshima and the Origins of the Arms Race* (New York: Knopf, 1975; Vintage, 1987); J. Samuel Walker, *Prompt & Utter Destruction: Truman & the Use of Atomic Bombs Against Japan* (Chapel Hill: University of North Carolina Press, 1997); Bird and Lifschultz, eds., *Hiroshima's Shadow*.

36. McGeorge Bundy, *Danger and Survival: Choices About the Bomb in the First Fifty Years* (New York: Random House, 1988), p. 88.

37. Ibid., pp. 94, 647. Bundy later wrote Barton J. Bernstein, "I agree that it is not at all clear where the 'million casualties' came from." (MB to Bernstein, Nov. 29, 1991, courtesy of Bernstein). See also Alperovitz, *The Decision to Use the Atomic Bomb,* p. 468.

38. McGeorge Bundy, *Danger and Survival,* p. 92. When the historian Barton Bernstein later wrote a scholarly article critical of Bundy's hidden role in the *Harper's* article, Bundy vigorously defended himself: "As for me, why should I not assist—as a law clerk might assist a judge—as long as the final document said what Stimson himself wanted to say. . . . I think the bomb article was much more like a political speech, where no one expects any draftsman to claim credit. . . . That of course does not excuse errors or overstatements, and the article contains both." (MB to Bernstein, Nov. 29, 1991, courtesy of Bernstein.)

39. McGeorge Bundy, *Danger and Survival,* pp. 92–93, 97.

40. *The MacNeil/Lehrer NewsHour,* Aug. 6, 1985, transcript #2572.

41. Bernstein, "Seizing the Contested Terrain," pp. 35–72.

42. Stimson and Bundy, *On Active Service,* p. xi.

6: PORTRAIT OF A YOUNG POLICY INTELLECTUAL, 1948–1953

1. Gerald T. Dunne, *Hugo Black and the Judicial Revolution* (New York: Simon & Schuster, 1977), pp. 261–64; MB to Frankfurter, July 20, 1947, Frankfurter Papers, LOC.

2. MB to Frankfurter, Sept. 30, 1947, Frankfurter Papers, LOC; MB interviews, Apr. 21, 1992; Nov. 3, 1994.

3. MB to Frankfurter, Sept. 30, 1947, Frankfurter Papers, LOC. "They were perfectly friendly," recalled Louis Auchincloss, "but there was nothing doing. . . . both Gregor and Mac were individuals who made up their own minds about things. But Helen Lippmann was distraught. " 'Why can't we snag him?' [she said.]" (Louis Auchincloss interview, Feb. 15, 1994.)

4. Ronald Steel, *Walter Lippmann and the American Century* (Boston: Little, Brown, 1980), p. 455; MB to Frankfurter, Sept. 30, 1947, Frankfurter Papers, LOC.

5. Walter Lippmann to MB, Jan. 8, 1948, Lippmann Papers, Yale.

6. Steel, *Walter Lippmann and the American Century,* pp. 322–26.

7. MB to Walter Lippmann, Jan. 19, 1948; June 6, 1949, Lippmann Papers, Yale.

8. Peter Grose, *Gentleman Spy: The Life of Allen Dulles* (Boston: Houghton Mifflin, 1994), p. 289.

9. MB interview, Dec. 2–3, 1992; Richard Norton Smith, *Thomas E. Dewey and His Times* (New York: Simon & Schuster, 1982), pp. 518–19.

10. Steel, *Walter Lippmann and the American Century,* pp. 454–55; Francis X. Sutton interview, Dec. 1, 1994; MB interview, Dec. 2–3, 1992.

11. Frankfurter to Bundy, Dec. 1, 1948; Bundy to Frankfurter, Dec. 3, 1948, Frankfurter Papers, LOC.

12. MB interview, Nov. 3, 1994.

13. MB to Frankfurter, Dec. 3, 1948, Frankfurter Papers, LOC.

14. Victor Navasky, *Naming Names* (New York: Viking, 1980), p. 52.

15. MB to Walter Lippmann, June 6, 1949, Lippmann Papers, Yale. "I was also more crusadingly anti-Stalinist than Mac," Schlesinger said, "because communism, Stalinism was not a problem for the Republican Party, but it was a problem for the liberal community, which is why, I guess, I was more engaged in it than they were" (Arthur Schlesinger, Jr., interview, June 6, 1995).

16. Richard Rovere, *Final Reports: Personal Reflections on Politics and History in Our Times* (Middletown, Conn.: Wesleyan University Press, 1984), pp. 132–36.

17. MB to Frankfurter, Apr. 19, 1949, Frankfurter Papers, LOC.

18. Martin Walker, "Gentleman Spies," *NYT Book Review*, Nov. 12, 1995, p. 55; Sallie Pisani, *The CIA and the Marshall Plan* (Lawrence: University Press of Kansas, 1991), p. 73.

19. Arthur Schlesinger, Jr., interview, June 6, 1995; Burton Hersh, *The Old Boys: The American Elite and the Origins of the CIA* (New York: Scribner's, 1992), pp. 307–308, 158.

20. Bundy argued that when he "stressed the importance of peace as a goal of policy he had in mind those people who want to drop bombs on the Russians in a preventive war. Their line of argument ignores the fact that a great deal has been achieved in just avoiding fighting." He also opposed the rearming of Germany. "To rearm the German nation," Bundy wrote in his council paper that summer, "because of the Russian danger would be monstrous folly. . . . Germany as a disarmed and neutralized area can become a stable element in a world at peace; no other kind of Germany can make this claim." (Meeting of Sept. 26, 1949, Records of Groups, vol. XXX 1948/51, CFR.)

21. MB handwritten undated letter to Dean Acheson, with Acheson's reply dated Jan. 18, 1949, Box 4, Folder 51, Acheson Papers, Yale. Dean Acheson, *Present at the Creation: My Years in the State Department* (New York: Norton, 1969), p. 251.

22. Philip M. Cronin, "Yale Man McGeorge Bundy Named Dean of Harvard's College Faculty," Harvard *Crimson*, registration issue, September 1953.

23. David Halberstam, *The Best and the Brightest* (New York: Random House, 1972), p. 56.

24. MB to Frankfurter, Sept. 29, 1949, Oct. 7, 1949, Frankfurter Papers, LOC.

25. MB interview, Dec. 2–3, 1992; Milton MacKaye, "Bundy of the White House," *Saturday Evening Post*, Mar. 10, 1962.

26. KLPB Oral History, p. 105; MB to John Mason Brown, Jan. 2, 1950; John Mason Brown to MB, Jan. 5, 1950, Brown Papers, HL; MacKaye, "Bundy of the White House."

27. Zeph and Diana Stewart interview, June 21, 1993; Ben Bradlee interview, Dec. 17, 1993.

28. Carl Kaysen interview, June 18, 1993. A gift from Kaysen and other of Bundy's White House staff, the silver dice were engraved with the words "A Decision Making Tool."

29. MB interview, Dec. 2–3, 1992.

30. Halberstam, *The Best and the Brightest*, pp. 56–57.

31. McGeorge Bundy, "The Attack on Yale," *The Atlantic*, November 1951, pp. 50–52.

32. William F. Buckley, Jr., "The Changes at Yale," *The Atlantic*, December 1951, pp. 78–83.

33. Lester Tanzer, ed., *The Kennedy Circle* (New York: Luce, 1961), p. 35; Michael Wreszin, *A Rebel in Defense of Tradition: The Life & Politics of Dwight Macdonald* (New York: Basic Books, 1994), p. 274.

34. McGeorge Bundy, ed., *The Pattern of Responsibility: From the Records of Dean Acheson* (Boston: Houghton Mifflin, 1952), p. vi.

35. MB interview, Apr. 5, 1993.

36. McGeorge Bundy, *The Pattern of Responsibility*, pp. vi–xi.

37. McGeorge Bundy, "Were Those the Days?" *Daedalus*, Summer 1970, p. 566.

38. McGeorge Bundy, *The Pattern of Responsibility*, p. ix.

39. Ibid., p. 34.

40. Ibid., pp. 26, 31–34.

41. Ibid., pp. 34–35.

42. MB interview, Nov. 3, 1994; McGeorge Bundy, "The Missed Chance to Stop the H-Bomb," *New York Review of Books*, May 13, 1982, p. 19; MB to Oppenheimer, Apr. 7, 1952, Box 191, Oppenheimer Papers, LOC.

43. When Mary Bundy gave birth to their second son, Oppenheimer wrote Mac a note of congratulations and enclosed a four-leaf clover, "for both of you and your new child" (Oppenheimer to MB, Sept. 14, 1955, Box 122, Oppenheimer Papers, LOC).

44. MB to James R. Killian, Jan. 20, 1953; "Panel of Consultants on Arms and Policy—Minutes of Meeting, May 16–18, 1952, Princeton, N.J.," Box 191, Oppenheimer Papers, LOC.

45. James B. Hershberg, *James B. Conant: Harvard to Hiroshima and the Making of the Nuclear Age* (New York: Knopf, 1993), pp. 602–603, 902.

46. Ibid., p. 604.

47. Ibid., p. 605.

48. McGeorge Bundy, "Early Thoughts on Controlling the Nuclear Arms Race," *International Security* 7:2 (Fall 1982).

49. Ibid., pp. 12, 15, 19–20.

50. McGeorge Bundy, "The Missed Chance to Stop the H-Bomb," *New York Review of Books*, May 13, 1982, p. 16.

7: DEAN BUNDY OF HARVARD, 1953–1960

1. See David Caute, *The Great Fear: The Anti-Communist Purge Under Truman and Eisenhower* (New York: Simon & Schuster, 1978); Victor Navasky, *Naming Names* (New York: Viking, 1980).

2. James Hershberg, *James B. Conant: Harvard to Hiroshima and the Making of the Nuclear Age* (New York: Knopf, 1993), p. 626.

3. Ibid., p. 638.

4. Richard Norton Smith, *The Harvard Century: The Making of a University to a Nation* (New York: Simon & Schuster, 1986), p. 186.

5. Milton Viorst, *Hustlers and Heroes: An American Political Panorama* (New York: Simon & Schuster, 1971), p. 278; Smith, *The Harvard Century*, p. 197; Lester Tanzer, ed., *The Kennedy Circle*, (Washington, D.C.: Luce, 1961), p. 31.

6. Smith, *The Harvard Century*, p. 187.

7. Ibid., p. 199.

8. Arthur Schlesinger, Jr., interview, June 6, 1995. When the overseers were asked to confirm Pusey's appointment in June 1953, two dissenting votes were cast by Joseph Alsop and J. Robert Oppenheimer, both good friends of Mac Bundy's. Oppenheimer thought it was "not a happy appointment" and in private he berated "the quality of the very few things he [Pusey] has written." (Telephone transcript of Oppenheimer and George Whitney, president of the Board of Overseers at Harvard, June 5, 1953, Box 126, Oppenheimer Papers, LOC.)

9. David M. Oshinsky, *A Conspiracy So Immense: The World of Joe McCarthy* (New York: Free Press, 1983), p. 322; Thomas C. Reeves, *The Life and Times of Joe McCarthy: A Biography* (New York: Stein & Day, 1982), pp. 507–508.

10. Nathan Marsh Pusey interview, Aug. 24, 1993.

11. MB interview, Apr. 5, 1993.

12. David Halberstam, *The Best and the Brightest*, (New York: Random House, 1972), p. 57.

13. *Boston Globe*, Aug. 23, 1953.

14. R. H. Winnick, ed., *Letters of Archibald MacLeish: 1907 to 1982* (Boston: Houghton Mifflin, 1983), p. 372.

15. Richard M. Freeland, *The Truman Doctrine and the Origins of McCarthyism: Foreign Policy, Domestic Politics, and Internal Security, 1946–1948* (New York: New York University Press, 1985). See Freeland's new preface, pp. xi–xviii.

16. Hershberg, *James B. Conant*, pp. 431–33, 621.

17. Ibid., p. 624.

18. Ibid., p. 625.

19. Sigmund Diamond, *Compromised Campus: The Collaboration of Universities with the Intelligence Community, 1945–1955* (New York: Oxford University Press, 1992), p. 125.

20. William L. Marbury, *In the Catbird Seat* (Baltimore: Maryland Historical Society, 1988), pp. 290–91.

21. J. Anthony Lukas letter to the author, May 24, 1997.

22. "There were some good people in the Communist Party," Bundy later said. "But party discipline sometimes could compel these people to be incompletely truthful about their views. I encountered this in the Cambridge chapter of the American Veterans Committee, which was run by Cord Meyer for quite a long time. This committee was supposed to be the liberal alternative to the American Legion. But it turned out that it contained a communist contingent. I joined in order to vote for the majority, in order to help Meyer retain control over the organization. The problem with these people was that they concealed their Communist Party membership; they had a hidden agenda." (MB interview, Apr. 5, 1993.)

23. Eric Bentley, ed., *Thirty Years of Treason* (New York: Viking, 1971), p. 610.

24. Seymour Martin Lipset and David Riesman, *Education and Politics at Harvard* (New York: McGraw-Hill, 1975), p. 199.

25. McGeorge Bundy, "Harvard and Government Security Policy," statement before the Subcommittee on Government Operations, U.S. Senate, Mar. 15, 1955, published in *School and Society*, July 9, 1955.

26. McGeorge Bundy letter to President Nathan Pusey, May 6, 1954, courtesy of Sigmund Diamond. Bundy retrieved this letter from the closed Harvard University archives after Diamond wrote his essay in *The New York Review of Books*. He gave a copy to Diamond. Sigmund Diamond letter to Francis H. Burr, Fellows of Harvard College, Sept. 22, 1970, courtesy of Diamond. Diamond also spent an afternoon in the spring of 1954 telling of his predicament to Perez Zagorin, a friend in Cambridge (Perez Zagorin phone interview, Aug. 5, 1996).

27. Diamond, *Compromised Campus*, pp. 18–22. Landes told Diamond in 1977, "What's he [Bundy] talking about, hallucination? He had the machine going while I was talking with him. He walked over to the window, and when he came back he pulled the switch. It was an old-fashioned machine with a record." (Diamond notes, Apr. 21, 1977, courtesy of Diamond.)

28. MB to David Landes, June 1, 1977, courtesy of Diamond and Landes.

29. Robert N. Bellah letter, *New York Review of Books*, July 14, 1977.

30. Ellen W. Schrecker, *No Ivory Tower: McCarthyism & the Universities* (New York: Oxford University Press, 1986), p. 263.

31. Robert N. Bellah letter and McGeorge Bundy letter, *New York Review of Books*, July 14, 1977.

32. Schrecker, *No Ivory Tower*, p. 261.

33. Bundy told Diamond, "There weren't very many cases like yours, Sig, only four or five that I can remember." Bundy went on to say he remembered one appointment offered to a young scholar that was withdrawn due to his party membership: "He went elsewhere, but he's back at Harvard now." (Sigmund Diamond notes, Apr. 21, 1977, courtesy of Diamond.)

34. MB interview, Apr. 5, 1993.

35. Schrecker, *No Ivory Tower*, p. 258.

36. Diamond, *Compromised Campus*, p. 21.

37. Ibid., 49.

38. Ibid., pp. 45–46, 49, 292, fn. 2.

39. Sigmund Diamond, "Kissinger and the FBI," *The Nation*, Nov. 10, 1979; Walter Isaacson, *Kissinger: A Biography* (New York: Simon & Schuster, 1992), p. 71; A July 15, 1952, FBI memo stated, "Steps will be taken, however, to make KISSINGER a Confidential Source of this Division" (Diamond, *Compromised Campus*, pp. 139–40); Herbert Mitgang, "When Academics Doubled as Intelligence Agents," *NYT*, July 29, 1992.

40. Bundy wrote David Landes, "The case was quite different with non-Communists, of whatever degree of radicalism, who also often refused to name names —why the American radical was usually serene and the ex-Communists so often disturbed is an interesting question that I cannot answer" (Bundy letter to Landes, June 1, 1977, courtesy of Sigmund Diamond).

41. MB to David Landes, June 1, 1977, courtesy of Sigmund Diamond.

42. Bellah letter, *New York Review of Books*, July 14, 1977.

43. Schrecker, *No Ivory Tower*, pp. 338–39; O. Edmund Clubb, "McCarthyism and Our Asian Policy," *Bulletin of Concerned Asian Scholars*, no. 4 (May 1969).

44. David F. Ricks telephone interview, Nov. 10, 1995.

45. "The Crimson Tide," *Newsweek*, May 28, 1962, p. 58.

46. Carl Kaysen interview, June 18, 1993; Viorst, *Hustlers and Heroes*, p. 278.

47. Arthur Schlesinger, Jr., interview, June 6, 1995.

48. Lipset and Riesman, *Education and Politics at Harvard*, pp. 197–98.

49. David Halberstam interview, May 15, 1995 (telephone), June 5, 1995.

50. J. Anthony Lukas letter to the author, May 24, 1997; Richard Ullman interview, Feb. 16, 1994; A. J. Langguth interview, Feb. 22, 1997.

51. Leslie Gelb interview, Feb. 17, 1994; A. J. Langguth interview, Feb. 22, 1997.

52. John Kenneth Galbraith, *A Life in Our Times: Memoirs* (Boston: Houghton, Mifflin, 1981), p. 363.

53. McGeorge Bundy, "Were Those the Days?" *Daedalus*, Summer 1970, pp. 532–533.

54. Lawrence S. Lifschultz, "Could Karl Marx Teach Economics in the United States?" in John Trumpbour, ed., *How Harvard Rules: Reason in the Service of Empire* (Boston: South End, 1989), pp. 279–86.

55. McGeorge Bundy, "Were Those the Days?," p. 531.

56. Carl Kaysen interview, June 18, 1993.

57. MB interview April 5, 1993; McGeorge Bundy, "Were Those the Days?," p. 543.

58. John Kenneth Galbraith interview, June 22, 1994.

59. Trumpbour, ed., *How Harvard Rules*, p. 51.

60. Smith, *The Harvard Century*, p. 219.

61. Lipset and Riesman, *Education and Politics at Harvard*, p. 302.

62. Mr. and Mrs. David F. Ricks telephone interview, Nov. 10, 1995.

63. Smith, *The Harvard Century*, p. 220.

64. McGeorge Bundy, "The Battlefields of Power and the Searchlights of the Academy," in E.A.J. Johnson, ed., *The Dimensions of Diplomacy* (Baltimore: Johns Hopkins Press, 1964), pp. 1–3.

65. Nathan Pusey interview, Aug. 24, 1993.

66. Jeff McConnell, "The CIA's Charles River Link," *Boston Globe*, Oct. 24, 1985; John Ranelagh, *The Agency: The Rise and Decline of the CIA* (New York: Simon & Schuster, 1986), p. 475.

67. Victor Marchetti and John D. Marks, *The CIA and the Cult of Intelligence* (New York: Dell, 1974), p. 225.

68. "Visiting Committee Meeting," May 18, 1957, C188, Box 13, Folder 490, MIT Archives. This transcript was inadvertently released to another researcher. The first four pages are missing.

69. Smith, *The Harvard Century*, p. 246.

70. McGeorge Bundy, "The Years of Indecision," *The Reporter*, Oct. 13, 1953.

71. Peter Novick, *That Noble Dream: The "Objectivity Question" and the American Historical Profession* (New York: Cambridge University Press, 1988), p. 305

72. Charles Beard, "Who's to Write the History of the War?" *Saturday Evening Post*, Oct. 4, 1947; William L. Langer, *In and Out of the Ivory Tower: The Autobiography of William L. Langer* (New York: Watson, 1977), p. 224.

73. Novick, *That Noble Dream*, p. 305.

74. McGeorge Bundy, "Were Those the Days?," pp. 535–37.

75. Stephen R. Graubard, *Kissinger: Portrait of a Mind* (New York: Norton, 1973), p. 175.

76. Isaacson, *Kissinger*, p. 97.

77. Ibid., pp. 94–95; Marvin Kalb and Bernard Kalb, *Kissinger* (Boston: Little, Brown, 1974), p. 57; Bruce Mazlish, *Kissinger: The European Mind in American Policy* (New York: Basic Books, 1976), p. 77.

78. Milton MacKaye, "Bundy of the White House," *Saturday Evening Post*, Mar. 10, 1962. MacKaye does not name the "foreign-born professor, able but overbearing," who had been "over the years, a tireless advocate of his own academic schemes," but the description could fit few men other than Kissinger.

79. Henry Kissinger, *White House Years* (Boston: Little Brown, 1979), pp. 13–14.

80. Francis X. Sutton interview, Dec. 1, 1994.

81. MB interview, Apr. 5, 1993.

82. Roger Rosenblatt, *Coming Apart: A Memoir of the Harvard Wars of 1969* (Boston: Little, Brown, 1997), p. 126.

83. Michael Maccoby interview, Dec. 13, 1993.

84. Phyllis Keller, *Getting at the Core: Curricular Reform at Harvard* (Cambridge: Harvard University Press, 1982), pp. 20–23.

85. David Riesman interview, June 21, 1994.

86. David Riesman, "The Innocence of *The Lonely Crowd*," *Society* 27:2 (January/February 1990), pp. 76–79.

87. Carol Brightman, *Writing Dangerously: Mary McCarthy and Her World* (New York: Harcourt Brace, 1992), p. 552.

88. Stanley Hoffmann interview, Feb. 15, 1995.

89. William Wright, *Lillian Hellman: The Image, the Woman* (New York: Simon & Schuster, 1986), p. 317.

90. Halberstam, *The Best and the Brightest*, p. 58.

91. MB interview, Apr. 5, 1993; Edmund Wilson, *The Fifties* (New York: Farrar, Straus & Giroux, 1986), pp. 410–11.

92. Oscar Handlin Oral History, 1981, p. 91, Widener Library, Harvard.

93. Victor Weisskopf, *The Joy of Insight: Passions of a Physicist* (New York: Basic Books, 1991), pp. 160–61.

94. Michael R. Beschloss, *The Crisis Years: Kennedy and Khrushchev, 1960–1963* (New York: HarperCollins, 1991), p. 96; *NYT*, Apr. 26, 1959; *Time*, May 4, 1959; Aleksandr Fursenko and Timothy Naftali, *"One Hell of a Gamble,": The Secret History of the Cuban Missile Crisis* (New York: Norton, 1997), pp. 10–11. Ted Szulc writes in the *WP Book World* (June 29, 1997) that Castro never applied to Harvard.

95. McGeorge Bundy, "Were Those the Days?," pp. 531–67.

96. Nathan Pusey interview, Aug. 24, 1993.

97. Stanley Hoffmann, interview, Feb. 15, 1995; McGeorge Bundy, "Were Those the Days?," p. 537.

98. MB interview, Apr. 5, 1993.

99. Draft of Harvard Club Speech, Senate Papers, Frederick Holborn Papers, Box 562, JFK.

100. Arthur Schlesinger, Jr., interview, June 6, 1995; Arthur Schlesinger, Jr., *A Thousand Days: John F. Kennedy in the White House* (Boston: Houghton Mifflin, 1965), pp. 16–17.

101. MB interview, Apr. 5, 1993.

102. Theodore Sorensen, *Kennedy* (New York: Harper & Row, 1965), p. 253.

103. John Morton Blum, ed., *Public Philosopher: Selected Letters of Walter Lippmann* (New York: Ticknor & Fields, 1985), p. 601. Two days after his meeting with Kennedy, Lippmann received a phone call from Mac Bundy, who was obviously feeling him out about Kennedy's intentions. He modestly told Lippmann that his candidate for the job of secretary of state was John J. McCloy. Lippmann responded, "I think you ought to be it," to which Bundy said, "Oh, that's all nonsense." (Walter Lippmann Oral History, p. 5, JFK.)

104. *Newsweek*, Mar. 4, 1963, p. 23.

105. MB interview, Apr. 5, 1993; *Boston Globe*, Dec. 31, 1960.

106. *Boston Globe*, morning edition, Dec. 31, 1960; Sorensen, *Kennedy*, p. 263

107. Halberstam, *The Best and the Brightest*, p. 59; David Halberstam interview, June 5, 1995.

8: WILLIAM BUNDY AND THE CIA, 1951–1960

1. WPB interview, Mar. 11, 1993.

2. WPB interview, Apr. 3, 1993; HB Oral History, p. 304. Harvey Bundy would always believe that Hiss had never handed over classified papers to a spy ring: "He was a highly intelligent man. My God, if he was going to take any papers and hand them over to [Whittaker] Chambers he could have found something better than what he did hand over." (HB Oral History, pp. 304–310.)

3. WPB letter to Peter Grose, undated 1993, courtesy of Bundy; Walter L. Pforzheimer interview, Apr. 12, 1993.

4. Willard Mathias interview, Dec. 3, 1993.

5. Dean Acheson, *Present at the Creation: My Years in the State Department* (New York: Norton, 1969), p. 360; *Washington-Times Herald*, July 10, 1953.

6. *Washington Star*, Apr. 14, 1950.

7. WPB interview, Mar. 11, 1993.

8. For an overview, see Bruce Cumings, *The Origins of the Korean War: The Roaring of the Cataract, 1947–1950*, vol. II (Princeton: Princeton University Press, 1990), and Melvyn P. Leffler, *A Preponderance of Power: National Security, the Truman Administration, and the Cold War* (Stanford: Stanford University Press, 1992).

9. WPB interview, Apr. 3, 1993.

10. WPB letter to Peter Grose, undated 1993, courtesy of Bundy; Walter L. Pforzheimer interview, Apr. 12, 1993; WPB interview, Apr. 3, 1993.

11. Harold Ford interview, June 24, 1993.

12. Russell Jack Smith, *The Unknown CIA: My Three Decades with the Agency* (Washington, D.C.: Pergamon-Brassey's, 1989), p. 121.

13. Ibid., p. 53.

14. Ibid., p. 54.

15. John Ranelagh, *The Agency: The Rise and Decline of the CIA* (New York: Simon & Schuster, 1986), p. 243.

16. Smith, *The Unknown CIA*, p. 134.

17. Robin Winks, *Cloak & Gown: Scholars in the Secret War, 1939–1961* (New York: Morrow, 1987), p. 450.

18. Smith, *The Unknown CIA*, p. 75.

19. Ibid., p. 135.

20. Ibid., p. 118.

21. WPB interview, Apr. 3, 1993.

22. Harold Ford interview, June 24, 1993; Willard Mathias interview, Dec. 3, 1993.

23. Rhodi Jeffreys-Jones, *The CIA & American Democracy* (New Haven: Yale University Press, 1988), p. 71.

24. Stewart Alsop, *The Center: People and Power in Political Washington* (New York: Popular Library, 1968), p. 204.

25. Chester Cooper interview, Oct. 29, 1993.

26. Harold Ford interview, June 24, 1993; Russell Jack Smith interview, June 7, 1993.

27. Harold Ford interview, June 24, 1993.

28. Chester Cooper interview, Oct. 29, 1993.

29. William L. Langer to WPB, May 26, 1953; David Owen to WPB, May 28, 1953, HU.

30. During World War II, Lewis Strauss had left his investment banking firm of Kuhn, Loeb to work as a high-ranking official in the Navy Department. Bill Bundy believed Strauss "had it in for Oppenheimer any which way." WPB interview, Apr. 3, 1993.

31. Ranelagh, *The Agency*, p. 239.

32. WPB interview, Apr. 3, 1993. In another account of this story, Bundy said he and Mansfield had helped their friend to "escape from government without publicity or disgrace—he [Mansfield] could not have saved him outright—in 1953." (Bundy letter to David Barrett, Mar. 12, 1989, courtesy of Barrett.)

33. Chester Cooper interview, Oct. 29, 1993; William Bundy letter to Peter Grose, undated 1993, courtesy of Bundy.

34. WPB letter to Peter Grose, undated 1993, courtesy of Bundy.

35. Walter L. Pforzheimer interview, Apr. 12, 1993; SECRET Memorandum for the Record, July 9, 1953, courtesy of Pforzheimer.

36. WPB letter to Peter Grose, undated 1993, courtesy of Bundy.

37. SECRET CIA Memorandum for the Record, July 9, 1953, courtesy of Pforzheimer.

38. Walter L. Pforzheimer interview, Apr. 12, 1993.

39. Walter L. Pforzheimer interviews, Apr. 12, 29, 1993.

40. Evan Thomas, *The Very Best Men* (New York: Simon & Schuster, 1995), p. 100.

41. Chester Cooper interview, Oct. 29, 1993.

42. SECRET CIA Memorandum for the Record, July 9, 1953, courtesy of Pforzheimer.

43. Chester Cooper interview, Oct. 29, 1993.

44. Ibid.

45. Walter L. Pforzheimer interview, Apr. 12, 1993; SECRET Memorandum for the Record, July 9, 1953, courtesy of Pforzheimer.

46. *NYT*, July 10, 1953; Associated Press, July 9, 1953, published in the *WP*, July 10, 1953, courtesy of the *Boston Globe* clip file.

47. *NYT*, July 10, 1953.

48. WPB letter to Peter Grose, undated 1993, courtesy of Bundy.

49. Ranelagh, *The Agency*, p. 241; Richard Nixon, *RN: The Memoirs of Richard Nixon* (New York: Grosset & Dunlap, 1978), pp. 139–40.

50. U.S. Senate Select Committee to Study Governmental Operations with Respect to Intelligence Activities (Church Committee), *Supplementary Reports on Intelligence Activities*, book VI (Washington, D.C.: Government Printing Office, 1976), p. 257; R. Harris Smith, *OSS: The Secret Story of America's First Central Intelligence Agency* (New York: Dell, 1973), pp. 370–71.

51. Nixon, *RN*, p. 140; Ranelagh, *The Agency*, p. 760.

52. McCarthy to Dulles, July 16, 1953; Dulles to McCarthy, July 22, 1953; McCarthy to Dulles, July 27, 1953; Dulles to McCarthy, Aug. 1, 1953; McCarthy to Dulles, Aug. 3, 1953; Dulles to McCarthy, Sept. 21, 1953 (courtesy of Walter Pforzheimer). McCarthy released these letters to the press on August 4, 1953; see *NYT*, Aug. 5, 1953.

53. Joe Alsop, *WP*, July 17, 1953. Afterwards, Alsop received a note of gratitude from Kay Bundy: "The world is a richer place because there are Alsops in it. Thank you!" (Alsop-Bundy, July 1953, Box 9, Alsop Papers, LOC.) Lippmann had criticized Allen Dulles for claiming the CIA was exempt from congressional oversight.

54. Jeffreys-Jones, *The CIA & American Democracy*, p. 75; *Chicago Tribune*, July 23, 1953.

55. Thomas Powers, *The Man Who Kept the Secrets: Richard Helms and the CIA* (New York: Knopf, 1979), p. 64; Walter L. Pforzheimer interview, Apr. 12, 1993. Pforzheimer said Dulles told this assembly, "The press is saying we beat Joe McCarthy. I don't want any of you saying this; do not discuss this case as a victory." See also Lyman Kirkpatrick, *The Real CIA* (New York: Macmillan 1968), p. 139.

56. WPB to William L. Langer, Feb. 11, 1954, HU.

57. WPB interview, Nov. 1, 1993; WPB letter to Peter Grose, undated 1993, courtesy of Bundy.

58. Cumings, *The Origins of the Korean War*, vol. II, pp. 126, 796.

59. Chester Cooper interview, Oct. 29, 1993.

60. WPB interview, Nov. 1, 1993.

61. WPB letter to Peter Grose, undated 1993, courtesy of Bundy; Leonard Mosley, *Dulles: A Biography of Eleanor, Allen, and John Foster Dulles and Their Family Network* (New York: Dial, 1978), p. 321.

62. Ranelagh, *The Agency*, p. 760; Godfrey Hodgson, "Cord Meyer: Superspook," in Philip Agee and Louis Wolf, eds., *Dirty Work: The CIA in Western Europe* (Secaucus, N.J.: Lyle Stuart, 1978), pp. 63–64.

63. David M. Oshinsky, *A Conspiracy So Immense: The World of Joe McCarthy* (New York: Free Press, 1983), p. 325; Lippmann's column appeared in the *Washington Post* on July 21, 1953. Dulles wrote Lippmann on August 7, 1953, claiming that previous congressional investigations had destroyed some CIA operations. Note also that in the autumn of 1952, two Agency officers were held in contempt of court for refusing to testify in a felony case and sentenced to fifteen days in jail. President Truman, believing the CIA should not be forced to talk about its activities, quietly pardoned them. (*NYT*, July 19, 1953.)

64. Joe Alsop–Kay Bundy, July 1953, Box 9, Alsop Papers, LOC.

65. Jeffreys-Jones, *The CIA & American Democracy*, p. 77.

66. *Supplementary Reports on Intelligence Activities*, book VI, p. 257.

67. William Bundy, "US Perceptions of Soviet Policy and Behavior," paper delivered at a symposium on the Cold War, Woodrow Wilson School, Princeton University, July 29, 1990, cited by Peter Grose, *Gentleman Spy: The Life of Allen Dulles* (Boston: Houghton Mifflin, 1994), pp. 347–48, p. 591, fn. 23.

68. Robert Amory Oral History, JFK, pp. 92–97.

69. Walter LaFeber, *America, Russia & the Cold War, 1945–1984* (New York: Knopf, 1985), p. 28; Michael McGwire, *Military Objectives in Soviet Military Policy* (Washington, D.C.: Brookings, 1987). Matthew Evangelista, "Stalin's Postwar Army Reappraised," *International Security* 7:3 (Winter 1982–83), pp. 110–38. Captain Gil-

berto Villahermosa, "Stalin's Postwar Army Reappraised: Déjà Vu All Over Again," *Soviet Observer* 2:1 (New York: W. Averell Harriman Institute for Advanced Study of the Soviet Union, Columbia University, September 1960). Villahermosa is citing Soviet army documents; see page 2, footnote 5 of his paper.

70. George Kennan, "Containment Then and Now," *Foreign Affairs*, Spring 1987, pp. 888–89. See also "Off the Record Discussion of the Origins of Cold War," an Oral History interview conducted by Arthur Schlesinger of Averell Harriman, Hamilton Fish Armstrong, Philip Mosely, John Campbell, Chester Cooper, John J. McCloy and George Stevens, May 31, 1967, AH, LOC. In 1971, McCloy looked back at the initial decision to deploy large numbers of American troops under NATO command and observed, "Contrary to some present contentions, we did not then fear a Soviet ground attack in spite of all the harassments in Berlin. . . . What we did fear was the political and psychological effect in Western Europe of the presence in Eastern Europe of large under-mobilized Soviet ground forces with nothing more convincing to offset their influence than the rather illusory commitments of the NATO pact alone." (McCloy letter to Hamilton Fish Armstrong, May 17, 1971, PU.)

71. WPB interview, Apr. 3, 1993. For a detailed discussion of the CIA's inflated estimates of Soviet military capabilities, see Evangelista, "Stalin's Postwar Army Reappraised," and Villahermosa, "Stalin's Army Reappraised."

72. "Probable Soviet Courses of Action to Mid-1952," NIE-25, declassified June 24, 1993, and published in Scott A. Koch, ed., *Selected Estimates on the Soviet Union: 1950–1959*, Washington, D.C.: Central Intelligence Agency Center for the Study of Intelligence, 1993).

73. "The Likelihood of General War Through 1957," SNIE 11–54, Feb. 15, 1954, published in *Selected Estimates on the Soviet Union: 1950–1959*, p. 199.

74. Willard Mathias interview, Dec. 3, 1993; Mathias dictated this excerpt from an NIE document into the author's tape recorder. Six years later Mathias wrote another estimate, dated June 9, 1964, which was even more explicit, arguing that this "evolution" was "probably irreversible."

75. Practically alone among the nation's pundits, Walter Lippmann had for some time been arguing that the Soviets were basically pursuing a defensive military posture. After an interview in October 1958 with Premier Nikita Khrushchev, Lippmann wrote, "They [the Soviets] cannot believe that we really think they will commit military aggression when they themselves are so sure that they must avoid a war." (Ronald Steel, *Walter Lippmann and the American Century* [Boston: Little Brown, 1980], p. 511.)

76. Willard Mathias interview, Dec. 3, 1993. Hal Ford wrote in his 1989 report that there were occasions when the "patriotism" of the authors of the estimates was directly questioned. (Harold P. Ford, *Estimative Intelligence: The Purposes and Problems of National Intelligence Estimating* [Washington, D.C.: Defense Intelligence College, 1989] p. 72.) See also Willard Mathias's forthcoming book, *The Long War: Triumphs and Tragedies in Strategic Intelligence*.

77. See Ford, *Estimative Intelligence*; Raymond Garthoff interview, Sept. 28, 1993.

78. WPB interview, Apr. 3, 1993.

79. Robert Amory Oral History, pp. 89–90, JFK.

80. See S-39, Mar. 10, 1953, "Consequences of the Death of Stalin," and NIE-81, May 22, 1953, "Soviet Courses of Action Regarding Germany Through 1954."

81. WPB interview, Apr. 3, 1993.

82. As Hal Ford later concluded, "ONE was slow in coming to these alerts, and for some time it did not stand up forcefully against strongly-held views in the community that Sino-Soviet squabbles were not likely to become serious" (Ford, *Estimative Intelligence*, p. 77).

83. Stephen E. Ambrose, *Eisenhower: The President* (New York: Simon & Schuster, 1984), pp. 209–10; Robert D. Schulzinger, *A Time for War: The United States and Vietnam, 1941–1975* (New York: Oxford University Press, 1997), p. 77.

84. Ranelagh, *The Agency*, p. 431; Dwight D. Eisenhower, *Mandate for Change* (Garden City, N.Y.: Doubleday, 1963), p. 372.

85. Chester Cooper interview, Oct. 29, 1993.

86. WPB interview, Apr. 3, 1993; Ranelagh, *The Agency*, pp. 431–32; Chester Cooper interview, Oct. 29, 1993.

87. See NIE-91, June 4, 1953, "Probable Developments in Indochina Through 1954." This estimate concluded, "If present trends in the Indochinese situation continue through mid-1954, the French Union political and military position may subsequently deteriorate very rapidly." Harold P. Ford interview, June 24, 1993; Ford, *Estimative Intelligence*, p. 78.

88. WPB Oral History, p. 2, LBJ; WPB interview, Nov. 1, 1993; WPB letter to Donald M. Wilson, Nov. 10, 1982.

89. Doris Kearns, *Lyndon Johnson & the American Dream* (New York: Harper & Row, 1976), p. 127; WPB interview, Nov. 1, 1993.

90. WPB interview, Nov. 1, 1993; Kearns, *Lyndon Johnson & the American Dream*, p. 127.

91. WPB interview, Nov. 1, 1993.

92. Mosley, *Dulles*, p. 457.

93. Willard Mathias interview, Dec. 3, 1993; When Mathias later complained about Bundy's editorship, Cremeans told him, "It's my fault; I introduced those two guys, and they've been buddy pals ever since."

94. WPB interview, July 15, 1993.

95. Ibid.

96. *Goals for Americans: Programs for Action in the Sixties, Comprising the Report of the President's Commission on National Goals* (New York: The American Assembly and Prentice-Hall, 1960), pp. 1–31.

97. *WP*, Dec. 11, 1960; WPB interview, July 15, 1993; WPB to Kennedy, Nov. 11, 1960, Senate Papers, Holborn Files, Correspondence 1960 "B", Box 566, JFK.

98. WPB interview, July 15, 1993; Lester Tanzer, ed., *The Kennedy Circle* (Washington, D.C.: Luce, 1961), p. 41.

99. WPB interview, July 15, 1993.

100. Thomas Hughes later said, "I think Bill [Bundy] expected, and I know Acheson expected, him to get what turned out to be Mac's job." Hughes interview, Feb. 11, 1993.

9: The Kennedy Years

1. David Wise, "Scholars of the Nuclear Age: McGeorge Bundy, Walt W. Rostow and Jerome B. Wiesner," in Lester Tanzer, ed., *The Kennedy Circle* (Washington, D.C.: Luce, 1961), p. 38.

2. John Prados, *Keepers of the Keys: A History of the National Security Council from Truman to Bush* (New York: Morrow, 1991), p. 97.

3. During Bundy's tenure, "no hard decision was ever taken in the formal National Security Council meetings." Michael V. Forrestal interview transcript by Joseph Kraft, Apr. 8, 1964, Secret, p. 40, MF. This transcript was obtained by the author from the late Averell Harriman.

4. Carl Kaysen interview, June 18, 1993.

5. Walter Isaacson, *Kissinger: A Biography* (New York: Simon & Schuster, 1992), p. 110.

6. MB interview, Nov. 17, 1993; Prados, *Keepers of the Keys,* pp. 114–15; Arthur Schlesinger, Jr., interview, June 6, 1995.

7. Robert Komer interview, Oct. 5, 1993.

8. This was a staff report prepared for Congressman Robert W. Kastenmeier and later published in *The Liberal Papers,* ed. James Roosevelt (New York: Doubleday Anchor, 1962).

9. Marcus Raskin interviews, June 4, Sept. 3, 1993; MB to David Riesman, Apr. 4, 1961, Bundy Papers, Chronological File, Box 398, JFK. There were limits to Bundy's New Frontier openness. Even before recruiting Raskin, he had tried to bring aboard Michael Maccoby, twenty-seven, his former aide from Harvard. But when Maccoby published an article with Erich Fromm in *Commentary* critical of the whole "counterforce" strategy of nuclear deterrence, Bundy sent him a note saying he could better advance the debate while serving outside the government. (Michael Maccoby interview, Dec. 13, 1993.)

10. Forrestal interview by Kraft, p. 58; Prados, *Keepers of the Keys,* p. 114.

11. Forrestal interview by Kraft, pp. 16, 21.

12. *Newsweek,* Mar. 4, 1963, p. 24; Stephen Birmingham, *The Right People: A Portrait of the American Social Establishment* (Boston: Little, Brown, 1968), p. 229.

13. *Newsweek,* Mar. 4, 1963; *WP,* Jan. 18, 1961; Michael R. Beschloss, *The Crisis Years: Kennedy and Khrushchev, 1960–1963* (New York: HarperCollins, 1991), p. 249.

14. *NYT,* Mar. 20, 1961.

15. MB to Stanley Hoffmann, Apr. 3, 1961, Bundy Chronological File, Box 398, JFK.

16. *Newsweek,* Mar. 4, 1963, p. 20.

17. Sidney Hyman, "When Bundy Says, 'The President Wants—' " *NYT Magazine* Dec. 2, 1962. See also Lloyd Gardner, "Harry Hopkins with Hand Grenades? McGeorge Bundy in the Kennedy and Johnson Years," courtesy of Gardner, on file at LBJ.

18. Max Frankel, "The Importance of Being Bundy," *NYT Magazine,* Mar. 28, 1965.

19. Robert Smith Thompson, *The Missiles of October* (New York: Simon & Schuster, 1992), p. 185.

20. Beschloss, *The Crisis Years,* p. 249.

21. *Newsweek,* Mar. 4, 1963, p. 23.

22. Roger Hilsman, *To Move a Nation* (Garden City, N.Y.: Doubleday, 1967), pp. 45–46.

23. Beschloss, *The Crisis Years,* p. 250.

24. Seymour M. Hersh, *The Dark Side of Camelot* (Boston: Little, Brown, 1997), p. 111.

25. *WP,* Oct. 5, 1961, and WPB interview, Nov. 1, 1993. Shortly before his assassination, President Kennedy's "persistent and not always gentle needling" persuaded Mac Bundy to resign his membership from the club in protest against its segregation. Mac regretted that he never got around to telling Kennedy that he had finally resigned. (William Manchester, *The Death of a President* [New York: Harper & Row, 1967], p. 581.)

26. Chester Cooper interview, Oct. 29, 1993.

27. Milton MacKaye, "Bundy of the White House," *Saturday Evening Post,* Mar. 10, 1962; Frankel, "The Importance of Being Bundy."

28. Walt Rostow interview, Dec. 16, 1992; Blanche Moore interview, Apr. 15, 1992.

29. Charles Moritz, ed, *Current Biography* (New York: Wilson, 1965), June 1964; Elise O'Shaughnessy interview, Nov. 17, 1993; Laurence Barrett, Herald Tribune News Service, Oct. 18, 1963; Thomas Hughes interview, Feb. 11, 1993.

30. Anonymous source.

31. Isaiah Berlin to Joe Alsop, Apr. 20, 1966, Box 73, Alsop Papers, LOC.

32. Hyman, "When Bundy Says, 'The President Wants—.' "

33. Frankel, "The Importance of Being Bundy."

34. James C. Thomson, Jr., interview, Feb. 13, 1995.

35. *WP*, Dec. 31, 1962.

36. Arthur Schlesinger, Jr., *Robert Kennedy and His Times* (New York: Ballantine, 1978), pp. 638–39; Nicholas Katzenbach interview, Dec. 2, 1994; Jean Stein, interviewer, and George Plimpton, ed., *American Journey: The Times of Robert Kennedy* (New York: Harcourt Brace Jovanovich, 1970), p. 87.

37. Harvard *Crimson*, Nov. 7, 1960.

38. Richard M. Bissell, Jr., with Jonathan E. Lewis and Frances T. Pudlo. *Memoirs*, (New Haven: Yale University Press, 1996), ch. 7.

39. Beschloss, *The Crisis Years*, pp. 104–105.

40. Richard Reeves, *President Kennedy: Profile in Power* (New York: Simon & Schuster, 1993), p. 70.

41. Piero Gleijeses, "Ships in the Night: The CIA, the White House and the Bay of Pigs," *Journal of Latin American Studies*, February 1995, p. 21. See also Tim Weiner, "CIA Bares Its Bungling in Report on Bay of Pigs Invasion," *NYT*, Feb. 22, 1998, p. 6, and Peter Kornbluh, ed., *Bay of Pigs Declassified: The Secret CIA Report* (New York: The New Press, 1998).

42. Ibid., p. 22; Bundy Memorandum of Meeting with the President, Feb. 8, 1961.

43. Gleijeses, "Ships in the Night," p. 23.

44. McGeorge Bundy, National Security Action Memorandum No. 31, Mar. 11, 1961, POF Staff Memo, Bundy, Box 62, JFK.

45. Gleijeses, "Ships in the Night," p. 26.

46. John Ranelagh, *The Agency: The Rise and Decline of the CIA* (New York: Simon & Schuster, 1986), pp. 362, 364.

47. Beschloss, *The Crisis Years*, p. 106.

48. MB to JFK, Feb. 25, 1961, POF Staff Memo, Bundy, Box 62, JFK.

49. Arthur Schlesinger, Jr., *A Thousand Days: John F. Kennedy in the White House* (Boston: Houghton Mifflin, 1965), pp. 251–52.

50. Harris Wofford, *Of Kennedys and Kings: Making Sense of the Sixties* (New York: Farrar, Straus & Giroux, 1980), p. 361.

51. WPB interview, July 15, 1993.

52. Wofford, *Of Kennedys and Kings*, p. 356.

53. Richard Goodwin, *Remembering America*, pp. 176–77; Schlesinger memos to the president, Apr. 5, 10, 1961, courtesy of Professor Philip Brenner. Schlesinger's dissent did not prevent him from later lobbying the editors of *The New Republic* to suppress a report on the Bay of Pigs. See Garry Wills, *The Kennedy Imprisonment: A Meditation on Power* (New York: Pocket Books, 1983), p. 152.

54. David Atlee Phillips, *The Night Watch* (New York: Ballantine, 1977), p. 135.

55. Beschloss, *The Crisis Years*, p. 121.

56. MB to JFK, undated, POF Staff Memo, Bundy, Box 62, JFK.

57. MB to Taylor, May 5, 1961, NSF Chronological File, Bundy, Box 398, and MB to Taylor, May 4, 1961, NSF, Box 61A–61B, JFK.

58. Richard Bissell interview, July 13, 1992.

59. Thompson, *The Missiles of Cuba*, p. 115; WPB interview, July 15, 1993.

60. MB interviews, Nov. 17, 1993; Sept. 19, 1995.

61. "JFK's McGeorge Bundy," *Newsweek*, Mar. 4, 1963, p. 24.

62. David Halberstam, *The Best and the Brightest* (New York: Random House, 1972), p. 68.

63. Saul Landau interview, Jan. 19, 1995; Scott Armstrong and Landau inter-

viewed General Escalante, who said his own information came from the capture years later of a man who at the time of the landings was the number two officer aboard the decoy ship. For more evidence on the plan to stage an attack on Guantanamo, see Warren Hinckle and William W. Turner, *The Fish Is Red: The Story of the Secret War Against Castro* (New York: Harper & Row, 1981), pp. 80–83.

64. MB interview, Sept. 19, 1995.

65. Bissell, *Memoirs;* Theodore Draper, "Is the CIA Necessary?" *New York Review of Books,* Aug. 14, 1997, p. 20.

66. MB interview, Sept. 19, 1995. See also *Operation Zapata: The Ultrasensitive Report and Testimony of the Board of Inquiry on the Bay of Pigs* (Frederick, Md.: Alethela Books, University Publications of America, Inc., 1981), pp. 96–97; Ranelagh, *The Agency,* p. 363; see also Bissell, *Memoirs,* ch. 7. In a 1984 interview by Lucien S. Vandenbrouke, Bissell also claimed, "Assassination was intended to reinforce the plan. There was the thought that Castro would be dead before the landing. Very few, however, knew of this aspect of the plan." (*Diplomatic History* [Fall 1984], cited by Hersh, *The Dark Side of Camelot,* p. 203.) Hersh suggests that Kennedy and Bundy may well have thought that Castro's assassination was part of the plan. In his memoir Bissell writes, "No doubt as I moved forward with plans for the brigade, I hoped the Mafia would achieve success."

67. Schlesinger, Jr., *Robert Kennedy and His Times,* p. 507.

68. *Newsweek,* Mar. 4, 1963, p. 23.

69. Years later Bill Bundy confronted Eisenhower's military aide General Andrew Goodpaster, whom Bundy thought to be a "soul of integrity," and asked him, "Andy, what did Ike intend to do with that exile force? Did he regard them as a tethered goat that would draw Castro's forces, and then the marines would clobber them? What did he have in mind? What was the strategy?"

Goodpaster replied quietly, "I asked him that question twice in the last ten days of his presidency and never got an answer." (WPB interview, July 15, 1993.) Historians would not learn until the mid-1980s how committed Eisenhower was to the operational notion of training Cuban exiles to invade the island. For instance, in a December 5, 1960, memo (not declassified until May 1983) Eisenhower told Dulles, Bissell and others that he thought "we should be prepared to take more chances and being more aggressive." (Memo of Meeting with the President, Dec. 5, 1960, DDE.)

70. WPB interview, July 15, 1993.

71. Randall Bennett Woods, *Fulbright: A Biography* (New York: Cambridge University Press, 1995), p. 269. MB to Lippmann, May 2, 1961, Lippmann Papers, Yale.

72. Halberstam, *The Best and the Brightest,* p. 69; "Notes on the 478th Meeting of the National Security Council, April 22, 1961," released at the Musgrove Plantation Conference on the Bay of Pigs, May 31–June 2, 1996.

73. Marcus Raskin interview, June 4, 1993.

74. MB to JFK, May 16, 1961, NSF Chronological File, Box 398, JFK.

75. Richard Goodwin memo to JFK, "Conversation with Commandante Ernesto Guevara of Cuba," Aug. 22, 1961, POF, Box 115, JFK, cited by Gleijeses, "Ships in the Night," p. 42; Goodwin, *Remembering America,* p. 201; Goodwin also interpreted Guevara's overture as a sign of weakness and urged the president to intensify covert actions against the regime.

76. Edwin O. Guthman and Jeffrey Shulman, eds., *Robert Kennedy: In His Own Words, The Unpublished Recollections of the Kennedy Years* (New York: Bantam, 1988), pp. 13, 247.

77. Neil Sheehan et al., eds. *The Pentagon Papers as Published by The New York Times* (New York: Bantam, 1971), pp. 89–91.

78. MB to Brigadier General J. B. Sweet, Apr. 21, 1961, Bundy Chronological File, Box 398, JFK.

79. Kai Bird, "Stalin Didn't Do It," *The Nation*, Dec. 16, 1996, a review essay of Carolyn Eisenberg, *Drawing the Line: The American Decision to Divide Germany, 1944–1949* (New York: Cambridge University Press, 1996).

80. Averell Harriman confidential memo with Mr. Khrushchev, June 23, 1959, AH, LOC.

81. Beschloss, *The Crisis Years*, p. 178.

82. Vladislav M. Zubok, "Khrushchev and the Berlin Crisis: 1958–1962," Working Paper No. 6, Cold War International History Project, Woodrow Wilson International Center for Scholars, Washington, D.C., May 1993. Hope M. Harrison, "Ulbricht and the Concrete 'Rose': New Archival Evidence on the Dynamics of Soviet–East German Relations and the Berlin Crisis, 1958–1961," Working Paper No. 5, Cold War International History Project, Woodrow Wilson International Center for Scholars, May 1993.

83. Georg M. Schild, "John F. Kennedy and the Berlin Crisis," unpublished essay, courtesy of William Burr, NS; C. L. Sulzberger, *The Last of the Giants* (New York: Macmillan, 1970), p. 415.

84. Marcus Raskin interview, Sept. 3, 1993. Raskin wrote Bundy a memo on July 6, 1961, urging recognition of the Oder-Neisse line. See Raskin to Bundy, July 6, 1961, Institute for Policy Studies archives, Box 7, Wisconsin Historical Society.

85. Gregg Herken, *Counsels of War* (New York: Knopf, 1985), p. 159; Beschloss, *The Crisis Years*, p. 256; Fred Kaplan, *Wizards of Armageddon* (New York: Simon & Schuster, 1983), p. 298; Peter Wyden, *The Wall*, (New York: Simon & Schuster, 1989), pp. 249–50.

86. Beschloss, *The Crisis Years*, p. 256; Marcus Raskin interview, June 4, 1993.

87. Carl Kaysen interview, June 18, 1993. Kaysen said that while it was an emotional argument with Raskin, "I doubt that I came to tears." A few weeks later Kaysen wrote Bundy about the war plan, SIOP-62, and described the "rigidity of the plan, especially in respect of targeting . . ." (Memorandum for General Maxwell Taylor . . . , Sept. 5, 1961, NSF, Carl Kaysen, Box 320, declassified Apr. 28, 1997).

88. Herken, *Counsels of War*, pp. 158–60; Beschloss, *The Crisis Years*, p. 256; Wyden, *The Wall*, p. 252.

89. Memorandum of Conference with the President, July 27, 1961, Conferences with the President, Joint Chiefs of Staff, NSF, Chester V. Clifton Papers, Box 345, JFK, declassified May 2, 1994.

90. McGeorge Bundy, *Danger and Survival: Choices About the Bomb in the First Fifty Years* (New York: Random House, 1988), pp. 375–76.

91. Daniel Ellsberg interview, Dec. 15, 1993; Herken, *Counsels of War*, p. 144.

92. Daniel Ellsberg interview, Dec. 15, 1993.

93. John Newhouse, *War and Peace in the Nuclear Age* (New York: Knopf, 1989), p. 162.

94. Bundy himself later wrote, ". . . it soon became clear to McNamara that it would be much easier to control strategic procurement if he did not at the same time challenge SAC's targeting doctrines" (McGeorge Bundy, *Danger and Survival*, p. 354). In the wake of the Berlin crisis, on October 23, 1961, Kennedy approved National Security Action Memorandum 109, which delineated four distinct, graduated steps in the event of a military conflict over Berlin. Only at phase four, after the failure of conventional force, would tactical nuclear weapons be used on a few targets to demonstrate Washington's willingness to use nuclear weapons. (*FRUS, Berlin Crisis, 1961–1962* [Washington, D.C.: Government Printing Office, 1993], pp. 521–23.)

95. McGeorge Bundy, *Danger and Survival*, p. 363.

96. State Department Memorandum to the President, June 28, 1961, *FRUS, Berlin Crisis, 1961–1962*, p. 141.

97. Walter Isaacson and Evan Thomas, *The Wise Men: Six Friends and the World They Made* (New York: Simon & Schuster, 1986), p. 611.

98. Douglas Brinkley, *Dean Acheson: The Cold War Years, 1953–71* (New Haven: Yale University Press, 1992), p. 139.

99. Schild, "John F. Kennedy and the Berlin Crisis"; Kenneth P. O'Donnell and David F. Powers, with Joe McCarthy, *"Johnny, We Hardly Knew Ye"* (Boston: Little, Brown, 1970), p. 338.

100. Kai Bird, *The Chairman: John J. McCloy/The Making of the American Establishment* (New York: Simon & Schuster, 1992), p. 509.

101. Theodore Sorensen, *Kennedy* (New York: Harper & Row, 1965), p. 591; McGeorge Bundy, *Danger and Survival*, p. 368.

102. W. W. Rostow, *The Diffusion of Power: An Essay in Recent History* (New York: Macmillan, 1972), p. 231.

103. Reeves, *President Kennedy*, p. 211 (Bundy memo to JFK, Aug. 14, 1961, NSF Box 82, JFK).

104. Brinkley, *Dean Acheson*, pp. 151, 196.

105. Carolyn Eisenberg, *Drawing the Line: The American Decision to Divide Germay, 1944–1949* (New York: Cambridge University Press, 1996), p. 485. See also Vladislav Zubok and Constantine Pleshakov, *Inside the Kremlin's Cold War: From Stalin to Khrushchev* (Cambridge: Harvard University Press, 1996), pp. 248–58.

106. Carl Kaysen to McGeorge Bundy, with attached twelve-page memo, "Thoughts on Berlin," Aug. 22, 1961, Germany-Berlin General, NSF Files, Box 82, JFK. Kaysen reiterated this argument two years later: "A certain stability for East Germany is, I believe, in our interests as well as the Soviet Union. . . . This is the time for some new thinking in regard to Eastern Germany and Eastern Europe. We will certainly gain with Poland and Czechoslovakia and help loosen the bonds between them and Moscow if they no longer fear attack by force on the Oder-Neisse line." (Kaysen memorandum, "Outlook for Future Discussions with USSR," July 28, 1963, NSF, Carl Kaysen Papers, Box 376, JFK.)

107. Averell Harriman to JFK, Sept. 1, 1991, Secret, AH. Harriman went on to say that a denuclearized West and East Germay "protects us against the possibility of Germany's getting independent nuclear capability with which she could blackmail both West and East."

108. An eminent historian of the Cold War, Melvyn P. Leffler, writes about many of these missed opportunities in his essay "Inside Enemy Archives: The Cold War Reopened," *Foreign Affairs*, Summer 1996. For a contrary view, see John Lewis Gaddis, *We Now Know: Rethinking Cold War History* (New York: Oxford University Press, 1997).

109. McGeorge Bundy, *Danger and Survival*, p. 385.

110. Ibid.

111. Beschloss, *The Crisis Years*, p. 310.

112. Ibid., p. 702. Kennedy's fiscal 1964 defense budget was 11 percent higher in real dollars than Eisenhower's 1960 defense budget. (H. W. Brands, *The Devil We Knew: Americans and the Cold War* [New York: Oxford University Press, 1993], pp. 78–79.)

113. Herken, *Counsels of War*, p. 155.

114. Carl Kaysen interview, June 18, 1993; Betty Goetz Lall interview, Feb. 23, 1985; Bird, *The Chairman*, pp. 515–16. Bundy himself does not even mention the Foster Panel's recommendations in his own book on the bomb. But he does report that when McNamara chose to build an initial thousand Minuteman missiles "he was choosing a number that Congress would find acceptably large, not a number that he himself could demonstrate as strategically necessary" (McGeorge Bundy, *Danger and Survival*, p. 547).

115. John Morton Blum, ed., *Public Philosopher: Selected Letters of Walter Lippmann* (New York: Ticknor & Fields, 1985), pp. 603–605.

116. David Riesman letter to author, July 5, 1994; Riesman letters to James Warburg, May 3, July 20, 1961, James Warburg Papers, Box 42, JFK.

117. Todd Gitlin, *The Sixties: Years of Hope, Days of Rage* (New York: Bantam, 1987), pp. 90–95. Peter Goldmark recalled, "Bundy defended the White House line, but he was a smart man—and he was listening very closely, as his comments during the meeting showed. . . . As a measure of how near 'the practical center' we were, nearly everything we recommended, which was denounced by Bundy in the meeting as 'impractical' and by opponents as traitorous, came to pass in the next few years—a test ban treaty, withdrawal of the Thor and Jupiter missiles good only for the first strike, etc." (Peter C. Goldmark, Jr., letter to author, Oct. 15, 1997.)

118. Joseph Kraft, "The Two Worlds of McGeorge Bundy," *Harper's*, November 1965, p. 110.

119. Ibid.

120. MB to Mr. President, Apr. 25, 1962, JFK.

121. Marcus Raskin interview, Sept. 3, 1993.

122. Beschloss, *The Crisis Years*, p. 338.

123. WPB "Memorandum for the Secretary," Oct. 10, 1961, Secret, obtained by the author under FOIA from Department of Defense, Jan. 5, 1994.

124. John Kenneth Galbraith, *Ambassador's Journal* (Boston: Houghton Mifflin, 1969), p. 212.

125. J. K. Galbraith to the President, Nov. 21, 1961, NSF Vietnam, Box 195, JFK.

126. Galbraith, *Ambassador's Journal*, p. 256. "I could always go to Mac with my views on Vietnam," Galbraith recalled. "The door was always open." (J. K. Galbraith interview, June 22, 1994.)

127. MB, "Top Secret Memorandum for the President," Nov. 15, 1961, declassified May 28, 1993, Bundy Chronological File, Box 399, JFK.

128. J. K. Galbraith, "SECRET Memorandum to the President," Apr. 4, 1962, AH.

129. Michael Forrestal, "TOP SECRET Memorandum of Conversation," Apr. 6, 1962, AH. Before his death in 1989, Forrestal removed his memorandums from the Harriman collection. The author retains copies of these materials.

130. U.S. Senate Select Committee to Study Government Operations with Respect to Intelligence Activities (hereafter cited as Church Committee) *Alleged Assassination Plots Involving Foreign Leaders*, Nov. 20, 1975, pp. 156, 186. Bissell initially told the Church Committee that any "urgings" for the creation of an assassination capability would have come from either Bundy or Walt Rostow. He later changed this testimony and claimed that Bundy at no time had "urged" him to establish ZR/RIFLE and that Bundy had merely not objected. But then, Bissell also went on to say, "I suspect that his reacton was somewhat more favorable than that . . ."

131. Church Committee, *Alleged Assassination Plots Involving Foreign Leaders*, p. 157. On April 7, 1975, Bundy also testified before the Rockefeller Commission on the CIA. According to Seymour Hersh, the next day Bundy sought out the commission's executive director, David W. Belin, and said, "as I reflected overnight about my answers to certain questions, my recollection was refreshed. . . . I recall the words 'executive action capability' more clearly than I did yesterday. . . . I think it was something like . . . a plan to have some kind of standby capability for actions against individuals." Belin told Hersh, "There is no doubt that Bundy lied to me." A veteran staffer of the Warren Commission investigation, Belin concluded that President Kennedy and Bundy both knew about the CIA's attempts to kill Castro. (Hersh, *The Dark Side of Camelot*, pp. 189–90.)

132. Church Committee, *Alleged Assassination Plots Involving Foreign Leaders*, pp. 211–15. (Bundy and Kennedy had specifically refused to give the assassins any additional U.S. weapons, but had not otherwise opposed the assassination.) Ranelagh, *The Agency*, p. 346.

133. Michael Forrestal to Mac Bundy, Sept. 7, 1962, Secret, "Proposed Tibetan Operations," AH; Ranelagh, *The Agency*, p. 335.

10: THE CUBAN MISSILE CRISIS

1. Dino A. Brugioni, *Eyeball to Eyeball: The Inside Story of the Cuban Missile Crisis* (New York: Random House, 1991), p. 207; Roger Hilsman, *To Move a Nation* (Garden City, N.Y.: Doubleday, 1967), p. 180.

2. MB memo to JFK, Mar. 4, 1963, in McGeorge Bundy, *Danger and Survival: Choices About the Bomb in the First Fifty Years* (New York: Random House, 1988), p. 684.

3. Richard E. Neustadt and Graham T. Allison, Afterword to Robert F. Kennedy's *Thirteen Days: A Memoir of the Cuban Missile Crisis* (New York: Norton, 1971), p. 122; Richard Reeves, *President Kennedy: Profile in Power* (New York: Simon & Schuster, 1993), p. 370; Brugioni, *Eyeball to Eyeball*, p. 220.

4. Brugioni, *Eyeball to Eyeball*, p. 223.

5. Barton J. Bernstein, "Reconsidering the Missile Crisis: Dealing with the Problems of the American Jupiters in Turkey," in James A. Nathan, ed., *The Cuban Missile Crisis Revisited* (New York: St. Martin's, 1992), p. 65; Raymond Garthoff, *Reflections on the Cuban Missile Crisis* (Washington, D.C.: Brookings, 1987), p. 142; Kai Bird, *The Chairman: John J. McCloy/The Making of the American Establishment* (New York: Simon & Schuster, 1992), p. 524. Bernstein suggests that at the time, the CIA mistakenly estimated the Soviets had about 75 launchers. See also Ernest R. May and Philip D. Zelikow, eds., *The Kennedy Tapes: Inside the White House During the Cuban Missile Crisis* (Cambridge: Harvard University Press, 1997), pp. 14, 32.

6. Robert McNamara, *Blundering into Disaster: Surviving the First Century of the Nuclear Age* (New York: Pantheon, 1986), pp. 44–45; General Anatoli I. Gribkov and General William Y. Smith, *Operation Anadyr: US and Soviet Generals Recount the Cuban Missile Crisis* (Chicago: edition q, inc, 1994), p. 157.

7. Transcripts of the first and second ExComm meetings, Oct. 16, 1962, 11:50 A.M.–12:57 P.M., and 6:30–7:55 P.M., in Laurence Chang and Peter Kornbluh, eds., *The Cuban Missile Crisis, 1962: National Security Archive Documents Reader* (New York: New Press, 1992), pp. 86–113. See also May and Zelikow, eds., *The Kennedy Tapes*, pp. 45–117.

8. Chang and Kornbluh, eds., *The Cuban Missile Crisis, 1962*, pp. 102–103. Kennedy also mused that the crisis "shows that the Bay of Pigs was really right." See Michael Beschloss, *The Crisis Years: Kennedy and Khrushchev, 1960–1963* (New York: HarperCollins, 1991), p. 443. In a 1987 conference on the crisis, Ted Sorensen flatly stated, "The President never mentioned a shift in the balance of power as his reason for wanting the missiles out." See J. Anthony Lukas, "Class Reunion: Kennedy's Men Relive the Cuban Missile Crisis," *NYT Magazine*, Aug. 30, 1987.

9. Transcript of the second ExComm meeting, Oct. 16, 1962, 6:30–7:55 P.M., in Chang and Kornbluh, eds., *The Cuban Missile Crisis, 1962*, p. 104; May and Zelikow, eds., *The Kennedy Tapes*, pp. 112–13.

10. Transcripts of the first and second ExComm meetings, Oct. 16, 1962, 11:50 A.M.–12:57 P.M., and 6:30–7:55 P.M., in Chang and Kornbluh, eds., *The Cuban Missile Crisis, 1962*, pp. 86–113.

11. Bernstein, "Reconsidering the Missile Crisis," pp. 59–64.

12. Reeves, *President Kennedy*, p. 377.

13. Douglas Brinkley, *Dean Acheson: The Cold War Years, 1953–71* (New Haven: Yale University Press, 1992), p. 163.

14. McGeorge Bundy, *Danger and Survival*, p. 400; Theodore Sorensen Oral History, p. 53, JFK; MB interview, Nov. 17, 1993.

15. Beschloss, *The Crisis Years*, p. 459; Chang and Kornbluh, eds., *The Cuban Missile Crisis, 1962*, pp. 123–27.

16. "Minutes of the October 19, 1962 Excomm mtg. 11:00 A.M.," taken by Leonard Meeker, Document 21, in Chang and Kornbluh, eds., *The Cuban Missile Crisis, 1962*, pp. 123–27. Bundy's position mirrored that of the Joint Chiefs, who throughout the crisis consistently urged a massive air strike to be followed by the invasion they had been planning for months. See Gribkov and Smith, *Operation Anadyr*, pp. 130–35. For more on Gen. Curtis LeMay's belligerent advice to President Kennedy, see Richard Rhodes, *Dark Sun: The Making of the Hydrogen Bomb* (New York: Simon & Schuster, 1995), pp. 574–576.

17. Arthur Schlesinger, Jr., *Robert Kennedy and His Times* (New York: Ballantine, 1978), p. 546. Schlesinger had exclusive access to RFK's papers and here he is citing "RFK handwritten notes, October 31, 1962," RFK Papers.

18. MB interview, Nov. 17, 1993.

19. Document 21, in Chang and Kornbluh, eds., *The Cuban Missile Crisis, 1962*, pp. 124–25.

20. Ibid., p. 126–27.

21. Roswell L. Gilpatric Oral History, p. 56, JFK.

22. "Second Interview of Michael V. Forrestal by Joseph Kraft on Tuesday, July 28, 1964, SECRET," pp. 71–72, MF, copy in author's files. This 171-page transcript has never been published or released for public inspection.

23. WPB interview, Feb. 16, 1994.

24. Beschloss, *The Crisis Years*, p. 485.

25. Document 34, Khrushchev's letter to Kennedy, Oct. 24, 1962, in Chang and Kornbluh, eds., *The Cuban Missile Crisis, 1962*, pp. 163–64.

26. Dean Rusk, *As I Saw It* (New York: Norton, 1990), p. 237.

27. WPB interview, Feb. 16, 1994.

28. Bird, *The Chairman*, p. 529.

29. Roswell L. Gilpatric Oral History, p. 61, JFK. Deborah Shapley, *Promise and Power: The Life and Times of Robert McNamara* (Boston: Little, Brown, 1993), pp. 176–77. Shapley reports that Anderson later denied that the exchange was acrimonious. Captain George Anderson was the navy officer who in 1954 had concluded that three tactical atomic weapons, properly employed, would be enough to smash the Viet Minh siege of Dien Bien Phu (McGeorge Bundy, *Danger and Survival*, p. 267). WPB interview, Feb. 16, 1994.

30. "Second Interview of Michael V. Forrestal by Joseph Kraft," pp. 63–64. This conversation may have occurred around the time that the commander in chief of the U.S. Strategic Air Command, when instructed to bring his units to the highest peacetime alert status, DefCon 2, decided to issue the orders in uncoded messages, precisely so that the Soviets would know that the United States was that much closer to a nuclear war. Raymond Garthoff has written that this was done without the knowledge of the president, ExComm or the chairman of the Joint Chiefs (Garthoff, *Reflections on the Cuban Missile Crisis*, p. 62).

31. Beschloss, *The Crisis Years*, pp. 526–27.

32. Chang and Peter Kornbluh, eds., *The Cuban Missile Crisis, 1962*, p. 376.

33. McGeorge Bundy, *Danger and Survival*, pp. 432–33. Bundy first wrote about this "secret diplomacy," as he called it, in *Time* magazine (Sept. 27, 1982) in an article he drafted and co-signed with Rusk, McNamara, Ball, Gilpatric and Sorensen.

34. Bernstein, "Reconsidering the Missile Crisis," p. 96. With the exception of Arthur Schlesinger, Jr., the Kennedy family has not made Robert F. Kennedy's diaries available to scholars of the missile crisis.

35. A. Dobrynin's Cable to the Soviet Foreign Ministry, Oct. 27, 1962, Russian Foreign Ministry Archives, in Richard Ned Lebow and Janice Gross Stein, *We All Lost the Cold War* (Princeton: Princeton University Press, 1994), pp. 523–26. See also James Hershberg, "Anatomy of a Crisis," *Cold War International History Project Bulletin*,

issue 5 (Spring 1995). Robert Kennedy's own memorandum on his interview with Dobrynin puts a rather more self-serving gloss on the encounter. See May and Zelikow, eds., *The Kennedy Tapes*, pp. 607–608.

36. Lukas, "Class Reunion." Shapley, *Promise and Power*, p. 181. According to General Taylor, the Joint Chiefs recommended an invasion for Monday. See "Summary Record of NSC ExComm Mtg. No. 8, October 27, 1962, 4:00 P.M., Top Secret," sanitized September 1987, NSF 316–317, JFK. May and Zelikow, eds., *The Kennedy Tapes*, p. 629.

37. Anatoly Dobrynin, *In Confidence: Moscow's Ambassador to America's Six Cold War Presidents* (New York: Times Books, 1995), pp. 86–89. General LeMay was quoted as saying later, "We Lost." See Lukas, "Class Reunion," *NYT Magazine*, Aug. 30, 1987; H. W. Brands, *The Devil We Knew: Americans and the Cold War* (New York: Oxford University Press, 1993), p. 83; Edwin O. Guthman and Jeffrey Shulman, eds., *Robert Kennedy: In His Own Words, The Unpublished Recollections of the Kennedy Years* (New York: Bantam, 1988), p. 14.

38. Beschloss, *The Crisis Years*, p. 541.

39. McGeorge Bundy, *Danger and Survival*, pp. 432–36; Bernstein, "Reconsidering the Missile Crisis," p. 100; May and Zelikow, eds., *The Kennedy Tapes*, p. 606.

40. McGeorge Bundy, *Danger and Survival*, p. 436.

41. Ibid., p. 416; James G. Hershberg, "Before 'The Missiles of October': Did Kennedy Plan a Military Strike Against Cuba?" in Nathan, ed., *The Cuban Missile Crisis Revisited*, pp. 238–39, 269–71.

42. Hershberg, "Before 'The Missiles of October,' " p. 245; Brigadier General Lansdale report "The Cuba Project," Feb. 20, 1962, in Chang and Kornbluh, eds., *The Cuban Missile Crisis, 1962*, p. 23.

43. Gribkov and Smith, *Operation Anadyr*, p. 107; McCone Memorandum of Meeting with the President, Aug. 23, 1962, with attached Memorandum, Proposed Plan of Action for Cuba, Aug. 21, 1962.

44. Arthur Schlesinger, Jr., Memorandum for the President, Sept. 5, 1962, Cuba General, September 1962, Box 36, NSF, JFK.

45. Marcus Raskin memo to Carl Kaysen, Sept. 24, 1962, Cuba General, September 1962, Box 36, NSF, JFK. Raskin was quoting from *The New Dealers*, by "Unofficial Observer" (New York: Simon & Schuster, 1934), pp. 280–81.

46. Bundy memo to Brigadier General E. G. Lansdale, Sept. 19, 1962; Congressman Ed Edmondson to JFK, Sept. 12, 1962, with attached memo to the president, "A Proposal for Liberation of Cuba," Sept. 12, 1962, declassified Feb. 29, 1996, Mandatory Review Case NLK-90-49, JFK.

47. Hershberg, "Before 'The Missiles of October,' " p. 249.

48. Ibid., p. 254. See also Elizabeth Cohn's essay, "Building Consensus in the ExComm," in the same volume, p. 221.

49. Gribkov and Smith, *Operation Anadyr*, p. 120.

50. Hershberg, "Before 'The Missiles of October,' " p. 271. Remarkably, Robert F. Kennedy left the first ExComm meeting on October 16, 1962, and that very afternoon chaired a meeting on Mongoose in which he berated the CIA's Richard Helms for "discouraging" results. Kennedy announced he was now going to give Mongoose his "personal attention" and would henceforth hold a meeting every morning at 9:30 A.M. to discuss the program. Referring to the news that morning about missiles in Cuba, he bluntly asked Helms what percentage of Cubans would fight for Castro "if the country was invaded." (Richard Helms, Memo for the Record, Oct. 16, 1962, released at Musgrove Plantation Conference on the Bay of Pigs, May 31–June 2, 1996.) Since James Hershberg's account was published, cursory notes have surfaced which indicate that McNamara told the Joint Chiefs on the afternoon of October 15, 1962 (before the missiles were discovered), that the president had decided that no military action should

be taken against Cuba in the next three months. See JCS Special Historical Study, "The JCS and U.S. Military Responses to the Threat of Castro's Cuba," Historical Division, Joint Secretariat, JCS, April 1981, Top Secret, pp. 11–12, declassified May 1996, courtesy of Hershberg.

51. Gribkov and Smith, *Operation Anadyr*, pp. 166, 177. Gribkov used a figure of 98 tactical warheads in his book, but later amended this to 158. Gribkov said that he believed the Soviet commander in Cuba would have used tactical nuclear weapons "in order to avoid the humiliation of defeat, regardless of Moscow's orders." In an April 4, 1994, seminar at the Woodrow Wilson Center in Washington D.C., Generals Gribkov and Smith warned, "It is hard to believe that they [the Soviet forces] would have held back any of their weapons and fought, in effect, with one hand tied behind their backs." Gribkov also revealed that Khrushchev did not order the removal from Cuba of the 158 tactical nuclear warheads until November 20, 1962. Technically, they were strictly defensive weapons and therefore were not covered by the U.S.-Soviet agreement to remove offensive weapons.

52. MB to Archibald MacLeish, Oct. 30, 1962, Box 4, MacLeish Papers, LOC.

53. Kennedy, *Thirteen Days*, p. 45.

54. Bernstein, "Reconsidering the Missile Crisis," pp. 106–107.

55. McGeorge Bundy, *Danger and Survival*, p. 453.

56. Brands, *The Devil We Knew*, p. 85.

57. Chalmer Roberts, *WP*, Nov. 3, 1962.

58. MB interview, Nov. 17, 1993.

59. Beschloss, *The Crisis Years*, p. 605; McGeorge Bundy, *Danger and Survival*, p. 390; MB interview, Nov. 17, 1993. Bundy later learned to his embarrassment that "ein Berliner" means a particular kind of pastry, and that he should have said, "Ich bin Berliner." "Fortunately," he told the historian Michael Beschloss, "the crowd in Berlin was untroubled by my mistake; no one in the square confused JFK with a doughnut."

60. Theodore Sorensen, *Kennedy* (New York: Harper & Row, 1965), p. 601.

61. Beschloss, *The Crisis Years*, pp. 598–99, 601.

62. Bird, *The Chairman*, p. 238. In 1963, according to a still-classified Top Secret State Department report, "The U.S. strategic retaliatory force is manifestly superior to the Soviet Union's. The U.S. force now contains at least 500 missiles—ATLAS, TITAN, MINUTEMAN, POLARIS—and will increase to over 2,000 missiles by 1968. In addition, the U.S. has 12 SAC bombers on air-alert and 561 more on quick-reaction alert. By comparison, the Soviets are estimated to have between 270 and 320 ICBM and sub-launched missiles today and their predicted 1968 missile force will number somewhere between 590 and 860. The consensus is that today the Soviets could place 200 bombers over North America on a first strike. Our missile force is deployed so as to assure that under any conceivable Soviet first strike, a substantial portion of it would survive." (Document in author's possession.)

63. Bundy had written Kennedy as early as September 1962, when negotiations had been deadlocked, "I do think it is getting to be time to consider a top-level and politically savvy visitor to Moscow, and my own candidate would be Harriman" (Beschloss, *The Crisis Years*, p. 588).

64. McGeorge Bundy, *Danger and Survival*, p. 461. See also SECRET "Instructions for Honorable W. Averell Harriman," July 10, 1963, AH. Bundy and Kaysen intervened to ensure that Harriman's instructions were framed so as to seek "the most comprehensive nuclear test ban treaty possible. . . ." See Memo of Telcon, Kaysen/Harriman, June 28, 1963, and TOP SECRET EYES ONLY, "To Mr. Bundy from Mr. Kaysen," June 28, 1963, AH, where Kaysen argues "there is something to be gained by serious and wide-ranging exploration of Soviet interest in test ban and broader security and disarmament measures." The State Department had attempted to formulate instructions for Harriman which would have prohibited him from exploring any of these broader security issues.

65. "Memorandum: The Moscow Negotiations," Aug. 1, 1963, SECRET. This document is unsigned, but the author obtained it from Harriman's personal archives. See also a 26-page SECRET EYES ONLY cable from Harriman to Secretary of State, reporting on his negotiations in Moscow on July 16, 1963.

66. Harriman thought Khrushchev wanted a formal nonaggression treaty in order to lessen tensions over a divided Germany: "Greater stability [in Eastern Europe and East Germany in particular] will tend to loosen them still further and permit these countries to look more to the West than they have in the past. West Germany has consistently tried to develop its relations with East Germans, but has insisted that we hold an umbrella over their activities in order to maintain the pretense that they are against acceptance of East Germany." Harriman memorandum, SECRET, July 30, 1963, AH.

67. For instance, the State Department's Policy Planning Council recommended on August 23, 1963, against a suggested agreement to cease production of tritium, a key bomb ingredient. See Henry Owen to "Members of the Tuesday Planning Group," Aug. 23, 1963, SECRET, AH, in author's possession.

68. Ray S. Cline to Averell Harriman, July 4, 1963, with attached SECRET CIA Memorandum, "Soviet Policies and Problems on the Eve of the Moscow Negotiations," July 3, 1963, AH. Note that U.S. defense spending in fiscal 1964 was $55.4 billion; the Arms Control and Disarmament Agency estimated in August 1963 that the United States could save some $18 billion of this if the U.S. Disarmament Treaty proposals of April 1962 had been implemented.

11: AUTUMN ASSASSINATIONS

1. Michael Forrestal interview transcript by Joseph Kraft, SECRET, Aug. 14, 1964, pp. 126–27, MF. This document has never been declassified.

2. Ibid., p. 128; Michael V. Forrestal, SECRET Memo for Mr. Bundy, Dec. 6, 1962. Forrestal reported to Bundy that he had been receiving indications "that there is a revival of the military tendency to resort to techniques of mass destruction in South Vietnam." As many as thirty-five "free zones" had been created where "indiscriminate bombing and use of napalm is permitted. . . ."

3. Townsend Hoopes and Douglas Brinkley, *Driven Patriot: The Life and Times of James Forrestal*, (New York: Knopf, 1992), pp. 480–81; "Michael V. Forrestal Dies at 61," *NYT*, Jan. 13, 1989; Forrestal "Biographical Data," Jan. 15, 1962, NSF, Box 320, JFK.

4. Roger Hilsman, *To Move a Nation* (Garden City, N.Y.: Doubleday, 1967), p. 6.

5. David Halberstam interview, June 5, 1995.

6. Frances FitzGerald, *Fire in the Lake: The Vietnamese and the Americans in Vietnam* (New York: Vintage, 1972), pp. 14, 242; Francis X. Winters, *The Year of the Hare*, (Athens: University of Georgia Press, 1997), p. 178.

7. Forrestal Oral History, pp. 136–37.

8. Ibid., pp. 141, 143.

9. Ellen J. Hammer, *A Death in November: America in Vietnam, 1963* (New York: Oxford University Press, 1987), p. 121. The French ambassador, Roger Lalouette, advised Diem to ask the Americans "gently" to withdraw some of their troops. Simultaneously, Lalouette was encouraging Diem to negotiate with the North. On September 18, 1963, Joe Alsop reported that Lalouette was serving as a catalyst for talks with the North. Alsop also quoted Nhu as saying that the North Vietnamese had "begged him to open negotiations." (Seymour M. Hersh, *The Dark Side of Camelot* [Boston: Little, Brown, 1997], p. 424.)

10. Anne E. Blair, *Lodge in Vietnam: A Patriot Abroad* (New Haven: Yale University Press, 1995), pp. 43–44.

11. William Prochnau, *Once Upon a Distant War: Young War Correspondents and the Early Vietnam Battles* (New York: Times Books, 1995), p. 403; Edwin O. Guthman and Jeffrey Shulman, eds., *Robert Kennedy: In His Own Words, The Unpublished Recollections of the Kennedy Years* (New York: Bantam, 1988), p. 403.

12. Prochnau, *Once Upon a Distant War,* p. 403; Guthman and Shulman, eds., *Robert Kennedy,* p. 403; Stanley Karnow, *Vietnam: A History* (New York: Viking, 1983), p. 288. On September 30, 1963, Bundy was given a Defense Department memo, addressed to the CIA director, which said of Halberstam that ". . . he is by and large accurate in terms of the facts that he includes in his articles." It concluded, nevertheless, that "reporting of this sort has contributed directly to the current state of affairs existing in South Vietnam." (Handwritten memo to Bundy, Sept. 30, 1963, with attached memo for Director of Central Intelligence, "David Halberstam's Reporting on South Vietnam," NSF, Box 209, JFK.)

13. "Memo on Washington Meeting in Aftermath of August Plot," Aug. 31, 1963, in Neil Sheehan et al., eds., *The Pentagon Papers as Published by The New York Times* (New York: Bantam, 1971), pp. 204–205.

14. Blair, *Lodge in Vietnam,* pp. 49–50; David Halberstam, *The Best and the Brightest* (New York: Random House, 1972), pp. 267–68.

15. Halberstam, *The Best and the Brightest,* p. 370.

16. Stanley Hoffmann interview, Feb. 15, 1995. Hoffmann lost Bundy's letter. This and another letter Bundy wrote about the French and NATO remained vivid in his memory as examples of Bundy's hubris. "There was this sense of infallibility, which I must say is what exasperated me about the Kennedy administration. I knew many of these people. They were arrogant bastards, Kaysen perhaps most of all, but also Schlesinger and Galbraith. . . . They always knew what the interest of another country was much better than the natives."

17. Paul M. Kattenburg, *The Vietnam Trauma in American Foreign Policy, 1945–1975* (New Brunswick, N.J.: Transaction, 1980), p. 120.

18. Bundy to Clifton and Salinger for the President, Sept. 1, 1963, Box 199, Vietnam, NSF, JFK; WPB Vietnam Manuscript, ch. 10, p. 9.

19. WPB interview, Feb. 16, 1994; WPB Vietnam Manuscript, ch. 9, p. 15.

20. WPB interview, Feb. 16, 1994. Halberstam confirmed meeting McNamara during this trip (David Halberstam, *WP,* May 14, 1995).

21. Forrestal Oral History, p. 163; WPB Vietnam Manuscript, ch. 9, p. 17.

22. Forrestal Oral History, p. 166.

23. WPB Vietnam Manuscript, pp. 9–20.

24. Bundy to Lodge, Eyes Only, Oct. 5, 1963, NSF Vietnam, Box 200, JFK.

25. Chester L. Cooper, *The Lost Crusade: America in Vietnam* (New York: Dodd, Mead, 1970), p. 216. Cooper in an interview (Oct. 29, 1993) disputed John M. Newman's interpretation of this incident in his book *JFK and Vietnam* (New York: Warner, 1992).

26. Robert S. McNamara interview, Mar. 7, 1990. Roswell Gilpatric made the same claim in a speech at the JFK Library. Roger Hilsman also claimed, "On numerous occasions President Kennedy told me that he was determined not to let Vietnam become an American war" (Roger Hilsman letter to the editor, *NYT,* Jan. 20, 1992). Schlesinger Jr., *NYT.*

27. Summary Record of NSC meeting, Oct. 2, 1963, 6:00 P.M., NSF Vietnam, Box 314, JFK.

28. See text of White House statement issued on Oct. 2, 1963, NSF, Vietnam, Box 200, JFK. For a full discussion of whether Kennedy intended to withdraw from Vietnam, see Newman, *JFK and Vietnam,* and Noam Chomsky, *Rethinking Camelot: JFK, the Vietnam War, and U.S. Political Culture* (Boston: South End, 1993).

29. WPB Vietnam Manuscript, ch. 10, p. 10.

30. TOP SECRET Memorandum of Conversation, The President, Governor Harriman, M. V. Forrestal, Apr. 6, 1962; J. K. Galbraith SECRET Memorandum for the President, Apr. 4, 1962, AH.

31. Jeff Shesol, *Mutual Contempt: Lyndon Johnson, Robert Kennedy and the Feud That Defined a Decade* (New York: Norton, 1997), pp. 385–86; Daniel Ellsberg interviews, May 7, 1996; Oct. 20, 1997. Arthur Schlesinger, Jr., *Robert Kennedy and His Times* (New York: Ballantine, 1978), pp. 98–99, 774.

32. Senator Mike Mansfield letter to Francis X. Winters, S.J., Oct. 24, 1989, courtesy of Winters; Winters, *The Year of the Hare*, pp. 21, 232.

33. Michael V. Forrestal interview transcript for CBS documentary "Vietnam Special," Dec. 21, 22, 1971, pp. 12–14, courtesy of Alexandra Whitney. CBS aired only a small portion of this interview.

34. Schlesinger, Jr., *Robert Kennedy and His Times,* pp. 764–70; Schlesinger, *NYT Book Review,* Mar. 29, 1992; Roger Hilsman letter to the editor, *NYT,* Jan. 20, 1992.

35. Hilsman, *To Move a Nation,* p. 501; Schlesinger, Jr., *Robert Kennedy and His Times,* p. 770. Michael Forrestal recalled Bobby Kennedy "beginning to have serious doubts about the whole effort in Vietnam . . ." in the summer of 1963 (Jean Stein, interviewer, and George Plimpton, ed., *American Journey: The Times of Robert Kennedy* [New York: Harcourt Brace Jovanovich, 1970], p. 207).

36. George McT. Kahin, *Intervention: How America Became Involved in Vietnam* (New York: Knopf, 1986), p. 177. Bundy was receiving numerous cables from the CIA reporting on various coup plots, including an assassination attempt on Ngo Dinh Nhu that "failed when the detonator of the explosive failed to work." (See CIA memos and cables, specifically CIA cable, Sept. 17, 1963, "Continued Operation of Tran Kim Tuyen's Coup d'Etat Group," NSF Vietnam, Box 200, CIA Reports, JFK.) For Bundy's worries, see Lodge cable to Bundy, Oct. 25, 1963, and Bundy to Lodge, Oct. 25, 1963, NSF Vietnam, Box 201, CIA Reports, JFK. Bundy's handwritten question can be found on an undated memo in NSF Vietnam, Box 201, Oct. 15–28, 1963, JFK.

37. See series of Lodge-Bundy eyes-only cables in NSF Vietnam, Box 201, Oct. 29–31, 1963, CIA Reports, JFK.

38. Blair, *Lodge in Vietnam,* p. 68.

39. Sheehan et al., *Pentagon Papers,* p. 232.

40. Rusk cable to Saigon embassy (drafted by Bundy and Hilsman), NSF Vietnam, Box 201, State Cables, Nov. 1–2, 1963, JFK. Just days before the coup, Diem had recalled his chargé d'affaires in Washington, D.C., Tran Van Dinh, and instructed him "to go to India to negotiate with the North." Dinh told Seymour M. Hersh that he believed Diem "was in the process of telling the United States to get out" when he was assassinated. (Hersh, *The Dark Side of Camelot,* pp. 433–34.) Mac Bundy would always deny that Nhu's secret contacts with Hanoi had been a motivation for the coup. He admitted to receiving the CIA's reports on Nhu, but said, "I don't think I gave them very heavy weight, because I didn't give Nhu very heavy weight." (MB interview, Feb. 15, 1994.)

41. Prochnau, *Once Upon a Distant War,* p. 473.

42. Hammer, *A Death in November,* p. 298; Blair, *Lodge in Vietnam,* p. 70.

43. Bundy Eyes Only for Lodge, NSF Vietnam, Box 201, CIA Reports, Nov. 1–2, 3–5, 1963, JFK. Maxwell D. Taylor, *Swords and Ploughshares* (New York: Norton, 1972), p. 301; Hammer, *A Death in November,* p. 300; Blair, *Lodge in Vietnam,* p. 75. In retrospect, Mac Bundy commented that the fact that he and Kennedy were shocked by Diem's murder "just says we hadn't thought very hard, because the notion that there would be a coup and that they would be glad to have a successful leader of nine years standing waiting around to reclaim the throne, I mean, that was dumb. But I shared in the stupidity." (MB interview, Feb. 15, 1994.)

44. Prochnau, *Once Upon a Distant War,* p. 482.

45. WPB Vietnam Manuscript, ch. 10, p. 6.

46. MB to WPB, Nov. 21, 1963, NSF Vietnam, Box 202, Memos & Misc., JFK.

47. WPB Vietnam Manuscript, ch. 9, p. 19; WPB interview, Feb. 16, 1994.

48. Blair, *Lodge in Vietnam*, p. 91.

49. KLPB Oral History, p. 108.

50. WPB interview, Feb. 16, 1994.

51. J. K. Galbraith to Kennedy, July 9, 1963, NSF India, Box 111, Galbraith Special File, Misc. Messages, JFK.

52. William Manchester, *The Death of a President*, (New York: Harper & Row, 1967), p. 271.

53. WPB Oral History, p. 11, LBJ; Manchester, *The Death of a President*, p. 402.

54. Chester Cooper interview, Dec. 3, 1993.

55. Manchester, *The Death of a President*, pp. 473, 476, 479–80.

56. Ibid., pp. 416, 445, 541.

57. Ibid., p. 550.

58. Ibid., pp. 559, 467, 581, 603. After the funeral Mac wrote Joe Alsop that "those of us who had the luck to be a part of it [Kennedy's presidency] had best be damned grateful. . . . Now we go on and while it will not be the same, it will certainly not be dull; and if he is watching, I'll bet he's amused." Alsop also suggested that Mac and Bill should donate one of their late father's Monet paintings to the White House "as double memorials to your father and the President—the two men you cared most about, both of whom you lost within the short space of a year" (Alsop to Mac Bundy, Dec. 16, 1963, Alsop Papers, LOC).

59. WPB interview, Feb. 16, 1994. Kay Bundy thought Johnson had "invented the whole story" about his mother because he "evidently thought that I was going to be able to make Mac stay with him . . ." (KLPB Oral History, p. 112).

60. Manchester, *The Death of a President*, p. 445.

61. Ibid., pp. 449–50.

62. Frederick L. Holborn interview, Nov. 20, 1996. Holborn was the presidential aide who handed Bundy's note to Kennedy as he left for Dallas.

63. Doris Kearns, *Lyndon Johnson & the American Dream* (New York: Harper & Row, 1976), pp. 177–78.

64. Lloyd Gardner, *Pay Any Price: Lyndon Johnson and the Wars for Vietnam* (Chicago: Dee, 1995), p. 93.

12: LBJ AND VIETNAM, 1964

1. McGeorge Bundy, "The Presidency and the Peace," *Foreign Affairs*, pp. 353–365, April 1964. Lloyd C. Gardner, *Pay Any Price: Lyndon Johnson and the Wars for Vietnam* (Chicago: Dee, 1995), pp. 93–94.

2. Roger Hilsman to the Secretary, with attached memo, Jan. 3, 1964, and Michael Forrestal to Bundy, Jan. 8, 1964, AH. The Forrestal document remains classified "Top Secret." See also Bundy to LBJ, Jan. 7, 1964, *Vietnam 1964*, vol. I of *FRUS, 1964–1968* (1992), p. 4.

3. Senator Mike Mansfield to the President, Jan. 6, 1964, *Vietnam 1964*, p. 2. Two days after becoming president, Johnson told Bundy and other officials that Southeast Asia was not going to go the way of China under his presidency. (Memorandum of Conversation, Nov. 24, 1963, LBJ, cited by Michael R. Beschloss, *Taking Charge: The Johnson White House Tapes, 1963–1964* [New York: Simon & Schuster, 1997], p. 73.)

4. Bundy to Johnson, Jan. 9, 1964, *Vietnam 1964*, pp. 8–9. Bundy warned Soviet ambassador Anatoly Dobrynin in December 1963 not to expect the United States to pull out of Vietnam because "this would be equivalent to Johnson's political suicide."

See Dobrynin's memoir, *In Confidence: Moscow's Ambassador to America's Six Cold War Presidents* (New York: Times Books, 1995), p. 117. Bundy told LBJ that on Vietnam, Galbraith's "views are like Mike Mansfield's, with perhaps a shade more understanding of the need for some firm position on the scene before we seek a political solution" (MB, Memorandum for the President, July 15, 1964, LBJ).

5. Ronald Steel, *Walter Lippmann and the American Century* (Boston: Little, Brown, 1980), pp. 549–50.

6. George Kahin, *Intervention: How America Became Involved in Vietnam* (New York: Knopf, 1986), pp. 188–89; Gardner, *Pay Any Price*, p. 113.

7. Forrestal to the President, Jan. 30, 1964, *Vietnam 1964*, pp. 42–43; WPB Vietnam Manuscript, ch. 12, p. 13.

8. Beschloss, *Taking Charge*, pp. 226–27.

9. LBJ tapes, WH 6403.01, PNO 9, #2309, Mar. 2, 1964; also cited by Beschloss, *Taking Charge*, pp. 262–63.

10. WPB Vietnam Manuscript, ch. 12, pp. 8–9.

11. LBJ tapes, WH 6403.01, PNO 9, #2309, Mar. 2, 1964; also cited by Beschloss, *Taking Charge*, pp. 262–63.

12. WPB Vietnam Manuscript, ch. 12, p. 17; McNamara-Ball Telcon, Feb. 22, 1964, 3:15 P.M., George Ball Papers, LBJ; David Halberstam, *The Best and the Brightest* (New York: Random House, 1972), p. 398; *Time*, Nov. 15, 1963, p. 33.

13. *NYT*, Mar. 1, 1964; *U.S. News & World Report*, Mar. 16, 1964, p. 19.

14. WPB Vietnam Manuscript, ch. 12, pp. 20–29; James C. Thomson, Jr., "How Could Vietnam Happen?: An Autopsy," *The Atlantic*, April 1968, p. 50; Thomson interview, Feb. 13, 1995.

15. Michael Forrestal to Mac Bundy, Mar. 18, 1964, Secret, AH.

16. Thomas B. Allen, *War Games* (New York: McGraw Hill, 1987), pp. 193–208; Harold P. Ford interview, June 24, 1993.

17. Halberstam, *The Best and the Brightest*, p. 462.

18. MB to LBJ, June 1, 1964, NSF, Box 2, LBJ.

19. WPB Vietnam Manuscript, ch. 13, p. 29; Randall Bennett Woods, *Fulbright: A Biography* (New York: Cambridge University Press, 1995), p. 391. In a memo briefing Bundy for his encounter with Fall, James C. Thomson, Jr., suggested, "I would force Fall to spell out precisely what would be negotiated and how South Vietnam would look after the negotiations had been implemented. I have heard him pushed on this before; he is generally forced to concede that his proposal will indeed lead to Communist takeover—and this will not be music to Senatorial ears." (Thomson to Bundy, May 12, 1964, Thomson Papers, Box 24, JFK.) When the bombing commenced a year later, Fall told Lawrence Spivak on national television that such tactics would be militarily ineffective (Dorothy Fall phone interview, Nov. 7, 1997).

20. A. J. Langguth interview, Feb. 22, 1997; Marguerite Higgins, *Our Vietnam Nightmare* (New York: Harper & Row, 1965).

21. WPB Vietnam Manuscript, ch. 13, p. 19.

22. Ted Gittinger, ed., *The Johnson Years: A Vietnam Roundtable* (Austin: University of Texas, 1993), pp. 24–25.

23. MB to LBJ, June 6, 1964, NSF, Box 2, LBJ.

24. MB to LBJ, June 10, 1964, NSF, Box 2, LBJ.

25. Michael Forrestal to John McNaughton, May 1, 1964, Secret. Bundy received a copy of this document, which was obtained from the Harriman Papers.

26. Michael Forrestal to Mac Bundy, May 26, 1964, AH, *Vietnam 1964*, p. 387.

27. Mac Bundy memo, May 26, 1964, *Vietnam 1964*, p. 390; Woods, *Fulbright*, pp. 346–47.

28. LBJ tape, WH 6405.10, #3522, May 27, 1964, LBJ; also quoted in Beschloss, *Taking Charge*, pp. 370–72.

29. Beschloss, *Taking Charge*, pp. 401–402. Two weeks earlier Russell had suggested, "If I was going to get out, I'd get the same crowd that got rid of old Diem to get rid of these people and get some fellow in there that said he wished to hell we would get out. That would give us a good excuse for getting out. . . ." When Johnson described McNamara's plan to interdict the flow of men and material down the Ho Chi Minh Trail with bombing, Russell said, "Oh, hell! That ain't worth a hoot. That's just impossible. . . . We tried it in Korea. . . ." (*Taking Charge*, pp. 363–70.)

30. Michael Forrestal to Jack Valenti, June 8, 1964, AH.

31. Michael Forrestal to the Secretary [Rusk], July 21, 1964, Top Secret, AH.

32. *NYT*, May 29, 1964.

33. James C. Thomson, Jr., Memorandum for McGeorge Bundy, July 22, 1964, Thomson Papers, Box 11, JFK.

34. Michael V. Forrestal letter to Alexandra Whitney, Apr. 6, 1964, courtesy of Alexandra Whitney.

35. Michael Forrestal to Mac Bundy, Secret and Personal, June 18, 1964, AH.

36. Allen Whiting interviews, Sept. 27, Oct. 2, 1995.

37. Marshall Green interview, Oct. 16, 1992.

38. James C. Thomson, Jr., interview, Feb. 13, 1995; Thomson, Jr., "How Could Vietnam Happen?: An Autopsy," p. 47. In the spring of 1964 one of the State Department's former China experts, O. Edmund Clubb, sent Thomson a twenty-four-page memo on "Why the War in Vietnam Cannot be Won." The choice, wrote Clubb, was clear: "to follow in French footsteps until overtaken by a similar fate or to adopt a new approach. . . ." Clubb argued that a negotiated end to the fighting, even if that led to reunification under the North, was the best outcome Washington could expect. "The Ho Chi Minh government was pushed into Communist China's arms by French military pressures and is currently held there by its need for military support against the United States . . . even a mildly Titoist North Vietnam . . . would be easier to live with than a North Vietnam bound tightly to Communist China. . . ." (Oliver E. Clubb, May 22, 1964, James C. Thomson, Jr., Papers, Box 24, JFK.)

39. WPB Vietnam Manuscript, ch. 14, pp. 13–14.

40. Memorandum from the Board of National Estimates (Sherman Kent) to Director John McCone, June 9, 1964, *Vietnam 1964*, p. 485.

41. Ibid. Bundy also admired Sherman Kent, who in turn once said of Mac, "That guy is absolutely the smartest guy I ever dealt with in my whole academic career . . ." (Willard Mathias interview, Dec. 3, 1993). Mac Bundy couldn't remember Kent's "Death of the Domino Theory" estimate; it was, he said, "a problem of palimpsest" (MB interview, Sept. 19, 1995).

42. WPB Vietnam Manuscript, ch. 14, pp. 10–11.

43. Ibid., p. 14.

44. Michael Forrestal memo to Secretary of State, Aug. 3, 1964, *Vietnam 1964*, pp. 598–600. A copy of this document was given to Mac Bundy.

45. WPB Vietnam Manuscript, ch. 14, p. 22.

46. The best account to date of the Gulf of Tonkin incident can be found in Edwin E. Moise's *Tonkin Gulf and the Escalation of the Vietnam War* (Chapel Hill: University of North Carolina Press, 1996). See also Joseph C. Goulden, *Truth Is the First Casualty: The Gulf of Tonkin Affair—Illusion and Reality* (Chicago: Rand McNally, 1969), pp. 51, 75.

47. Ray Cline reported his doubts to the President's Foreign Intelligence Advisory Board on August 6, 1964. When interviewed by Moise in 1992, Clifford said he couldn't recall the details, but that if Cline had conveyed this information he would have passed it on directly to President Johnson. (Moise, *Tonkin Gulf and the Escalation of the Vietnam War*, pp. 198–99; Eric Alterman phone interview with Moise, June 9, 1994, courtesy of Alterman.)

48. WPB letter to Eric Alterman, May 13, 1993, courtesy of Eric Alterman; Kahin, *Intervention*, p. 222; "The Phantom Battle That Led to War," *U.S. News & World Report*, July 23, 1984. A CIA analyst concluded just a few days after the August 4, 1964, attack that the North Vietnamese radio communications cited by McNamara were actually messages about the first attack. See Gardner, *Pay Any Price*, p. 137, and Woods, *Fulbright*, pp. 350–52.

49. WPB letter to Eric Alterman, May 13, 1993; Moise, *Tonkin Gulf and the Escalation of the Vietnam War*, p. 254.

50. WPB Vietnam Manuscript, ch. 14; George Ball Oral History, I, p. 23, LBJ.

51. Kahin, *Intervention*, pp. 220, 224; Deborah Shapley, *Promise and Power: The Life and Times of Robert McNamara* (Boston: Little, Brown, 1993), p. 305; Woods, *Fulbright*, p. 353.

52. Transcript of VOA interview with William P. Bundy taped for release on Aug. 15, 1964, and reprinted in *The Department of State Bulletin*, Sept. 7, 1964, p. 335.

53. Actually, the information Bundy and others were withholding from the American public was an open secret to anyone who wanted to know. See Thomson memorandums, Aug. 5, 6, 1964, James C. Thomson, Jr., Papers, Box 11, JFK. See also Moise, *Tonkin Gulf and the Escalation of the Vietnam War*, p. 66.

54. MB interview, Sept. 19, 1995.

55. William J. Duiker, "Hanoi's Response to American Policy: 1961–1965: Crossed Signals?," unpublished manuscript, Feb. 2, 1994, pp. 15–17. See also Moise, *Tonkin Gulf and the Escalation of the Vietnam War*, pp. 251–52. Immediately after the Tonkin incident, Mike Forrestal estimated that there were 28,000 to 34,000 regular Viet Cong forces, supplemented by 60,000 to 80,000 part-time guerrillas. "Infiltrees," he wrote, "are believed to make up 30 percent of the regular Viet Cong forces." (Michael Forrestal to the Secretary, Aug. 8. 1964; SECRET, AH.)

56. Gardner, *Pay Any Price*, p. 144.

57. SNIE 53-2-64, Oct. 1, 1964, *Vietnam 1964*, p. 806.

58. MB, Memorandum to the President, Oct. 1, 1964, LBJ.

59. Robert S. McNamara, with Brian VanDeMark, *In Retrospect: The Tragedy and Lessons of Vietnam* (New York: Times Books, 1995), pp. 156–57; David L. DiLeo, *George Ball: Vietnam and the Rethinking of Containment* (Chapel Hill: University of North Carolina Press, 1991), p. 103.

60. DiLeo, *George Ball*, p. 120.

61. William P. Bundy, Memorandum for Secretary Rusk, Secretary McNamara, Mr. Ball, Mr. McGeorge Bundy, "Attached Think-Piece on Our Choices in Southeast Asia," Oct. 19, 1964. This forty-two-page memo was released to the author under FOIA on Dec. 17, 1996. Bundy quotes portions of it in WPB Vietnam Manuscript, ch. 17, pp. 15–26. It is also briefly described in *Vietnam 1964*, pp. 812–13.

62. William P. Bundy, Memorandum for Secretary Rusk et al., "Attached Think-Piece on Our Choices in Southeast Asia," and WPB Vietnam Manuscript, ch. 17, pp. 15–26.

63. WPB Vietnam Manuscript, SO-1.

64. Ibid., ch, 18, p. 1.

65. Ibid., pp. 16–17; SO-le. On November 21, 1964, Bill Bundy and McNaughton drafted a document which stated, "The so-called 'domino' theory is oversimplified" (*Pentagon Papers*, Senator Gravel Edition, vol. 3, p. 658).

66. Thomson, Jr., "How Could Vietnam Happen?: An Autopsy," p. 51.

67. WPB Vietnam Manuscript, SO-1f; ch. 18, p. 17; WPB interview, Nov. 12, 1996; Dan Ellsberg interview, May 7, 1996; Feb. 21, 1997. See also *Vietnam 1964*, pp. 812–13.

68. Daniel Ellsberg interview, May 7, 1996; WPB interview, Nov. 12, 1996; Jonathan Moore could not recall this incident.

69. WPB Vietnam Manuscript, ch. 18, p. 37; Kahin, *Intervention*, p. 248.

70. Woods, *Fulbright*, p. 362.

71. James C. Thomson, Jr., Memorandum to MB, June 11, 1965 (Thomson quotes from his Nov. 28, 1964, paper to Bundy), Thomson Papers, Box 11, JFK.

72. James C. Thomson, Jr., interview, Feb. 13, 1995. Thomson retold this story anonymously to David Halberstam, and after Bundy's death published it in the *New York Times* (Sept. 22, 1996).

73. Halberstam, *The Best and the Brightest*, p. 517.

74. Eric F. Goldman, *The Tragedy of Lyndon Johnson* (New York: Knopf, 1969), p. 199; *Boston Globe*, Aug. 5, 1964; Edwin O. Guthman and Jeffrey Shulman, eds., *Robert Kennedy: In His Own Words, The Unpublished Recollections of the Kennedy Years* (New York: Bantam, 1988), p. 415.

75. MB to LBJ, Aug. 24, 1964, Bundy Memos to the President, LBJ.

76. Thomas Hughes interview, Oct. 27, 1997.

77. MB to Rusk, McNamara and Ball, Nov. 25, 1964, LBJ.

78. MB, Memorandum for the Record, Sept. 15, 1964, Memos to the President, Folder 6, Item 20, LBJ. See also Gordon Chang, *Friends and Enemies: The United States, China, and the Soviet Union, 1948–1972* (Stanford: Stanford University Press, 1990).

79. Joe Alsop letter to Avis Bohlen, undated, Autumn 1964, Box 69, Alsop Papers, LOC.

80. Halberstam, *The Best and the Brightest*, pp. 517–18; Doris Kearns, *Lyndon Johnson & the American Dream* (New York: Harper & Row, 1976), pp. 241–42.

81. Louis Auchincloss interview, Feb. 15, 1994.

82. MB memorandum for the President (two memos, both dated Dec. 2, 1964), LBJ.

83. MB interview, Sept. 19, 1995.

13: VIETNAM: THE DECISION, 1965

1. MB to LBJ, Feb. 2, 1965, Bundy Memorandums to the President, LBJ.

2. Thomas L. Hughes, "Experiencing McNamara," *Foreign Policy*, Fall 1995, pp. 155–71.

3. WPB Vietnam Manuscript, ch. 22, p. 11.

4. Lloyd C. Gardner, *Pay Any Price: Lyndon Johnson and the Wars for Vietnam* (Chicago: Dee, 1995), p. 153.

5. WPB Vietnam Manuscript, ch. 20, p. 21.

6. George W. Ball, *The Past Has Another Pattern*, (New York: Norton, 1982), p. 389.

7. James C. Thomson, Jr., "How Could Vietnam Happen?: An Autopsy," *The Atlantic*, April 1968, p. 51; George Kahin, *Intervention: How America Became Involved in Vietnam* (New York: Knopf, 1986), p. 272.

8. MB, "Memorandum for the President," Jan. 27, 1965, Bundy Memos, LBJ; Kahin, *Intervention*, pp. 272–74, 505; Gardner, *Pay Any Price*, pp. 166–67.

9. Gardner, *Pay Any Price*, p. 167.

10. Kahin, *Intervention*, p. 275.

11. Chester Cooper, *The Lost Crusade: America in Vietnam* (New York: Dodd, Mead, 1970), p. 257.

12. Gardner, *Pay Any Price*, p. 168.

13. Cooper, *The Lost Crusade*, p. 259; Gardner, *Pay Any Price*, p. 169; WPB Vietnam Manuscript, ch. 22, B-6.

14. Stanley Karnow, *Vietnam: A History* (New York: Viking, 1983), p. 412; David

Halberstam, *The Best and the Brightest* (New York: Random House, 1972), p. 521; *Washington Star*, Feb. 8, 1965. Ironically, only a month before, Bundy had advised against a similar retaliatory strike, telling Johnson, "It is easy for advisers to be brave, but it is the President who must live with the decision." (Robert D. Schulzinger, *A Time for War: The United States and Vietnam, 1941–1975* [New York: Oxford University Press, 1997], p. 169.)

15. Neil Sheehan et al., *The Pentagon Papers as Published by The New York Times* (New York: Bantam, 1971), pp. 423–27; Kahin, *Intervention*, pp. 281–83; Lyndon Johnson, *The Vantage Point: Perspectives of the Presidency, 1963–1969* (New York: Holt, Rinehart and Winston, 1971), pp. 126–27. Bundy also came back from Vietnam with a new respect for the enemy: "They can appear anywhere—and at almost any time. They have accepted extraordinary losses and they have come back for more. They show skill in the sneak attacks and ferocity when cornered." Even so, he forced himself to conclude, "[T]he weary country does not want them to win." (Michael H. Hunt, *Lyndon Johnson's War: America's Cold War Crusade in Vietnam, 1945–1968* [New York: Hill & Wang, 1996], pp. 90–91.)

16. WPB Vietnam Manuscript, ch. 22B, p. 25.

17. Halberstam, *The Best and the Brightest*, pp. 533, 515.

18. William Conrad Gibbons, *The U.S. Government and the Vietnam War*, part III (Princeton: Princeton University Press, 1989), pp. 60, 96–97. In late March 1965, Thomson concluded that the "long-run consequences" of disengagement "will be far less costly" than to "push on in search of full—and elusive—victory." ("Courage, Vision and the Vietnam Future," Mar. 30, 1965, Thomson Papers, Box 25, JFK.)

19. Ronald Steel, *Walter Lippmann and the American Century*, (Boston: Little, Brown, 1980), p. 558. Regarding Joseph Kraft's December 1964 *Harper's* essay, see "Secret Interview of Michael V. Forrestal by Joseph Kraft," Apr. 8, July 28, Aug. 14, 1964, AH, in the author's possession.

20. Edward Weeks, ed., *Conversations with Walter Lippmann* (Boston: Little, Brown, 1965), pp. 197–210.

21. Karnow, *Vietnam*, p. 410.

22. Eric F. Goldman, *The Tragedy of Lyndon Johnson*, (New York: Knopf, 1969), p. 404.

23. Gibbons, *The U.S. Government and the Vietnam War*, part III, pp. 156–57.

24. Robert D. Schulzinger, *A Time for War*, p. 171. Todd Gitlin, *The Whole World Is Watching: Mass Media in the Making and Unmaking of the New Left* (Berkeley: University of California Press, 1980), p. 73. Simultaneously, Bill Bundy cabled the U.S. embassy in Saigon that approval had been given to increase U.S. troop levels to 82,000 over the next two months. He warned, however, that it "remains most important that these deployments receive no publicity prior to actual arrival." (WPB TOP SECRET cable, Apr. 22, 1965, FOIA document declassified Jan. 14, 1997.)

25. *WP*, Feb. 18, 1965.

26. Harriman/Schlesinger memorandum of conversation, Mar. 20, 1965, AH, author's archives.

27. I. F. Stone, *In a Time of Torment* (New York: Vintage, 1967), pp. 212–18; WPB Vietnam Manuscript, ch. 22B, pp. 35–40; Andrew Patner, *I. F. Stone*, (New York: Pantheon, 1988), p. 101.

28. Marcus G. Raskin and Bernard B. Fall, eds., *The Viet-Nam Reader* (New York: Random House, 1965), p. 135; Marcus Raskin interviews, May 30, 1991, and Apr. 5, 1997; WPB to Raskin, Jan. 11, 1965, and Raskin to WPB, Jan. 25, 1965; James C. Thomson, Jr., Papers, Box 25, JFK.

29. Lloyd C. Gardner, "Harry Hopkins with Hand Grenades? McGeorge Bundy in the Kennedy and Johnson Years," p. 29, courtesy of Gardner, on file at LBJ.

30. Steel, *Walter Lippmann and the American Century*, pp. 558–63.

31. Melvin Small, *Johnson, Nixon and the Doves* (New Brunswick, N.J.: Rutgers University Press, 1988), p. 42.

32. Judith Clavir Albert and Stewart Edward Albert, eds., *The Sixties Papers: Documents of a Rebellious Decade* (New York: Praeger, 1984), p. 222; Todd Gitlin, *The Sixties: Years of Hope, Days of Rage* (New York: Bantam, 1987), pp. 183–84.

33. Greg Lawless, *The Harvard Crimson Anthology*, (Boston: Houghton Mifflin, 1980), p. 159; Gardner, "Harry Hopkins with Hand Grenades? McGeorge Bundy in the Kennedy and Johnson Years," p. 30; Gardner, *Pay Any Price*, pp. 204–205.

34. That spring Bill Bundy compared the youthful critics of the war to his own naive support for the Loyalists during the Spanish Civil War. "It happens," he wrote Jim Rowe, Jr., "that I just finished reading George Orwell's *Homage to Catalonia*, which pretty well brings out how fallacious the liberal view of the Spanish fight was after the opening months." The New Left, he thought, was making the "same type of error" in its romanticization of the National Liberation Front. (WPB to James H. Rowe, Jr., Apr. 17, 1965, FOIA document declassified Jan. 14, 1997.)

35. Eli S. Zaretsky–McGeorge Bundy correspondence, Apr. 21, 28, 1965, Box 71, WH Central File Subject File, LBJ; Eli S. Zaretsky phone interview, Mar. 27, 1997.

36. *WP*, May 15, 1965.

37. *Boston Globe*, May 13, 1965; *WP*, May 15, 1965.

38. Gardner, *Pay Any Price*, p. 215; *NYT*, May 16, 1965.

39. Thomas Powers, *The War at Home* (New York: Grossman, 1973), pp. 57–62. That spring Bill Moyers reported to Johnson: "Schlesinger is also with you on Vietnam. . . . He says with enough troops on the ground you might start winning the jungle war and surely will have stronger muscle for any discussions that emerge." (Undated, spring 1965, Moyers to LBJ, LBJ.)

40. *NYT*, May 17, 1965; *WP*, May 16, 1965.

41. *WP*, May 16, 17, 1965.

42. *NYT*, May 17, 1965.

43. Stone, *In a Time of Torment*, p. 238.

44. MB letter to Joseph Alsop, Feb. 15, 1971, Box 135, Alsop Papers, LOC; MB interview, Feb. 15, 1994.

45. Robert A. Scalapino letter to MB, June 3, 1965, Box 71, WH Central File, Subject File, LBJ.

46. MB interview, Feb. 15, 1994. Bundy first met broadcast executive Fred Friendly at this time. Bundy later recruited him to work on public television at the Ford Foundation.

47. James Thomson, Jr., interview, Feb. 13, 1995.

48. CBS News Special Report, "Vietnam Dialogue: Mr. Bundy and the Professors," June 21, 1965, James C. Thomson, Jr., Papers, JFK. The hour-long debate included not only Bundy and Morgenthau, but also Professor Zbigniew Brzezinski, Professor O. Edmund Clubb, Dr. Guy J. Pauker and Professor John D. Donoghue.

49. David L. Schalk, *War and the Ivory Tower: Algeria and Vietnam* (New York: Oxford University Press, 1991), pp. 53–54; Powers, *The War at Home*, pp. 67–69.

50. Richard N. Goodwin, *Remembering America* (Boston: Little, Brown, 1988), pp. 400–401. Moyers later told the historian Robert Dallek that he consulted a psychiatrist in a preliminary effort to determine if a name could be attached to Johnson's behavior.

51. MB interview, Feb. 15, 1994.

52. *Time*, June 25, 1965; *WP*, June 15, 1965.

53. Small, *Johnson, Nixon and the Doves*, p. 51; MB interview, Feb. 15, 1994; *Time*, June 25, 1965.

54. Randall Bennett Woods, *Fulbright: A Biography* (New York: Cambridge University Press, 1995), p. 377.

55. Goodwin, *Remembering America*, p. 406.

56. Woods, *Fulbright*, pp. 377, 381, 390.

57. MB interview, Feb. 15, 1994.

58. Halberstam, *The Best and the Brightest*, p. 46.

59. Henry Kissinger–McGeorge Bundy correspondence, Apr. 12, 13, 1965, Bundy correspondence, LBJ.

60. Goldman, *The Tragedy of Lyndon Johnson*, pp. 446, 457; Small, *Johnson, Nixon and the Doves*, p. 53.

61. *Saturday Review*, July 3, 1965.

62. William Bundy himself acknowledged in a SECRET memo on April 15, 1965, that the administration had a "problem" with their official line that the United States had been prepared in "principle" to support free elections in 1956. "Actual belief at this time," Bundy wrote, "was that such elections would probably have produced pro-Communist majority, and there are unfortunately quotations in Eisenhower book and other literature making this point clear." (FOIA document declassified Jan. 14, 1997.) A month later Bundy nevertheless gave a speech at Berkeley in which he asserted that the North Vietnamese, "all propaganda to the contrary notwithstanding, simply were not willing to risk the loss of South Viet-Nam in elections." (W. P. Bundy, "Draft Berkeley Speech," Mar. 24, 1965, FOIA document declassified, Jan. 14, 1997).

63. Walter Lippmann–McGeorge Bundy correspondence, Apr. 20, 23, 28, 1965, Lippmann Papers, Yale.

64. Steel, *Walter Lippmann and the American Century*, pp. 574–75.

65. Thomas L. Hughes notes of meetings, April 21, April 22, April 26, May 7 and May 13, 1965, courtesy of Hughes, who discovered these notes in his papers in June 1998. Robert W. Merry, *Taking on the World: Joseph and Stewart Alsop—Guardians of the American Century* (New York: Viking, 1996), p. 419; Steel, *Walter Lippmann and the American Century*, p. 560.

66. Not surprisingly, Mac's letter "pleased" Alsop greatly "and meant a great deal" to him "in all sorts of different ways." Even so, while Joe was touched by Mac's declaration of "love," he was still rankled that Bundy would not talk to him about the war. (MB to Joseph Alsop, undated, General Correspondence "B" 1964, Alsop Papers, LOC. The letter is probably from January or February 1965. See also Merry, *Taking on the World*, p. 419.)

67. MB memorandum for the president, Mar. 31, 1965, Box 3, NSF, LBJ.

68. MB to LBJ, June 3, 1965, Box 3, NSF, LBJ; Woods, *Fulbright*, p. 385.

69. Robert S. McNamara, with Brian VanDeMark, *In Retrospect: The Tragedy and Lessons of Vietnam* (New York: Times Books, 1995), p. 186.

70. Larry Berman, *Planning a Tragedy: The Americanization of the War in Vietnam* (New York: Norton, 1982), pp. 71–74.

71. Ibid., pp. 77–80.

72. Ibid., pp. 187–89.

73. McNamara claims in his 1995 memoir, *In Retrospect*, "I shared all his [Bundy's] views and concerns. But the challenge was to lay out the answers—not just the questions" (p. 194).

74. MB interview, Nov. 3, 1994.

75. David L. DiLeo, *George Ball: Vietnam and the Rethinking of Containment* (Chapel Hill: University of North Carolina Press, 1991), p. 235.

76. MB interview, Nov. 3, 1994.

77. Clark Clifford, with Richard Holbrooke, *Counsel to the President* (New York: Random House, 1991), p. 410. Clifford favored a negotiated settlement: "It won't be what we want, but we can learn to live with it."

78. WPB Vietnam Manuscript, ch. 26, p. 25.

79. Brian VanDeMark, *Into the Quagmire: Lyndon Johnson and the Escalation of the Vietnam War* (New York: Oxford University Press, 1991), pp. 169–70.

80. Berman, *Planning a Tragedy*, pp. 86–87.

81. Gibbons, *The U.S. Government and the Vietnam War*, part III, pp. 330–42.

82. WPB Vietnam Manuscript, ch. 26, p. 26, and Halberstam, *The Best and the Brightest*, p. 580.

83. Allen Whiting interviews, Sept. 27, Oct. 2, 1995.

84. Gibbons, *The U.S. Government and the Vietnam War*, part II, pp. 330–42; WPB Vietnam Manuscript, ch. 27, p. 8. See also draft WPB memo, June 25, 1965, "Ideas and Possible Outline for Project," TOP SECRET, FOIA document declassified Jan. 14, 1997.

85. WPB Vietnam Manuscript, ch. 27, p. 1; Berman, *Planning a Tragedy*, p. 90.

86. Berman, *Planning a Tragedy*, p. 88.

87. Ibid., pp. 93–94.

88. Nicholas Katzenbach interview, Nov. 12, 1996.

89. Gibbons, *The U.S. Government and the Vietnam War*, part III, pp. 347–50. Walter Isaacson and Evan Thomas, *The Wise Men: Six Friends and the World They Made* (New York: Simon & Schuster, 1986), pp. 650–52; Kai Bird, *The Chairman: John J. McCloy/The Making of the American Establishment* (New York: Simon & Schuster, 1992), p. 578.

90. WPB Vietnam Manuscript, ch. 27, p. 20.

91. MB letter to Larry Berman, cited in Berman, *Planning a Tragedy*, p. 145.

92. Thomas Hughes interview, Feb. 11, 1993.

93. Gibbons, *The U.S. Government and the Vietnam War*, part III, pp. 403–404; WPB Vietnam Manuscript, ch. 27, pp. 26–33.

94. WPB Vietnam Manuscript, ch. 27, p. 33; McNamara, *In Retrospect*, p. 201.

95. Gibbons, *January–July 1965*, part III of *The U.S. Government and the Vietnam War*, p. vii.

96. Merle Miller, *Lyndon: An Oral Biography* (New York: Ballantine, 1980), p. 508.

97. McNamara, *In Retrospect*, pp. 219–20.

98. Lieutenant General Harold G. Moore (Ret.) and Joseph L. Galloway, *We Were Soldiers Once . . . and Young: Ia Drang, the Battle that Changed the War in Vietnam* (New York: HarperCollins, 1992), pp. 400–401.

99. Ted Gittinger, ed., *The Johnson Years: A Vietnam Roundtable* (Austin: University of Texas, 1993), p. 107; Small, *Johnson, Nixon and the Doves*, pp. 68–69.

100. Gardner, "Harry Hopkins with Hand Grenades? McGeorge Bundy in the Kennedy and Johnson Years." Gardner cites Bundy to Johnson, Nov. 27, 1965, Boxes 91–95, NSF Vietnam, LBJ.

101. Benjamin Bradlee interview, Dec. 17, 1993; Harriet Bundy Belin and Gaspard d'Andelot Belin interview, June 20, 1993.

102. MB interview, Nov. 3, 1994.

103. John J. McCloy–McGeorge Bundy correspondence, Apr. 4, 9, 25, 20, 1962, JJM. See also Bird, *The Chairman*, p. 440.

104. *Newsweek*, Mar. 7, 1966.

105. Judge Charles Wyzanski memorandum (sent to Jack McCloy), Nov. 13, 1965, Box C1, Folder Ford Foundation 1, JJM.

106. MB interview, Feb. 15, 1994.

107. MB interview, Sept. 19, 1995; MB, Memorandum for the President, Nov. 30, 1965; MB memo to LBJ re: "Letter of Resignation," Dec. 4, 1965, Box 1, Office of the President Files, LBJ; *Newsweek*, Dec. 20, 1965.

108. McNamara, *In Retrospect*, p. 235.

109. Clifford with Holbrooke, *Counsel to the President*, pp. 434–35.

110. Arthur Schlesinger, Jr., *Robert Kennedy and His Times* (New York: Ballantine, 1978), p. 792.

111. Benjamin Bradlee interview, Dec. 17, 1993. Note that Bradlee did not inform

readers of the *Washington Post* that McNamara was shedding tears over the war as early as the end of 1965. Tom Hughes recalled, "McNamara was telling people at dinner parties all over town what he really thought about the war" (Thomas Hughes interview, Feb. 11, 1993).

112. James C. Thomson, Jr., interview, Feb. 13, 1995.

113. MB to LBJ, Jan. 24, 1966, NSF Vietnam, Boxes 91–95, LBJ.

114. Gardner, *Pay Any Price*, pp. 291–92; Untitled Notes, Feb. 15, 1966, Bundy Papers, Box 2, LBJ.

115. *WP*, Feb. 21, 1966; Schlesinger, Jr., *Robert Kennedy and His Times*, p. 794.

116. Maxine Chesire, *WP*, Mar. 1, 1966.

117. Walter Lippmann, *WP*, Mar. 1, May 3, 1966.

118. Joseph Kraft, *WP*, Mar. 2, 1966; Merry, *Taking on the World*, p. 447.

119. Arthur Schlesinger, Jr., "McGeorge Bundy: The End of an Era," *WP*, Feb. 27, 1966.

120. MB interview, Sept. 19, 1995; MB to LBJ, Feb. 2, 1965, Bundy Memoranda to the President, LBJ.

121. Halberstam, *The Best and the Brightest*, p. 627; *The New Republic*, Apr. 16, 1966.

122. Fulbright letter to Lewis Douglas, Jan. 9, 1968, Douglas Papers, University of Arizona, Tuscon; Townsend Hoopes, *The Limits of Intervention* (New York: McKay, 1973), p. 61; secret memorandum of conversation with the president, May 30, 1966, AH, author's archives.

123. McNamara, *In Retrospect*, p. 186.

124. Gibbons, *The U.S. Government and the Vietnam War*, part II, pp. 330–42; Berman, *Planning a Tragedy*, pp. 187–89.

14: VIETNAM QUAGMIRE, 1966–1969

1. WPB interview, Feb. 16, 1994.

2. Thomas Hughes interview, Feb. 11, 1993.

3. WPB Oral History, Tape 3, p. 30, May 29, 1969, LBJ.

4. John Prados, *The Hidden History of the Vietnam War* (Chicago: Dee, 1995), pp. 96–97.

5. Deborah Shapley, *Promise and Power: The Life and Times of Robert McNamara* (Boston: Little, Brown, 1993), p. 475.

6. Frederick Bunnell, "American 'Low Posture' Policy Toward Indonesia in the Months Leading Up to the 1965 'Coup,' " *Indonesia* no. 50 (October 1990), p. 49.

7. Marshall Green (Foreword by William P. Bundy), *Indonesia: Crisis and Transformation, 1965–1968* (Washington, D.C.: Compass, 1990), pp. xi–xii; WPB letter to David Johnson, Jan. 22, 1996, courtesy of Johnson.

8. Francis Underhill letter to David Johnson, Nov. 9, 1995, courtesy of Johnson.

9. Adam Schwartz, *A Nation in Waiting: Indonesia in the 1990s* (Boulder: Westview, 1994); Jeri Laber, "Smoldering Indonesia," *New York Review of Books*, Jan. 9, 1997; Benedict R. Anderson and Ruth T. McVey, "A Preliminary Analysis of the October 1, 1965 Coup in Indonesia" (Ithaca: Cornell Modern Indonesia Project, 1971).

10. Peter Dale Scott, "The United States and the Overthrow of Sukarno, 1965–1967," *Pacific Affairs*, Summer 1985, pp. 239–64; Geoffrey Robinson, *The Dark Side of Paradise* (Ithaca: Cornell University Press, 1995). See also David T. Johnson's unpublished paper "Gestapu: The CIA's 'Track Two' in Indonesia," courtesy of Johnson. Francis Underhill later wrote Johnson, "I was never convinced that it was a Communist coup attempt. . . . I am sure, however, that the U.S. was not involved." Underhill letter to Johnson, Nov. 9, 1995, courtesy of Johnson. See also Mark Curtis, "British Role in

Slaughter," *The Observer*, July 28, 1996; "Democratic Genocide," *The Ecologist*, vol. 26, no. 5 (September–October, 1996); letters from Ambassador Robert L. Barry, Kathy Kadane and Jeri Laber in "Smoldering Indonesia: An Exchange," *New York Review of Books*, Apr. 10, 1997. For a contrary view, see Paul F. Gardner, *Shared Hopes, Separate Fears: Fifty Years of U.S.-Indonesian Relations* (Boulder: Westview, 1997). A retired U.S. Foreign Service officer, Gardner was commissioned by the United States–Indonesia Society to write this book.

11. H. W. Brands, "The Limits of Manipulation: How the United States Didn't Topple Sukarno," *Journal of American History*, December 1989, p. 786; Audrey R. Kahin and George McT. Kahin, *Subversion as Foreign Policy: The Secret Eisenhower and Dulles Debacle in Indonesia* (New York: New Press, 1995), p. 228; Geoffrey Robinson, "Some Arguments Concerning U.S. Influence and Complicity in the Indonesian 'Coup' of October 1, 1965," unpublished manuscript, Dec. 20, 1983, courtesy of Robinson; Scott, "The United States and the Overthrow of Sukarno, 1965–1967." A "Secret" six-page State Department document on Indonesia reported that "at least 300,000 Indonesians were killed" from October 1, 1965 through mid-March 1966. (AH Papers, author's archives.)

12. Daniel Ellsberg interview, May 7, 1997.

13. Brands, "The Limits of Manipulation," pp. 785–808; Kahin and Kahin, *Subversion as Foreign Policy*, p. 230.

14. Green, *Indonesia*, p. 69.

15. Bunnell, "American 'Low Posture' Policy Toward Indonesia in the Months Leading Up to the 1965 'Coup,' " p. 60. U.S. military aid to the Indonesian military amounted to $39.5 million in the years 1962–65. When Congress attempted in 1963 to cut off military aid to Indonesia, Assistant Secretary of State Roger Hilsman told a key congressman, "This would be very silly. . . . Our military aid to Indonesia is designed to strengthen the Western position. When Sukarno leaves the scene, they can put up a fight." (Memorandum of telephone conversation, June 25, 1963, James C. Thomson, Jr., Papers, Box 21, JFK.) Significantly, the Johnson administration persuaded Congress to treat this aid as a covert matter. In 1976 the Church Committee investigations into the intelligence community demonstrated that Lockheed Corporation made political payoffs to Indonesian personalities, who in turn passed these funds to General Suharto. See Scott, "The United States and the Overthrow of Sukarno, 1965–1967," pp. 253, 256.

16. Robert Martens gave the list to Tirta Kentjana Adhyatman, an aide to Adam Malik, an Indonesian politician allied with General Suharto. Adhyatman later wrote Martens, "I remember how you supply me with the names of the Politburo members and CC, including photographs." (Adhyatman to Martens, Nov. 20, 1988, courtesy of David Johnson.)

17. Kathy Kadane, "U.S. Officials' List Aided Indonesian Bloodbath in '60s," *WP*, May 21, 1990; Roger Kerson, "The Embassy's Hit List," *Columbia Journalism Review*, November–December 1990; Michael Wines, *NYT*, July 12, 1990; Green, *Indonesia*, p. 154. Kadane's story was subsequently criticized by Michael Wines of the *New York Times*. Wines reported that Green "had no recollection that Mr. Martens [the political officer] had compiled lists of Communist Party members. . . ." Kadane's December 18, 1989, transcript, however, clearly shows that Green was aware of the list. When Kadane said that "the decision to have Bob [Martens] disseminate the names to an army emissary was made by a group of you, yourself, the station chief Hugh Tovar, Ed [Masters] himself, the defense attaché and Jack Lydman [Green's deputy]," Green replied, "Well, I wouldn't gainsay it—in other words, if he said that were so, I would agree with it." Earlier in the interview Green had said, "The extent to which we had any hand in it, that's something I wouldn't know. Maybe you could ask Bob [Martens] whether or not we furnished the information. I know that Bob has told me that we had a lot more information than the Indonesians themselves." When Kadane sug-

gested that the list "became quite relevant later on after the army attack," Green said, "Oh, that's right. It did. That's right." Obviously, Green was aware that such a list had been compiled. Wines failed to grasp the remarkable thing about Green's memory of these events which was that the decision to hand over the list was clearly made as a matter of course, with little or no deliberation over the bloody consequences. Green was not denying Kadane's reporting of what his colleagues had done. (See transcripts of Kathy Kadane interviews, July 1990 Memo to Editors from States News Service, NS.)

18. WPB interview, Nov. 12, 1996.

19. Bunnell, "American 'Low Posture' Policy Toward Indonesia in the Months Leading Up to the 1965 'Coup.' " When confronted with the theory of U.S. involvement in the coup, Mac Bundy said, "My memory is a blank on the subject. . . ." MB to David Johnson, Jan. 19, 1996, courtesy of Johnson. On the other hand, James Reston wrote in the *New York Times* on June 19, 1966, that "there was a great deal more contact between the Indonesian high command and Washington before September 30 [the coup] than is generally realized."

20. *Department of State Bulletin*, Feb. 5, 1968.

21. MB to Joseph Alsop, Jan. 22, 1967; Alsop to MB, Jan. 25, 1967 and MB to Alsop, Jan. 27, 1967, Box 76, Alsop Papers, LOC. See also Arthur Schlesinger, Jr., *The Bitter Heritage: Vietnam and American Democracy, 1941–1966* (Boston: Houghton Mifflin, 1966), p. 75. A CIA investigation concluded, "We have searched in vain for evidence that the US display of determination in Vietnam directly influenced the outcome of the Indonesian crisis in any significant way." Suharto's war on the PKI "appears to have evolved purely from a complex and long-standing domestic political situation. Nevertheless, events in Indonesia might have developed differently if the US had withdrawn from Southeast Asia." (CIA Intelligence Memorandum, The Indonesian Crisis and US Determination in Vietnam, May 13, 1966, NSF, Box 248, LBJ.)

22. Green, *Indonesia*, pp. 152–53; In retrospect, Green argued, "After 1967, Bundy should have gone for a political accommodation in Vietnam. Elections would probably have led to a communist victory, but we should have risked this. It was hopeless anyway." (Green interview, Oct. 16, 1992.)

23. Townsend Hoopes, *The Limits of Intervention* (New York: McKay, 1973), p. 119.

24. Allen Whiting interviews, Sept. 27, Oct. 2, 1995; Qiang Zhai, "Beijing and the Vietnam Conflict, 1964–1965: New Chinese Evidence," *Cold War International History Project*, issues 6–7 (Winter 1995–96), p. 237.

25. *Department of State Bulletin*, June 20, 1966.

26. PERSONAL-SECRET Memo of Conversation with Secretary McNamara, May 30, 1966, AH.

27. SECRET, Memos of Conversation with Secretary McNamara, Oct. 10, Nov. 26, 1966, AH.

28. Marilyn B. Young, *The Vietnam Wars: 1945–1990* (New York: HarperCollins, 1991), p. 177.

29. Shapley, *Promise and Power*, p. 410; Paul Hendrickson, *The Living and the Dead: Robert McNamara and Five Lives of a Lost War* (New York: Knopf, 1996), p. 265.

30. Stanley Karnow, *Vietnam: A History* (New York: Viking, 1983), p. 11.

31. SECRET State Department memo of conversation, Aug. 5, 1966, AH. Harriman was told this by a RAND Corporation expert, Leon Goure, whose report was based on interviews with eight hundred Viet Cong and North Vietnamese prisoners of war.

32. *The Pentagon Papers: The Defense Department History of United States Decisionmaking on Vietnam*, Senator Gravel Edition, vol. 4 (Boston: Beacon, 1971), p. 420.

33. Karnow, *Vietnam*, p. 602; William Colby and Peter Forbath, *Honorable Men: My Life in the CIA* (New York: Simon & Schuster, 1978), p. 272.

34. SECRET State Department memo of conversation, Aug. 2, 1966, AH.

35. Bill Moyers to WPB, Jan. 13, 1967, Bill Moyers Papers, LBJ.

36. *Pentagon Papers*, Gravel ed., vol. 4, pp. 138, 156–59.

37. Sheehan described the U.S. effort in Vietnam as "a killing machine" and he wondered "whether the United States or any nation has the right to inflict this suffering and degradation on another people for its own ends" (Noam Chomsky, *American Power and the New Mandarins* [New York: Pantheon, 1969], pp. 245–46). Chomsky's essay "The Logic of Withdrawal" was originally published in *Ramparts* magazine, September 1967; David M. Barrett, *Uncertain Warriors: Lyndon Johnson and His Vietnam Advisers* (Lawrence: University Press of Kansas, 1993), pp. 71–72.

38. Michael Wreszin, "Arthur Schlesinger, Jr., Scholar-Activist in Cold War America: 1946–1956," *Salmagundi*, Spring–Summer 1984, p. 274; Schlesinger, Jr., *The Bitter Heritage*, pp. 105–106.

39. Joseph Alsop letter to MB, Jan. 30, 1967, Box 76, Alsop Papers, LOC.

40. Robert W. Merry, *Taking on the World: Joseph and Stewart Alsop—Guardians of the American Century* (New York: Viking, 1996), pp. 447, 451; Joseph Alsop to Sir Isaiah Berlin, Mar. 18, Apr. 14, 1966, Box 73, Alsop Papers, LOC.

41. McGeorge Bundy, "The End of Either/Or," *Foreign Affairs*, January 1967, pp. 200–201.

42. Shapley, *Promise and Power*, pp. 366, 418.

43. Ibid., pp. 420–21.

44. Daniel Ellsberg interview, May 7, 1996.

45. TOP SECRET—PERSONAL—LITERALLY EYES ONLY GOVERNOR HARRIMAN, Memorandum of Conversation with Secretary McNamara, July 1, 1967, 2:00 P.M., AH.

46. Richard Ullman interview, Feb. 16, 1994; Leslie Gelb interview, Feb. 17, 1994.

47. WPB interview, Feb. 16, 1994.

48. Melvin Small, *Johnson, Nixon and the Doves* (New Brunswick, N.J.: Rutgers University Press, 1988), p. 151; WPB interview by Tom Wells, May 27, 1986, courtesy of Wells.

49. KLPB, Oral History, p. 114. Katharine Bundy died on June 6, 1983.

50. *WP*, Aug. 16, 1967; *NYT*, Aug. 16, 1967.

51. William P. Bundy, "Bundy Comments on Galbraith's Plan," *NYT Magazine*, Nov. 12, 1967.

52. Thomas Powers, *The War at Home* (New York: Grossman, 1973), pp. 192–93; David L. Schalk, *War and the Ivory Tower: Algeria and Vietnam* (New York: Oxford University Press, 1991), p. 44; "A Call to Resist Illegitimate Authority," in Marvin E. Gettleman et al., eds., *Vietnam and America: A Documented History* (New York: Grove, 1985), pp. 308–309; Marcus Raskin phone interviews, June 19, July 25, 1997.

53. Sam Adams, *War of Numbers: An Intelligence Memoir* (South Royalton, Vt.: Steerforth, 1994), pp. 94, 109.

54. Prados, *The Hidden History of the Vietnam War*, p. 124. When Sherman Kent learned how the military had cooked the books, he told Adams, "Sam, have we gone beyond the bounds of reasonable dishonesty?" (Adams, *War of Numbers*, p. 122).

55. Adams, *War of Numbers*, p. 218. Bundy's old friend Joe Alsop was an eternal optimist. That autumn he wrote Donald Graham's wife (Donny, Jr., was then serving in the 1st Air Cavalry in Vietnam), "Contrary to what you read in the *New York Times* the war is going very well indeed and our progress should begin to show in a very dramatic way by next spring or early summer." (Alsop to Mrs. Donald Graham, Oct. 19, 1967, Box 130, Alsop Papers, LOC.)

56. Walter Isaacson and Evan Thomas, *The Wise Men: Six Friends and the World They Made* (New York: Simon & Schuster, 1986), pp. 679–80.

57. Lloyd C. Gardner, *Pay Any Price: Lyndon Johnson and the Wars for Vietnam* (Chicago: Dee, 1995), pp. 401–403; William Conrad Gibbons, *The U.S. Government and the Vietnam War*, part IV (Princeton: Princeton University Press, 1955), pp. 878–880; Small, *Johnson, Nixon and the Doves*, p. 121.

58. Shapley, *Promise and Power*, p. 439.

59. Adams, *War of Numbers*, pp. 144, 219.

60. WPB interview, Nov, 12, 1996.

61. WPB interview with Tom Wells, May 27, 1986; WPB interview, Feb. 16, 1994.

62. Randall Bennett Woods, *Fulbright: A Biography* (New York: Cambridge University Press, 1995), p. 476.

63. Clark Clifford, with Richard Holbrooke, *Counsel to the President* (New York: Random House, 1991), pp. 484–85; Hendrickson, *The Living and the Dead*, pp. 344–345; Joseph A. Califano, Jr., *The Triumph and Tragedy of Lyndon Johnson* (New York: Simon & Schuster, 1991), pp. 262–63; Barrett, *Uncertain Warriors*, p. 126; WPB interview, Nov. 12, 1996.

64. W. P. Bundy, "Negotiating Posture Options and Possible Diplomatic Actions," Second Draft, Mar. 3, 1968, Clark Clifford Papers, Box 1, National Objectives (1), declassified Apr. 15, 1986, LBJ.

65. Gardner, *Pay Any Price*, pp. 449–50.

66. WPB interview, Nov. 12, 1996.

67. Ibid.

68. Gardner, *Pay Any Price*, pp. 452–53; Isaacson and Thomas, *The Wise Men*, pp. 699–700.

69. Gardner, *Pay Any Price*, p. 454; Clifford, *Counsel to the President*, pp. 516–518.

70. Gardner, *Pay Any Price*, p. 458.

71. WPB interview, Feb. 16, 1994.

72. WPB interview, Nov. 12, 1996; *NYT*, July 28, 1968; WPB letter to Donald M. Wilson, Nov. 10, 1982, James Rowe Papers, LOC.

73. WPB interview, Nov. 12, 1996; Rudy Abramson, *Spanning the Century: The Life of W. Averell Harriman, 1891–1986* (New York: Morrow, 1992), p. 666.

74. WPB letter to the editor, *NYT*, June 13, 1991; Clifford, *Counsel to the President*, pp. 581–84; Walter Isaacson, *Kissinger: A Biography* (New York: Simon & Schuster, 1992), pp. 130–32.

75. *NYT*, Oct. 13, 1968.

76. *NYT*, Apr. 2, 1968.

77. Stanley Hoffmann interview, Feb. 15, 1995.

78. James C. Thomson, Jr., "Getting Out and Speaking Out," *Foreign Policy*, Winter 1973–74, p. 61.

79. James C. Thomson, Jr., "How Could Vietnam Happen?: An Autopsy," *The Atlantic*, April 1968, pp. 47–53.

80. Thomson, Jr., "Getting Out and Speaking Out," p. 64; WPB Oral History, May 29, 1969, LBJ.

81. David Halberstam, *The Best and the Brightest* (New York: Random House, 1972), p. 625.

82. WPB interview, Nov. 12, 1996.

15: THE FORD FOUNDATION

1. Martin Mayer, *NYT*, Nov. 13, 1966, p. 149.

2. *Ford Foundation Annual Report, 1967*, p. 11; Nicholas von Hoffman, *Left at the Post* (Chicago: Quadrangle, 1970), pp. 195–97.

3. Milton Viorst, *Hustlers and Heroes: An American Political Panorama* (New York: Simon & Schuster, 1971), p. 269.

4. Mayer, *NYT*, Nov. 13, 1966.

5. *NYT*, Feb. 28, 1966.

6. Mayer, *NYT*, Nov. 13, 1966, p. 142.

7. Merrimon Cuninggim, *Private Money and Public Service: The Role of Foundations in American Society* (New York: McGraw-Hill, 1972), p. 137; Mayer, *NYT*, Nov. 13, 1966, p. 152; Viorst, *Hustlers and Heroes*, p. 268.

8. MB to John J. McCloy, Apr. 4, 1962, JJM.

9. Mayer, *NYT*, Nov. 13, 1966.

10. Richard Armstrong, "McGeorge Bundy Confronts the Teachers," *NYT Magazine*, Apr. 20, 1969, p. 27.

11. Mayer, *NYT*, Nov. 13, 1966.

12. James Day, *The Vanishing Vision: The Inside Story of Public Television* (Berkeley: University of California Press, 1995), p. 103.

13. Ibid., pp 108–109, 140–41; Richard Magat, *The Ford Foundation at Work*, (New York: Plenum, 1979), pp. 172–76.

14. Day, *The Vanishing Vision*, p. 249.

15. *NYT*, Aug. 3, 1966.

16. Tamar Jacoby, "McGeorge Bundy: How the Establishment's Man Tackled America's Problem with Race," *Alicia Patterson Foundation Reporter*, Fall 1990, p 2.

17. "A Foundation Decade: An Interview with McGeorge Bundy," *Black Enterprise*, September 1975.

18. Jacoby, "McGeorge Bundy," p. 2.

19. Mayer, *NYT*, Nov. 13, 1966; Jacoby, "McGeorge Bundy"; *Fortune*, April 1968.

20. Jacoby, "McGeorge Bundy"; Fritz F. Heimann, ed., *The Future of Foundations* (Englewood Cliffs, N.J.: Prentice-Hall, 1973), p. 49; Joseph C. Goulden, *The Money Givers* (New York: Random House, 1971), p. 264. The Cleveland voter registration drive probably added some 20,000 new black voters to the rolls. Carl Stokes won the primary race by a margin of 18,000 votes and then defeated his Republican opponent by a margin of only 1,600 votes. Though King's SCLC and Stokes's own campaign organization also participated in the voter registration drive, the Ford Foundation funds to CORE obviously had a major impact on the electoral outcome. (Lawrence Stern and Richard Harwood, "Ford Foundation: Its Works Spark Backlash," *WP*, Nov. 2, 1969; Leonard Silk and Mark Silk, *The American Establishment* [New York: Basic Books, 1980], p. 141.)

21. Stephen E. Ambrose, *Nixon: The Triumph of a Politician, 1962–1972* (New York: Simon & Schuster, 1989), p. 265. Apparently, the IRS was not persuaded to act, though the bulk of the Nixon presidential papers are still not open for research so scholars cannot know this definitively.

22. Irwin Ross, "McGeorge Bundy and the New Foundation Style," *Fortune*, April 1968, p. 107.

23. Joseph Alsop letter to MB, Nov. 16, 1967, and MB letter to Alsop, Dec. 6, 1967, Box 76, Alsop Papers, LOC. This was not the first time Alsop had drawn attention to the role radicals played in the civil rights movement. In April 1964 he wrote a column, almost certainly based on information passed to him by J. Edgar Hoover, which charged that Dr. King had "accepted and almost certainly still is accepting Communist collaboration and even Communist advice." *(New York Herald Tribune, Apr. 15, 1964; Chauncey Eskridge letter to Whitney, Apr. 24, 1964, and Alsop letter to Whitney, May 18, 1964, Box 70, Alsop Papers, LOC.)

24. Goulden, *The Money Givers*, p. 253.

25. Joseph Alsop to MB, Jan. 5, 1968. Alsop also told Bundy that he believed "there really was conspiracy behind last summer's troubles in the cities . . ." Alsop letter to MB, Nov. 16, 1967, Box 76, Alsop Papers, LOC.

26. Norman Podhoretz, "A Certain Anxiety," *Commentary*, August 1971, p. 8; Norman Podhoretz, *Breaking Ranks: A Political Memoir* (New York: Harper & Row, 1979), pp. 247–48; Louis Harp, "Commentary Moves to the Right," *Jewish Currents*, December 1971, pp. 5–9, 27–30.

27. Armstrong, "McGeorge Bundy Confronts the Teachers"; Gary Dorrien, *The Neoconservative Mind: Politics, Culture, and the War of Ideology* (Philadelphia: Temple University Press, 1993), p. 166; Alan M. Wald, *The New York Intellectuals: The Rise and Decline of the Anti-Stalinist Left from the 1930s to the 1980s* (Chapel Hill: University of North Carolina Press, 1987), pp. 354–55.

28. Jacoby, "McGeorge Bundy," p. 7; Armstrong, "McGeorge Bundy Confronts the Teachers," p. 121; Thomas C. Reeves, ed., *Foundations Under Fire* (Ithaca: Cornell University Press, 1970), p. 22.

29. Jason Epstein, *New York Review of Books*, Oct. 10, 1968; Maurice R. Berube and Marilyn Gittell, eds., *Confrontation at Ocean Hill–Brownsville: The New York School Strikes of 1968* (New York: Praeger, 1969), pp. 188, 192.

30. David Halberstam, "The Very Expensive Education of McGeorge Bundy," *Harper's*, July 1969, pp. 38, 40.

31. Jeffrey Hart, "Foundations and Social Activism: A Critical View," in Heimann, ed., *The Future of Foundations*, p. 50; Joseph Alsop, *WP*, July 2, 1969.

32. Armstrong, "McGeorge Bundy Confronts the Teachers"; Goulden, *The Money Givers*, p. 256.

33. Jacoby, "McGeorge Bundy," p. 7.

34. Irwin Ross, "McGeorge Bundy and the New Foundation Style," *Fortune*, April 1968, p. 105.

35. Viorst, *Hustlers and Heroes*, p. 271; Goulden, *The Money Givers*, pp. 277–78.

36. Armstrong, "McGeorge Bundy Confronts the Teachers."

37. Silk and Silk, *The American Establishment*, p. 134; *WP*, Nov. 2, 1969.

38. Judge Charles Wyzanski memo to John J. McCloy, Nov. 13, 1965, Box C1, Ford Foundation 1, JJM.

39. Heimann, ed., *The Future of Foundations*, p. 51.

40. Arthur Schlesinger, Jr., *Robert Kennedy and His Times* (New York: Ballantine, 1978), pp. 848–49.

41. Jacoby, "McGeorge Bundy," p. 8.

42. Francis X. Sutton interview, Dec. 1, 1994; *A Selected Chronology of the Ford Foundation* (New York: Ford Foundation).

43. Scott Allen, "The Greening of a Movement," *Boston Sunday Globe*, Oct. 19, 1997.

44. *The Public Interest Law Firm: New Voices for New Constituencies* (New York: The Ford Foundation, 1973), p. 39. Silk and Silk, *The American Establishment*, p. 136.

45. Thomas C. Reeves, ed., *Foundations Under Fire*, p. 15.

46. Hoffman, *Left at the Post*, pp. 198–99.

47. Bruce Oudes, ed., *From the President: Richard Nixon's Secret Files* (New York: Perennial Library/Harper & Row, 1989/1990), p. 565.

48. Francis X. Sutton interview, Dec. 1, 1994; *Ramparts* March 1967; John Ranelagh, *The Agency: The Rise and Decline of the CIA* (New York: Simon & Schuster, 1986), p. 216. The Congress for Cultural Freedom was renamed the International Association for Cultural Freedom. See also *Ford Foundation Annual Report, 1968*, p. 64.

49. Viorst, *Hustlers and Heroes*, pp. 271–72.

50. Harold Howe interview, June 21, 1994.

51. Peter Collier and David Horowitz, *The Fords: An American Epic* (New York: Summit, 1987), pp. 363–64; Harold Howe interview, June 21, 1994.

52. MB interview, Nov. 3, 1994; *Ford Foundation Annual Report, 1966*, p. 94; Joseph Alsop letter to Sir Isaiah Berlin, Apr. 25, 1966, Box 73, Alsop Papers, LOC.

53. Silk and Silk, *The American Establishment*, pp. 147–48; Waldemar A. Nielsen, *The Golden Donors: A New Anatomy of the Great Foundations* (New York: Dutton, 1985), p. 72.

54. McGeorge Bundy, "The President's Review," *Ford Foundation Annual Report, 1978*, p. viii.

55. McGeorge Bundy, "The Issue Before the Court: Who Gets Ahead in America," *The Atlantic*, November 1977, pp. 41–54; Jacoby, "McGeorge Bundy." If the Supreme Court was persuaded by Bundy's brief on behalf of affirmative action, the *Bakke* ruling nevertheless remained controversial. It turned out that Bundy's stand was something of a rear-guard action: affirmative action programs were allowed to remain in place for another two decades, but by the late 1990s, they were once again under attack both from Congress and the judiciary.

56. Harold Howe interview, June 21, 1994.

57. *WP*, May 24, 1979.

16: VIETNAM AFTERMATH

1. WPB interview, Feb. 16, 1994.

2. Gloria Emerson, *Winners and Losers: Battles, Retreats, Gains, Losses and Ruins from the Vietnam War* (New York: Harcourt Brace Jovanovich, 1978), pp. 331–32.

3. Richard Ullman interview, Feb. 16, 1994. Ullman, who sat next to Halberstam, said the lectures were "bad.... They were simply a defense of the administration's actions in Vietnam." Bundy's lecture texts are missing from the council's archives.

4. Godfrey Hodgson, *America in Our Time* (Garden City, N.Y.: Doubleday, 1976), p. 354.

5. Harrison E. Salisbury, *Without Fear or Favor* (New York: Times Books, 1980), p. 192.

6. *Washington Star*, Oct. 18, 1971; *WP*, Dec. 31, 1971.

7. WPB interview, Feb. 16, 1994.

8. Salisbury, *Without Fear or Favor*, p. 345. WPB to Joe and Stew Alsop, July 8 (undated), Box 214, Alsop Papers, LOC. By the time Ellsberg leaked the papers to the *New York Times*, Marcus Raskin had already used his own copy of the Pentagon Papers to write a history of the war with his Institute for Policy Studies colleagues. *Washington Plans an Aggressive War* was published about the same time as the *New York Times* published the Pentagon Papers. (Raskin interview, June 19, 1997.)

9. *WP*, Mar. 10, 1973; Salisbury, *Without Fear or Favor*, pp. 345–46; Daniel Ellsberg phone interview, Feb. 14, 1998; David Rudenstine, *The Day the Presses Stopped: A History of the Pentagon Papers Case* (Berkeley: University of California Press, 1996), pp. 341–42.

10. *WP*, Apr. 27, 1971.

11. Harold Howe interview, June 21, 1994.

12. Carl Kaysen interview, June 18, 1993.

13. Richard Ullman interview, Feb. 16, 1994; Richard Barnet interview, Dec. 1, 1989; Richard Falk interview, Mar. 28, 1985; Leonard Silk and Mark Silk, *The American Establishment* (New York: Basic Books, 1980), p. 206.

14. *Boston Globe*, Aug. 23, 1971; *WP*, Aug. 23, 1971. "If the ruling class had to depend on David Rockefeller it would be in pretty bad shape," Carl Kaysen later said. "David is not very bright, just dogged." (Carl Kaysen interview, June 18, 1993.)

15. Mac Bundy called Kissinger's memoir, *White House Years*, an "apologia" and vigorously attacked Kissinger's thesis that but for Watergate, he and Nixon could have succeeded in saving South Vietnam from collapse in 1975. McGeorge Bundy,

"Reconsiderations: Vietnam, Watergate and Presidential Powers," *Foreign Affairs,* Winter 1979–80; William P. Bundy, "Dictatorships and American Foreign Policy," *Foreign Affairs,* October 1975; William P. Bundy, "Who Lost Patagonia? Foreign Policy in the 1980 Campaign," *Foreign Affairs,* Fall 1979; McGeorge Bundy, "High Hopes and Hard Reality: Arms Control in 1978," *Foreign Affairs* 57: 3 (1979). Bill Bundy also was not afraid to offend the man who had hired him. In 1979–80, Bundy rejected an essay from David Rockefeller defending the Shah of Iran. (James Chace phone interview, Aug. 8, 1997.)

16. Heyden White Rostow interview, Dec. 2, 1993.

17. David Talbot, "And Now They Are Doves," *Mother Jones,* May 1984, pp. 26–60.

18. James C. Thomson Jr., "A Memory of McGeorge Bundy," *NYT,* Sept. 22, 1996; Thomson phone interview, May 7, 1997.

19. William Bundy, *A Tangled Web: The Making of Foreign Policy in the Nixon Presidency* (New York: Hill & Wang, 1998), pp. 500, 529.

20. Talbot, "And Now They Are Doves," p. 33.

21. Gordon Goldstein lecture on McGeorge Bundy's unfinished manuscript, Woodrow Wilson Center, Washington, D.C., Apr. 5, 1997; Francis M. Bator, "Glimpses of Mac," *Groton School Quarterly,* May 1997, p. 6. Just two weeks before he died, Mac Bundy told Brown University scholar James G. Blight that Kennedy "would not have sent the army in" and Johnson "was determined to send the army in." "Let's imagine for a minute," Bundy said, "that George Ball had been secretary of state. Would that have changed the outcome, knowing what we know about George's views? Not one bit, because there was no way he could have persuaded LBJ. It's not that LBJ was a super-hawk. It's that he had no equal as a manipulator. . . . In the discussions in the summer of 1965, on whether or not to send in the army: did LBJ really want to know the truth? Was he capable of changing his mind? Were the debates we think we see in the minutes of those meetings *really* debates? I don't think so. LBJ was going to send in the army, period." According to Bundy, given LBJ's views, there were no missed opportunities, except the "opportunity" that was irretrievably lost when Kennedy was assassinated. Had Kennedy lived, Bundy believed, there would have been no Vietnam War. With Johnson in the White House—and Hanoi's determination to unify the country—the war was destined to unfold as the tragedy it became. Bundy confessed to Blight that given his views on LBJ the most difficult task facing him in writing his Vietnam memoir was to write what he had to say "without sounding self-serving." (James G. Blight memorandum, Aug. 28, 1996, courtesy of Blight.)

22. *WP,* May 14, 1967.

23. WPB letter to General Bruce Palmer, Jr., Nov. 24, 1987, courtesy of Stanley Resor.

24. WPB letter to Professor David Barrett, May 13, 1993, courtesy of Barrett, author of *Uncertain Warriors: Lyndon Johnson and His Vietnam Advisers.* Bundy wrote a blurb for Barrett's book.

25. James Chace interview, Oct. 6, 1992. In a private seminar, Bill Bundy said much the same thing to Jim Thomson and Dan Ellsberg: "We would have fought a better war—as Thomson says—if we had been prepared to keep 300,000 [troops] over there for ten years—but that would have been very difficult to sell to the American public." (Handwritten notes from Dec. 16, 1970, seminar, courtesy of Daniel Ellsberg.) In a confidential memo of "Working Notes" for the same meeting, Bundy concluded, "An implacable country in our position could probably have succeeded; we are not implacable unless aroused more than this war could do." (William P. Bundy, "Working Notes for December 16 Meeting," courtesy of Daniel Ellsberg.)

26. G. d'Andelot Belin, ed., *Fifty Years Out: Published by the Class of 1939, on the Occasion of Its 50th Reunion, June 1989, Yale University,* pp. 33–36.

27. Gordon Goldstein telephone interview, Sept. 27, 1996.

28. Harold Howe II phone interview, Sept. 27, 1996; Gordon Goldstein phone interview, Sept. 27, 1996; text of Howe's eulogy, "McGeorge Bundy: 'A Man For All Seasons,' " Sept. 20, 1996, courtesy of Howe.

29. *WP,* unsigned editorial, Sept. 18, 1996.

30. John Kifner, "McGeorge Bundy Dies at 77; Top Adviser in Vietnam Era," *NYT,* Sept. 17, 1996. Afterwards, "Doc" Howe circulated a letter to "Friends of McGeorge Bundy" in which he reported that "some were outraged" by the "stumbling effort" of the *New York Times'*s obituary writer. (Harold Howe II, Memorandum to "Friends of McGeorge Bundy," Sept. 23, 1996, courtesy of Howe.)

31. Walter Isaacson, "The Best and the Brightest," *Time,* Sept. 30, 1996.

32. Arthur Schlesinger, Jr., "A Man Called Mac," *George,* December 1996, p. 104.

33. James C. Thomson, Jr., "A Memory of McGeorge Bundy," *NYT,* Sept. 22, 1996.

Interviews

David C. Acheson
Louis S. Auchincloss
William Barnes
Richard J. Barnet
Francis M. Bator
Gaspard d'Andelot Belin, Jr.
Harriet Bundy Belin
Richard M. Bissell, Jr.
William McCormick Blair, Jr.
Benjamin Crowninshield Bradlee
Andrew Bundy
Harvey H. Bundy, Jr.
McGeorge Bundy
Mary Lothrop Bundy
Stephen Bundy
William Putnam Bundy
James Chace
Blair Clark
Ray Cline
William Colby
Chester L. Cooper
John C. Culver
Daniel I. Davidson
Sigmund Diamond
Daniel Ellsberg
Gloria Emerson
Richard Falk
Dorothy Fall
Ramsey Forbush
Franklin Ford
Harold P. Ford
John Kenneth Galbraith
Raymond L. Garthoff

Leslie H. Gelb
Gordon Goldstein
Gordon Grayson
Marshall Green
David Halberstam
Richard McGarrah Helms
Richard Hewlett
Stanley Hoffmann
Frederick Holborn
Townsend Hoopes
Marshall Hornblower
Harold Howe II
Thomas L. Hughes
Richard K. Irons
Ron Javers
Nicholas Katzenbach
Carl Kaysen
Robert Komer
William Kunstler
Betty Goetz Lall
Saul Landau
A. J. Langguth
Arthur Levenson
J. Anthony Lukas
Robert S. McNamara
Michael Maccoby
Charles Maechling, Jr.
Willard Mathias
Blanche Moore
Jonathan Moore
Elise O'Shaughnessy
Walter Pforzheimer
Charles Porter

Nathan M. Pusey
Marcus G. Raskin
Stanley Resor
David F. Ricks
David Riesman
Heyden White Rostow
Walt Rostow
Arthur Schlesinger, Jr.
Russell Jack Smith
Peter O. A. Solbert
Diana Stewart

Zeph Stewart
Francis X. Sutton
James C. Thomson, Jr.
Richard Ullman
Paul Warnke
Allen Whiting
Alexandra Whitney
Donald Malcolm Wilson
Adam Yarmolinsky
Perez Zagorin
Eli S. Zaretsky

Select Bibliography

Abramson, Rudy. *Spanning the Century: The Life of W. Averell Harriman, 1891–1986.* New York: Morrow, 1992.

Acheson, David C. *Acheson Country: A Memoir.* New York: Norton, 1993.

Acheson, Dean. *Present at the Creation: My Years in the State Department.* New York: Norton, 1969.

Adams, Sam. *War of Numbers: An Intelligence Memoir.* South Royalton, Vt.: Steerforth, 1994.

Agee, Philip, and Louis Wolf. *Dirty Work: The CIA in Western Europe.* Secaucus, N.J.: Lyle Stuart, 1978.

Albert, Judith Clavir, and Stewart Edward Albert, eds. *The Sixties Papers: Documents of a Rebellious Decade.* New York: Praeger, 1984.

Allen, Thomas B. *War Games.* New York: McGraw-Hill, 1987.

Alperovitz, Gar. *The Decision to Use the Atomic Bomb and the Architecture of an American Myth.* New York: Knopf, 1995.

Alsop, Joseph W., with Adam Platt. *"I've Seen the Best of It": Memoirs.* New York: Norton, 1992.

Alsop, Stewart. *The Center: People and Power in Political Washington.* New York: Popular Library, 1968.

———. *Stay of Execution: A Sort of Memoir.* Philadelphia: Lippincott, 1973.

Ambrose, Stephen E. *Nixon: The Triumph of a Politician, 1962–1972.* New York: Simon & Schuster, 1989.

Amory, Cleveland. *The Proper Bostonians.* New York: Dutton, 1947.

Ashburn, Frank D. *Peabody of Groton: A Portrait.* Cambridge, Mass: Riverside, 1967.

Auchincloss, Louis. *A Writer's Capital.* Minneapolis: University of Minnesota Press, 1974.

Baker, Leonard. *Brandeis and Frankfurter: A Dual Biography.* New York: Harper & Row, 1984.

Baker, Liva. *Felix Frankfurter.* New York: Coward-McCann, 1969.

Ball, George W. *The Past Has Another Pattern.* New York: Norton, 1982.

Baltzell, E. Digby. *The Protestant Establishment: Aristocracy & Caste in America.* New York: Random House, 1964.

Barnet, Richard J. *Roots of War: The Men and Institutions Behind U.S. Foreign Policy.* New York: Atheneum, 1972.

Barrett, David M. *Uncertain Warriors: Lyndon Johnson and His Vietnam Advisers.* Lawrence: University Press of Kansas, 1993.

Beard, Charles A. *President Roosevelt and the Coming of the War, 1941.* New Haven: Yale University Press, 1948.

Bentley, Eric, ed. *Thirty Years of Treason.* New York: Viking, 1971.

Berman, Edward. *The Influence of the Carnegie, Ford and Rockefeller Foundations on American Foreign Policy: The Ideology of Philanthropy.* Albany, N.Y.: State University of New York Press, 1983.

Berman, Larry. *Lyndon Johnson's War.* New York: Norton, 1989.

———. *Planning a Tragedy: The Americanization of the War in Vietnam.* New York: Norton, 1982.

Berube, Maurice R., and Marilyn Gittell, eds. *Confrontation at Ocean Hill–Brownsville: The New York School Strikes of 1968.* New York: Praeger, 1969.

Beschloss, Michael R. *The Crisis Years: Kennedy and Khrushchev, 1960–1963.* New York: Edward Burlingame Books/HarperCollins, 1991.

———, ed. *Taking Charge: The Johnson White House Tapes, 1963–1964.* New York: Simon & Schuster, 1997.

Biddle, George. *An American Artist's Story.* Boston: Little, Brown, 1939.

Bill, James A. *George Ball: Behind the Scenes in U.S. Foreign Policy.* New Haven: Yale University Press, 1997.

Bird, Kai. *The Chairman: John J. McCloy / The Making of the American Establishment.* New York: Simon & Schuster, 1992.

Bird, Kai, and Lawrence Lifschultz, eds. *Hiroshima's Shadow: Writings on the Denial of History and the Smithsonian Controversy.* Stony Creek, Conn.: Pamphleteer's Press, 1998.

Birmingham, Stephen. *The Right People: A Portrait of the American Social Establishment.* Boston: Little, Brown, 1968.

Bissell, Richard M., Jr., with Jonathan E. Lewis, and Frances T. Pudlo. *Memoirs.* New Haven: Yale University Press, 1996.

Blair, Anne E. *Lodge in Vietnam: A Patriot Abroad.* New Haven: Yale University Press, 1995.

Blight, James G., and David A. Welch. *On the Brink: Americans and Soviets Reexamine the Cuban Missile Crisis,* 2nd ed. New York: Noonday, 1990.

Blum, John Morton, ed. *Public Philosopher: Selected Letters of Walter Lippmann.* New York: Ticknor & Fields, 1985.

Brands, H. W. *Cold Warriors: Eisenhower's Generation and American Foreign Policy.* New York: Columbia University Press, 1988.

———. *The Devil We Knew: Americans and the Cold War.* New York: Oxford University Press, 1993.

Brightman, Carol. *Writing Dangerously: Mary McCarthy and Her World.* New York: Harcourt Brace, 1992.

Brinkley, Douglas. *Dean Acheson: The Cold War Years, 1953–71.* New Haven: Yale University Press, 1992.

Brown, John Mason. *Many a Watchful Night.* New York: Whittlesy House, 1944.

Brugioni, Dino A. *Eyeball to Eyeball: The Inside Story of the Cuban Missile Crisis.* New York: Random House, 1991.

Bundy, McGeorge. *Danger and Survival: Choices About the Bomb in the First Fifty Years.* New York: Random House, 1988.

———, ed. *The Pattern of Responsibility: From the Records of Dean Acheson.* Boston: Houghton Mifflin, 1952.

Bundy, McGeorge, et al. *Zero Hour: A Summons to the Free.* New York: Farrar & Rinehart, 1940.

Bundy, William. *A Tangled Web: The Making of Foreign Policy in the Nixon Presidency.* New York: Hill & Wang, 1998.

Burch, Philip H., Jr. *Elites in American History: The New Deal to the Carter Administration.* New York: Holmes & Meier, 1980.

Burns, James MacGregor. *Roosevelt: The Lion and the Fox.* New York: Harcourt, Brace & World, 1956.

Buzzanco, Robert. *Masters of War: Military Dissent & Politics in the Vietnam Era.* New York: Cambridge University Press, 1996.

Califano, Joseph A., Jr. *The Triumph and Tragedy of Lyndon Johnson.* New York: Simon & Schuster, 1991.

Calvocoressi, Peter. *Top Secret Ultra.* New York: Pantheon, 1980.

Carbonell, Nestor. *And the Russians Stayed.* New York: Morrow, 1989.

Caute, David. *The Great Fear: The Anti-Communist Purge Under Truman and Eisenhower.* New York: Simon & Schuster, 1978.

Chang, Gordon. *Friends and Enemies: The United States, China, and the Soviet Union, 1948–1972.* Stanford: Stanford University Press, 1990.

Chang, Laurence, and Peter Kornbluh, eds. *The Cuban Missile Crisis, 1962: National Security Archive Documents Reader.* New York: New Press, 1992.

Chernow, Ron. *The House of Morgan: An American Banking Dynasty and the Rise of Modern Finance.* New York: Atlantic Monthly Press, 1990.

Chomsky, Noam. *American Power and the New Mandarins.* New York: Pantheon, 1969.

———. *Rethinking Camelot: JFK, the Vietnam War, and U.S. Political Culture.* Boston: South End, 1993.

Clifford, Clark, with Richard Holbrooke. *Counsel to the President.* New York: Random House, 1991.

Colby, William, and Peter Forbath. *Honorable Men: My Life in the CIA.* New York: Simon & Schuster, 1978.

Collier, Peter, and David Horowitz. *The Fords: An American Epic.* New York: Summit, 1987.

Conant, James B. *My Several Lives: Memoirs of a Social Inventor.* New York: Harper & Row, 1970.

Cooper, Chester. *The Lost Crusade: America in Vietnam.* New York: Dodd, Mead, 1970.

Cumings, Bruce. *The Origins of the Korean War: The Roaring of the Cataract, 1947–1950.* Princeton: Princeton University Press, 1990.

Cuninggim, Merrimon. *Private Money and Public Service: The Role of Foundations in American Society.* New York: McGraw-Hill, 1972.

Current, Richard N. *Secretary Stimson: A Study in Statecraft.* New Brunswick, N.J.: Rutgers University Press, 1954.

Day, James. *The Vanishing Vision: The Inside Story of Public Television.* Berkeley: University of California Press, 1995.

Dellinger, David. *From Yale to Jail: The Life of a Moral Dissenter.* New York: Pantheon, 1993.

Diamond, Sigmund. *Compromised Campus: The Collaboration of Universities with the Intelligence Community, 1945–1955.* New York: Oxford University Press, 1992.

DiLeo, David L. *George Ball: Vietnam and the Rethinking of Containment.* Chapel Hill: University of North Carolina Press, 1991.

Dobrynin, Anatoly. *In Confidence: Moscow's Ambassador to America's Six Cold War Presidents.* New York: Times Books, 1995.

Donaldson, Scott. *Archibald MacLeish: An American Life.* Boston: Houghton Mifflin, 1992.

Dorrien, Gary. *The Neoconservative Mind: Politics, Culture, and the War of Ideology.* Philadelphia: Temple University Press, 1993.

Dunne, Gerald T. *Hugo Black and the Judicial Revolution.* New York: Simon & Schuster, 1977.

Eisenberg, Carolyn. *Drawing the Line: The American Decision to Divide Germany, 1944–1949.* New York: Cambridge University Press, 1996.

Ellsberg, Daniel. *Papers on the War.* New York: Simon & Schuster, 1972.

Emerson, Gloria. *Winners and Losers: Battles, Retreats, Gains, Losses and Ruins from the Vietnam War.* New York: Harcourt Brace & Jovanovich, 1978.

FitzGerald, Frances. *Fire in the Lake: The Vietnamese and the Americans in Vietnam.* New York: Vintage, 1972.

Ford, Harold P. *Estimative Intelligence: The Purposes and Problems of National Intelligence Estimating.* Washington, D.C.: Defense Intelligence College, 1989.

Foreign Relations of the United States, 1961–1963, vol. I, *Vietnam 1961.* Washington, D.C.: Government Printing Office, 1988.

――, vol. II, *Vietnam 1962.* Washington, D.C.: Government Printing Office, 1990.

Foreign Relations of the United States, 1964–1968, vol. I, *Vietnam 1964.* Washington, D.C.: Government Printing Office, 1992.

――, vol. II, *Vietnam, January–June 1965.* Washington, D.C.: Government Printing Office, 1996.

――, vol. III, *Vietnam, June–December 1965.* Washington, D.C.: Government Printing Office, 1996.

Freeland, Richard M. *The Truman Doctrine and the Origins of McCarthyism: Foreign Policy, Domestic Politics, and Internal Security, 1946–1948.* New York: New York University Press, 1985.

Fursenko, Aleksandr, and Timothy Naftali. *"One Hell of a Gamble": The Secret History of the Cuban Missile Crisis.* New York: Norton, 1997.

Gaddis, John Lewis. *We Now Know: Rethinking Cold War History.* New York: Oxford University Press, 1997.

Galbraith, John Kenneth. *Ambassador's Journal.* Boston: Houghton Mifflin, 1969.

――. *A Life in Our Times: Memoirs.* Boston: Houghton Mifflin, 1981.

Gardner, Lloyd C. *Pay Any Price: Lyndon Johnson and the Wars for Vietnam.* Chicago: Dee, 1995.

Gardner, Lloyd C., and Ted Gittinger, eds. *Vietnam: The Early Decisions.* Austin: University of Texas, 1997.

Gardner, Paul F. *Shared Hopes, Separate Fears: Fifty Years of U.S.-Indonesian Relations.* Boulder: Westview, 1997.

Gettleman, Marvin E., et al., eds. *Vietnam and America: A Documented History.* New York: Grove, 1985.

Gibbons, William Conrad. *The U.S. Government and the Vietnam War,* parts II, III and IV. Princeton: Princeton University Press, 1989, 1995.

Gitlin, Todd. *The Sixties: Years of Hope, Days of Rage.* New York: Bantam, 1987.

――. *The Whole World Is Watching: Mass Media in the Making and Unmaking of the New Left.* Berkeley: University of California Press, 1980.

Gittinger, Ted, ed. *The Johnson Years: A Vietnam Roundtable.* Austin: University of Texas, 1993.

Goldman, Eric F. *The Tragedy of Lyndon Johnson.* New York: Knopf, 1969.

Goodwin, Richard. *Remembering America.* Boston: Little, Brown, 1988.

Gosse, Van. *Where the Boys Are: Cuba, Cold War America and the Making of a New Left.* New York: Verso, 1993.

Goulden, Joseph C. *The Money Givers.* New York: Random House, 1971.

――. *Truth Is the First Casualty: The Gulf of Tonkin Affair—Illusion and Reality.* Chicago: Rand McNally, 1969.

Graubard, Stephen R. *Kissinger: Portrait of a Mind.* New York: Norton, 1973.

Green, Marshall (Foreword by William P. Bundy). *Indonesia: Crisis and Transformation, 1965–1968.* Washington, D.C.: Compass, 1990.

Grew, Joseph C. *Turbulent Era: A Diplomatic Era of Forty Years,* vol. II. Boston: Houghton Mifflin, 1952.

Gribkov, General Anatoli I., and General William Y. Smith. *Operation Anadyr: US and Soviet Generals Recount the Cuban Missile Crisis.* Chicago: edition q, inc., 1994.

Grose, Peter. *Gentleman Spy: The Life of Allen Dulles.* Boston: Houghton Mifflin, 1994.

Gunther, John. *Roosevelt in Retrospect.* New York: Harper & Bros., 1950; Pyramid, 1962.

Guthman, Edwin O., and Jeffrey Shulman, eds. *Robert Kennedy: In His Own Words, The Unpublished Recollections of the Kennedy Years.* New York: Bantam, 1988.

Halberstam, David. *The Best and the Brightest.* New York: Random House, 1972; Ballantine, 1992.

Hamilton, Ian. *Robert Lowell: A Biography.* New York: Random House, 1982.

Hammer, Ellen J. *A Death in November: America in Vietnam, 1963.* New York: Oxford University Press, 1987.

Heimann, Fritz F., ed. *The Future of Foundations.* Englewood Cliffs, N.J.: Prentice-Hall, 1973.

Hendrickson, Paul. *The Living and the Dead: Robert McNamara and Five Lives of a Lost War.* New York: Knopf, 1996.

Herken, Gregg. *Counsels of War.* New York: Knopf, 1985.

Herring, George C. *America's Longest War: The United States and Vietnam, 1950–1975,* 2nd ed. New York: Knopf, 1986.

————. *LBJ and Vietnam: A Different Kind of War.* Austin: University of Texas Press, 1994.

Hersh, Burton. *The Old Boys: The American Elite and the Origins of the CIA.* New York: Scribner's, 1992.

Hersh, Seymour M. *The Dark Side of Camelot.* Boston: Little, Brown, 1997.

Hershberg, James. *James B. Conant: Harvard to Hiroshima and the Making of the Nuclear Age.* New York: Knopf, 1993.

Higgins, Marguerite. *Our Vietnam Nightmare.* New York: Harper & Row, 1965.

Hilsman, Roger. *To Move a Nation.* Garden City, N.Y.: Doubleday, 1967.

Hinckle, Warren, and William W. Turner. *The Fish Is Red: The Story of the Secret War Against Castro.* New York: Harper & Row, 1981.

Hodgson, Godfrey. *America in Our Time.* Garden City, N.Y.: Doubleday, 1976.

————. *The Colonel: The Life and Wars of Henry Stimson, 1867–1950.* New York: Knopf, 1990.

Hogan, Michael J., ed. *America in the World: The Historiography of American Foreign Relations Since 1941.* New York: Cambridge University Press, 1995.

Hoopes, Townsend. *The Limits of Intervention.* New York: McKay, 1973; Norton, 1987.

Hoopes, Townsend, and Douglas Brinkley. *Driven Patriot: The Life and Times of James Forrestal.* New York: Knopf, 1992.

Humphrey, Hubert H. *The Education of a Public Man: My Life and Politics.* Garden City, N.Y.: Doubleday, 1976.

Hunt, Michael H. *Lyndon Johnson's War: America's Cold War Crusade in Vietnam, 1945–1968.* New York: Hill & Wang, 1996.

Isaacson, Walter. *Kissinger: A Biography.* New York: Simon & Schuster, 1992.

Isaacson, Walter, and Evan Thomas. *The Wise Men: Six Friends and the World They Made.* New York: Simon & Schuster, 1986.

Jeffreys-Jones, Rhodri. *The CIA & American Democracy.* New Haven: Yale University Press, 1988.

Johnson, E.A.J., ed. *The Dimensions of Diplomacy.* Baltimore: Johns Hopkins Press, 1964.

Johnson, Lyndon Baines. *The Vantage Point: Perspectives of the Presidency, 1963–1969.* New York: Holt, Rinehart and Winston, 1971.

Kahin, Audrey R., and George McT. Kahin. *Subversion as Foreign Policy: The Secret Eisenhower and Dulles Debacle in Indonesia.* New York: New Press, 1995.

Kahin, George McT. *Intervention: How America Became Involved in Vietnam.* New York: Knopf, 1986.

Kalb, Marvin, and Bernard Kalb. *Kissinger.* Boston: Little, Brown, 1974.

Kaplan, Fred. *Wizards of Armageddon.* New York: Simon & Schuster, 1983.

Karnow, Stanley. *Vietnam: A History.* New York: Viking, 1983.

Kattenburg, Paul M. *The Vietnam Trauma in American Foreign Policy, 1945–75.* New Brunswick, N.J.: Transaction, 1980.

Kearns, Doris. *Lyndon Johnson & the American Dream.* New York: Harper & Row, 1976.

Keller, Phyllis. *Getting at the Core: Curricular Reform at Harvard.* Cambridge: Harvard University Press, 1982.

Kelley, Brooks Mather. *Yale: A History.* New Haven: Yale University Press, 1974.

Kennedy, Robert F. *Thirteen Days: A Memoir of the Cuban Missile Crisis.* New York: Norton, 1971.

Kirkpatrick, Lyman. *The Real CIA.* New York: Macmillan, 1968.

Kissinger, Henry. *White House Years.* Boston: Little, Brown, 1979.

Kramnick, Isaac, and Barry Sheerman. *Harold Laski: A Life on the Left.* New York: Allen Lane/Penguin, 1993.

LaFeber, Walter. *America, Russia & the Cold War, 1945–1984.* New York: Knopf, 1985.

———. *The American Age: United States Foreign Policy at Home and Abroad Since 1750.* New York: Norton, 1989.

Laney, Al. *Prep Schools.* Garden City, N.Y.: Doubleday, 1961.

Langer, William L. *In and Out of the Ivory Tower: The Autobiography of William L. Langer.* New York: Watson, 1977.

Lebow, Richard Ned, and Janice Gross Stein. *We All Lost the Cold War.* Princeton: Princeton University Press, 1994.

Leffler, Melvyn P. *A Preponderance of Power: National Security, the Truman Administration, and the Cold War.* Stanford: Stanford University Press, 1992.

Leffler, Melvyn P., and David Painter, eds. *Origins of the Cold War: An International History.* New York: Routledge, 1994.

Leuchtenburg, William E. *Franklin D. Roosevelt and the New Deal: 1932–1940.* New York: Harper & Row, 1963.

Lipset, Seymour Martin, and David Riesman. *Education and Politics at Harvard.* New York: McGraw-Hill, 1975.

McCarthy, Mary. *The Seventh Degree.* New York: Harcourt Brace Jovanovich, 1974.

McCormick, Thomas J. *America's Half-Century: United States Foreign Policy in the Cold War.* Baltimore: Johns Hopkins University Press, 1989.

McCullough, David. *Truman.* New York: Simon & Schuster, 1992.

McNamara, Robert S. *Blundering into Disaster: Surviving the First Century of the Nuclear Age.* New York: Pantheon, 1986.

McNamara, Robert S., with Brian VanDeMark. *In Retrospect: The Tragedy and Lessons of Vietnam.* New York: Times Books, 1995.

Magat, Richard. *The Ford Foundation at Work.* New York: Plenum, 1979.

Manchester, William. *The Death of a President.* New York: Harper & Row, 1967.

Marbury, William L. *In the Catbird Seat.* Baltimore: Maryland Historical Society, 1988.

Marchetti, Victor, and John D. Marks. *The CIA and the Cult of Intelligence.* New York: Dell, 1974.

Mariani, Paul. *Lost Puritan: A Life of Robert Lowell.* New York: Norton, 1994.

May, Ernest R., and Philip D. Zelikow, eds. *The Kennedy Tapes: Inside the White House During the Cuban Missile Crisis.* Cambridge: Harvard University Press, 1997.

Mazlish, Bruce. *Kissinger: The European Mind in American Policy.* New York: Basic Books, 1976.

Merry, Robert W. *Taking on the World: Joseph and Stewart Alsop—Guardians of the American Century.* New York: Viking, 1996.

Meyer, Cord. *Facing Reality: From World Federalism to the CIA.* New York: Harper & Row, 1980.

Miller, Merle. *Lyndon: An Oral Biography.* New York: Ballantine, 1980.

Moise, Edwin E. *Tonkin Gulf and the Escalation of the Vietnam War.* Chapel Hill: University of North Carolina Press, 1996.

Monagan, John S. *The Grand Panjandrum: The Mellow Years of Justice Holmes.* Lanham, Md.: University Press of America, 1988.

Moore, Lieutenant General Harold G., and Joseph L. Galloway. *We Were Soldiers Once . . . and Young: Ia Drang, the Battle that Changed the War in Vietnam.* New York: HarperCollins, 1992.

Morison, Elting E. *Turmoil and Tradition: A Study of the Life and Times of Henry L. Stimson.* Boston: Houghton Mifflin, 1960.

Mosley, Leonard. *Dulles: A Biography of Eleanor, Allen, and John Foster Dulles and Their Family Network.* New York: Dial, 1978.

Muggeridge, Malcolm. *Chronicles of Wasted Time: The Infernal Grove.* New York: Quill, 1982.

Nathan, James A., ed. *The Cuban Missile Crisis Revisited.* New York: St. Martin's, 1992.

Navasky, Victor. *Naming Names.* New York: Viking, 1980.

Newhouse, John. *War and Peace in the Nuclear Age.* New York: Knopf, 1989.

Newman, John M. *JFK and Vietnam.* New York: Warner, 1992.

Nielsen, Waldemar A. *The Golden Donors: A New Anatomy of the Great Foundations.* New York: Dutton, 1985.

Nixon, Richard. *RN: The Memoirs of Richard Nixon.* New York: Grosset & Dunlap, 1978.

Novick, Peter. *That Noble Dream: The "Objectivity Question" and the American Historical Profession.* New York: Cambridge University Press, 1988.

O'Donnell, Kenneth P., and David F. Powers, with Joe McCarthy. *"Johnny, We Hardly Knew Ye."* Boston: Little, Brown, 1970.

Oren, Dan A. *Joining the Club: A History of Jews and Yale.* New Haven: Yale University Press, 1985.

Oshinsky, David M. *A Conspiracy So Immense: The World of Joe McCarthy.* New York: Free Press, 1983.

Oudes, Bruce, ed. *From the President: Richard Nixon's Secret Files.* New York: Perennial Library/Harper & Row, 1989/1990.

Palmer, Bruce. *The 25-Year War: America's Military Role in Vietnam.* New York: Simon & Schuster, 1985.

Parrish, Thomas. *The Ultra Americans: The U.S. Role in Breaking the Nazi Codes.* New York: Stein & Day, 1986.

Patner, Andrew. *I. F. Stone.* New York: Pantheon, 1988.

Pearson, Drew, and Robert Allen (published anonymously). *Washington Merry-Go-Round.* New York: Liveright, 1931.

Pells, Richard H. *The Liberal Mind in a Conservative Age: American Intellectuals in the 1940s and 1950s.* Middletown, Conn.: Wesleyan University Press, 1989.

The Pentagon Papers: The Defense Department History of United States Decisionmaking on Vietnam, Senator Gravel Edition, 5 vols. Boston: Beacon, 1971–72.

Phillips, David Atlee. *The Night Watch.* New York: Ballantine, 1977.

Pierson, George Wilson. *Yale: The University College, 1921–1937.* New Haven: Yale University Press, 1955.

Pisani, Sallie. *The CIA and the Marshall Plan.* Lawrence: University Press of Kansas, 1991.

Podhoretz, Norman. *Breaking Ranks: A Political Memoir.* New York: Harper & Row, 1979.

Powers, Thomas. *The Man Who Kept the Secrets: Richard Helms and the CIA.* New York: Knopf, 1979.

———. *The War at Home.* New York: Grossman, 1973.

Prados, John. *The Hidden History of the Vietnam War.* Chicago: Dee, 1995.

———. *Keepers of the Keys: A History of the National Security Council from Truman to Bush.* New York: Morrow, 1991.

———. *The Soviet Estimate: U.S. Intelligence Analysis and Russian Military Strength.* New York: Dial, 1982.

Prochnau, William. *Upon a Distant War: Young War Correspondents and the Early Vietnam Battles.* New York: Times Books, 1995.

Ranelagh, John. *The Agency: The Rise and Decline of the CIA.* New York: Simon & Schuster, 1986.

Raskin, Marcus G., and Bernard B. Fall, eds. *The Viet-Nam Reader.* New York: Random House, 1965.

Reeves, Richard. *President Kennedy: Profile of Power.* New York: Simon & Schuster, 1993.

Reeves, Thomas C. *The Life and Times of Joe McCarthy: A Biography.* New York: Stein & Day, 1982.

———, ed. *Foundations Under Fire.* Ithaca: Cornell University Press, 1970.

Rhodes, Richard. *Dark Sun: The Making of the Hydrogen Bomb.* New York: Simon & Schuster, 1995.

Robinson, Geoffrey. *The Dark Side of Paradise.* Ithaca: Cornell University Press, 1995.

Roosevelt, Archie. *For Lust of Knowing: Memoirs of an Intelligence Officer.* Boston: Little, Brown, 1988.

Roosevelt, James, ed. *The Liberal Papers.* New York: Doubleday Anchor, 1962.

Rosenblatt, Roger. *Coming Apart: A Memoir of the Harvard Wars of 1969.* Boston: Little, Brown, 1997.

Rostow, W. W. *The Diffusion of Power: An Essay in Recent History.* New York: Macmillan, 1972.

Rovere, Richard. *Final Reports: Personal Reflections on Politics and History in Our Time.* Middletown, Conn.: Wesleyan University Press, 1984.

Rudenstine, David, *The Day the Presses Stopped: A History of the Pentagon Papers Case.* Berkeley: University of California Press, 1996.

Rusk, Dean. *As I Saw It.* New York: Norton, 1990.

Salisbury, Harrison E. *Without Fear or Favor.* New York: Times Books, 1980.

Schalk, David L. *War and the Ivory Tower: Algeria and Vietnam.* New York: Oxford University Press, 1991.

Schlesinger, Arthur, Jr. *The Bitter Heritage: Vietnam and American Democracy, 1941–1966.* Boston: Houghton Mifflin, 1966.

———. *Robert Kennedy and His Times.* New York: Ballantine, 1978.

———. *A Thousand Days: John F. Kennedy in the White House.* Boston: Houghton Mifflin, 1965.

————. *The Vital Center: The Politics of Freedom.* Boston: Houghton Mifflin, 1949.

Schrecker, Ellen W. *No Ivory Tower: McCarthyism & the Universities.* New York: Oxford University Press, 1986.

Schulzinger, Robert D. *A Time for War: The United States and Vietnam, 1941–1975.* New York: Oxford University Press, 1997.

Schwartz, Adam. *A Nation in Waiting: Indonesia in the 1990s.* Boulder: Westview, 1994.

Shapley, Deborah. *Promise and Power: The Life and Times of Robert McNamara.* Boston: Little, Brown, 1993.

Sheehan, Neil. *A Bright Shining Lie: John Paul Vann and America in Vietnam.* New York: Random House, 1988.

Sheehan, Neil, et al., eds. *The Pentagon Papers as Published by The New York Times.* New York: Bantam, 1971.

Sherwin, Martin. *A World Destroyed: Hiroshima and the Origins of the Arms Race.* New York: Knopf, 1975; Vintage, 1987.

Shesol, Jeff. *Mutual Contempt: Lyndon Johnson, Robert Kennedy and the Feud That Defined a Decade.* New York: Norton, 1997.

Silk, Leonard, and Mark Silk. *The American Establishment.* New York: Basic Books, 1980.

Small, Melvin. *Johnson, Nixon and the Doves.* New Brunswick, N.J.: Rutgers University Press, 1988.

Smith, R. Harris. *OSS: The Secret Story of America's First Central Intelligence Agency.* New York: Dell, 1973.

Smith, Richard Norton. *The Harvard Century: The Making of a University to a Nation.* New York: Simon & Schuster, 1986.

————. *Thomas E. Dewey and His Times.* New York: Simon & Schuster, 1982.

Smith, Russell Jack. *The Unknown CIA: My Three Decades with the Agency.* Washington, D.C.: Pergamon-Brassey's, 1989.

Sorensen, Theodore. *Kennedy.* New York: Harper & Row, 1965.

Stavins, Ralph, Richard J. Barnet, and Marcus G. Raskin. *Washington Plans an Aggressive War: A Documented Account of the United States' Adventure in Indochina.* London: Davis-Poynter, 1972.

Steel, Ronald. *Walter Lippmann and the American Century.* Boston: Little, Brown, 1980.

Stein, Jean, interviewer, and George Plimpton, ed. *American Journey: The Times of Robert Kennedy.* New York: Harcourt Brace Jovanovich, 1970.

Stillwell, Paul, ed. *Assault on Normandy: First-Person Accounts from the Sea Services.* Annapolis: Naval Institute Press, 1994.

Stimson, Henry L., and McGeorge Bundy. *On Active Service in Peace and War.* New York: Harper & Bros., 1948.

Stone, I. F. *In a Time of Torment.* New York: Vintage, 1967.

Sulzberger, C. L. *The Last of the Giants.* New York: Macmillan, 1970.

Sussman, Warren I. *Culture as History: The Transformation of American Society in the Twentieth Century.* New York: Pantheon, 1984.

Tanzer, Lester, ed. *The Kennedy Circle.* Washington, D.C.: Luce, 1961.

Taylor, Maxwell D. *Swords and Ploughshares.* New York: Norton, 1972.

Thomas, Evan. *The Very Best Men.* New York: Simon & Schuster, 1995.

Thompson, Robert Smith. *The Missiles of October.* New York: Simon & Schuster, 1992.

Trumpbour, John, ed. *How Harvard Rules: Reason in the Service of Empire.* Boston: South End, 1989.

VanDeMark, Brian. *Into the Quagmire: Lyndon Johnson and the Escalation of the Vietnam War.* New York: Oxford University Press, 1991.

Views from the Circle: Seventy-five Years of Groton School. Groton, Mass.: The Trustees of Groton School, 1960.

Viorst, Milton. *Hustlers and Heroes: An American Political Panorama.* New York: Simon & Schuster, 1971.

Vogelgesand, Sandy. *The Long Dark Night of the Soul: The American Intellectual Left and the Vietnam War.* New York: Harper & Row, 1974.

Von Hoffman, Nicholas. *Left at the Post.* Chicago: Quadrangle, 1970.

Wald, Alan M. *The New York Intellectuals: The Rise and Decline of the Anti-Stalinist Left from the 1930s to the 1980s.* Chapel Hill: University of North Carolina Press, 1987.

Weeks, Edward, ed. *Conversations with Walter Lippmann.* Boston: Little, Brown, 1965.

Welchman, Gordon. *The Hut Six Story: Breaking the Enigma Codes.* New York: McGraw-Hill, 1982.

Weisskopf, Victor. *The Joy of Insight: Passions of a Physicist.* New York: Basic Books, 1991.

Wills, Garry. *The Kennedy Imprisonment: A Meditation on Power.* New York: Pocket Books, 1983.

Wilson, Edmund. *The Fifties.* New York: Farrar, Straus & Giroux, 1986.

Winks, Robin. *Cloak & Gown: Scholars in the Secret War, 1939–1961.* New York: Morrow, 1987.

Winnick, R. H., ed. *Letters of Archibald MacLeish: 1907 to 1982.* Boston: Houghton Mifflin, 1983.

Winters, Francis X. *The Year of the Hare.* Athens: University of Georgia Press, 1997.

Wofford, Harris. *Of Kennedys and Kings: Making Sense of the Sixties.* New York: Farrar, Straus & Giroux, 1980.

Woods, Randall Bennett. *Fulbright: A Biography.* New York: Cambridge University Press, 1995.

Wreszin, Michael. *A Rebel in Defense of Tradition: The Life & Politics of Dwight Macdonald.* New York: Basic Books, 1994.

Wright, William. *Lillian Hellman: The Image, the Woman.* New York: Simon & Schuster, 1986.

Young, Marilyn B. *The Vietnam Wars: 1945–1990.* New York: HarperCollins, 1991.

Zubok, Vladislav, and Constantine Pleshakov. *Inside the Kremlin's Cold War: From Stalin to Khrushchev.* Cambridge: Harvard University Press, 1996.

Acknowledgments

IN MY PERSONAL LIFE I have surrounded myself with the kind of people McGeorge Bundy once called the "verbally minded," those quick-witted, opinionated characters from the "chattering class." They are impatient people, and I have sorely tried their patience.

One day recently my son, Joshua, came home from school and proudly announced that he had written a "long book," longer, he said, "than Daddy's." It had brightly colored drawings, long rows of handcrafted letters and a great many pages stapled together. As I admired his "good work," Joshua said with the precious honesty of a five-year-old, "Daddy, you know what? I can write a book faster than you. So when you finish your book, we can play, right, and all the time?"

In the seven years it has taken me to write this book, Joshua was only the first of many who waited impatiently for me to finish. My wife, Susan Goldmark, has now made it possible for me to write two biographies, and for this I will forever be grateful. For many years she has enriched my life with her intelligence, beauty and sassy wit.

In the world of publishing, Alice Mayhew is a legendary editor; her name is attached to literally scores of important and wonderful books. Over the last seventeen years, she has waited with inordinate patience for me to write first *The Chairman*, a biography of John J. McCloy, and now this biography. I thank her, and also Roger Labrie, an associate editor at Simon & Schuster. Their extensive editorial suggestions on a long and complicated manuscript were always astute. Charlotte Gross's copyediting was superb.

Gail Ross is everything an author's agent should be: smart, irreverent, commonsensical and honest with her opinions. She made me do the work to sell this book, and then she too had to wait too long for the result.

Eric Alterman, Barton J. Bernstein, Philip Brenner, Carolyn Eisenberg, Thomas L. Hughes, A. J. Langguth, Melvyn P. Leffler, the late J. Anthony Lukas, former congressman John Monagan, Paula Newberg, John Prados, Marcus Raskin, Geoffrey Robinson, Ellen Schrecker, Peter Dale Scott, James Thomson, Jr., Don Wilson and Francis X. Winters, S.J., read portions of the manuscript. Bruce Cumings and Daniel Ellsberg took time away from their own book projects to read the entire manuscript. Their expert comments have improved the narrative immeasurably.

Many other friends and colleagues have sustained me over the years: Gar and Sharon Alperovitz, Scott and Barbara Armstrong, David Berick and Ellen Selonick,

Wayne Biddle and Mimi Harrison, Shelly Bird, Nancy Bird, Norman Birnbaum, Jim Boyce and Betsy Hartmann, Frank Browning, David Corn, Joseph Eldridge and Maria Otero, Thomas Ferguson and Elizabeth Anne McCauley, Helma Bliss Goldmark, Richard Gonzalez and Tara Siler, Bill Goodfellow and Dana Priest, Christopher Hitchens and Carol Blue, Amy Janello, Brennon Jones, Jim and Elsie Klumpner, William Lanouette, Lawrence Lifschultz and Rabia Ali, Ed Long and Pamela Norick, Priscilla Johnson McMillan, Christina Macaya, Paul Magnuson and Cathy Trost, Leo C. Maley III, Uday Mohan, John and Rosemary Monagan, Jim Morrell, Anna Nelson, Tim Noah and Marjorie Williams, Caleb Rossiter (a future U.S. congressman) and Maya Latynski, Arthur Samuelson, Michael Schwartz and Emily Medine, Martin Sherwin, Steve Solomon, John Tirman, Sanho Tree, James Wilkins III, Adam Zagorin and Mary Carpenter. Victor Navasky, the publisher and editorial director of *The Nation*, continues to shine as my best and funniest Wise Man.

McGeorge and William Bundy did not welcome the prospect of a critical biography, but when I came knocking on their doors they nevertheless took time away from their own book projects to answer my questions, many of which must have dredged up difficult memories. I thank them for their patience. I also want to thank Mary Lothrop Bundy, Harriet Bundy Belin and Mary Acheson Bundy for graciously responding to my requests for photographs from their family albums.

No book of this scope can be researched without the assistance of young and energetic students of history. I was fortunate to have as researchers Ross Dunbar, Dean Engle, David Huang, Katarina Jerinic, Ronald A. Lapid, Dawn Nakano, Robert M. Radick, Jeffrey M. Rosa, Jeff Schutts, Robert J. Sierralta, Jean Y. Suh and Will Winter. Without their diligence, this book would have taken many more years to write.

A legion of archivists helped me to unearth thousands of pages of Bundy correspondence, diary items and other primary sources for this book. I am grateful to Stephanie Fawcett, Suzanne Forbes, Maura Porter, June Payne, William Johnson and Allan Goodrich at the John F. Kennedy Presidential Library; David C. Humphrey at the U.S. State Department's Office of the Historian; Regina Greenwell, Linda Hanson and Mary Knill at the Lyndon B. Johnson Presidential Library; Ben Primer at the Princeton University Archives; Tom Blanton and Bill Burr at the National Security Archive; Harley P. Holden at the Harvard University Archives; David Haight at the Dwight D. Eisenhower Library; Lee Gust at the Council on Foreign Relations Archives, Alan Divack, Faith Coleman and Gloria Walters at the Ford Foundation Archives; Wilbur Mahoney and David Langbart of the National Archives; John N. Jacob of the George C. Marshall Foundation Library; Daria D'Arienzo of the Amherst College Archives; Mary Wolfskill, James H. Hutson, David Wigdor, Fred Bauman, Michael Klein, and Ernest Emrich at the Library of Congress Manuscript Reading Room; Peter Sheils, Margaret Rowman, Rosemary Melendy and Margaret Grafeld of the State Department's Office of Freedom of Information; and finally, Dwight M. Miller and Dale C. Mayer at the Herbert Hoover Presidential Library.

Biographies are easily the most expensive form of history to research, so I am particularly grateful to the John D. and Catherine T. MacArthur Foundation for its generous support of this book project. The Lyndon Baines Johnson Foundation funded part of my research in the Johnson Presidential Library. The Rockefeller Foundation gave me the extraordinary opportunity to spend five weeks in the Villa Serbelloni, a writer's paradise in the Italian village of Bellagio.

This book is dedicated to my wife and son—but also to my parents, Eugene and Jerine Bird, who have spent much of their lives trying to bring an end to the wars of the Middle East. They taught me the importance of history.

Index